OFFICIAL

Netscape
Communicator 4

BOOK
WINDOWS EDITION

An imprint of
Ventana Communications Group

The Definitive Guide
to Navigator 4 & the
Communicator Suite

PHIL JAMES

VENTANA

Official Netscape Communicator Book, Windows Edition
Copyright © 1997 by Phil James

Library of Congress Cataloging-in-Publication Data

James, Phil.
Official Netscape communicator book / Phil James. —Windows ed.,
1st ed.
p. cm.
Includes index.
ISBN 1-56604-723-4
1. Netscape. 2. World Wide Web (Information retrieval system)
3. Internet (Computer network) I. Title.
TK5105.883.J3498 1997
005.7'13769—dc21   97-3502

First Edition 9 8 7 6 5 4 3 2

Printed in the United States of America

Published and distributed to the trade by Ventana Communications Group
P.O. Box 13964, Research Triangle Park, NC 27709-3964
919.544.9404
FAX 919.544.9472
http://www.vmedia.com

Ventana Communications Group is a division of International Thomson Publishing.

Netscape Publishing Relations
Suzanne C. Anthony
Netscape Communications Corporation
501 E. Middlefield Rd.
Mountain View, CA 94043
http://home.netscape.com

President
Michael E. Moran

**Vice President of
Content Development**
Karen A. Bluestein

**Director of Acquisitions and
Development**
Robert Kern

Managing Editor
Lois J. Principe

Production Manager
John Cotterman

Art Director
Marcia Webb

**Technology Operations
Manager**
Kerry L. B. Foster

Brand Manager
Jamie Jaeger Fiocco

Creative Services Manager
Diane Lennox

Acquisitions Editor
JJ Hohn

Project Editor
Amy E. Moyers

Copy Editors
Suzanne Hayes Rose
Chuck Hutchinson

Technical Reviewer
Richard F. Jessup

Desktop Publishers
Patrick Berry
Jaimie Livingston

Proofreader
Jessica Ryan

Indexer
Ann Norcross

Interior Designer
Patrick Berry

Cover Illustrator
Elena Skrinak

About the Author

Phil James is a software design consultant, performance artist, part-time musician, and author of the best-selling *Official Netscape Navigator Books*, which have sold over 300,000 copies worldwide and have been translated into more than 10 languages. As a literary writer, his stories have appeared in a variety of print and electronic zines.

Acknowledgments

A big thank you to the people at Netscape who provided me the early information I needed, especially Edith Gong, Suzanne Anthony, and Sandy Cold Shapero.

I also want to thank my very excellent technical editor, Richard Jessup, as well as Tara Calishain for some much needed last minute help.

Then there's my awesome Internet service provider, Computerland (**http://www.computerland.net**). I don't think they've been down even once since I started this book.

Of course it's the staff at Ventana who really make projects like this happen. I'd like to thank Patrick Berry, Kristin Miller, Becky Steele, John Cotterman, Lois Principe, Lance Kozlowski, Caroline McKenzie, Jaimie Livingston, Christine Cleveland, Meredith Blackwelder, Bob Kern, Karen Bluestein, and especially JJ Hohn for all her hard work. A skilled cook as well as editor, she added the food-related site listings to Chapter 14. Then there's Amy Moyers, the project editor on this book. For handling some very crazy last minute problems calmly and effectively, she deserves all kinds of medals, ribbons, and statuettes. Thanks, Amy, for making it all the way through June 11 without quitting or strangling anyone. Oh, and of course thanks to Melanie Stepp for participating in the Friday afternoon e-mail conferences that have helped shape this project.

Lastly, a great big thank you to my wife and kids, who still put up with me through the crazy deadlines.

Contents

Foreword

While Netscape is without question one of the most visible software companies, we are also working hard to make our client-end products increasingly *invisible*. We don't believe software should dictate a user's experience, so we spend much of our time creating tools that enable content providers present media-rich information in their own creative, innovative ways. Netscape software works quietly—but powerfully—behind the scenes, providing the needed foundation. We recognize that the emphasis in desktop computing has shifted from arcane procedures to content itself, and Netscape has taken a leadership role in reinforcing this shift.

Nowhere is this more apparent than in Netscape Communicator 4. Communicator gives content providers more flexibility than ever before in shaping and presenting information. Dynamic HTML and enhanced Java and JavaScript enable interactive user interfaces—limited only by a designer's imagination. And of course you can extend Communicator's multimedia power with a huge variety of plug-ins. Clearly, Communicator stretches way beyond the world of text links and Back and Forward buttons.

One of the most exciting components of Communicator is *Netcaster*. Netcaster takes this new content-based model a step further by letting you subscribe to information channels that may be updated at regular intervals. And because channel information is stored locally on your system rather than on a distant server, it may include large multimedia files that you access instantaneously. This feature has already inspired content providers to create forward-looking user interfaces that we wouldn't have dreamed of a few years ago.

But Communicator is not just about innovative approaches to presenting information—it's also about integrating online tasks. With Communicator, your computer becomes a communications center. Its components work together to provide a single seamless approach to communicating with your coworkers or with the world. You use the same tools to create HTML e-mail as you use to create a full-blown Web page; the same Address Book lets you initiate a conference call or fire off a quick message; and you no longer need separate applications to surf the Web and receive Web channels. Thanks to this integration, Communicator is much more than the sum of its parts.

Of course anyone in business knows that growth entails risk, and now that intranets and the Internet have become household words, the security of online communications is an important consideration. In its earlier Navigator products, Netscape took the lead in providing world-class SSL security. Now Communicator adds unprecedented *flexibility* in dealing with security issues. Object signing lets you know what entity is sending you a Java applet or JavaScript code; you can then choose to allow or disallow any actions such as disk access that may compromise the security of your system. S/MIME e-mail enables digitally-signed messages that assure you of the identity of your correspondent. And a new Security Advisor lets you tailor a broad range of security settings for your exact needs. Security has become as configurable as the rest of Communicator.

The *Official Netscape Communicator 4 Book* provides a broad, step-by-step introduction to the world's most innovative communications and collaboration product. As we enter a new era in desktop computing—an era in which *information* takes precedence over *procedure*—Communicator insures that you stay way ahead of the curve.

Marc Andreessen
Netscape Communications Corporation

Introduction

Each new release includes some new bells and whistles and perhaps even a change or two that really matters. But what *doesn't* change is your relation to the program. Familiar procedures result in familiar output.

Other applications, especially in the area of communications, evolve more quickly because they must keep pace with technological and social changes in the world at large. For example, as consumers started to shop electronically from home, software vendors had to come up with flexible new security protocols and schemes to protect online transactions.

Then there are programs that leap-frog themselves dramatically with each new version. Netscape Navigator was like that, jumping from a graphical Web browser to an integrated set of communications tools in just one upgrade. Now its successor—Netscape Communicator 4—moves us even further toward a new model of desktop computing.

In the new model I'm talking about, *information* takes precedence over *procedures*. It's really a very simple idea. Information is what you're interested in, so why not make it the program's central focus? Communicator supports a wealth of new capabilities that let content providers embed highly interactive elements or even entire user interfaces right into the information they send you. The information itself becomes your workspace, supported by simple software procedures and flexible configuration options.

What Is Communicator 4?

Communicator is more than the successor to Navigator 3. In fact, Navigator 4 is just one part of Communicator. Communicator is really a tightly integrated communications suite made up of the following components:

- **Navigator 4**—your window on the Web. Navigator 4 lets you experience and interact with a huge variety of multimedia documents on the Internet or on your office intranet. As you'll learn in this book, Navigator 4 includes many significant advances over previous Navigator versions.

- **Netcaster**—your desktop "channel tuner." With Netcaster you can subscribe to information channels that are updated on a regular basis, providing you with everything from up-to-the-minute stock quotes to weekly movie reviews to the latest paperwork from your HR department. Channels can even automatically update your software. And because channels are stored locally on your machine, you can access the media-rich information they provide instantaneously.

- **Messenger**—your e-mail link to the world. E-mail has rapidly become a commonplace means of getting in touch and staying in touch, and Communicator's Messenger component provides full-featured e-mail support. You can send and receive messages that look just like Web pages, with embedded links, graphics, animations, and even sound. In addition, Messenger supports the S/MIME standard for digitally signed messages, ensuring the security of information you send and receive.

- **Collabra Discussion Groups**—your key to specialized information and collaborative work. Communicator's Discussion Groups component lets you read and respond to messages in the thousands of specialized newsgroups on the Internet, forums for in-depth discussion of everything from astrophysics to zydeco. In addition, you can participate in private discussion groups on your own office intranet, bouncing ideas around with coworkers without leaving your desk.

- **Composer**—your page creation workshop. With Communicator's Composer component, you can create your own HTML documents quickly and easily, even if you're a beginner. Specialized page templates make it easy, whether you're creating a simple home page for yourself or publicly accessible material promoting your company. A variety of *WYSIWYG* tools help you tailor your page to your exact needs, and you can even extend Composer's power with special Composer plug-ins.

- **Conference**—your Internet phone. Actually, the Conference component is much more than a phone. Yes, it lets you make long distance voice calls using the Internet, but it also lets you chat (type messages back and forth) or transfer files at the same time you talk. Using a unique white board feature you can even share graphical information, marking up or changing each other's ideas, and a collaborative browsing feature lets Conference participants view the same Web sites simultaneously. Not only does Conference save on phone charges, it might save you from having to buy a couple of plane tickets!

But Communicator 4 is more than the sum of its parts. The components are integrated in such a way that you don't need to learn new commands or procedures for each new task. If you know how to use Messenger, you already know how to use the Discussion Groups component, and if you know how to find an e-mail address in the Address Book you already know how to place a Conference call.

Who Can Use This Book

This book is aimed at anyone who is reasonably familiar with some version of Windows and wants to get busy on the Net or on an office intranet. It's also aimed at anyone who's been communicating electronically for a while but wants to upgrade to Netscape Communicator 4. Here's what you need:

- A 486 or better PC with at least 16MB of RAM and Windows 95, Windows 3.1, or Windows NT installed.

- If you haven't already installed Communicator, about 16MB of space on your hard drive.

- For the version of this book that comes with a CD-ROM, a CD-ROM drive.

- A TCP/IP local area network (intranet) or a way to get on the Internet.

- For home access via an Internet access provider, a modem, preferably one that can run at 28.8 Kbps or greater.

The last two requirements need some explanation. First of all, you can gather from what I said earlier that Internet access is not really necessary in all cases. Thousands of people are using Netscape Communicator to share multimedia information within their own companies. This use relies not on the Internet but on intranets, enterprise-wide networks that a local system administrator sets up.

But let's say you're a home user who wants to get out into the big Internet ocean. Chances are that unless you're a very ambitious and wealthy computer nerd, you don't have a direct connection to the Net. That means you need a modem and an account with an Internet service provider. Neither is hard to get or very expensive any more. Of course, you should get the fastest modem you can afford, preferably one that can run at 28.8 Kbps, but a 14.4 Kbps modem will still do the job.

For those of you who bought the version of this book that has a CD-ROM inside the back cover, here's something you *don't* need: Communicator itself. That's right, the CD includes the official software right from Netscape!

How This Book Is Organized

Chapter 1, "Intranets, the Internet, & Communicator 4," provides an overview of the technology we're dealing with: where it came from, some of its features, and where it's going. You'll learn what the difference really is between the Internet and the World Wide Web, and you'll learn enough about the technical underpinnings of the Net or your office intranet to understand any other technical discussions in the book.

In **Chapter 2, "Introducing Communicator 4,"** you will learn how this communications suite fits together. In addition, I will introduce you to all the Communicator-specific terminology you'll need. Once you read this chapter, you'll be ready to work through the step-by-step procedures for Communicator's individual components.

Chapter 3, "Browsing & Beyond," introduces you to the Navigator 4 component and the basics of browsing HTML and multimedia documents. In a few short minutes, you'll be cruising, surfing, or whatever the term is this year.

Web channels and "push" technology have garnered about as much media attention this year as Whitewater, and **Chapter 4, "Netcaster,"** shows you how to become part of an exciting trend. Follow the simple directions in this chapter and in moments you'll know how to subscribe to and configure a variety of information channels.

Electronic mail is one of the most important "meat and potatoes" Internet and intranet applications, and **Chapter 5, "Netscape Messenger,"** covers it fully. Step-by-step tutorials guide you through all the procedures you need, and in no time you'll be zipping off messages as if you'd been doing it for years.

Chapter 6, "Discussion Groups," introduces you to one of the most fascinating services available on the Net or on your intranet. Discussion groups are forums where you can read or post about specialized information; they also let you work collaboratively with teams of coworkers. This chapter shows you how.

Of course the real *fun* of the new information technologies are their multimedia capabilities. **Chapter 7, "Media on the Move: Working With Graphics, Sound & Video,"** explains how Communicator makes your computer screen look more and more like a TV screen. I show you some of what's available out there, and I walk you through configuring Communicator so that it uses your system optimally in dealing with these new types of information.

Chapter 8, "The Ancestors: FTP, Gopher & Telnet" introduces you to three old Internet friends. These Internet services have been around for quite a while, but are still extremely useful tools. You'll learn how to explore file archives and download files via FTP, the standard file transfer protocol on the Net. You'll also learn how to use text-based systems to research highly specialized information.

Chapter 9, "Creating Your Own Page," covers Communicator's Composer component. This chapter leads you step-by-step through the process of designing and publishing a Web page, whether for your own use or for public access.

In **Chapter 10, "Power Communicator 4,"** we go beyond the basics and show you some of the more forward-looking extensions to a forward-looking piece of software. Don't be scared off by the word "advanced": none of these features are difficult to use. In this chapter we explore VRML, Java, JavaScript, and plug-ins.

Chapter 11, "Netscape Conference," covers one of the most exciting Communicator components. Thanks to Conference you no longer have to watch the clock when making long distance calls—they don't need to cost any more than regular Net access. This chapter includes simple step-by-step procedures for Conference's many other features as well.

Want to do your banking on the Net? Before you do, you might want to read **Chapter 12, "Communicator 4 Security."** This chapter gives you the lowdown on Communicator's impressive security features, including encryption, digitally signed e-mail, and signed Java and JavaScript. After reading or working through this chapter you may worry less and sleep more soundly.

Chapter 13, "The Professional Edition," is a special bonus chapter that briefly introduces the features of Netscape Communicator, Professional Edition. You may or may not need the extra features provided in the Professional Edition; this chapter will help you find out.

In **Chapter 14, "Favorite Sites,"** I tell you about some of my own favorite Internet resources. This list is not exhaustive, since that would require volumes—and literally constant updating. Instead, these are a few attractions that I've found exciting, informative, fun, or just plain weird. You can also think of them as jumping off places for your own explorations. If you have purchased the version of this book that has a companion CD-ROM inside the back cover, you also have an electronic version of Chapter 14. You can browse the listings using Communicator's Navigator 4 component, simply clicking the links to visit sites you're interested in.

In **Appendix A**, you'll find instructions for installing Communicator 4, as well as highlighted options for navigating the CD-ROM contents.

Navigate!

To further enhance this book, we're providing a place to go for the latest information about this and other Netscape Press titles. Connect via the World Wide Web to http://www.netscapepress.com to access a complete catalog of Netscape Press titles, technical support, updated information related to this book, and areas where you can download a Web version of Chapter 14, so that you don't have to type in all the Internet addresses we provide.

Netscapepress.com is also the home of *Navigate!*—the official electronic publication of Netscape Press and your best source for articles and reviews aimed at Netscape users. *Navigate!* features interviews with industry icons and experts as well as articles excerpted from upcoming Netscape Press titles.

Netscape Press is a joint effort between Ventana and Netscape Communications Corporation and serves as the publishing arm of Netscape.

OK, enough introduction. Let's get busy exploring the vast new world of multimedia information!

CHAPTER 1

Intranets, the Internet & Communicator 4

Last time I was stuck in an airport I conducted an experiment. I wanted to see how long I could wait at the gate passively listening to the buzz of conversation around me before I heard the word *intranet*. Or *Internet*. Or any of the myriad phrases associated with the new information technology. It was less than two minutes before I overheard a man and a woman quietly, almost clandestinely, trading e-mail addresses. Moments later some guy with a power suit and a bad haircut was screaming into the pay phone that if so-and-so wouldn't even meet him in a private virtual chat space to discuss the matter, why the @#$% would he respond to that @#$%^&* Usenet post!

Toto, we're not in Kansas anymore.

Just about everywhere you go these days you hear these cyber-buzzwords. If you spend much time in airports or reading magazines, you'd think most people spend a significant portion of their time "cruising the Web" or "engaging in online transactions" or even "exploring virtual 3-D worlds." But as with most new technologies, jargon precedes popular understanding. New terminology makes it possible to share new ideas, but it also exacerbates the epidemic of Geek Answer Syndrome. There is no shortage of people who will blab on authoritatively but incorrectly about anything to do with information technology, flashing their vocabulary like bright plumage. (Yes, I know, it's mainly the men.)

Now you can tell the know-it-alls to pipe down because after reading this chapter, you'll *really* understand what intranets are, what the Net and the Web are, and how you can tap the power of these exciting new resources using Netscape Communicator. In other words, you'll be well on your way to full cybergeek status! By the time you've finished this chapter, you may not have the technical knowledge of a Bill Gates, but you'll be able to answer the following questions and probably more:

- Just what *is* an intranet? What's the difference between an intranet and the Internet?
- What kinds of services and information are available on the Internet?
- How do Internet and intranet addressing work?
- What is the World Wide Web? How is it related to the Net?
- What is hypertext? How about hypermedia?
- What exactly can you do with Netscape Communicator?
- Are there any general guidelines for using intranets and the Internet?

What Are Intranets?

It's really a lot simpler than you'd guess. A *network* is a collection of computers that are connected together so they can share information, such as database files or programs in an office setting. An *intranet* is simply a network that lets people within an organization share the kind of information you can experience—and create—with Netscape Communicator: pages full of text, graphics, sound, and video; fill-out forms; e-mail with pictures; specialized newsgroups and interactive conferences; directories full of files you can download; and a broad range of custom-tailored resources for research, education, or entertainment.

Netscape Communicator may be the best piece of software you can use to access information on an intranet, but it's not the only one. In fact, the whole idea behind intranets is that they use standardized methods, or *protocols*, for moving information from one computer to another. That means an entire office, or even a company with many physically remote sites, can communicate using an intranet without worrying about specific hardware or software. Hot-shot programmers at a San José office can use their UNIX server machine to provide an animated demo program that you view in Sheboygan using a vintage Mac.

No two intranets are alike because the content varies—and varies extremely—from business to business. And yet, in a way, all are identical because the underlying protocols, the ways information is packaged and relayed from one machine to another, are always the same. Later in this chapter, in the sidebar called "Under the Hood: TCP/IP," you'll learn a little about some of these underlying protocols. But before that, I'd like to introduce you to the important concept of *clients and servers*.

Clients & Servers

In order to distribute information efficiently, intranets rely on two different kinds of software or hardware. When you are sitting at your desk looking at information that's out there on your intranet, the machine you're using is acting as a *client*. But where does this information really reside? You guessed it: on a *server*. A server is a computer or software program that "dishes up" information in a particular format. For instance, a Web server makes Web pages available, and a mail server acts like a post office that delivers your mail.

One machine on an intranet may house several different types of servers, and a computer can even act as a server and a client at the same time. You could run a small Web server on your desktop PC, letting people access multimedia pages you've created, while you're busy cruising around to other sites using a Web client like Netscape Communicator. In all but the smallest enterprises, however, servers are usually dedicated machines that do nothing but serve up information.

In Figure 1-1, you see a typical office intranet with several clients and servers.

Figure 1-1: An intranet.

What Is the Internet?

The Internet is like an office intranet on steroids: it is a huge worldwide *public* network of networks. The Internet lets individuals on one network share information with users on another network that may be thousands of miles away. As with an intranet, the shared information can take many forms. For instance, you can use the Internet to send e-mail messages, download files, view video clips, or listen to music. You can even use the Net for banking and shopping. The Internet is just like an intranet in another way, too: it uses the same client-server model and the identical protocols! That's why intranets can extend outward and blend seamlessly with the Internet. At your office computer you may not even know when you're getting information from a local intranet server or when you're getting it from an Internet server halfway around the world.

The physical Internet looks like a vast net of wires. A few high-speed "backbone" cables branch out into other cables, which in turn radiate outward into finer strands. Most of the developed areas of the world have already been wired, so by routing your information or requests through this vast system you can reach other Internet users all over the world. Fortunately, the routing happens automatically, just as it does with telephone calls, so you don't need to know *how* data gets from your computer to a computer in Timbuktu.

And the system is democratic. Anyone can use it. You don't really need to have your own network in order to connect—you can communicate using the current infrastructure by plugging into somebody else's network. Maybe you're already doing this. If you have a *Serial Line Internet Protocol* (SLIP) or *Point-to-Point Protocol* (PPP) account, you simply connect via modem and phone line to your Internet Service Provider's network site (known as a "point of presence"). The actual transmission of data is free to you, but you'll probably need to pay the service provider for the time you spend accessing their equipment.

There are hundreds of thousands of users sitting at their PCs right now, gathering information from far-flung reaches of the globe. A very basic diagram of the Internet is shown in Figure 1-2.

Figure 1-2: The Internet.

Under the Hood: TCP/IP

You could probably get through life just fine without understanding the technical underpinnings of intranets and the Net. But if you like the nuts and bolts stuff, boy have I got a sidebar for you!

TCP/IP really means "the TCP/IP protocol suite." It is a group of protocols that allows data to be transmitted correctly from one machine to another over an intranet or the Net. And what exactly is a protocol? It's simply a set of standardized conventions for communication. In the human world, a typical protocol is saying "Your Honor" when you talk to a judge. In the world of data communications, a protocol might require that a sending machine include a special string of characters before and after every chunk of data so that the receiving machine can determine where that data begins and ends.

The TCP part of TCP/IP stands for Transmission Control Protocol. It divides any information you send into manageable blocks; conversely, it reconstructs received blocks into a stream of information. TCP does not require that all the blocks be received in the right sequence, since it attaches sequence numbers for reassembly. TCP also includes error checking; if blocks are missing or garbled, it requests that they be resent. When you run Internet applications, you remain blissfully unaware of all of this activity because the TCP software layer "sits below" the application software. Information is passed from the application software to TCP without any human intervention; at the other end, reassembled information is passed *from* TCP to the appropriate software program.

The IP part of TCP/IP stands for Internet Protocol. The Internet Protocol is the real workhorse of the Internet. When you send something over an intranet or the Internet, TCP passes its packets on to IP. This is roughly like dropping a letter off at the post office because IP repackages the data and makes sure that all of it gets delivered from point to point on the intranet or Internet on its way to the final destination: the specified IP or domain name address. Conversely, when IP receives packets, it "delivers" them up to TCP. There are other low-level Internet protocols, but these are the two most important ones, the basis of most intranet and Internet communication.

History of the Internet

We're going to breeze through this section quickly, because the way most books do it is a big *Y A W N*.

One: the paranoid phase.

It's the early 1970s: a time of menace, leisure suits, platform shoes, Sonny Bono, and nuclear buildup. The U.S. Defense Department implements a network called ARPAnet that's cleverly designed so that even if part of its physical structure is destroyed, information can still be sent to any remaining destination. This *packet-switching* technology will become the foundation of the Internet.

Two: the academic phase.

It's the early 1980s now. Local area networks at a variety of research institutions start hooking into ARPAnet. Fast forward to a few years later: The National Science Foundation (NSF) establishes five supercomputer centers and connects them via their own network, NSFnet. This network-of-networks uses the same protocols as ARPAnet. Educational institutions and government agencies start plugging into NSFnet, and faster lines are installed all over the place. What is now known as the Internet opens its virtual doors to most of the academic and government community, who quickly put all kinds of boring things on it.

Three: the hobbyist phase.

With great difficulty, individuals can get on the Net, even from home. Gradually, thanks in part to improved software from the founders of Netscape, access becomes easier. People who enjoy communicating with others share all sorts of things—haikus and pictures of their pet cat. It's Internet as show-and-tell. Andy Warhol predicted a time when everyone would enjoy 15 minutes of fame. While that hasn't quite yet happened, at least everybody can enjoy 15 *kilobytes* of fame.

Four: the commercial phase.

In America it isn't long before a good thing becomes a profitable thing. It's the mid-90s. Thousands of companies have started to promote and sell products over the Net, and we're all trying to figure out how to filter junk e-mail (also known as *spam*). At the same time, businesses are discover that they can streamline operations and increase productivity by connecting their in-house networks to the Internet. Almost overnight, the Net grows from a nerdy back-water into an ocean of Capitalist dreams.

And that's the history of the Internet so far.

> **TIP**
>
> *In addition to* Internet *and* intranet, *you might hear or read the word* extranet *from time to time. What is an extranet? It's simply a TCP/IP network that links businesses to customers, suppliers, etc. You can also think of it as part of an enterprise intranet that is made available to the outside world for marketing or other specific purposes.*

What Is the Web?

There is a lot of confusion among the general public about what the World Wide Web really is and especially about how it relates to the Internet as a whole. Let's clarify these issues right now.

The World Wide Web is, quite simply, a global hypermedia document that resides on and stretches across intranets and most of the Internet. Whoa! What's this boy talking about? To understand the Web you really need to know what we mean by hypertext and hypermedia.

Hypertext & Hypermedia

Imagine you are reading this book on your computer screen instead of on the page. As you read along, you notice that some of the words are underlined and may appear in a different color or *font*, just like that. In this example, you try clicking your mouse on the word "font." Magically, a new document appears on your screen, explaining what fonts are. This new document also contains words and phrases that you can click on, taking you to yet other documents or to other places in the same document. That's what *hypertext* is all about: the nonlinear presentation of text, letting you jump from idea to idea following your own associative pathways. The clickable words and phrases are known as links, and the activity of moving around through these linked documents is known as *browsing*.

Now imagine that when you click on the *font* link you don't just get a text explaining fonts. Instead, a fancy picture pops up, a colorful depiction of fonts through the ages from Guttenberg to Adobe. Perhaps you're even presented with a video clip complete with Charlton Heston narration and a corny John Williams score. Congratulations! You've just learned what *hypermedia* is: the nonlinear presentation not just of text, but of a variety of other media including graphics and sound.

Hypermedia on the Net & on Intranets

So what does this have to do with intranets and the Internet? When you click on a link, the document that you get—whether it's text, graphics, sound, or full-motion video—does not have to be on the same machine as the original document. Thanks to a special protocol known as *HyperText Transfer Protocol* (HTTP), the primary protocol for the World Wide Web, you can access documents from a server on your office intranet—or from any public World Wide Web server on the Internet! The basic Web page might be on your own computer or on a server run by your publications department; the video clip about fonts might reside on a machine in Hollywood or Timbuktu. Now here's the conceptual leap that makes this new technology so exciting: you can think of the collection of all the documents linked together as one big hypermedia document.

Let's go back to our original definition of the Web: a global hypermedia document that resides on and stretches across intranets and most of the Internet. Make sense now?

About Hypermedia?

Suppose you're reading one of those wonderful but frustrating Russian novels in which 36 major characters are introduced during the first two chapters. If you're anything like me, you'll continually find yourself flipping back and forth trying to keep track of who's who. Was Natasha Galanskaya the one who ran away with the Count against her father's wishes, or was that Natalia Balanchina? Wouldn't it be great if you could just push a button on a character's name and instantaneously be transported to a full description of that character's relevant history? Well, you can't do that in a book or a magazine or even a regular computer document, but the magic of hypermedia makes it possible.

Let's look at another example of how hypermedia can improve the communication process, and even make learning more fun and interesting. Suppose you're a high school student studying astrophysics. One option is to open your textbooks and review the mathematics of planetary motion in the abstract. Even if you enjoy solving a few motion problems, it's still a fairly boring exercise. But what if your physics lab computer is linked to the Web and takes you to a virtual textbook with animations that show the orbits of the bodies, in full color and motion? Or plays back short lectures on the day's exercises, by the foremost authority in the field? Educators and trainers know the power of multimedia to speed learning and increase students' retention levels. This type of presentation has become popular in education and corporate training environments, as it presents information in an interesting and entertaining format.

When we click on the graphics, video, and sound objects embedded in a compound-document Web page, we are fulfilling prophesies made years ago for a global information system. When you're up and running with Netscape Communicator, you'll see exactly what all the excitement's about.

Servers & Browsers

Remember how I said that both intranets and the Internet use what is called a client-server model? The Web is a great example of this. Special machines or software known as World Wide Web servers make the linked hypermedia documents available to the public or, in the case of intranets, to coworkers in your office. Individuals then move around through these documents using software known as Web clients or, more commonly, Web *browsers*. Obviously a Web browser has to be able to display or "play" a wide variety of hypermedia formats. The Web browser Netscape Navigator 4 is one component of Netscape Communicator.

Because the World Wide Web uses a standardized protocol (HTTP) for transferring the information across intranets and the Internet, and because all Web software adheres to this protocol, any kind of Web browser will work with any kind of Web server. For instance, a site may decide to use one of the server packages developed by Netscape, but any World Wide Web browser will be able to access the information available at that site. Conversely, the browser we are discussing in this book can access hypermedia documents on any Web server anywhere in the world.

What's a Home Page?

Once you start exploring the World Wide Web, you'll encounter the term *home page* over and over again, and it won't always be used the same way. Here are some of the things it can mean:

- A home page is the document that's displayed by a Web browser such as Netscape Communicator when you first load the program. This document may be located on your local machine, on an office intranet machine, or at a remote site. In the case of Netscape Communicator, the default home page is a document located at Netscape's own Web site, but as with most other browsers, you can change this.

- A home page is the top-level document at a particular Web site. For instance, a typical small business's home page would contain a title, a logo, some introductory information, and a bunch of links to more detailed marketing information.

- A home page is a personal Web document created by an individual and made available to the public (Joe Blow's 15 kilobytes of fame). Many access providers now let users copy Web documents to their public Web servers, and the Net sprouts hundreds of new personal home pages every day. You'd be surprised who's out there!

- In some contexts, a home page is simply any hypertext Web document, though I have to admit it bugs me when I hear people use the term this way.

What You Can Do on the Internet or Intranets

What advantages do office intranets and the Internet offer you right now? What can you actually *do* with Netscape Communicator? Let's take a deeper look at a few of the services and resources that can have a real impact on your life.

Electronic Mail

Thanks to intranets and the Internet, you can send messages not only to your coworkers but to just about anybody who has a computer and a network connection, either direct or via a modem. If the individual you want to contact is not directly on your intranet or on the Net, you can use Netscape Communicator to send a message to him or her on one of the popular online services such as CompuServe or America Online. The great thing about e-mail in Communicator is that you don't do anything different to send messages to your coworker two cubicles away or your Congressperson in Washington. The only difference is that your coworker may send you a more sensible response.

There are a number of advantages to sending messages via e-mail instead of the U.S. Postal Service (known affectionately as "snail mail" by e-mail advocates). First of all, there's the speed. It may take only seconds for your message to reach somebody on the other side of the world. The recipient can read your text immediately on the screen, respond to it right away, save it for later, print it out, or quickly forward it to somebody else. You can create electronic mailing lists for sending notices to hundreds or even thousands of people at once. Messages you receive can be organized into convenient electronic folders and saved for as long as you want without taking up any office space. And with Netscape e-mail, you can format your e-mail message to look just like a Web page. Because of these advantages, and several others that you'll learn about in Chapter 5, e-mail has become my principal means of communicating with the world. I receive several dozen e-mail messages a day and send about as many. In a two-week period I generate more messages than all the old-fashioned paper letters I've written in my life!

On the Net, you send e-mail instead of snail mail. On an intranet, you use e-mail instead of routing paper memos or trotting down to your boss' office to explain the latest screw-up. E-mail can increase the efficiency of any office that employs more than three or four people. Of course it's a double-edged sword. I've known businesses where unbelievable amounts of time are wasted on e-mail gossip and "humor." Thanks to human nature, every new communications technology has the potential both for increased efficiency and for more creative ways of slacking off.

Netscape Communicator includes full-featured e-mail support, and Figure 1-3 shows what the main e-mail window looks like, whether you're on an intranet, the Net, or both. By the way, Communicator not only lets you include HTML code in your e-mail messages (see the sidebar below called "What's HTML"), it also lets you include pictures, sound, and even Java applets. (You'll learn more about Java in Chapter 10.)

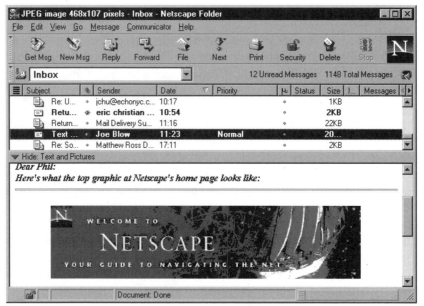

Figure 1-3: An e-mail message that includes text and a picture.

Enterprise-wide Documents

Netscape Communicator provides organizations with a standardized front-end for viewing policies and procedures documents, company news, sales charts, and customer information. I know of several companies that put a new multimedia "Web page of the day" on their servers each morning. When employees fire up their desktop machines, they are greeted with an up-to-date office newsletter, complete with digital photos of top management that can be saved and manipulated in a graphics program!

Netscape Communicator can help an office insure that everyone is using the same paperwork; that in-house information is disseminated quickly and reliably; and that data is presented as effectively as possible using the new technologies. Communicator can add impact to your job, making it a little flashier and more interesting. Imagine a monthly sales report appearing on your screen with animated 3-D graphs—or a division-wide layoff notice with a soundtrack by Yanni!

Figure 1-4 shows an example of a colorful office newsletter that is viewed by the entire staff of an organization using Netscape Communicator.

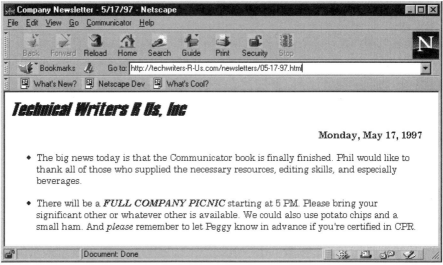

Figure 1-4: An office newsletter, updated daily.

Conferencing & Real-Time Collaboration

Netscape Communicator lets you share ideas and plans with other individuals in specialized company-wide discussion groups—or in public Internet newsgroups. Instead of calling meeting after meeting, you can consult with a group of coworkers electronically. You jot down an idea that everyone in your group sees and responds to; then you sift through their suggestions and post another message. The group conversation continues along these lines without requiring any kind of scheduling. Or instead of tracking down expensive experts in a particular field, you can use Communicator to find knowledge-able people right on the Net, in online discussion groups that work exactly the same way. I'll cover these Communicator features in Chapter 6. Meanwhile, Figure 1-5 shows what this discussion group feature looks like.

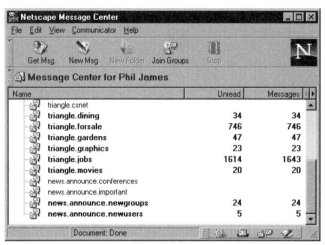

Figure 1-5: Some discussion groups in Netscape Communicator.

But Communicator also lets you collaborate in *real-time* with coworkers or friends. It means you can actually use your intranet or the Net to converse with people, either by voice or typed "chat"; it means you can send text or other files to each other as you speak; it means that as you cruise the Web, you can make the pages you view appear in a friend's browser at exactly the same time; and it means that no matter how far apart you are, you can add text, drawings, sketches, and other materials to a special shared workspace supplied by Communicator. Imagine collaborating with somebody in another country on the layout of a newsletter or the design of a jet engine. If you're less ambitious, imagine playing tic-tac-toe with your coworker down the hall while trying to get your boss off the phone. You'll learn more about these powerful collaboration tools in Chapter 11.

Research

Locating specific information used to be a tedious and time-consuming process. Remember digging through library card catalogs and then wandering through dusty stacks of books, only to discover that what you needed wasn't even at this library? Now finding references to topics can be as simple as typing in a keyword and clicking a button—from the privacy of your own home or office! The Internet includes entire libraries of specialized information, and thousands of these are accessible, free of charge, to the general public.

The Internet also supports a variety of research techniques and styles.

Suppose you're trying to come up with a topic for a speech you have to deliver. At first you might want to browse a variety of materials to refine your subject area. This process is much like going to an area in a library and starting to pull books off the shelf, except that on the Internet you can leap from library to library, following associative links or trains of thought. Once you've determined the exact subject of your speech, you may need to track down some very specific information, such as statistics to back up a particular point. Once again there are Internet services that will help you; powerful search tools that will scurry around the Net and quickly find your needle in the information haystack. Netscape Communicator gives you access to these tools through the Net Search feature on the Netscape home page, shown in Figure 1-6.

Figure 1-6: Net Search gives you access to a variety of search tools from the Netscape home page.

News & Information

This is the age of information, and success in many fields depends on getting the latest news as quickly as possible. The Internet provides numerous sources for specialized, up-to-date information. You may want to subscribe to an electronic mailing list, for instance, that keeps you posted on the latest developments in nanotechnology; you may want to get stock prices more current than those you can read in your local newspaper; or you may want to participate in a Usenet newsgroup where specialists in some arcane area of knowledge keep you abreast of what you need to know. Because of its scope and speed, the Internet is by far the most efficient way to make sure you maintain expert status in your little corner of the information universe. Netscape Communicator gets you the information you need!

Software

One of the most astounding features of the Internet is the availability of thousands and thousands of software programs that you can download at no charge. In fact, until recently you couldn't even buy commercial Internet client programs for PCs that were anywhere near as good as the freeware and shareware available on the Net. (For more information about freeware and shareware, see Chapter 8.) That situation is starting to change, but there still are times when you need a program dedicated to a very specific task, such as playing a new kind of sound or video file.

Many of the sites that allow you to download programs are large, and most do not include descriptions of the files. Fortunately, Netscape Communicator helps you locate and download exactly what you need.

Figure 1-7 shows you some of the directories of files available at Netscape's own FTP site.

And special new AutoInstall features in Communicator allow software to be updated automatically. Fall asleep struggling with version 2 and wake up in the morning to a brand new version 3!

Figure 1-7: The Netscape FTP site.

Promotion, Shopping & Online Transactions

For years the Internet was a commerce-free zone. It was funded and monitored by dedicated bureaucrats and academicians who instituted strict usage policies restricting anything that smelled vaguely of money. Well, all that's changed. Now there are vast regions of cyberspace that look less like research libraries and more like your local mall, and most major corporations maintain Web sites where they promote their products and services. Figure 1-8 shows a portion of the Yahoo's directory of companies (http://www.yahoo.com/Business_and_Economy/Companies/Directories/). From here you can browse to a wide variety of commercial Web sites.

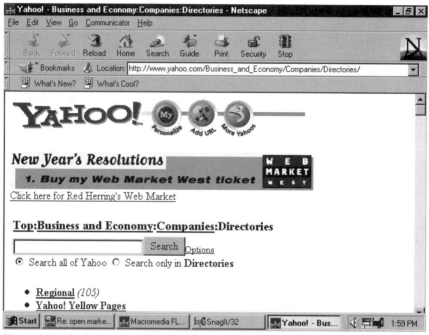

Figure 1-8: Yahoo's directory of companies.

Until recently, marketing types were up against a serious problem when it came to getting promotional information out to users: people had to know how to go out and find the stuff. That's changed. Netscape's Inbox Direct feature lets you subscribe to services that automatically send hypermedia information directly to you via e-mail. With Inbox Direct you can get graphs of your stock activity four times a day, charts of current weather conditions in your area, or a dazzling variety of carefully, and sometimes not so carefully, targeted electronic junk mail. In addition, Communicator supports *netcasting*, which allows a distant server to update areas in your browser window automatically. The commercial applications for this are obvious, but it's also a useful tool for keeping employees up to date in a corporate setting.

Lastly, Communicator includes a special "kiosk mode" for libraries, lobbies, and other publicly accessible areas. This special configuration is programmable with JavaScript (see Chapter 10.) and displays the browser window without the usual toolbars and other "window dressing."

Recreation

Planning a vacation? The Internet can provide current travel information on just about any area of the globe. Considering taking up a new sport? Want to find out about the latest foreign movies? The Internet can point you to the resources you need.

But the Internet not only supplies information *about* recreational activities, it also provides its own diversions and amusements. If you like interactive online games, for instance, you may be in danger of staying glued to your keyboard and monitor well into the wee hours. Figure 1-9 shows one of the many games sites available to you via the Web.

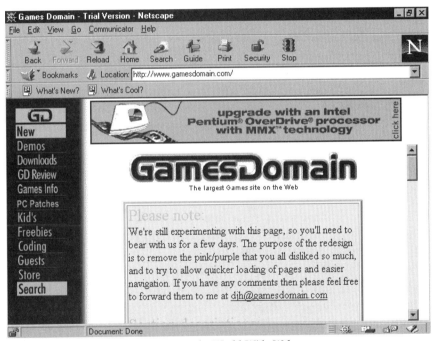

Figure 1-9: The Games Domain site on the World Wide Web.

By the way, the accessibility of all these recreational sites is one of the reasons why your office intranet may not be connected to the Net!

OK, so there's all this great stuff out there and exciting things you can do with your computer. How do you get to it? Let's take a quick look at how information actually moves from one place to another on an intranet or the Net. A basic understanding of *addressing* will make it easier for you to find the servers or sites with information you're interested in.

Netcasting

One of the most exciting new ways of working with Internet and intranet information is known alternatively as *netcasting*, *webcasting*, or *push technology*. Netcaster is the Communicator component that gives you access to this new technology, and I cover it thoroughly in Chapter 4. But it may be helpful to get a brief overview in advance.

With netcasting, you subscribe to various *channels* that provide you with information. A channel is simply a collection of media-rich information stored on your computer and displayed on your desktop. You receive this information by *subscribing* to a channel. Once you subscribe, the information is downloaded to your machine. You may choose to have the material updated at regularly scheduled intervals. For instance, you can configure a weather channel to update itself a couple of times a day, or a stock ticker to update itself with new financial information every twenty minutes.

A channel may be full of text, graphics, and links, or it may be written in Java (see Chapter 10) and provide a completely novel user interface. Of course it can include sound, animation, video, and interactive elements that are limited only by the imagination of the content provider. And since these elements are stored locally, they display or play immediately. You avoid the "click-and-wait" procedure so common on today's crowded Internet.

What kinds of channels will you be able to access preview using Netcaster? Here are a few of the exciting possibilities:

- Online magazines delivered directly to your screen on a regular basis.

- Entertainment channels that include not only articles, listings, and multimedia previews, but interactive games and educational activities for children. Imagine a puzzle-of-the-day channel.

- Promotional channels that keep you updated on the latest product releases, add-ons, or technical information. You could even subscribe to a channel that automatically upgrades a piece of software as new versions become available.

- Informational channels that provide up-to-the-minute news in your area of interest, whether it's politics, finance, or sports.

In short, netcasting provides you with the same rich variety of information as the Web itself, but it's presented in a way that doesn't require you to explicitly seek it out. Once you subscribe to a channel, updated information comes directly to you at intervals you specify.

Internet & Intranet Addressing

The whole basis of intranets and the Internet is that machines are constantly sending messages to other machines. Some of these messages are software commands, some are requests for data, and some include the human-readable data itself. Obviously there has to be a way for information to get to the proper recipient, and so the underlying suite of communications protocols includes an addressing scheme. At the heart of the addressing scheme is the concept of domains.

Domains & Domain Names

By *domain*, we simply mean where a computer resides. For instance, a specific computer at the University of Missouri is in the *missouri* domain, which in turn is within the top-level *edu* domain, the domain that includes all Internet-connected colleges and universities in the United States. The complete domain name of a machine called *bigcat* at the University of Missouri, for instance, would be *bigcat.missouri.edu*. No other machine anywhere on the Internet has the same domain name. Every name is registered with a special Internet organization to ensure that it is unique.

I have an e-mail account on vmedia.com. To reach my account, all you need to do is add my username to the domain name. My username is pjames, so my full e-mail address is *pjames@vmedia.com*. If you wanted to visit the Web pages at vmedia.com, however, you'd simply tell Netscape Communicator to get a document from the Web server machine at that site, www.vmedia.com.

But suppose you're on an intranet. It works the same way on a private network as it does on the public Net. Every server has a particular name. If I run a company called Geek Books R Us, for instance, my Web server machine might be called www.geekbooks.com. The only difference is that people from the world outside my company are not be able to reach this server—unless I connect my intranet to the Net.

At first these addresses may look impossible to pronounce, but pronunciation conventions have developed. Pjames@vmedia.com is pronounced "p-james at v-media dot com," and ftp.vmedia. com is pronounced "f-t-p dot v-media dot com." Of course usernames don't have to be as simple as mine. If your LAN administratoror Internet service provider lets you choose your own name, you might want to be zzzx_12_qwerty@serviceprovider.com. Then again you might not. Keep in mind that people who send you e-mail need to remember your address.

Fortunately, the Internet almost never cares about case-sensitivity in e-mail addresses. In all cases the domain names are case-insensitive, and generally the actual e-mail Ids are as well. You can send a message to pJaMeS@vMEdiA.cOm, and I will still get it. But most experienced Internet users stick with lowercase when typing addresses—it's just easier. If you use both uppercase and lowercase letters in your addresses, some of the more experienced users will chuckle at the newcomer, more often called a "clueless newbie."

TIP

Even though Internet e-mail addresses usually aren't case-sensitive, remember that pathnames for URLs for Web pages and FTP directories are!

As I mentioned earlier, the last part of a domain name address is called the top-level domain. There are six standardized domain names currently in use, corresponding to types of organizations as shown in Table 1-1.

Domain	Type of Organization
com	Commercial entity
edu	Educational institution
gov	Government agency or department
mil	Military organization
net	Network resource
org	Other type of organization, usually a not-for-profit

Table 1-1: Top-level domains.

TIP

The IAHC, the committee in charge of these naming standards, recently added seven more top-level names to the list. These may also be used by anyone register-ing a new name:

.firm	*for businesses*
.store	*for online stores*
.web	*for Web-related organizations*
.arts	*for cultural and entertainment organizations*
.rec	*for organizations emphasizing recreational activities*
.info	*for organizations that provide information*
.nom	*for individuals who want to be identified as such*

In addition, Internet sites outside the United States are identified by a special two-letter, top-level domain name. For instance, a computer in Finland would have a top-level domain name of *fi*, and a computer in Germany would have a top-level domain name of *de* (for Deutschland). As you start cruising around the Net, you will run into these foreign domain names on a daily basis. There is even a two-letter designation for the United States (you guessed it, *us*), but it is rarely used since the six "organization type" names are more descriptive.

IP Addresses

Pretty simple, isn't it? Well, luckily for those of us who make a living explaining such things, it's not *quite* that simple. Domain name addresses are really easy-to-remember translations of the kind of addresses intranets and the Internet really uses, numeric *IP addresses*. IP stands for "Internet Protocol." You may have read about IP in the earlier sidebar, "Under the Hood: TCP/IP." For now, it's only important to understand the difference between the two kinds of addresses.

If you're my age, you may remember when phone numbers always began with the name of the exchange, as in "Murray Hill Seven, Five Five Five Five." The Murray Hill Seven exchange, which you dialed as MU7, corresponded with a particular geographic area, in this case the Murray Hill neighborhood of Manhattan. But in fact your telephone didn't really care about Murray Hill, it simply transmitted down the line the fact that you had dialed the *numbers* 687. If you think of Murray Hill Seven as roughly equivalent to a top-level domain name, you can think of 687 as the top-level portion of the *IP address*.

Here's the point: an IP address is not only the numeric equivalent of a domain name, it's the form of address that really matters to the computers, routers, and other equipment that comprise an intranet or the Net. You could get by without all the friendly understandable domain names, but not without cold, hard IP addresses. And so when you use a domain name address to attach to some resource such as a Web server, a special *Domain Name Service* (DNS) on your intranet or on the Net looks up the name and replaces it with an IP number. And as long as you're connected to an intranet or to the Net, you have your own IP address so that remote machines know how to send you the information you request.

IP addresses are structured very much like domain name addresses, but backwards. They consist of four numbers, each less than 256, separated by periods. The rightmost number specifies the actual machine, while those to the left identify the network and subnetwork. When I link to the Net via my PPP account with the service provider ThoughtPort, for instance, my IP address is 199.171.225.100. The "100" part of that address is my actual computer on the ThoughtPort network.

URLs

Besides e-mail addresses, domain names, and IP addresses, there's just one other kind of address you need to know about: the *Uniform Resource Locator*, or *URL*. URLs are like signs pointing to hypermedia documents on the Web. They provide the protocol and addressing information that Netscape Communicator or another browser uses to connect to the target document, whether it's on the Internet or your local intranet. The first part of a URL specifies the type of data or the protocol necessary to retrieve the data, the second part is the domain name that specifies the server where the information is located, and the optional third part specifies the pathname or directory where that data is stored. For instance, the URL http://www.vmedia.com/vvc/index.html tells Netscape Communicator to retrieve the file index.html from the vvc directory at www.vmedia.com (Ventana Online's Web server) using the HTTP protocol, the protocol for Web pages. (See Chapter 8 for information about accessing other kinds of resources available via other major Internet protocols, including FTP and Gopher.)

URLs are used in several different ways. First of all, they are part of the hidden information that tells your browser to jump to a remote document when you click on a link. In the middle of a Web document, for instance, the above URL might be used like this:

```
<a href="http://www.vmedia.com/vvc/index.html">Click here to go to the
Ventana Online home page!</a>
```

Only "Click here to go to the Ventana Online home page!" appears on the screen; all that other stuff is not visible, but Netscape Communicator reads it out of the file and uses the information as directions to a target document. You can also type or paste URLs directly into the location field of Netscape Communicator to jump immediately to a remote document. And finally, you can add URLs to Netscape Communicator's configurable toolbar or as "bookmarks" for easy access at some later time.

What's HTML?

All Web pages that contain text are written in a language called HTML, which stands for HyperText Markup Language. HTML is simply ordinary ASCII text with embedded codes (usually referred to as *tags*) that represent instructions for displaying the text or for linking to other Web documents. For example, *<I>italic</I>* or *<B>bold</B>* in a Web document tells the browser to display the phrase "italic or bold" with the word "italic" in italics and the word "bold" in boldface. It is important to understand that HTML does *not* indicate exactly what the resulting text should look like—that is up to the browser software. On a system that can't display true italic or bold fonts the browser might just display the words in a different color. This makes HTML a universal language, ensuring that Web pages are displayable in one way or another on any machine or operating platform that can run a Web browser.

Figure 1-10 shows a typical Web page, and Figure 1-11 shows what some of the HTML source for it looks like.

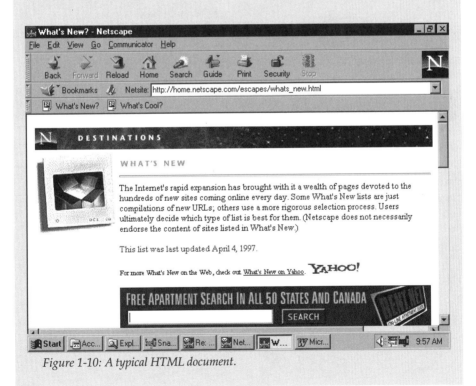

Figure 1-10: A typical HTML document.

```
Source of: http://home.netscape.com/escapes/whats_new.html - Netscape

<HTML>
<HEAD>
<TITLE>What's New?</TITLE>
<SCRIPT LANGUAGE="JavaScript">

<!--
function Go_Dest(form)
{   var
http='http://home.netscape.com'+form.destinations[form.destinations.selected]
    top.location.href=http;
        return;
}



//-->

</SCRIPT>
</HEAD>
<BODY BGCOLOR="#FFFFFF" TEXT="#000000">
<TABLE BORDER="0" WIDTH="600" CELLPADDING="2">
<TR>
<TD HEIGHT="2" WIDTH="120"><IMG SRC="/escapes/images/white.gif" ALIGN=MIDDLE
<TD HEIGHT="2" WIDTH="120"><IMG SRC="/escapes/images/white.gif" ALIGN=MIDDLE
<TD HEIGHT="2" WIDTH="120"><IMG SRC="/escapes/images/white.gif" ALIGN=MIDDLE
<TD HEIGHT="2" WIDTH="120"><IMG SRC="/escapes/images/white.gif" ALIGN=MIDDLE
<TD HEIGHT="2" WIDTH="120"><IMG SRC="/escapes/images/white.gif" ALIGN=MIDDLE
</TR>
```

Figure 1-11: The HTML source, viewed using the Document Source command from Communicator's View menu.

HTML is an evolving language. No sooner had version 1 of the HTML specification been released than work began on a level 2 that would contain more advanced text-handling capabilities. HTML 2.0, completed and approved by a standards body known as the Internet Engineering Task Force (IETF), also includes support for interactive forms and image maps. Interactive forms let you enter data on the screen that is then sent to the host site, and image maps let you link to other documents by clicking on "hot spots" within an image.

The latest proposed upgrade to HTML is HTML 3.2. Netscape has been at the forefront of the collaborative design process in proposing *and implementing* new features for HTML 3.2. Many of these exciting new extensions are covered later in this book.

> **TIP**
>
> *Files that contain HTML tags are known as HTML files, and they always have an extension of either .HTM or .HTML. On UNIX and other systems that support long filenames, the extension is .HTML; on DOS-based systems, it's .HTM. This extension tells the browser it is dealing with a hypertext document rather than some other type of hypermedia document, such as an image or audio file.*

Some Pointers on Using the Net

We've talked about intranets, the Internet, the Web, and some of the technical underpinnings of all this new communications technology. We're going to end the chapter by focusing on something a little different: *you*.

The Internet is more than a collection of wires and computers; it's a culture. And like any culture it has its own unwritten rules of behavior, its own *shoulds* and *shouldn't*s and even outright taboos. But unless you're very young and come from a very geeky family, your mother never taught you any of this. Not to worry, I can probably keep you from getting into serious trouble.

There aren't many laws or cops on the Net, and the best way to keep it that way is with generosity, sensitivity, and common sense. The online culture has developed its own guidelines, and before actually exploring the Net it's a good idea to get familiar with some of these rules of the road. Here are just a few that will make your Internet travels more efficient and pleasant. I think these guidelines are so important that I try to include the following subsections in every book I write. (Sure took that Harlequin Romance editor by surprise!)

Avoid Traffic Jams

They stopped calling it a superhighway because sometimes it's more like driving through Bombay. Every day several thousand clueless newbies start exploring the Net. (Don't worry, you're not one of them: you bought this book!) Servers can support only a certain number of clients, and routers start to seem "sludgy" when they're called upon to transfer packets of data for thousands of users. Certain sites are practically impossible to reach, especially those distributing the latest free software or pictures of naked people.

To avoid traffic jams, and to avoid creating them, follow these simple rules of thumb:

- Connect during nonbusiness hours whenever possible. (Since this is a world-wide system, remember to compensate for different time zones!)

- If you're unable to connect with a particular server—for instance, if you get an "unable to connect with host" message when you try to access a Web page—wait a while before trying again. Bombarding the Net with unsuccessful connection attempts only adds to the problem.

- Use what are known as "mirror sites" for downloading files via FTP. Since some of the large anonymous FTP servers are so busy, a number of hosts sprinkled around the Net have been kind enough to "mirror" the exact contents, keeping their file lists completely up-to-date. The original site usually informs you about these mirror sites in its sign-on message. FTPing to a mirror is just like FTPing to the original host, except that you'll be out of the heaviest traffic.

- Find the closest site that has what you need. Don't Telnet to Timbuktu if you can get the same information by FTPing to Peoria. When you access far-flung reaches of the globe, your packets of information must travel point-to-point through dozens of locations.

- Don't create unnecessary message traffic. This is especially important in Usenet newsgroups (see Chapter 6). If you have something to say, by all means say it, but the Net provides a useful venue for practicing eloquent restraint. Don't send the text of your Great American Novel to the whole world, simply tell users where they can find it. And remember that even a short message like "Ha ha ha!" expands to several hundred bytes of control and addressing information, and may require the services of dozens of routers. Sending a message like this may look free to you, but it definitely costs the community as a whole.

- Follow any instructions that are given to you for logging off a particular site. If you don't follow the proper procedures for logging off from a Telnet site, for instance, a connection may be left open, perhaps making it difficult for others to log in.

Understand Acceptable Use

Certain networks on the Internet, including the large backbones, have published standards for information that may be transmitted via their equipment and cabling. When you sign up with an access provider, you are mailed or e-mailed a document that outlines the acceptable use policies in effect for the networks used by that provider. You must adhere to these strictly! Besides the obvious prohibitions against using the network for trafficking in drugs and bombs, these policies usually make clear what kinds of commercial activities are permitted.

Here's a typical list of prohibitions from an acceptable use policy statement:

- Users may not transmit any data or programs that cause disruption of service for others.

- Users may not transmit any form of computer worm or virus.

- Users must not use the network to violate intellectual property laws by distributing copyrighted or otherwise protected information, documents, or software programs.

- Users may not distribute unsolicited advertising.

But the written policies are really only the beginning of acceptable use. Common sense and respect for others should be your guiding principles when communicating over the Net. The Internet is not a good place for personal attacks and threats, as they frequently escalate into full-blown "flame wars" that waste resources. It's not always a good place for challenging local community ethical standards, either, since various factions are looking for excuses to impose more stringent regulation. Make sure that you post your materials at the appropriate sites.

Respect & Protect Privacy

Privacy is the big hot topic on the Internet today. To what extent should government agencies have access to private Internet communications? Should the content of public sites be regulated? Should there be safeguards against commercial entities adding you to electronic mailing lists? It remains to be seen how all of these issues will be decided, but it is very clear that the Internet community expects its citizens to respect the privacy of other individuals. Nothing will get you in more trouble than trying to "hack" somebody else's account, trying to take advantage of technological loopholes to access private data, or publishing confidential information.

At the same time, you should realize that in a culture as large as the Internet there are going to be occasional problems with privacy, and you should do what you can to protect yourself and others by keeping your accounts secure:

- Always use good, specific passwords; your spouse's name or the name of a *Star Trek* character just won't cut it.

- Change your passwords often.

- Always inform the appropriate network administrators when you think there may have been a security breach.

- If you're worried about particularly sensitive information, make sure that you're conducting communicating with secure Web servers that support the SSL protocol built into Communicator (see Chapter 12).

- And just in case, don't make any information available on the Net if you wouldn't want it to appear on the front page of *USA Today* or your home-town newspaper. Yes, I learned this lesson the hard way once, but we're not going to talk about that!

Be Willing to Ask for Help

In my experience, the most annoying Internet—and intranet—users are those who "know just enough to be dangerous." They go crashing around leaving a mess for others to clean up. Look, the Internet is full of *real* experts; if you don't know how to do something, just ask. You'll be amazed at how helpful and friendly the seasoned Net veterans can be. I've asked some pretty stupid questions on the Internet, but only rarely have I received a snooty response.

Of course, before asking questions of other users, you should look for available resources such as help files or appropriate technical documents. The Netscape site, which appears as soon as you load Netscape Communicator if you're attached to the Net, is full of useful information. Many Usenet newsgroups even maintain files of frequently asked questions, called FAQs. But if you've exhausted other resources, there's nothing wrong with a plea for help.

Don't Be Afraid to Explore

On the other hand, one of the most valuable ways to learn how to use the Net is simply to explore. As long as you're not trying to do something too tricky or arcane, common sense will usually get you where you want to go. Half the fun of the Internet is wandering around, guided as much by your instincts as by a conscious plan. Certainly you can do no harm by getting out there and seeing the world!

Moving On

What makes Netscape Communicator the premier product for accessing both the Internet and office intranets is not its slick interface, or its availability on a variety of platforms, or its solid reliability, or even its early support of forward-looking Web features. What really sets this product apart is that it lets you do *everything you need to do on the Net or on your intranet*. In addition to browsing the Web, you can use Netscape Communicator to send and receive e-mail; to read and post newsgroup messages; to gather files; to collaborate with coworkers; and to explore a wide range of specialized Internet services. In the following chapters, we'll be exploring all aspects of this versatility using a hands-on approach, and pretty soon *you'll* be the one that answers your friends' Netscape questions.

We'll start in Chapter 2 with a quick overview of Communicator, and then in Chapter 3 we'll move on to Netscape Navigator 4, the Web browser itself.

Introducing Communicator 4

In Chapter 1 you learned about intranets and the Internet, as well as some of the services and resources they offer. Now it's time to get down to business and start using Netscape Communicator to really *experience* what's available. First, though, let's take a look at what you need before you run Communicator.

Requirements

Before you install Netscape Communicator you should make sure you have the following:

- A 386sx or better PC with at least 16 Megabytes of RAM and running Windows 3.1, Windows 95, or Windows NT.
- At least 20 Megabytes of free space on your hard drive.
- A CD-ROM drive to install the software from CD.
- If you want to use Communicator's Conference component, a 486 or better PC, a sound card, speakers, and a microphone. Though any sound card will work; one that offers full-duplex operation is preferable.
- A direct (hard-wired) connection to an intranet or to the Internet, or a dial-up SLIP or PPP connection to an intranet or the Internet.

If you're directly connected to an intranet or the Internet via an office network, that's probably all you need. Of course your network administrator may have to configure your system for proper access, but once that has been accomplished, you are ready to install and run Communicator.

But if, for instance, you want to use a dial-up SLIP or PPP connection from home, this next section is for you.

Requirements for SLIP & PPP Connections to the Net

Obviously, if you want to connect to the Internet via a phone line, you need a phone line! There are a few additional requirements:

- A modem with a data rate of at least 14.4 Kbps (known as a "14.4 modem"). A faster modem, with a rate of at least 28.8 Kbps, is preferable, especially for browsing the World Wide Web. If you want to use ISDN, you need a special ISDN card or external ISDN adapter.

- A SLIP or PPP account with an ISP (Internet Service Provider). One of the best ways to find an ISP is through Netscape's ISP Select page at http://home.netscape.com/assist/isp_select/. Yes, I know, it's a chicken/egg situation—how do you access that page if you don't already have an ISP? Fortunately, these days you can often find a friend who is already on the Net and will help you get to the ISP Select page. Or maybe you can check it out at work. If not, there are lots of national ISPs advertised in computer and Internet magazines, and your local yellow pages may list some ISPs in your area. If you purchased your computer recently, it may even have come with pre-installed startup packages from a few ISPs such as AT&T WorldNet.

> **TIP**
>
> *If you want to connect to the Net via ISDN, both your local phone company and your Internet Service Provider must support the technology. Often your phone company can help you find an ISP that supports ISDN. Make sure to research this carefully before buying any ISDN hardware!*

- Dial-up software for connecting to your ISP. Windows 95 and Windows NT have this software built right in, and your ISP will tell you how to configure it. If you're running Windows 3.1, you need some supplemental software, but this is usually distributed by the ISP you choose, often fully configured. If your ISP seems unwilling or unable to help you get set up properly, find a new ISP!

OK, now that you know what you need, it's time for an overview of Communicator itself.

What *Is* Communicator 4?

Netscape Communicator is not really a single program; rather, it is a tightly integrated software *suite*. And what the heck does that mean? It means it's a group of programs, each with a specialized purpose, designed to work together cooperatively. For example, if the software component that browses the Web encounters a link that lets you send e-mail, it automatically launches the e-mail component. In Figure 2-1, the large circle is Communicator as a whole. The arrows that connect the individual components show how information may be shared cooperatively among the components so that you can move from task to task without ever needing to launch a separate application.

Figure 2-1: Communicator 4 and its components.

In subsequent chapters you'll learn about the various parts of the Communicator suite one at a time, working through step-by-step procedures that show you how to take advantage of highly specialized features. But to really harness Communicator's power, you need to get a clear picture of how it all fits together. There won't be many detailed procedures in this chapter; I'll just show you some features that affect operation of the suite as a whole and introduce you to some terminology so that everything makes sense when we get down to the nitty-gritty. But first, let's fire the program up!

Startup Options

Technically, you cannot really launch Communicator—you can only launch one of its components. So when you double-click the Communicator icon, how does the program know which of its components you really want?

By default, Communicator launches its Web browser component, Navigator 4, when you click the Communicator icon. But you can change this behavior if you want. Once you are in any one of the component programs, select Preferences from the Edit menu. A Preferences dialog box appears. From the Category list at the left, select Appearance if it's not already selected. The Appearance options on the right include four check boxes that let you choose to launch Navigator, Netcaster, Messenger, Collabra Discussions, or Page Composer at startup. You can select any combination of these four—Communicator has no problem with launching several of its components at once. Whatever you do, though, don't try *un*checking all four boxes—you may never get back to this dialog box again!

I'll include some more information on the Appearance preferences in Chapter 3.

Starting Communicator 4 the First Time

The first time you launch Communicator after installing it, it runs a Wizard that lets you enter some essential configuration information. In fact, it sets up what's known as a *user profile* for you—a set of configuration options that's specific to your individual use of the suite as a whole and its various components. For instance, you can enter your e-mail address, the address of your discussion groups server, etc. etc. Most of this is information you've probably received already from your network administrator or ISP, but if you don't know all these details right now, don't worry about it. You can add or change any of the configuration options later on, and the chapters on the individual components will show you how.

But if you do want to enter everything correctly right away, here's the information you need:

- Your e-mail address.

- The username you use to access your e-mail server. If you use your ISP for e-mail, this is usually the same as your regular SLIP/PPP login name.

- Your e-mail password.

- The address of the server you use to send e-mail, which is also known as the outgoing mail server or SMTP server.

- The address of the server you use to receive e-mail (incoming mail server). This is usually the same as your outgoing mail server.

- Whether your incoming mail server uses POP3 or IMAP4 protocol (if you're using a commercial ISP it's probably POP3).

- The address of your discussion groups server.

OK, let's get busy:

1. Double-click the Communicator icon on your desktop. The Profile Setup Wizard appears, as shown in Figure 2-2. To open the Profile Setup Wizard after you have run Communicator for the first time, double-click the Profile Manager. If you are already running Communicator you will be asked to exit in order for the Wizard to run.

Figure 2-2: The Profile Setup Wizard.

2. Click Next. The second page of the Wizard appears, as shown in Figure 2-3.

Figure 2-3: The second page of the Profile Setup Wizard.

3. Fill in your name. If you know your e-mail address, fill that in as well. Click Next again.

4. In the Profile Name field that appears on the next page, type in a name for your profile. Typically this will be your own name or a simple nickname (my user profile is "phil"). Don't bother changing the directory in the bottom edit box unless you plan to set up multiple user profiles and want a separate directory for each user. (See the section later in this chapter called "Adding User Profiles to Communicator 4.")

5. Click Next. The Mail and Discussion Groups Wizard appears, as shown in Figure 2-4.

6. Enter your name, your e-mail address, and the domain name address of your outgoing e-mail (SMTP) server.

TIP

Don't worry if you don't know the address of your SMTP server—or even what one is! E-mail configuration is covered in depth in Chapter 5. The information is usually provided by your network administrator or Internet Service Provider, but if you don't have all the answers now you'll have the opportunity to enter the configuration information later. Just leave any fields blank and click Next.

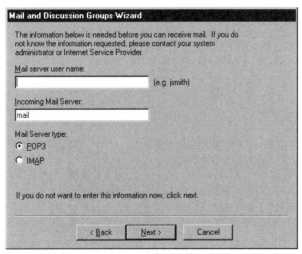

Figure 2-4: The Mail and Discussion Groups Wizard.

7. After entering the information, click Next. The second page of the Mail and Discussion Groups Wizard appears, as shown in Figure 2-5.

Figure 2-5: The second page of the Mail and Discussion Groups Wizard.

8. Enter your username for your incoming mail server. Often, this is the same as your regular login name for your SLIP/PPP account. Then fill in the domain name address for your incoming mail server. (Typically, this will

be the same address as your *outgoing* e-mail server.) Finally, select one of the option buttons depending on whether your e-mail server uses the POP3 protocol or the IMAP protocol for mail retrieval. Most ISPs use POP3.

TIP

Again, ask your ISP or system administrator for this information. If you can't get it or simply don't understand, just click Next and wait for Chapter 5.

9. Click Next. On the final page of the Mail and Discussion Groups Wizard, enter the address of your discussion group server. If you're not planning on using Communicator's discussion groups feature or if you don't know the correct address, just leave the field alone.

TIP

For more information on discussion groups, please see Chapter 6.

10. When you have finished entering information in the Wizard, click Finish. Netscape Navigator 4, the Web browser component of Communicator, appears on your screen.

As I mentioned before, you can configure Communicator so that it displays other components instead of or in addition to Navigator 4 when you launch it. Once you are in any one of the component programs, select Preferences from the Edit menu. A Preferences dialog box appears. From the Category list at the left, select Appearance if it's not already selected. The Appearance options on the right include four check boxes that let you choose to launch Navigator, Netcaster, Messenger, Collabra Discussions, or Page Composer at startup. You can select any combination of these four.

A Quick Look Around

Now that you've got the software up and running, let's take a quick look around. The next few sections of this chapter give a brief overview of some of Communicator's interface features that make it a fully integrated suite.

The Component Bar

Communicator integrates its components in a variety of interesting ways, but the most basic is via a special Component Bar, as shown below in Figure 2-6.

Figure 2-6: The Component Bar.

The Component Bar appears on your desktop whenever you launch one of Communicator's components. Let's say you want to send a quick e-mail message, so you start up Messenger by double-clicking the Netscape Messenger icon in your Netscape folder. When Netscape Messenger appears, the Component Bar appears right along with it.

And what can you do with the Component Bar? You use it to launch any of the following Communicator components: the Navigator Browser, the Messenger e-mail Inbox, Collabra discussion groups, or Composer. Simply click the appropriate icon and the associated component appears immediately. Or if the component is already loaded, clicking its icon in the Component Bar will put the focus on its window, letting you continue your work without having to search for the window you need.

TIP

Two Communicator components are not included in the Component Bar: Netcaster and Conference. To access either of these, simply double-click the appropriate icon in the Netscape Communicator folder. You can also select Netcaster or Conference from the Communicator menu item in any Communicator component.

By default, the Component Bar is what is known as a *floating* or unanchored control. That means you can move it anywhere on your desktop, just like a program window. Simply click and drag its title bar. And you can make it either horizontal or vertical: just right-click on it and choose the orientation you want from the context menu that pops up.

But what happens if you click the Component Bar's Close button? If you're running the software now, give it a try. At first it might seem that the Component Bar has disappeared. But if you hunt around a little, you'll find that it has simply been transformed into a smaller *anchored* control, one that doesn't float but sits at the right hand side of the status line in any Communicator component that is currently running. Take a look at Figure 2-7.

Figure 2-7: The Component Bar as an anchored control within a Communicator program.

The Component Bar looks different when it's anchored in a status line, but it works exactly the same way. Click any one of the icons within it and you're transported to the associated component.

Once you've turned the Component Bar into an anchored control, it stays that way until you click the maximize icon (the left-most icon on the bar, which looks like a gray page with horizontal lines). It appears as an anchored control in every new Communicator component you launch, and it even persists in this form after you close down all Communicator components and re-launch. Similarly, once you click the maximize icon it maintains its "floating" form until you click its Close button.

TIP

> *Why choose one or the other of the Component Bar's formats? A floating control is useful if you keep your Communicator components minimized, so that an anchored control would not always be available to you. An anchored control in the status line, on the other hand, saves you the trouble of finding a floating control on a busy screen if you're already working in a Communicator component.*

The Communicator 4 Menu

Netscape has provided another method of moving among the different Communicator components. Every Communicator component includes a Communicator item on its menu bar. When you click the Communicator item, you'll see something like the menu shown in Figure 2-8.

Figure 2-8: The Communicator menu in Navigator.

As you can see, the choices at the top of this menu let you access the other Communicator components with a simple click of the mouse. And if you prefer using the keyboard, Ctrl+1, Ctrl+2, Ctrl+3, etc. will move you around from component to component.

Shared Resources in Communicator 4

Remember how I called Communicator a *tightly integrated* software suite? Besides obvious interface elements such as the menus and the Component Bar, there are a number of other manifestations of this tight integration. Several important features, for instance, are used by more than one component.

The Address Book

Let's say you and your significant other have the same friends. (Unlikely, I know.) Do you really need two address books? No, you can each use a single one when you need to make a call or address a letter.

Similarly, Communicator components that require address information don't all need to have separate electronic address books. Instead, there is a single Communicator Address Book that may be accessed by all components when needed. That saves you from having to enter data more than once.

Figure 2-9 shows the Communicator Address Book.

TIP

You access the Address Book by choosing Address Book from the Communicator menu, or simply by pressing Ctrl+Shift+2.

Figure 2-9: The Address Book.

Notice that there is a New Msg button *and* a Call button. Click the New Msg button and you can send an e-mail message to an individual using Messenger; click the Call button and you can initiate voice communications with the same individual using Conference. The Address Book even lets you enter supplemental information that is not required by any of the Communicator components, making it the only electronic rolodex you need. And if you're on an intranet, you can import your company's address book right into your own Address Book.

The Message Center

Communicator's Message Center is another example of a shared resource; in this case one that's used by both Messenger and Collabra. Let's take a look at it in Figure 2-10.

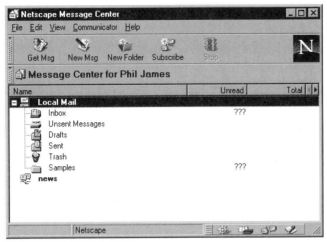

Figure 2-10: The Message Center.

TIP

You can access the Message Center by choosing Message Center from the Communicator menu, or simply by pressing Ctrl+Shift+1. You can also access it by clicking the Message Center button at the right side of the Messenger or Discussion Group window, just below the large Netscape icon.

The Message Center is a highly organized storage system for all your e-mail messages *and* all your discussion group (newsgroup) messages. At the top of the window you can see the mail category, and below it several folders in which e-mail messages are filed away. But below the last of the e-mail folders there is the name of a discussion group server, secnews.netscape.com, and arranged hierarchically under that are several discussion groups available on that server.

Figure 2-11 shows what you get if you double-click one of the mail folders, in this case the Inbox. As you can see, my Inbox folder contains a list of messages I've received via e-mail.

Figure 2-11: My Inbox e-mail folder, accessed from the Message Center.

Now let's double-click one of the discussion groups, for instance netscape.devs-javascript. This time I get a list of messages that have been posted to that particular discussion group, as shown in Figure 2-12.

Thus the Message Center provides a sort of headquarters for all message-related activity in Communicator. Not only that, but as you can see from the last two illustrations, the user interface for accessing your e-mail is very similar to the user interface for accessing discussion groups. You don't have to learn a new set of keystrokes or mouse clicks to move from one Communicator component to another.

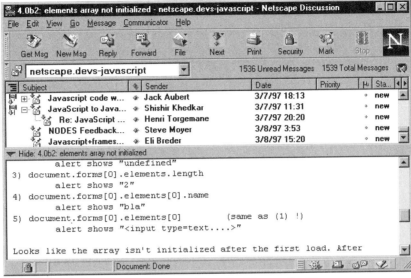

Figure 2-12: A discussion group accessed from the Message Center.

Security

Security is yet another area that is shared among the various Communicator components. Many of Communicator's windows include a Security button. Click it and Figure 2-13 shows what you get.

As you may be able to tell from the long list of security features on the left, this is a window that is shared by all the Communicator components, and that provides access to security features in Navigator and Netcaster as well as in e-mail and discussion groups. Again, there is no need to learn separate interfaces for the different components.

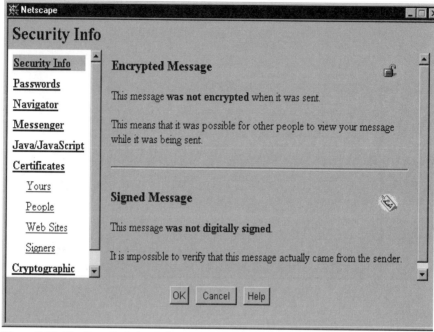

Figure 2-13: The Security Info window.

Preferences

Communicator is a very full-featured suite, and so there are many configuration options. Don't worry, most of these you never need to touch. The most important ones are set up for you automatically when you install the program, and other very specialized ones provide entertainment for the propeller-heads among us. Fortunately, Netscape has provided unified access to the preferences for all Communicator components, as shown in Figure 2-14. These are all available by choosing Preferences from the Edit menu of a Communicator component.

The designers at Netscape have grouped these settings very sensibly, but until you get used to this integrated way of working, some of the groupings may throw you off. The preferences are not divided up by component, but organized according to the *type* of option they affect. For instance, on one preferences page you might find a color setting that affects the backgrounds of both outgoing e-mail messages and new Web pages you create; on another page you might find an option that affects the network performance of several different components. You have to get used to thinking of Communicator as more than the sum of its parts.

Figure 2-14: The Communicator preferences.

OK, I've been talking for a while about *integration*, and that is one of the features that sets Communicator apart from simple Web browsers and even from other Internet suites. Now we'll move on to a concept that may seem alien at first and which affects the entire Communicator suite, not just individual components. You already know about user profiles, but did you know that Communicator lets you set up more than one of them?

Adding User Profiles to Communicator 4

Let's say you're using Communicator at home, and everyone in your family uses it a little differently. Your son likes to hear a beep whenever new e-mail arrives on your mail server (see Chapter 5), but you don't. Your daughter likes a visual background composed of hundreds of little pictures of LL Cool J, but you prefer Winona Ryder. Your visiting cousin has set up a Wayne Newton site as the home page that comes up when you launch Navigator; you don't want to be rude, but you're much more into Beck and get pretty embarrassed when your friends keep seeing Wayne on your screen.

Well, the Netscape programmers had your domestic harmony in mind when they designed Communicator. Communicator allows several different user profiles, each of which may have its own bookmarks (see Chapter 3), mail and discussion settings (see Chapter 5), preferences, and message folders that are completely separate from the others. It's almost like running the program on completely separate machines.

When you have several different user profiles configured for Communicator, Figure 2-15 shows what you'll see after launching any one of the components.

Figure 2-15: The Profile Manager dialog box.

At this point simply choose the correct profile and click Start Communicator.

As you saw earlier, when you first start Communicator it creates a single profile for you based on your responses to questions it asks, your name and e-mail address, for instance. So how do you create an additional profile in Communicator? Just follow the steps outlined below:

1. In the Netscape Communicator folder, double-click the Utilities sub-folder.

2. In the Utilities folder that opens up, double-click User Profile Manager. Then click New to create a new profile. The Profile Setup Wizard appears, just as it did when you first launched Communicator. If you are currently running Communicator you will be asked to exit in order for the Wizard to run.

3. Work through the questions in the Profile Setup Wizard, this time entering information that's appropriate to this new user.

TIP

If you are creating an alternate profile for your own use, make sure to fill in your actual name and e-mail address again, even if you have already configured these in your main user profile.

4. In the Profile Name that appears in the Wizard, type in a name for your alternate profile. If you want a separate directory for each user, change the name of the directory in the bottom edit box of this page.

5. When you have finished entering information in the Wizard, click Finish. Communicator returns you to the Select a Profile dialog box, which now contains two profiles: your original one and the new one. You can now select from the list and click OK to launch Communicator.

Once you fire up a Communicator component using a new user profile, you can make whatever changes you want to the preferences, bookmarks, etc. without fear of screwing up any other profiles that exist. For simplicity's sake, I'll assume throughout the rest of this book that you have a single user profile—in other words, I won't mention the Select a Profile dialog box every time I outline a procedure that includes launching the program. But now you know how to use this powerful Communicator feature to help keep your intranet or Internet wanderings more organized.

Working With Communicator Online & Off-line

Unless you are hard-wired into an office network, your computer is probably not on an intranet or the Net at all times. If you have a dial-up SLIP or PPP connection that you pay for on an hourly basis, you may want to cut costs by minimizing your online time After you collect your latest e-mail messages, for instance, it is wasteful to leave your machine sitting on the Net while you read them all.

If you want to be online some of the time and off-line at other times, there are a couple of ways you can configure this: The first involves settings in your network dialer to control the amount of time your computer is idle before you are automatically disconnected. Note that your ISP may allow a maximum idle time before it initiates a disconnect. You cannot extend that time, of course, but you may wish to disconnect earlier.

■ If you are using Windows 95, the operating system can be configured so that your Dial-Up Networking connection is initiated whenever you launch Communicator or other Internet programs, and so that your connection hangs up if you are idle for a certain amount of time. To configure this, click Internet in Control Panel and check the Use AutoDial and Auto disconnect check boxes. You can also change the amount of idle time before Dial-Up Networking automatically terminates your connection.

■ If you are using Windows 3.1, the dialer provided by your ISP may include similar options for automatic connection and disconnection.

The second online and off-line control is in Communicator itself. Communicator has three modes for dealing with online and off-line operation in order to keep switching between them under your control. You'll learn more about them in Chapter 3, but see Figure 2-16 for a quick preview.

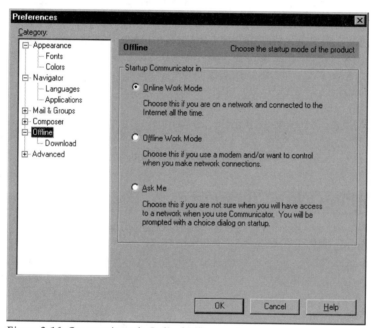

Figure 2-16: Communicator's Online/Offline modes.

To get to this preferences tab, select Preferences from the Edit menu of any Communicator component, then click the Offline category. The choices here are fairly self-explanatory. If you select Online Work Mode, Communicator assumes you are connected to the Net or to an intranet at all times. When you send an e-mail message, for instance, Messenger will try to try to deliver your message to the specified address. If you are not currently connected, it will huff and puff and finally return an error message.

What happens if you choose Offline Work Mode and try to send a message when you're not connected? In this case Messenger simply stores your message in a special Outbox folder, queued for delivery when you eventually go online.

And how about clicking the "Ask Me" choice? In this mode Communicator will ask you if you want to go online when you first start one of its components. If you say you do, your Dial-Up Networking connection will be initialized (assuming you're using Windows 95 or Windows NT) and you will be connected to the Net.

TIP

If you have configured any Netcaster channels to update themselves on a regular basis (see Chapter 4), Communicator goes online automatically to download the new information unless you're in Offline mode. If you're in Online mode but not connected to the Net, Communicator attempts to establish a connection.

Moving On

In this chapter I've tried to give you a brief overview of Communicator as a whole, highlighting a few features and terms that could be confusing if they weren't explained before discussing the individual components.

But by now I'm sure you're ready to dive right in. In the following chapters we'll go through step-by-step procedures that will get you fluent with all aspects of using Communicator for browsing the Web, subscribing to Netcaster channels, sending and receiving e-mail, participating in discussion groups, creating your own Web pages, and talking or collaborating in real-time with other Communicator users. Let's start with the most popular of all Net and intranet activities, Web browsing.

CHAPTER 3

Browsing & Beyond

Now that you have a basic understanding of what Netscape Communicator as a whole is all about, it's time to take a look around your office intranet or the Net itself. In this chapter, you'll be using Netscape Navigator 4, which is the Web browser component of Netscape Communicator. You'll learn some of the best ways to use this tool to navigate effectively and efficiently. For instance, you'll learn:

- How to move around a Web document, and how to get from one document to another.

- How to work with forms and other unique Web documents.

- How to use navigation aids such as the configurable toolbar, bookmarks, and desktop shortcuts.

- How to take advantage of exciting Web resources like Yahoo!, where you can easily search for specific topics and keywords on pages all around the world.

- How to optimize the software so that it works exactly the way you want it to.

Netscape Navigator 4 is so simple to use that you could actually master the program by trial and error. Recently I taught our neighbor's son how to use it by saying, "When you see some words that are underlined and in another color, click on them. That takes you to other places." After an hour he was whizzing around the Web like a seasoned veteran. Of course, he is seven years old and learns this kind of stuff a lot faster than those of us who were born before PCs and Nintendo. By the end of this chapter, you may not quite be a pre-adolescent Web-geek, but you'll know how to use the main features of Netscape Navigator 4 and how to find what you're looking for quickly and easily.

One quick note to avoid any confusion. Remember how I said that Netscape Navigator 4 is the Web browser component of Communicator? That means I'll be using the terms "browser window" and "Navigator 4 window" interchangeably. They're exactly the same thing.

OK, now let's get going.

The Browser Window

We'll start by taking a closer look at the Netscape Navigator 4 window:

1. Make sure you are connected to your intranet or the Internet, either directly or through a SLIP or PPP connection with your access provider.

   ■ In this tutorial I'll assume you're connected to the Internet itself, not just your corporate intranet. That way the text and illustrations will be correct for most readers. If you're not on the Internet, the principles discussed below will still be valid, but Navigator will not display the pages depicted in the illustrations. Your initial home page, for instance, will be the one set up by your network administrator rather than the Netscape home page shown below.

2. Double-click the Netscape Communicator icon to launch the program. If you have a SLIP or PPP account with an Internet Service Provider but are not currently connected, a dialog box may pop up asking you if you want to connect. Click Yes. The browser window appears, and the Netscape home page starts loading as shown in Figure 3-1.

Figure 3-1: The browser window with the Netscape home page.

TIP

Communicator can be configured so that instead of or in addition to the browser window, other Communicator components appear when you launch the program. You can make this change in the Appearance category, after selecting Preferences from the Edit menu.

■ By default, Netscape Navigator 4 uses the Netscape home page as your personal home page (in this context your *home page* is the document that loads automatically when you launch the program). Depending on the speed of your Internet connection and how busy the Netscape site is, this may take a few moments. Later in the chapter, you'll learn how you can select a different Web document as your home page in the sidebar "Changing Your Home Page." *Note: If you are on an intranet, your network administrator may already have changed your home page.*

- If you configured Communicator so that it requires a password, you will be asked to enter your password when you launch the program. For more about passwords, see Chapter 12.

Like any other Windows program, Navigator arranges many of its user-accessible features in a menu bar across the top of the window. I'll cover the commands available in the menus as they come up in using the program. But except for a few specialized commands, the menu bar is generally not the most efficient way to run the program. Let's take a look instead at the toolbars, the rows of buttons and icons just below the menu bar.

The Toolbars

I'm not talking about the floating gray thing at the top of your window with four icons on it. That's the Component Bar, and if you don't know what it does you haven't read Chapter 2. You can go back and check the section called "The Component Bar" if you want, but in brief: you click the icons in the floating gray thing to access Communicator's various modules such as your Mailbox, Collabra discussion groups, Composer, and of course Navigator. You can move the Component Bar around your screen, and you can shrink it and anchor it to the Navigator status line (at the bottom of the window) by closing it. Clicking the left-most icon in the minimized Component Bar makes it expand and "float" again, but you can use all its icons to access other Communicator components even when it's minimized.

But right now we're in Navigator 4, and the bars full of icon buttons just under the menu are the toolbars I'm talking about. In a toolbar you click individual buttons or icons to control different program functions. Toolbars are so convenient that Netscape threw in three of them!

The Navigator toolbars are a little fancier than your average toolbar. For instance, you can move them around. Try this: click on the top toolbar, the one with the Back and Forward buttons, and drag it down the screen an inch. Notice how it changes places with the middle toolbar, as shown in Figure 3-2.

Not only can you move these toolbars around, you can roll them up and down like window shades. To the left of each toolbar there's a small tab with a down arrow in it. Just click one of these tabs and watch what happens. Yep, if you click all three you end up with something like Figure 3-3.

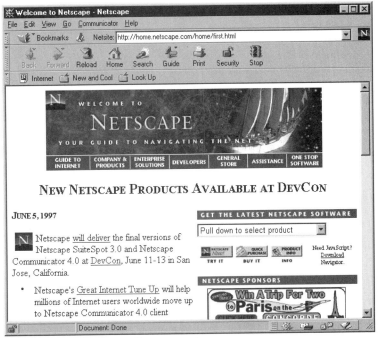

Figure 3-2: The top two toolbars reversed.

Figure 3-3: Navigator window with all three toolbars minimized.

To expand a minimized toolbar, simply click the up arrow.

> **TIP**
>
> *Don't want any toolbars at all? You can choose which ones you want to hide right in the View menu. This is a good way to maximize the amount of screen space available for displaying large Web documents or graphics.*

So you can understand what I'm talking about in the next couple of pages, I'm going to give these three toolbars names. I'm going to call the large toolbar with all the icons in it the Command Toolbar. The Toolbar that contains the Bookmarks and Location/Netsite features I'll call the Location Toolbar, and the toolbar that's at the bottom I'll call the Personal Toolbar. Each of these toolbars has a very different function, so let's go over the components of each one individually.

The Command Toolbar

The Command Toolbar gives you access to all of the Navigator functions via standard icon buttons. And here's what all these buttons do, starting from the left:

- **The Back and Forward buttons.** Clicking these buttons allows you to cycle through the documents you have already viewed. You can revisit these documents in reverse order (relative to the order in which you originally viewed them) by pressing the Back button, and then you can retrace your path using the Forward button. If you simply place your mouse pointer on either button, a tool-tip shows you where the button will take you if you click it.

- **The Reload button.** When you click Reload, Navigator 4 reloads the current document from the Web or from its location on your intranet. What's the point? Please see the "Reloading & Refreshing" sidebar.

- **The Home button.** Clicking this button returns you to your home page.

- **The Search button.** Clicking this button takes you to Netscape's Net Search page, where you search the Web or Usenet newsgroups for particular information using a variety of search engines. I'll talk a lot more about searching later in the chapter, but Figure 3-4 shows what you get when you press the Search button.

Reloading & Refreshing

Navigator's Reload command makes the browser go out on your intranet or the Net and reload the Web document that's currently displayed.

Well, it's not *quite* that simple. First Navigator checks to see if the page has changed at all, and it only reloads it if it's different from the one stored in its cache from the last time you loaded it. This can be useful if you want the latest information from a site that changes daily, for instance. But since reloading means reconnecting with the remote site and possibly downloading files, it can also be slow, especially when the Net is particularly busy. If you want to redisplay a page in Netscape Navigator 4 but don't particularly care if it's the very latest version, you can use the Refresh command that's located in the View menu. This command loads the most recent version of the URL that has been saved to the program's cache.

You can also force a reload, in other words make Navigator go out and get a fresh copy of a page even if it hasn't changed. To do this, hold down the Shift key while clicking the Reload button.

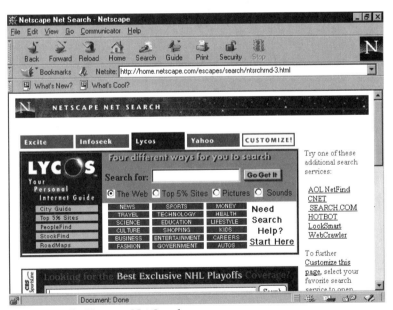

Figure 3-4: The Netscape Net Search page.

■ **The Images button.** This button isn't always present on the Command Toolbar. It only appears if you have configured Navigator 4 so that the program does not automatically display images it encounters in Web pages. This configuration can save you time on slow connections. The Images button becomes available so that you can *explicitly* request that graphics be displayed for the page you're currently viewing. Clicking the button won't change the program configuration; the next page you view will still display without images unless you click the button again.

To configure Navigator 4 so that it does not automatically display images, and so that the Images button appears on the Command Toolbar, please see the section below entitled "Advanced Preferences."

■ **The Guide button**. Click this button and a submenu appears, as shown in Figure 3-5.

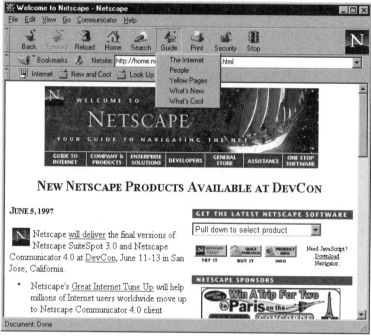

Figure 3-5: The Guide submenu.

Just click one of the top three choices and you are transported to a specialized directory where you can browse for Web sites by category, search for individuals on the Net, or look for software that's available for free downloading. And the bottom two choices take you to special pages on the Netscape site that list some of the latest and greatest links.

- **The Print button**. This is pretty self-explanatory. Click this button to print the currently displayed document.

- **The Security button**. This button shows you the security status for any document you view in Navigator. If you are currently viewing a secure document, one that is protected by Netscape's SSL security protocol (see Chapter 12), the button displays a locked paddle lock; otherwise, it displays an unlocked paddle lock. If you click the button, you can view detailed security information about any secure document. Additionally, the Security button lets you change the security configuration for Navigator itself. Don't worry if this sounds alien to you at this point: I'll cover all you need to know about security in Chapter 12.

- **The Stop button**. If you are in the process of receiving a Web document, you can stop it from loading by pressing this button. Why would you want to do this? Often you don't really know what a document contains until you see some of it. Or perhaps you've already received the textual information you're interested in and simply want to stop the download of graphics, which can be quite slow in the case of large images.

- **The Netscape button**. The Netscape button appears at the far right of the Command Toolbar. When the icon becomes animated and shows a bunch of meteors whizzing by the big N, you know that the program is busy retrieving a document. While the meteors are falling, your Reload button changes to a Stop button as well. In fact if you click the Netscape button while a document is loading into the browser window, it works just like the Stop button; the document immediately stops loading. In addition, however, you are transported to Netscape's own home page. You can also use the Netscape button to get to the Netscape page when the program is *not* busy loading a document.

TIP

If you're on a corporate intranet, your system administrator may have changed the Netscape button to a different icon, perhaps your corporate logo. In this case clicking the button may take you to your own company's home page. Similarly, if your ISP supplied your copy of Communicator, the button may take you to that ISP's site.

Now let's work our way down the screen to the next of the three toolbars.

The Location Toolbar

The program is called Navigator. It's about going places. And the Location Toolbar provides you with a few great tools for getting there.

- **Bookmarks.** At the left of the Location Toolbar you see the word "Bookmarks" and a book icon. This is called the Bookmarks QuickFile icon. When you click it, a menu appears that includes the items Add Bookmark, File Bookmark, and Edit Bookmarks. (If you already have a bookmarks file, for instance from an earlier version of Netscape Navigator, other items might appear in the menu as well.) At the bottom of the menu is a Personal Toolbar Folder item that lets you access the bookmarks you've added to the Personal Toolbar even if the Personal Toolbar is currently hidden. I'll be talking about bookmarks at length later in this chapter, but for now all you need to know is that they are shortcuts that let you navigate in one click to a location you've saved. Add Bookmarks stores the location of the currently displayed document for easy access right from this toolbar, and Edit Bookmarks lets you to organize your bookmarks in convenient groupings. File Bookmark does the same thing as Add Bookmark, except that it lets you choose from several Bookmark folders if you have more than one. It also lets you add a bookmark to the Personal Toolbar Folder even if the Personal Toolbar is hidden.

- **The Netsite/Location box.** This text box has a label that changes according to how you use it. When Netscape Navigator 4 displays a Web document retrieved from a site that uses a Netscape Web server product, such as FastTrack or the Netscape Enterprise Server, the box is labeled Netsite; when it displays information retrieved from a non-Netscape server, the box is labeled Location. If you want to enter a URL manually, you can either type it or paste it directly into this field (the label changes to Go To while you're typing the new URL). Press Enter when you've finished entering the URL, and Netscape Navigator 4 jumps to that page.

TIP

You'll notice an arrow button directly to the right of the Netsite box. You can click this button to display a drop-down list of the sites you've recently visited. Click any site in the list to return to it. (Note: This list only shows pages whose URLs you have entered in the Netsite/Location box and URLs you've opened using the Open Page command on the File menu. It does not display the URLs for sites you've visited by following links within Web documents.)

Entering URLs the Easy Way

You learned in Chapter 1 that a URL, or the address of a particular resource such as a Web page, includes three parts: the protocol used to retrieve the resource (such as HTTP, Gopher, or FTP), the name of the server where the information you want is located, and optionally, a directory or file name. For instance, the URL for the Netscape home page is http://home.netscape.com, and the URL for one of its FTP sites is ftp://ftp.netscape.com. Both of these examples include a protocol specification and a server name.

Most often you get to a site by clicking a link within a Web page, but sometimes you need to type the URL itself into the Netsite or Location box. Wouldn't it be nice if you didn't always have to type that "http://" or "ftp://"?

Well, you don't! Netscape Navigator 4 is intelligent. You can leave off the protocol specification and the program will do its best to figure out what kind of resource you had in mind. For instance, if you type in **home.netscape.com**, Navigator 4 knows you really mean http://home.netscape.com. If you type in **gopher.well.com**, you are automatically transported to gopher:// gopher.well.com. For names that start with the standard "www" you can even leave the www off. For instance, for the URL http://www.echonyc.com you can type as little as echonyc.com! It's a great time saver.

Throughout this book I'll tell you to type in complete URLs, including the protocol specification. I'm doing that so you get used to the format and to make very clear what kind of resource we're talking about. But after a while, you'll almost certainly want to take advantage of this handy shortcut.

■ **The Page icon.** The Page icon is a little picture of a page and a bookmark just to the left of the Netsite/Location box. This icon is really a shortcut representation of the current URL. You can drag the Page icon onto the Windows 95 desktop to create a shortcut to the URL, and you can drag it onto the Bookmarks QuickFile icon or onto the Personal Toolbar to create a new bookmark (see upcoming section on Bookmarks). You can even drag the Page icon into a Netscape Composer window to edit the document.

The Personal Toolbar

This is one of the nicest new features in Netscape Navigator 4. Notice that the Personal Toolbar contains three buttons: Internet, New and Cool, and Look Up. Clicking these buttons transports you to Netscape's own Netscape Guide What's New, What's Cool White pages and Yellow pages, where you will find links to a variety of interesting Web resources. But that's not what makes the Personal Toolbar exciting. Its real power is in its *customizability*. When you encounter a link in a document, you can drag it up to the Personal Toolbar to create a brand new icon button that sits next to the two default ones. Then all you need to do is click that icon button to access the link. Let's give it a try:

TIP

A link is simply some text or graphic element in a Web document which, when clicked, takes you to a different site. Text links, by default, are underlined and colored differently from the surrounding text. Graphics links are sometimes not as easy to differentiate from other components of the page, but when you place your cursor over either a text or graphics link the cursor changes into a pointing hand.

1. Make sure you're connected to the Internet.
2. Make sure your Personal Toolbar is open or maximized. If not, click the up arrow tab to its left.
3. If Navigator 4 is not currently displaying the Netscape home page, click the Home button and wait for the page to appear.
4. On the Netscape home page, scroll down and locate the link "Customer Service," as shown in Figure 3-6.

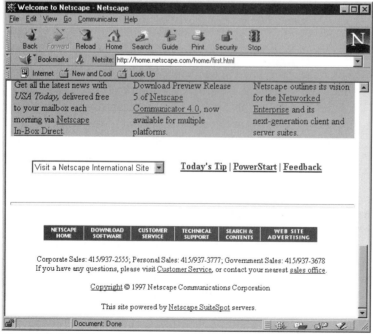

Figure 3-6: The Netscape home page, with Customer Service link.

If you were to click the link, Netscape's customer service page would appear. But you don't need customer service right now, so instead of navigating to the link, let's save it to the Personal Toolbar in case we need it later:

1. Click the Customer Service link and drag it up to the Personal Toolbar. Once you let go of the mouse button, the link appears there as a new button, as shown in Figure 3-7.

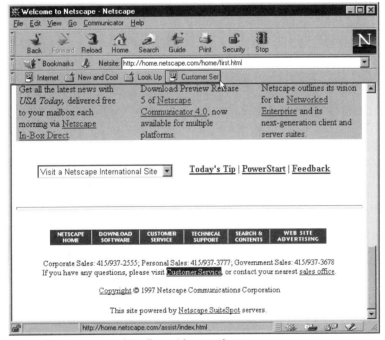

Figure 3-7: The Personal Toolbar with a new button.

2. Want to change the order of the icon buttons in the Personal Toolbar? Just click and drag them right or left.

Customizing the Personal Toolbar

Suppose you don't want the Internet, New and Cool, and Look Up buttons in your Personal Toolbar. Or suppose you want to change how a particular button reads, without changing the link itself. For instance, you might want the button that accesses the Netscape customer service simply to read "HELP!!!"

Here's the trick to remembering how to customize the Personal Toolbar: it's really just a Bookmarks folder that's presented in a different way, and the links in it are really just bookmarks. That means you customize the Personal Toolbar the same way you customize any other Navigator bookmarks.

Ah, but I haven't covered bookmarks yet. Well, let me give you just enough information to get started with your Personal Toolbar. This will help make bookmarks clearer to you, too, when you get to the Bookmarks section of this chapter.

1. Click the Bookmarks icon and then select Edit Bookmarks. The Bookmarks window appears, as shown in Figure 3-8.

Figure 3-8: The Bookmarks window.

- If no items appear under the Personal Toolbar Folder, double-click it to expand it, or simply click the "plus" icon.

2. Select one of the items under the Personal Toolbar Folder (What's New?, for instance), then right-click. A submenu appears, which includes the items Delete Bookmark and Bookmark Properties, among others.

3. To get rid of a bookmark from the Personal Toolbar, click Delete Bookmark.

4. To change the text that appears on the button, or to modify its URL or description, select Bookmark Properties and then edit the appropriate fields in the Bookmark Properties dialog box that appears, as shown in Figure 3-9.

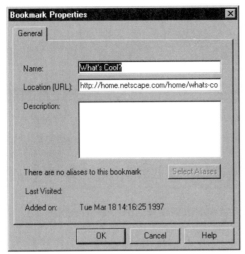

Figure 3-9: The Bookmark Properties dialog box for a Personal Toolbar button.

If you keep in mind that these convenient buttons are really bookmarks just like any other bookmarks, you'll never forget how to customize the Personal Toolbar.

Navigator's toolbars offer some extremely powerful tools for navigating to and viewing Web documents, either on the Net or on an office intranet. Now let's continue this overview by moving down the screen to the document display area itself.

The Display Window

The display window is the most important area within Netscape Navigator 4. This is where Navigator 4 displays the formatted text, links, hotspots, form fields, graphics, and other items that make up a Web page. Some of these fields and controls are "static," like a standard paragraph of text, while others are "active" and actually perform a function. Some controls may be immediately obvious, like a button, while others may be hidden. For example, the Netscape page in Figure 3-10 includes a Welcome to Netscape graphic with hotspots. When you click these hotspots, you are magically teleported to other Web pages, just as if you'd clicked a text link. You'll learn more about these components of a Web page later in this chapter. For now, though, just remember that if your mouse cursor turns into a hand with a pointing finger, you can click there to do something or go somewhere!

Figure 3-10: A graphic menu with hotspots.

TIP

> *Netscape Navigator 4 includes standard scroll bars along the right and bottom edges of the display window. If you resize the window (or if a Web page is longer than one screen length, which is usually the case), these controls let you scroll the display so that you can view the entire page.*

Canvas Mode

Netscape Navigator is the perfect tool for displaying marketing or other information in a public setting such as on a public access terminal in a mall, library, or doctor's waiting room. But in settings like this, it looks a lot slicker if the actual information—perhaps a succession of static images or a video clip—takes up the entire screen, without any menu bars and window borders. And if the display is interactive, allowing viewers to click buttons to access new information, it is essential to eliminate or hide any user interface elements that will let them customize the display—for instance by scrolling an image out of view, or resizing the browser window, or even navigating to other Web sites!

Navigator provides a special kiosk mode that Netscape also refers to as *Canvas mode.* When in Canvas mode, you cannot affect the display except through interface elements specifically programmed by the author of the Web page. For example, take a look at Figure 3-11:

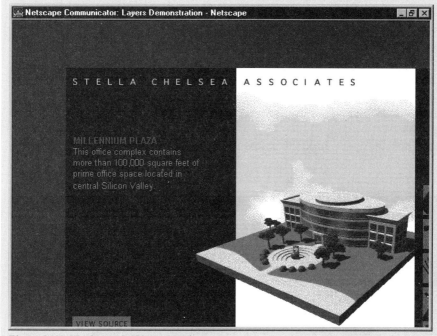

Figure 3-11: Navigator in Canvas mode.

A viewer can click any of the buttons or icons on the screen to access more detailed information but is effectively "locked out" of the Navigator software itself until he or she presses the Close Demo button (in an actual public setting this button would not exist). You won't suddenly find a nude photo of Strom Thurmond on the screen instead of your carefully crafted promotional material.

So how do you put Navigator into Canvas mode? That's easy: you don't do anything at all. The Web page *itself* includes specially programmed instructions to Navigator that tell it to "get out of the way." These instructions are written in an easy-to-use programming language called JavaScript that may be mixed in with regular HTML code. In Chapter 10 I'll show you how to create a page that puts any Navigator browsers that access it into canvas mode.

The Status Line

At the very bottom of the browser window lives the Navigator status line. What's it for? That's right, it displays current status information. For example, the paddle lock icon at the far left works the same way as the Security button on the Command Toolbar: it shows you the security status of the current document. If it is a locked paddle lock, you are viewing a secure document; if it's an unlocked paddle lock, you are viewing an ordinary document that's not protected by encryption (see Chapter 12). And if you click the paddle lock icon, you can see more detailed security information.

But the status line shows you lots more information as well, in the form of text messages. If you're currently receiving a picture from a Web site, for example, Navigator 4 fills in the status line with the name of the image file and a status bar that indicates the progress of the transfer. Or if you move your mouse pointer over a link, the status line shows its URL, as you can see in Figure 3-12.

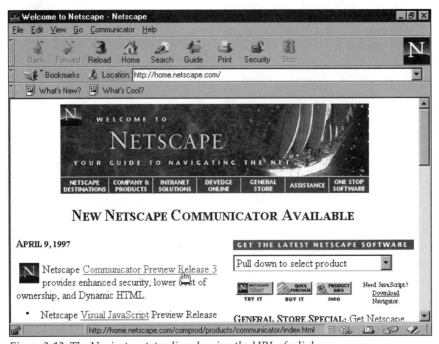

Figure 3-12: The Navigator status line showing the URL of a link.

In addition, if you've closed your Component Bar, it appears in minimized form at the right side of the status line, as shown in Figure 3-13. You can click any of the icons to access other Communicator features such as e-mail or discussion groups, and you can re-expand the Component Bar by clicking the left-most icon.

Figure 3-13: The Component Bar minimized on the status line.

Local Area URLs

As I mentioned in Chapter 1, you don't need the Internet to use Netscape Communicator effectively. In fact, you don't even need an intranet! If you're on a local area network (LAN), you can use the program to access documents within your own organization or your own computer. For instance, employees could call up the latest sales data or view a fancy multimedia demonstration of a new product or service. There are lots of things you *can't* do without an intranet and a real Web server, but in a very small office viewing stored documents may be all you need.

To access a document that is stored locally rather than at a remote site, press Ctrl+O or select Open Page from Navigator 4's File menu. An Open Page dialog box pops up. Now you can click Browse to look around your own computer or another computer on your LAN for the document you want. HTML documents appear with the Netscape logo, but you can also choose to view text or graphic files.

You can also access a locally stored document by clicking a link to it within another document. For instance, you may want to construct a home page that contains links to a variety of important files on your LAN. The URL for a locally stored file looks a little different from other URLs, and you should know how to construct one in case you ever need to enter one directly in the Netsite/Location box. A local file URL starts with *file:*. Next, as with all complete URLs, there are *two* forward slashes, then the exact path to the file. Got all that? Here's an example—an HTML file called PRODUCT.HTM that's located in the Public directory on the Q drive of your LAN: file://Q:/Public/PRODUCT.HTM. Of course if this file were on your own computer, you would specify one of your local drives, for instance C, instead of Q.

TIP

You can enter the path for the file using backslashes if you want; Navigator automatically converts them to forward slashes, which are the standard for Web browsers.

Netscape Communicator supports most of the same media on a LAN as it does on the Net or a true intranet. You can use the program to play sound files, run video clips, and even gather information from other employees using HTML forms (see "Forms on the Web" later in this chapter). And of course a document can contain a mix of links to Internet sites and to local files. This power and flexibility make Netscape Communicator an excellent tool for disseminating enterprise-wide information even without a Web server!

Links & Hotspots

Let's continue our discussion of Web navigation with the most common active control found within Web pages: the *link*. We've already discussed links a little bit, but now it's time to get into it a little deeper. OK, review time: a link is a special text string or image embedded within a document. It tells Navigator to jump to another document or to a different place in the current document. Linked documents may be physically stored at the same site or another site halfway across the world. As I explained in Chapter 1, this is the essence of hypertext.

Links are considered "followed" once you click them to display the new information. Navigator 4 changes the color of a followed link to indicate that you've used it before. This color coding can help you retrace your steps.

To use a link, simply move your mouse pointer over the link text and click. But how can you be sure you're on a link? You already know one visual cue, the pointing hand cursor, but there are others as well.

How Can I Tell I'm on a Link?

Navigator 4 provides a number of visual cues to indicate the presence of a link:

- By default, text links are underlined and appear in blue, while regular inactive text is not underlined and appears black. If you return to a page after using one of its links, the link then appears in red to indicate that you've been there. You can always click the same link again; it does not become inactive once you've clicked it. The change in color is only a helpful reminder.

- As I mentioned earlier, if you rest your mouse cursor on a link, the status line changes to indicate the link's URL. No URL in the status line, no link!

- As I also mentioned earlier, your mouse cursor changes to a pointing hand when it rests on a link.

Figure 3-14 shows a section of Netscape's own online handbook that contains a number of links.

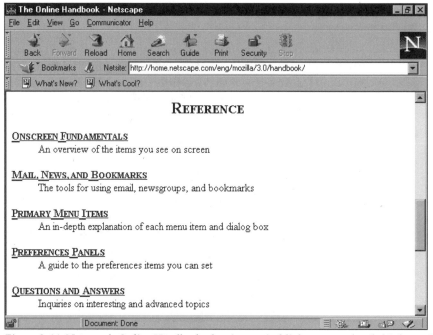

Figure 3-14: Netscape's Online Handbook, showing typical links to more detailed information.

TIP

Often the content of the text containing the link indicates what the link will do. For instance, "download PROGRAM.ZIP now" and "jump to the index" are self-explanatory.

Changing What Links Look Like

If you don't like blue or underlines, you can change the properties of link text. Click Preferences on the Edit menu and then choose Colors under the Appearance category at the left side of the window. (If you don't see the Colors item, double-click Appearance to expand the list.) In the Colors window, you can change the default colors for links you've used (Visited Links) and for those you haven't tried yet (Unvisited Links). You can also check a box to tell Navigator whether or not links should be underlined.

In this same dialog box you can also change the default background color for Web pages as well as the default color of regular (non-link) text. To change these settings, uncheck the Use Windows colors checkbox and then click the respective buttons. To force Navigator to display these colors no matter what a Web page specifies, check the checkbox at the very bottom of the dialog box.

Using Hotspots

Hotspots are just like links, except they are embedded within graphical information rather than text. Like links, hotspots perform an action when you click
them. You might click one to jump to another page or to view an image or
even to play a piece of music. Sometimes hotspots are smaller "thumbnail"
versions of full-size images that you can download, or they may be beautifully
designed arrows pointing to the next in a series of linked documents. Many
sites also use hotspots as "menu items" within larger images that serve as
menu systems. In the Netscape home page, for instance, you can click on
various areas within the same graphic to jump to different documents. Let's
give this a try:

1. Make sure you are connected to the Internet.

2. Double-click the Netscape Communicator or Navigator icon to launch
   the program. The main window appears, and the Netscape home page
   starts loading, as shown earlier in Figure 3-1.

3. In the large graphic near the top of the page, click the General Store
   section. The General Store appears, as shown in Figure 3-15.

Figure 3-15: The General Store.

Congratulations! You just used a hotspot to get from the Netscape home page to the General Store. Traveling sure is simple in cyberspace.

TIP

Usually, clicking a link causes the text and graphics currently displayed in the Navigator window to be replaced with new text and graphics. Sometimes, however, your current window will stay the same and an entire new window opens up to display the new information. The command to open a new window is part of the control information in the HTML file itself.

In this example, it was easy to find the hotspots in the graphic because they included text. But there are other ways to indicate hotspots as well. Sometimes they are displayed with a colored border, or the author of a Web page might refer to a hotspot in a line of text such as "Click the right arrow to move to the next page."

Right-Clicking Links & Images

Normally you click with your left mouse button on links and hotspots. But by clicking your *right* mouse button instead, you can access a wide range of ways to manipulate these interactive elements.

When you click a link with the right mouse button, a context menu appears that lets you:

- **Open in New Window**. This opens a new browser window that displays the document specified in the link. Your original window remains open. Navigator lets you keep multiple browser windows open, each displaying different Web documents or even the same document.

- **Open Link in Composer**. This opens the link in Netscape Composer, letting you modify the contents of the document.

- **Back**. Selecting this item is the same as clicking the Back button on the Command Toolbar.

- **Forward**. Selecting this item is the same as clicking the Forward button on the Command Toolbar.

- **Reload**. Selecting this item is the same as clicking the Reload button on the Command Toolbar.

- **Stop**. Selecting this item is the same as clicking the Bookmarks icon on the Location Toolbar. Not really, I just wanted to see if you're paying attention. Yep, it's the same as clicking the Stop button.

- **View source**. Want to see the actual HTML code for the current document? Click here.

- **View Info**. This option shows you lots of useful information about the current document, including the various graphic components it contains and when it was created.

- **Add Bookmark**. This lets you add the link to your Bookmarks without actually having to navigate to the target document.

- **Create Shortcut**. This lets you create a desktop shortcut to the link. It is equivalent to dragging the Link icon out to the desktop, except you do not currently need to be displaying the target document.

- **Send Page**. If you click this item a New Message window appears, letting you address an e-mail to any recipient you want. The message already includes the currently displayed document as an attachment (please see Chapter 5 if you don't understand this terminology).

- **Save Link as**. This lets you save the target HTML file on your hard drive or network drive.

- **Copy Link Location**. This copies the link to the Windows clipboard. It is the same as double-clicking the Page icon, except you do not need to be currently displaying the target document.

When you click a hotspot or graphic with the right mouse button, you see many of the same menu items, plus these additional specialized choices:

- **View Image**. This allows you to view the current image by itself, without the surrounding text or other graphics.

- **Set as Wallpaper**. This lets you use the current image as your Windows wallpaper.

- **Save Image as**. This lets you save the graphic to your hard drive or a network drive.

- **Copy Image Location**. This copies the URL of the image to the Windows clipboard.

- **Add Bookmark**. This lets you create a new bookmark for the graphic (see the later section on Bookmarks).

Using the Navigator 4 Controls

As I mentioned earlier, Navigator's topmost toolbar is the program's control center. You can use these buttons like the forward and reverse gears of a car, moving back and forth through Web documents. You can also use them to print the contents of any page or even to locate specific information on the Internet.

Of course, all these functions are also available from the menu bar, but most Internet surfers find that the graphical nature of the Web lends itself to mouse control, making the toolbar the easiest and most convenient method for harnessing the power of Netscape Navigator 4.

In this section, we'll discuss the buttons you'll use the most as we navigate through Netscape's own Web site.

TIP

Note that pages on the Netscape Web site may change from time to time, so the screens and links we use may not agree exactly with what you see on your screen. However, you should still be able to follow the steps in a general fashion.

The Forward & Back Buttons

You've already seen how easy it is to get to a new document by clicking a link or hotspot. But what if you need to return to a previously viewed page? Maybe you forgot to download a file, or you suddenly decide to back up and follow a different information trail. This is where the first two buttons on the toolbar come into play. Back and Forward allow you to retrace your steps to a previous page or, if you've already backtracked, to jump forward to the last page you accessed.

To see how this works, follow these steps:

1. Make sure you are connected to the Internet. If Navigator 4 is not currently running, launch it by double-clicking its icon or the Communicator icon.

2. In the Netscape home page, click the hotspot for the General Store. If you're already at the General Store because you're a good student who followed the last set of directions, just stay there!

3. Now click the Back button. We're back where we started, at the Netscape home page. Guess what the Forward button does? Go ahead and click it now. As you probably guessed, the General Store page pops up once more.

TIP

If you simply place your mouse cursor on either the Forward or Back button, a tool-tip shows you where the button will take you to when you click it. This can help you stay oriented when working with a page that has multiple frames (see the section called "Understanding Frames."

4. Now click a new link or hotspot. It doesn't really matter which one. Once the new document appears, click the Back button twice. As you probably expected, the Back button can lead sequentially back through all the pages you have visited. And of course Forward works the same way, in reverse.

Multiple Connections

You can display several Web documents at once with Netscape Navigator 4. Select New from the File menu, then Navigator Window from the submenu that appears. You can also simply press Ctrl+N. Another window pops up, and you can use it, like the first window, to navigate to any site. As I mentioned before, some sites automatically open new browser windows to display information, so you may have several windows open already.

And why would you want to connect to more than one site at a time?

- If you're researching a specific topic and you've found more than one page with pertinent information or links, it's a good idea to load each page in a separate window if you need to compare them.

- Certain sites may be particularly slow, and opening an additional window allows you to continue exploring while you wait for the display of the first page to finish.

- Extra-large files like .MOV or .AVI animations may take several minutes to download. With a second window, you can continue surfing while you wait.

When you first open a new browser window, it "inherits" the history of the original window and displays the oldest page in that history, which is usually the Netscape home page. If you're wondering what I mean by *history*, it will all make sense after the section on "The History List & Bookmarks." Don't worry about it for now—all you need to know is that the new window is just like the old one, and you can use it to get anywhere you want on the Web.

The Reload Button

You already know about the Reload button, but here are some hints on when to use it:

- Use the Reload button to redisplay the current page if you originally pressed Stop while it was still loading. The Reload button will enable you to get the entire document.

- Use the Reload button to redisplay the current page if you originally displayed it in text-only mode and now want to see the graphics. Note: you may need to press Shift while clicking Reload in order to force Navigator to go back to the original source of the document rather than to a locally stored copy.

- Use the Reload button to redisplay the current page if some of the text is garbled or there are other obvious display errors. Again, you may need to press Shift while clicking Reload in order to force Navigator to go back to the original source of the document.

The Home Button

You can click new links and dance around with the Forward and Back buttons as long as you want, but eventually you might get dizzy and long for home. To return to the Netscape home page, or to your corporate intranet's home page:

1. Click the Home button.

That's it. (I love one-step procedures.)

Your Home Page

Why do you even need a home page? There are several reasons:

- A home page helps you stay oriented with a familiar starting point. Imagine what surfing would be like if you started without a home base—or, even worse, jumped to a random page every time you started the program!

- Many seasoned Web surfers set their home pages to their favorite site, especially if the contents of the page change often. This way, you can check your favorite page each time you begin a Navigator session. If you have your own personal Web page, for example, you could set it as your home page.

- Some pages are especially designed to offer as much as possible for new Web surfers, making them ideal launching pads for Web exploration. For example, the Netscape home page offers links to the newest and most popular pages, Web search tools, and a wealth of exciting Internet resources—all from one screen.

At some point, though, you may want to change your home page. Why? First, a purely practical reason: if your current home page is particularly busy or it's operated on a slower connection, it may take 30 seconds or so to load the page! Delays like that can get quite tiring after a few sessions, so you'd probably want to select a faster site (or perhaps even use a page you've created on your local hard disk). If you're really interested in saving time, you can even set your home page as "blank," so there's no load time at all.

Additionally, your interests are likely to change. You can save valuable Internet time by constructing a customized home page and including in it the sites you access the most. (To learn how to do this, see Chapter 9.)

To change your home page, follow these steps:

1. Select Preferences from the Edit menu, then select Navigator from the Category list at the left of the window.

2. In the Home Page section, enter the URL of your new home page. Make sure you spell the address correctly! If you've saved or created a page on your local hard drive or a network drive, you can use the Browse button to find the HTML file you want to use. You can also click the Use Current Page button to set the document currently displayed as your new home page.

3. Click OK.

I'm going to cover the Search and Guide buttons a little later in this chapter, when I talk about finding information on the Web, so for now, let's move ahead to the Print button.

The Print Button

Okay, so you've found the Secret to Life's Eternal Mystery on a particular Web page, and you'd like to save it for future reference. You could highlight the text with your mouse and copy the text to the Windows clipboard, but why not print out the whole thing? That way you can keep a hard copy of all of the contents of the page, including the images.

To print the contents of a page, click the Print button. Like most Windows applications, Navigator provides standard options that you can access from within the Print dialog box, and you can change the appearance of printed documents by selecting Page Setup from the File menu.

You can also display a preview image of the output before you print it by selecting the Print Preview option from the File menu. Figure 3-17 shows a print preview of the Netscape General Store.

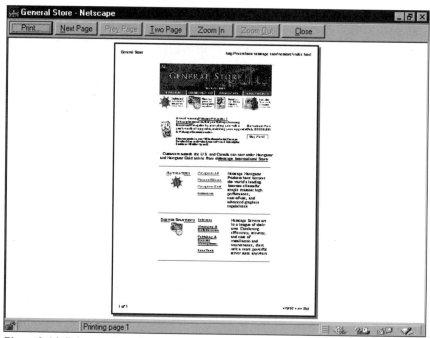

Figure 3-16: Print preview of the Netscape General Store.

The Security Button

When you click the Security button while displaying a regular non-encrypted Web document, you get something like Figure 3-17:

Figure 3-17: The Security Info page.

Basically, this page tells you that the current document is not a secure one. But when you connect to a secure site, one that's protected by encryption (see Chapter 12), all kinds of things change. First, a dialog box like the one in Figure 3-18 appears.

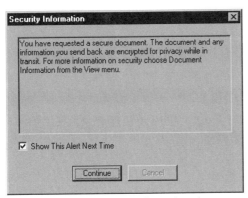

Figure 3-18: The Security Information alert.

By default, Navigator shows alerts like this both when you retrieve a secure document *and* when you return to a non-encrypted document after viewing a secure one. (To learn about changing these defaults, see Chapter 12.) Once you click continue, the secure document appears in the browser window and the Security button changes to depict a locked paddle lock. This indicates that you are currently viewing a secure page, as shown in Figure 3-19.

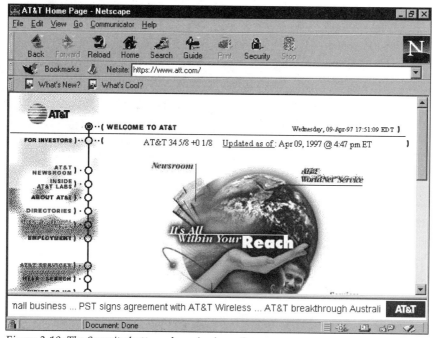

Figure 3-19: The Security button when viewing a Secure page.

TIP

The Security icon at the far left of the status line behaves just like the Security button, changing to a locked paddle lock when you access a secure site. You can also click this icon, just like the Security button, for additional information and settings.

What happens now when you click the Security button? Take a look at Figure 3-20.

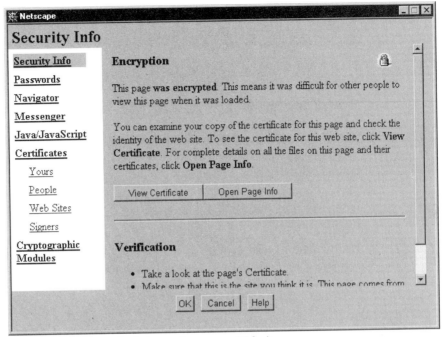

Figure 3-20: The Security Info page for a secure Web site.

As you can see, the Security button lets you display Security information for the current page. In addition, it lets you view and configure a wide variety of security settings. I'll cover those in Chapter 12, but for now let's move on to the final Command Toolbar button.

The Stop Button

OK, here are some hints on when to use the Stop button:

- Click the Stop button when you notice that the document you've requested is not the one you really want.

- Click the Stop button when a document seems to be taking too long to display—perhaps the remote Web server isn't operating properly.

- Click the Stop button when you're in the middle of retrieving that "Babes and Hunks on the Web" page and you suddenly realize your boss is standing right behind you.

I use the Stop button all the time to stop retrieving documents that are loading slowly. And why do some pages seem to take forever to load? Possible reasons for a long wait can include:

- **Heavy usage on the Web site you're calling.** Try calling during low-traffic hours—late at night or early in the morning.

- **Heavy usage on the system that provides your Internet connection.** Check with your access provider to see when the system is being used the least. Remember that the server where a particular page is located may be in another part of the world, so you may have to make allowances for time differences.

- **Extra-large graphics or files you're receiving.** (Remember, you can always keep track of where you are in the transfer process by watching the progress bar that appears in the Navigator status line.)

- **A slow data pipeline.** In plain English, this means that some sites are connected to the Web by leased modem lines or older networks, and these slower connections can be bottlenecks.

TIP

If Navigator is attempting to receive a Web page or a file and the transfer seems stuck, you can often retrieve the data successfully by aborting the current transfer with the Stop button and immediately trying the same link again.

Here's a good rule of thumb: the best time to surf the Net is when you really should be sleeping.

So far you've learned the basics of navigating a simple Web page. In most cases, it's as easy as clicking links and using the Forward, Back, and Home buttons. But besides plain old vanilla Web pages, there are a few different kinds of documents you'll encounter from time to time. First we'll take a look at fill-out forms and then at frames.

Forms on the Web

"Please fill in your name, address, and phone number." You've been doing it your whole life on paper, and now you can do it electronically too.

Forms are scattered all over the Web. Some let you fill in a search word and then find it for you in a collection of documents; some let you buy a CD or new software product; some even engage you in a real-time conversation.

Whatever their purpose, World Wide Web forms share a common look and feel when displayed in Netscape Navigator 4. Here's an example:

1. Make sure you are connected to the Internet.

2. In the Netsite/Location box enter **http://hoohoo.ncsa.uiuc.edu/ archie.html** and hit Enter. The Archie request form appears, as shown in Figure 3-21.

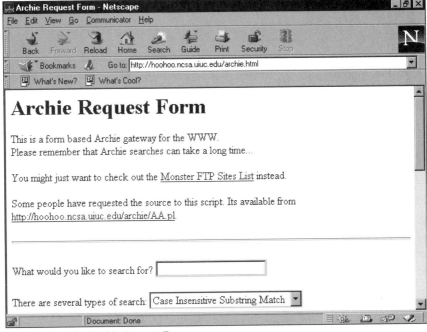

Figure 3-21: The Archie Request Form.

TIP

> *Remember, you don't need to type in entire URLs. Entering*
> ***hoohoo.ncsa.uiuc.edu/archie.html*** *will do the trick.*

Archie is an Internet service that's been around much longer than the Web. It is a tool for finding files at FTP sites (see Chapter 8). But until the Web came along and provided convenient fill-out forms like this one, Archie was much more difficult to use.

Take a few minutes to scroll through this page and examine its various forms elements. There are boxes you can type text into, drop-down lists, and radio buttons. There is also a Submit button that lets you send your request once you have completed filling in the information. If you want, type something in the What would you like to search for? box and then click the Submit button. Let's say you typed the word test and left all the other fields alone. In a few seconds you'd be presented with something like Figure 3-22.

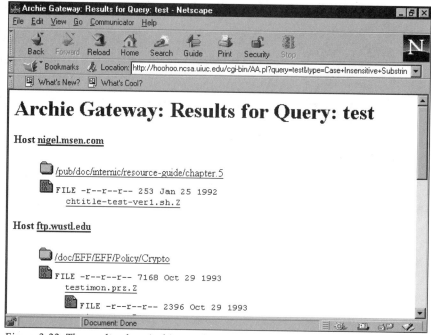

Figure 3-22: The results of an Archie search.

As the commercial uses of the Internet become more prominent, we'll see more and more forms for actual transactions. Already you can buy all kinds of products directly over the Net, and the Web's forms interface makes it easy. By the way, Netscape has been a leader in Internet security, and Netscape Navigator 4 indicates when a form is not secure by a special alert message. The message informs you that any information you submit is unencrypted and could be observed by a third party while it's in transit.

This may sound a bit frightening, but security is typically not a problem with the vast majority of forms you'll fill out online. As a rule, simply take the same precautions that you would if someone were asking similar questions over the telephone. If you feel uncomfortable providing a particular piece of private information, you'll probably want to follow Navigator's recommendation and cancel the form without submitting it. Chapter 12 discusses security issues in more detail.

As more and more companies start collecting data and even selling products via the Internet, online forms may become the bread-and-butter interface on the Web. But fortunately the Web is not all bread and butter, it's champagne and Jell-O, too. Let's take a look at something a bit more fun than forms: *frames*.

Understanding Frames

One of the coolest features of Netscape Navigator 4 is its support for frames. Frames are distinct areas within the Navigator display area. Special HTML commands in a Web document tell the program to partition the display. Each frame is a stand-alone environment that recognizes mouse clicks, has its own scroll bars, and can include all the features of any Web page. Each frame has its own distinct URL. In short, each frame is actually a window displaying its own Web page. Netscape Navigator 4 can actually "freeze" one of the frames so that it stays onscreen all the time while you interact with the links and hotspots in another frame. You may see logos, advertisements, or tables of contents handled in this fashion.

And not all frames look alike. Using Netscape Navigator 4 you may see frames with wide borders, narrow borders, or even no borders at all.

Let's take a look at an example of frames, as shown in Figure 3-23. This figure is the Netscape Web site at http://developer.netscape.com/. As you can guess from the URL, this is a more technical site. Home.netscape.com is where you hang your hat—developer.netscape.com is where you proudly display your pocket protector.

Figure 3-23: An example of a Web page with frames.

Because each frame is its own entity, make sure you select the appropriate frame (by clicking) when you decide to print something. Only the contents of the selected frame, and not the entire display window, print. In addition, you can reload the contents of individual frames by selecting Reload from the View menu, and you can even e-mail the contents of a frame by selecting Send Frame from the File menu.

The way developers use frames makes Web sites very flexible and dynamic for the user. At this Netscape site, notice how each of the two frames is used differently. The left-hand frame displays a clickable table of contents, while the larger right-hand frame displays the actual content. Also, notice how each frame has its own scroll bars.

Other sites use frames to display different types of elements. One frame, for instance, may contain text, while another contains graphics. As you click and read through the text, the graphics can change or rotate based on the text displayed. Frames are also used with multimedia or 3D objects. One pane may contain instructions or a story about how to navigate a VRML world with Cosmo or Live3D, while the other contains the actual VRML objects. (Don't know what Cosmo, VRML, and Live3D are? Please turn to Chapter 10.)

TIP

You can go back and forward in frames just as you do in the browser window as a whole. To go back to the information previously displayed in a frame, select that frame (by clicking in it) and click the Back button. To go forward, select the frame and click the Forward button. You can also right-click in the frame and choose the Forward or Back options from the context menu that appears.

Dynamic HTML

In Chapter 1 you learned a little bit about HTML, the language that's used to compose Web pages. But Navigator 4 supports some exciting new extensions to HTML that Netscape groups together as *Dynamic HTML*. Dynamic HTML gives Web designers more flexibility in making pages look exactly as they want them to look—and in making them more interactive. Here are a few of the features that comprise Dynamic HTML:

- **Dynamic Fonts.** Web pages can now specify exact fonts, font sizes, and font weights that Navigator will then display correctly in your browser window. If you don't already have the specified font on your system, it will be sent to you automatically along with the rest of the HTML information.

- **Style Sheets.** Web page developers can create style sheets that specify sets of design elements such as layout, fonts, bullet styles, etc. These style sheets can then be applied to multiple pages, allowing for a unified look and feel. This not only makes it faster to develop new pages, it means that you will be presented with a consistent user interface when navigating a particular site.

- **Dynamic Layers.** HTML developers may design pages that have multiple layers of information. Text may be overlayed on graphics, or vice versa. Layering also provides a simple way to enhance Web pages with animation.

With Dynamic HTML, various *HTML objects*—such as fonts—may be stored locally. When a Web page calls for the object, it doesn't have to be downloaded anew. Dynamic HTML also means that a Web page may quickly adapt aspects of its design to suit the needs of *your* system.

We've covered a lot of material so far. You should be pretty good at navigating Web documents at this point, either on the Internet or on an office intranet. You may be feeling a bit lost, however. As a technical writer I feel compelled to use clichéd automotive analogies—using clichéd automotive analogies is a lot of what we do for a living—so here goes: you now know how to operate the car, but do you know where you're going? Never fear, the next few sections of this chapter are focused on getting to places and finding things.

Finding Information in a Web Page

From time to time you'll encounter huge documents that are crowded with text and links. Scrolling slowly through a mountain of text line by line is one method of locating that link you remember, but Netscape Navigator 4 makes it much easier with the Find command.

Let's look for a specific string of text on Netscape's own home page:

1. Make sure you are connected to the Internet. If Netscape Navigator 4 is not currently running, launch it by double-clicking its icon or the Communicator icon.

2. If the Netscape home page is not currently displayed, click the Home button or enter **home.netscape.com** in the Netsite/Location box and hit Enter. In a few seconds, the Netscape page appears. Click the Company and Products link that's part of the large image at the top of the page. Netscape's Company and Products page appears.

3. Hit Ctrl+F or select Find in Page from the Edit menu. Navigator displays the Find dialog box, as shown in Figure 3-24.

Figure 3-24: The Find dialog box.

4. Let's say you're sick of flipping burgers and want a job as a Netscape programmer. OK, enter the word **work** in the Find what: field and click the Find Next button. In a flash, Navigator locates the "A Cool Place to Work" link, highlights it, and displays the surrounding section of the document, as shown in Figure 3-25. Simply click the link if you want more information about employment opportunities at Netscape.

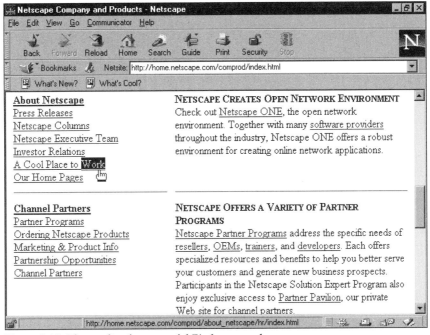

Figure 3-25: The results of a successful Find command.

- If you need a case-sensitive search, enable the Match case option; Navigator 4 will display only those instances in which the capitalization matches your entry. You can also specify in which direction the program should search—click the Up radio button to search upward through the document or on the Down radio button to move downward. The search begins at the current cursor position.

5. To search for more occurrences of the same string, click the Find Next button again.

Finding Information on the Web

Now you know how to find words or phrases in a single Web document. That's great, but don't set up shop as a research expert just yet. There are hundreds of thousands of people who know how to find information not just in a single document, but across all the publicly available documents on the Internet! That sounds impressive, but using Navigator 4 it's almost a no-brainer.

There are two different methods for finding specific information on the Web: *searching* and *browsing*. Searching means explicitly requesting documents containing specific words or phrases; browsing, in the sense we are using it here, means looking through subject indexes of documents as you refine your search. It's like looking for a needle in a haystack that gets smaller and smaller as you work your way down through categories of information. Let's try some searching first, using Navigator's Search button.

The Search Button

As I mentioned earlier, the sheer size of the World Wide Web makes it extremely difficult to locate a particular piece of information or a specific Web page by simply fishing for the right URL. For this reason, topical search engines have been around for as long as the Web itself.

Search engines usually look through an index of documents for a query string that you specify. Some search tools also allow you to add logical operators like "and," "either," and "or" so that you can perform more sophisticated searches.

Netscape Navigator 4 provides you with links to all the search engines you're likely to need. Clicking the Search button brings up the Net Search page, shown in Figure 3-26.

Figure 3-26: The Net Search page.

You can access a variety of search engines such as Infoseek, Lycos, Excite, and Yahoo! directly from this page. Simply click the appropriate tab near the top of the page.

The Fifth Tab

The Netscape Search page not only provides access to four of the most powerful search engines available, it also lets you add another! If you click the Customize tab, you can add AOL NetFind, HOTBOT, LookSmart SEARCH.COM, or WebCrawler. Not only that, Customize lets you determine which of these engines launch automatically whenever you click the Search button.

Navigator also provides a convenient shortcut to searching. If your search phrase consists of two or more words, just enter it in the Netsite/Location box and hit Enter. Navigator passes this phrase on to the current default search engine. You'll receive your result in seconds, without even needing to visit the Search page!

And why does your search phrase need two or more words in order for this convenient shortcut to work? Otherwise, Navigator thinks you are specifying a URL. If I enter **phil** in the Netsite/Location box, Navigator 4 tries to connect to phil.com or www.phil.com. But if I enter **"Phil James"**, it looks for my name on the Web using one of the search engines.

Let's search for a specific topic using Infoseek:

1. Click the Infoseek button.

2. Enter the string **Wittgenstein** in the search field and then click the seek now button. Infoseek returns the search results shown in Figure 3-27.

3. To jump directly to one of the pages, simply click the corresponding link.

A Net search is not guaranteed to locate every site on a particular topic, but if you're hunting for reference material or just surfing because you're interested in the subject, you'll probably find more than enough sites to keep you busy.

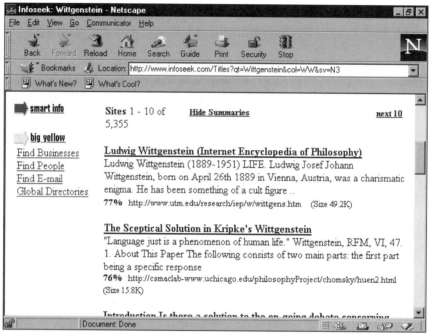

Figure 3-27: Search results from an Infoseek query.

Searching Newsgroups

In Chapter 6 you'll learn all about Usenet newsgroups, which are large discussion groups among Internet users who are often experts in a particular field. Newsgroups are especially useful for ferreting out very specific or very timely information. There are groups where you can get in-depth analysis of everything from Wittgenstein's philosophy to Antonio Banderas's abdominals.

Several of the search engines available from the Net Search button let you find concepts, ideas, or phrases in this ever-changing morass of Usenet information. Once a week, for instance, I look up my own name to see what people are saying about my books—and I've even made some changes based on this information.

Let's try it. Press the Net Search button and then select Alta Vista from the list of search engines at the bottom of the page. Once the Alta Vista page appears, type in your request and select Usenet from the drop-down list to the right of the word "Search." Your browser window will look something like the one in Figure 3-28.

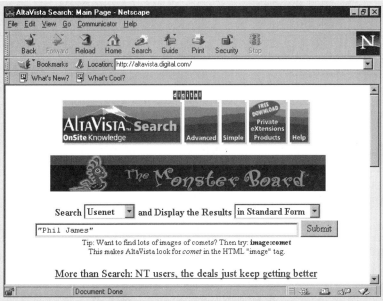

Figure 3-28: The author in search of himself. If you're looking for a phrase that includes spaces, put the whole phrase in quotes.

And Figure 3-29 shows what your window will look like after clicking Alta Vista's Submit button:

Figure 3-29: The results of a Usenet search.

Now let's move on to browsing for specific information using Navigator's Guide button.

The Guide Button

If you click the Guide button, a submenu appears, as shown below in Figure 3-30.

Figure 3-30: The expanded Guide button.

You've already seen the What's New? and What's Cool? links: they are bookmarks in your Personal Toolbar. The Internet item takes you to the Netscape Guide by Yahoo, which is a great front-end for searching out specific kinds of information on the Web; the People item is good for finding your long-lost Uncle Zelig; and the Yellow Pages item can provide you with the electronic and street addresses of businesses all around the world. You should take some time to explore these resources on your own, but for now let's take a quick look at two of them: Netscape Guide and People.

Exploring the Netscape Guide

For a taste of the limitless expanse of information available on the Web today, there's no better place to begin than the Netscape Guide, developed by Yahoo! Yahoo! started as a hobby project by Stanford University students David Filo and Jerry Yang in April 1994. Since then, Yahoo! has mushroomed into a profitable business that's become a career, but Filo and Yang still offer their original service free of charge to everyone, and their own site has become the home page for uncounted Web surfers. Their latest creative venture is this collaboration with Netscape on the Netscape Guide.

What are we waiting for? Let's start exploring! To access the Netscape Guide, make sure you are connected to the Net and then just click the Guide button. Next, select The Internet from the submenu that appears. The main Netscape Guide page appears, as shown in Figure 3-31.

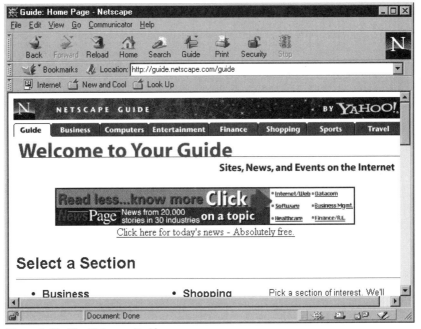

Figure 3-31: The Netscape Guide page.

You can see that the Guide is divided into several broad sections, accessible by clicking the tabs across the top of the page. For instance if you click the Business tab, you are taken to a page that includes several more subcategories such as Employment, Small Business, and Web Business. But Netscape Guide is much more than a simple hotlist of links. If you scroll down the top Business page, you'll discover daily news headlines related to business, a listing of Web events, an economic calendar, and even a facility for tracking FedEx letters and packages!

But the most interesting feature of the Netscape Guide is that you can customize it to display the information you're most interested in. To do this, simply click the Customize This Page link in any one of the categories.

TIP

Want a special front-end site like Netscape Guide for your kids? Try Yahooligans. You can get to it at www.yahooligans.com.

People

The Web is not just pages, it's also *people*. Behind every great URL, there's a living, breathing human being, or at least a Cro Magnon with some minor technical savvy.

How do you find people on the Net? There are a number of "Internet phone books," specialized listings, and search facilities available to anyone with a Web browser. Netscape's People facility gives you access to several of these. If you're looking for your long-lost Aunt Prudence and you know she likes to surf the Net, this is the place to start. And Netscape is committed to adding new directories and search tools to the page as they become available.

Figure 3-32 shows the "white pages" resources that are available through the People feature.

Some of these tools are good for finding a friend's e-mail address, others are good for finding a phone number or snail mail address. Most often I use them when I'm really bored and want some bittersweet what's-she-doing-now information on high school girlfriends.

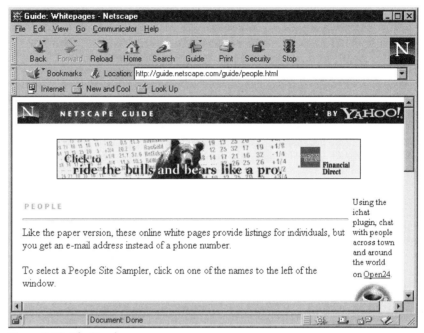

Figure 3-32: The People page.

So now you're an intrepid Net explorer, cruising through documents from around the world. You know how to search for obscure information, how to leap from idea to idea in great hypermedia bounds, and best of all, how to waste lots of time on the Web looking at groovy but useless sites. The rest of this chapter is devoted to *organizing* this huge mass of information. Using Navigator 4's history and bookmarks features, you can not only save the URLs of sites that you want to revisit, you can store them in categories and subcategories that make sense to you.

The History List & Bookmarks

As you travel around the World Wide Web, you'll often find yourself jumping back to the same pages over and over again. From time to time you may also need a specific URL that you visited two or three sessions ago. And you're certain to find a number of Web pages that become your favorites, so you'll want to visit them often.

Netscape Navigator 4 provides several methods for keeping track of where you are on the Web—and where you've been. In this section, we'll discuss the two important features that help you maintain your own Web road map: the history list, which keeps track of where you've been in the current session, and bookmarks, which are permanent pointers to your favorite Web pages.

Using the History List

The history list is actually a collection of entries automatically maintained by Navigator 4. Each entry represents a single site you have visited. Each time you load a new Web page, the URL for that site is saved. This makes the history list an excellent tool for jumping among pages while you check references.

There are three ways to access a list of sites you've visited, and they each show slightly different information. First, the simplest:

1. After you have viewed several documents using Navigator 4, click the down arrow just to the right of the Netsite/Location box. A history list appears right there, as shown in Figure 3-33. Note that the list is scrollable, with only the most recent ten pages showing.

2. Click any entry in the list to return to that document.

Figure 3-33: The drop-down history list.

This Netsite/Location box history list includes only URLs you've entered in the box itself or by using the Open Page command on the File menu; it does not include any sites you've visited by clicking a link.

You can also return to a previously viewed page by clicking Go on the menu bar. The menu that appears includes a history list at the bottom, as shown in Figure 3-34. Once again, you can simply select one of the entries to jump to it immediately.

Figure 3-34: The Go menu.

The history list in the Go menu displays all the sites you've visited during this Navigator session. It includes pages that you've navigated to by clicking links as well as those you've visited by entering URLs in the Netsite/Location box. It does not, however, display any sites you've visited in previous Navigator sessions.

Lastly, you can display the history list within a dialog box, which allows for a neater and more complete presentation of each entry:

1. Select History from the Communicator menu, or simply press Ctrl+H. Navigator 4 displays the History dialog box, as shown in Figure 3-35.

Figure 3-35: The History dialog box.

- Notice that each entry appears as a single line, complete with both the page title and its URL address as well as lots of other information you may or may not want. You can add or eliminate informational fields by clicking the arrow buttons to the right of the column labels, and you can adjust the size of the columns by placing your cursor on the edges of the labels and dragging right or left.

2. To jump to a particular page, simply double-click the entry.

3. To make a bookmark out of a link from this window, right-click the entry and select Add to Bookmarks from the context menu that appears. (I'll cover bookmarks in the next section.)

This very thorough view of your navigational history includes pages you've visited by clicking links and pages you've visited by entering URLs in the Netsite/Location box. But unlike the list at the bottom of the Go menu, it is persistent: it includes your history from previous Navigator sessions as well as your current session. In other words, quitting the program doesn't erase the list.

But how many previous sessions does it record? That depends on a setting that you can change. Read on.

Changing the History List Expiration Time

To configure how long the history list persists and accumulates new entries before it is cleared, follow these steps:

1. Select Preferences from the Edit menu, then click the Navigator category as shown in Figure 3-36.

Figure 3-36: Navigator options.

2. In the History section of the right-hand dialog box, enter the number of days you want your history list to persist before it is cleared. If you are an active Web surfer, you may want to reduce the number.

3. To clear your history list immediately, click the Clear History button.

Bookmarks

Now that you're familiar with the history list, you may be saying to yourself, "Well, that's great for finding places I've been, but I want a more selective list of sites. And I don't want the entries to expire unless I erase them." Luckily, you don't have to resort to paper and pencil or try to maintain a text file of your favorite sites—Navigator 4 provides you with bookmarks, which are saved permanently in your own "Web page directory." You can also create a simple Web page of your own that includes your favorite sites; we'll discuss this in Chapter 9.

Adding & Using Bookmarks

The two actions you'll perform most often with bookmarks are (1) adding them and (2) using them to jump to a stored URL. There are four different ways to add a bookmark for the document that's currently displayed:

- Click the Bookmarks QuickFile icon and select Add Bookmarks from the menu.

- Right-click in the display window, then select Add Bookmark from the menu that appears.

- Drag the Page icon (the one just to the left of the Netsite/Location box) over to the Bookmarks QuickFile icon.

- Hit Cntl+D.

TIP

When you drag the Page icon to the Bookmark icon, you can add the new bookmark directly to any subfolder of the Bookmarks file (see the section called "Organizing Your Bookmarks" to learn about Bookmark subfolders).

You can also add a bookmark for a link within a document by right-clicking the link and then choosing Add Bookmark from the context menu that appears.

Using bookmarks to jump to a document is just as easy:

- Click the Bookmarks QuickFile icon, then select one of the bookmarks that appears at the bottom (see Figure 3-37). You are immediately teleported to the selected URL.

Figure 3-37: The Bookmarks menu, showing list of bookmarks at the bottom.

As with the history list, Netscape Navigator 4 also provides a fuller, alternative interface to your bookmarks: the Bookmarks window.

The Bookmarks Window

Now that you know how to use bookmarks at the simplest level, let's advance a bit. Just as history entries can be displayed in the History dialog box, you can also display a bookmark list that offers a lot more functionality than the Bookmarks menu. To open the Bookmarks window, click the Bookmarks QuickFile icon and then select Edit Bookmarks. The Bookmarks window appears, as shown in Figure 3-38.

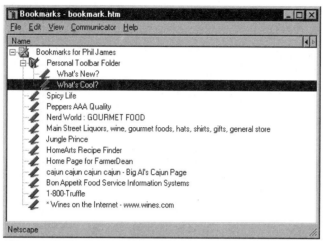

Figure 3-38: The Bookmarks window.

Depending on what sites you've already added to your bookmarks list, your window may look different from mine.

TIP

You can change the name of any bookmark folder, including the top-level one, by right-clicking it and selecting Properties from the context menu that appears. You can also change the name of individual bookmarks this way.

As you can see, Navigator 4 displays the contents of the current bookmark file in a tree format, with entries appearing under the folder icon. The Bookmarks window has its own menu bar, which we'll refer to as we explain the other bookmark functions. But to jump to the document represented by a bookmark entry you don't even need the menu. Simply double-click the entry itself.

TIP

Netscape Communicator lets you use more than one bookmark file and also makes it easy to switch between files. From the File menu in the Bookmarks window, you can choose Open to select a new file, or Save As to save the current file under a new name.

The Personal Toolbar Folder

You'll notice right away that one of the folders in the Bookmarks window is the Personal Toolbar folder. This includes all the bookmarks that you've placed on Navigator's Personal Toolbar, typically by dragging links onto it. Remember, the Personal Toolbar folder is just like any other Bookmarks folder. You modify any items within it exactly as you modify the items in any other folder, and the changes you make will be reflected automatically in the appearance of the Personal Toolbar.

Organizing Your Bookmarks

If you're familiar with the Windows drag-and-drop function and the tree structure common in Windows 95 applications like Explorer, you'll have no problem organizing your bookmarks any way you like.

For example, let's say you'd like to categorize your bookmarks by subject matter, with each subject represented by its own folder. For the purposes of this exercise, we'll add a new folder called Computers under the existing Main Bookmarks folder.

First, to create a new bookmark folder:

1. Select and then right-click the existing folder under which the new folder should be created. In this case, the existing folder is Phil James's Bookmarks.

2. Choose New Folder from the context menu. Navigator 4 displays the Bookmark Properties dialog box shown in Figure 3-39.

Figure 3-39: The Bookmark Properties dialog box.

3. Enter **Computers** in the Name field. If you like, you can add a simple text description that will display when you right-click the folder and select Properties.

4. Click OK to save the folder.

Now that you've added the Computers folder, you can either create new bookmark entries within it or move existing entries into it.

To create a new bookmark:

1. Right-click the folder under which the new entry should be created. In this case, we'll click Computers.

2. Select New Bookmark from the context menu that appears. Navigator 4 displays the Bookmark Properties dialog box, shown before in Figure 3-39.

3. Enter the name for your new bookmark in the Name field. As an example, let's use **A nifty Computer URL**. If you like, you can add a simple text description that displays when you right-click the entry and select Properties.

4. Enter the URL into the Location (URL) field.

5. Click OK to save the entry. Your Bookmarks window should now look something like Figure 3-40.

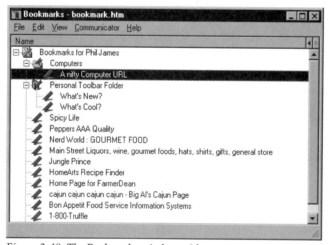

Figure 3-40: The Bookmarks window with new entry.

TIP

You can also insert folders and bookmarks by selecting the respective items from the File menu.

It's even easier to move an existing bookmark into a folder. Click and drag the entry icon (which looks like a sheet of paper with the edge folded down) and drop it on top of the desired folder. Notice that your cursor changes appearance to indicate you're dragging the entry to a new spot. The entry will now appear as a sub-branch under the folder.

When you add entries under a folder, Netscape Navigator 4 also displays the entries and folder hierarchy as part of the Bookmarks menu. Folders with entries in them appear with arrows on the right side of the menu; when you select the folder, the folder name expands to show the bookmark entries within it. And by dragging the Page icon over to the Bookmarks QuickFile icon, you can add the currently displayed page into any one of these folders!

If you'd like to separate your entries or folders on the Bookmarks menu, right-click the name in the Bookmarks window and select New Separator from the context menu. When you return to the Bookmarks QuickFile icon, you'll see a line separating that entry or folder from the others on the menu.

TIP

Once you've expanded your entries within several folders, it may be harder to find a particular entry. Of course, you can use the Find command in the Bookmarks window, but it also helps to close folders you're not using. Closing a folder hides all the bookmark entries under it. To close a folder, double-click its icon; to expand it and display the entries it contains, double-click its icon again. You can also single-click the plus or minus icon to the left of the folder icon. In addition, you can sort the display of your bookmarks in a variety of convenient ways by clicking the available choices on the View menu.

What's an Alias?

You'll notice that the context menu which pops up when you right-click a particular bookmark contains a *Make Alias* command. This command lets you create an alternate bookmark that links to the same URL as the original one. In addition, if you change the original bookmark in any way, the alias changes along with it.

What's the point? Using aliases, you can have the same bookmark in more than one folder. Simply move the aliases you create into whatever folder locations you want. If you simply *copy* the bookmark to a different folder, any changes in the original are not reflected in the copy. Aliases ensure that even multiple instances of the same bookmark remain up-to-date.

Changing Where New Bookmarks Get Added

There is another way to stay organized. You can configure Netscape Navigator 4 so that new bookmarks are always placed in a folder you specify. By default, when you click Add Bookmarks, the new bookmark is added to the end of the top-level bookmark folder. But let's say you want all new bookmarks to go into a subfolder called New. Here's how you do it:

1. In the Bookmarks window, select and right-click the folder you want to use for all newly added bookmarks.

2. Select Set as New Bookmarks Folder from the context menu. A page icon appears on top of the file icon for that folder, as shown in Figure 3-41.

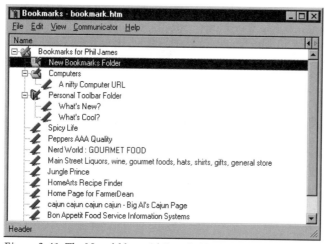

Figure 3-41: The New folder, with icon indicating it is the default New bookmarks folder.

There can be only one New bookmarks folder at a time, at least within the same bookmarks file. If you want to change it, simply select a different folder and repeat step 2. Remember, you can always return the program to its default mode of operation by selecting the top-level folder as the default New bookmarks folder.

Customizing the Bookmarks Menu Display

As you collect dozens or even hundreds of bookmarks, all neatly categorized within their folders, the Bookmarks menu starts looking pretty long. You probably don't need to see all these bookmarks every time you run the program, so why not limit what's displayed in the menu? Navigator 4 makes this easy:

1. In the Bookmarks window, select the folder that you want to have displayed on the Bookmarks menu, then right-click.

2. Select Set as Bookmark Menu from the context menu.

Now only the items in that folder (and any of its subfolders) will appear in the Bookmarks menu. You can always change back to the program's default display of all bookmarks by selecting the top-level folder and repeating step 2.

> **TIP**
>
> *Want to be able to switch among several different Personal Toolbars, each containing different bookmarks? That's easy. You can make ANY bookmark folder your Personal Toolbar folder. Simply right-click the folder you want to use, then choose Set as Toolbar Folder from the context menu.*

Importing & Exporting Bookmarks

As you build your collection of bookmarks, you may want to share your favorite Web sites with others. In fact, many Web surfers keep a "favorite sites" file or "hotlist" in HTML format that they can share with others through Internet mail. Navigator 4 makes it simple to import a bookmark file (bring new entries from some other HTML file into your bookmark file) or export your entries (create an HTML hotlist that others can use).

Remember, an HTML file is simply a text document that contains links to other Web documents. HTML documents are standardized so that all Web browsers can interpret them correctly. That's why importing and exporting allow you to trade files with any Web user, whether or not they have Netscape Communicator.

From the browser window, follow these steps to *import* a bookmark file:

1. Select Edit Bookmarks from the Bookmarks QuickFile icon menu. The Bookmarks window appears, as shown earlier in Figure 3-41.

2. From the Bookmarks window File menu, select Import. Navigator 4 displays a standard Windows or Windows 95 Import bookmarks file dialog, as shown in Figure 3-42.

Figure 3-42: The Import bookmarks file dialog box.

3. Navigate to the directory where the HTML file is stored and then double-click it.

From the Navigator display window, follow these steps to *export* a bookmark file:

1. Select Edit Bookmarks from the Bookmarks menu. The Bookmarks window appears, as shown earlier in Figure 3-37.

2. Select the bookmark file you want to export.

3. From the Bookmarks window's File menu, select the Save As command. Navigator displays the standard Windows or Windows 95 save bookmarks file dialog box, as shown in Figure 3-43.

Figure 3-43: The Save bookmarks file dialog box.

4. Save the file in any location and under any name you want. Make sure the file type is set to HTML files.

Navigator 4 Shortcuts for Windows 95/NT

By far the easiest way to create convenient shortcuts to your favorite Web sites is to drag the Page icon into the Personal Toolbar, as explained earlier in the section called "The Personal Toolbar." But if you're running Netscape Navigator 4 under Windows 95 or Windows NT 4.0, you can also create iconized *desktop* shortcuts that will make connecting to your favorite Web page as easy as a click of your mouse—even when Communicator isn't running.

There are several ways to create desktop shortcuts:

- If you click and drag a link, the pointer will change to indicate that the link can now be dropped onto your desktop. A highlighted link is shown in Figure 3-44, while the new desktop shortcut should look something like Figure 3-45.

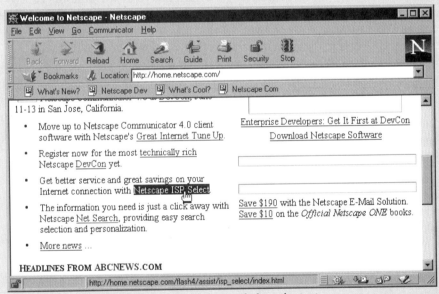

Figure 3-44: A highlighted link, soon to become a desktop shortcut.

Figure 3-45: A Netscape shortcut icon on the desktop.

- You can click your right mouse button on a link and then select Create Shortcut from the context menu that pops up.

- You can drag the Page icon (just to the left of the Netsite/Location box) out onto the desktop. This creates a desktop shortcut to the current URL, just as it would have created a Custom shortcut if you'd dragged it to the Personal Toolbar.

Once you've created a desktop shortcut, all you have to do is double-click it to access the site. Netscape Communicator doesn't even have to be running—clicking the shortcut will automatically launch Navigator 4 with the correct URL.

As you've seen, Netscape Communicator's browser window is pretty painless to use "right out of the box." You didn't have to spend hours configuring the software before you could start exploring, and in fact, you could just keep on Web-trucking without ever delving into the setup menus. But I know you too well—you're the kind of person who will never be satisfied with anything less than fully optimized software. In the final section of this chapter, you'll learn how to do a little bit of tweaking so that Navigator 4 works exactly as you want it to.

Tweaking Your Browser

If you select Preferences from the browser window's Edit menu, you'll see a Category list of six different Preference choices: Appearance, Navigator, Mail & Groups, Composer, Offline, and Advanced. The Composer Preferences are covered in Chapter 9, and Mail & Groups are covered in Chapters 5 and 6, so we won't bother looking at those right now. Let's start by glancing at the Appearance options. You'll quickly get a sense of what kind of customization is possible in Navigator 4.

Appearance Preferences

To access the Appearance preferences, simply select Appearance from the Categories list, as shown in Figure 3-46.

Figure 3-46: The Appearance options.

In the top section of this window, you can choose which Communicator components you want to launch automatically when you click the Communicator icon. If you select all five, for instance, you will have five different windows on your screen when you start Communicator, including an e-mail window, a Web page editing window, a Netcaster window, the Navigator browser window, and the Collabra discussion groups window.

In the bottom section of this page, you can choose how to display the buttons in the Command Toolbar. Until you get familiar with the program, Pictures and Text is probably the best choice.

There are two more Appearance windows: Fonts and Colors. To access these, the Appearance item in the Category list on the left must be expanded. If they are not in your list, double-click the Appearance item or simply click the plus icon. Fonts and Colors appear in the list, and you can click them to access the respective settings.

Fonts

Back in the Category list on the left, click the Fonts item. The window that appears lets you associate incoming data with particular display fonts, as shown in Figure 3-47.

Figure 3-47: The Fonts options.

In the United States, just about all the Web information you receive will be in the Western, or ISO-Latin-1, character set, and this character set will be displayed using the default Times New Roman and Courier New fonts. However, you can change these fonts—and their sizes—if you want. Just click the appropriate drop-down list and make your choice.

If a Web page specifies a font that you don't currently have on your system, it may be downloaded to you automatically—without any intervention on your part—so that the document appears as intended in your browser window. Netscape calls this feature Dynamic Fonts. To take advantage of Dynamic Fonts, you must select the bottom option button; the top option button forces Navigator to use the fonts you have selected even if the Web page specifies a very different font, and the middle button lets Navigator display the special fonts specified in a document only if they're already on your system.

TIP

You can also change your font size right within the browser window. Simply select Increase Font or Decrease Font from the View menu. You can also hit Ctrl+] to increase the font size or Ctrl+[to decrease the size.

Colors

We already visited here earlier in the chapter. The Colors window lets you change the default colors for text and links that are displayed in Navigator 4 as well as in HTML information displayed in Messenger and other Communicator components. In addition, it lets you specify a new background color or even a .GIF file for the display background. You can also decide here whether or not you want Navigator 4 to always use these colors rather than responding to the special color requests in Web documents.

Now let's move on to the Navigator preferences.

Navigator 4 Preferences

In the Category list on the left, select Navigator. The Navigator options appear, as shown in Figure 3-48.

Figure 3-48: The Navigator options.

Here you can choose which Web document, if any, Navigator 4 displays when you launch the program. The default is the Netscape home page, located at the Netscape site. Earlier in the chapter we discussed why you may want to change this.

The top section of this page lets you elect to start Navigator with a blank page, with a specific home page, or with whatever the last page was that you visited before closing the program. This last option is a real convenience if you're doing research at a variety of specialized sites and want to continue where you left off.

In the middle section you specify what site Navigator will access when you click the Home button, or when you start the program if you chose Home page in the top section. Just type in the URL. You can also use the Browse button to find and specify a local HTML file you want to use, and you can use the Use Current Page button to use the currently displayed document as your home page.

In the bottom section you can set how long you want the URLs in your history list to stick around, and you can also click the Clear History button to delete all these saved URLs immediately. If you visit a lot of sites, your history list may get very long and too unwieldy to work with, so this button can really simplify your online life.

There is a Languages tab underneath the Navigator category on the left. If it is not displayed, double-click Navigator or simply click the plus icon.

Languages

In the Languages window you can specify which languages you want Navigator 4 to accept from a Web server. Just click the Add button and choose which languages you want to add. Let's say you access a site that includes separate versions of the lyrics to LL Cool J's "Doin' It" in Chinese, Dutch, and Swedish. You could view the Chinese lyrics properly only if you've added Chinese to the list. You can also use the up and down arrow buttons to prioritize the languages you add. If Chinese is first on your list, Navigator will attempt to display the page using Chinese characters first.

And now we move on to the Applications window.

Applications

Not all files that are placed on the Internet or on your office intranet are meant to be viewed in a Web browser. For instance, you wouldn't use Navigator 4 to view a Microsoft Word document or to uncompress a ZIP file (see Chapter 8 for more information on ZIP files). But Navigator *can* launch the correct program when it encounters a file that it is not designed to handle itself. For instance, you might click a link to a file called MORTGAGE.XLS. Because of the .XLS extension, Navigator knows it's an Excel file and launches the spreadsheet program (if it's available on your system) with the information correctly displayed. In this case, Excel is considered a *helper application*.

Let's take a closer look. Still in the Preferences window, select the Applications category under Navigator, as shown in Figure 3-49. If Applications is not displayed, double-click Navigator, or simply click the plus icon.

Figure 3-49: The Applications window.

TIP

When Navigator encounters a file type on the Net or on your office intranet that it doesn't "know about," it may pop up an "Unknown File Type" dialog box. This dialog box includes a button labeled Pick App. If you click the button, you are taken to the Applications window shown above in Figure 3-50. Follow the directions below to tell Navigator what helper application should be associated with this unfamiliar file.

This looks like a fairly complicated dialog box at first, but once you understand the concepts, it's really pretty simple. The large scrolling list includes the names of different kinds of files you might encounter as you cruise the Net or your office intranet with Navigator 4. As you click each file type from the list, the bottom section of the window changes to display details about the particular file type. For instance, Figure 3-50 shows the file type details for WRI (Microsoft Write) files.

Figure 3-50: The Applications window, with file type details for Write files.

The bottom includes three fields:

- **Extension**. This is simply the extension for this kind of file. When Navigator encounters a file called CHAPTER3.DOC, for instance, it knows it's a Windword file because of the .DOC extension. An icon to the left of the field provides a graphical representation of the file type, just as it would appear on your Windows 95/NT desktop.

- **MIME Type**. MIME, or Multipurpose Internet Mail Extensions, is a universal standard for naming file types. Usually the MIME designations make sense, as in the case of Winword files, which are classified as application/msword.

- **Handled By**. This field specifies the helper application that will be launched when Navigator encounters a file of this type. An icon to the left represents the program. In this case, when Navigator encounters a file with the extension .WRI, it launches the program Write, which then displays the file correctly.

But what if you don't want Microsoft Word to start up every time Navigator encounters a .WRI file? What if you want to view the contents of the file in some other application such as WordPad or WordView—or what if you simply want to save it to disk?

No problem. Just click the Edit button. The Edit Type dialog box appears, as shown in Figure 3-51.

Figure 3-51: The Edit Type dialog box.

In the Handled By section, select Save to Disk if you simply want files of this type saved rather than displayed or otherwise processed. Or if you want them handled by a different application, make sure the Application option button is selected and then click the Browse button to select a different program.

TIP

If you want Navigator to ask you before it automatically opens files of this type in a helper application, check the checkbox at the bottom of this Window. This is useful, for example, if you sometimes want to view Winword files immediately and sometimes simply want to save them to disk.

What about the top option button, the one labeled Navigator? In this case it's grayed out (made unavailable) because Navigator itself cannot display Winword files—it must call upon the services of a helper application such as Microsoft Word. But take a look at Figure 3-52, which shows the Edit Type dialog box for GIF Image files.

Figure 3-52: The Edit Type dialog box for GIF Image files.

Since Navigator *can* display GIF files without any outside help, the Navigator option button is available—and selected by default. If you click a link to a GIF file, it will be displayed using the browser window. But you may want a different program, such as a full-featured graphics program, to display any GIF files you encounter. In that case, simply select the Application option button and browse for the program you want to use. In any case, click OK when you're finished editing this file type.

TIP

Settings in the Applications window affect every Communicator component, not just Navigator 4. For instance, they affect the way attached files are handled in Netscape Messenger (see Chapter 5).

If you want to get fancy, you can even add new file types and subtypes to Communicator's default list. However, this is truly a propeller-head option: you should not even be thinking about it except to add a new standardized MIME type, and unless you really know what you're doing. Assuming you have the proper geek credentials, though, it's pretty easy. In the Applications window, click New Type. Then just fill in the blanks.

And yes, you can even delete file types by clicking the Remove button. I do not recommend this. There is no harm in having extra file types listed, even ones you'll never encounter, but unless you're pretty technical it may be hard to add back a type you've deleted.

Now let's move on to the Offline category.

Offline Preferences

Still in the Preferences window, select the Offline category, as shown in Figure 3-53.

Figure 3-53: The Offline Preferences.

The choices here are fairly self-explanatory. If you select Online Work Mode, Communicator assumes you are connected to the Net or to an intranet at all times. If you choose Offline Work Mode, Communicator assumes you are not always connected. These choices affect the behavior of Messenger and Discussion Groups more than Navigator (see Chapters 5 and 6).

And how about clicking the "Ask Me" choice? In this mode Communicator will ask you if you want to go online when you first start one of its components. If you say you do, your Dial-Up Networking connection will be initialized (assuming you're using Windows 95 or Windows NT) and you will be connected to the Net.

Now let's advance to the last of the Preference categories, Advanced Preferences.

TIP

You may have noticed that I'm skipping the Download category under Offline. That's because the settings that appear there only relate to e-mail and discussion groups, and they are covered fully in Chapters 5 and 6.

Advanced Preferences

Don't worry, this is not a geeks-only zone by any means. The folks at Netscape throw in the word Advanced so you can feel good about yourself, but it's really pretty easy.

Go ahead and click Advanced in the Category list on the left of the Preferences window. The Advanced preferences window appears, as shown in Figure 3-54.

Figure 3-54: Advanced preferences.

Let's cover the options in the top section one at a time:

- **Automatically load images**. If you leave this checked, Navigator will automatically load all the images that are part of the Web page you are currently visiting. On very slow connections this may be tedious, and you may want to uncheck this box to experience the Web in much faster "text only" mode. If this box is unchecked, a Show Images button becomes available on the Control Toolbar. Using Show Images, you can force Navigator to display the graphics at particular sites, on a case-by-case basis, even though *automatic* display is disabled.

- **Enable Java**. You'll learn about Java in Chapters 4 and 10, but for now, all you need to know is that it's a programming language that extends the abilities of Navigator and makes your computer do amazing things. Java programs, or "applets," that are included in a Web page are downloaded by Navigator and then run locally on your machine. Because you are in effect running a new program that you know nothing about, Java may in rare cases create havoc on your system or pose security risks. If you are worried about this, uncheck this box and read Chapter 12, where I discuss security in detail.

- **Enable JavaScript**. Same idea here. JavaScript is a simpler language than Java, though, and it has more built-in security. It is used for lots of small "special effects" within the browser window, things like scrolling marquees and kiosk mode. Go ahead and uncheck this box if you want, but you will be missing out on some of the graphical niceties of the Web pages you visit.

- **Enable style sheets**. I mentioned style sheets earlier. They are collections of formatting and layout information that may be stored for reuse by multiple Web pages. In most cases you should leave this item checked.

- **Enable AutoInstall**. Communicator includes an exciting new feature whereby new plug-ins (see Chapters 7 and 10), upgrades, or other extensions to the program may be installed automatically. You don't need to request or install the software yourself. Once you've approved an electronic security certificate that appears on your screen identifying the source of the software, the files simply download, unpack their virtual bags, and makes themselves at home on your computer. A typical example: Navigator encounters a multimedia file that requires a special plug-in in order to display properly. You are asked to approve the installation of the new plug-in, which then installs itself automatically on your system. Within minutes or even seconds, the multimedia file is displayed correctly in the browser window. In rare cases where this imposes a security risk, you may want to uncheck this checkbox.

■ **Send e-mail address as anonymous FTP password**. When you log onto anonymous FTP sites to browse and download files (see Chapter 8), the convention is to send your e-mail address as the password. In most cases you should not check this box; Navigator will generate one for you.

The bottom section of this window deals with *cookies*, and whether or not you want Navigator to accept them. Cookies, in this case, are bits of information that a Web site stores on your own hard drive. This enables the site to "remember," from session to session, information that's specific to your use of the site. For instance, you may have chosen a particular color configuration on the site, or a category of information that you want to access each time. Cookies enable Web page designers to do things that would be very clumsy otherwise, but not everybody likes the idea of them. They may be used, for instance, to provide advertisers and other collectors of demographics with information about the trail of pages at their site you have visited.

This dialog box lets you deal with cookies in one of three ways. You can accept them; you can accept them only if the information they contain is sent back to the originating Web site, not to some other URL; or you can reject them. My personal advice: unless you have a specific reason to worry about cookies, let Navigator accept them and don't lose any sleep.

If you expand the Advanced category in the list on the left, you'll see that there are two other subcategories: Cache, Proxies, and Disk Space. The last of these items is covered in Chapters 5 and 6, but let's take a look at the first two now.

Cache Settings

Bear with me for a few minutes, we're going to get a little bit technical. Don't worry, it won't hurt much. If you're not too concerned about performance right now, you can just skip the rest of this chapter and come back here later. But if you want to make sure Navigator 4 is operating as efficiently as possible—and this can be important when you're paying for Internet access on an hourly basis—read on.

A *cache* (pronounced just like the green stuff) is a reserve area (a file) on your computer that houses information downloaded from the Internet as you navigate. You can think of it as a temporary holding cell that Navigator uses to store data between the time it is downloaded and the time it is displayed. If your cache is large enough, it can store entire Web pages and even graphics. That way, when you return to a previously visited site, Navigator doesn't have to download the information all over again; it can simply grab it from the cache.

There are actually two caches, a memory cache and a hard disk cache. The memory cache holds text and graphics only as long as you run any component of Communicator. The hard disk cache, on the other hand, is persistent: it holds information even after you exit the program. That way you can retrieve large documents quickly, without having to re-download them from the original site on the Net.

TIP

> *The Navigator 4 Refresh command (available from the View menu) redisplays the current document using information stored in the cache. The Reload button, on the other hand, actually goes back to the original document site, checks to see if it has changed since the last time you accessed it, and then reloads it from the Internet if there are any changes. So if you think that a document may have changed since the last time you visited it during the current session, you should use the Reload button to view any updates.*

There are advantages and disadvantages in setting high cache sizes for both types of caches. Even though memory caches are much quicker than disk caches, devoting more RAM to this type of cache can slow down your computer's overall performance. On the other hand, higher disk cache settings eat up your hard disk space.

Follow these steps to change your settings for cache sizes:

1. Click the Cache category under Advanced to display the Cache settings window, shown in Figure 3-55.

Figure 3-55: The Cache settings.

2. You can set the size of the memory cache in the Memory Cache field. The default setting is 1024K of RAM. Unless you have a large amount of memory on your system, such as 32MB or more, you may want to keep this setting where it is. Otherwise, you can try setting it at 1200K to see if your browsing speeds increase.

3. Set the amount of hard disk space that you want to reserve for a disk cache. This value is entered in the Disk Cache field; its default is set to 7680K (7M) of hard disk space. On most newer computers that come with hard disks of 450MB or more, you should have no problem reserving even more for this cache if you want.

TIP

Experiment with both the memory cache and hard disk cache sizes to determine the best settings for your system. If you tend to use Communicator without other applications running at the same time, such as a word processor or spreadsheet, you can set the memory cache much higher to make Netscape Navigator 4 run quicker. If you generally run Netscape Communicator with other applications that need large amounts of memory, keep the memory cache low, around 600K. This ensures that each application has ample RAM to run properly.

4. To clear the current content from your disk or memory caches, click Clear Memory Cache or Clear Disk Cache. When you click either of these buttons, a confirmation box pops up, asking if you are sure you want to clear the selected cache. Click OK to confirm that you do; click Cancel if you change your mind.

Why Would I Want to Clear a Cache?

Depending on how much navigating you do or how often you visit a site, you may want to periodically clear a cache setting. Having a cache decreases the time it takes to access sites that you've recently visited, but it does increase the strain on your local computer. When your memory cache is set to a high value, the amount of memory devoted to Communicator cannot be used by other resources. This slows down your machine when you run these other applications. Also, you may want to clear the memory cache if you've been online for several hours and you feel your machine responding sluggishly to Navigator 4. After you clear the cache, you should notice an improvement in your PC's performance.

5. Click one of the radio buttons toward the bottom of the page. If a document stored in cache has been revised, you'll want to see the revision instead of the old document. These buttons specify how Netscape Navigator 4 checks the Web for document revisions:

- **Once per Session.** Checks for page revisions only once during the time you start and quit Communicator. This is the default setting, and you will probably find it adequate unless you are trying to keep up with late-breaking news on CNN.

- **Every Time.** Checks for changes each time you request a Web document rather than relying on data stored in the cache. Because Navigator 4 is constantly checking the cached item against the Web page, you encounter a little performance degradation when you use this option.

- **Never.** Performs no verifications; a page available in cache is always brought from cache. Not a good selection if you want to see the latest-and-greatest offerings at a particular Web site.

Proxies

The next category under Advanced is Proxies. Let's take a quick look at the Proxies settings page shown in Figure 3-56.

Figure 3-56: The Proxies page.

Some corporate networks do not let you access Internet resources directly. Instead, you send your requests for information to a special *proxy server*, which then relays your request on to its intended site—if you have the right permissions. Similarly, incoming information is collected by the proxy, and you access it from there. Some networks have different proxy server addresses for different types of Internet resources. If your Proxies page is set up correctly, however, all this buck-passing is completely transparent to you. When you try to access home.netscape.com, for instance, it looks to you like you're accessing it directly, even though all the information goes through an intermediary address that keeps track of everything you do.

If you don't think you have a proxy server, leave the top option button selected. If you think you *do* have a proxy server, ask your network administrator how to fill in this page. The Manual proxy configuration choice lets you set up a different network address for each type of Internet resource, and the Automatic proxy configuration choice lets you specify the URL for a special configuration file on your network that includes all the necessary proxy information.

The last category under Advanced is Disk Space. The options in this window only apply to e-mail and discussion group messages, however, and so I will cover them in Chapters 5 and 6. When you are done with the other categories in the Preferences window, simply click OK to return to Navigator 4.

Moving On

In this chapter, you learned the basics of navigating Web pages, as well as how to operate the major features of Communicator's browser component, Netscape Navigator 4. You now know how to search for a particular site, as well as where you can find the newest and coolest pages on the Web. You also know how to change some of the program's settings so that it operates exactly the way you want it to.

Now let's move on to something everybody's talking about: Netscape Netcaster and what's commonly known as *push technology*. In the next chapter you'll learn how to subscribe to information *channels* that give you quick access to media-rich information that updates itself automatically!

CHAPTER 4

Netcaster

Without a doubt, Netcaster is the Communicator component that has received the most media attention. With its new flexible approach to multimedia information, it has stirred the imaginations of content providers, Information System (IS) managers, and end users.

Netcaster is so new, in fact, that content providers are constantly coming up with new ways to exploit its power. This chapter shows you how to use Netcaster and introduces you to some of the exciting possibilities it inspires.

What is Netcaster?

In a nutshell, Netcaster is the Communicator component that delivers information to you automatically—you don't need to search the Web or your office intranet for what you want. With Netcaster, the information comes to *you*. (Yes, this is the "push" technology that you may have heard about.)

In addition, Netcaster lets you download and then later browse Web sites offline, without being connected to the Net or your intranet. Not only does this save you money in online charges, it saves you time as well. Instead of waiting for a large image to display, for example, you see it immediately when you click its link.

To really understand Netcaster, though, you need to understand the concept of channels.

What is a Channel?

In the context of Netcaster, a channel is a Web site that is delivered automatically to your desktop. Or, you can think of it as a collection of media-rich information in a particular area of interest. You *subscribe* to a channel, which is then downloaded to your machine and stored locally so that you can access it quickly. Netcaster can also update your channels automatically, going online and collecting the latest information at regular intervals that you specify.

What Kind of Channels are Available?

Back in the early and mid 80's, the number and variety of cable channels on television was dazzling. There was the Weather Channel, the Golf Channel, and of course millions of different shopping channels.

The Web makes the variety available on cable seem dull by comparison. Since any Web site can be a channel, the possibilities of Netcasting are almost endless. You can have channels on sports, news, movies, Pez, lighthouses, haiku— the list goes on and on!

But trying to consider that amount of variety might blow your mind. So in the interest of saving a few neurons, let's look at some of channels that are set up specifically for Netcasting.

- **ABCNEWS.Com**. Instead of waiting for the ABC news to come on in the evening, let the news come to you. The ABCNEWS.Com channel dishes up stories and updates around the clock, as you can see in Figure 4-1.

- **The Sporting News**. Do you want sporting news, statistics, and scores? The Sporting News channel pushes it your way, as shown in Figure 4-2.

- **Lycos Direct.** With a more Internet-centric content, Lycos Direct offers you not only news and updates, but also site reviews and coverage of what's best on the Internet (see Figure 4-3).

Figure 4-1: ABCNEWS.Com means you don't have to wait for the news.

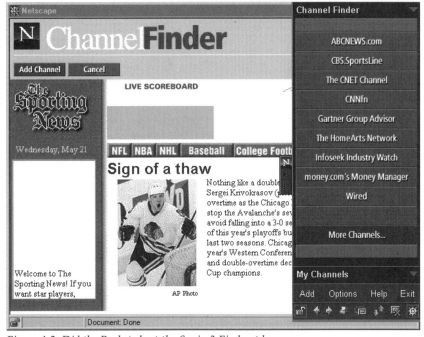

Figure 4-2: Did the Rockets beat the Sonics? Find out here.

Figure 4-3: Lycos cuts down your surf time by bringing you the best of the Internet.

What is a Webtop?

A *webtop* is a channel that appears full-screen and is anchored to your desktop. In other words, a webtop remains on your screen all the time. You may work in other windows, or open other channels, on top of the webtop. It actually serves as a temporary replacement for your Windows desktop.

A webtop may be updated automatically at regular intervals, just like any other channel. That means it can provide you with late-breaking news as you work in other applications. This ability to update automatically can be a great help in a corporate intranet, to ensure that everyone is on "the same page." Figure 4-4 shows a typical corporate webtop.

Sounds great, doesn't it?

So how do you actually get into Netcaster?

I thought you'd never ask.

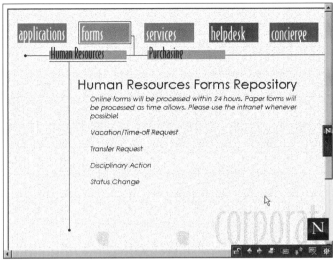

Figure 4-4: A typical corporate webtop.

Starting Netcaster

To start Netcaster, either choose the Netcaster icon from the Communicator program group, or choose Netcaster from any component's Communicator menu. You'll get the Netcaster drawer, which looks like Figure 4-5.

Figure 4-5: The Netcaster drawer.

> **TIP**
>
> *At the time of this printing, Netcaster is available for download from the Netscape Home Page. Once you have downloaded it from the Netscape Home Page and installed it, Netcaster will automatically integrate itself into your Communicator software.*

Java Security

When you first start Netcaster, a Java Security alert pops up like the one shown in Figure 4-6.

Figure 4-6: The Java Security alert.

The text here sounds pretty threatening, but not to worry. All it means is that Netcaster is what is known as a *signed Java* application—an application written in the Java programming language that needs your explicit approval before it is allowed to perform certain tasks such as accessing your hard drive.

As a language, Java includes a variety of safeguards. Typically, it *cannot* access your hard drive without special permission. JavaScript, a simpler but related language, is even more secure. And that's where *signed* Java and JavaScript comes in. With signed Java or JavaScript, an application presents you with a special *security certificate* that positively identifies its creator or distributor. You can approve or reject the certificate. If you reject it, the application will not run at all. You are also given the option of allowing or disallowing specific types of access to your system that may compromise security. These types of access are outside the usual security restrictions of regular unsigned Java and JavaScript. In other words, in accepting a certificate you are agreeing to loosen security.

In the alert shown above, you can accept the certificate (grant full access to the application) by clicking Grant, or you can reject it (deny the necessary access) by clicking Deny. Be warned, though, that if you click Deny, Netcaster won't run. You may as well just move along to Chapter 5! If you check the Remember this Decision… checkbox you will never have to see this alert again.

Before choosing Grant or Deny, you can view in detail what types of access to your system Netcaster is requesting. Go ahead and click the Details button. The Java Security's Target Details window appears, as shown in Figure 4-7.

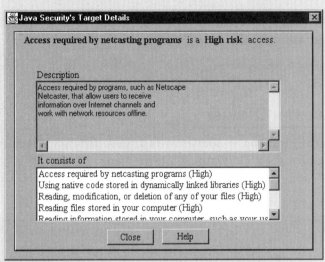

Figure 4-7: The Java Security's Target Details window.

Since you probably got this copy of Netcaster from a trusted source, you don't have to worry too much about granting "high risk access" to the program. After all, other Communicator components have been accessing your hard disk already. But in the case of *other* signed Java or JavaScript objects that you might encounter in cruising the Web, you should weigh the pros and cons of granting high risk access very carefully.

You can learn more about Java and JavaScript in Chapter 10, and about dealing with Java and JavaScript security issues in Chapter 12.

Looking at the Netcaster Drawer

The Netcaster drawer is a separate entity from the channels that display beside it. The Netcaster drawer remains available all the time, even when you're moving between channels or choosing a new channel.

In this book I'll be using the terms Netcaster drawer and Netcaster window interchangeably, depending on context. They are the same thing.

Sometimes, however, you might want to hide the drawer in order to allow a channel—or even another program—more screen real estate. The next section tells you how.

Hiding the Netcaster Drawer

About halfway down the Netcaster window there's a small textured tab on its left side. You can see a picture of it in Figure 4-8.

Figure 4-8: The tab on the Netcaster drawer.

To hide the Netcaster drawer, just click the tab. All of the Netcaster drawer will vanish except for the small tab, as you can see in Figure 4-9.

To retrieve the Netcaster drawer, simply click the tab again. The Netcaster drawer reappears complete with tab.

As you explore the Netcaster drawer you might find yourself somewhat confused because of the two lists that are presented in the drawer; the Channel Finder and the My Channels lists. Here's how they work.

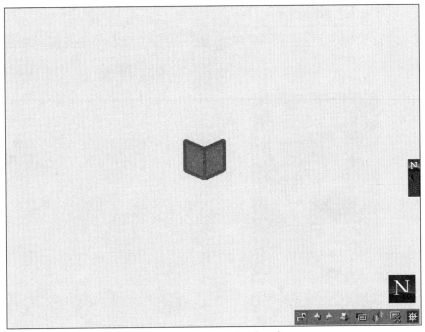

Figure 4-9: The Netcaster drawer hidden except for the tab.

The Channel Finder & My Channels Lists

Netcaster's Channel Finder lists a number of interesting channels that are available, and it lets you preview them to see if you want to subscribe. The Channel Finder is somewhat similar to the "preview channels" that cable companies use to interest you in subscribing to HBO or a sports network, for instance.

Once you've actually subscribed to a channel, it appears in another Netcaster list, the once called *My Channels*. These are channels that have already been stored on your hard drive and that you can access immediately.

Let's take a closer look at these two different lists.

The Channel Finder

The Channel Finder is an integral part of the Netcaster drawer, as you can see in Figure 4-10.

Figure 4-10: The Channel Finder listing.

As I mentioned earlier, the Channel Finder listing is sort of like a preview channel. It includes several of the channels available through Netcaster, with an option to see more by clicking on the "More Channels" button. If you click a channel in the Channel Finder, you can see some sample content for that channel. You are then given the opportunity to subscribe.

But although your cable provider may offer the "People Who Chew With Their Mouth Open Channel," that doesn't mean you want to watch it. Your cable guide doesn't have any way to customize a list by showing only the channels you want to watch, but Netcaster does. It's called My Channels.

My Channels

To access the My Channels list—that is, the list of channels to which you've actually subscribed—click the black box towards the bottom of the screen that says My Channels. The My Channels list pops up, looking like what you see in Figure 4-11.

Figure 4-11: The My Channels listing.

Initially the only channel on your list is the Netscape Channel. As we continue through this chapter you'll learn how to add channels and configure them to update when you want. Soon you too will have "57 channels and nothing on"! (By the way, if you want to get back to the Channel Finder list, just click the Channel Finder button above the My Channels button.)

TIP

The channels listed on Channel Finder are there only to let you know about the major channels available. They will not update automatically—only those channels you've added to your "My Channel" list will update.

Now that you know how to start Netcaster and how to tell the difference between the My Channels and Channel Finder lists, let's talk about what you can do with Netcaster itself.

There are two toolbars on the Netcaster drawer. The top one is a text toolbar and the bottom one is an icon toolbar. In the next section I'll cover the text tool bar only. The icon toolbar is for moving around webtops and will be covered later in this chapter.

The Text Toolbar

To use any of the commands on the text toolbar, just click it. The tools are Add, Options, Help, and Exit.

Add

Click Add to add a channel to your My Channels list. (More about that shortly.)

Options

The Options command lets you set your options for individual Netcaster channels that you've subscribed to as well as for the program as a whole. When you click the Options button you'll see a box like the one in Figure 4-12.

Figure 4-12: The Options dialog box..

The Options dialog box has three tabs: Channels, Layout, and Security. The first tab, Channels, lets you:

- Set the properties for individual channels in the My Channels list. To do this, select a channel from the list and click the Properties button.

- Manually update individual channels so that any new information is automatically downloaded to your hard drive. To do this, click the Update Now button.

- Add a new channel (click the Add button). Later in this chapter we'll walk through the process of adding a channel this way.

- Delete a channel. To do this, select a channel and click Delete.

We'll talk more about adding channels and setting channel properties later in the chapter.

Now, click the layout tab to set the layout options for the program as a whole. You'll see a screen like that in Figure 4-13.

Figure 4-13: The layout options in Netcaster.

The first two options in this tab let you decide where you want the Netcaster drawer and actual channel information—or the webtop—to appear on your screen. Netcaster's default setting is for the Netcaster drawer to appear on the right side of the screen and the actual channel information to appear on the left. But by using the pull-down menu beside "Attach Netcaster drawer to" and "Attach Webtop to" you can change the placement of the Netcaster drawer and the webtop.

Below these two pull-down menus is a checkbox labeled "Automatically hide Netcaster window." When this box is checked, the Netcaster drawer will hide itself automatically every time you choose a channel. (The drawer tab will remain, however, so you can click on it and cause the drawer to reappear.)

The last option in this tab is the default channel selector. The default channel is the channel that automatically appears when you first launch Netcaster; it's kind of like the home page preference you set when you use Netscape Navigator. The default channel for Netcaster is no channel at all. If you want to keep it that way, just leave the "None" button under this option checked. If you want to have a default channel, however, click on the "Set default to" radio button and use the pull-down menu to choose any of the channels in the My Channels listing as your default channel.

Help

Help brings up the help file for Netcaster.

Exit

Exit quits the Netcaster program.

By now the Netcaster drawer is probably feeling more familiar to you. Let's get down to business and add some channels to your My Channels list. You've already seen two ways to add new channels:

- You can click the Add button in the text toolbar.
- You can click the Add button in the Channels tab of Options.

But perhaps the most convenient way to add new channels is through the Channel Finder. That's where we're going next.

Using the Channel Finder

As I mentioned at the beginning of this chapter, *any* Web site can be a Netcaster channel. However, not all Web sites are suited to this form of presentation. Fortunately, the Channel Finder can get you started examining a few choice sites that were specifically designed as Netcaster channels.

Let's walk through the process of previewing and adding a channel from the Channel Finder list.

Adding a Channel

Look at the Channel Finder list and find a channel that you think might be interesting. In this example we'll use the CNNfn channel. When you click on the button that says CNNfn, a *descriptor card* pops up with a logo for CNNfn, as you can see in Figure 4-14.

Figure 4-14: The CNNfn descriptor card in the Channel Finder list.

Click the Add Channel button in this descriptor card, or just double-click the card itself. A Navigator window appears with preview information on the CNNfn channel. You can see it in Figure 4-15.

Figure 4-15: The preview window for CNNfn.

Look over the information in the preview window. If you decide you want to subscribe to it, click the Add Channel button in the upper left hand corner of the preview window. A dialog box pops up so you can set the properties for this channel.

Setting Channel Properties

In the Name box, make sure the name of the channel is as you want it to appear in the My Channels list—CNNfn, perhaps, or CNN Financial. Below that, in the Location field, the URL should already be filled in. (If you're adding a channel manually, you'll have to type it in yourself. Just type in the URL as you would type it to go to a Web page.) Below the name and location field, there's a pull-down menu to specify how often you want this channel to be updated with new information from the Web. You have several choices, ranging from every 30 minutes to every week. For this example, choose every day.

Now that you've got all the basic information down, you need to establish how you want this channel to look on your screen. Click the Display tab to bring up the Display properties dialog box, as shown in Figure 4-16.

Figure 4-16: Setting display properties.

The only thing you have to decide within this tab is whether you want the channel to appear as a default window (a standard Navigator window) or as a webtop, which takes up the whole screen. For the sake of this example, let's set the channel to appear in a default window.

The final setting you'll want to establish is the size of the channel's cache. The cache is the amount of space the channel will take up on your hard drive to store its text, pictures, and other multimedia. Obviously if you have a small hard drive, you'll want to be conservative in assigning cache space to your channels. On the other hand, assigning too little cache space to a channel means that you won't be able to download the entire channel for offline browsing. (We'll go over offline browsing at the end of the chapter.)

To access the cache settings, click the cache tab. You'll get a screen that looks like the one in Figure 4-17.

Figure 4-17: Setting the cache properties for a channel.

First, decide how many informational *levels* of the channel you want to download and store. What do I mean by levels? Here's how it works:

- The first level is the first page of the channel, including any graphics or other multimedia files it contains.

- The second level consists of all the pages to which the first page links.

- The third level consists of all the pages to which the second page links, and so on.

If the first level has five links, while all the pages in the second level have ten links, and the third level has twenty links—well, you can see that going deeper than just two or three levels can take up a lot of space on your hard drive. For the sake of this example, click the field next to the word level(s) and enter the number 2. This indicates that you want to download and store two levels of the CNNfn site.

Finally, you're going to have to indicate the maximum amount of space you want to give this channel on your hard drive. The option here reads "Don't store more than ____ KB of information." Click the KB field and type in the amount of space you want to devote to this channel's cache. Bear in mind that 1000KB of space equals a full megabyte, while 2KB of space is hardly enough for the average text file. For this example, enter 1000 in the KB field. That'll devote 1MB of your hard drive space to the CNNfn channel.

TIP

Once you indicate the number of levels you want to download and the amount of diskspace you want to reserve, Netcaster begins to download the channel to your hard drive. To stop this process, click the Stop Update button in the cache tab.

Once you've set the options in the cache tab, click the OK button. CNNfn now appears on your My Channels list, as you can see in Figure 4-18.

Figure 4-18: CNNfn in the My Channels list.

TIP

You can hide the CNNfn description box in the Channel Finder listing simply by clicking it.

Now that you know how to add a channel, let's talk some more about working with channels—specifically, how to add them manually and adjust their properties. After that, we'll discuss how to move around in webtops.

Manually Adding a Channel

We've walked through adding a channel in the Channel Finder, but eventually you're going to want to add a channel that isn't listed in the Channel Finder.

Why? Because as was mentioned in the beginning of this chapter, any Web site can be a channel. Of course, there's no way that the Channel Finder can list every Web site in existence—heck, not even the search engines can do that. Now let's manually add a channel and set its properties. It's almost as simple as doing it with the Channel Finder. These channel properties you set, by the way, are the same ones that you see when you add a channel through the Channel Finder and when you adjust settings using the Options button, so you are already familiar with much of this process.

To begin adding a channel manually, click Add in the Netcaster drawer. The Add channel dialog box appears, as shown in Figure 4-19.

Figure 4-19: Manually adding a channel.

From here, you set the properties just like you did when you added a channel in Channel Finder. The only difference is that you'll have to specify the name and the URL of the channel. Remember, any URL will work!

But what if you decide you want to change a channel's properties, or if you want to delete a channel altogether?

Changing Channel Properties & Deleting Channels

Eventually you're going to change your mind about a channel. You may want to change how much space you want to devote to it, or how often you want it to update. You may even decide to delete it, freeing up valuable hard drive space for other information.

Changing channel properties or deleting channels is easy. Click Options in the Netcaster drawer. You'll see the dialog box we discussed earlier in the chapter, as shown in Figure 4-20.

Figure 4-20: The Options dialog box.

To remove a channel, follow these steps:

1. Scroll through the list of channels in the dialog box until you find the channel you want to delete.

2. Click it to highlight it.

3. Click the Delete button.

To change the properties of a channel, do the following:

1. Scroll through the list of channels in the dialog box until you find the channel you want.

2. Click it to highlight it.

3. Click Properties. The Properties dialog box appears, as shown in Figure 4-21.

Figure 4-21: The Properties dialog box.

4. Modify any of the properties and click OK.

You now know how to add channels, change channel properties, and even delete channels you no longer want to use. So you're a great administrator of your desktop system, but we've left something out. How do you actually *access* a channel once you've added it to your My Channels list?

Accessing Channels

To access a channel, click the My Channels button in the Netcaster drawer. A list of the channels available to you pops up. Find the channel in which you're interested and click it. The channel appears on your screen, and depending on how you've set your options your Netcaster drawer may vanish.

A channel works a lot like a Navigator page. There are hypertext links and hot spots—places on the channel that link to other pages in the channel when they're clicked. However, sometimes moving around in the anchored full-screen channels—what we've been calling webtops—can get confusing. To alleviate that confusion, Netcaster offers a icon bar for moving around on the webtop.

Moving Around in a Webtop

At the beginning of the chapter we discussed webtops. Since webtops take up the entire screen, and since they act as as a temporary replacement for the Windows desktop, navigating within one can be confusing. You do not have the usual Navigator toolbars available as navigational aids. To solve this problem, Netcaster provides a special icon bar at the bottom corner of the screen. It contains icons that are very similar to the ones you're used to in Navigator 4 (see Chapter 3).

TIP

Webtops have hyperlinks just like other Web pages do. You can click these hyperlinks to move around within a channel just as you would use hyperlinks to move around in a Web page.

If you're using the Webtop mode to display a channel, and you've got your options set so that the Netcaster drawer disappears when you open a channel, you might find yourself with the webtop, the drawer tab, and an icon bar in the lower corner of the screen, as shown in figure 4-22.

Figure 4-22: The icon bar.

Using the Icon Bar

The webtop may contain links, buttons, and other navigational objects, but the icon bar provides a convenient external interface. Here's what the icons in the bar represent, from left to right:

 Security. This is an icon of a lock. If the lock is in an unlocked position, it means that this webtop (or any channel) is "insecure" and any information sent between your computer and this webtop is unencrypted (see Chapter 12). On the other hand, if the icon is in a locked position, this channel is "secure" and suitable for sensitive communications like commerce and online purchasing. Please see Chapter 12 for more information on security issues.

 Back arrow. Goes to the previous page on the webtop.

 Forward arrow. Goes to the next page on the webtop.

 Printer. Prints the webtop.

Webtops. Hides or displays the webtop. Click once on this icon to hide the webtop; click it again to display it. This is convenient for switching between viewing the current channel and getting some other work done.

 Up and Down Arrows. Sends the webtop to the front or the back. When you have several screens active on your computer at once—say, one screen for e-mail, one screen for the Web, and your webtop—it might be inconvenient to have the webtop as the primary item on your screen. Clicking this button moves it to the "back," showing the other screens first. Later, when you want to access the webtop again, you click this button to bring it to the front, making it the primary user interface.

 Screen and X. Closes the webtop.

 Navigator logo. Opens a new Netscape Navigator window.

Using Netcaster Offline

In the last 20 or so pages, you have learned the basics of using Netscape Netcaster. Now let's see how you can leverage its features to save time and connection fees.

You don't have to be connected to the Internet all the time to take advantage of Netcaster. Once you've updated the channels you're interested in, you can disconnect from the Internet and browse them just as if you were still online.

But how do you tell if your channels are updated, and how do you update your channels manually? Read on.

Manually Updating Channels

Make sure you're connected to the Internet or your office intranet and then launch Netcaster. Open the My Channels list. Under some of your channels you may see a red and gray animated progress bar.

Figure 4-23: The progress bar.

This progress bar shows that new material is still being "pushed" to your channel from the Internet or your intranet. Until this bar disappears, the download is still in progress, and any effort to browse this channel offline won't be completely successful.

Sometimes you'll want to force an update to a particular channel. For example, you may have a site that you want to update only weekly, but before you browse it offline you want to make sure it contains all the latest information. To manually update a channel follow these steps:

1. Click the Options button in the Netcaster drawer. The Options dialog box appears as shown in Figure 4-23.

Figure 4-23: The Options dialog box.

2. Scroll through the list of channels in the box and highlight the channel you want to update.

3. Click the Update Now button. Assuming you're connected to the Net or your office intranet, the channel immediately begins to update.

4. Click OK to dismiss the Options box.

Again, wait until the progress bar vanishes to make sure the entire channel has been updated.

Offline Browsing

Once the progress bar has disappeared, how do you browse offline? Simply disconnect your Internet or intranet connection, click the My Channels button, and choose a channel from the list. You'll be able to browse a channel just like you would online—only a lot faster since the information is already on your hard drive.

TIP

If you've imposed small cache sizes on your channels, then you might not be able to completely browse a downloaded channel. The channels will download updates only until their allotted space on your hard drive has been filled. If you repeatedly try to browse channels offline but find that the channels have not been completely downloaded, try increasing the cache size for your channels.

And remember, you can do this any time with any Web page you wish. If there's a Web page that you like to check regularly for updates, it's a real time-saver to download the information in advance and browse it at your leisure. For example, say you checked in on the Netscape Press site every Monday, poking around to see what new books are on the horizon. With Netcaster, you could set up the Netscape Press What's New page as a channel that updates weekly. Once a week Netcaster would grab any new material, insuring that you don't miss out on any book announcements. This can save you a lot of time. You don't have to do surf to the site or wait for the page to load; instead, it's sent to you.

Moving On

As you can see, Netcaster is one of the most exciting and flexible communications facilities available, whether you're connected to a corporate intranet or the Net as a whole. And since it's a brand new feature, you can expect the software to evolve and grow as information providers stretch its limits.

Now let's look at one of the oldest and best known bread-and-butter communications applications: e-mail. The next chapter is a complete tutorial on using Netscape Messenger to send and receive electronic messages that can even look like complete Web pages!

CHAPTER 5

Netscape Messenger

Netscape isn't content with just making the world's best Web browser. In Netscape Communicator, Netscape has created a multipurpose software product that can do much more than just display Web documents.

The most basic of all Internet tools is electronic mail, or *e-mail*. E-mail is the most widely used software tool of any kind, and Netscape Communicator provides a separate interface called *Messenger* just to handle this service. In this chapter, we'll show you how to use the Netscape Messenger window to send, receive, read, and store e-mail. This window, shown in Figure 5-1, is accessed by clicking the Mailbox icon in the Component Bar, by clicking the Messenger icon on your desktop, or by selecting Messenger Mailbox from any component's Communicator menu.

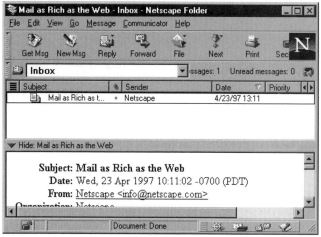

Figure 5-1: The Messenger window, with the Inbox folder selected.

Before we get into that, however, let's begin with a few words about e-mail itself.

What Is E-mail & How Does It Work?

E-mail, as you probably know, is the electronic messaging service of intranets and of the Net. When you send a message to a friend via e-mail, that message travels from your machine over your office intranet or the Internet itself until it arrives at your friend's machine, or to a special electronic post office on a machine he or she can access. The message is then kept there until your friend retrieves and reads it.

How does the intranet or Internet know how to get a piece of e-mail from your machine to your friend's post office account? It works just about like regular old-fashioned snail mail: all the necessary delivery information is contained in your friend's e-mail address.

When you write a piece of e-mail, it's essential to get the address right. There's no friendly Mr. Postman to figure out that you really meant the house down the block from the address you indicated. Every character counts. If there is a mistake in the address you enter—even one wrong letter—the mail will simply be returned to you as undeliverable.

The standard form for an address is *user@domain*. This address is in two parts, separated by an @ sign (press Shift+2 on your keyboard). The part before the @ is the username, and the part after the @ is the domain name—the name of the machine where that user has an e-mail account. It is important that e-mail addresses not have any spaces in them.

Usernames are how individual users are identified on systems that may be accessed by many people. For instance, the username part of Count Dracula's e-mail address, dracula@transylvania.com, is *dracula*. Domain names are the names of the machines themselves. The domain name in the address, *transylvania.com*, identifies the name of a machine, transylvania. The *.com* at the end of the domain name means that this is a commercial service. There are also *.gov* services, which are governmental institutions; *.edu* services, which are at educational institutions; and so on. We touched on some of this in Chapter 1. Sometimes addresses will end with information about a country or network instead of or in addition to a type of service. For example, addresses ending in .ca are in Canada, and addresses ending in .uk are in the United Kingdom.

What's My E-mail Address?

Your e-mail address is your identity in the online world; you were probably given your e-mail address by the people who provide you with Internet access. If you are on an office intranet, your e-mail address may be your network login name followed by an @ sign and the domain name of your company. Then again, it may not—you really need to check with your system administrator.

If you get on the Net using a SLIP or PPP account, you can usually figure out your e-mail address. If your login name is *frank* and your Internet access provider is *graveyard.com*, then your e-mail address is probably frank@graveyard.com. If this isn't correct, then you will have to call your access provider to figure out what your address is.

TIP

If your Internet service provider doesn't provide you with an e-mail account, you should seriously consider switching service providers!

Exchanging Messages With Online Services

What if you have friends who are not connected directly to the Internet via a LAN or a SLIP or PPP account, but are users of some online service such as America Online (AOL) or CompuServe? Can you exchange e-mail messages with them?

Sure! Users of CompuServe, MCI Mail, AT&T Mail, Prodigy, or AOL can send you e-mail using your regular Internet address. Typically, the procedure is no more complex than sending a message to another user of the service. You can also send e-mail to a user on any of these services, using Netscape Navigator 4 in the same way you would when communicating with another individual on the Net. The only difference is the addressing. If an online service user gives you his or her ID, you have to know how to turn it into a valid Internet address so that any message you send can be delivered. The method for translating addresses varies from service to service.

CompuServe

User IDs on CompuServe take the form of two numbers separated by a comma, as in 71234,5678. To send e-mail to a CompuServe subscriber, you address it to that ID number at (@) the domain compuserve.com. The only trick is that the comma between the two numbers must be replaced by a period. Thus the Internet e-mail address for the user whose ID is 71234,5678 would be:

```
71234.5678@compuserve.com
```

That's all there is to it; you send the message just like any other e-mail.

MCI Mail

MCI Mail users really have three IDs: a number; a "handle," or abbreviated name; and a normal full name. For instance, the user Jake Barns might have the following set of IDs:

```
123-4567
jbarns
Jake Barns
```

To send e-mail to Jake, you could use any of the following Internet e-mail addresses:

```
1234567@mcimail.com
jbarns@mcimail.com
jake_barns@mcimail.com
```

Please note that in the user number, you drop the hyphen, and in the full name you have to add an underscore (_) character between the first and last names.

America Online

All you need to know is the AOL user's "screen name"; you just add the at sign (@) and the domain aol.com. A valid Internet e-mail address for an AOL user might be, for instance:

```
aoluser@aol.com
```

Note that even if the AOL user has a space in his or her AOL name—John Doe, for instance—you can ignore that space and simply address your e-mail to johndoe@aol.com.

Prodigy

This is just like America Online. You send e-mail to a particular user ID at prodigy.com. Here's an example:

```
abc123@prodigy.com
```

AT&T Mail

As with AOL and Prodigy, each AT&T Mail user has a unique username. To address a message, you simply append @attmail.com to the username. A valid address might be as follows:

```
msmuffet@attmail.com
```

OK, you've learned a little about e-mail addressing and how e-mail works. Now it's time to look at Netscape Messenger itself. We'll start by getting a brief overview of the program, examining the features of the Messenger window, and then by actually working through the common e-mail tasks: sending and receiving messages, organizing folders, and keeping track of addresses.

Getting Started

Make sure that you are connected to the Net or to your office intranet. Now go ahead and double-click the Messenger icon on your desktop, or select the Mailbox icon from the Component Bar. As soon as the component starts running, a Password Entry dialog box appears asking for your e-mail password, as shown in Figure 5-2.

Figure 5-2: The Password Entry dialog box.

Your e-mail password is the password your incoming e-mail server requires in order for you to retrieve new messages. If you're not currently connected to your office intranet or the Net, you can still use Messenger offline. In this case, click Cancel when asked for your password. You should also click Cancel if you don't know what your current password is.

Your E-mail Password

Once you type in your password, Messenger remembers it for as long as any of the Communicator components is running. If you quit Communicator altogether, you will have to enter your password again the next time Messenger tries to access your incoming mail server. If you're on a relatively secure computer and want Messenger to always remember your e-mail password, even after you've quit and restarted the program, select Preferences from the Messenger's Edit menu and then select the Mail Server category on the left side of the dialog box that appears. On the right, in the Mail Server window, click the More Options button and then check the "Remember my mail password" checkbox. Click OK to save your changes.

Once you click OK after entering your e-mail password, Messenger logs into your incoming mail server and checks for any new messages. You are left in the Messenger window, with your Inbox folder (a folder for storing new e-mail) selected, as shown in Figure 5-3.

Figure 5-3: The Messenger window, with the Inbox folder displayed.

We'll examine this window in detail in a few minutes, but first a section for those of you who didn't enter your e-mail account information the first time you ran Communicator (see the section in Chapter 2 called "Starting Communicator the First Time"). If you need to add or modify e-mail account information such as your e-mail address or the address of your server, read on. Otherwise, jump to the section called "The Messenger Window."

Adding or Modifying Account Information

Before getting started, you need to have the following information handy:

- Your e-mail address.

- The username you use to access your e-mail server. If you use your ISP for e-mail, this is usually the same as your regular SLIP/PPP login name.

- Your e-mail password.

- The address of the server you use to send e-mail, which is also known as the outgoing mail server or SMTP server.

■ The address of the server you use to receive e-mail (incoming mail server). This is usually the same as your outgoing mail server.

■ Whether your incoming mail server uses POP3 or IMAP4 protocol (if you're using a commercial ISP it's probably POP3).

Once you have all this information on hand, click Preferences in the Messenger's Edit menu and then select Identity from the category list on the left. The Identity dialog box appears, as shown in Figure 5-4.

Figure 5-4: The Identity dialog box.

Enter your actual name and e-mail address in the appropriate fields. You may also enter a reply-to address if it is different from your e-mail address, as well as an optional organization name.

TIP

You may want to use a different reply-to address if you have several e-mail accounts, for instance one at home and one at work.

Don't worry about the Signature File and Address Book Card options—those will be explained later in this chapter.

Once you have completed the Identity dialog box, click the Mail Server category on the left. The Mail Server dialog box appears, as shown in Figure 5-5.

Figure 5-5: The Mail Server dialog box.

In this dialog box, enter your e-mail account name (often the same as your login name on your intranet or for your SLIP/PPP account), the address of your outgoing mail (SMTP) server, and the address of your incoming mail server. In most cases, these two addresses will be the same. In the bottom section of the dialog box, select whether your incoming e-mail server is of the POP3 or IMAP variety.

SMTP, POP3 & IMAP

Like all Internet and intranet programs, Netscape Communicator relies on established protocols to send and receive data. As explained earlier in this book, protocols are simply conventions that allow one piece of software to exchange data with another. For instance, a client program might expect a particular kind of acknowledgment after it sends a packet of data. Both sender and receiver need to play by the same rules.

Internet mail programs use SMTP (Simple Mail Transport Protocol) to *send* messages. The client, Netscape Messenger, first establishes a connection with the remote SMTP server, the machine that acts as host for the recipient's e-mail account. Once the link is established, Messenger sends the recipient's name. If the server can accept mail for that user, it responds with an OK. If there are several intended recipients, this negotiation continues for each of them. Finally Messenger sends the actual body of the e-mail message.

To *retrieve* messages from your e-mail server, Netscape Messenger uses one of two different protocols, depending on how the server is configured. The more common and older protocol is called POP3 (Post Office Protocol, version 3). Recently, IMAP (Internet Message Access Protocol) has become very popular. IMAP stores all your messages, in their correct folders, on the mail server. This means that if you access your mail from several different machines, you will always see exactly the same thing. (You may also keep local copies of your messages for offline reading, though.) I won't go into the details of POP3 and IMAP because they're somewhat complex, but it's important to make sure that your e-mail account is on a server that supports one of these protocols (most do). And if you have a choice between POP3 and IMAP, choose IMAP.

If you are using a POP3 server, notice that you can elect to leave your messages on the server after you retrieve them. That way you can retrieve them again, perhaps from a different computer. This option is useful if you travel, or if you sometimes work from home.

And if you are using an IMAP server, notice that you have a couple of extra options:

- **Keep copies of messages locally for offline reading.** As I mentioned in the sidebar above, IMAP servers store all your messages so that you can re-access them at any time, and from any computer. However, you can also keep copies of these messages on your local machine in case you want to read them when you're not connected to your IMAP server. To do so, check this checkbox.

■ **Server supports encrypted connections (SSL).** Some IMAP servers support special encryption that assures the privacy of your messages. If the IMAP server on your intranet supports encrypted connections, check this checkbox.

Now click the More Options button. The More Mail Server Preferences dialog box appears, as shown in Figure 5-6.

More Mail Server Preferences   ☒

    Local mail directory: `C:\Program Files\Netscape\Users\pjames\mail`   Choose...

    IMAP mail directory:

    ☐ Check for mail every `10`   minutes
    ☐ Remember my mail password.

    ☐ Use Netscape Messenger from MAPI-based applications

                                                   OK   Cancel

Figure 5-6: The More Mail Server Preferences dialog box.

The top two edit fields let you specify directories for local storage of your e-mail messages. If you're using POP3, you should probably leave the top field alone unless you have a very specific reason for changing the directory; if you're using IMAP and have specified that you want to store messages locally, you need to complete the second field.

You'll learn more about how Messenger checks for new mail messages later in the chapter, so for now you can ignore the second set of options. As for the bottom checkbox, check it if you want IMAP-enabled Windows applications always to use Netscape Messenger when they let you send an e-mail message.

Once you have completed the Mail Server preferences, click OK to return to the main Messenger window.

The Messenger Window

The top pane of the Messenger window shows a summary list of the messages you've received, while the bottom pane shows the actual contents of any message that you select in the top pane. Right away you can see that you've already received one e-mail, an introductory message from Netscape. (This message wasn't actually delivered to you via your e-mail server, it was "built into" the program.) Let's examine the top pane, the message list pane, first.

If you see only one pane, click the blue up-arrow at the bottom left of the window. This will make the message content pane appear. You can hide it again by clicking the down-arrow marked Hide between the two panes. You can also resize the panes by placing your cursor in the area between them and then clicking and dragging up or down.

> **TIP**
>
> *You can create a desktop shortcut to your Inbox folder—or to any e-mail folder or discussion group in the drop-down list—by clicking and dragging the icon to the left of the list out onto the Windows 95/NT desktop.*

The Changing Mailbox Icon

The Mailbox icon in the Component Bar will not always look the same. Before you send or retrieve any messages, it may look like an envelope next to an empty inbox. This form of the Mailbox icon indicates that Messenger has not accessed your e-mail server to retrieve new messages. Either you are not connected to the Net or your office intranet, or you have not yet entered your e-mail password. Once Messenger has your password and can access your server to check for mail, and once you actually have some messages in your Inbox, the icon changes to an inbox with an envelope *inside* it.

The Mailbox icon in the Component Bar changes in another way, too. Messenger periodically checks your mail server to see if new messages have arrived there. If there *are* any new messages, the Mailbox icon contains a green down arrow. You can then retrieve your new messages if you wish.

The Message List Pane

Notice the envelope icon to the left of each message. It changes according to the status of the message:

- When you first receive a message, before you select it for viewing, the icon depicts a vertical envelope with a green arrow next to it. This is the "unopened" icon.

- Once you've viewed the contents of a message, the icon changes to depict an opened letter next to its horizontal envelope. This is the "opened and read" icon.

- Even after you've viewed the contents of a message, Messenger lets you "flag" it as unread (see the sidebar below called "Flagging Messages as Unread"). If you flag a previously read message as unread, the icon changes to a simple horizontal envelope. There is no separate letter to indicate "opened" or green arrow to indicate "unopened."

Notice that there are several informational fields for any messages you've received, including the pre-installed message from Netscape:

TIP

For now, ignore the button to the left of the Subject label. I'll talk about that later in the chapter, in the section called "Threading."

- **Subject:** This shows the subject of the message, as specified by the individual who sent the message.

- **Sender:** Typically this will be an e-mail address or the name of the sender.

- **Date:** This is when the message was sent to you. If it was sent today, this field contains the *time* it was sent. If it was sent before today, this field contains the *date* it was sent. Thus you can see at a glance which messages are very recent.

- **Priority:** The author of a message you receive may have marked it as urgent, as normal, or as low-priority. Not all messages contain this information.

In addition, there is a green diamond between the Subject and Sender fields. When you see a green diamond next to a particular message, it means that the message hasn't been read yet. Typically, you will have more than one message in the top pane. When new messages arrive, they will always have the green diamond next to them. Once you select a particular message from the list, however, the contents appear in the lower pane and the green diamond disappears, indicating that the message has been read. In addition, the Subject, Sender, and Date information no longer appear in bold font.

Flagging Messages as Unread

Even after you read a message, you can mark it as unread by clicking in the "green diamond" field. The green diamond reappears and the Subject, Sender, and Date become bold again. This is a useful reminder if you want to reread a particular message later. Besides marking messages as unread, there are also a variety of marking options available in the Mark submenu of the Message menu:

- **Thread read.** Select this option to mark an entire subject *thread* as read (see the section below called "Threading").

- **All Read.** Select this option to mark all the messages in your Inbox as read.

- **by Date.** This option lets you specify a date before which all messages will be marked as read. In other words, it will make Messenger display only newer messages as unread.

- **for Later.** This option marks a message or set of messages as read for the duration of the current Messenger session. After that, they return to unread status.

To mark or unmark multiple messages, select them using Ctrl+click, then choose the appropriate action from the Mark submenu. You can select just your flagged messages to mark or unmark, or even all your messages, by clicking the appropriate choice in the Select submenu of the Edit menu.

There are several other informational fields for every message you receive, but they do not show up automatically. You can access them by clicking the left arrow that's just to the right of the Date label. Try it now:

1. Click the arrow just to the right of the Priority label. As you click repeatedly, new informational fields appear, squeezing into the window as shown in Figure 5-7. Each click adds one new field.

2. Now click the right arrow. The fields disappear one by one as you click, and the original fields stretch to fill the window.

3. Using the left and right arrows, adjust the label bar until it appears as it did initially, with the Date field as the rightmost field.

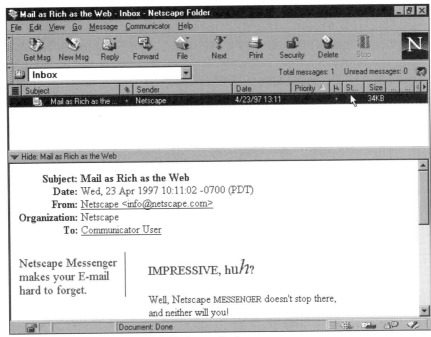

Figure 5-7: New informational fields for received messages.

And what are these additional informational fields? They are:

■ **Status:** This field may contain a variety of information about the message. If you haven't read the message yet, it contains the word "New." It also tells you whether or not you've replied to a message. If you've replied, it contains the word "replied." As I get older and more forgetful, I grow more and more fond of the Status field.

■ **Size:** This is the actual number of bytes in the message.

■ **Unread:** This field is useful only when you are viewing messages in *threaded* order. It indicates how many messages in a particular thread are still unread. For instance, if you reply to a message that you receive and then the original sender responds to your reply, you'll have a thread containing two messages in your Inbox. This field indicates how many of them are unread. Don't worry if you don't completely understand this right now, there's a whole section on threading later.

■ **Total:** This is the total number of messages in a particular thread.

Now look at Figure 5-7 again. That's right, I left something out of my description. There's a "red flag" field between Priority and Status. The red flag works pretty much like the green diamond: if you click the red flag column to the right of a message, the flag appears; click again and it's gone. Figure 5-8 shows a message that has been red-flagged.

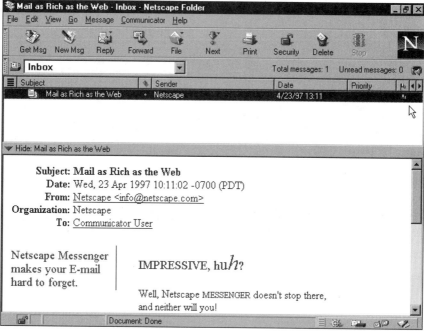

Figure 5-8: A red-flagged message.

What's the point? The red flag is exclusively for your own purposes. You can use it as a reminder, for instance, to read a message more thoroughly later, or to forward it to another recipient.

TIP

You can change the order of the informational fields by dragging the labels (Subject, Sender, Date, etc.) to the right or left. On my own system at home, I have moved the red flag field to the left, next to the green diamond, since I use it often and don't want to scroll to the right to find it.

That's the Message List pane in a nutshell. I'll go over the buttons and commands that are useful here when we actually get into sending and receiving e-mail, but for now, let's take a quick look at the bottom pane of the window, the Message Content Pane.

The Message Content Pane

The bottom section of the Messenger window is where all the excitement happens. This pane contains the actual content of any message you select from the Message List Pane. As soon as you click *any* informational field for a message at the top, you have in effect opened its envelope and the contents are revealed below.

Using the scroll bar to the right of the Message Content Pane, take a few moments to scroll down through the sample message from Netscape. Probably the first thing you notice is that four headers near the top indicate the subject of the message, its date, who it's from, and who it's intended for, as shown in Figure 5-9.

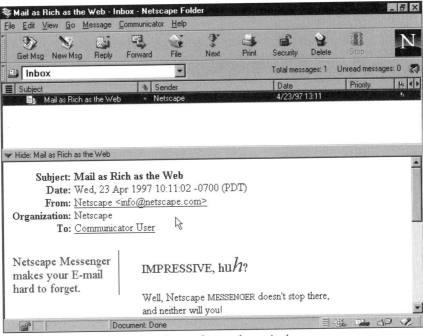

Figure 5-9: The informational headers at the top of a received message.

TIP

If you want, you can configure Messenger so that it displays more informational headers as part of each message. The additional headers provide technical details about the message's addressing, content type, etc. To make this change, select Headers from the View menu and then click All in the submenu that appears. Or if you prefer the lean clean look, click Brief.

Notice that the To and From headers are blue and underlined, just like links in a Web page. In fact, they *are* links. If you click either one, the name and e-mail address is added to a personal Address Book Card, which you can use later to automate the process of addressing new messages. I'll cover that in depth later, in the section called "The Address Book," but for now scroll a little further down in the Message Content Pane.

Take a look at Figure 5-10, which depicts more of the contents of the sample message from Netscape.

Figure 5-10: A little further down in the sample message.

As you can see, this doesn't look like a regular old-fashioned e-mail message at all, it looks like a Web page! That's right, Messenger supports formatted text, graphics, links, and other HTML features just like a Web browser. If you click a link in the message, Messenger launches Netscape Navigator 4 with the appropriate URL. And you can even replay the animation included in this message by clicking the Replay button!

TIP

> *As you can see in the above example, Messenger displays images and HTML files as part of the message itself, or inline. But if you don't like this behavior and just want to deal with the enhanced material as separate attachments to any messages you receive, select Attachments from the Messenger's View menu and then click As Links from the submenu that appears. You'll learn more about attachments in the section called "Dealing With Attached Files You Receive."*

One last thing about the Message Content Pane: you can make it disappear. To do this just click the down arrow in the area between the two panes, just to the left of the word Hide. As expected, the beautifully formatted message vanishes, and all you are left with is your message list. To display the message now, double-click one of its informational fields. It appears in a separate window, as shown in Figure 5-11.

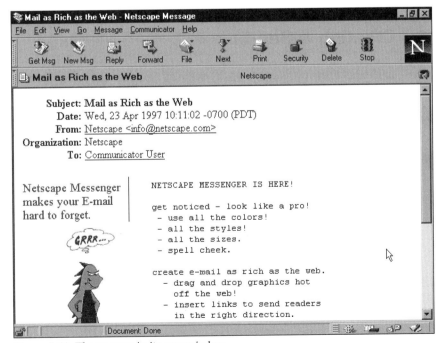

Figure 5-11: The message in its own window.

Why would you want Messenger to display only the message list instead of the message contents as well? There are several possibilities:

- It may be easier to get an overview of messages you've received, or to organize them into folders and threads, if you display as much of the list as possible.

- Messages that contain a lot of graphics may take time to display. You can often work more quickly with your message list by foregoing the actual message contents.

- Your boss often wanders by your desk, and you don't necessarily want him or her to see the contents of all your messages.

To display both panes again, simply click the up arrow at the bottom left of the window.

Now that you've configured your account information and gotten the lay of the land, or at least the lay of the main window, you're ready to start sending and receiving e-mail with Netscape Messenger. Of course there are a number of options that could dramatically enhance your use of the program, but I'll cover most of these as they come up in the context of actual tasks, and then I'll talk about a few advanced options near the end of the chapter. But for now let's get busy with the nitty-gritty of sending and receiving e-mail messages. This is where it gets fun.

Creating & Sending an E-mail Message

In the next few sections you will actually compose an e-mail message to yourself, send it, and retrieve it from your mail server. Why send a message to yourself? It's not just because you're such a fan of yourself, it's also because this is the easiest way to learn and test Messenger's capabilities. But first, there's something I need to explain. Messenger lets you send two different kinds of messages: Plain Text and HTML.

Plain Text and HTML Messages

As you saw in Figure 5-10 above, formatting and graphics can greatly enhance e-mail messages, giving them more impact and letting them convey information more flexibly. Netscape calls messages that include HTML formatting and other typical features of a Web page *HTML Messages*. Unfortunately, though, not all e-mail programs are created equal, and so there are quite a few people out there who will not be able to fully appreciate the careful creative work you've put into an HTML message. In fact, it will look like a bunch of confusing HTML code on their screen.

If you know the recipient of your message uses Messenger or some other browser that supports HTML messages, feel free to get creative. But of course Messenger also lets you send Plain Text e-mail, messages that do not include all the multimedia bells and whistles. Messenger even lets you specify in your Address Book (see the section below called "The Address Book") which recipients can receive HTML messages and which can only receive Plain Text. If you try to send an HTML message to somebody who is configured as unable to view it properly, Messenger will give you the option of sending your message as Plain Text. You can even send the same message to multiple recipients in different formats: HTML for those who can handle it, Plain Text for those who can't. Again, this will be covered in more depth in the section called "The Address Book."

Messenger has two different windows for composing new messages, one that's suited to Plain Text messages and another that includes features which help you create HTML. By default, Messenger presents you with the more universal Plain Text menu. But if you think you will generally be sending HTML messages, you can configure Messenger so that it brings up the HTML window for new messages by default. To do this:

1. Select Preferences from the Messenger's Edit menu, then click the Messages category.

2. In the Messages dialog box that appears, check the top checkbox, labeled "By default, send HTML messages."

But Messenger allows even more flexibility in dealing with HTML/Plain Text messages. In the same dialog box, click the More Options button. The More Messages Preferences dialog box appears, as shown in Figure 5-12.

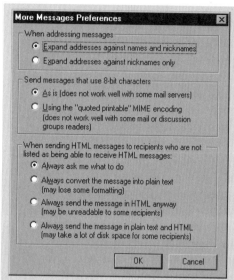

Figure 5-12: The More Messages Preferences dialog box.

Take a look at the bottom section of this dialog box, which deals with the HTML/Plain Text issue. Carefully read all the choices. Obviously, the first choice is the most flexible, allowing you to choose "on the fly" whether to send an HTML or Plain Text message to a particular recipient. (Remember, this option will only work if your *default* is to send HTML messages.)

In the next few sections all the screenshots will show the HTML window for creating new e-mail messages, but the principles discussed in the text will be the same if you're sending Plain Text.

OK, let's send a message:

TIP

You do not need to be connected to the Internet (or your office intranet) right now. You can compose your message without being connected, then connect some time before you actually send it.

1. Start Messenger, if it's not already running. Remember, you can do this by double-clicking the Netscape Messenger icon on your desktop or by clicking the Mailbox icon in the Component Bar. If Navigator or some other component is already running, you can also select Messenger Mailbox from the Communicator menu.

2. In the Inbox window, click the New Msg button. The Message Composition window appears, as shown in Figure 5-13.

Figure 5-13: The Message Composition window (HTML).

As you can see, this window is divided into two parts. The top part contains the addressing and other header information for your message, the text that will appear at the very beginning of the message when it is received. Netscape calls this the Addressing Area. The bottom part is the pane where you actually create your message.

In the top line of the Addressing Area, there's a To button and a bunch of blank space to the right of a little "person" icon. That blank space is where you type in the name of your message recipient. In this case, type in your own e-mail address. You'll end up with something like Figure 5-14.

Figure 5-14: The To field filled in.

TIP

You don't have to compose your message in any particular order. If you want to create the body of your message in the bottom pane before you address it, that's fine. It's just the same as snail mail: you can address an envelope either before or after you write your letter.

Suppose you want your message to go to more than one person? Well, you can include as many addresses as you want on the same line, separating them with commas. Messenger will automatically add new To fields to accommodate the new recipients. But there are other ways you can send your message to more than one person. Try this:

1. Click the space just below your original To button. A new To button appears, as well as a new person icon.

2. Click the new To button. A drop-down list appears with six different options. If you click Cc, for instance, the To button becomes a Cc button, as shown in Figure 5-15.

Figure 5-15: Mail message with a new Cc field filled in.

And what do these various addressing options mean? Each of the headers in the top pane has a specific function. The To field you already know about, so here are the others:

■ **Cc.** The Cc field works like carbon copies in the old-fashioned world of paper and typewriter—a copy of your message is sent to everyone listed on the Cc line. Typically, the message is sent to these recipients for their information, and they don't need to reply. Note that the designated recipient or recipients of the mail will see who has been Cc'ed.

TIP

Instead of typing in e-mail addresses, click the Address button to select addresses from your Address Book. You can read about setting up your Address Book later, in the section called, unsurprisingly, "The Address Book."

■ **Bcc.** Bcc, for *Blind Cc*, is used when you want to send a copy of a letter to someone but do not want that person's name to appear in the Cc line. The recipient or recipients of the mail who are listed on the To and Cc lines will not know who has been Bcc'ed.

■ **Groups.** In this field, you can list the names of any Usenet newsgroups or Collabra discussion groups you'd like your epistle posted to. You will learn more about newsgroups and discussion groups in Chapter 6.

- **Reply-To.** The Reply-To line is where you can put the e-mail address of another account where you want responses sent. This is useful if you want to receive replies at a different mail account from the one you are currently using.

- **Followup-To.** This field is also for use with Usenet newsgroups and Collabra discussion groups. For more information, please see Chapter 6.

Now it's time to fill in the Subject line. The Subject is whatever you want it to be—it tells the recipient what your message is about. Try to keep your Subject lines, which are optional, short and informative. In this case, just enter **Letter from me.**

Now let's move down the window and create the actual body of your message:

1. Place your cursor in the large bottom pane of the Message Composition window and click.

2. Start typing. For the purpose of this tutorial, simply type in the phrase **I'm reading this like totally awesome book about Netscape Communicator**, as shown below in Figure 5-16.

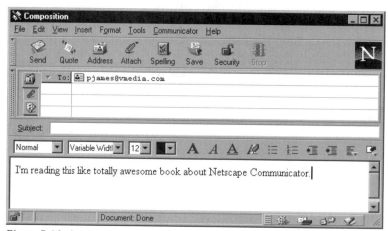

Figure 5-16: A message to yourself.

- If you need to edit your message, use the cursor, backspace, and delete keys just as with any text editor. You can also drag with your mouse to select portions of the text that you want to cut, copy, or paste. These operations use the default Windows key combinations, or you can select the commands from the Edit menu.

> **TIP**
>
> *You can give yourself more room to create your message by hiding the Addressing Area and even the toolbar. To do this, click the arrow icons just to the left of these areas. You can re-expand (or unhide) them later by clicking the "closed" icons. This works just like the toolbars in Navigator 4.*

You could send this test message just as it is, but remember that Netscape Messenger lets you make your message look like a Web page! Using the toolbar that's just above the message content area, you can control the formatting and color of your text and even insert links, horizontal lines, tables, and graphics. Let's try some of this.

> **TIP**
>
> *The next section is about editing your message using HTML features. If you don't think you'll be sending any HTML messages in the near future, feel free to skip ahead to the section called "Sending Your Message." You might want to catch the sidebar called "Check Your Spelling," though. The spelling checker works for both HTML and Plain Text messages.*

Beautifying Your Message

OK, your message is nice and honest, but it's kind of plain. In Chapter 9 you'll learn many ways to add graphical (and sonic) interest not only to e-mail messages but to entire Web pages you create yourself, but for now I'll just work across the toolbar and show you a few interesting tricks.

> **TIP**
>
> *In creating HTML messages, Messenger uses the services of another Communicator component, Netscape Composer. That means that some of the interface for creating HTML messages may be affected by your Composer preferences (see Chapter 9).*

Select a Style

The first control on the message composition toolbar is a drop-down list of *HTML styles*. Styles are tags that tell a Web browser or e-mail viewer to display text in a particular way. For instance, a Heading 1 style tells the client program to display the corresponding text as a large header, usually surrounded on the top and bottom by some empty space. Let's add a header to the test message:

1. Place your cursor at the beginning of the phrase you typed, click, and hit Enter. You now have a blank line above your original text.

2. Move your cursor up to the blank line and click. Enter the words **News Flash**.

3. Click the arrow to the right of the drop-down style box (which now contains the Normal style tag) and select the Heading 1 item. Your Message Composition window should now look like Figure 5-17.

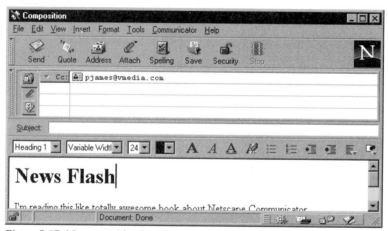

Figure 5-17: Message with a Heading 1 style added.

Change Fonts

You can also change the fonts that are used in your message. To do this, you select a new item from the Font list, the second control on the toolbar.

1. Click and drag your mouse across the words News Flash so that the entire phrase is selected (appears in reverse).

2. Click the arrow to the right of the Font list and select Fixed Width. Your Message will now look something like Figure 5-18.

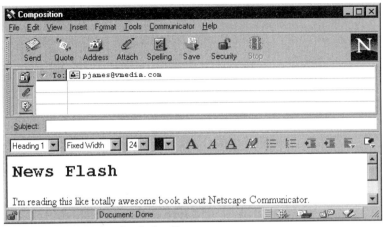

Figure 5-18: A new font for the heading.

Change Font Size

The next control lets you manipulate very precisely the relative or absolute size of text in your message. Depending on how you've configured Composer (see Chapter 9), the font sizes that appear in this list may be:

- Relative HTML sizes—with 0 as normal, positive (plus) values as increasingly larger, and negative values as progressively smaller.

- Absolute point sizes, such as 10 or 12 points.

- A combination of relative and absolute units. In this case, the list will be divided into two clear sections.

Experiment a little with custom font sizes to get the feel of how this control works. You can even select individual letters to create dramatic effects. In the following illustration, Figure 5-19, I've selected individual letters of the word awesome. I've given the "a" a value of +2, the next letter a +3, and so on.

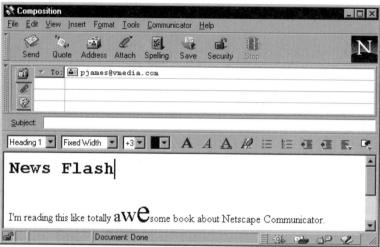

Figure 5-19: Fun with font sizes.

Change Font Color

If this book were printed in color, you could see what the next control does. Try it on your own. Select some text from your message and then drop down the list of colors, as shown in Figure 5-20.

Figure 5-20: The color list.

Now simply choose a new color for the text you've selected. You can have your message looking like an ad from the 60s in no time.

Add Bold, Italic & Underline

Messenger makes it easy to add bold, italic, and underline text to your message. You do it with the three "A" buttons to the right of the color list. Here we go:

1. Click and drag your mouse to select the word awesome once again.

2. Click the first two A buttons (bold and italic). Your window will now look something like Figure 5-21:

Figure 5-21: The word awesome in bold and italic.

Character Styles

Besides bold, italic, and underline, Messenger supports a number of other character styles such as subscript, superscript, and blinking text. To format text with these special attributes:

1. Select the text.

2. Select Style from the Format menu.

3. Choose the character style you wish to apply.

Don't like some of the character style changes you've made? You can always remove any styles you've added. Simply select the text you wish to "unstyle" and click the Remove All Styles button, just to the right of the Underline button. This feature not only removes character styles, it also removes any HTML links in the selected text.

Make a Bulleted or Numbered List

Now let's add some more text to our message:

1. In your message, place your cursor after the word Communicator and click. Enter the phrase **Here's why:**

2. Press Enter and add three new very brief paragraphs like the ones shown in Figure 5-22.

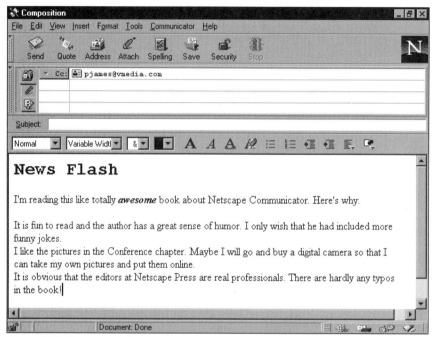

Figure 5-22: Some new text.

3. Click and drag to select all three of the new paragraphs.

4. Click the Bullet button. You'll get something resembling Figure 5-23.

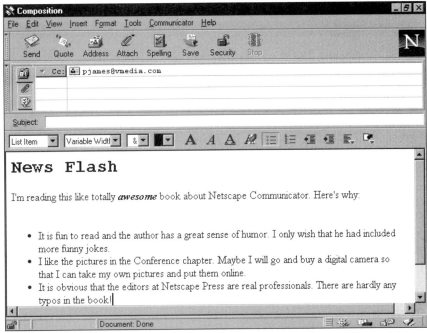

Figure 5-23: A bulleted list.

Want a numbered list instead? Reselect the three new lines and click the Numbered List button, just to the right of the Bullet button. Voilà! Instant high-impact presentations for that quarterly sales meeting.

Adjust Indents

Communicator lets you adjust how far a paragraph is indented. This is especially useful if you want to create multi-level lists. Check it out:

1. Select the numbered list you just created and make it a bulleted list again. (Click the Bullet button.)

2. Go to the end of the It is fun to read line, click, and press Enter.

3. Enter **Humor** and press Enter.

4. Enter **Light-hearted**.

5. Using your mouse, select these last two lines you typed.

6. Click the second of the two Indent buttons, the one with the *right* arrow indicating more indent. Figure 5-24 shows what you get.

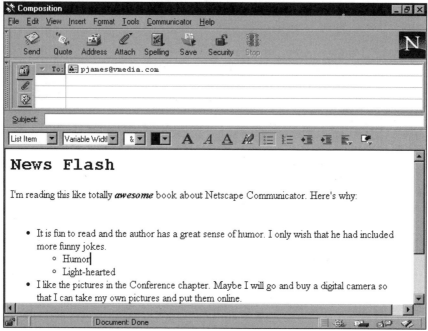

Figure 5-24: A multi-level list.

You can use the leftmost Indent button to return the new items to the same level as the original three bulleted phrases if you want, or you can create yet deeper levels for your list. Feel free to experiment.

Change Alignment

The second to last button on the toolbar lets you specify the alignment for particular paragraphs. For example:

1. Scroll back up to the beginning of your message and click your cursor anywhere in the phrase News Flash.

2. Click the Alignment button, then select the bottom of the three new buttons that appear, the Right Alignment button. The beginning of your message now looks like Figure 5-25.

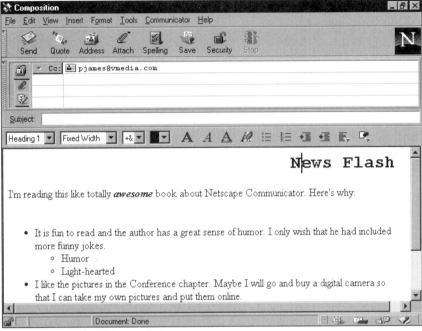

Figure 5-25: The header aligned right.

Netscape Messenger lets you choose Left Alignment, Center Alignment, and Right Alignment. HTML does not currently support full or block justification, in which both the right and left edges of text are perfectly lined up.

Check Your Spelling

Speling chalenjed? No problum!

See that button with the ABC and the checkmark on it? That's your personal spelling assistant. Click it and you can make all your e-mail messages read like they've been thoroughly worked over by Netscape Press' crack editorial team.

Figure 5-26 shows a message with a few problem words in it.

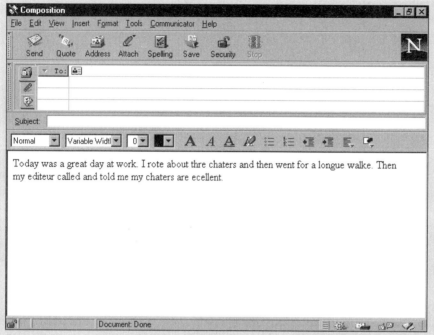

Figure 5-26: A message with spelling mistakes.

Click the Check Spelling button and you see something like Figure 5-27.

Figure 5-27: The spelling checker at work.

The spelling checker has found the first of the errors. If you've used Microsoft Word or any other major word processing program, this dialog box should look pretty familiar to you. It offers you an alternate spelling for the word, or in some cases a list of possible spellings. If you don't like the choice or choices it offers you, type in the correct spelling in the Change To box yourself. Here's what the various buttons do:

- **Replace**. The spelling checker changes the currently selected word to the spelling that is highlighted in the Suggestions box. Highlight the spelling you want to use before clicking the Replace button. You can also type a new spelling directly into the Word box before clicking the Replace button.

- **Replace All**. The spelling checker changes every instance of this particular misspelling within your message.

- **Ignore**. If you click this button, the spelling checker doesn't bother correcting the selected word and instead goes on to the next misspelling it finds, if any.

- **Ignore All**. If you click this button, the spelling checker won't stop at any further words in your message that are spelled this way.

- **Stop**. Click this button to exit the spelling checker. It will not look for any further errors in your message unless you press the Check Spelling button again.

- **Learn**. If you click this button, the spelling checker adds the selected word, as it is currently spelled in your message, to a custom dictionary. Once it is added to the dictionary, the spelling checker will no longer consider it a misspelling when it encounters this word in *any* message you write. This can be useful for unusual proper nouns and specialized technical words that you use frequently.

- **Edit Dictionary**. This button lets you edit your custom dictionary directly, adding words that the spell checker will not flag as errors when it encounters them. For instance, if you often spell check messages that include your own e-mail address as a signature, you might want to add that address to the dictionary, as shown in Figure 5-28.

Figure 5-28: Adding your e-mail address to the Personal Dictionary.

You can also use this feature to *delete* words from your dictionary.

Figure 5-29 shows the e-mail message after Communicator's spelling checker has done its job:

Figure 5-29: The message after spell checking.

Add a Link

Now scroll back down to the bottom of the message. Hit Enter a couple of times, but make sure the Bullet button is not depressed or all your blank spaces will be bulleted! At the very bottom of your message you'll add a link to the electronic version of this book. Here's how:

1. Click the rightmost button on the toolbar. A vertical row of five new buttons drops down, as shown in Figure 5-30.

Figure 5-30: The Insert Object buttons.

2. Click the Link button, the one with a chain link on it. A Properties dialog box appears, as shown in Figure 5-31.

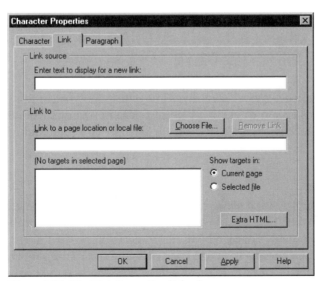

Figure 5-31: The Link Properties dialog box.

3. In the Link source field enter the words **Ad for a Great Book**.

4. In the Link to field enter **http://www.vmedia.com/communicator**.

5. Ignore the other options. They will make more sense to you after you read Chapter 9. For now, just click OK. You are returned to your message, which now contains a link as shown in Figure 5-32.

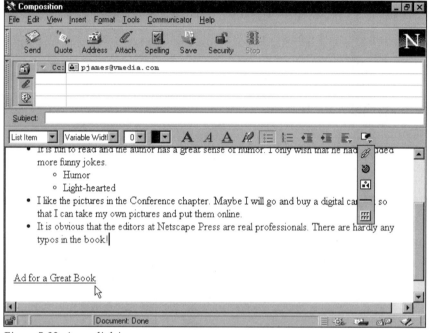

Figure 5-32: A new link in your message.

I love this feature. Whoever receives your message (you, in this case) can simply click this link to travel to a Web site, either on your corporate intranet or on the Net itself. You can give it a try later, after you send and receive your new e-mail.

Add a Target

Targets (sometimes called *anchors*) are a different kind of link. Instead of referring to a different HTML document, they refer to a particular location within the current document. This can be useful in very long e-mail messages. Your recipient clicks on a link and is transported to the concluding remarks at the end of your message or back to the executive summary at the beginning.

Chapter 9 covers targets in depth, so I'm not going to get into that here. But when you're ready to use this feature, just press the second of the Insert Object buttons, the one with the arrow and target.

Add a Picture

If you click the third of the Insert Object buttons, a pretty threatening dialog box pops up as shown in Figure 5-33.

Figure 5-33: The Image Properties dialog box.

Don't worry, it's not as bad as it looks. In the Image location field you simply enter or paste the URL of a remote picture you want to include in your message, or you can click the Choose File button and select a graphics file from your own hard drive or a network drive. Then select one of the Text alignment buttons in the middle of the dialog box. Each button provides a different option for how the graphics will be integrated with surrounding text. I'm not going to go into any more detail right now since it's all covered in Chapter 9, but an example of what you can do with graphics in an e-mail message is shown in Figure 5-34.

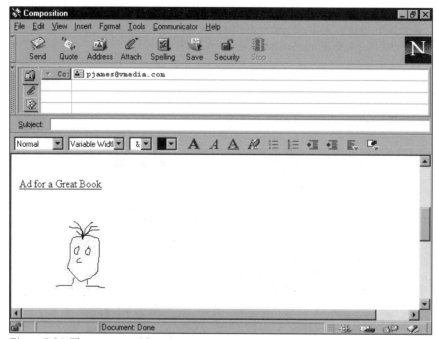

Figure 5-34: The message with an image.

TIP

There's an even easier way to add pictures to your messages: just drag them in. That's right, you can click any image on your desktop or in a folder and drag it right into the Composition window. If the original is in a format other than GIF or JPEG, Messenger will even convert it to one of these Net-friendly formats.

Add a Horizontal Line

Your message is starting to get that *all fluff, no substance* look that's so familiar in this Age of the Image. Hey, that's *good*! You're on your way to becoming a typical Web designer. But let's add just a little more fluff for good measure.

1. Scroll back up to the top of your message.

2. Put your cursor at the end of the News Flash line and press Enter.

3. In the Insert Object button list, click the second to last button, which depicts a horizontal line. What you get is shown in Figure 5-35.

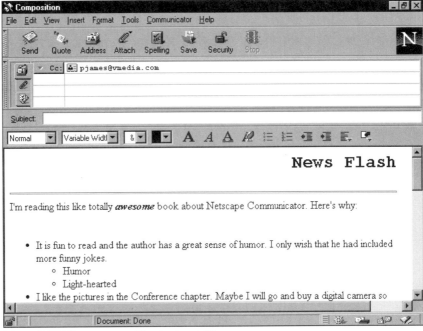

Figure 5-35: The message with a horizontal line.

Don't like the way that horizontal line looks? You can change it! Right-click the horizontal line and select Horizontal Line Properties from the context menu that appears. Then play around with the settings until you get something you like. You can save these settings as your default for horizontal lines by checking the "Save settings as default" checkbox.

Add a Table

Yes, you can even add tables to your e-mail messages, although if you're putting tables into your casual notes to friends you may be in serious need of a life. I'll cover tables in Chapter 9 (you knew that), but if you're a die-hard HTML geek and want to start experimenting right away, just press the last of the Insert Object buttons and get busy.

By the way, here's an interesting use of tables in e-mail. Figure 5-36 shows a report I get a couple of times a day from the Mercury Mail service called Closing Bell. It is formatted as a table showing the ups and downs of various stocks I'm interested in.

Figure 5-36: An example of tables in e-mail.

Page Colors and Properties

We're not quite done tweaking the message yet. This next set of configuration options, accessible only through the menus, affects various characteristics of the message as a whole, not just individual elements within it. Let's take a look:

1. Still in the Message Composition window, select Page Colors and Properties from the bottom of the Format menu. The Colors and Background tab appears, as shown in Figure 5-37.

2. To change the overall color scheme of your message, select from the drop-down Color Schemes list. The Use custom colors option button is automatically selected, and you are shown a sample of your new colors.

3. To change individual elements within the chosen color scheme, click any of the buttons for Normal Text, Link Text, etc. and then select a new color from the palette that appears. Note that you can also change the background color of your message.

4. If you want to return to eliminate these changes, click the option button at the top labeled "Use viewer's browser colors." With this option selected, colors you add to your e-mail will not be saved; when your recipient displays your message, it will appear with his or her default browser colors.

Figure 5-37: The Colors and Background tab.

You can also specify an image, rather than a solid color, to use as the background for your message. To do this:

1. Check the Use Image checkbox in the Background Image section.

2. Enter the URL of the image you want to use, or click the Choose File button. A Choose Image File dialog box appears, as shown in Figure 5-38.

Figure 5-38: The Choose Image File dialog box.

3. Choose a GIF or JPEG file from your local hard drive or network drive and click Open.

TIP

If you check the "Leave image at the original location" checkbox, the message you send will download the image from the location you specified each time your recipient views the message. That means it should be located at an accessible Web site.

As you work with these appearance changes, you can click Apply at any time to see what they look like in your actual message. Remember, reverting to your original look is as simple as choosing an option button, so there's no real danger. If you like what you've done, though, and want to use your customized color scheme as a default in future rich text messages, check the check box labeled "Save these settings for new pages."

When you're done with the Colors and Background settings, click OK to return to your message.

MAILTO: Tags

Besides calling up the Message Composition window, Netscape Communicator offers another way to send mail. Web pages can include special HTML tags called MAILTO: tags. They look just like ordinary links, although often they appear in italics. When you click one of these, Netscape Communicator automatically pops up the Message Composition window, allowing you to send a message to the recipient indicated in the MAILTO: tag.

MAILTO: tags provide a convenient way to solicit feedback or comments in a Web document.

Sending Your Message

This is where the virtual rubber finally hits the virtual road. For this exercise, you'll need to be connected either to your office intranet or to the Net. If you connect to the Net via a dial-up SLIP or PPP connection, go ahead and establish that link now. Once you're connected, return to the Netscape Messenger window and the message you just composed.

Actually putting your message "in the mail" is very simple.

1. Make sure you're connected to the Net or to your office intranet.

2. Click the Send button. Depending how you configured Messenger for handling HTML vs. Plain Text recipients, a dialog box may appear asking you which format you want to use, as shown in Figure 5-39.

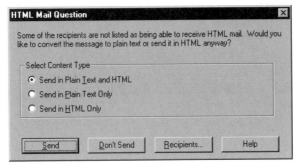

Figure 5-39: The HTML Mail Question dialog box.

TIP

The dialog box won't appear if you've already entered yourself in the Address Book as a recipient who prefers HTML e-mail (see the section below called "The Address Book").

- Most of the options in this dialog box are pretty obvious. The first one tells Messenger to send two copies of the message, one in Plain Text and one in HTML, to each recipient; the second one tells Messenger to send the message in Plain Text only; and the third tells Messenger to send the message in HTML format only.

3. Once you've selected an option, click the Send button. Or, if you want even more flexibility, click the Recipients button. A dialog box appears letting you specify different formats for different recipients of the same message, as shown in Figure 5-40.

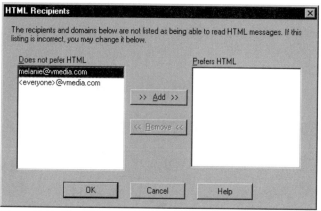

Figure 5-40: The HTML Recipients dialog box.

TIP

Messenger automatically creates the entry <everyone> followed by the domain address of your recipient(s). If you move this over to the Prefers HTML box, Messenger will assume that every e-mail ID on that server prefers receiving HTML. In the example shown above in Figure 5-40, let's say I add <everyone>@echonyc.com to the Prefers HTML list. Since my e-mail address includes echonyc.com, I am assured of receiving all the formatting and graphics in this HTML message I send to myself. But if I had cc'd Joe_Blow@echonyc.com, he would get the message in HTML format too, even though I didn't explicitly add him to the list.

4. Once you've indicated in this dialog box which of your recipients should receive your message in HTML format and which should receive it in Plain Text, click OK.

5. Back in the HTML Mail Question dialog box, click Send.

Please realize that there won't always be this many steps to sending a message. In many cases, as soon as you click Send in the New Message window your message is on its way. That's the way it works if you create a message without any HTML formatting, or if you have already specified in the Address Book that your recipients prefer HTML e-mail.

Sending Options

The US Postal Service lets you send letters in a variety of ways. You can send packages third class and save money, or you can pay a little extra to insure a valuable gift, or you can send your Dear John letters by certified mail so you're absolutely certain that someone-who-used-to-be-special knows you're ditching him. Similarly, Netscape Messenger offers a variety of sending options.

In the Message Composition window, there are three small tabs at the left of the Addressing Area. The top one depicts an address book with a stylized human figure on it, the middle one depicts a paper clip, and the bottom one depicts a checklist. This bottom one is what we're interested in right now, because it lets you access the sending options. Click it and what you get is shown in Figure 5-41.

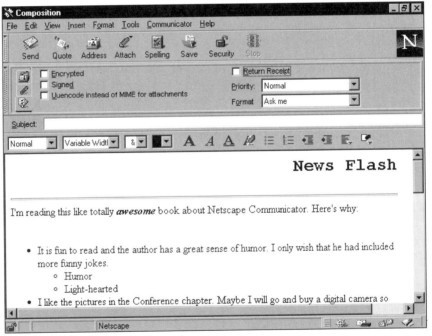

Figure 5-41: The Sending Options tab.

You can check any or all of the check boxes prior to clicking the Send button. Your message will receive the "special handling" you specify:

■ **Encrypted.** If you check this, your message is sent in a form that is unreadable until it is decrypted at the other end by the recipient's copy of Messenger. This privacy feature only works if you already have a copy of your recipient's Security Certificate, which includes the key used to encrypt the message. Please see the section on "E-mail Security" later in this chapter.

■ **Signed.** If you check this, Messenger will automatically "sign" your message with the special unique digital signature that's part of your Personal Security Certificate. That means the recipient of the message knows it's really you who sent it, or at least that it was sent using your computer. It also means that your recipient can now send you encrypted messages, since your signature includes your encryption key. Again, you must have a Personal Security Certificate to use this feature. Please see the section on "E-Mail Security" later in this chapter.

■ **Uuencode instead of MIME for attachments.** Uuencoding and MIME are two different standards for transferring binary (non-text) data across networks or the Internet. Typically, if you want to attach a non-text file such as a spreadsheet, graphic, or program to your message, it is automatically MIME-encoded (please see the section below called "Attaching Files to Messages"). But if a particular recipient does not have a MIME-enabled e-mail program that can decode the information correctly, try checking this box. Uuencoding is a less flexible but more universal older standard.

■ **Return receipt.** If you check this, you will automatically receive (via e-mail, of course) a confirmation that your message has arrived at its destination.

In addition to the check boxes, there are two drop-down lists:

■ Use the **Priority** list to indicate just how important you think your message is. If you select Highest, for instance, the message will include that designation in its headers, letting your recipient know that this is no idle chit chat. Some e-mail client programs will graphically flag messages that are given specific priorities; as you've already seen, Messenger has a special Priority field that indicates any special priority for incoming messages.

■ The **Format** list is available only if Messenger is configured so that you send HTML messages by default. In this case, you can select *Plain Text* from the list, overriding the HTML formatting, or you can choose *Ask me*, so that when you send the message you are presented with the HTML Mail Question dialog box shown earlier in Figure 5-39.

Signatures & Sig Files

Many Internet users attach special *signatures* to the end of each message. A signature is really just a line or two of text, typically something you might put on a business card. *Phil James, Bon Vivant and General Man-About-Town*. Stuff like that. You don't want to type in this same information each time you create a message, though, so Messenger lets you create a text file that automatically gets appended to every e-mail you create. Seasoned Internet users call this a *sig file*.

How do you create a sig file? It's no different from creating any other text file. Just start typing in Notepad or some other editor and then save your work with a file name like SIG.TXT. Select Preferences from Messenger's Edit menu and click the Identity tab. In the Signature File field, specify the exact location and name of your sig file. (You can use the Browse button to find it and fill in the field for you.) Now whenever you send a message, the contents of your sig file are appended at the end.

If you want to move quickly and come back later to some of the niceties of sending e-mail, as well as some of Messenger's advanced features, you can jump ahead for now to the section called "Retrieving Your E-mail."

Saving Copies of Sent E-mail

By default, a copy of every message you send is stored in a folder called Sent. In the Messenger window, click the down arrow to the right of the word Inbox. You'll see a list of available folders. Select Sent to see the contents of that folder. The message you just e-mailed should appear in the Messenger window.

If you want to store your sent messages in a different folder, if you want to e-mail them to yourself as well as to your recipient, or if you don't want to bother storing them at all, select Preferences from the Edit menu, then click the Messages category under Mail & Groups. Let's go over the options available in the Copies of outgoing messages section of this dialog box, as shown below in Figure 5-42.

Figure 5-42: The Messages preferences, showing options for copies of outgoing mail.

■ **Automatically email a copy of outgoing messages to.** One way to keep copies of your outgoing messages is to actually send yourself the same message. If you click the Self box, all outgoing e-mail will be sent not only to your recipient, but back to you as well. If you have several different e-mail accounts, you may want to e-mail a copy of your outgoing correspondence to a different address. In this case, simply fill in the Other address box.

TIP

Note that there is a setting here for discussion group messages as well. I'll tell you all about discussion groups in Chapter 6.

■ **Automatically copy outgoing messages to a folder.** Instead of actually e-mailing outgoing messages back to yourself, you can simply copy them to a Messenger folder (see the section "Working With Folders" later in the chapter). As I mentioned earlier, you'd normally use the Sent folder for this purpose, but you may want to select a custom folder you've created. And to keep Messenger from saving any sent messages, just uncheck the box.

Drafts

Let's say you don't want to send your message right away but want to keep working on it in subsequent Messenger sessions. In the Message Composition window, just click the Save button. Your work-in-progress is moved to a folder called Drafts that you can select from the drop-down folder list at any time. Then simply click your message in the Drafts folder, work on it some more, and click the Send button when you're finally ready to send it.

8-bit Encoding and Long Lines

There are two more rather technical options for e-mail messages you send. You can leave these options alone unless you get complaints that your messages aren't arriving properly, or that portions of them are unreadable.

Some recipients of your messages may claim that they cannot read the end of the lines of text of messages you send, or that lines of quoted text are wrapping before a new quote character (>) appears. (Please see the section below called "Replying to E-mail" if you don't know what I'm talking about.) If this is the case, select Preferences from the Edit menu, then the Messages category under Mail & Groups. Change the value in the "Wrap long lines..." field.

In addition, for some mail servers, it may be necessary to encode your messages with a special encoding called "8-bit MIME." This will only be the case if your message text contains "high bit" characters such as symbols and if these are not displayed properly by your recipient's mail reader. You can make this change by going to the same Messages dialog box and then clicking the More Options button. In the center section of the dialog box that appears, select the second option button.

Retrieving Your E-mail

Remember, e-mail is a little different from snail mail in that it doesn't come right to your house. When somebody sends you a message, it is stored on a mail server until Messenger goes out and grabs it. That means the message you just sent to yourself doesn't appear automatically in your Inbox—you have to click the Get Msg button.

Let's give it a try:

1. Make sure you're still connected to the Internet or to your office intranet. Back in the Messenger window, click the Get Msg button.

2. If you have quit Messenger since you sent your message, you may encounter the Password Entry dialog box again. Simply enter your e-mail password.

Once you enter your password, Netscape Messenger logs you in to your post office account to retrieve your mail. Your Messenger window now looks something like Figure 5-43.

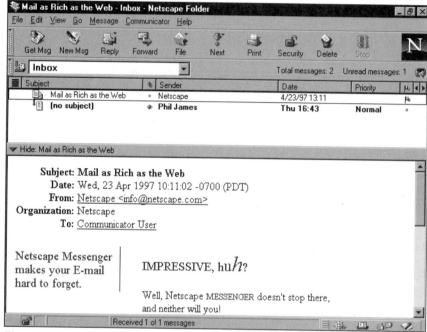

Figure 5-43: The Messenger window with your newly received e-mail message.

Mail Retrieval Options

If your incoming e-mail account is on a POP3 server, you can choose to handle retrieved messages in one of two different ways. Once you've retrieved your messages, they may be deleted from the server or they may be stored there indefinitely. If they are not deleted, you can access the same messages again. This is useful if you access your e-mail account using two different computers, for instance one at home and one at work.

To select whether or not messages will be deleted from your POP3 server once they are retrieved, select Preferences from Messenger's Edit menu and then click the Mail Server category. If you want your messages left on the server after retrieval, check the "Leave mail on server after retrieval" checkbox.

➡

What if you're accessing your e-mail via an IMAP server? With IMAP, messages are *always* kept on the server. You *re*-access them every time you go online. But you can elect to store copies of your messages locally as well, so that you can view them even when you're not online. To configure the program this way, select Preferences from Messenger's Edit menu and then click the Mail Server category. Check the "Keep copies of messages locally for offline reading" checkbox.

If you are new to e-mail, your test message is probably the only one that will be retrieved. But if you have already been using this e-mail account, Messenger will get the rest of your e-mail stored at that address as well.

Replying to E-mail

Replying to a piece of e-mail differs from sending new mail in several important ways. First of all, when you reply, Netscape Messenger fills in the To field automatically, since the intended recipient is usually the sender of the original message. The program also fills in the Subject field with "Re:" and the subject of the mail you are replying to.

There is another important difference: the program lets you use a special quote feature to include the text of the e-mail you are responding to right in the body of your reply.

Let's try it. In the Messenger window, select a received message and click the Reply button, then choose either Reply to Sender or Reply to Sender and All Recipients from the submenu that appears.

TIP

If you want to respond only to the individual who sent the message, click Reply to Sender; if you want your response to go to any people who were Cc'd on the message, select Reply to Sender and All Recipients. If you choose this second option, the To field will be filled in automatically with the address of the sender and the Cc field will be filled in automatically with the names of any individuals who were Cc'd.

Once you click either Reply to Sender or Reply to Sender and All Recipients, the Message Composition window appears with the correct fields filled in. In addition, the original message is included in the content area. Notice that every line of the original message text begins with a vertical blue bar, indicating that this is quoted material.

> **TIP**
>
> *If you have configured Messenger so that you send Plain Text messages by default, the quote character that begins each line of quoted text will be ">" instead of a blue bar. This is the Internet standard for indicating quoted material in Plain Text messages.*

To Quote or Not to Quote

Maybe you don't want the quoted original message to appear in the Composition window *every* time you create a response. To change this, select Preferences from Messenger's Edit menu and then click the Messages tab. Uncheck the check box labeled "Automatically quote original message when replying."

This doesn't mean that you can never include original messages in your replies, just that you have to tell Messenger to do so explicitly. That's a piece of cake. In the Composition window, simply click the Quote button. I find it more convenient to use the program this way. It just takes a second to click the Quote button, but it's tedious to edit out automatically quoted messages when you *don't* want to include them.

At this point, you can add whatever text you like below—or above—the quoted text. You can also add other people to the To or Cc fields if you like. If the message you have quoted is long, or if you want to respond to only one or two sentences of a letter, it is considered polite to delete the portions not relevant to your reply, although it is bad etiquette to delete or alter quoted text without indicating removals by inserting [...] or (snip) or some other indication that you edited the quoted material.

Following these steps for replying to your test message, you should end up with a Composition window like the one shown in Figure 5-44.

Once you've completed your reply, sending it is just like sending a new message: simply click the Send button. The status line will display messages telling you about the status of your message transmission.

> **TIP**
>
> *To reply quickly to a message, right-click it and select Reply to Sender or Reply to Sender and All Recipients from the context menu that appears.*

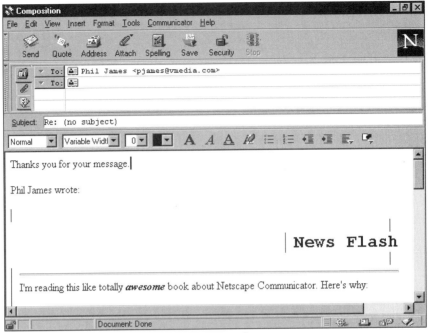

Figure 5-44: A reply including quote of the original message.

Forwarding Messages

You use the Forward button when you want to send a letter along to someone other than the people listed in the From or Cc fields. Forward is similar to Reply, with a couple of differences. The Subject line is filled in with the subject line of the letter labeled Fwd instead of Re (with the entire field enclosed in square brackets), and the To field is not filled in. It's up to you to fill in the To field with a new recipient for the message.

The message being forwarded is automatically included as an attachment to the mail rather than as text in your actual message. (You'll learn more about attachments in the section called "Attaching Files to Messages.") Clicking the Quote button will include the text of the forwarded letter, bracketed by the quote character, but if you use this feature to annotate the forwarded letter, remember to delete the attachment so that you don't send two copies of the same text. To forward a message quickly, right-click it and select Forward or Forward Quoted from the context menu that appears.

Mail Checking & Notification

Wouldn't it be nice if you didn't have to click the Get Msg button periodically to check for new messages? Well, Messenger can handle even this task for you. All you really have to do is tell Messenger how often you want it to check the server. Here's how:

1. Select Preferences From Messenger's Edit menu.

2. Click the Mail Server category.

3. Click the More Options button near the bottom of the dialog box. A new dialog box appears, as shown in Figure 5-45.

Figure 5-45: The More Mail Server Preferences dialog box.

4. Make sure the "Check for mail every" check box is checked, and enter the number of minutes for how often you want Messenger to log onto the mail server to check for new messages.

You may also want to check the "Remember my mail password" checkbox—as long as you're not worried about other people using your computer to send gag e-mail on your behalf! With this box checked, Messenger will no longer ask for your password the first time you send an e-mail or retrieve new messages. This can be a real convenience if you're letting Messenger check for mail automatically.

When you're done with this dialog box, click OK. Click OK once more in the Preferences dialog box to return to the main Messenger window.

So how do you know that new e-mail has arrived at your server? As long as your machine can connect to your mail server, Messenger gives you three different signals that new mail has arrived there:

■ It makes a "ding" sound in your PC's speakers.

TIP

If you don't like dings, you can turn this feature off by selecting Preferences from the Edit menu of any other Communicator component, clicking Mail & Groups category, and unchecking the "Enable sound alert when messages arrive" option.

■ It puts a green down-arrow next to the Messenger icon in the Component Bar.

■ It puts an envelope icon in your Windows 95 or NT 4.0 taskbar tray.

To retrieve your new messages, you can simply click either of these icons. Within moments, the new mail appears in your Inbox. The envelope icon disappears from the taskbar tray and the green arrow disappears from the Component Bar icon.

But what if you don't want to keep Communicator running all the time just to see if you have new mail? With Communicator, Netscape provides a special supplemental program that can tap you on the virtual shoulder when you have new mail on your server—without even running Communicator. In fact, this special Mail Notification program does more than tap you on the shoulder. If you want, it can play selections from your favorite Broadway show when you get a message. On a more practical level, it can also launch Messenger if there's a message. Check it out:

1. Make sure you are connected to your office intranet or to the Net itself.

2. In the Netscape Communicator folder on your desktop, double-click the Utilities subfolder. Then, click the Netscape Mail Notification icon. A small envelope icon appears in your Windows 95 or Windows NT taskbar tray.

   ■ If Notification cannot automatically check your server—for instance, if you're not connected to an intranet or the Net, or if you have not told Messenger to remember your password following the instructions above—you will see a red X through the icon until you remedy the problem.

3. Place your cursor on the tray icon. A tool tip pops up indicating that "There are no new messages waiting."

- If the program is currently checking for new mail, the icon looks like a spinning blue disc.

4. Now right-click the icon. A context menu appears with the following choices:

- **Check Now.** Typically, you set Notification to check your server for new mail at regular intervals (you'll find out how in a minute). But if you want the program to go out and look for new mail right now, click this command.

- **Run Mail.** Click this to start Messenger if it's not currently running, or to switch to it if it's already loaded.

- **New Message.** Click this to create a new e-mail message in Messenger.

- **Exit.** Click this to shut down Mail Notification.

You can also check or uncheck the Enabled item to enable or disable e-mail notification.

Oops, I left one description out: Options. I left it out because that's where we're going right now, and we're going to look at it in some detail. To configure Mail Notification:

1. Click the Options item on the Mail Notification context menu. The Netscape Mail Properties dialog box appears, as shown in Figure 5-46.

Figure 5-46: Netscape Mail Properties.

2. In the Notification tab, enter a number of minutes for the frequency with which the program will check for new mail on your server.

3. Click one of the "Notification When Mail Arrives" options. (Yes, this is where you can enter PHANTOM_OF_THE_OPERA.WAV or the name of any other sound file.)

■ If you elect not to have Notification holler at you when it discovers new mail on your server, you'll still find out pretty quickly. The icon in your Windows taskbar tray sports a bright red flag that waves back and forth when you have new mail. I have Notification check my server every couple of minutes, so leaving the sound on would drive me batty.

4. Click the Launching Mail tab, as shown below in Figure 5-47.

Figure 5-47: The Launching Mail tab.

■ In the top half of this dialog box, you can tell Notification how to find Messenger—obviously it needs to find the program in order to launch it. You should do fine leaving the top option button selected.

■ In the bottom half of this dialog box, you can tell Notification to launch Messenger with the Inbox window displayed or the Folder window displayed. So far in this chapter we've only looked at the Inbox window, which is the one that makes the most sense in this option unless you're automatically routing certain incoming messages to particular custom folders (see the section on "Working with Folders" below). For now, leave this set to Open Inbox Window.

5. Click the Mouse tab, as shown in Figure 5-48.

Figure 5-48: The Mouse tab.

- This is pretty self-explanatory: simply decide what action you want to initiate by double-clicking (or Ctrl+double-clicking) the Mail Notification icon.

6. You can ignore the Mail Server Configuration tab at this point—it is only useful for trouble-shooting if Notification doesn't seem to be working. Just click OK. The Properties dialog box disappears and you are ready to use Notification.

That's all there is to it. Now you simply wait for Notification to do its job. Periodically, at the interval you've configured, it goes out and checks for new messages on your mail server. If it finds any, you may hear a sound, and the icon in your taskbar tray suddenly looks like the one in Figure 5-49.

Figure 5-49: The Notification icon indicating that there is a new message on the mail server.

When you place your cursor over the icon it indicates exactly how many messages it found. To launch or return to Messenger and retrieve those messages, simply double-click the Notification icon (assuming that's the way you've configured the Mouse tab).

With Mail Notification loaded, you'll know right away when you receive new mail. And since you know right away, you'll be able to respond quickly. The next section shows you how.

The Address Book

So far we've been addressing messages manually, by typing actual e-mail addresses into the To and Cc fields. But that's a tedious process, and you're bound to incorporate some mail-stopping typos from time to time. Wouldn't it be great if instead of entering dracula@transylvania.com you could pick the address from a list, or even just type in drac? Well, both of these shortcuts are available thanks to Messenger's Address Book facility.

The Address Book is actually a collection of informational "cards" about individuals. It's like a giant electronic Rolodex. The Address Book has two options—it allows you to enter single addresses and groups of addresses, or custom mailing lists. And there are several ways to enter new individuals into the Address Book. Let's start with the simplest first.

1. Select any message in the Message List pane. Once its content appears in the Message Content pane, click the blue underlined link in the To, From, or Cc header at the top of the message. A window like the one in Figure 5-50 pops up.

Figure 5-50: A new card.

TIP

The Address Book is also used by Netscape Conference, which I cover in Chapter 11. That's what the Netscape Conference tab is for. You can ignore it for now.

2. Fill in any fields you want. You may want to edit the First Name and Last Name fields, but the Email Address field is already correct. It doesn't matter what you enter in the Nickname field as long as it's easy for you to remember and to associate with this entry. This is the shortcut name (like drac) that you'll be able to enter in the To field when you create a new message. The completed Name tab should look something like Figure 5-51.

Figure 5-51: The completed Name tab.

- If you check the Prefers to receive HTML check box, any HTML messages you send to this individual will automatically be sent in HTML format—Messenger will not ask you if you want to convert it to Plain Text.

3. Click the Contact tab and fill in as many of the fields as you wish. This information is optional, but if you complete it, the Address Book becomes a handy reference as well as an e-mail addressing tool.

4. Click OK. Your Address Book now contains a new entry.

Let's see how it works:

1. Back in the Messenger window, click New Msg. The Composition window appears.

2. In the To field, enter **drac**. Notice that as you start to type, Messenger completes the word for you. You only need to type the first few letters of long nicknames.

TIP

*By default, Messenger expands not only nicknames you type in, but also actual names. In other words, typing **drac** and typing **Count** will both result in the e-mail address dracula@transylvania.net. But you can configure the program so that only nicknames get expanded into e-mail addresses, not names. To make this change, select Preferences from Messenger's Edit menu and click the Messages category. Then click the More Options button. In the top section of the More Messages Preferences dialog box that appears, select the option "Expand addresses against nicknames only."*

Now you can simply complete the actual text of your message and click Send. But that's only one way to do it. There is an alternate and equally convenient approach to addressing your e-mail using the Address Book:

1. From the Messenger window, click New Msg. The Composition window appears.

2. Click the Address button. The Select Addresses window appears, as shown in Figure 5-52.

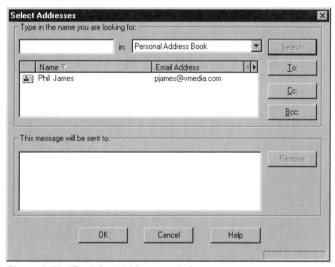

Figure 5-52: The Select Addresses window.

3. Select a name from the list in the top pane and click the To button. The address is added to the bottom pane.

- You can keep adding addresses to the bottom pane by selecting them and pressing the To, Cc, or Bcc buttons. You can also remove recipients for your message by selecting them in the bottom pane and clicking Remove.

TIP

To find names quickly in a long Address Book, start typing the name in the top left box. Messenger will take you right to it.

4. When you're done adding recipients for your message, click OK. You are returned to the Composition window, with the To, Cc, and Bcc fields correctly filled in.

Address Lists

You can also add lists of recipients to the Address Book. That way, a single nickname can represent as many addresses as you want. For instance, you could create an Address Book entry called Congress Critters that lets you automatically send the same message to Jesse Helms, Al D'Amato, and Dick Armey. To create a list, you need to access the Address Book window.

1. Select Address Book from the Communicator menu, or simply press Ctrl+Shift+2. The Address Book window appears, as shown in Figure 5-53.

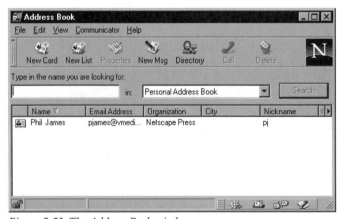

Figure 5-53: The Address Book window.

TIP

Notice that you can add individuals from this window as well: simply click the New Card button. Remember, too, that the Address is used by Netscape Conference (see Chapter 11). That's what the Call button is for.

2. Click the New List button. A dialog box like the one in Figure 5-54 appears.

Figure 5-54: The Mailing List dialog box.

3. Fill in the List Name field with the "official" name of this list, **Congress Critters**.

4. Fill in the List Nickname field with an easy-to-type nickname like **con**.

5. Optionally, fill in the Description field. This field is just for your reference.

6. Now start adding nicknames from your Address Book to the bottom pane. They will be expanded automatically into full names. You can also type in actual e-mail addresses that are *not* already in your Address Book, and you can remove names by selecting them and clicking the Remove button.

7. When you are finished adding names to your address list, click OK. Your Address Book window now contains a new list, as shown in Figure 5-55. Lists are designated with a "two person" icon to distinguish them from regular individual entries.

Figure 5-55: The Address Book with a new address list.

You use lists exactly the same way you use other Address Book entries. You can either type the list's nickname in the To field of the Message Composition window, or you can click the Address button and select it. In either case, your message will go out to every member of the list.

I've shown you how to click the Address button from the Composition window in order to address a new message. But you can do it the other way around, too. You can go to the Address Book window without ever calling up the Composition window. Then, select an individual or list name and click Compose. You'll be taken to the Composition window with the To field already filled in.

TIP

You can save your Address Book as a file, and you can import other people's Address Book files into your personal Address Book. These Save As and Import options are both available in the Address Book's File menu.

Adding Your Address Card to Messages

Earlier in the chapter I showed you how you can add a special signature to all your outgoing e-mail messages. But there's an even cooler feature. You can automatically add your own Address Book Card to every message you send. As you know, this card includes information such as your home or business address and your phone number. When other Messenger users receive a message which includes this information, Figure 5-56 shows you what they see.

Figure 5-56: A message with added Address Book Card information.

If recipients click the View Complete Card button, they see lots more information about you, as shown in Figure 5-57.

Figure 5-57: A message with complete Address Book Card information.

Obviously the amount of information that appears depends on how much information you've entered in your own Address Card.

But here's where it gets interesting. When the recipient of your message clicks the Add to Address Book button, all of the information about you is copied to a new Address Card on that user's system. In effect you're giving your recipient an electronic rolodex card that can be used to automate any e-mail he or she wants to send you.

Creating or editing your own Address Card, the one you include with outgoing e-mail messages, is the same as creating or editing anyone else's card. You can access it from the Address Book window, or click your name in the To field of any message you receive. Then just fill in whatever fields you want. But how do you tell Messenger to include this information in outgoing e-mail messages? That's easy:

1. From Messenger's Edit menu, select Preferences, then select the Identity tab.

2. Check the "Always attach Address Book Card to outgoing messages" check box.

3. If you want to create a new card or edit your current one, click the Edit Card button.

TIP

Checking the "Always attach..." box means that your Address Book Card will be appended to every message you send. You may not want the program to behave this way. To publish your Address Book Card selectively, adding it to some messages but not to others, leave this box unchecked. Then you can use the Attach command to add it to particular e-mail messages. For information on how to do this, see the section called "Attaching Files to Messages" below.

Searching Directories for E-mail Addresses

The Address Book is a great way to organize and access information that you already know. But let's say you want to send a message to your Uncle Waldo in Minnesota and you don't remember his e-mail address. Fortunately, the Address Book contains a facility that lets you search special "lookup" directories located on the Net or on your corporate intranet. Straight out of the box (or rather straight off the CD) Communicator supports Bigfoot, Four11, InfoSpace, WhoWhere, and Switchboard, all excellent address search databases. It even supports the FedEx package tracking system—instead of searching for an individual, just type in a tracking number!

There are two ways to search for individual e-mail addresses:

1. Select Address Book from the Communicator menu of any component.

2. Once you're in the Address Book, enter the name you are looking for (or part of it) in the field in the upper left corner of the window.

3. Click the down arrow next to the field that now contains the phrase "Personal Address Book." From the list that appears, select a different database or lookup service such as Bigfoot.

TIP

To use the listed directories, you must be connected to the Net. Your list, however, may contain additional intranet databases configured by your network administrator.

4. Click Search. In a few seconds Communicator retrieves a list of names that contain the string you specified. For instance, Figure 5-58 shows a bunch of Phil Jameses listed on Bigfoot.

Figure 5-58: And all these years I thought I was unique!

Want to send a message to one of these Phil James impostors? Select the name, right-click, and select New Message from the context menu that appears. You will be transported immediately to the Message Composition window, with the appropriate e-mail address already filled in. This is a major convenience and one of my favorite Messenger features.

In the second and more robust method of searching for e-mail addresses, you still start from the Address Book window. This time, however, click the Directory button. A Search dialog box appears, as shown in Figure 5-59.

Figure 5-59: The Search dialog box.

TIP

You can also access this search facility by clicking the Directory button in the Message Composition window.

Here's how to use this facility:

1. Drop down the "Search for items" list and select a database such as Four11 or Bigfoot.

TIP

You can reorder the directories in this list. To do so, select Preferences from the Edit menu, then the Directory category under Mail & Groups. Use the up and down arrows to change the positioning of directories in the list.

2. Using the three boxes in the middle of the dialog box, restrict your search based on what you know about the individual you are looking for.

Hmm, this may need some explaining. Let's pretend you're looking for a friend named Bill Clinton who unfortunately is not *the* Bill Clinton. (Or fortunately, you decide.) Since you know the exact name, just drop down the middle list (which now reads "contains") and select "is" instead. Then simply enter Bill Clinton in the rightmost edit box.

But wait a second: you know of at least one other Bill Clinton, and there may be many more. You should restrict your search further so that you don't get the addresses of thousands of these guys. Click the More button and you are given some extra fields to narrow down your search, as shown in Figure 5-60.

Figure 5-60: Extra fields to narrow the search.

You can keep adding fields to restrict your search until you're comfortable that the results will be useful. Then hit Search. After a few minutes of huffing and puffing, you should get something that looks like Figure 5-61.

Figure 5-61: The search results.

Want your search results to display last name first? Select Preference from Messenger's Edit menu, then click the Directory category. Select the last option button on the page and click OK.

Notice the buttons along the bottom of the window. From right here you can select an individual and add him or her to your Address Book. You can even pop an address right into the Message Composition window by clicking the Compose Message button.

Can't find somebody using Messenger's Search utility? Try using Navigator 4 to access some other large search services on the Web. Just click Navigator's Places button and select People from the submenu that appears.

Adding Search Directories

Warning: You have just entered a geeks-only zone. If acronyms make you queasy and you'd rather read a good novel than track down obscure technical information, get out of this sidebar quickly and proceed to the section called "Working with Folders."

By default, Messenger includes your Address Book, the Four11 Directory, and the Bigfoot Directory, InfoSpace, Switchboard, and WhoWhere in its list of searchable databases. These are all excellent services. But you—or your intranet administrator—can add other services to the list as well. These databases may be located on your local intranet or out in some faraway corner of the Net, it doesn't matter. There is only one rule: they must be configured as *Lightweight Directory Access Protocol* (*LDAP*) *servers*.

LDAP is a special protocol that lets Messenger, as a client, "talk" to one of these database servers. Using established conventions, it can post queries like the ones we've looked at. Using the same LDAP protocol, the server returns the information to Messenger via the Net or an office intranet.

To add an LDAP server to Messenger's list, you need to know its domain name, its port number, and whether or not it requires a password. If you're fairly technical and can get this information (and if you have a password if it's on a secure server), here's how you configure Messenger:

1. Select Preferences from Messenger's Edit menu.

2. Click the Directory category under Mail & Groups.

3. In the Directory category, click the New button. An Add Directory Server dialog box appears.

4. In the Description field, enter a name for the server that will appear in Messenger's list.

5. In the LDAP Server field, fill in the domain name address of the LDAP server.

6. In the Search Root field, fill in the search root, if any, given to you by the LDAP administrator.

7. Fill in the Port Number field with the correct port number for the server.

8. In the Maximum Number of Hits field, enter the maximum number of results you'd like to receive in response to your query.

9. If this is a secure server, check the Secure box. You can also check the Save Password box if you don't want to enter your password each time to initiate a search.

10. When you've completed the LDAP Server Properties dialog box, click OK. The new server will appear in Messenger's list.

Searching Your E-mail

As you start to receive more e-mail messages, you may lose track of what each one is about. Subject lines are often vague or misleading, and it can take hours to look through dozens or even hundreds of messages for the one piece of information you really need. Fortunately Messenger provides a powerful search feature. To use it, select Search Messages from Messenger's Edit menu. A Search dialog box appears, as shown in Figure 5-62.

Figure 5-62: The Search dialog box.

To use this tool, press the down arrow to the right of the first box and select where you want to search. To search your e-mail rather than newsgroup articles (see Chapter 6), you'd select either in Inbox or in All mail folders. (You'll learn more about folders in the section below called "Working with Folders.")

Next, construct a search criterion by completing the three boxes in the middle of the dialog. In the first box, select from the list which part of the messages you want to search. Perhaps you want to search the From field for a particular name or the body of the message for a particular word. Next select an item from the second box. Does the area of the message you've chosen contain the word? Or does it begin or end with the word? Lastly, type in the word (or partial word) you're interested in. If you need to make your search more precise by specifying more search criteria, press the More button and keep working. This lets you develop very complex searches. You could look, for instance, for a message that contains the word Windows but *wasn't* sent by Microsoft.

When you've completed your search criteria, simply click the Search button. If it exists, Messenger finds what you're looking for.

Messenger also supports a much simpler kind of search for text within individual messages. With a message selected, simply hit Ctrl+F or select Find in Message from the Edit menu. To find subsequent occurrences of the same word, simply press Ctrl+G or select Find Again from the Edit menu.

Attaching Files to Messages

Besides including HTML tags and inline images in messages, you can also include entire HTML files or attach any kind of file, whether it's text or binary. There are no restrictions on the type of material you can include with your message. You can send spreadsheets, graphics, sounds, word processor files, programs, you name it. You can even attach files that are not on your own computer by sending the URLs for the files as attachments to your message!

To attach a file to an e-mail message:

1. Follow all the steps outlined earlier for creating a new e-mail message or replying to one.

2. Before sending the message, click the Attach button. A submenu pops up with several choices:

   ■ **File.** Select this to attach a file.

   ■ **WEB Page.** Select this to attach the URL for a remote Web page.

   ■ **My address book card.** You can select this on its own or in addition to either of the other choices. With this item checked, your own Address Card will be appended to the message, as explained earlier in the section called "The Address Book."

3. For the purposes of this exercise, click File. An Enter file to attach dialog box appears, as shown in Figure 5-63.

Figure 5-63: The Enter file to attach dialog box.

4. Select a file from your computer (or your network) and then click Open. You are returned to the Messenger window, with the Attachment tab selected in the Addressing Area and a file listed as an attachment, as shown in Figure 5-64.

Figure 5-64: Message with a file attached.

5. To add more files, click the Attach button again. Or, as a shortcut, you can simply click within the area that displays the attached files.

6. Once you have attached all the files you want, you send the message like any other, by clicking the Send button.

TIP

When your message includes attachments, the paper clip icon on the Attachments tab is red rather than blue.

Pretty simple, isn't it? But there's an even easier way to attach files to your e-mail messages:

1. Again, follow all the steps outlined earlier for creating a new e-mail message or replying to one.

2. At the left side of the top pane, click the Attachments tab, the one that depicts a paper clip. You should now see a big empty Attachments area in the top pane, as shown in Figure 5-65.

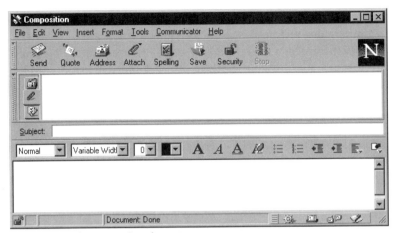

Figure 5-65: The empty Attachments area.

3. Now click and drag the icon for any file on your system into this area. You can select files from your desktop, from any folder on your system, or from Windows Explorer, for example. Once you've dragged the file into the area, it appears in the Attachments list, as shown above in Figure 5-65. You can even drag multiple files into the Attachments area all at once. Don't worry, the files aren't deleted from your system—only *copies* are sent with your e-mail.

Attaching Web Pages

Instead of attaching a locally stored file to your message, you can attach the URL for a Web page or other multimedia file that's located somewhere else. To do this, click the Attach button and then select Web Page instead of File from the submenu that appears. A dialog box like the one in Figure 5-66 appears.

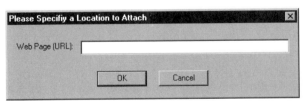

Figure 5-66: The Please Specify a Location to Attach dialog box.

Just enter a URL and click OK, then complete and send your message. Assuming your recipient is using Messenger or another HTML-enabled e-mail program, he or she will see the Web page right within the message. And by the way, just as with files you can drag Internet shortcuts right into the Attachments area.

TIP

You can send messages with attached URLs right from the Navigator window, too. Let's say you're viewing an awesome graphic and you want to send it to a friend. Just click Send Page from Navigator's File menu. A new message Composition window pops up with the URL for the file already attached. Once again assuming your friend is using Messenger or another HTML-enabled e-mail program, he or she will see the graphic immediately in the message.

Making Sure Your Attached Files Arrive Safely

E-mail is a system designed primarily for exchanging text messages, and attached files require special handling by Internet and intranet software. Netscape Communicator's default settings will work fine in most cases, but if somebody complains that a binary file you attached to a message was corrupt or wouldn't run, click the Sending Options tab before sending your message (the tab with the checklist on it, just under the Attachments tab) and select "Uuencode instead of MIME for attachments." This makes Netscape Messenger use an older alternate method of encoding for the attachments to this message.

Dealing With Attached Files You Receive

Not only does Netscape Messenger let you attach all kinds of files to e-mail messages, it also includes special options for dealing with attached files that you receive. For instance, as I mentioned before, when you receive an image file, it is automatically displayed as an image, and attached HTML files are automatically displayed just like Web pages. If you don't want images and HTML formatting displayed inline (as part of the message), select Attachments from Messenger's View menu and then click As Links from the submenu that appears.

TIP

Every message that includes at least one attachment also contains a paper clip icon near the top. If you click this icon, a new frame opens up that includes icons for each of the attachments. Clicking the attachment icons displays them in separate windows, or, in the case of a binary file, opens it or saves it to disk. More about attached binary files coming right up!

What if you receive an attachment that cannot be displayed automatically in the Message Contents pane, for instance a spreadsheet file or Word document? Figure 5-67 shows what you'll see at the bottom of the message:

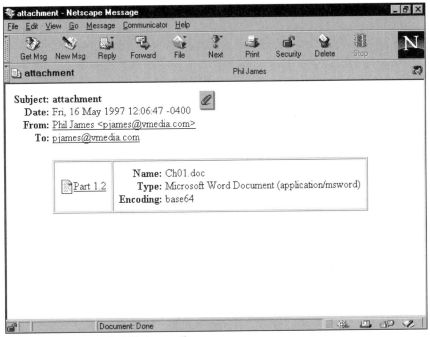

Figure 5-67: An attached file in a mail message.

As you can see, the fields on the right inform you of the name of the file, what MIME type it is (more about MIME in a moment), and what method was used to encode it. At the left, there is a clickable link. In most cases, if you click on this link Messenger will automatically launch the correct application on your system for viewing or otherwise processing the attached file. For instance, if the attached file is a Word document, Messenger will launch Microsoft Word. Within seconds, you'll see the attached file displayed right within Word. In some cases, the file may be saved to disk instead of displayed within another program. Don't worry, you'll be asked where you want to save it!

MIME Types

MIME, or Multipurpose Internet Mail Extensions, includes a universal standard for naming file types. Usually the MIME designations make sense, as in the case of Winword files, which are classified as application/msword. The first part of the designation lets you know that the file is associated with an application, the second part specifies the exact application. By knowing the MIME type of a file it encounters, a program such as Communicator can know what application to launch.

Messenger cannot automatically handle every type of file you might receive. Obviously, there are thousands of different file formats, and new ones come along every day. Figure 5-68 shows the dialog box that appears when you click an attached file that Messenger doesn't know how to handle.

Figure 5-68: The Unknown File Type dialog box.

Let's go over each of these buttons:

- **More Info.** If you're connected to the Net, clicking this button takes you to Netscape's Plug-In Finder page. There you can download a special plug-in application that will extend Communicator's capabilities so that it can handle this type of file properly (please see Chapter 10).

- **Pick App.** If you click this button, a new dialog box appears, as shown in Figure 5-69.

Figure 5-69: The Configure External Viewer dialog box.

TIP

"External Viewer" is just a synonym for helper application.

If you have an application on your system that can deal with this type of file, enter its path and name here. You can use the browse button to find the helper application if you want.

- **Save File.** This button lets you save the file to disk so that you can deal with it later in another application.

- **Cancel.** Even if you click cancel, the file will still be available to you later whenever you view the e-mail message it's attached to.

You can also use a special configuration facility for customizing the way Netscape Communicator associates particular types of files with different helper applications, but that topic is beyond the scope of this chapter. For a full discussion, turn back to the section called "Applications" in Chapter 3. All of the information there applies to Messenger as well as to Navigator 4 and other Communicator components.

Working With Folders

You've been using e-mail for a week and your Messenger window is clogged with thousands of messages. These include pep talks from the CEO, dire warnings from the people in Accounting, and some *very* interesting gossip about your immediate supervisor. Do these messages really all belong together in the same Inbox?! *Kids, it's TIME TO GET ORGANIZED!*

Let's take another look at the Messenger window, as shown below in Figure 5-70.

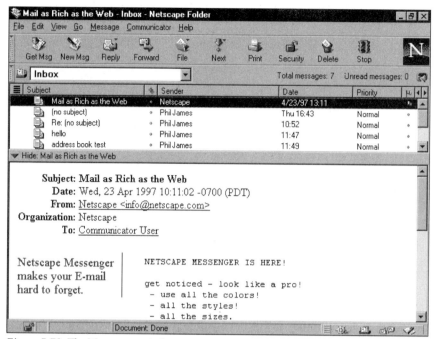

Figure 5-70: The Messenger window.

The drop-down folder list at the left of the window displays the word Inbox. This is because the Inbox is the default folder where all new mail is stored. Now press the down arrow to the right of the listbox. You'll see something like Figure 5-71.

There are five default mail folders in addition to one or more news folders. Don't worry about the news folders for now; I'll cover those in the next chapter. The five mail folders are:

■ **Inbox.** You already know all about this one.

■ **Unsent Messenges.** If you are working offline, this is where messages are stored before they are actually sent. Please see the sidebar ahead on "Working Offline."

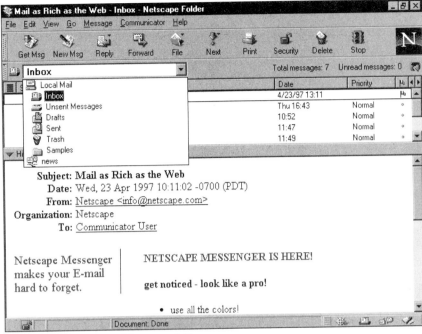

Figure 5-71: Some more Messenger folders.

- **Drafts.** As I mentioned earlier, this is a folder in which you can store messages that you are still working on. From the Message Composition window, you click the Draft button and your current message is moved to the Drafts folder. From there, you can work on your message some more and simply click the Send button when you're finally satisfied with your work.

- **Sent.** This folder, by default, stores a copy of all messages that you send.

- **Trash.** When you delete a message using the Delete button, it's not gone forever. It's simply moved to the Trash folder. That way you can recover messages you've deleted accidentally. Messages are only really gone when you delete them from the Trash folder. By the way, you can empty your Trash folder quickly by selecting Empty Trash from the Message Center's File menu.

> **TIP**
>
> *Not all of these folders may exist when you run Messenger the very first time. Some of them are created the first time they're needed, for instance when you send or delete your first message.*

You can move to a particular folder simply by clicking it in the drop-down list. Then only the messages in that particular folder are displayed.

Working Offline

If you think of your messages as *belles-lettres* and like to polish your prose until it sparkles with wit and wisdom, you need this sidebar—especially if you're a SLIP or PPP user paying for all that time connected to the Net. Messenger lets you create as many messages as you want without being connected. Later, you can send them in a batch all at once.

How does this work? Well, you create a message offline—without being connected to the Net. Then, instead of clicking the Send button, you select Send Later from the File menu. The Composition window disappears. Your message has been copied to the Outbox folder, a temporary storage area for messages waiting to be shipped off on their journey across the Internet.

So some time later you connect to the Net and want to send whatever messages you've stored in the Outbox. From Messenger's File menu, simply click Send Unsent Messages. Messages in your Outbox are also sent when you retrieve new messages.

Of course you can use the Send Later option even if you're permanently connected to an intranet, but it becomes especially valuable for dial-up Internet connections when you're paying by the minute.

This is also a good time to talk about Messenger's configuration options for working online or offline. Select Preferences from Messenger's Edit menu and then click the Offline category. What appears is shown in Figure 5-72.

➡

Figure 5-72: The Offline dialog box.

The choices here are fairly self-explanatory. If you select Online Work Mode, Messenger assumes you are connected to the Net at all times. When you click the Send button, for instance, it will try to send your message to the specified address. If you are not currently connected, it will huff and puff and finally return an error message.

What happens if you choose Offline Work Mode and try to send a message when you're not connected? Messenger simply places your message in the Outbox folder, queued for delivery when you eventually go online. By the way, when you're in Offline mode, the Send button automatically becomes a Send Later button.

Messenger behaves the same way when you have selected Ask Me and are not connected, placing outgoing messages in the Outbox and ignoring requests to retrieve new mail. The difference here is that in Ask Me mode Communicator will ask you if you want to go online when you first start the program.

Moving Messages Between Folders

The whole idea of folders is that they help you organize your messages, sort of like files in a file cabinet. That means you have to be able to move messages from one folder to another. It's easy in Netscape Messenger:

1. Select a message in your Inbox (or any other folder). Optionally, select several messages using Ctrl+click.

2. Click the File button. A submenu appears with the names of all your folders, as shown in Figure 5-73.

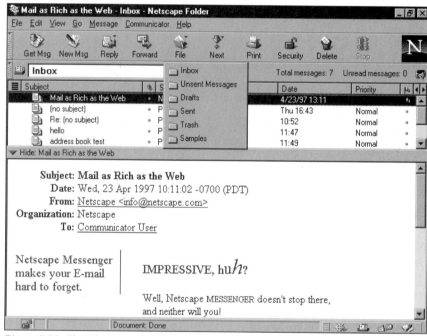

Figure 5-73: The File command submenu.

3. Click the folder to which you want to move your selected message(s).

You can also copy (rather than move) selected messages by selecting the Copy Message command from the Message menu.

TIP

When you want to move a message to a folder quickly, just right-click it and select File Message from the context menu that appears.

Of course you can also simply *delete* messages by selecting them and clicking the delete button. As a safety precaution, they are stored in your Trash folder until you explicitly delete them from there.

Creating New Folders

It's great to know how to move messages from folder to folder, but there's not much to be gained in moving them around among Messenger's default folders. To really get organized, you need to create new folders. Let's create one called Office Gossip:

1. In the Messenger window, with any folder displayed, click the small button at the far right on the toolbar, just underneath the Netscape logo. This is the Message Center button. The Message Center window appears, as shown below in Figure 5-74.

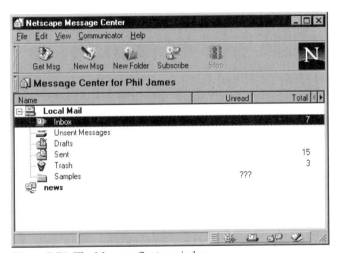

Figure 5-74: The Message Center window.

- The Message Center window displays a hierarchical view of all your folders, including discussions you've subscribed to (see Chapter 6).

2. Select the top level folder, called simply Local Mail. Right-click and select New Folder from the context menu that appears. A dialog box pops up asking you to enter a name for the new folder.

TIP

If you don't want to make this a top-level mail folder but instead a sub-folder of some already existing folder, select from the list at the bottom of this dialog box.

3. Enter **Office Gossip** and click OK.

Voilà! Look at the Message Center window now, as shown in Figure 5-75.

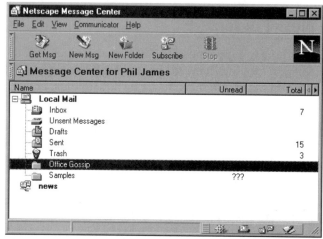

Figure 5-75: The Message Center window with a new folder.

Your new folder will appear in the regular Messenger window folder list. You can now move individual messages from your Inbox into this new folder, following the instructions in the previous section "Moving Messages Between Folders."

By the way, you can create sub-folders of folders, too. For instance, if you select the Office Gossip folder in the Message Center window and then click New Folder in the File menu, you can create a sub-folder called Really Hot Office Gossip. You can hide or reveal sub-folders in the Message Center window by clicking the plus and minus signs to the left of the parent folder. Only the hierarchical location of a sub-folder differentiates it from any other folder—otherwise it's exactly the same.

TIP

The Message Center window is a great place to empty your Trash folder in one fell swoop. Simply select Empty Trash Folder from the File menu. And there's one other small housekeeping chore you should do periodically. From the same file menu, select Compress Folders. This gets rid of any extra disk space that's being used up unnecessarily as a result of deleting messages from folders.

Mail Filtering

What if a friend of yours at work *only* sends you gossipy messages? No work-related stuff, no weather reports, just hard-core who's-doing-what-with-whom. Maybe you get so many of these messages that it becomes a pain to move them to your Office Gossip folder. Hey, no problem. Messenger can do the work for you!

Yes, Messenger includes a special filtering feature that automatically moves incoming mail into particular folders—instead of the Inbox—based on certain criteria such as the sender, the subject, or even a word that appears in the body of the message! If you don't want any messages with the word broccoli in them, you can get Messenger to move them into the Trash folder as soon as they come in.

Here's how it works:

1. From Messenger's Edit menu, select Mail Filters. The Mail Filters window pops up, as shown in Figure 5-76.

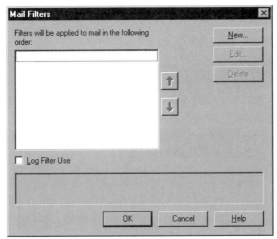

Figure 5-76: The Mail Filters window.

2. Since you don't have any filters yet, click the New button. A new Filter Rules dialog box appears, as shown in Figure 5-77.

Figure 5-77: The Filter Rules dialog box.

3. Fill in a name for your filter, replacing the word Untitled in the first edit box. For instance, you might call it Broccoli.

4. Now start filling in your filter rules. For this example, drop down the first list box and select the item body. You can leave the word "contains" in the next box, but in the last box to the right enter **broccoli**. This means that the filter will be triggered whenever it encounters the word "broccoli" in the body of a message.

TIP

If you want to make your rule more precise, you can click the More button and add further criteria. For instance, you might want the filter to be triggered only if it encounters the word broccoli AND the date is after next week some time. I don't know why you might want that, but you might.

5. Next, tell Messenger what action to take when it encounters the criteria you've specified. For this example, leave the Move to folder command, but in the right-hand box select the Trash folder.

- Instead of moving these messages to the Trash folder, you could simply select delete from the drop-down list on the left. The effect would be the same.

- Two of the actions available in the drop-down list are Ignore Thread and Watch Thread. You'll understand what these mean after reading the section below, "Sorting and Threading Messages."

6. Fill in a description for your filter so that you can see at a glance what it's all about. Your completed Filter Rules dialog box should look something like Figure 5-78.

Figure 5-78: A completed Filter Rules dialog box.

7. Click OK. You are returned to the Mail Filters dialog box with your new rule displayed, as shown in Figure 5-79.

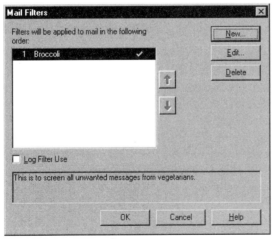

Figure 5-79: A new rule.

- As you can see, the Mail Filters dialog box lets you edit or delete any filter you've created. But more importantly, it lets you toggle filters on and off. To turn any filter off without deleting it, simply click in the On column. The checkmark changes to a dot, and the filter becomes inactive. To turn it back on, click again.

- If you have several filters, you may need to experiment with the order in which they're activated. You can do this by using the arrows at the left side of the dialog box. For instance, you have a filter that deletes all incoming messages that contain broccoli and another one that moves messages from your coworker Jack into the Gossip folder. Jack sends you some gossip about your boss and some broccoli—should it be deleted or moved to the Gossip folder? This is where the order of the filters becomes important.

- You can create a log file of filter use by checking the Log Filter Use check box. Messenger will create a file that details every time a filter was "fired." This can be useful for debugging your filters—or for figuring out why you have all those messages in your Trash folder.

In this section you've learned how to organize your e-mail messages by filing them away in folders. But Messenger also provides several features that help you organize your messages *within* individual folders, and that's what we'll examine next.

Hiding Old Messages

Messenger provides a convenient trick that will make you *look* organized even if you're not. Let's say you have lots and lots of messages in your Inbox folder, some read and some unread. You can force Messenger to display only the unread, or new, messages in the message list pane. To do this, simply select Messages from the View menu, then New from the submenu that appears. Messenger now only displays messages that you haven't yet read, or that you've marked as unread. To switch back to viewing all your messages, select All from the same submenu.

You'll notice that the submenu also includes several other choices related to *threads*. You'll learn all about threads and threading in just a few minutes.

Sorting & Threading Messages

Take a quick look at my actual real life Inbox folder shown in Figure 5-80:

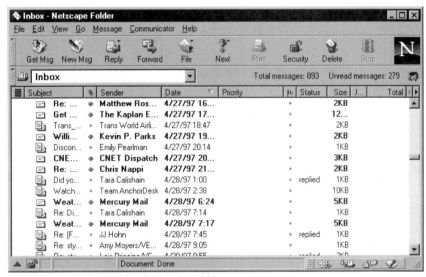

Figure 5-80: Phil's actual real life Inbox folder.

You can probably tell from the subject fields that there are all kinds of messages: personal notes, business correspondence, weather, and stock reports, etc. Yes, I'll admit it: I'm an e-mail slob. I'm just not very good about creating tidy folders and efficient filters. And because my Inbox gets so crowded, I rely heavily on Messenger's sorting and threading features. Sorting and threading affect the order and hierarchy of messages within individual folders. Instead of wandering through a huge random list of e-mail you've received, you can move efficiently through a list you've unrandomized in useful ways.

TIP

The Next button is an effective way to navigate large lists of messages. The Next button takes you to the next unread *message.*

Sorting

By default, mail in a folder is sorted in chronological order, with the earliest mail at the top of the folder and the latest mail at the bottom. To sort alphabetically by subject, click the Subject bar (column label), as shown in Figure 5-81. Note that Messenger places a small arrow in the Subject bar indicating that this is the current sort criterion.

Figure 5-81: Mail sorted by subject.

You can also sort by sender name, as shown in Figure 5-82. To do this, simply click the Sender bar.

In fact, you can sort by *any* of the informational fields available.

Let's go back to sorting by date for a moment. Suppose you want the most recent messages at the top of the list rather than at the bottom? You can reverse the order of any sort tools by selecting Ascending in the Sort menu under View. This makes date sorting run from most recent to earliest, and alphabetical sorting run from Z to A, as shown in Figure 5-83.

Figure 5-82: Mail sorted by sender.

Figure 5-83: Mail sorted by sender in reverse order.

Threading

I bet you're wondering, "What's that button with the lines on it to the left of the Subject, Sender, and Date bars? And when is this @#$%^&* book going to explain it?"

Then there are the Curious George types among you who've already clicked the button. The lines on the button became indented when you clicked it, but unless you've collected a bit of e-mail already you didn't notice any other change.

This is the *Thread* button. When you click it, your messages are sorted in thread order. That means any messages which have the same subject line are grouped together, and then each of those *groups* is placed in the list in order by date.

Confused?

Let's say that on January 1 you get a message from your mother. On January 2 you get a message with the subject line "Make Big Bucks on the Internet." On January 3 you get a message from your father. On January 4 you get another message labeled "Make Big Bucks on the Internet." If you are currently sorting by date but don't press the Thread button, here's the order of messages:

Jan 1 - letter from Mom
Jan 2 - "Make Big Bucks on the Internet"
Jan 3 - letter from Dad
Jan 4 - "Make Big Bucks on the Internet"

But after you press the Thread button, here's the order of messages:

Jan 1 - letter from Mom
Jan 2 - "Make Big Bucks on the Internet"
Jan 4 - "Make Big Bucks on the Internet"
Jan 3 - letter from Dad

Notice that I indented the second "Make Big Bucks" message. That's the way Messenger does it, too. The January 2 message is the initial message in the thread; subsequent messages with the same subject are grouped *underneath* it, not only spatially but hierarchically as well.

Let's see what this looks like in the Messenger window. Figure 5-84 shows a portion of my Inbox with Threading turned on.

Figure 5-84: My Inbox after clicking the Thread button.

Notice the item Yahoo!'s Picks of the Week. That's the initial message of a thread. To see all the messages in that particular thread, simply click the plus sign to the left of the initial message, as shown below in Figure 5-85.

Figure 5-85: The expanded view of the Yahoo!'s Picks thread, showing all the messages I've received with the same subject.

One of the best things about threading is that the subject lines don't always have to be *exactly* the same for two messages to be considered part of the same thread. *Replies* to messages are automatically put in the same thread with the original message. Let me explain:

Your delinquent son writes you a message from Las Vegas with the subject "Need Money Quick." You respond, and your message is automatically titled "Re: Need Money Quick." Since you've told him No way, he responds urgently to your response, begging and making promises he'll never keep. What's the subject line of his response? Right, once again it's "RE: Need Money Quick" or perhaps even "Re: Re: Need Money Quick." So you've received two messages now from your son: "Need Money Quick" and "Re: Need Money Quick." Even though the subject lines are not exactly the same, Messenger knows to stick them together in the same thread.

TIP

> *To exit "thread mode" and return to a different sorting order for your messages, simply click one of the label bars such as Sender or Date.*

Selecting Threads

Often it is useful to select all the messages in a particular thread, for instance if you want to move them to a different folder. Of course you can click the plus sign to expand a thread, then individually select each message using Ctrl+click, but Messenger provides a much simpler technique:

1. Scroll down the message list to the initial message of the thread you want to select.

2. Click the small blue icon to the very left of the message. This is the thread selection control. The entire thread is selected, as shown in Figure 5-86.

You do not need to expand the thread (by pressing the plus sign) before clicking the thread selection control.

TIP

> *Messenger puts a blue-green down arrow next to the icon of any thread that contains messages you haven't read yet. This is a convenient way to find newly retrieved messages when you are sorting by thread rather than by date.*

Figure 5-86: A thread after pressing the blue thread selection control.

Watching & Ignoring Threads

Maybe not all threads are equally important to you. You'd better stay pretty aware of messages from the boss about a project you're working on, but you can probably live without some of that juicy office gossip. Fortunately, Messenger lets you mark individual threads as *watched* or *ignored*. Watched threads are ones you really care about. You can choose to view *only* watched threads if you want, thus filtering out anything you don't want to see right now. Ignored threads are the opposite. When new messages arrive in ignored threads, Messenger doesn't even alert you by putting the green arrow next to the thread icon.

To mark a thread as watched:

1. Make sure your messages are currently sorted by thread. If they are not, click the Thread button.

2. Select the initial message of the thread you want to mark as watched. Or, mark a "lone" message if you want to see if responses to it come in.

3. From the Message menu, select Watch Thread. Optionally, you can just type **W**.

To view just the new messages in your watched thread(s):

1. Select Messages from the View menu, then Watched Threads with New from the submenu that appears.

2. To return to viewing all your messages, select All from the same menu.

   - Note that you can also choose to view *all* threads with new messages.

And to *ignore* threads:

1. Make sure your messages are currently sorted by thread. If they are not, click the Thread button.

2. Select the initial message of the thread you want to mark as ignore. Or, mark a "lone" message if you want to ignore any future responses to it.

3. From the Message menu, select Ignore Thread. Optionally, you can just type **K**.

That's all there is to it. Now you won't be alerted by the green arrow icon when new messages arrive in the thread. You can, however, choose to see messages in ignored threads by selecting Messages from the View menu and then Ignored from the submenu that appears.

Mailing Lists

By now you're pretty good at using Netscape Messenger. In fact if you've tried everything I've suggested so far in this chapter, you probably qualify as a power user. Wear that pocket protector with pride! But now I'd like to move away from the technical aspects of e-mail and back into the realm of *content*. This is a section about how to get more mail, for those of you who don't get enough.

TIP

This section is only useful if you can send and receive Internet e-mail. If you're on an intranet that doesn't allow you to exchange messages outside your own company domain, skip ahead to the section on "E-mail Security."

Internet e-mail is not just for exchanging private messages. It can also be used for gigantic group conversations among Internet users via an Internet service known as *mailing lists*.

A mailing list is simply a list of the e-mail addresses of everyone who wants to send and receive mail about a certain topic. There are mailing lists for discussing bonsai trees, rap music, adoption, cars, computer software, folk dancing, and on and on. There are thousands of lists, with new ones being created every week.

Adding your e-mail address to a mailing list is a way of joining these conversations. This is called *subscribing*, and removing your e-mail address from such a list is called *unsubscribing*. Once you've subscribed to a list, any mail you send to the list address gets sent back out to all the other e-mail addresses included on the list, and any mail from any of the other subscribers also gets sent to you.

When you subscribe to a mailing list, you immediately begin receiving mail from the other subscribers. If, after reading what other people on the list are talking about for a few days, you have something to add, you can send mail back to the list address, and everyone else on the list sees your message.

So how do you find out what mailing lists are out there, and how to subscribe to them? The closest thing the Net has to an official list is Stephanie da Silva's list of *Publicly Accessible Mailing Lists*, originally created by Chuq Von Rospach. This list is an impressive compendium of mailing lists with a name, a short description, and information on how to subscribe for each one. The list itself is currently in 22 parts, arranged alphabetically and stored on a machine at MIT.

How do you retrieve this list of lists? Simple, you use Netscape Messenger:

1. In the Messenger window, click the Compose button. The Message Composition window appears.

2. Enter **mail-server@rtfm.mit.edu** in the To field.

3. Enter **Mailing Lists** in the Subject field. (Do this for your own information. The MIT mail-server doesn't care what's in the Subject field.)

4. Type only one line in the body of the message:

```
send pub/usenet/news.answers/mail/mailing-lists/part01
```

Your completed message should look like the one in Figure 5-87.

Figure 5-87: Mail ready to go to the MIT mail server.

This message instructs the MIT mail server, a kind of electronic file clerk, to send you Part 1 of the list. The list is large, and Part 1 is only the beginning! If you want to see more of the list, send another piece of mail to mail-server@rtfm.mit.edu with just this line:

```
send pub/usenet/news.answers/mail/mailing-lists/part*
```

You need to replace the asterisk shown above with the number for the part of the list you're interested in. To get to Part 7, for instance, enter **part07** after the final slash.

Using Mailing Lists

There are a few differences between sending and receiving mail from a mailing list and sending and receiving personal mail, because mailing lists are a public forum. When you send a message to a mailing list, you don't even know how many people are reading it, much less who all of them are. This changes the way people read and write e-mail. Mailing lists are famous for long-running, voluminous, and often quite heated exchanges of e-mail, and because they are public forums, there are different rules of conduct there.

Mailing List Etiquette

- **Read before you write.** This is Rule #1. Before you send e-mail to a mailing list, remember that you are writing for a particular audience, and make sure that what you have to say is relevant. The rule of thumb when dealing with mailing lists is to read what other people are saying for about a week before sending any mail yourself, to make sure that any questions or comments you may have are pertinent. (Reading a list without posting is called *lurking*.)

- **Don't waste people's time.** This advice seems self-evident, but you will often see people posting mail that adds nothing to the discussion. Don't jump into a conversation just to tell everyone you agree with what someone else has said. If you are quoting another person's message, only quote what is relevant to your point. Nothing wastes people's time more than scrolling through screen after screen of a message they have already read once, only to read "I think you are completely correct" at the end.

- **Use private e-mail when appropriate.** When you read something posted to a mailing list, you have a choice between replying to the writer in private or sending your reply to the entire list. If you merely want to say you agree, or ask where you can get a copy of something mentioned in the post, send e-mail to the writer instead of to the list.

- **Use the Subject line carefully.** As with private e-mail, the Subject line is the first thing anyone sees in mail from you, and it tells people whether they are interested in what you have to say. Use the Subject line to describe, as succinctly as possible, the contents of your mail.

- **If you are no longer interested in a particular mailing list, use the proper procedure for unsubscribing.** When you signed up for the list, you were probably sent a message that included thorough instructions. Now's the time to follow them! In most cases, you send your *unsubscribe* command to an address that's different from the one where you send regular messages. Nothing annoys mailing list recipients more than getting *unsubscribe* messages along with the usual information.

One of the main differences between mailing list mail and personal mail is that when you want to reply to a message, you have a choice between replying only to the author of the article or sending the reply out to the whole list. If you have something to add to the debate, you should send your mail to the list, but if you just want to say that you agree with what someone has said, send it to the author only. The best way to tell what's appropriate is to read what other people are posting to the list to see what kinds of things are being discussed in public.

When replying to something you have read on a mailing list, make sure to examine the To field of your outgoing mail. Different mailing lists handle the return address differently. On some lists, when you use the Reply function, the To field is set up assuming that you want to send mail out to the whole mailing list, while on others it is set up assuming that you want to reply only to the author of the original post. If you want to reply to the whole group, you would select Reply to All.

TIP

Checking the To line of your mail before you reply will prevent you from sending mail you meant to be private to everyone on the list, or from sending mail you meant to be public only to one other person.

One concept that you will sometimes hear discussed on mailing lists is the *signal-to-noise ratio*. This is an engineering term that has been pressed into service to describe the percentage of messages sent to any given mailing list that are useful or interesting. Lists where there is generally an engaged and articulate discussion going on are said to have a high signal-to-noise ratio, while lists where the subscribers are posting messages needlessly are said to have a low signal-to-noise ratio. Good mailing list etiquette helps create a high signal-to-noise ratio.

Inbox Direct

Netscape Messenger also supports a very different kind of mailing list called *Inbox Direct*. With Inbox Direct you still subscribe to services that send you specialized messages, but typically these are not messages you'd respond to. For instance, my Inbox Direct subscriptions include a local weather report and stock quotes several times a day.

But the main difference between Inbox Direct messages and regular old mailing list messages is that they are all HTML-enhanced, with colorful graphics and even sound. In fact, when you subscribe to an Inbox Direct service, you are really asking for specialized Web pages to be delivered directly to your Messenger Inbox on a regular basis, just as paper magazines are delivered to your house via snail mail. You can think of Inbox Direct as the e-mail version of Netcaster. In fact, services like Inbox Direct are often referred to as *mailcasting*.

To subscribe to Inbox Direct services, use Navigator 4 to go to the Netscape home page (http://home.netscape.com) and click the Inbox Direct link.

TIP

If you subscribe to many mailing lists, your Messenger folders will get pretty crowded pretty quickly. Not only that, you might start using up more hard drive space than you want to! Netscape Messenger lets you control the "runaway Inbox" problem not only through the filtering options covered earlier in the chapter, but also by restricting the size of messages you can receive.

If you don't want to receive e-mail larger than a particular size (which may often be junk e-mail anyway), select Preferences from the Edit menu of any Communicator component, then expand the Advanced category by double-clicking it or by clicking the plus sign. Select Disk Space from the new categories that appear. Now check the first check box and in the edit field type the upper size limit of messages you want to receive.

In this same dialog box, you can also require Messenger to ask you if you want to compact your folders when it will save a certain amount of disk space. Just check the second check box and set the minimum space saved.

Lastly, you can save disk space by configuring Messenger so that it deletes the bodies of old messages, saving just the headers. This is especially useful if you're saving messages on your mail server as well as locally. To access this feature, click the More Options button in the Disk Space dialog box. Check the check box in the dialog box that appears and set the minimum age for deleting the bodies of messages.

E-mail Security (S/MIME)

I'll end this chapter with a very brief discussion of one of the hottest topics in the online world: e-mail security. As we start using e-mail for financial transactions and other sensitive communications, the privacy of our messages becomes increasingly important. There's a whole chapter later in the book on security (Chapter 12), so we're not going to get into too much detail here. But it's important to understand the basics.

Messenger supports a standard known as S/MIME (Secure MIME) for digitally signed and encrypted e-mail messages. S/MIME can assure you that messages you send and receive are authentic and have not been read anywhere between their point of origin and their final destination. In this section I'll cover the basic features of S/MIME as implemented in Messenger.

TIP

If your incoming e-mail server is an IMAP server (rather than POP3), it may support encrypted connections, automatically encrypting information it sends you. If your network administrator has told you that this is the case, select Preferences from Messenger's Edit menu and then click the Mail Server category. Check the very last checkbox, "Server supports encrypted connections," in the Mail Server dialog box.

Let's start with sending signed and encrypted messages.

Sending Signed and Encrypted Messages

Messenger lets you send *signed messages* that include a digital security certificate assuring the recipient that the message did in fact come from you, or at least from somebody sitting at your computer. Digital security certificates are issued by special certifying organizations. Getting a personal security certificate can be compared with getting a passport from the Post Office, except this is a "cyber-passport" and you can obtain one electronically, using Netscape Communicator of course. In Chapter 12, I show you how to get a new personal security certificate, but for now let's assume you already have one. Let's see how you attach it to your e-mail:

1. Follow the steps outlined earlier in this chapter for creating a new e-mail message.

2. In the Composition window, click the Sending Options tab, as shown in Figure 5-88.

Figure 5-88: The Sending Options tab.

3. Check the checkbox labeled "Signed."

4. Send your message by clicking the Send button.

TIP

After you check the Signed checkbox, a signature tag appears as part of the icon on the Security button.

That's it! And what does the recipient see when they look at a signed message? I'll cover that in the section below called "Receiving Signed and Encrypted Messages," but for now let's move on to sending encrypted messages.

Encrypted messages are ones that are scrambled using a special *algorithm,* or formula, so that they cannot be read at any point between your computer and your recipient's computer. In encrypting your message, Messenger uses a key that's part of your recipient's digital security certificate—that's how your recipient can *de*crypt it at the other end. Yes, you have to have received a signed message from an individual before you can send that individual an encrypted message. Or you have to have received the individual's certificate some other way, perhaps from a directory server. You do not necessarily need your *own* digital certificate in order to send encrypted e-mail, but without one nobody will be able to send *you* encrypted messages.

To send an encrypted message:

1. Follow the steps outlined earlier in this chapter for creating a new e-mail message.

2. In the Composition window, click the Sending Options tab, as shown earlier in Figure 5-88.

3. Check the checkbox labeled "Encrypted."

4. Send your message by clicking the Send button.

TIP

After you check the Encrypted checkbox, the paddle lock icon on the Security button appears locked rather than open.

Receiving Signed and Encrypted Messages

What happens when you receive a signed and/or encrypted message? Check out Figure 5-89.

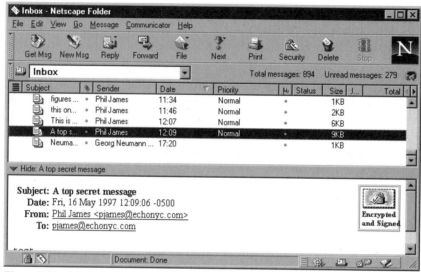

Figure 5-89: A signed and encrypted message selected in Messenger.

The Messenger window looks different in several ways:

- The Security button now depicts a locked paddle lock (indicating an encrypted message) with a tag hanging from it (indicating that it's also a signed message).

- The status line paddle lock is now locked, and the "signed" icon appears to its right.

- Just to the right of the usual headers, the message itself contains a special "Encrypted and Signed" icon.

TIP

Remember, signing and encryption are related but independent S/MIME features. You may receive messages that are just encrypted, or just signed. In these cases the icon will of course be slightly different.

The whole idea of signed messages is that you can verify the identity of the sender. Obviously the mere presence of these new icons doesn't necessarily give you the assurance you need. When Immigration agents ask you to verify your identity, they usually want to see a bit more than your passport's blue and gold cover. Well, go ahead and click the new icon within the message, or the Security button, or the paddle lock icon on the status line. Any one of these actions has the same result: it opens up the message sender's electronic passport. A new Security Info window appears, providing detailed security information as shown in Figure 5-90.

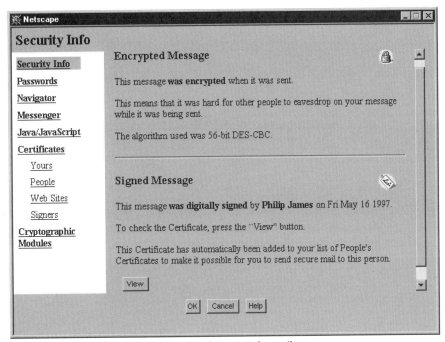

Figure 5-90: Security Info for a signed and encrypted e-mail message.

To see more identifying information about the message sender, simply click the View button. The details of the individual's security certificate appear in a new window, as shown in Figure 5-91.

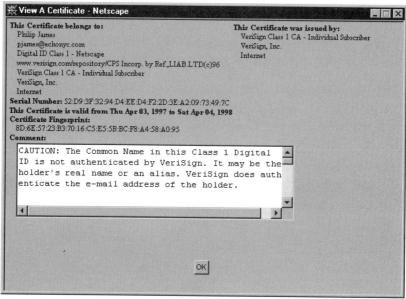

Figure 5-91: The View A Certificate window.

TIP

> *Much of the information in this window will make more sense after reading Chapter 12, but in a glance you can at least ascertain who really sent the message—or at least whose computer it was sent from.*

Click OK when you've finished viewing the sender's security certificate.

Messenger Security Options

Back in the Security Info window shown in Figure 5-90, notice that there are a variety of configuration categories in the left-hand frame. To reconfigure any Messenger security options, you would click the Messenger category. But that is beyond the scope of this chapter. If you want to get busy with e-mail security settings now, please turn to Chapter 12 for very thorough information.

Moving On

E-mail is a big subject, and at some point in this chapter you were probably wondering if it would ever end. But the perseverance was worth it, wasn't it? I mean, now you can go around saying things like "just e-mail me, babe."

In the next chapter, you'll learn another way to communicate with others on your office intranet or on the Net: discussion groups. Like Messenger, the discussion groups feature is a tool for sending and receiving messages. But where mail is usually private, discussion groups provide shared or even fully public forums where you can bandy about ideas or work on projects collaboratively. Collabra uses much of the same user interface as Messenger, so this next chapter is going to be an easy one.

CHAPTER 6

Discussion Groups

Only a few human urges are stronger than the urge to "put in your two cents," and you'll find few better correctives to narrow thinking than encouraging the expression of varied opinions. Of all the new communications technologies, discussion groups are perhaps the clearest example of a tool that enhances participation in decision making, in learning, and even in focused entertaining chit-chat.

> **TIP**
>
> *Many of the techniques you'll use in working with discussion groups are identical with procedures you're already familiar with from Communicator's e-mail facilities. Chapter 5 contains large chunks of material that I could repeat here, but in the interest of keeping this book under 20 pounds and sparing a few trees, I'll instead assume that you're already familiar with the basics of Messenger. At times I may steer you toward the appropriate sections in Chapter 5.*

What Are Discussion Groups?

Discussion groups share some basic features with e-mail. In fact, both facilities are based around sending and receiving messages. There's a big difference, though. When you send messages to a discussion group rather than to an individual e-mail recipient, those messages are read by several people, potentially by every member of the group. And when you receive discussion group messages, you aren't the only one reading them. Again, every member of the group gets the same messages. Ten people might respond to one message, and you will see not only the original message but all ten responses. You can respond to the original message yourself, or to any one of the responses, and everyone will see your message too.

So a discussion group is really a group of people engaged in an electronic conversation. The conversation may be fast- or slow-paced. A controversial message may elicit dozens of immediate responses, or an informational message may elicit no responses at all. And the conversation may be more or less focused depending on the goals of the group. For instance, you might have a small discussion group within your company dedicated to reworking personnel policy. But you can also find very large discussion groups that feature endless debates about TV shows or the latest supermodel—which brings up the whole issue of *public* versus *private* discussion groups.

Private Discussion Groups

Private discussion groups are, unsurprisingly, groups that the general public can't access. Earlier, I used the example of a discussion group dedicated to reworking personnel policy. That would be a private group within the company, open only to certain employees.

On intranets, private discussion groups are often established and configured using Netscape's Collabra server. This special program handles the message traffic. All messages are actually sent to the Collabra server, which acts as a central clearing house. Individual members of a particular discussion group use Communicator to "grab" any new messages from the Collabra server as well as to send any responses or new messages.

A single Collabra server may service many different discussion groups. But when your copy of Communicator logs on to a Collabra server to grab new messages, it accesses messages only from the groups you belong to. The Collabra server may be set up to allow you to join new groups, however, and you may even have permission to create new discussion groups.

Discussion Group Terminology

Although discussion groups have some similarities with e-mail, experienced users generally use slightly different terminology. Instead of *sending* a message, for example, you *post it to the group*, or simply *post* it. And the message itself is often referred to as a *posting* or a *post*.

The large public discussion groups that comprise Usenet (see the sidebar called "What Is Usenet?" below) are almost always referred to as *newsgroups*, and the entire system that makes these public groups available is known as *Usenet, Netnews,* or *network news*. Client programs (like Communicator) that let you access discussion groups are often called *news readers*. When you join a discussion group or newsgroup, you *subscribe* to it, and when you quit the group, you *unsubscribe* from it. Subscribing to a discussion group simply means that Communicator will "remember" the group from session to session so that you may click on its name to open it rather that having to rejoin each time.

You need to know one other important term: *threads*. You may remember this word from Chapter 5. In the context of discussion groups, threads are individual trains of conversation posted to a particular group. I post a message. You post a response. Ten people respond to your response, and so on. Generally speaking, threads share a common theme, so you could refer, for instance, to "the Whitewater thread" in a newsgroup dedicated to Bill Clinton. Large public discussion groups sometimes have several simultaneous threads.

Public Discussion Groups

Public discussion groups are groups that anyone can join. Generally, they are slightly less focused than private discussion groups. You won't find a public discussion group about your company's personnel policy (unless you work for the government), but you can probably find a newsgroup devoted to personnel policy in general—or even personnel policy within a particular industry. Some public newsgroups cover broad areas like photography, aviation, and alternative health practices. Public discussion groups provide a public town square where you can get together with people of like interests to say what's on your minds.

No single server exists for all public discussion groups. Instead, the messages are duplicated among many servers. A discussion group server *subscribes* to various public groups from what is called a news feed, which is simply a computer on the Net that distributes discussion group messages to other servers. Then you, in turn, subscribe to particular discussion groups from your server. (See the sidebar called "What Is Usenet?" below.) When you read messages from the alt.rec.photography public discussion group, for instance, you are downloading the messages from your discussion group server, but they are the same messages people are downloading from different servers all around the world. Conversely, when you respond to a message in a public discussion group, you are actually uploading the message to your discussion group server, but from there it travels across the Net and is distributed to thousands of other discussion group servers.

What Is Usenet?

The most prominent system of public discussion groups is *Usenet*, also known as *Netnews*. Usenet is simply a huge collection of discussion group servers that make their groups available to other servers and to the general public. Public discussion groups disseminated via Usenet are known as *Usenet newsgroups*.

Usenet was originally developed for UNIX systems in 1979. It has become a worldwide network of thousands of Usenet sites (discussion group servers) running many operating systems such as UNIX, MS-DOS, and Windows NT on various types of computers. Millions of people share messages electronically over these Usenet sites. The messages are sent from server to server using the UNIX-to-UNIX Copy Protocol (UUCP).

Usenet servers don't have to be connected to the Internet, since UUCP doesn't require the Internet for the transport of messages. But because thousands of Usenet sites *do* have access to the Internet, it has become the most commonly used electronic postal route for public discussion groups. The total number of distinct newsgroups on the Internet is in the thousands and growing daily. Consequently, millions of people who may have started using the Internet to gain access to the World Wide Web or to e-mail find that they can participate in Usenet newsgroups as well, provided they have Netscape Communicator or other client software.

Although UUCP is used to transfer discussion group messages from server to server, the servers use a different protocol to communicate with client programs such as Communicator. When your computer logs on to a discussion group server to read messages or post responses, it uses the Network News Transfer Protocol (NNTP) to communicate with the server.

In Netscape Collabra, Communicator's discussion group component, private and public groups look alike. You don't need to learn different interfaces for the two types of groups. Figure 6-1 shows the Message Center window (one of the two main discussion group windows) with a combination of public and private groups. The groups listed under the server news.computerland.net are all public groups that I have subscribed to, and the groups listed under secnews.netscape.com are private groups. Remember, private groups exist only on the server itself, whereas public groups "live" on many servers at once.

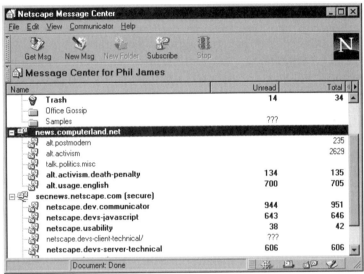

Figure 6-1: The Message Center window with a combination of public and private discussion groups.

TIP

Notice that the public discussion groups (newsgroups) are named according to a convention that looks a little like that for domain names, with descriptive words separated by dots. (You'll learn more about this convention in the section called "How Many Public Groups Can I Get?") The private discussion groups, on the other hand, do not necessarily adhere to this format because Netscape's Collabra server, the server for these private groups, allows for alternate "friendlier" names.

TIP

> *Notice also that the list of private discussion groups includes various folders, which in turn contain other groups. The Collabra server allows discussion groups to be categorized like this in a hierarchical tree fashion.*

Discussion groups are differentiated in one more way. Both types, public and private, may be either *moderated* or *unmoderated*.

Moderated & Unmoderated Discussion Groups

You've probably heard the term "signal to noise ratio." It's an engineering term used to describe how much of the data that's being communicated is usable information. For instance, if you have a very bad phone connection, you're getting lots of data in the form of hiss but very little usable information in the form of spoken words.

The term applies to discussion groups as well. Because of the human "two cents" urge I mentioned at the beginning of this chapter, people sometimes talk (or type) when they really have nothing much to contribute. This scenario is especially true in large public newsgroups where some of the participants suffer from chronic cases of Male Answer Syndrome.

To help improve the signal to noise ratio, some discussion groups (whether public or private) are *moderated*. In this case, the discussion group server does not automatically and immediately make all postings available to the group as a whole. If you post a new message or a response to a moderated group, somebody—yes, an actual human—reads what you wrote and determines whether your message is germane to the ongoing discussion. Send a message about Johnny Depp's hair to a moderated newsgroup on particle physics and nobody but the moderator will ever see your words. Well, maybe some of the moderator's friends.

How Many Public Groups Can I Get?

How many angels can dance on the head of a pin? Nobody knows, and the same is true regarding the total number of Usenet newsgroups available at any time via the Internet. To impose some order on the basically anarchic structure of Usenet, newsgroups have a fairly strict hierarchical naming convention.

Newsgroup names look similar to Internet addresses; they are a series of words or abbreviations separated by dots, as in this example:

`rec.arts.movies.reviews`

The first word in the name denotes the major category to which the newsgroup belongs. A few of the major, hierarchical categories of Usenet newsgroups are:

- **alt.** *Alternative* newsgroups contain articles that are often very interesting but can be on the controversial side, if not downright disgusting. Reader beware! This major category alone accounts for thousands of Usenet newsgroups.

- **comp.** *Computer* newsgroups discuss computer-related issues.

- **misc.** The *miscellaneous* newsgroups category (as you no doubt have guessed) is a catchall category for discussions that don't fit into one of the other categories.

- **news.** The *news* category is for newsgroups discussing Usenet network news itself. These newsgroups are great sources of information about Usenet.

- **rec.** *Recreation* newsgroups discuss recreation, sports, and the arts.

- **sci.** *Science* newsgroups cover scientific topics.

- **soc.** *Social* newsgroups focus on issues of perceived social importance.

- **talk.** If you like good arguments, *talk* newsgroups are the place for you.

Newsgroups in these categories are usually distributed worldwide. Other major categories that may be distributed throughout the world include bionet (biology newsgroups), biz (business newsgroups), and vmsnet (discussions about the VMS computer operating system). Geographical, organizational, and commercial newsgroups are usually distributed only within their areas of interest.

Newsgroups in the *bit* major category are actually an alternative distribution method for Bitnet listserv mailing lists. Conversely, many newsgroups also distribute articles via mailing lists to users who don't have access to a news server. In effect, the pertinent messages are mailed to the user's electronic mailbox, enabling the user to get network news via a simple dial-up Internet e-mail account.

Because of the sheer volume of Usenet traffic, and due to the timely nature of much of the newsgroup content, most newsgroup servers put a limit on the number of days an article will be available for reading. Past the time limit, an article is said to have expired and is removed from the server. The time limit varies from server to server, but many long-standing newsgroups keep archives of expired articles.

TIP

There are special newsgroup search services that let you search for information in newsgroup archives. The most popular of these is DejaNews, which you can access via Navigator 4 at http://www.dejanews.com.

Do you have access to all the newsgroups on the Internet? Maybe, maybe not, depending on your server. Later in this chapter, we'll see how to get a list of all the newsgroups available through your server.

The best way to gain an understanding of Usenet newsgroups is to browse through several of them, reading the messages but not responding. This practice is affectionately known as *lurking*. In this case, lurking for a while makes a lot of sense. Before you know it, you'll feel compelled to jump in there and participate in the conversation.

Usenet Pictures

One of the more popular pastimes unique to the Internet is the trading of digital pictures of all kinds—pictures of animals, cartoons, heavenly bodies of various sorts, you name it. Whereas digital pictures can be made available on FTP sites or attached to electronic mail, Usenet has become a widely used method of sharing favorite electronic images. Most such files are posted in the newsgroups that have names beginning with *alt.binaries.pictures;* however, they may appear in postings in any newsgroup.

Because of its high resolution and the relatively high data compression, the Joint Photographic Experts Group (JPEG) file format is the current favorite for storing high resolution digital pictures for transmission over the Internet.

If a discussion group message contains either a GIF file or a JPEG file, Communicator displays the image, along with the rest of the article, in the message content pane.

You can even save the images to disk in a viewable form. Simply right-click on the graphic and select Save Image as... from the context menu that appears.

Specifying Your Discussion Group Server

You're probably eager to try your hand at reading discussion groups right away, but we still need to take care of a little housekeeping. Before the Collabra discussion group component of Communicator can access messages, you have to give it the name of your discussion group server.

TIP

Most ISPs provide access to a news server along with their e-mail and HTTP servers. Often, the name of the news server will take the form news.myserviceprovider.com.

You can give the name in two different ways. You may have already entered the address of your discussion group server when you installed Communicator, or when you created a new profile. Or you may have entered the information when editing your profile using the Profile Manager. But if not, you can access this configuration option from any Communicator window.

TIP

Before you can use discussion groups effectively in Communicator, you also need an e-mail account. If you have not configured Netscape Messenger to send and receive e-mail, please read Chapter 5.

To configure a discussion group server in Communicator:

1. From any Communicator component, select Preferences from the Edit menu. Then Click the Mail & Discussion Groups category to expand it, as shown in Figure 6-2.

2. Click the Groups Server category, as shown in Figure 6-3.

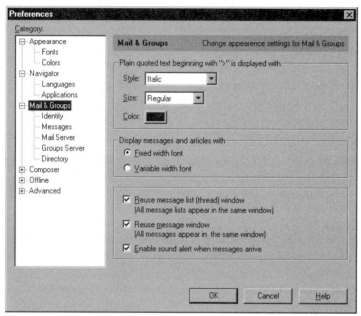

Figure 6-2: The expanded Mail & Groups category.

Figure 6-3: The Groups Server dialog box.

3. Enter the address of your Discussion groups (news) server. You should get this information from your network administrator if you're on an intranet or from your ISP if you're connecting to the Net by modem.

4. Leave the Discussion group folder field alone unless you want to change the location on your system where discussion group messages will be stored.

Perhaps I need to explain the last option in this dialog box. The more popular Usenet newsgroups are very busy, and it is not unusual for several hundred new messages to appear each day. When you tell a client program you want to get all new messages for a particular group from the server, you might not know what you're asking for! Thousands of messages may have accumulated since the last time you checked. Fortunately, Communicator lets you know when there are a high number of new messages. As long as you keep this option checked, the program will not only inform you when you're about to download more than 500 new messages, it will also give you the option of *limiting* the download to 500. And in the box to the right of the check box, you can change that limit of 500 to any number you want.

Figure 6-4 shows a completed Groups Server dialog box.

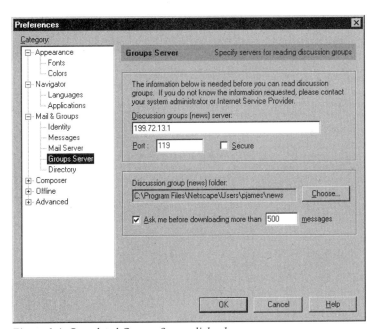

Figure 6-4: Completed Groups Server dialog box.

Simply click OK to return to save your changes and return to Communicator.

Getting Started: The Message Center

In Communicator, discussion groups are accessed via a window called the Message Center. You can make that window appear in three different ways:

- Click the Discussion Groups icon in the Communicator Component bar.

- Click the Discussion Groups icon in the Communicator folder on your desktop.

- From Messenger (see Chapter 5), click the Message Center button, which is at the far right, just underneath the large Netscape icon as shown in Figure 6-5.

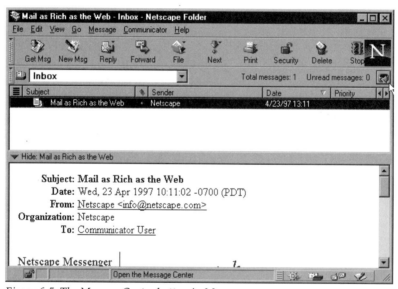

Figure 6-5: The Message Center button in Messenger.

TIP

You can also access a specific discussion group directly from the Navigator 4 window, either by clicking a link to that group or by entering its URL in the Location/Netsite box. URLs for newsgroups always begin with the prefix news://. For instance, to access the public discussion group alt.activism on the Computerland server, I would type news://news.computerland.net/alt.activism. This would bypass the Message Center window. Instead, I'd be taken directly to the discussion group window for alt.activism, showing the messages in that group.

No matter which of these methods you use, the results are the same. The Message Center window appears, as shown in Figure 6-6.

Figure 6-6: The Message Center window.

You may remember this window from the discussion of e-mail folders in Chapter 5. Notice that it contains not only your e-mail folders (Inbox, Drafts, Sent, and so on) but also the name of your discussion group server. You can see that I use four different discussion servers: secnews.netscape.com, news.computerland.net, edda.vmedia.com, and localhost (this last one is on my own machine and is just for testing). Using this number of servers is somewhat unusual—chances are, you use just one server for all your discussion group needs, but in the sidebar called "Adding Servers," I'll show you how you can access several different servers.

Discussion Host Properties

If you right-click a discussion group server in the Message Center window and then select Discussion Group Server Properties from the context menu, a dialog box appears giving you some added information about the server, as shown in Figure 6-7.

Figure 6-7: The Discussion Group Server Properties dialog box.

In this example, information from the discussion group server is encrypted, meaning that it is a special secure server (see Chapter 12). Additionally, it uses a different port from the standard 119 that is used by most public servers.

Notice the options at the bottom of the dialog box. If you are using a publicly accessible server that permits anonymous login, you would select the bottom option; otherwise, select the top option to transmit your username and password each time you log on to send or retrieve messages.

Why do some of the discussion group servers I use have plus signs to their left? The plus signs indicate that I have subscribed to one or more discussion groups on those servers. To expand the list, showing the actual discussion groups I've subscribed to, I simply click the plus signs (or double-click the server names). Figure 6-8 shows the expanded view of the servers, in which the discussion groups are listed.

Figure 6-8: The Message Center window, showing discussion groups I've subscribed to.

To collapse this view, hiding the names of the actual discussion groups, click the minus signs or double-click the server names.

And, of course, this action brings up the next topic: how do you subscribe to discussion groups?

Subscribing to Discussion Groups

Communicator provides two different ways to subscribe to new discussion groups. If you know the name of the group, you can simply specify it. If, on the other hand, you don't know exactly which group or groups you want to join, you can browse a list of all available discussion groups on the server and make your choice from the list.

To specify a discussion group to join, follow these steps:

1. Make sure you are connected to your intranet or to the Net.

2. Using any of the methods outlined in the preceding section, open the Message Center window, as shown earlier in Figure 6-6.

3. Select your discussion group server by clicking its name.

4. Click the Subscribe button. The Subscribe to Discussion Groups window appears, as shown in Figure 6-9.

Figure 6-9: The Subscribe to Discussion Groups window.

You can also access this window by selecting the discussion server in the Message Center window, right-clicking, and selecting Subscribe to Discussion Groups from the context menu that appears.

TIP

Each of the tabs in the Subscribe to Discussion Groups window includes a drop-down Server list that lets you select a different discussion group server if you've configured more than one. You can even add a new server from here by clicking the Add Server button. See the sidebar called "Adding Servers."

After a few minutes, the window starts to fill with the list of all the discussion groups available on this server. If the list is long, this process might take a while. Finally, it looks something like the one in Figure 6-10.

Figure 6-10: A complete list of discussion groups available on this server.

TIP

As Communicator retrieves the list of available groups, it immediately displays them. If the group or groups you're interested in have already appeared in the window, you can halt the retrieval of additional groups by clicking the Stop button. If you want to retrieve a more complete list some time later, simply click the Get Groups button.

Notice that some of the groups contain a wildcard character and may be expanded by clicking the plus sign to the left of the name. You can't subscribe to alt.*, for instance, but you could subscribe to any of the 2,632 *alt* groups that become available when you expand the hierarchy.

Let's give it a try:

1. Click the plus sign next to alt.*, or simply double-click the item itself. An expanded list appears, as shown in Figure 6-11.

Figure 6-11: The expanded list of alt groups.

- Notice that some of the alt groups may be expanded to yet another level.

- You can also expand and collapse the display of groups using the Expand All and Collapse All buttons. Expand All, however, expands the display to include *all* levels underneath the selected level, not just the next level. Once you click Expand All, you won't need to click any more plus signs. Conversely, Collapse All shrinks the display of the discussion groups so that only the selected level appears.

2. When you find a discussion group you want to subscribe to, select it and click the Subscribe button. Or just click the dot in the Subscribe column next to any groups you want to subscribe to. In either case, a checkmark appears in the Subscribe column. Figure 6-12 shows the list of *alt* groups with several checked for subscription.

- To *un*subscribe from a group, simply click the checkmark.

Figure 6-12: Subscribing to several discussion groups from the list of all available groups.

Searching for Groups

Maybe you don't know the exact name of a discussion group you want to subscribe to, but browsing through a long list of available groups could be very tedious. Communicator provides a search utility to help you find a group you're interested in.

To find a discussion group in a particular area of interest, follow these steps:

1. Still in the Subscribe to Discussion Groups window, select the Search for a Group tab, as shown in Figure 6-13.

Figure 6-13: The Search for a Group tab.

2. Enter a word to search for and click the Search Now button. Figure 6-14 shows the results of searching for any groups that contain the word "aviation."

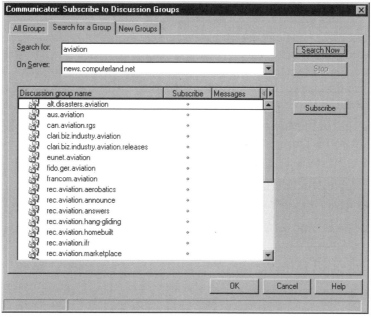

Figure 6-14: Aviation-related groups available on the server.

You can subscribe to groups right in this search window by selecting them and clicking Subscribe. Alternatively, you can just click the Subscribe column for any groups you're interested in. And remember, you can *un*subscribe from any group by clicking the checkmark in the Subscribe column.

Other Ways to Find Public Discussion Groups

There are a number lists of public discussion groups available online. One of the best is at http://home.netscape.com/escapes/newsgroups/index.html. This list organized by category and includes brief descriptions of each group. If you're using Navigator 4 to view this site, clicking a group name automatically opens a discussion group window and displays current messages in the group. Another such service with descriptions and a search feature is provided by http://tile.net/news/.

Some sites, including Netscape's own, host discussion groups about their products. At the Netscape site (http://home.netscape.com), for example, click Assistance and then User Groups. This will take you to http://help.netscape.com/nuggies/,where you can click on a discussion group of interest and not only open the group but also add its server.

Displaying New Discussion Groups

Periodically, most discussion group servers add new groups. They may be private groups that somebody in your company has created, or they may be new Usenet newsgroups that have become available on the Net. Communicator provides a separate view of any discussion groups that have been added since the last time you clicked the Clear New button. Let's take a look:

1. Still in the Subscribe to Discussion Groups window, click the New Groups tab, as shown in Figure 6-15.

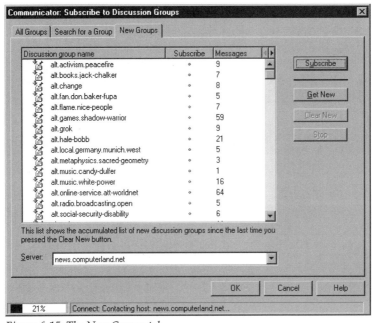

Figure 6-15: The New Groups tab.

2. Subscribe to any new groups following the procedures outlined in the preceding two sections.

3. To clear the list of new groups, click Clear New.

If no new discussion groups are listed, you may not have retrieved a list since the last time you clicked the Clear New button. Try clicking Get New and see what appears.

Adding Servers

As I mentioned earlier, Communicator lets you participate in discussion groups on more than one server. And adding a server is simple:

1. In the Message Center's File menu, clkD´ New Discussion Group Server. Or, in the Subscribe to Discussion Groups window discussed in the preceding sections, click the Add Server button. In either case, the New Discussion Groups Server dialog box appears, as shown in Figure 6-16.

Figure 6-16: The New Discussion Groups Server dialog box.

2. Enter the domain name of the server in the Server field.

3. Unless your network administrator or ISP has given you specific instructions, leave the Port field set to 119.

4. If your network administrator has told you this server is secure, check the Secure check box.

5. If this server requires a name and password for access, check the Always use name and password check box. Most servers maintained by ISPs do not require this option to be checked.

After you have completed the dialog box, click Add. Your new server now appears in the Message Center window as well as in the drop-down list of servers in the Subscribe to a discussion group window.

Retrieving Discussion Group Messages

We're up to the fun part.

OK, you've subscribed to a discussion group or two and are ready to see what people are talking—or typing—about. Here goes:

1. Make sure you're connected to your intranet or to the Net.

2. Launch Collabra Discussion Groups by clicking its icon on the desktop, by clicking the Discussion Groups button on the Component bar, or by clicking the Message Center button in Messenger. The Message Center appears, as shown earlier in Figure 6-6.

3. Click the plus sign to the left of the discussion server you want to use. The display now includes a list of all the discussion groups you've subscribed to on that server, as shown in Figure 6-17.

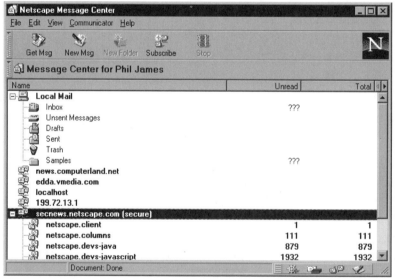

Figure 6-17: The Message Center, showing subscribed-to discussion groups listed under the server name.

4. Double-click the name of the discussion group you want to retrieve.

Right-clicking a Discussion Group

As in most areas of Communicator, right-clicking the name of a discussion group from the list brings up a context menu that provides access to a variety of commands and features. In this case, Figure 6-18 shows what you get:

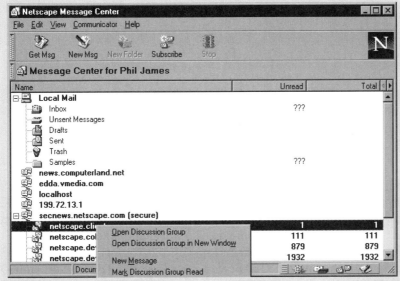

Figure 6-18: The context menu for a discussion group.

Most of these options are self-explanatory. You can open the group (the same as double-clicking it), remove the group (unsubscribe from it), create a new message, or mark all the messages in the group as read. You can also view the properties of the particular group and search for text within its messages. See the section called "Searching Your Discussion Group Messages" later in this chapter.

As soon as you double-click the name of a discussion group, a couple of different windows may pop up.

- You may be presented with a dialog box that indicates more than a certain number of new message headers appears in the group, as shown in Figure 6-19.

Figure 6-19: The Download Headers dialog box.

- If you want *all* the new messages to appear in the message list pane, simply click Download. If you want to download only a certain number, select the second option button; you also can change the number. If you select the second option button and specify 100, for instance, Communicator will display only the 100 newest messages in the discussion group.

- The bottom check box lets you automatically mark all the remaining messages—the ones you don't download—as read. They therefore will not be downloaded the next time you click Get Msg or double-click the discussion group. After you have decided how you want to limit incoming messages, if at all, just click Download.

- And why message *headers?* Communicator's Discussion Groups component does not immediately download actual message content, but only the information to include in the message list pane. When you select a message, the actual content is immediately downloaded. Obviously, this feature conserves disk space.

TIP

You can prevent the Download Headers dialog box from appearing by changing the default limit (500 messages) that triggers it or by disabling this feature altogether. To make these changes, select Preferences from the Edit menu of any Communicator component. If the Mail & Discussion Groups category is not expanded to show its subcategories, double-click it or click the plus sign. Next, click the Groups Server category. You'll find the options I'm talking about at the bottom of the right-hand dialog box. Simply select the Ask me... check box to remove the checkmark or change the number to its right.

■ If you're connecting to a private discussion group that requires a username and password, dialog boxes requesting these elements may appear. Simply enter the information and click OK for each of the dialog boxes.

Once you have responded to any of these message limit or security dialog boxes, you're in the main discussion group window, as shown in Figure 6-20.

Figure 6-20: The main discussion group window displaying message headers from the alt.activism newsgroup.

Downloading all the message headers might take a while. A progress bar on the status line indicates the progress of the download. You can halt the download at any time by clicking the Stop button.

The new window looks almost exactly like your e-mail Inbox window, but a few significant differences are apparent:

- The Delete button has been replaced with a Mark button. That's because marking messages in various ways is a very important function when you're dealing with discussion groups, since the volume of messages may be much greater than it is with personal e-mail. You may want to select large batches of messages to mark as read, for example.

- Message size is indicated as a number of lines rather than a number of bytes.

- The messages are automatically sorted in thread order. Of all the different ways you can sort messages in Communicator, thread order makes the most sense for discussion groups. Especially in large groups, many different conversations may be going on at once, and you need to be able to isolate these threads so that you can work with them effectively. Remember, the initial message of each thread is indicated by a plus sign and a special icon to its left. If you click the plus sign, it expands the thread, revealing all the subsequent messages; if you click the icon, it selects the entire thread.

Marking Discussion Group Messages

Due to the volume of messages in public discussion groups, marking them may be your key to staying organized. Clicking the Mark button lets you mark messages or groups of messages in a variety of ways:

- **as Read:** This option marks the selected message or messages as read.

- **as Unread:** This option lets you return a message marked as read to its original unread status.

- **Thread Read:** This option lets you mark an entire thread as read, even though you have selected only the initial message of the thread.

- **Category Read:** Categories are subfolders within a discussion group. They are supported by Collabra servers. For example, a Human Resources discussion group on your intranet may include a Personnel Policies category. This option lets you mark an entire category as read.

- **All Read:** This option lets you mark all the messages in the discussion group as read.

- **by Date:** This option lets you mark as read all messages before a particular date so that you don't have to read through old material. When you select this option, a dialog box appears asking you to specify the cut-off date.

- **for Later:** This option marks selected messages as read for this session only. In subsequent sessions, they will appear as unread.

Reading Messages

The process of reading messages works just like e-mail. To read a message, simply select it by clicking. Communicator immediately downloads the message content and displays it in the bottom pane of the window. Clicking the Next button always takes you to the next *unread* message.

Just as with e-mail, you can hide the content pane by clicking the arrow between the two panes, and you can display a message in its own window by double-clicking it. And just like e-mail messages, discussion group postings may include links to Web pages or to other discussion groups. In fact, every discussion group message includes a header with clickable links to all the different groups to which this particular message has been posted. You can see an example of these links in Figure 6-21.

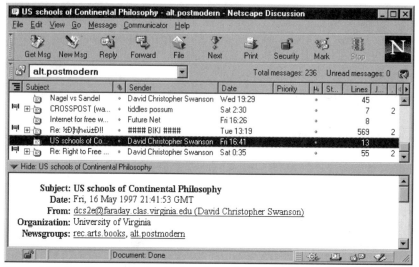

Figure 6-21: The Newsgroups header in a discussion group message, showing all the groups to which this message has been posted.

Click one of these links and you are transported to the new discussion group—as long as it's available on your server. As for the numbers in the References header, they are simply links to other messages in the same discussion thread. The numeral *1* denotes the original message in the thread; the numeral *2* denotes the second message; and so on. You can go directly to the referenced message by clicking the numeral.

TIP

Just as with e-mail messages, you can choose to see more or less of this header information. Click Headers in the View menu and then select All, Normal, or Brief from the submenu that appears.

From the discussion group window, you can collect new messages from the server at any time by clicking the Get Msg button.

Saving Disk Space

Since discussion groups may include hundreds or even thousands of active messages, Communicator provides a number of options for storing them.

Select Preferences from the Edit menu of any Communicator component, then expand the Advanced category and select Disk Space, as shown in Figure 6-22.

Figure 6-22: The Disk Space dialog box.

- To restrict the retrieval of messages to those smaller than a certain size, check the first check box and specify a size.

- Communicator includes a facility for compacting folders (eliminating wasted space from deleted messages). You use this facility by choosing Compact Folders from the File menu, but you can also configure the program so that it prompts you to compact folders when the resulting savings in disk space would be greater than a specified amount. To activate this prompting feature, check the second check box and enter an amount in kilobytes.

- To limit the time that messages are stored, select the first option button in the Discussion Groups Messages Only section of this dialog box, and then specify the maximum time that messages should stay on your system.

- To keep all messages until you explicitly delete them, select the Keep all messages option button.

- To keep only a certain number of new messages for each discussion group, click the next option button and specify a number.

- If you want to keep only unread messages and automatically discard all read messages whenever you leave the discussion group window, check the bottom check box. **Note:** If you check this check box, the previous three options affect only unread messages.

- Now click the More Options button for more disk space choices, as shown in Figure 6-23.

Figure 6-23: The More Disk Space Options dialog box.

Remember that when you select a message in the message list pane, it is downloaded to your computer. But if you check the check box here, Communicator will automatically delete the contents of all discussion group messages older than a specified number of days. The message description remains in the message list pane, but the contents are re-downloaded if you select the message.

Caution: Obviously, discussion group servers don't keep messages forever— they are periodically removed or "scrolled off." If you configure Communicator so that it automatically deletes the contents of old messages, you might not be able to retrieve those messages later from the server even though they still appear in the message list. Of course, old messages may still be accessible via a newsgroup search service which has its own archive database. For example, see DejaNews at http://www.dejanews.com/forms/dnq.html.

Replying to Messages

Again, the process of replying to messages works almost exactly like e-mail. Select a message you want to respond to, and then follow these steps:

1. Click the Reply button. A submenu appears with several reply options, as shown in Figure 6-24.

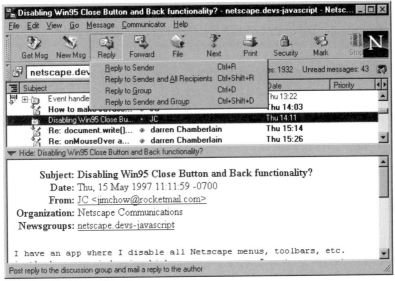

Figure 6-24: The Reply submenu.

2. Select one of the options:

- To send a private "offline" e-mail response to the author of the original message, click Reply to Sender. In this case, your message will *not* be available to other members of the discussion group.

- To send a private "offline" e-mail response to the author of the original message *and* to all of his or her intended recipients, click Reply to Sender and All Recipients.

- To reply to the discussion group as a whole (in other words, to make your response available to everyone in the group), click Reply to Group.

- To make your response available to this group as a whole *and* to send it privately to the message originator, click Reply to Sender and Group. This option assures that the message originator reads your response in a timely fashion.

- After you've selected an option, the Message Composition window appears, as shown in Figure 6-25.

JC wrote:

I have an app where I disable all Netscape menus, toolbars, etc. in the browser window in which my app appears. I want my users to use only the back and exit
functionality I have built into my app.

Sorry if this has been asked before (I checked and did not see anything), but:

(1) Is there a way to disable the Close button (the one with the X) on the system title bar of a Netscape browser window through Javascript or any other means?

(2) Is there a way to disable the "Back" functionality on the right mouse button or keyboard quick key?

Thanks.

Figure 6-25: The Message Composition window after clicking Reply to Sender and Group.

TIP

Notice that the address fields include all the groups to which the original message was posted. If you leave these fields alone, you will be continuing the same thread in each of these discussion groups. If you do not think your response is appropriate to any of the groups, simply delete that address.

3. Enter your response just as you would enter an e-mail message. Although Communicator lets you beautify your message with all kinds of HTML formatting, I recommend avoiding this in messages intended for public Usenet groups. Many readers will have client software that cannot interpret the HTML commands correctly. However, you should have no problem with attaching images to your messages. In fact, thousands of JPEG images are distributed in public newsgroups every day.

TIP

You may want to edit the quoted message in your response, saving only those portions that you are responding to directly. Discussion group messages are often composed of original text interspersed with brief quoted sections of the original posting.

4. When you finish addressing and writing your message, click Send. Your message is delivered to your discussion group server. If you're responding to a public Usenet group, your message then makes its way to thousands of other discussion group servers.

Initiating a New Thread

In addition to responding to messages that already exist in discussion groups, you can start a new thread yourself. Doing so is as simple as sending an e-mail message.

1. In Communicator's Message Center, click a discussion group. Alternatively, if you're already in Messenger, you can simply select the discussion group from the drop-down list of mail folders and discussion groups.

2. Once the discussion group window is displayed, click the New Msg button. A blank Message Composition window appears, as shown in Figure 6-26.

Figure 6-26: A new Message Composition window.

- ▪ Notice that the first address field is automatically filled in with the name of this group. You can add other groups for your message as well, or you can click the Group button and then select To or CC to send your message simultaneously to an individual via e-mail.

3. Using any of the procedures you learned in Chapter 5, create a new message.

4. Once you have completed your message, click the Send button.

That's all there is to it! Your new message is transferred to your discussion server as well as to any e-mail recipients you've specified. If you're posting your message to a public Usenet group, within hours it will start appearing on servers all around the world. The next time you get new messages you might have several responses in your thread.

Searching Your Discussion Group Messages

As you start to receive more discussion group messages, you may lose track of what each one is about. Fortunately, Communicator provides a powerful search feature. To use it, select Message Search from the Edit menu. A Search dialog box appears, as shown in Figure 6-27.

Figure 6-27: The Search Messages dialog box.

Notice that the Search for items in field already contains the name of the current discussion group. To broaden the scope of the search, click the down arrow to the right of the field. From the submenu that appears, you can choose to search any group you want.

Next, construct a search criterion by completing the three boxes in the middle of the dialog. In the first box, choose whether you want to search the sender field or the subject header of the message. Next, select an item from the second box. Does the area of the message you've chosen contain the word? Or does it begin or end with the word? Finally, type in the word (or partial word) you're interested in. If you need to make your search more precise by specifying more search criteria, click the More button and keep working. Clicking this button lets you develop very complex searches.

After you've completed your search criteria, simply click the Search button. If the item you're searching exists, Communicator finds what you're looking for.

The software also supports a much simpler kind of search for text within individual messages. With a message selected, simply press Ctrl+F or select Find in Message from the Edit menu. To find subsequent occurrences of the same word, simply press Ctrl+G or select Find Again from the Edit menu.

Going Offline

Communicator lets you go offline—i.e., disconnect from your intranet or the Net—simply by clicking Go Offline in the File menu. But you may want to finish some discussion group business before actually disconnecting. Luckily, when you click the Go Offline item a Download dialog box appears, as shown in Figure 6-28.

Figure 6-28: The Download dialog box before going offline.

As you can see, this dialog box lets you retrieve new mail and send any messages in your Outbox before actually disconnecting. It also lets you get the latest discussion group messages from any groups you specify using the Select Discussion Groups button. Simply check or uncheck the Choose field in the list that appears.

Moving On

Discussion groups are one of the most flexible new communications tools. You can use them to collaborate on projects at work, to ferret out arcane information, to confer with experts in particular areas of interest, and to participate in giant slow-motion conversations. Discussion groups provide both increased efficiency and virtually endless opportunities for slacking.

In the next chapter, you'll learn more about what makes Communicator a real multimedia program, as we cover the basics of graphics, sound, and video.

CHAPTER 7

Media on the Move: Working With Graphics, Sound & Video

By now you have some idea what Netscape Communicator has to offer. Unlike simple browser programs, you can use Communicator not only to gather information but also to subscribe to Web channels, exchange e-mail, read discussion groups, and collaborate with coworkers. That's great, but when we talk about it in the abstract it doesn't sound all that exciting, does it? To understand why the Web and related resources have generated so much excitement, you really have to take a look—and a listen! It's the multimedia aspects of the new communications technology that have insured its acceptance beyond the world of government offices and college labs. We all like pictures, we all like sound. Pictures and sound are how we amuse ourselves—and how people sell us stuff. Yes, multimedia junk e-mail is now a part of our lives!

Netscape Communicator offers fuller support for multimedia than any other communications program to date. As a Communicator user, you now have at your fingertips a vast assortment of multimedia documents that virtually come to life when you view them.

Multimedia Mail

In this chapter I'll generally depict multimedia documents in Navigator 4, Communicator's browser window. But Messenger, Netcaster, and Collabra discussion groups support the same kinds of graphics, video, and sound. The only difference is what window they appear in. I've viewed some amazing video clips out on the Web, but I've also received a couple of pretty surprising singing telegrams in my e-mail!

Graphics on the Web

Pictures play an important role in our lives: we hang them on our walls; we pay money to stand and look at them in museums; we take snapshots of our loved ones and favorite places. Pictures are perhaps the most common form of communication in our society, and that is becoming true for online communications as well. In fact, much of the growth and popularity of the Web and of intranets is a result of people like you and me having a new way to gather and disseminate information in a colorful and creative way.

In the following sections, you'll read about the types of graphics that are available on the Internet or your office intranet. And of course you'll learn how you can view and download them with Netscape Communicator.

What Kinds of Images Are Available?

Each month, thousands of new Web pages are created and placed online. Almost all of them contain some sort of graphic. Graphics can be small or large, colorful or black and white, tasteful or tasteless. You can probably find the exact image you're looking for on the Web, if you look long enough. It may not be legally posted there, but it will be there (I discuss copyright infringement later in this chapter).

So what kinds of images can you expect to find on the Web? Almost anything. There are:

- Paintings by Renoir, Van Gogh, and little Jimmy from Ms. Wharton's first grade class.

- Publicity shots of your favorite movie and television stars, including Moe Howard, Jim Carrey, and Wynona Rider.

- Detailed weather maps like the ones you see your local weather man pointing at cluelessly on the 11 o'clock news.

- More *Star Trek* and *Deep Space Nine* photos than we care to know about.

- Colorful advertisements from IBM and Microsoft and Absolut and Ford and... and...

- Cartoons and animations.

- And yes, even pictures of naked people, if you look in the right places.

Graphics in Netscape Communicator 4: An Overview

Fortunately for all you picture lovers, Communicator includes features that let you view the vast majority of graphics on the Web. Graphics appear in a variety of sizes, shapes, and formats. In one way or another, Netscape Communicator can either display them or provide an easy way for you to view them in another application. The best way to understand the types of graphics and how they display is to link to a fairly typical site.

TIP

In this chapter I'll be using examples from the Internet, but the principles and procedures are the same on an office intranet. In other words, you should probably go ahead and read this chapter, even if you're not connected to the Net.

To view a graphic in Netscape Communicator:

1. Make sure you are connected to the Internet.

2. Double-click the Netscape Navigator 4 or Communicator icon to launch the program. The Navigator 4 window appears, and the Netscape home page starts loading.

3. Click your mouse inside the Netsite/Location field at the top of the window to select the URL http://home.netscape.com/.

4. Replace the URL with the one for the Ventana Online page by entering **http://www.vmedia.com** (or simply **vmedia**). Then press Enter. Navigator 4 retrieves the Ventana Online page, as shown in Figure 7-1.

Figure 7-1: The Ventana Online page.

Notice that Navigator displays text first, then fills in the graphics. Sometimes you see a description of the graphics, before it starts loading, in the top left corner of its frame. On the Ventana page, the big "Ventana" is really a graphic image. In fact, although there are plenty of words, there is very little actual text on this page: almost everything is done with graphics. Notice also the animated gears. Simple animation like this has become a common special effect in Web pages.

TIP

Animations add life to a Web page, but they can also slow down the display of other information. Navigator 4 makes it easy to disable animations. Simply select Stop Animations from the View menu.

Have I Got the Entire Document?

Many Web pages take some time to download to your computer. How can you be sure you've received the whole thing? Navigator 4 provides several clues.

First, you can look at the status line at the bottom of the browser window. This area indicates the transfer progress of the Web document. Toward the left side of the status line, just to the right of the paddle lock icon, a gray bar moves horizontally whenever Navigator is in the process of downloading information. And to the right of the progress bar, in the central portion of the status line, a readout displays the size, percentage downloaded, and the rate at which Navigator 4 is retrieving the document or components it references. You may have a difficult time reading this line because it's constantly changing as different graphics or other elements of the page start to download, but it will give some idea of how fast things are going. When the document has completely transferred, the gray bar disappears and the status line laconically reads Document: Done.

Another way to see if a document is still transferring is to watch the animated Netscape logo in the top right corner of the window. As the document transfers, a meteor shower streams across the big Netscape *N*. When the shower ends, the document has finished downloading and all the graphics are displayed.

On a Web page like the one shown in Figure 7-1, you may see several different graphics and notice that they're used in a variety of ways. By far the most prevalent type of image you encounter in Web pages is an *inline graphic*. Inline graphics are part of the Web document itself; they appear alongside the text. Inline graphics can include photos, buttons, icons, cartoons, and many other types of pictures. They are used for the following purposes:

- Logos
- Decorations
- Bullet points
- Illustrations
- Separators

Sometimes graphics are not inline, but exist only as a separate image file that you can download to your hard disk for later viewing, or one that you need to view in a separate application from Netscape Communicator. One common external viewer is LView Pro, which was used to display the graphic shown in Figure 7-2. You'll learn more about these types of images and how to view them in the section entitled "Graphics on Demand," later in this chapter.

Figure 7-2: A graphic displayed in LView Pro.

When you connect to a site, such as http://www.vmedia.com (Ventana's Web site), the Web document begins to transfer to your computer and appears in the browser window. As the document displays, you usually see some text first, and then the graphics begin to appear. Depending on the speed of your connection, images may seem to flow in line by line or pop right up along with the text. It all has to do with the amount of data that your modem or dedicated line can transmit to your computer monitor. For example, high-speed connections, such as ISDN or T1 lines, can transmit more data per second than modem connections.

TIP

Tired of waiting for a document's images to display? Click the Stop button on the Navigator 4 Control Toolbar to stop the transfer. If you want to re-initiate the transfer later, click Reload.

Or turn off the automatic display of graphics entirely, as described later in this chapter under "Text-Only Mode."

To accommodate users with all kinds of connections, some sites offer two different versions of the same page. One page usually includes a lot of graphics that a typical modem user will not want to wait to download to his or her computer. The other usually has very few images and mostly text. When you link to a site that has these options, such as the Internet Underground Music Archive (IUMA), you must make a choice to view the page with a lot of images, or one that has been toned down a little to avoid unnecessary waiting.

Figure 7-3 shows you the site when you choose to see the graphics-intensive pages. Figure 7-4 shows what you'll see if you choose the same pages with fewer graphics. Running with a 14.4 Kbps modem, the graphics-intensive page took more than 2 minutes to display. The "lite" version took only 12 seconds!

Figure 7-3: The IUMA site with lots of graphics.

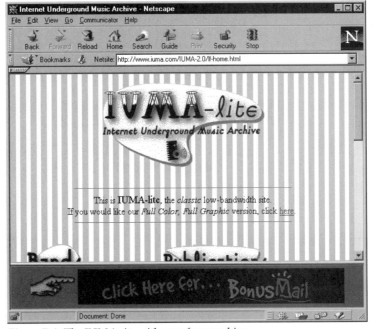

Figure 7-4: The IUMA site with very few graphics.

Most sites include the same textual information in both their graphics version and their text-only pages—the only thing you'll miss is the images themselves.

Later you'll learn how to optimize the display of graphics in Netscape Communicator, but first, let's discuss a couple of special-purpose graphics often used in Web pages: background images and icons.

Background Images

Background images do just what their name implies—they provide the background to the text and other graphics in a Web document. Background images typically are very small images that are repeated again and again over the entire background. (This technique sometimes is referred to as *texture mapping* in graphics design programs.) The images can be solid colors, textures, patterns, or whatever the Web author comes up with. For example, the Graphion home page pictured in Figure 7-5 shows a gray granite background. Some other backgrounds that you may encounter include marble, wood grain, and metallic, but occasionally you'll even see some company's logo repeated a hundred times across your screen. *Blech!!*

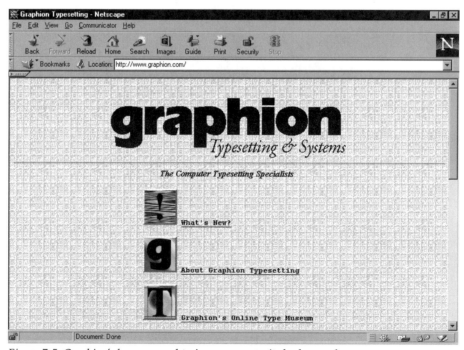

Figure 7-5: Graphion's home page, showing a gray granite background.

When you create a Web page with Composer or some other HTML editor, you can specify an image to be used as the background. (As you saw in Chapter 5, you can even add an image background to your e-mail!) Not all Web sites use backgrounds, but it's fast becoming the norm. Backgrounds offer the Web author a way to set a standard color, texture, or image for the entire Web site.

Icons

Icons are another type of graphic you'll encounter on almost all Web pages. Icons are small images or buttons, sometimes miniatures of larger images you can find at that site. Icons are used to highlight certain points on the page, lead you to another Web page or site, or let you view or download a larger image. Let's look at each of these uses.

In Figure 7-6, you see a set of icons to the left of some text on the Web page. These icons serve the same purpose that bullets do in a book or business document: to distinguish key points. Icons can also be used to highlight special text on a page.

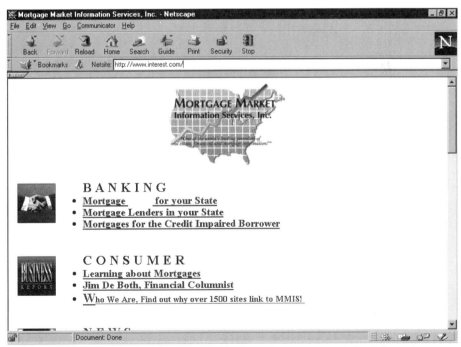

Figure 7-6: Icons emphasize important text on the page (© Mortgage Market Information Services, Inc.).

The second type of icon is actually a hotspot that links to another page or another site, sometimes to graphics of products or announcements. This type of icon works the same as linked text on a page—when you click it, you connect to that other site or page. Icons of this type sometimes have a small blue border around them to indicate that they are links. Figure 7-7 shows examples of icons that you click to advance to another related site.

Figure 7-7: Icons that provide links.

Icons are also used as small "try-before-you-download" versions of larger graphics. When you click this kind of icon, often called a *thumbnail*, the larger image begins to transfer. The advantage of this approach is obvious: the smaller thumbnails transfer to your machine much more quickly than full images you may not even be interested in.

For example, the Web page in Figure 7-8 shows small icons of Renoir paintings (http://sunsite.unc.edu/wm/paint/auth/renoir/). You can scroll down the page and click the painting you'd like to see in full size. Now a larger painting displays in Navigator 4, as shown in Figure 7-9.

Figure 7-8: Thumbnail of a painting.

Figure 7-9: Full view of the same painting.

TIP

Some conscientious Web page authors include file sizes and estimated transfer times next to icons or thumbnails. Use these estimates to determine if the wait is going to be worth it. When I am on these sites, I find the smallest file and download it first. If I don't like the quality, I probably will not download another one.

Graphics Formats Supported by Netscape Communicator 4

The graphics in Web documents typically come in standard file formats that most Web browsers, such as Navigator 4, can understand and display on your computer. The standard file formats include Graphics Interchange Format (GIF), Joint Photographic Experts Group (JPEG), and XBM. GIF and JPEG are the most common graphics you'll encounter in Web pages. XBM is a UNIX graphics format and is more likely to be found at university or research areas that generally work with high-speed computing applications. Navigator 4 natively supports these three graphics formats. That means that when the program encounters a GIF, JPEG, or XBM file, it displays it automatically in the browser window.

Though GIF and JPEG are the most common, many other types of graphics formats appear occasionally on the Web, including Macintosh PICT, BMP, PCX, TIFF, and encapsulated PostScript (EPS). A brand new standard called PNG (Portable Network Graphics) is starting to become prominent as well. Later in this chapter, in the section on plug-ins, you'll learn how to extend Communicator's multimedia powers so that it supports some of the less-common image formats. With plug-ins, you don't have to run another program to view these graphics—they are displayed right within the Navigator window.

Both GIF and JPEG as well as other image files are compressed to save transmission time and to limit their storage size. It is beyond the scope of this book to get into the technical differences between JPEGs and GIFs, but the two formats excel in different areas. JPEG compression is often used for ultra-realistic photographic images, while GIF is used for colorful graphics. GIF images may also be *transparent*. Transparent GIFs are graphic files that have been customized to eliminate the background color of the image. Thus they appear to "float" on top of the Web page instead of being stuck inside a rectangular prison. There are even animated GIFs, files which contain a set of images that are automatically and repeatedly "flipped through" like a card deck to provide a simple simulation of motion.

TIP

JPEG files generally have an extension of .JPG; GIF files always have an extension of .GIF.

PNG Graphics

JPEG and GIF files have been *the* Web standard for a long time, but it may not last forever. The new PNG (Portable Network Graphics) standard offers some significant advantages:

- More colors—PNG images may contain literally trillions of colors.

- Smaller file size—due to new compression techniques, PNG images may be up to 30% smaller than equivalent GIF images.

- Enhanced transparency—PNG graphics may contain several layers or levels of transparency.

- Searchable content—PNG images may contain special embedded "meta" information about content or authorship. A viewer can search for this information just like text.

Graphics on Demand

Some Web sites offer images you can download to your computer for subsequent viewing. These differ from inline graphics because they are not part of the text of the Web page display, but are only *linked to* the document. You can still view many of these files in Navigator 4, using it simply as a file viewer instead of a Web browser. Or, if you want to edit the file or save it in a different format, you can view it in a stand-alone graphics application such as Paint Shop Pro.

At the Saturn Web site shown in Figure 7-10, for example, you can download a picture of one of the auto maker's new models and then view it in the Navigator 4 window.

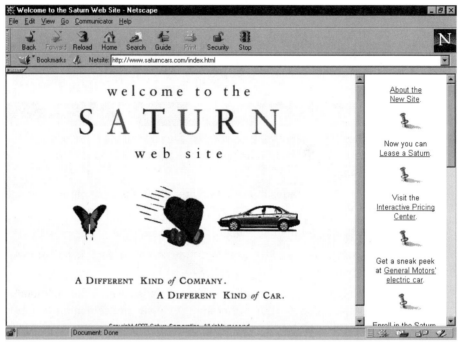

Figure 7-10: The Saturn Web site.

To download a picture:

1. Make sure you are connected to the Internet. If Netscape Navigator 4 is not currently running, launch it by double-clicking its icon or the Communicator icon.

2. In the Netsite/Location box at the top of the window, select the currently displayed URL and replace it with the following address on the Saturn Web site: **http://www.saturncars.com/car/97-Models/SL/index.html**. Press Enter.

TIP

Remember, you can abbreviate URLs. Leave off the http:// if you want.

3. After the Web document transfers to your computer and displays, you'll see that the right-hand frame contains small pictures of the Saturn SL/ SL1 taken from various angles. Click on any one of these photos to view a full-size picture. Now Navigator displays the larger picture in the left-hand frame, as shown in Figure 7-11.

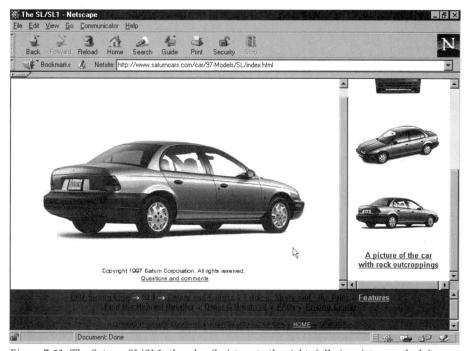

Figure 7-11: The Saturn SL/SL1: thumbnail picture to the right, full-size picture to the left.

TIP

Want to see the image on its own, without the frames? Right-click it and select View Image from the context menu that appears. The image is now displayed in the browser window on its own. To return to the frames, simply click the Back button.

Who Owns the Image?

The easy answer to this question is "probably not you." Almost every image on the World Wide Web and the Internet is owned by someone or by a legal corporation. Don't think that just because you can download an image to your computer's hard disk you own the rights to the file. In most cases, you do not. In fact, some images have been placed on the Web illegally, without permission from their owners. By downloading these images, you may also be breaking the law.

Fortunately, most sites comply with international copyright laws and make available only those images they own or have legally licensed from another party. These images are provided for you to view but typically are not for reuse in any form.

Some sites legally allow you to download graphics for use in commercial or noncommercial ways. Clip-art images, for example, fall into this category. Many sites offer downloadable images that you can incorporate in business documents, Web documents, and other sources. But remember, you are still responsible for making sure that the images you download are indeed owned or licensed by the person providing them.

Other sites require that you first pay a fee to acquire the rights to view and download images. Sites such as MTV, Sony, and Playboy offer repositories like this. Again, copyright laws restrict you from reselling these images as your own. You can only look at them; you can't plaster them all over Usenet newsgroups.

Now that the full-size image is onscreen, what can you do with it? Not much, since Netscape Communicator is designed only as a *viewer* of certain graphics types, not as a full-featured graphics editor. But what you *can* do is save the image to your hard disk for later viewing, editing, or other processing. If you enjoy a particular image and you've waited several minutes for it to transfer to your machine, you owe it to yourself to save it to disk.

To save an image to disk:

1. Right-click the image and then select Save Image As from Navigator 4's File menu. The Save As dialog box appears, as shown in Figure 7-12.

Figure 7-12: The Save As dialog box.

2. Choose a location for the file and then click the Save button. The Saving Location dialog box appears, showing the progress of the file transfer.

   ■ Because the file has already been downloaded to your computer, it takes only a few seconds to save it to the appropriate location on your disk.

3. Click the Back button to return to the previous Web page.

Redecorating Your Desktop

Not only can you save any image you encounter on the Web, you can even set it as your Windows wallpaper. Netscape Communicator makes this so easy that you may end up with all kinds of wacked-out designs on your screen. You should see my "At Home with Dom DeLuise" wallpaper.

To save an image as your Windows wallpaper:

1. Place your cursor over the image.

2. Click the right mouse button.

3. Select Set As Wallpaper from the context menu that appears.

Once you have set your new wallpaper, you may want to configure your system so that the image is tiled instead of centered. To make this change, click the Display icon in Control Panel, select the Background tab, and set the Netscape Wallpaper to Tile rather than Center.

Text-Only Mode

They say a picture is worth a thousand words, but we writers have never bought that. In spite of all the dire warnings of bow-tied professors, we have not degenerated into an illiterate society that worships only images. In fact as technology gets better and better at surrounding us with imagery, more and more *words* get published! Just look at how thick this book is. I use the Macintosh version of the book as a platform for my monitor.

You really see how important words are when you have a modem connection to the Net. If you have a slow modem and have been following the various links in this chapter, you're probably growing tired of waiting for some of the documents to transfer. In fact, if you have a modem that operates at less than 28.8 Kbps, you may already be working on next year's letter to Santa. But besides speeding up your Internet connection, there is another approach: you can bypass graphics altogether.

Navigator 4 gives you the option of turning off the automatic display of graphics by deselecting the "Automatically load images" option in Advanced settings. When this option is turned off, a small icon appears as a placeholder wherever an image is supposed to display. Figure 7-13 shows a Web document in text-only mode, with several placeholders for graphics.

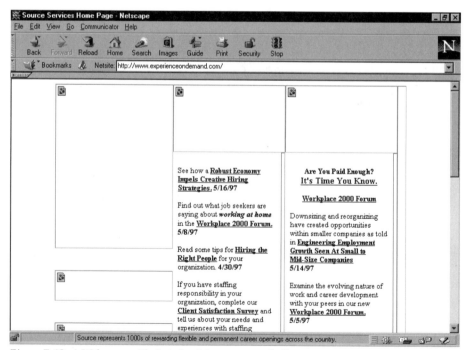

Figure 7-13: A Web page with Auto Load Images turned off.

And how exactly do you turn off the automatic loading of images? Easy:

1. Select Preferences from Navigator's Edit menu. The Preferences window appears.

2. From the list on the left, select Advanced. The Advanced preferences appear in the right section of the window, as shown in Figure 7-14.

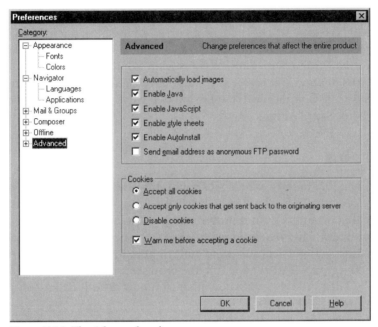

Figure 7-14: The Advanced preferences.

3. Uncheck the "Automatically load images" check box and click OK.

Even with this change to Communicator's image-viewing default, you can still view graphics at particular pages on a case-by-case basis. If you come across a particular document whose graphics you want to view, just click the Images button. This reloads the document with graphics displayed. Graphics are turned on for that page only; the Images button does not affect the "Automatically load" option.

> **TIP**
>
> **Important note:** *The Images button is available on the Navigator 4 Command Toolbar only when "Automatically load images" is deselected in Advanced preferences.*

As I mentioned earlier, though, Netscape Communicator cannot display every kind of graphic file that might exist out there on the Net. The programmers at Netscape work hard to support all of the most common types of graphics, but every day independent computer scientists are working on new file formats, some with better compression, some with more precise rendering of colors. If you want to display graphics other than those supported directly by Netscape Communicator, there are two ways to extend its power: plug-ins and helper applications.

Plug-ins

I'm not going to say a whole lot about plug-ins here, because they're covered more completely in Chapter 10. Basically, a plug-in is a special piece of software that extends Communicator's power. It seamlessly adds new features to the program. Plug-ins designed to display particular types of graphics make it look as though the features were built right in to Communicator—in most cases the graphics display within the browser window, just like ordinary GIF or JPEG files. You'd never know that Communicator is calling on any other software to do the work.

Plug-ins don't just display graphics. There are plug-ins that display particular word processor files as well as spreadsheets and databases. There are even plug-ins that play sound and animation files and a variety of full-motion video formats. Just about anything that extends Communicator's multimedia features can be implemented as a plug-in, and dozens of new ones appear every month.

Let's say that in the process of browsing the Web or your office intranet, you come upon a link to a graphics file that Communicator doesn't support out of the box. What happens? There are a variety of different scenarios, depending on the programming of the Web page containing the link and on whether or not the file type is one that has been registered with Netscape. (Registration with Netscape allows a new plug-in for the file type to be installed automatically, via a special "SmartUpdate" feature.) If it *is* a file type that has been registered with Netscape:

- You may be asked to agree to a license and approve the installation of a particular plug-in. Once you approve the installation, the plug-in may be installed on your system automatically.

Some plug-ins include a special digital security certificate that you can view before the plug-in is installed on your system. This certificate assures you that you are getting the plug-in from its rightful vendor. Plug-ins that include a digital certificate are known as signed plug-ins. *For more information on digital certificates, please see Chapter 12.*

- The plug-in may be installed automatically right away, if you previously approved a digital security certificate (see Chapter 12) from the plug-in vendor. As soon as the plug-in is installed, you can see the Web page with the multimedia information rendered correctly.

- You might be transported to Netscape's Plug-in Finder page with the appropriate plug-in selected from Netscape's list. Just follow the directions that appear, which will vary from plug-in to plug-in.

If the file type is *not* one that has been registered with Netscape, Figure 7-15 shows what you'll get. For this purposes of this example I've chosen a TIFF file, a fairly common older graphics format that you might encounter on an intranet.

Figure 7-15: The Unknown File Type dialog box.

What's that Pick App button? That's for setting up helper applications, not plug-ins. For more information on helper applications, see the section below, cleverly titled "Setting Up Helper Applications."

There's still a good chance you can get a plug-in that will let you view this file type. Simply click More Info. Netscape's Plug-in Finder page appears, as shown below in Figure 7-16.

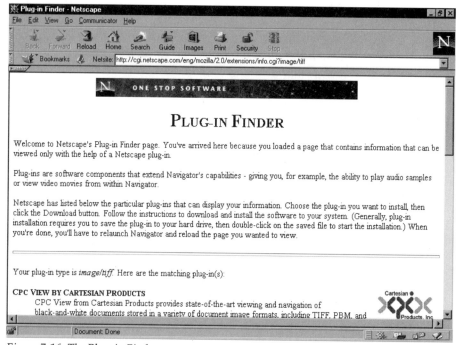

Figure 7-16: The Plug-in Finder page.

Make sure to read the text at the top of the Plug-in Finder page, then scroll down for a list of appropriate plug-ins, as shown in Figure 7-17.

Note that the Plug-in Finder page lists only those plug-ins that will display TIFF files. It's easy to find an appropriate plug-in when you don't have to search through a huge list of plug-ins you're not interested in.

When you read about the various plug-ins that are designed to display TIFF files, they all sound pretty good. So how do you choose one? Well, perhaps one of them supports more graphics types than the others that lets you view encapsulated postscript files, for instance, as well as TIFFs. Or perhaps one was written by a company with a reputation for quality products. Choosing a particular plug-in doesn't mean you have to stick with it for the rest of your life. You can try one out and see how it works. If you don't like it, you can download and install a different plug-in to display TIFF files at any time.

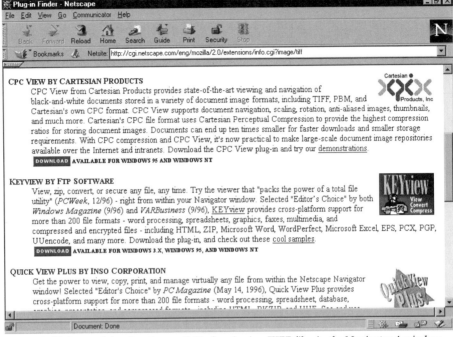

Figure 7-17: Some of the plug-ins available for viewing TIFF files in the Navigator 4 window.

TIP

For a complete list of all kinds of available plug-ins, check out Netscape's Plug-in page at http://home.netscape.com/comprod/mirror/navcomponents_download.html. You can also get to this page by selecting About Plug-ins from Navigator's Help menu and then clicking the click here link near the top of the Help page.

To download one of the plug-ins, simply click the Download button next to the text description. A new page appears. Follow all the directions. The process varies quite a bit from plug-in to plug-in, so I'll leave you on your own here. Some plug-ins are free, others are available in special try-before-you-buy versions, and for some, you'll have to get out your credit card right away. But if you follow the directions carefully for installing a particular plug-in, you'll end up with what's almost like a new version of Communicator, one that's now able to automatically display TIFF files, as shown below in Figure 7-18.

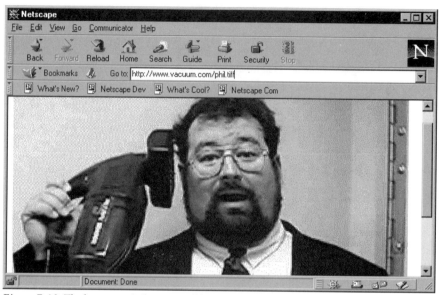

Figure 7-18: The browser window, now able to display TIFF files.

TIP

> *After you've downloaded a new plug-in, make sure to read any readme files very carefully. The installation process may require that you exit Netscape Communicator while the new software updates your system. Even if the instructions just tell you to exit Navigator, make sure to close down all Communicator windows!*

In a perfect cyberworld, there would be built-in support or a plug-in for every type of graphic available on the Internet. We're almost there, but not quite. If Netscape doesn't automatically support a particular graphic type, and if there is no plug-in available, you may need to set up what is known as a Helper application.

Setting Up Helper Applications

You read earlier in this chapter about how you can download images to view in another application, such as LView or Paint Shop Pro. When configured to work with Netscape Communicator, these applications are called *helper applications*. Virtually *any* program that can run on your system can be used as a helper application in Communicator. For instance, you could make any files with a .DOC extension appear in Microsoft Word, or any XLS files appear in Excel. But to make applications like these work with Communicator, you may need to set them up manually using the Applications catgory (under Browser) in the Communicator Preferences window.

Helpers vs. Plug-ins

Let's say there's a plug-in available to display a particular type of file. Is there any good reason to set up a helper application instead? Sure! Although plug-ins are ultra-convenient and ultra-cool, helper applications have their own advantages:

- You may already have an appropriate application for dealing with a particular kind of media file. Why crowd your hard drive with a plug-in—particularly one that isn't free—if you already have what you need?

- You may not want the file to display within the Navigator 4 window, but in a separate application with controls and commands that you're used to.

- Often a helper application offers more features than a plug-in. Obviously you can do a lot more with a spreadsheet in Excel than you can in a plug-in designed simply to display the data.

First, obtain a helper application and install it on your system—or decide on one that you already have. Applications that let you view or edit graphics are available from various sources, including third-party books, software stores, FTP and Gopher sites, and World Wide Web sites. Some of the applications that you may want to obtain are listed in Table 7-1.

Viewer Name	Supports File Types
LView Pro	GIF, JPEG/JPG, TIFF, BMP
Paint Shop Pro	GIF, JPEG/JPG, TIFF, BMP
GhostView	PostScript

Table 7-1: Some graphics viewers that can be used as helper applications.

Since Netscape Communicator automatically displays GIF and JPEG files, unless you're interested in editing or format conversion, you won't gain much with a helper application that supports only these formats. You need one that offers the capabilities to read those formats and others, such as TIFF and BMP.

These file types are fairly common, and some Web sites may include them in their documents or file archives.

Once you acquire and install a helper application on your system, use the following steps to configure it to work with Netscape Communicator to display any TIFF files you encounter:

1. Select Preferences from Navigator's Edit menu.

2. Select the Applications category under Navigator, as shown in Figure 7-19. If Applications is not displayed, double-click Navigator, or simply click the plus icon.

Figure 7-19: The Applications window.

TIP

You can access this same window by clicking the Pick App button in the Unknown File Type dialog box shown earlier in Figure 7-15.

This looks like a fairly complicated dialog box at first, but once you understand the concepts, it's really pretty simple. The large scrolling list includes the names of different kinds of files you might encounter as you cruise the Net or your office intranet with Navigator 4. As you click each file type from the list, the bottom section of the window changes to display details about the particular file type. For instance, Figure 7-20 shows the file type details for GIF files.

Figure 7-20: The Applications window, with file type details for GIF files.

The bottom includes three fields:

- **Extension**. This is simply the extension for this kind of file. When Navigator encounters a file called SOMETHING.GIF, for instance, it knows it's a GIF file because of the .GIF extension. An icon to the left of the field provides a graphical representation of the file type, just as it would appear on your Windows 95/NT desktop.

- **MIME Type**. MIME, or Multipurpose Internet Mail Extensions, is a universal standard for naming file types. Usually the MIME designations make sense, as in the case of GIF files, which are classified as image/msword.

- **Handled By**. This field specifies the helper application that will be launched when Navigator encounters a file of this type—or, it simply reads "Netscape (internal)" if it's a file type that Netscape can display without a plug-in or helper application.

Now scroll down the list of file types and select TIFF Image. Unless you've already configured a helper application or plug-in for TIFF files, your window will look something like Figure 7-21.

Figure 7-21: The Applications window, with file type details for TIFF files.

Notice that the "Handled by" field is blank; no application has been configured to view TIFF files, and when Navigator encounters one it will present you with the Unknown File Type dialog box shown earlier in Figure 7-15. Here's how to add a particular application that will be launched automatically whenever Navigator encounters a TIFF file:

1. Still in the Applications window with TIFF Images selected, click the Edit button. The Edit Type dialog box appears, as shown in Figure 7-22.

Figure 7-22: The Edit Type dialog box.

2. In the Handled By section, notice that the Navigator option button is unavailable, since Navigator cannot handle this file type on its own. Make sure the Application option button is selected and then click the Browse button to select a program on your system that can display TIFF files. For instance, you might choose the program **C:\LVIEW\LVIEWPRO.EXE** as the helper applicaiton for TIFF files. Optionally, select Save to Disk if you simply want files of this type saved rather than displayed or otherwise processed.

TIP

If you want Navigator to ask you before it automatically opens files of this type in a helper application, check the check box at the bottom of this Window. This is useful, for example, if you sometimes want to view TIFF files immediately and sometimes simply want to save them to disk.

The subject of graphics on the Internet is a very large one, and we've covered only the basics in this chapter. Chapter 10 will go into more advanced uses of graphics through VRML and advanced plug-ins as well as Java and JavaScript, but for now let's see—or rather, hear—what's up with sound in Netscape Communicator.

Simple Animation: Server Push & Layering

Most Web pages require that you interact with them in some way. They usually include links to other pages, graphics to click, animations to view, or sound objects to download and listen to. All of these items are initiated in some way by the user, the person using the client application (Netscape Communicator, in this case).

Another type of HTML instruction enables Web authors to design pages that deliver an updated version of the page without interaction from the user. This technology is called *server push*. Using server push, the server transmits Web page instructions and information to your browser window. As you navigate to various Web sites that support server-push technology, the connection between you and the server on the other end remains open. The server can continue to "push" updated information and data to your computer continuously. By pushing several different images into the same location on a Web page, for instance, a server can give the impression of a single animated image. The connection between you and the server closes when you leave the site.

An example of a Web site that supports server push is the Word site at http://www.word.com. It uses server push in a variety of ways, often to display advertisements during the time you are moving from one page to another. The advertisement appears, gives you a few moments to read it, and then disappears so that you can continue on to the item that you originally selected.

Throughout Word, there are clever icons that rely on server push for animation. But there are all kinds of uses for server push. A sports site, for instance, can use server push to keep a scoreboard updated with the latest scores and team highlights.

Starting with the current version, Navigator also supports a new HTML feature called *Dynamic Layers*, or simply *layering*. Layering lets HTML developers design pages that have multiple layers of information. Text may be overlayed on graphics, or vice versa. Layering provides yet another way to enhance Web pages with animation.

Sound on the Web

Many computers you purchase today come with sound cards and speakers. This has fueled the growth of sound capabilities on the Net as well as on office intranets. Thousands of Web sites now include sound files that offer a new way to experience online content. Radio stations, public television stations, and network news shows are providing sites that feature sound recordings. Some sites even include *live* performances of rock bands or the play-by-play of weekly football games. As the Web matures, you'll be able to sit back and listen as you work on that marketing proposal or college term paper. The history of technology is a history of distractions, and the good folks at Netscape are doing their best to distract you by enabling Communicator to play the sounds of the Net.

Why Can't I Use My PC's Speaker?

You can, but you'll be disappointed with the results. Every PC comes equipped with a tiny speaker in it that you may hear beep every once in awhile. You'll hear it beep a few times, for instance, when you start up your computer. You can make this speaker play some of the sound files you find on the Internet by acquiring a speaker driver from Microsoft (called SPEAKE.EXE) and loading it on your system. You also need to acquire an application that plays different sound files. For many users, the reigning champion during the past year or so has been WPLANY.EXE, which is short for "We Play Anything." You can download WPLANY.EXE from ftp://ftp.cam.org/systems/ms-windows/slip-ppp/viewers/wplny09b.zip.

SPEAKE.EXE is part of Microsoft's Windows Driver Library, an archive file that includes other drivers as well. The URL is ftp://ftp.microsoft.com/Softlib/softlib.exe.

Supported Sound Files in Netscape Communicator 4

Netscape Communicator includes built-in support for the following sound file formats: AU, SND, AIF, AIFF, AIFC, MIDI, and WAV. It's not important to know what all these acronyms mean, but you *should* know that the three most popular sound types on the Web are AU, SND, and WAV. MIDI (Musical Instrument Digital Interface) files are really music files rather than sound files, digital "scores" that can be played correctly on any electronic musical instrument that supports the General MIDI standard. And that probably includes your sound card.

Listening to Sound in Netscape Communicator 4

When you connect to a Web site that contains sound files, you will generally see a speaker icon or some similar icon indicating that it is a sound file. If the sound file is of a type that Netscape Communicator supports, you can click the icon and Communicator automatically plays the file. Or if a sound file is embedded directly into an HTML page, you may not even have to click a link.

Now let's look at a typical example of a sound file on the Web. We'll return to the IUMA site to check out the experimental/spoken word band Asbestos Removal Crew.

1. Make sure you are connected to the Internet. If Netscape Navigator 4 is not currently running, launch it by double-clicking its icon or the Netscape Communicator icon.

2. In the Netsite/Location box at the top of the window, select the currently displayed URL and replace it with **http://www.iuma.com/IUMA-2.0/ftp/volume3/Asbestos_Removal_Crew/**. Press Enter. After a few moments, the page appears, as shown in Figure 7-23.

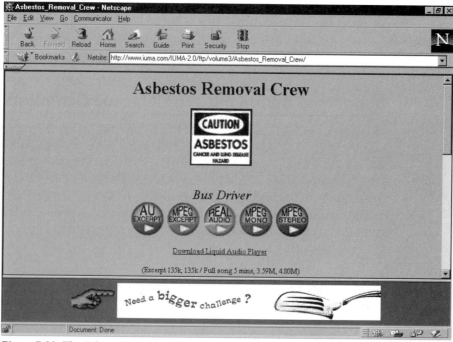

Figure 7-23: The Asbestos Removal Crew page on IUMA.

Since Navigator supports AU sound files right out of the box, scroll down and click the icon labeled "AU Excerpt." A sound control panel pops up. The controls are pretty much like those on any electronic device: click the arrow button to start playing, click the other button to stop. You can adjust the volume of the selection by dragging the slider to the right or left.

TIP

The sound controls will not display until the entire sound file has been downloaded. If it's a large file, or if you are on a slow connection, the sound control panel may be empty and gray for a while.

When the sound file ends, it stops automatically and you can do one of two things: play it over and over again or get a life.

Using RealAudio With Netscape Communicator 4

As I'm sure you just discovered, sound files can take a while to download to your machine. But fortunately, there are some new *streaming* standards that speed up the process. What do I mean by streaming? Suppose the sound file starts playing over your computer's speakers before it's completely downloaded. That's streaming. Instead of clicking a link and twiddling your thumbs, you can click a link and start shaking your booty. Not quite instant gratification, but close.

By far the most prominent streaming sound format on the Web is RealAudio. Using the RealAudio plug-in, which is available from the RealAudio Web site at http://www.realaudio.com, you can hear news, sporting events, music, and much more. The RealAudio format almost makes you feel as though you're listening to the radio, right on the Net. In fact, some traditional radio stations have started to supplement their broadcasts with RealAudio files on the Web.

The complete RealAudio system consists of two pieces. The first piece is one you'll probably never have to use unless you become a Web site administrator. The *RealAudio Server* is the software that enables Web sites to offer RealAudio files.

The other piece of the RealAudio puzzle is the client software that enables users like you to listen to RealAudio recordings. In this case, it's a plug-in that works seamlessly with Netscape Communicator, just as if it were a built-in feature.

Obtaining RealAudio

The RealAudio plug-in, which is what you want to install on your system, is currently free of charge. To get a copy of RealAudio, connect to RealAudio's Web site (http://www.realaudio.com/) and download the software to your computer. You will be asked to fill out a short form before downloading it.

TIP

Currently the RealAudio people are distributing two different plug-ins that will play RealAudio files: the plain old RealAudio plug-in, and a new one called RealPlayer. What makes RealPlayer different is that it also lets Communicator display a new kind of streaming video files called RealVideo (more about this in the section on video, later in the chapter). If you think you might want to experiment with RealVideo as well as RealAudio, you should download RealPlayer.

Make sure to read the list of system requirements to run the program. The requirements include 2MB of free disk space and a sound card with a Windows Sound driver. (The RealAudio Player and RealPlayer are not compatible with the PC Speaker program or other software programs that emulate a sound card.)

Installing & Configuring RealAudio

So you've completed the forms, chosen the correct version of RealAudio or RealPlayer, and downloaded it to your computer. It's sitting on your computer and ready to install. To install RealAudio or RealPlayer, run the file you just downloaded by double-clicking it in the Windows Explorer (or in the File Manager if you are using Windows 3.1). The installation program starts doing its thing. Simply follow the instructions that appear on your screen. When asked, make sure to indicate that you want to install the plug-in version of the program. At the conclusion of the setup process, the RealAudio player or RealPlayer launches and plays a welcome message. If the message sounds distorted, see the "Sound" section of the RealAudio Release Notes, which are stored on your system where you installed RealAudio or RealPlayer.

Can I Create My Own RealAudio Files?

Yes, you can, but you'll need some extra software. Specifically, you must download a copy of the RealAudio Encoder from the Progressive Networks Web site. Using Encoder, you start with a WAV or AU audio file and convert it to the RealAudio file format, with the extension .RA. Within the RealAudio file you can insert a name of the file, author, and copyright information. This information is displayed on the user's machine when he or she is playing it back. Of course, the file you've created doesn't do you much good unless you have a way to distribute it to the public. You must copy it to a site that has the RealAudio server software. For more information on RealAudio servers, see the RealAudio Web site at http://www.realaudio.com/.

Trying Out RealAudio

When you connect to sites that contain RealAudio links, you can listen to a link by clicking it. It's that easy. The RealAudio player or RealPlayer first contacts the host computer that contains the audio file. After a few moments during which it downloads the initial section of the file, it starts to play it over your system speakers. You can adjust the volume of the playback by using the slider control on the right side of the player.

TIP

RealAudio links are often indicated with an icon of a radio or boom box, sometimes with the letters "RA" on it. Take a look at Word magazine (http://www.word.com) for a typical use of iconized links like this, and for an example of RealAudio used effectively in conjunction with articles and stories.

So that you can try out RealAudio, Table 7-2 lists some sites that include RealAudio files. In the future, look for events such as football games, rock concerts, speeches, and the like to be simulcast as RealAudio events that you can listen to live.

Site Name	Address
National Public Radio	http://www.npr.org/
ABC Radio Network	http://www.abcradionet.com/
Delta Dream Vacations	http://pwr.com/LEISURE/DELTA.html
Advanced Digital Services	http://206.65.169.39/
Grace Hour	http://www. ggwo.org
Nightstand	http://www.nightstand.com/
Tabernacle Baptist Church	http://www.tabernacle.org/~tbc/
Toyota Motor	http://www.toyota.co.jp/
North Carolina News Network	http://www.capitolnet.com/ncnn/
Tech Talk Radio Network	http://ttn.nai.net/
BBC Radio 3: Facing the Radio	http://www.bbc.co.uk/ftr/
Black Cat Radio	http://www.memphiscat.com/
MusicNet	http://www.man.net/~musicnet/
OneWorld	http://www.oneworld.org/realaudio/index.html

Table 7-2: Some sites that have RealAudio files.

The RealAudio President

Politicians of every stripe are clamoring over the new telecommunications technologies, though they frequently misunderstand them. It is no surprise that several of President Clinton's speeches are available on the Web via RealAudio. Just point Navigator 4 to http://www.whitehouse.gov/WH/EOP/OP/html/OP_Speeches.html and start looking around—or listening around. If you have a good sound card and listen carefully enough, you might even hear Bill inhale.

Netscape's Own Streaming Sound

RealAudio may be the most prominent streaming sound protocol, but it's not the only game in town. Netscape has developed its own Media Server and Media Player to play sounds across the Net in real time, and best of all the player is included right within Communicator. Let's give it a try:

1. For the sake of this exercise, make sure you're on the Net.

2. Replace the current URL in the Netsite/Location box with **http:// 207.24.196.98/default.htm**. This is the main demo page for *elemedia*, a telephony and media project under development by Bell Labs (R&D folks who used to be with AT&T but are now part of Lucent Technologies). Take a look at Figure 7-24.

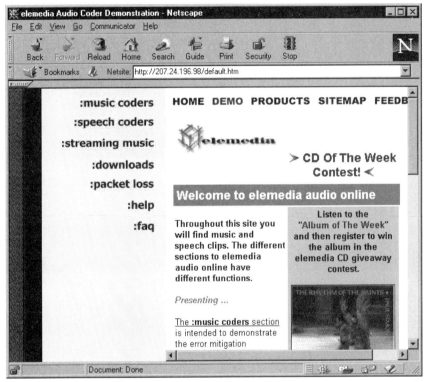

Figure 7-24: The elemedia page.

3. In the left-hand frame, click :streaming music. The frame on the right now contains some instructions that you don't need. Scroll to the bottom and click the "On to the Music" link. Now if you scroll down the right-hand frame you'll see a choice of musical selections.

4. Click anything except Hootie and the Blowfish. Being a classical kind of guy, I go for Bach's Brandenburg Concertos, so this is what I see next in the right-hand frame shown in Figure 7-25.

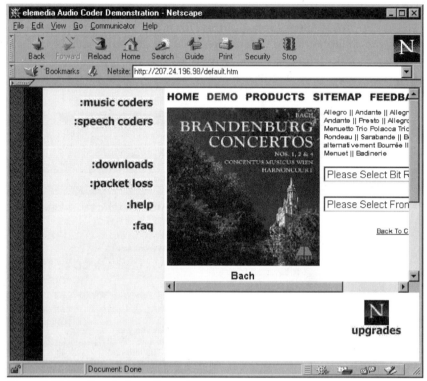

Figure 7-25: The Brandenburg Concertos.

5. There are two drop-down lists. From the top one choose a mono or stereo bit rate and from the bottom one choose the actual selection you want to hear. The bit rate you choose should be close to the maximum that is possible for your computer. For instance, if you're connected to the Net via a 28.8 Kbps modem, choose a bit rate of about 28800 bps; if you're on a fast hard-wired connection, choose a faster rate. Immediately, a sound control appears in the right-hand frame, as shown in Figure 7-26.

6. Again, this is just like a standard tape or CD player. Click the Play button to play your selection. You'll see some flashing dots on the button as the Media Player initiates the download of the file. Then you should start hearing music. The Play button becomes a Pause button.

7. Adjust the volume with the plus and minus buttons. When you want to stop listening, click the Stop button.

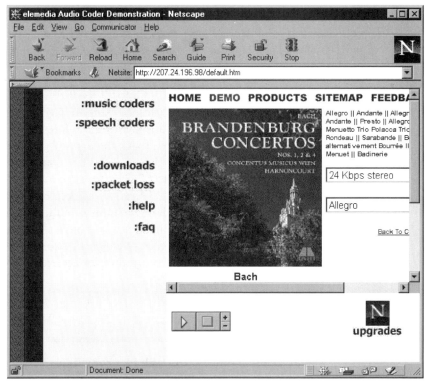

Figure 7-26: The Media Player sound control.

Media Player Settings
If you right-click the Media Player control and then select Properties from the context menu that appears, what you get is shown in Figure 7-27.

Figure 7-27: Netscape Media Player Properties.

> **TIP**
>
> *You can also access the Media Player Properties dialog box by double-clicking the Configure Media Player icon in the Utilities subfolder of the Communicator folder.*

It is beyond the scope of this book to get into all the settings; many of them only apply if you're on an intranet that uses the Netscape Media Server, and you should consult with your network administrator before changing them. But in the bandwidth tab, it's a good idea to set the maximum bandwidth for any audio streams you receive. If you're using a 28.8 Kbps modem with a PPP connection, for instance, you should select 28800 from the drop-down list. On the other hand, if you're on a fast T1 or T3 hard-wired connection, select the fastest speed available from the list. If there are pauses in the audio as you listen, you may need to try a different rate. Once you have selected your rate, you can set it as the default by clicking the Set Default button. The Media Player will use this bit rate every time Communicator accesses a streaming sound file on a Netscape Media Server.

Video in Netscape Communicator 4

Some of us spend so much time on the Web that sometimes we forget what real life is. Real life is an operating environment that includes mountains, oceans, trees, crying babies, barking dogs, Big Macs, and the Menendez brothers. It's not the greatest user interface, but it sure beats anything Bill Gates could come up with. And one of the most interesting features of real life is that things move! We do not experience life as a succession of still images such as those you usually encounter on the Net, but as a constant ebb and flow of matter through space.

Now you can come a little closer to real life on the Web. One of Netscape Communicator's most exciting new features is LiveVideo, the technology that lets you view video clips, often called movies, right within the browser window.

Let's give it a try:

1. Make sure you are connected to the Internet. If Navigator 4 is not currently running, launch it by double-clicking its icon or the Netscape Communicator icon.

2. In the Netsite/Location box at the top of the window, select the currently displayed URL and replace it with **http://home.netscape.com/comprod/ products/navigator/version_3.0/multimedia/video/index.html**. Press Enter. After a few moments, the Netscape LiveVideo page appears.

3. Scroll about a third of the way down the page and you'll see a video clip in progress at the left side of the page. It depicts various international flags superimposed over scenes of the various countries, as shown below in Figure 7-28.

Figure 7-28: Netscape's LiveVideo page with a video clip.

4. To stop the motion of the images, simply click the small video window; to start the clip up again, click once more.

5. Now click your right mouse button on the video. A context menu appears letting you pause, rewind, or fast forward the video, as shown in Figure 7-29. It also lets you step through the movie frame-by-frame using the Frame Forward and Frame Back commands.

Figure 7-29: The LiveVideo context menu.

How does this work? When Netscape Navigator encounters what is known as an AVI file (AVI is Microsoft's format for video files), LiveVideo automatically kicks in and lets you view the image the way it was meant to be viewed. No need for external programs or helper applications—just sit back and enjoy.

Video With Sound

Wait a minute! Something is very wrong. Here we are using the slickest newest technology, and all we're getting is silent movies. Weren't talkies invented around 1928?

Not to worry: LiveVideo supports soundtracks as well as moving images. Not all AVI files include sound, but when you click on one that does, Netscape Communicator will make you feel like you're sitting at Loewe's Cineplex staring up at the big screen. Just add popcorn.

Here's a nice example of an AVI clip that includes sound, put out by the government of Newfoundland and Labrador. Of course in order to hear the soundtrack, you'll need a sound card supported by your version of Windows.

1. Make sure you are connected to the Internet. If Navigator 4 is not currently running, launch it by double-clicking its icon or the Netscape Communicator icon.

2. In the Netsite/Location box at the top of the window, select the currently displayed URL and replace it with **http://www.gov.nf.ca/itt/business/ people.avi**. Press Enter. After a few moments, the first image of an AVI file appears in your browser window, as shown in Figure 7-30.

Figure 7-30: An AVI video clip by the government of Newfoundland and Labrador.

TIP

Large AVI files and AVI files that include sound may take a while to download. And I mean quite *a while. Keep that crossword puzzle and knitting project nearby.*

3. Click the image. Immediately it begins playing, complete with music and voice-over.

Other Video Formats

AVI is one of the most common video formats on the Web, but it's not the only one. As you venture into the far reaches of cyberspace you may encounter:

- QuickTime movies (with the extension .MOV, .MOOV, or .QT)
- MPEG movies (with the extension .MEPG, .MPG, .MPE, or .MP2)
- Flick files (with the extension .FLI or .FLC)
- IFF/ILBM files (with the extension .IFF)

The current version of Communicator only plays AVI and QuickTime files automatically, but the Netscape developers were smart enough to make the program extensible. If you want Communicator to play other animation formats right in the browser window, all you have to do is find a plug-in for that particular media type. We've talked about plug-ins earlier in the sections on graphics and on RealAudio, and we'll come back to them in the Chapter 10.

TIP

To play QuickTime movies on your system, you need to have the latest version of Apple QuickTime for Windows installed. The software is available at http:// quicktime.apple.com/qt/sw/sw.html. Make sure to follow all instructions for installing it. Once QuickTime is on your system, you're ready to go. Try QuickTime out at http://www.wandering.com, which makes excellent use of video clips in presenting information about Italy.

Streaming Video

One of the most exciting new developments in multimedia on the Web is streaming video. This works pretty much like streaming audio: instead of waiting for an entire file to arrive at your computer, you start viewing the moving images on your screen as the stream of information is downloaded. Earlier in the chapter, in the section on RealAudio, I mentioned RealPlayer, a plug-in that handles not only RealAudio but also the RealVideo streaming standard. RealPlayer is available at **http://www.realaudio.com**. That same site offers many links to RealVideo sites so that you can try out your new multimedia toy once you've installed it.

Moving On

In this chapter, you've learned the basics of viewing graphics and listening to sound in Netscape Communicator. You've also learned how to play video clips or movies, right in the browser window. By now you should have a sense of how vast the possibilities are when it comes to incorporating new media into Web pages. Advertising executives are jumping up and down with excitement, scheming all kinds of ways to inundate you with the latest multimedia innovations.

But in the next chapter we go back to basics again, to some of the ancestral text-based protocols that enrich intranets and the Internet as much as all this flashy stuff. If you do any kind of very thorough research using Communicator, you're bound to bump into three old friends of the cyber-traveler: FTP, Gopher, and Telnet.

CHAPTER 8

The Ancestors: FTP, Gopher & Telnet

I hope by now you have found a few ways that Netscape Communicator can simplify and enrich your life. Through its many easy-to-use features, you can access the Internet or your office intranet for sending and receiving multi-media e-mail; for viewing a wide variety of information maintained not only from your own workplace but by educational and government institutions around the world; for reading the subject-specific information contained in local or Usenet newsgroups; and perhaps simply for relaxing and having some fun.

The advanced features of Netscape Communicator plunge you into an electronic world full of bright images and sounds, and they let you jump around from link to link, blazing new information trails. Communicator's hypermedia browsing facilities provide a whole new approach to research, an approach that's very different from the plodding linear methods we grew up with. Some say that hypermedia browsing more closely models the way our brain really works, encouraging us to integrate knowledge by associative leaps rather than by carefully planned logical stitching.

However, there are some research tasks that call for a more traditional approach to the great volume of data available on the Net; there are also some wonderful repositories of knowledge that were put on the Internet before the WWW and have not been converted or are not even candidates for the Web. Fortunately, Communicator supports the older Internet services that are still very useful tools. The most important of these are *FTP*, *Gopher*, and *Telnet*.

FTP

FTP is one of the simplest and most obvious acronyms you'll come across on the Net: it simply stands for File Transfer Protocol. That sounds pretty generic, but every implementation of FTP follows the same very specific rules for sending and receiving data. The file must be broken up into pieces at one end and reassembled properly at the other; the data has to be checked for errors and stamped with the correct filename and date; and the FTP software has to enable users to navigate through the host system's directories to find the right file.

Throughout the Internet are scattered literally thousands of servers that provide files to users via FTP, and they all do their job in much the same way. Many of these sites are known as *anonymous* FTP sites, which means they allow any Internet user to log on specifically for the purpose of retrieving files. You don't need to be a registered user on the system. Typically, when logging in to anonymous sites, you specify *anonymous* as your username and your e-mail address as the password (see the sidebar, "Your Anonymous Password"). Netscape Communicator takes care of the login process automatically; you don't even see any prompts from the remote system.

Your Anonymous Password

When you log onto an anonymous FTP site, the server asks your software for a name and password. Communicator sends the username "anonymous" and automatically generates a password. Some FTP servers, however, require that you use your e-mail address as the password when you log on anonymously, and it used to be considered "good form" to do this even when it wasn't required. As more and more direct e-mail marketeers scour server logs for potential new customers, however, it may be wise not to spread your e-mail address around too widely.

To configure Communicator so that it sends your e-mail address as your password when you log on to anonymous FTP sites, select Preferences from the Edit menu and then click the Advanced category. Simply check the check box labeled "Send email address as anonymous FTP password" and click OK.

Of course Communicator needs to *know* your e-mail address before it can use it. If you followed the instructions in Chapter 5, you're all set. But if for some reason you decided not to use Netscape Messenger, you can still enter your e-mail address into the program. From the Edit menu, select Mail and Discussion Preferences. Then go to the Identity tab, fill in the informational fields, and click OK. Now Navigator's FTP feature can send your e-mail address to anonymous FTP sites.

Are there FTP sites that are not anonymous? Sure! Many corporations, for instance, maintain non-anonymous FTP sites so that employees can trade work-related files while on the road. Of course, you need an account and a real password to access files on these FTP servers. But for the sake of keeping our examples general in this chapter, we'll be dealing primarily with anonymous sites. If you think you need FTP access to your office intranet, please talk to your system administrator—and see the sidebar later in the chapter called "Non-Anonymous FTP."

What's Out There?

So what kinds of files are available at these anonymous FTP sites? You name it! There are:

- Fully functional software programs, including spreadsheets, text editors, modem programs, databases, and a dazzling variety of utilities.

- Updates and patches to most major retail software programs.

- Electronic texts ranging from Shakespeare's complete works to David Letterman's latest *Top Ten list*.

- Thousands of images, sounds, video clips, and animations.

- Technical reports, journals, electronic magazines, news summaries, and archives of user messages.

- Books and tutorials like this one that will help you get started with just about any software task.

Figure 8-1 shows some of the directories at a well-known FTP site, the University of North Carolina SunSITE. We'll explore this site more thoroughly later in the chapter.

Figure 8-1: Some of the directories of files at SunSITE.

"And I can do whatever I want with all this stuff?" I hear you asking. Well, yes and no. To understand why I'm waffling on this question, you need to understand that there are three broad categories of files on the Internet, and each of these categories has different rules and guidelines for usage.

Public Domain

Public domain files are files that have no copyright, and there are no restrictions whatsoever on their usage. For instance, you can do whatever you want with Shakespeare's *Hamlet* or *A Winter's Tale*. Modern texts are sometimes released into the public domain as well, by authors who care more about wide distribution than about collecting any royalties or other fees. Many political polemics, for instance, are public domain.

But what about software? Sure, there's lots of public domain software on the Net. This has often been created by altruistic developers as a resource for the good of the community. The old adage "you get what you pay for" doesn't always hold true on the Net. For instance, until recently, some of the very best Internet client software was public domain. Of course, there are developers who release unfinished or buggy programs into the public domain to collect feedback, as part of their development process or simply because they don't want to go through the process of refining their work. But programs like these are usually clearly marked, and in some situations they can provide a cost-effective way of dealing with very specific software tasks. And some public domain software is a true group effort: perhaps a programmer started a project years ago, and then somebody downloaded it and worked with it a bit more, then somebody else added new features, and so on. Since there are no restrictions on the redistribution or modification of public domain software, a program may evolve over the course of many years, forged as much by public scrutiny and feedback as by the work of any single designer.

Freeware

Freeware files are copyrighted, but there are no charges for using them. Let's say you write a program that you are very proud of, but you want to make sure anybody can use it for free. You place it on the Internet with a copyright notice and perhaps a text file explaining any restrictions on its use. For instance, you may want to make sure the software is always distributed in its original form, unmodified, and bearing your name as the sole author. You may want to make it clear that nobody else may sell the software, but may only distribute it freely as you have.

Many people misunderstand freeware, confusing it with public domain files. No, they are very different. Freeware is free, but you have to play by the rules.

Shareware

Shareware is a great marketing innovation that came into being almost concurrently with PCs. Shareware files or programs are distributed on a trial basis: you can download them and use them for free, but only for a short evaluation period. If you like the resource and want to keep using it, you must pay a fee (usually small) to the author or delete it from your machine. Generally it's OK to make copies for your friends to evaluate, but you, of course, can't charge for the software.

Shareware files and programs are copyrighted. You must not copy them except as specifically allowed by the author, and you must abide by any restrictions detailed in the license or accompanying documentation. There has been plenty of litigation over misuse of shareware materials!

The advantages of shareware for the user are obvious: you get to try something without spending a penny. But there are advantages for shareware authors as well. Distribution costs are kept to a minimum, and there are no middlemen to eat profits. The author also enjoys a direct relationship with the customer and often refines the product based on individual feedback rather than distributors' charts and graphs.

What About Viruses?

In spite of all the hype it gets, the Net is no utopia—it is more like a microcosm. Just as there is a slight chance you could get mugged on your way to the corner store, there is a slight chance that you will someday download a file that "crashes your hard drive" or otherwise messes with your system, causing you that peculiarly modern form of grief known as "restoring everything from backups." (That's assuming you bothered to keep an up-to-date backup like everyone told you to!)

How common are viruses? Certainly much less than sensationalistic mass media stories would have you believe, but there are some out there. The best defense, of course, is making sure that at any given moment you could restore everything you need from backup tape or disks. If this is not the case at your house, I suggest you put this book down and get busy backing up files.

There are other precautions you can take as well. Virus-checking programs such as McAfee Associates' SCAN are available at most major FTP sites, and there are a number of excellent commercial products as well, such as Norton Anti-Virus. It's a good idea to check your entire system once in a while using one of these programs. If you do discover a problem, delete all infected files from your hard drive, or follow any instructions that came with your antivirus software. You will probably also need to completely restore your hard drive from backup.

Yes, this can be a serious inconvenience. But in the interest of alleviating some of the techno-paranoia that flares up whenever the news weeklies don't have a juicy enough scandal, let's debunk a few myths:

- You cannot get viruses from pure ASCII text files or e-mail messages that contain only text. Generally speaking, something has to be *run* on your computer to infect it. Of course, this includes macros such as those that are sometimes included with Word documents or Excel spreadsheets.

- Most viruses do not destroy hardware, they only mess up your software so badly that it seems as though your hardware is faulty. Getting rid of all infected software and then completely restoring your system from backup will usually solve the problem.

- Viruses do not jump from disk to disk across your office.

- You won't catch any viruses by hanging around in particular Usenet newsgroups, though at times it *can* feel like you're coming down with something nasty!

For more information about viruses, here are a few Web sites to check out:

- The Frequently Asked Questions (FAQ) file for the VIRUS-L/comp.virus mailing list (http://www.cis.ohio-state.edu/hypertext/faq/usenet/computer-virus-faq/faq.html). This FAQ contains a lot of basic information about viruses, including common symptoms and how to proceed if your system is infected.

- Virus Information (http://csrc.ncsl.nist.gov/virus/). This page contains a comprehensive set of links to additional virus-oriented sites, as well as reviews of antivirus software.

How to Know What You're Getting

FTP sites are really just directories full of files, much like the directories on your own computer. The FTP protocol itself includes no provisions for describing the files or providing additional information, although it does let you view file details such as size, time, and date. So how do you know what all the files in an FTP directory really are? There are two ways:

- Many of the larger FTP sites have Web "front ends." In other words, you initially access them via a Web document that explains a little about the site and what it contains. When you're ready to download a file, you click on a link that fires up the actual FTP protocol, showing you lists of files and directories or going right ahead and transferring the file you want. Figure 8-2 shows an example of a Web front end to an FTP site, on the Netscape server itself.

- Most well-established FTP sites include informational files that describe the rest of the available files. These informational files are often named README or INDEX (sometimes in lowercase), or sometimes they have names that begin with a dot, as in .INDEX. You may also encounter informational files called something like WELCOME.TXT.

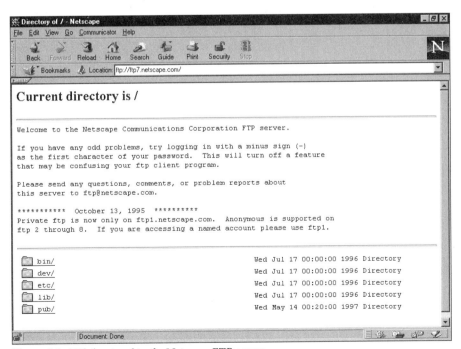

Figure 8-2: Web front end to the Netscape FTP server.

Tip

> *By default, Navigator 4 displays text files at FTP sites rather than automatically saving them to your hard drive. But what if you want to save a text file after viewing it? No problem. Just press Ctrl+S or select Save As from the File menu.*

Now let's click the WELCOME.TXT file link at Ventana's own FTP site to view its contents, shown in Figure 8-3.

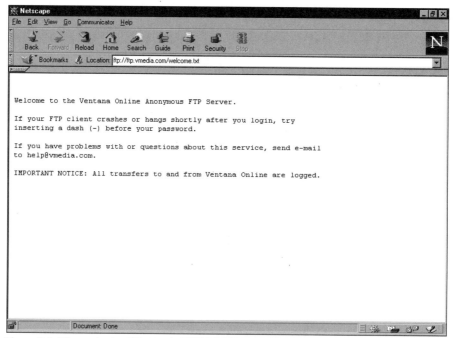

Figure 8-3: The contents of Ventana's WELCOME.TXT file.

As you can see, the WELCOME.TXT contains important information about the system itself.

Common Filename Extensions

Knowing somebody's last name won't necessarily tell you anything about the person, but the few characters that compose the extension to a filename are packed with information. For instance, if a file ends with .TXT, you can be pretty sure it's an ASCII text file, readable on virtually any system by using a simple text viewing program. But not all extensions are so obvious, so I've compiled a table of some of the most common ones you'll come across. Table 8-1 is by no means complete, but it's a good reference to keep handy as you start exploring FTP sites.

Extension	Type of File
.TXT	Simple text file, readable using Notepad, WordPad, or even the DOS type command.
.ASC	Probably a simple ASCII text file as well.
.DOC	May be a text file or a Microsoft Word document.
.EXE	An executable file (DOS or Windows program) that can be run from the command line or from the Windows Run command (or by double-clicking the file's icon in Windows 95). Often it is a *self-extracting archive* file; when you run it, it is decompressed into several files.
.ZIP	An archive file that has been compressed using the PKZIP compression program. You can use PKUNZIP or WinZip to extract the separate files that are part of the archive (see "Understanding Compression" later in this chapter).
.HQX	A file that has been archived using the BinHex compression program; you must use BinHex to decompress it. This compression standard is more common in the Macintosh world, and chances are good that an .HQX file is really intended for Mac use.
.SIT	A compressed, or "stuffed," Macintosh file. Probably not useful on your PC, although if you need one of these files, several good PC unstuffers are available on the Net.
.ARJ	Another type of compressed file. Several compression and decompression programs such as WinZip and DRAG AND ZIP can handle these files.
.LHA	See note on .ARJ above.
.ARC	See note on .ARJ above.
.ZOO	See note on .ARJ above.
.Z	A file compressed using the UNIX Zip. You can use the program GZIP, or a general purpose utility such as WinZip or DRAG AND ZIP, to decompress it.
.GZ	A file compressed using the GNU Zip program for UNIX. See note on .Z above.
.TAR	An archive file that has been compressed using the UNIX tar facility. It may be decompressed using a PC version of tar or a general purpose utility such as WinZip or DRAG AND ZIP.

Table 8-1: Common filename extensions on FTP sites.

Understanding Compression

You no doubt noticed that many of the notes in Table 8-1 refer to compression. When you look at the staggering number of files on the Internet (or, if you have Windows 95 or NT, at the staggering number of files on your hard drive!), it is clear that it's important to shrink files so that they are as small as you can possibly make them. And of course the smaller the file, the quicker it travels from one machine on the Internet to another, reducing overall transfer time and network traffic. But what exactly is file compression?

Think about the number 20,000,000,000,000,000,000,000. Now imagine trying to read this number to another person so that he or she can write it down. You *could* say "two zero zero zero zero zero zero zero zero zero zero zero zero zero zero zero zero zero zero zero zero zero zero zero," but that's the stupid way to do it. If you want to maintain your friend's respect, you'll probably say "two followed by 22 zeros." You have effectively compressed the information into fewer words, and your friend can decompress it by actually writing out the 22 zeros.

There are 256 different characters that may appear in a computer file in any order, or just half that number in the case of ASCII text files. In some files, there are no repeated characters and no repeated patterns of characters, but most are full of repetitions even if the repetitions are accidental. This means that most files can be compressed. Think of a database, for instance, in which there are lots of spaces that fill out fixed-length fields. It's easy to see how you can compress a file like this by indicating the space character and the number of times it should be repeated.

Of course, I'm oversimplifying. Compression techniques have become very sophisticated and use a variety of subtle approaches, or *algorithms*, that go far beyond merely tallying repeated characters. Some try to maximize the amount of saved disk space; others try to speed up the process of compressing and decompressing files. Most try for some sort of balance between these two aspects of the process.

You have to decompress most compressed files before they can be used; compressed files are good only for transferring and storing the information. The exceptions to this are compressed graphics and sound files, which you can view or listen to directly, without running any decompression software. In this case, Netscape Communicator (or some other viewing program) is automatically decompressing the file for you.

Clearly, you really need a compression program to deal with all the files you collect from the Net. In the next section, you'll kill two birds with one virtual stone: you'll learn how to use Netscape Communicator's FTP features as you download a copy of WinZip 6, one of the best compression/decompression programs available.

Smaller + Smaller = Bigger

As you travel around to different FTP sites, you'll notice that even large graphics files such as GIFs are rarely "zipped up" into archives; they're often left just as they are, with their original extension. Why?

Well, GIF files are *already* compressed. The graphics standard includes an algorithm for storing these files in as few bytes as possible. Images are obvious candidates for compression, since so many pixels are repeated. Think of the background, for instance, or large patches of color. If a graphics file contained position and color information for each individual pixel that appeared onscreen, it would be gigantic!

OK, so a GIF file is already compressed. But couldn't you make it even smaller by compressing it again? Nope. Curiously, by running a GIF file through a compression program such as PKZIP or WinZip, you actually make it *bigger*!

Kind of strange, huh? Well think about it: assuming that GIF compression is pretty tight (which it is), you're only going to eke out a few more bytes of space savings. But this added compression actually costs more space than it saves, for PKZIP has to add to the file the information about how to decompress it. In other words, it has to announce "this file has been compressed using PKZIP version *x*" as well as a bunch of other technical information. For this reason, it may not always be worth compressing small files that are known to contain lots of nonrepeating information. However, it may be worth it.

Downloading Your First File

In this example, you'll access a Web page that serves as a front end for an FTP site. You will be able to download the WinZip 6 file simply by clicking a link on the Web page, without wading through the actual directories on the FTP server itself. Later in the chapter, you'll see how Netscape Communicator displays this more "raw" FTP information.

To download WinZip 6 using Netscape Communicator's built-in FTP:

1. Make sure you are connected to the Internet.

2. Double-click the Netscape Communicator icon to launch the program. If it's already running, make sure you're in the browser window (Navigator 4). If you're not, click the browser icon on the Component Bar. The browser window appears, and the Netscape home page starts loading as shown in Figure 8-4.

   - If Navigator 4 is already running and is displaying a different document, you may need to click the Home button or the Netscape icon.

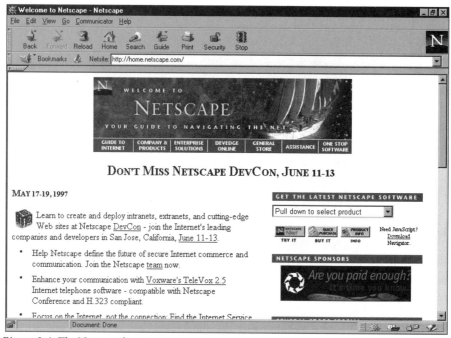

Figure 8-4: The Netscape home page.

3. Click your mouse inside the Netsite field at the top of the window to select the URL http://home.netscape.com/.

TIP

Remember, you don't always have to type in entire URLs; in many cases you can leave off the two slashes and everything that comes before them. If you simply enter home.netscape.com, Communicator is smart enough to figure out that you mean a Web site and will automatically use the HTTP protocol. Similarly, if you enter ftp.vmedia.com, Communicator knows you are trying to connect to an FTP site and will use FTP.

4. Replace this URL with the one for the WinZip home page by entering **http://www.winzip.com/** or just **winzip** . Once you have typed in the new URL, press Enter. Navigator 4 retrieves the WinZip home page, as shown in Figure 8-5.

Figure 8-5: The WinZip home page.

5. You may want to take some time to look around the WinZip home page. When you are ready, scroll down the page and click the Download Evaluation Version link. The WinZip:Download Page appears, as shown in Figure 8-6.

TIP

You can save FTP sites as bookmarks just like any Web document. Select Add Bookmark from the menu that appears when you select the Bookmarks Quickfile button, or drag the Page icon over the Bookmarks Quickfile icon. You can also simply type Ctrl+D. This is convenient if you don't have time to download a long file immediately but want to be able to find it easily later on.

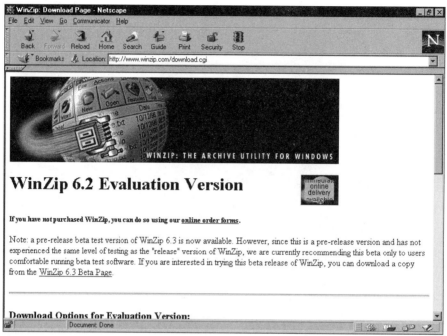

Figure 8-6: The Download WinZip page.

6. Now scroll down to the link that actually lets you download the correct file for your system—Windows 95/NT or Windows 3.1 (don't click just yet). Notice that the status line indicates the URL pointed to by the link, for instance ftp://ftp2.winzip.com/winzip/winzip95.exe. The *ftp* at the beginning of the URL tells Netscape Communicator to use the FTP protocol to connect with the site ftp2.winzip.com, switch to the *winzip* directory, and download the file *winzip95.exe*.

7. Click the appropriate link, depending on whether you are using Windows 95/NT or Windows 3.1.

Depending on various Communicator settings that will be discussed later in the section called "Helper Applications," there are a couple of different messages you might get at this point when you attempt to download a file. A warning box might pop up, like the one shown in Figure 8-7.

Read the text carefully. This dialog box appears if the type of file you're downloading is configured in Communicator as a type that should be opened or run automatically as soon as it is downloaded, *and* if Communicator is configured to ask you before opening this kind of file. As you'll find out in the "Helper Applications" section, it's easy to change this option.

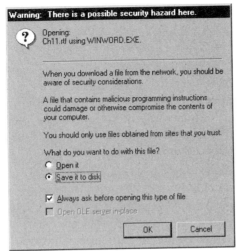

Figure 8-7: The possible security hazard warning box.

But sometimes when you attempt to download a file you may get a message like the one shown in Figure 8-8.

Figure 8-8: The Unknown File Type dialog box.

This simply means that no special action, helper application (viewer), or *plug-in* has been configured for this kind of file, and you can choose what to do with it. Netscape Communicator can automatically run a file like this as soon as it has been received, or it can automatically pop up a Save As dialog box that lets you save the file to disk for later viewing or processing. To learn how to make these configuration changes, see "Helper Applications" later in this chapter.

As you learned in Chapter 7, Communicator also supports special programs known as plug-ins. Plug-ins, like helper applications, may be associated with particular kinds of files you find on FTP sites. But unlike helper applications, which are really separate applications from Communicator, plug-ins let you view or otherwise act on files right within the browser window. By clicking the More Info button in the dialog box shown above in Figure 8-8, you are taken to

Netscape's Plug-In Finder page, and you may decide to install a plug-in designed specifically for the "unknown file type" you are trying to download.

If you *don't* get one of the two dialog boxes shown in the previous illustrations, one of two things will happen:

- The file will be downloaded and automatically run. This means it may be executed on its own or it may appear in an associated application that Communicator launches automatically. For example, the type of compressed executable file you're downloading may simply run, whereas a Word document may appear in a Word window.

- A typical Windows Save As dialog box may appear. In this case, choose a location (such as your C:\TEMP or C:\Download directory) for the file, and then click the Save button. The Saving Location dialog box appears, showing you the progress of the file transfer. Once Netscape Communicator has finished downloading the file, the Saving Location dialog box disappears.

Congratulations! You've just downloaded your first file via FTP, and you now have an important tool for dealing with files you will download in the future. To install WinZip 6, simply run the executable file that you saved on your hard drive (unless Communicator has already launched it automatically). You can run it from the DOS command line or using the Windows Run command. You can also double-click it in Windows Explorer or File Manager. Be sure to read any informational files included with the program, and please remember that WinZip 6 is shareware: if you continue to use it, you must register it. The WinZip package contains complete information on how to do this.

Now let's visit an anonymous FTP site the more traditional way, without relying on a Web page as the front end.

TIP

Once an FTP transfer has started, you can go back to browsing in the browser window. The file will keep downloading as you work. You can even start another FTP transfer and download several files at once.

Smart Resume

The new communications technologies are pretty amazing, but they're not perfect. You can expect occasional minor glitches. Here's something that has happened to me many times: I'm downloading a huge file via FTP when suddenly my Internet connection is dropped. The download stops, and I am left with a file that is absolutely useless.

But thanks to Communicator's Smart Resume feature, you don't need to start the download all over again. When you're back online, click on the link or file once more. Communicator determines that you already have part of the file and resumes the download right at the point it was cut short. In other words, it appends the rest of the data to the end of the partial file that you've already received. This can be a huge time saver!

Navigating FTP Sites

For this tutorial, we'll look at the very large anonymous Oak site at Oakland University in Rochester, Michigan. Primarily a mirror of the Simtel collection of files, this site houses literally thousands of programs of interest to the Internet community, from casual Net surfers to seasoned experts. I use Oakland as an example because it is fairly typical of some of the large public FTP sites scattered around the Net—and because you usually don't run into too much of a traffic jam trying to get on.

1. Make sure you are connected to the Internet and displaying Communicator's browser window (Navigator 4).

2. In the Location box at the top of the window, select the currently displayed URL and replace it with **ftp://oak.oakland.edu/**. Press Enter. After a few moments, the top-level directory at the Oak site appears, as shown in Figure 8-9.

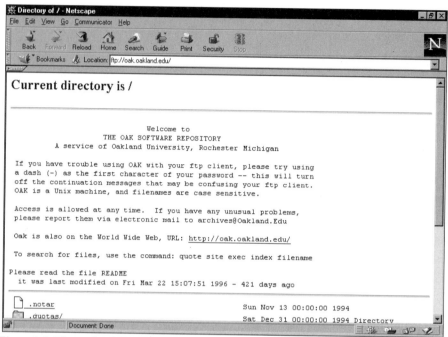

Figure 8-9: The top-level directory at Oak.

3. If there is any information at the top of the page, read it. Then scroll down. You can now see a list of several subdirectories of this top-level directory. Notice that Navigator 4 indicates directories with a Folder icon.

4. Most of the good stuff on Oak is under the /pub directory, so let's go there. (Pub directories often contain files that are useful to the general public.) Scroll down and click the /pub link. The /pub directory appears, as shown in Figure 8-10.

From here you can cruise around on your own for a while—Communicator makes it so easy that you don't need me to hold your virtual hand any more. If you're interested in ham radio files, click the link to the hamradio/ directory; if you're a Macintosh person, click macintosh/. You can always back up a level using the Back button, or you can return to any level you've already seen via the Go menu.

TIP

*If you know where you want to go on an FTP server, you can include the directory right in the URL. For instance, you could enter **ftp://oak.oakland.edu/pub/** right in the Location box in Netscape Navigator 4. And if you know what file you want to retrieve, you can even include the filename in the URL!*

Figure 8-10: The Oak /pub directory.

FTP Traffic Jams

FTP sites are among the busiest resources on the Net. They may not get as many users as the most popular Web pages, but because of the way FTP works, there is a built-in traffic problem.

When you access a Web page, you quickly download the document and are off. Click a link on the page, and you bop back to the site, or to a different site. You flit from site to site, never staying longer than it takes to get the requested information. But with FTP, you remain logged in to the server while cruising and perusing its directories at your own pace, and of course you remain logged in as you download files which typically are much larger than Web pages. The Web is like a fast-food joint, or like the old-fashioned automats where you walked around grabbing the dishes you wanted; FTP is like a real restaurant, with its share of customers who just never seem to stop eating!

Because of this inherent traffic problem, you may sometimes get a message telling you that too many users are already logged on when you connect with an FTP site. Sometimes, however, you will simply be unable to connect at all, and the browser window will just seem to be spinning its wheels. The solution to either of these problems is simple: try again later. In fact, try again *much* later, at a time when there are likely to be fewer info-junkies cruising the Net (3 A.M. works pretty well).

You say you like to sleep at night? Fortunately, there is another solution. For many of the larger public FTP servers, there are also *mirror sites*, FTP servers that contain the exact same files and directory structure but may experience less traffic. These mirror sites are kept in sync with the original: anything you can get at the original you can get at its mirror, and you can be sure that you're downloading the same version. Often the "sorry, we're too busy" message you get when trying to log on to an FTP server includes a list of mirror sites.

Some of the most useful files on Oak are the Windows 95 utilities contained in the pub/simtelnet/win95/util/ directory. You already know that you can get there by clicking your way down, level by level. But since you already know how to navigate this way, let's accelerate the process by taking a shortcut:

1. In the Location box near the top of the browser window, change the currently displayed URL so that it reads **ftp://oak.oakland.edu/pub/simtelnet/win95/util/**.

   ■ A long URL like this is an excellent candidate for a bookmark. I, for one, don't want to type it again!

2. Press Enter. Navigator 4 automatically takes you to the correct directory, as shown in Figure 8-11.

Notice the 00_index.txt file at the top of the directory list. You should read this file for capsule descriptions of all the files in this directory.

Now take a few moments to scroll down the list of files. Notice that Netscape Navigator 4 labels each one with a special blank file icon that has a bunch of 0s and 1s on it. This means that Navigator knows it's a binary (non-text) file but doesn't recognize the .ZIP extension. When you click on one of these filenames, the program will pop up the Unknown File Type dialog box mentioned above. If you want, though, you can have WinZip automatically extract .ZIP files. See "Helper Applications" later in this chapter.

You can also send, or upload, files to some anonymous FTP servers, though this is unusual on public sites. To upload a file to the FTP directory currently displayed in the browser window, select Upload File from Navigator's File menu. An Upload File dialog box appears. Simply select from your system the file you want to upload, then click the Open button. Assuming you have permission to upload files to the site, your file is transferred.

Figure 8-11: The ftp://oak.oakland.edu/pub/simtelnet/win95/util/ directory at Oak.

What Are Symbolic Links?

As you look around FTP sites, you'll notice that in any given directory there are files, subdirectories, and something called "symbolic links." What exactly are they?

A symbolic link is really just a nickname or, more exactly, a pointer to another directory or file. Imagine you are the administrator of an FTP site, and you just put a brand new evaluation version of Netscape Communicator in the directory */pub/pc/windows/win95/www/apps/netscape*. That's buried pretty far down in the directory structure, and people are going to take quite a while navigating down to that level. In addition, if they type in the entire URL, they are likely to make mistakes, taking even more time and further adding to the traffic problem. You want to make sure that users get to the new Netscape file quickly and efficiently. What to do? Create a symbolic link in the top-level directory, and call it, for instance, new_netscape. When a user clicks new_netscape, he or she is automatically transported to the directory where the file *really* lives.

The administrators of FTP sites can create symbolic links to directories or to files. If you click a link that's associated with a directory, you "teleport" to that directory; if you click a link to a file, Navigator 4 views the file or begins the download process. Symbolic links make it quicker, and much more pleasant, to navigate FTP sites that have complex directory structures.

Searching for Files

FTP is great if you know what you're looking for and where to find it. But what if all you know is that you need a particular kind of program, and you have no idea where to start looking? Or what if you can only remember part of the name of a file you want? Fortunately, the Net offers a wide variety of services for locating files in the FTP haystack. One of the old standbys, and still one of the most useful tools on the Net, is a service known as Archie.

Archie

Archie is an Internet service that lets you search indexes of most of the files available at anonymous FTP sites. These indexes are maintained on special Archie servers located around the world. To use Archie effectively, you need to know part of a file's name, or at least be able to make a reasonable guess about what characters might be in its name. For instance, let's say you want to find WinZip 6 but don't remember the exact name of its self-extracting archive file. Archie lets you specify a string of characters that appear anywhere in the name. It would be safe to guess that the string "winzip6" appears somewhere in the filename, so you can use that as your Archie search criterion and find the correct file even if its name is "latestwinzip600z.exe."

For advanced users interested in specifying very precise search parameters, Archie even supports the full set of regular expressions that let you search for all kinds of patterns within filenames. For instance, you could look for a file that begins with a lowercase letter, followed by any number of digits, followed by the string "zsa-zsa," followed by a number greater than five, followed by an extension of either .TAR or .SH, followed by another extension of . . . well, you get the idea. It is beyond the scope of this book to provide a tutorial on regular expressions, but I like to think of them as wildcards on steroids. If you want more information, why not use some of the Internet search tools you've learned about so far?

OK, let's give Archie a try:

1. Make sure you are connected to the Internet. If Netscape Navigator 4 is not currently running, launch it by double-clicking its icon or the Netscape Communicator icon.

2. In the Netsite/Location box at the top of the Navigator 4 window, re-place the currently displayed URL with **http://www-ns.rutgers.edu/htbin/archie** and press Enter. In a few moments, the Rutgers University Archie Request Form page appears, as shown in Figure 8-12.

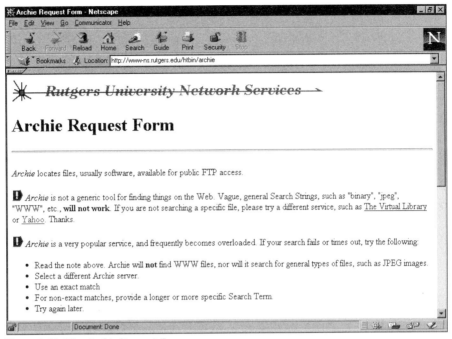

Figure 8-12: The Archie Request Form page.

3. Scroll down the page until you get to the search form itself. Fill it out as follows:

   ▪ In the Search By section, click the top radio button, Looking for Search Term in File Names (Ignore UPPER/lowercase).

   ▪ In the Search Term box, enter **winzip**.

   ▪ Leave the other settings alone.

   ▪ Your completed search form should look like Figure 8-13.

4. Now click the Start Search button. In a few moments, the Archie Search Results page appears, as shown in Figure 8-14, providing you with links to a few different FTP sites where you can get WinZip.

Figure 8-13: The completed Archie search request.

Figure 8-14: The Archie Search Results page.

As you can see, Archie is great if you know something—*anything*—about the name of the file you are looking for. But what if you're looking for a particular *kind* of file—a mortgage calculator, for instance—that could have any name at all? Luckily, the Internet provides other search utilities for this situation as well. One of the best is the c|net shareware page.

The c|net Shareware Page

To get to the c|net Shareware Page:

1. Make sure you are connected to the Internet. If Netscape Navigator 4 is not currently running, launch it by double-clicking its icon.

2. In the Netsite/Location box at the top of the Navigator 4 window, replace the currently displayed URL with **http://www.shareware.com/** (or just **shareware**) and press Enter. In a few moments, the shareware.com page appears, as shown in Figure 8-15.

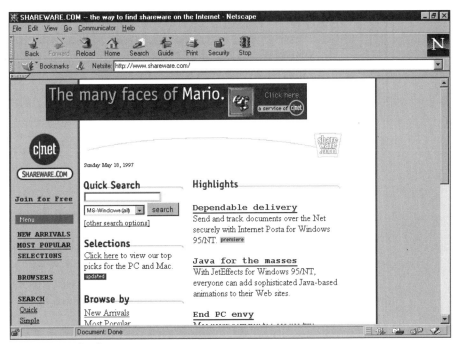

Figure 8-15: The shareware.com page.

3. After reading the introductory information on this page, scroll down to the search form.

4. Since we are interested in mortgage calculators for Windows, leave the drop-down list of file categories set to MS-Windows (all). In the search word box, enter **mortgage**. Your completed search form should look like Figure 8-16.

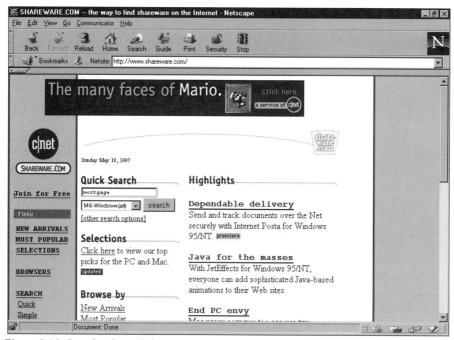

Figure 8-16: Completed search form.

5. Click the search button. In a few moments, the Search Results page appears as shown in Figure 8-17, with links to several different mortgage programs for Windows. You can click any one of these to retrieve the file from its FTP site.

The shareware.com page provides such a powerful search tool that you'll probably want to add it to your bookmarks, or maybe even to the Custom Toolbar.

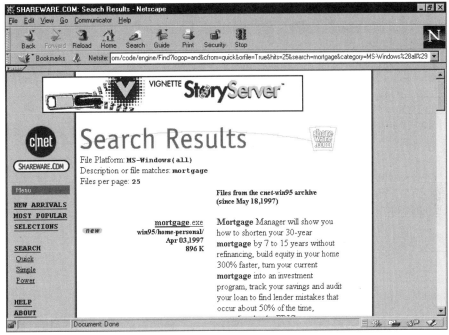

Figure 8-17: The search results.

Using Web Tools to Find Files

While there are other specialized tools for finding files on FTP sites, you may not actually need them. The World Wide Web is becoming more and more prominent as a front end for FTP servers. This means that you can find many files without specialized FTP search services; you simply use the same search engines you use for locating other types of information on the Web itself. The best of these utilities are available by clicking the Navigator 4 Search button. While an Infoseek search, for instance, may not get you directly to a particular file, it will probably take you to a Web page with a link to the file you're interested in. And of course, you can find lots of files by browsing through the dozens of categories that appear when you click the Places button and choose Destinations.

As I mentioned earlier, Netscape Communicator does more than just go out and retrieve files for you—it can actually help you start working with them right away. In the next section, you'll learn how to take advantage of this powerful feature.

What Are RFCs?

Just when you thought we were done with acronyms!

RFC stands for Request for Comment, and that's exactly what it is: a document put out on a public FTP site so that other Net users can read it and comment on the content. But an RFC contains very specialized information, technical information about the Internet itself. In fact, many of the Internet standards that have developed over the years are the result of this RFC process.

Most RFC files are slow, tedious reading, and nobody's turned them into a musical yet. But they are invaluable to anybody wanting to learn more about the Net, and a few of them are even fun. (Well, if you're a geek like me.) RFC 1208, for example, is a large glossary of networking terminology, and RFC 1325 has lots of tips for new Internet users.

How do you know what the different RFC files cover? Here are two URLs:

- ftp://isi.edu/in-notes/rfc-retrieval.txt

- ftp://isi.edu/in-notes/rfc-index.txt

The first file provides instructions on locating and downloading RFCs, and the second contains short descriptions of all the RFCs that currently exist.

Helper Applications

You've already seen that when you click on a text file at an FTP site, Navigator 4 automatically displays the contents rather than simply downloading the file to your hard drive. But that's only a small example of the automation that's possible. To understand how all of this works, let's go back to an FTP site we looked at earlier and associate WinZip with files that have the .ZIP extension.

1. Make sure you are connected to the Net.

2. In Navigator's Netsite/Location box, enter **ftp://oak.oakland.edu/pub/ simtelnet/win95/util/** and press Enter. (If you're on a Windows 3.1 machine, go instead to **ftp://oak.oakland.edu/pub/simtelnet/win3/**.)

3. Navigate down to a directory that interests you, then click a ZIP file to download. The Unknown File Type dialog box appears, as shown earlier in Figure 8-8. This time, click the Pick App button. A Configure External Viewer dialog box pops up.

4. If you want all ZIP files to be handled automatically by WinZip 6 as soon as they are retrieved, click the Browse button and find the WinZip program on your hard drive. For instance, if you are using Windows 95 or NT 4, you'd navigate to C:\Program Files\WinZip, select Winzip32.exe, and click the Open button.

5. Back in the Configure External Viewer dialog box, click OK. Now Communicator will download the file you've chosen and immediately launch WinZip 6 when the entire file has been saved to your hard drive.

Communicator also provides a separate and more powerful interface for associating particular types of files with appropriate actions or applications. Select Preferences from the Edit menu, then select the Applications category under Navigator, as shown in Figure 8-18. If Applications is not displayed, double-click Navigator, or simply click the plus icon.

Figure 8-18: The Applications window.

This looks like a fairly complicated dialog box at first, but once you understand the concepts, it's really pretty simple. The large scrolling list includes the names of different kinds of files you might encounter as you cruise the Net or your office intranet. As you click each file type from the list, the bottom section of the window changes to display details about the particular file type. For instance, Figure 8-19 shows the file type details for Winword (Microsoft Word) files.

Figure 8-19: The Applications window, with file type details for Winword files.

The bottom includes three fields:

- **Extension**. This is simply the extension for this kind of file. When Navigator encounters a file called CHAPTER3.DOC, for instance, it knows it's a Windword file because of the .DOC extension. An icon to the left of the field provides a graphical representation of the file type, just as it would appear on your Windows 95/NT desktop.

- **MIME Type**. MIME, or Multipurpose Internet Mail Extensions, is a universal standard for naming file types. Usually the MIME designations make sense, as in the case of Winword files, which are classified as application/msword.

- **Handled By**. This field specifies the helper application that will be launched when Navigator encounters a file of this type. An icon to the left represents the program. In this case, when Navigator encounters a file with the extension .DOC or the MIME designation application/msword, it launches the program Winword, which then displays the file correctly.

But what if you don't want Microsoft Word to start up every time Navigator encounters a .DOC file? What if you want to view the contents of the file in some other application such as WordPad or WordView—or what if you simply want to save it to disk after retrieving it via FTP?

No problem. Just click the Edit button. The Edit Type dialog box appears, as shown in Figure 8-20.

Figure 8-20: The Edit Type dialog box.

In the Handled By section, select Save to Disk if you simply want files of this type saved rather than displayed or otherwise processed. Or if you want them handled by a different application, make sure the Application option button is selected and then click the Browse button to select a different program.

TIP

If you want Communicator to ask you before it automatically opens files of this type in a helper application, check the checkbox at the bottom of this Window. This is useful, for example, if you sometimes want to view Winword files immediately and sometimes simply want to save them to disk. When Communicator encounters this file type, it will pop up a dialog box like the one shown earlier in Figure 8-6.

What about the top option button, the one labeled Navigator? In this case it's grayed out (made unavailable) because Navigator itself cannot display Winword files—it must call upon the services of a helper application such as Microsoft Word. But take a look at Figure 8-21, which shows the Edit Type dialog box for GIF Image files.

Figure 8-21: The Edit Type dialog box for GIF Image files.

Since Navigator *can* display GIF files without any outside help, the Navigator option button is available—and selected by default. If you click a link to a GIF file, it will be displayed using the browser window. But you may want a different program, such as a full-featured graphics program, to display any GIF files you encounter or download via FTP. In that case, simply select the Application option button and browse for the program you want to use. In any case, click OK when you're finished editing this file type.

TIP

> *Settings in the Applications window affect every Communicator component, not just Navigator 4. For instance, they affect the way attached files are handled in Netscape Messenger (see Chapter 5).*

If you want to get fancy, you can even add new file types and subtypes to Communicator's default list. However, this is truly a propeller-head option: you should not even be thinking about it except to add a new standardized MIME type, and unless you really know what you're doing. Assuming you have the proper geek credentials, though, it's pretty easy. In the Applications window, click New Type. Then just fill in the blanks.

TIP

And yes, you can even delete file types by clicking the Remove button. I do not recommend this. There is no harm in having extra file types listed, even ones you'll never encounter, but unless you're pretty technical it may be hard to add back a type you've deleted.

Netscape Communicator's Applications facility lets you deal efficiently with just about any file on any Internet FTP site. And if you want to further automate the program with new viewers, sound players, editors, or any kind of helper application, guess how you get these programs? By FTP, of course!

Non-Anonymous FTP

Grabbing files from anonymous FTP sites may be the most entertaining use of Netscape Communicator's built-in FTP facility, but there are other practical applications as well. For instance, when I finish writing this chapter, I will FTP it to Netscape Press, where an editor will massage the text and then place it back on the FTP server so I can look over her changes. To do this, I have to log onto an FTP site which requires that I enter a login name and a password.

Here's how to log onto a non-anonymous FTP site to exchange files:

In Navigator's Netsite/Location box, enter the URL for the site you want to connect to via FTP, but include your login name as part of the URL. For instance, when I want to log onto the WELL for the purposes of anonymous FTP, I type **ftp://pjames@well.com** and hit Enter. Immediately a dialog box appears asking me for your login password. Once you enter it, your home directory appears—or the directory you've been given access to by the system administrator. You navigate around the site just as you would navigate around a public (anonymous) FTP site, and the procedure for downloading files is identical. To send a file, select File Upload from Navigator's File menu. Using the Upload File dialog box that appears, choose a file from your local system to upload.

Some systems even let you include your password as part of the URL for a non-anonymous FTP connection. Simply type a colon after your login name, and then your password for the account. Using the example we looked at earlier, I would enter **ftp://pjames:mypassword@well.com**.

Now you've got the basic scoop on navigating FTP sites and downloading files. You've also learned some strategies for finding files on the Net by name or by subject area, and you've seen how Netscape Communicator can be customized to help you deal with your new files more efficiently. Now all you need is a bigger hard drive!

But before heading off to the computer store, why not take a few minutes to learn about two of the other ancestral tools that can still help make your online life easier and more rewarding? The first of these is Gopher.

Gopher

What if you don't know exactly what you're looking for on the Net and want to refine your search carefully as you explore? What if you want to delve deeply into a particular area of interest, for instance constitutional law? Typical Web sites may not help you, for often the links to other information are as arbitrary, whimsical, and wild as the imagination of the page's author.

Gopher servers, on the other hand, serve up information in tidy hierarchical menus and submenus, sticking to a subject and presenting it in top-down, outline format. Using World Wide Web documents, you leap rapidly from peak to peak. Using Gopher, you follow logically related information trails.

How Do They Come Up With These Names?

Most of the Internet services were developed not by commercial software companies, but by individuals in academia, often graduate students. This evolution is reflected in some of the jargon. If the marketing division of a software company had been involved, we'd probably be talking about Super UltraSearch Max Plus instead of Gopher. But the Golden Gopher is the mascot of the University of Minnesota where this powerful tool was developed, and there were no people in suits calling the shots.

Once you name something "Gopher," you have to extend the metaphor. If you visit many Gopher sites, you'll discover that they are sometimes called Gopher *holes*. And avid Gopher users often talk about *burrowing* to other sites. It's all kind of quaint in this age of cyber this and surf that.

In addition to extending metaphors, computer people have a compulsive need to mix them, and so it is very common on the Net to talk about *GopherSpace*. (You can put yourself into an altered state trying to visualize that one.) GopherSpace is simply the total collection of hierarchically organized resources available to you via Gopher.

In the old days (about three years ago), Gopher servers were usually accessed with specialized Gopher client programs, but Web browsers like Netscape Navigator 4 make extra software unnecessary. The Navigator component of Communicator can log you on to a Gopher server and then present you with the information so that it looks very much like any Web page. Menu items are colored like other Web links, and clicking on them brings up the appropriate submenus. Let's give it a try using the *WELL Gopher* as an example.

Using Gopher

The WELL is a large information service known for the variety of its online forums and the lively interactions of its users. It also maintains a very interesting Gopher site that's accessible to anyone on the Net. To begin exploring it:

1. Make sure you are connected to the Internet.

2. Double-click the Navigator 4 or Netscape Communicator icon to launch the program. The browser window appears, and the Netscape home page starts loading, as shown in Figure 8-22.

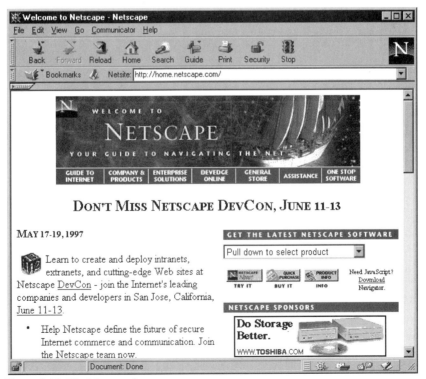

Figure 8-22: The Netscape home page.

3. Click your mouse inside the Netsite/Location field at the top of the window to select the URL http://home.netscape.com/.

4. Replace this URL with the one for the WELL Gopher site by entering **gopher://gopher.well.com/**. Then press Enter. Navigator 4 retrieves the top-level WELL Gopher menu, as shown in Figure 8-23.

   - Notice that when you connect to a Gopher server, virtually all the text in the browser window is composed of links. In the top level of the WELL Gopher, these are links to submenus rather than files, as indicated by the folder icons. The exception is the Search All Menus on the WELLgopher item, which brings up a searchable index of the entire Gopher server.

Figure 8-23: The WELL Gopher.

*Remember that you can type in partial URLs—Netscape Navigator 4 is smart enough to figure them out. Instead of entering **gopher://gopher.well.com/**, for instance, you could simply enter **gopher.well.com**. Because your abbreviated URL has the word "gopher" in it, Navigator assumes this is a Gopher site.*

5. Click the top menu item, About This Gopherspace. A new submenu appears, as shown in Figure 8-24.

   ▪ Notice that most of the links are to actual text files now, as indicated by the icons.

6. Click on the top item, What Is This Place? (The Basic Story). This time a text file appears, as shown in Figure 8-25.

Figure 8-24: The About This Gopherspace submenu on the WELL Gopher.

Figure 8-25: The WELL Gopher welcome file.

7. After reading the file, click Navigator 4's Back button to return to the About This GopherSpace menu. You may want to read some of the other articles here, such as "How to use Gopher to get about," or the "extended ramblings" version of the "What is this place?" file. (The WELL is famous for its extended ramblings.)

8. When you're done reading, click Back again to return to the top-level WELL Gopher menu. From there you can begin to explore many different areas. Feel free to browse. The WELL Gopher is especially known for its information on media, communications, cyberpunk literature, and music.

TIP

Gopher menus can be saved, printed, copied, or made into bookmarks and shortcuts just like any other kinds of pages. In most cases, you needn't pay attention to whether you're at a Web, Gopher, or File Transfer Protocol (FTP) site. If you can see it in the browser window, you can work with it using any of the techniques you learned in Chapter 3.

Although the hierarchy of all Gopher sites is similar, their content varies greatly. There are Gopher sites that specialize in just about any academic field you can think of, from art to astrophysics. In addition, there are Gopher sites that are just plain fun.

But the great thing about Gopher is that it allows a site to include links to other sites on its menus as well. In other words, you are not restricted to the information available only on that particular server. Gopher is really the precursor of the Web in letting sites link to one another in a vast information net.

As you start burrowing from one site to another, you are actually creating a customized hierarchical pathway for yourself, and you can move backward and forward along it to find the information you need. Let's see how this works.

Stretching Gopherspace

To demonstrate how you can "stretch" GopherSpace, let's use the WELL Gopher site again as a starting point (if the WELL Gopher is already displayed in your browser window, skip ahead to step 3 below):

1. Make sure you are connected to the Internet. If Navigator 4 is not currently running, launch it by double-clicking its icon or the Communicator icon.

2. In the Netsite/Location box at the top of the window, select the currently displayed URL and replace it with **gopher://gopher.well.com/**. Press Enter. After a few moments, the top-level menu at the WELL Gopher site appears, as shown earlier in Figure 8-24.

3. This time, click the Internet Outbound (Links We Think Are Cool) link. The Internet Outbound Gopher menu appears, as shown in Figure 8-26.

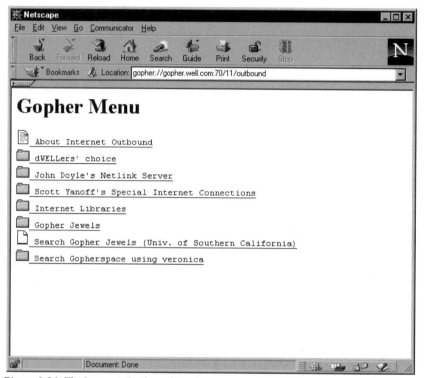

Figure 8-26: The Internet Outbound Gopher menu on the WELL.

4. All of the links on this menu provide useful starting points for Gopher burrowing. For this tutorial, click Scott Yanoff's Special Internet Connections. The Special Internet Connections Gopher menu appears, as shown in Figure 8-27.

■ Notice the icons depicting a computer terminal next to some of the links. This is how Navigator 4 indicates a Telnet connection. If you click on one of these links, Navigator launches a Telnet session with the host site. (More about Telnet later in this chapter.)

The Yanoff List, as it is sometimes known, offers you a wide variety of new jumping off points—or digging down points—for further Gopher burrowing. You should feel free to explore, and you may want to save this menu as a bookmark.

But before you descend into the Gopher tunnels, note that the Location box contains the URL gopher://gopher.well.sf.ca.us:70/11/outbound/Yanoff. *WELL* is still part of the site address because you've never really left the

WELL. No matter how far or deep you burrow through the menus, *WELL* will still form the initial part of the URL. The URL provides a map of the path you took to get to the target information.

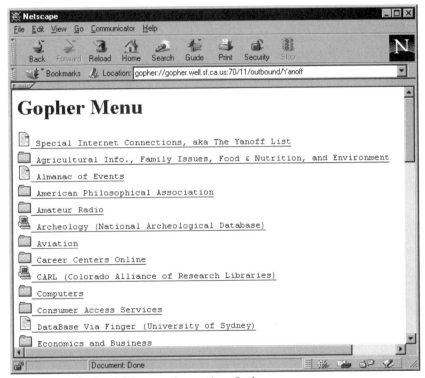

Figure 8-27: The Special Internet Connections Gopher menu.

There are many ways to get to The Yanoff List, but you have constructed a tunnel that begins at the WELL and passes through the Internet Outbound menu. What this means is that you have a complete record of your travels, and in saving a particular URL as a bookmark, you are actually saving a map of your entire journey. With this kind of hierarchical structure, there is really no way to get lost.

This is what I mean by stretching GopherSpace. With each new link you click, you are further extending a *customized* information pathway. You can see why Gopher is a useful research tool when you're trying to refine your quest for particular information.

The WELL is only one of many tunnel entrances. In the next section, I'll list some interesting Gopher sites to begin your explorations.

Great Gopher Holes I Have Known

Table 8-2 lists a few of the best-known Gopher sites.

URL	Description
gopher://gopher.uis.itd.umich.edu/	University of Michigan archive
gopher://ashpool.micro.umn.edu/	University of Minnesota archive
gopher://wx.atmos.uiuc.edu/	Weather maps
gopher://gopher.eff.org/	Electronic Frontier Foundation archive
gopher://gopher.well.sf.ca.us/	Whole Earth 'Lectronic Link (WELL) archive
gopher://wiretap.spies.com/	The Internet Wiretap
gopher://siggraph.org/	Conference proceedings and materials from the graphics special interest group (SIGGRAPH) of the Association for Computing Machinery
gopher://gopher.cpsr.org:70/11/cpsr	Computer Professionals for Social Responsibility archive
gopher://akasha.tic.com/	Sample issues of John Quarterman's Matrix News Internet newsletter, several works from Bruce Sterling
gopher://gopher.echonyc.com	Interesting information about New York City and media

Table 8-2: Some well-known Gopher sites.

Now that you know something about Gopher, let's take a brief look at another faithful old workhorse of the Internet, Telnet.

Telnet

The World Wide Web is the showroom of the Net. It's where you'll find information in all the latest styles and colors. If you want to show a newbie what the Net is all about, you'll almost certainly start with the Web.

But a fancy new car right off the showroom floor isn't always the best way to travel. Sometimes you need an all-terrain vehicle, a rugged tool that will take you places you can't access using the newer Web protocols. Telnet dates back to the days when the information superhighway was just a two-lane blacktop, and fortunately, you can still take advantage of its raw power through Netscape Communicator. And please slap me if I use another driving metaphor.

Using Telnet, you log in to other computers on the Net interactively. Once you log in, the Telnet host presents you with a command line or with text-based menus; you type menu choices or commands. Typical public Telnet sites include library card catalogs, weather information services, and a variety of specialized databases. You can also Telnet to text-based online services such as the WELL or Echo. And if you have a UNIX account on another computer on the Net, you can use Telnet to log in and run any UNIX program available on the host machine.

MUDs & MOOs

It's great to be able to access vast libraries of esoteric information via the Internet, but at some point we have to step back and take stock again of what computers are really for: playing games!

Some of the most interesting games spawned by modern information technology are MUDs and MOOs. MUDs are *Multiple-User Dimensions*, real-time, interactive role-playing games. MOOs are the object-oriented version, in which users can create their own objects, such as new rooms or features of the landscape. There are also variants of MUDs known as MUCKs, MUSHes, and MUSEs.

What all these games have in common is that several players at a time use the Internet to interact with one another as characters in a fictional world. Some of these text-based virtual worlds are full of magic and dragons, others are more like discussion forums, and some are meeting places for playing out group fantasies. Here are a couple of Web pages to get you started:

- MUDs, MOOs, and Other Virtual Hangouts
  (http://jefferson.village.virginia.edu/iath/treport/mud.html). Lots of information about MUDs and MOOs, and links to several sites.

- MUDs, MOOs, and MUSHes, "Hip-Waders in the CMC Swamp"
  (http://www.oise.on.ca/~jnolan/mud.html). Links to information and games.

Also check out the Usenet newsgroups under rec.games.mud. It's important to read the FAQs and whatever other information you can get before trying these games, as each has its own culture and rules of etiquette.

How does this remote login process work? Telnet is really a *terminal emulation* protocol. That means it makes your PC behave like a terminal that's directly connected to the host computer. What is a terminal? A terminal is a device that can't really do anything on its own, but when it is attached to a computer it provides users with a display screen and a keyboard. In other words, a terminal provides the user interface to a host computer. Normally, terminals are attached to the host by means of cable, but terminal emulation programs allow you to connect remotely using a PC and phone lines. With terminal emulation programs like PROCOMM PLUS and Hyperterm, you dial directly into a host; with Telnet, you connect via the Internet or a corporate intranet.

Figure 8-28 shows a typical Telnet session. In this example, I am logged in to the Echo online service, and you can clearly see the interactive nature of this kind of connection.

Figure 8-28: A Telnet session with Echo.

Telnet & Netscape Communicator 4

Let's see how observant you are: what's wrong with Figure 8-28?

That's right, it depicts some other software instead of Netscape Communicator. Instead of the usual toolbar and Netscape logo, you see a much simpler window. Did the author make a mistake? Did the editors miss it?

No. The fact is that Netscape Communicator does not actually include built-in Telnet. In fact, Web browsers almost *never* include built-in Telnet. Let me explain.

Terminal emulation programs and Web browsers are two very different kinds of software. Terminal emulation programs concentrate on providing direct access to the host computer operating system and its applications, while Web browsers concentrate on displaying multimedia documents.

Since these two functions are not a good fit, the authors of most World Wide Web programs have decided to support Telnet by launching an external helper application when necessary. If you click a link that represents the URL for a Telnet connection, Navigator 4 launches your Telnet session by executing a separate program, passing to it the address of the site. As soon as you're finished with the Telnet session, you can return to the browser window and to whatever document was last displayed in it. In fact, you don't even have to wait. If you're the kind of person who likes to do several things at once, you can go back and forth between active Telnet sessions and Navigator 4.

In order for Telnet to work, you have to have a program available on your system called **telnet.exe**. Fortunately, Windows 95 and NT come with this Telnet application, so Communicator can launch it automatically when necessary.

TN3270

Almost all public Telnet sites whose host computer is running the UNIX operating system these days support the standard version of the protocol that uses the VT100 terminal emulation. However, if the host is an IBM mainframe running an IBM operating system you may need a variant of Telnet known as *TN3270*. TN3270 sites require that you use a program that makes your PC act like an IBM 3270 terminal instead of a DEC VT100.

Your regular Telnet program probably does not include TN3270 capabilities. If you plan to connect to TN3270 sites, you'll need to get the Professional Edition of Netscape Communicator, which includes a full-featured 3270 facility. Please see Chapter 13 for more information on the Professional Edition.

Using Telnet

As with any other Internet service supported by Netscape Communicator, you can get to a Telnet site by any one of several methods. You can:

- Click a Telnet link in a Web document or at a Gopher site.
- Type a URL in Navigator 4's Netsite/Location box.
- Select a Telnet link from Bookmarks.
- Select a Telnet site from your Personal toolbar.
- Double-click a desktop shortcut to a Telnet site.

Any one of these actions will have the same result: Navigator 4 launches your Telnet application, which then logs you in to the site specified in the URL.

Let's give it a try by going back to a Telnet link you may have noticed earlier in a Gopher menu, the National Archeological Database. You may not be the slightest bit interested in archeology, but I have chosen this site because it is very typical of research sites that are publicly accessible via Telnet.

For the sake of this tutorial, I'm assuming you're using the Windows 95 Telnet application. The basic instructions should be close to accurate even if you're using a different program:

1. Make sure you are connected to the Internet. If Netscape Navigator 4 is not currently running, launch it.

2. In the Netsite/Location box at the top of the window, select the currently displayed URL and replace it with **gopher://gopher.well.sf.ca.us:70/11/ outbound/Yanoff**. Press Enter. (Hey, if you'd saved the Yanoff menu as a bookmark, you wouldn't have to type in the URL again.)

3. Click the Archeology (National Archeological Database) link. After a few seconds, the Telnet application appears with a login prompt from the remote site, as shown in Figure 8-29.

   ■ In addition, a small message box pops up telling you to log in to this site as "nadb," as shown in Figure 8-30.

Figure 8-29: Windows 95 Telnet program with login prompt from the National Archeological Database.

Figure 8-30: Login information message box.

TIP

Not all sites supply you with login instructions like this, but many do. Depending on the exact timing of data received from the remote site, the Telnet window might cover the informational message box so that it is invisible to you. Before experimenting with different logins to see what will work, move or temporarily minimize the Telnet window to make sure you didn't miss an important message.

*If the remote system presents you with a login prompt but no information about what to enter, try entering **guest** and pressing Enter.*

4. Click on OK in the message box. It disappears.

5. At the login prompt in the main Telnet window, enter **nadb**. You are now logged in to the National Archeological Database, as shown in Figure 8-31.

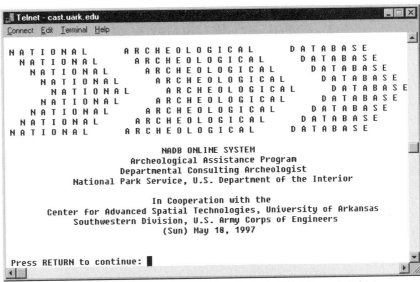

Figure 8-31: You're logged in to the National Archeological Database via Telnet.

6. As directed by the remote system, press Return (Enter) to continue. The NADB Connection Menu appears. Since you are connected via the Internet, select item 4, Internet to NADB, and press Return.

7. Continue following any directions that appear in the Telnet window. As is typical with research sites like this, you are asked to enter some information about yourself and to choose an ID number. Once you've gotten through this process, the NADB Main Menu appears, as shown in Figure 8-32.

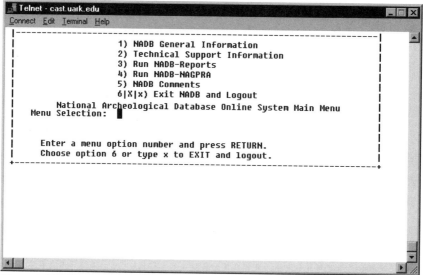

```
Telnet - cast.uark.edu                                              _ □ X
Connect  Edit  Terminal  Help
|-----------------------------------------------------------------|
|                  1) NADB General Information                     | ▲
|                  2) Technical Support Information                |
|                  3) Run NADB-Reports                             |
|                  4) Run NADB-NAGPRA                              |
|                  5) NADB Comments                                |
|                  6|X|x) Exit NADB and Logout                    |
|        National Archeological Database Online System Main Menu   |
|  Menu Selection: █                                               |
|                                                                  |
|                                                                  |
|    Enter a menu option number and press RETURN.                 |
|    Choose option 6 or type x to EXIT and logout.                |
+-----------------------------------------------------------------+
 ◄                                                               ► ▼
```

Figure 8-32: The NADB Main Menu.

8. At this point, you can choose an item from the menu to get more information about the NADB or to access its search tools immediately. If you're interested in archeology, feel free to return to this site later, but for now let's select menu option 6 (or enter the letter **x**), Exit NADB, and log out. If you are using the Windows 95 Telnet program, a message box pops up explaining that your connection to the host has been lost, as shown in Figure 8-33.

Figure 8-33: The Connection to Host Lost message.

9. Once you are disconnected from the remote host, you can simply quit your Telnet program.

That's all there is to it. At first it may seem awkward that Navigator 4 needs to launch a separate helper application for Telnet access, but there are several advantages to this system. The most significant bonus is that you can use any Telnet application you want, including ones that are much more configurable and full-featured than the program included with Windows 95.

Speaking of configuration, let's take a quick look at some ways to tailor your Telnet application so that it works most efficiently for you.

Logging Off Remote Systems

Your Telnet program probably provides a way to disconnect from a remote site at any point, without even telling the remote host that you are leaving. In the Windows 95 Telnet program, you simply choose the Disconnect option from the Connect menu.

Whenever possible, however, you should end your session cleanly by logging out from the remote Telnet site, choosing the appropriate menu options or following instructions for quitting. Otherwise, the software at the remote Telnet site may not immediately realize you are gone and may keep the connection open for several minutes, exacerbating Net traffic jams.

Unless you're having technical problems with the connection, disconnecting without logging out is considered poor online etiquette.

Customizing Your Telnet Application

Most Telnet applications offer a variety of options to make your online life easier and more productive. Since the Windows 95 Telnet program is typical of the simple applications that are available, we'll use it as an example. If you're using a different program, you may have to look around a little for the configuration options we're examining, but they should be there somewhere.

1. Launch Telnet by clicking its icon on the desktop or by using the Windows 95 Run command. The main Telnet window appears, as shown in Figure 8-34.

   - Most Telnet applications don't require you to be connected to the Net to change preferences or configuration options.

Figure 8-34: The Windows 95 Telnet application.

2. Select Preferences from the Terminal menu. The Terminal Preferences dialog box appears, as shown in Figure 8-35.

Figure 8-35: The Terminal Preferences dialog box.

The options in this dialog box are pretty typical of what's available in Telnet programs. Here are some tips for configuring these settings:

- **Local Echo**. Most remote Telnet sites echo back to you all the characters you type so that you can see what you are doing. Generally you should leave this check box unchecked; check it only if your typing is invisible to you.

- **Blinking Cursor**. Check this box if you want your cursor to blink while you are in Telnet. This can help you find the cursor on remote systems that include lots of lines or underscores in their screens.

- **Block Cursor**. Check this option if you want a block cursor instead of the usual cursor. This may be much easier to see on some systems.

- **VT100 Arrows**. The VT100 terminal emulation includes two different sets of character sequences ("mappings") that can be sent to the remote Telnet host when you press the arrow keys. Unless your arrow keys don't seem to be working properly at a particular site, leave this box unchecked. (For the propeller heads out there, unchecked means Keypad Application Mode, and checked means Keypad Cursor Mode. The remote site may send sequences that temporarily change your default setting.)

- **Buffer Size**. This option lets you specify how many lines you can scroll back to see text that has scrolled out of the Telnet window. Since the VT100 terminal displays 25 lines of text at one time, this option should be set to 25 or greater.

- **Emulation**. Unless a remote Telnet host explicitly requires VT52 emulation, you should keep this set to VT100/ANSI. Other Telnet programs may let you choose from a wider variety of terminal emulations, but VT100 is the most commonly supported one on publicly accessible sites.

- **Fonts**. Click this button to change the font of the text that appears in your Telnet window.

- **Background Color**. Click this button to change the background color of your Telnet window.

Once you have made your configuration changes, click OK to return to the main Telnet window.

Moving On

This has been the "back to basics" chapter—a quick look at some of the older workhorse Net services available through Netscape Communicator. In its support of FTP, Gopher, and Telnet, Communicator provides you with some of the most dependable tools available for gathering information. But enough of looking into the past. In the next chapter, we explore the future—or at least *your* future as a designer of your own Web pages! This may sound daunting at first, but not to worry. Netscape Composer makes it very, very easy.

CHAPTER 9

Creating Your Own Page

So far in this book, I've covered lots of ways to gather information from your intranet or from the Net itself. With Communicator, you can experience everything from plain-vanilla office memos to videos of John Travolta doing that sort of twist thing he does. But gathering information—or even sitting back and receiving it in e-mail—is only one side of the Communicator coin. Communicator includes a special module called Netscape Composer that lets you create your own beautifully formatted multimedia documents that others can then access.

Why Your Own Page?

I'm glad you asked. You might want to create your own Web pages for several reasons:

- **Presentations for work.** Instead of carrying those ubiquitous PowerPoint transparencies into your next meeting, why not create fully formatted and illustrated documents that co-workers can access right from their own computers? An example of a typical business document in HTML format is shown in Figure 9-1.

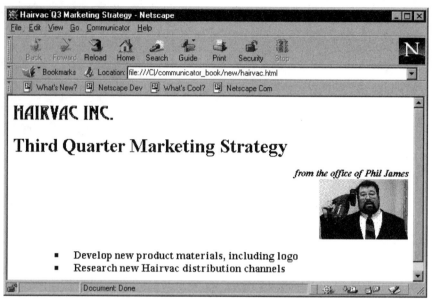

Figure 9-1: A business presentation in HTML format.

■ **Slicker e-mail.** When you use the HTML editing window to create e-mail in Netscape Messenger (see Chapter 5), you are actually accessing Netscape Composer. That's why you can make your messages look like Web pages: they really *are* Web pages. But you can also work separately in Composer and then add the results later to your e-mail messages. For example, you may want to include some fancy letterhead in every message or a page that includes pictures of your kids.

■ **A home base.** Remember how Navigator lets you choose a home page, the page that displays initially when you load the program? Well, you can make that home page your *own* home page, a special document that includes links to your favorite sites, formatted to your own exact specifications as shown in Figure 9-2. You can store this special starter page on a Web server or simply on your own machine.

Figure 9-2: A personal home base.

PowerStart

In this chapter, you'll learn several different ways of creating Web pages, but I *don't* cover one very useful tool: Netscape's *PowerStart* facility. PowerStart uses a Wizard very similar to the Page Wizard described later in this chapter. However, it helps you create a slightly different kind of Web page, a sort of home base that includes not only your most-used links, but also a personal notepad and access to various services that automatically update the information in your browser window. For example, without even a mouse click, your PowerStart page can display the latest technology news, stock quotes, or weather reports for your area.

So why don't I cover PowerStart in this chapter? Because configuring PowerStart is almost identical with using the Page Wizard described later in the chapter, and Netscape includes very thorough instructions as well. To access PowerStart, simply click the PowerStart link on Netscape's home page at http://home.netscape.com. Just follow the directions to create your PowerStart page. Once it's created, you access it the same way—by clicking the PowerStart link. Of course, you'll probably want to set it as your startup home page or create a link to it on your Personal toolbar.

Note: PowerStart requires an Internet connection—it will not work on an intranet alone.

■ **Setting up shop.** Do you have something to sell? Thousands of Internet users each day are setting up commercial sites that advertise products and services, and that even allow customers to make purchases. With pages created in Netscape Composer, you can tap into a whole new market.

■ **Self-publishing.** Maybe instead of something to sell, you have something to *say*. Sure, you can publish the company newsletter on your intranet, but the Web also makes it possible for individuals to publish their own artwork, literary pieces, and even music. If Doubleday won't give you that half-million dollar advance you deserve, why not put your Great American Cyber-Novel up on a Web server?

■ **Coordinating and organizing.** Thousands of organizations, large and small, keep members informed of activities through Web pages. Whether you're planning a Little League picnic or a march on Washington, you can disseminate the necessary information and work out the logistics through a well-designed Web site. Figure 9-3 shows the Web site maintained by the American Civil Liberties Union. It is a good example of well-planned HTML.

Figure 9-3: The ACLU Web site.

I probably haven't thought of many, many uses for Web pages. Let me know about some interesting ones you've discovered, and my publisher will send you lots of fabulous prizes. *NOT!*

What You Need

If you're creating a Web page that only you will see—for example, a special "hot list" composed of links to your favorite sites—all you really need is Netscape Communicator and a little bit of space on your hard drive or on a network drive. You create the file using Composer and then save it locally, in any directory you want. You can then view it in Navigator 4 by pressing Ctrl+O or selecting Open Page from the File menu. Alternatively, you can register it as your default home page (the page that is displayed when you start Navigator 4 or when you click the Home button) by selecting Preferences from the Edit menu, clicking the Navigator category, and then customizing the fields as shown in Figure 9-4.

Figure 9-4: The Navigator configuration window with a local home page specified.

Notice the unusual format of the URL for a local file (as opposed to one that resides on an actual Web server). The URL for a local file starts with the word *file*. Next, as with all complete URLs, there is a colon and two forward slashes, then the exact path to the file. Got all that? Here's an example—an HTML file called PRODUCT.HTM that's located in the Public directory on the Q drive of your LAN: file://Q:/Public/PRODUCT.HTM. Of course if this file were on your own computer, you would specify one of your local drives, for instance C, instead of Q.

You can enter the path for the file using backslashes if you want; Communicator automatically converts them to forward slashes, which are the standard for Web browsers.

Even if you want others to be able to view your home Web page, you may not need to do any more than copy it to a directory on your intranet where your audience has read permission. They would then simply go through the same steps as above to view the document, but instead of specifying a drive on their machine, they'd specify the correct network drive. This method is the simplest way of publishing a Web page. But it's not necessarily the best way. Many features, such as built-in security, forms, streaming multimedia, and Java, only become available to you as an HTML author if you put your work up on an actual Web server. In addition, publishing your page via a Web server is the only way to make it available to those people who can't access directories on your local area network.

Your Web Server

So do you need to run out and buy a Web server if you want to publish Web pages? *Absolutely not!* In fact, unless you're at least as much of a geek as I am, you shouldn't even consider getting your own server.

Why? You can find Web servers all over the place just waiting to provide a home for your latest creation. Maybe there's one on your intranet right now. If not, try convincing your network administrator to get one. Or if you log on to the Internet from home, your ISP (Internet Service Provider) may maintain a Web server that customers can use at no extra charge. If all else fails, plenty of commercial entities will be happy to house your pages for a small monthly fee.

In choosing a Web server for your pages, you should think about these few basic considerations:

- **Are you charged for using extra disk space?** HTML files are generally pretty small, but if your Web page includes many graphics, sound, or video files, you may go beyond the free storage limit. Check with the administrator of your Web server to make sure you won't receive unexpected bills.

TIP

Of course, being as efficient as possible in your use of graphics and other large media files is always wise. This way, you not only reduce storage charges, but you also assure that clients can load your pages quickly, even on slow connections.

- **Can you easily update your files?**   Information is as relative and dynamic as anything else. Yesterday's truth is today's theory and tomorrow's superstition. If the Web server you use doesn't make updating your files easy—for example, if you have to get permission from the administrator every time you make a change—you need to find a new Web server.

- **Does the Web server provide the features you need?**   Don't assume that just any Web server will support all the services you need. For example, if you want to collect information via HTML forms, make sure that your Web server can do this job for you. It will probably take some extra work on the part of the server administrator to set up this service for you. Or, if you need SSL security, make sure that you're placing your pages on a machine running one of Netscape's security-enhanced server applications. Starting a Web radio station? You'll need to put your sound files on a Netscape Media Server or a RealAudio server. In short, think about what kinds of bells and whistles you may want to add to your Web page in the next year or so, and then make sure your Web server supports them.

- **Is the server reliable?**   As the Net grows, Web servers sometimes have a hard time keeping up with the traffic. Your local ISP may have been the most reliable one in the world until somebody posted those nude pictures of Brad Pitt. Now, with two hundred thousand hits a day tying up the lines, sometimes nobody can get through to your modest little numismatics page. If the administrators of your Web server are not committed to upgrading hardware as necessitated by traffic, or if they are unable to maintain their equipment and software in top-notch condition, it's time to look elsewhere.

OK, you've chosen a Web server that will store and make available the documents you create. Later, in the section called "Publishing Your Page," I'll show you how to put these documents up on the server. But first you have to *create* a document or two. And before you do that, you have to configure Composer so that it works exactly the way you want it to.

Configuring Composer

Let's breeze through this configuration so we can get to the fun stuff:

1. Click the Netscape Composer icon on your desktop. Alternatively, from any other Communicator module, click the Composer button in the Component bar. The Composer window appears, as shown in Figure 9-5.

Figure 9-5: The Composer window.

2. From the Edit menu, select Preferences and then, if necessary, click the Composer category in the left-hand pane. The Composer preferences dialog box appears, as shown in Figure 9-6.

Figure 9-6: The Composer preferences dialog box.

3. In the Author Name box, fill in your name.

4. While you're working through this chapter, you may want to *un*check the Auto save check box. That way, you can always revert to the original file you're working on if you make a big mess of it while editing. But once you've worked through this chapter and are actually creating your own Web pages, you should probably come back and check the Auto save check box. If Composer automatically saves your work every 10 minutes or so, you can't lose *too* much of your hard work in the event your computer crashes.

5. In the next two fields, enter the full path and program names of any external editors you want to use for editing HTML code or graphics images directly. You can use the Choose buttons to locate these programs on your system.

External Editors??

Wait a second: Composer is supposed to be an HTML editor. Why do you need to specify additional external editors here?

Netscape Composer is known as a *WYSIWYG* editor—What You See Is What You Get. That means you can manipulate text and graphics directly on the screen, and you see pretty much what your page will look like at all times. As you adjust the size of fonts or move graphics around on your page, Composer is busy behind the scenes generating the actual HTML source code that will tell other people's browsers how to display your page. For example, when you select some text and click the Bold button, you see bold text on your screen. But Composer, behind the scenes, has changed the actual HTML file you're generating so that the text you selected is now surrounded by the standard HTML bold on and bold off tags, like this:

<B>your selected text here</B>

You are insulated from these programming details by the graphical interface Composer provides.

Sometimes, however, you may want to manipulate the HTML source directly. For example, you may want to add some advanced or specialized HTML commands that are not available through the Composer interface. (If Composer covered *every* tag and option available in the HTML specification, your screen would be covered with dozens of buttons and toolbars!) Or you may want to tweak the spacing of some elements on your page very precisely, which is sometimes easier to do by changing a value than by moving a mouse around.

Remember, the actual HTML files generated by Composer, like all HTML files, are text files. So to edit HTML code directly, you need a text editor. Chances are you already have one you like. Rather than making you learn a new program, the Netscape programmers decided to let you specify your *own* editor for working directly with HTML code. Then to edit your HTML source code using an external editor, you simply choose HTML Source from Composer's Edit menu. You'll learn more about this topic in the section called "Editing Your HTML Source."

TIP

Composer also lets you specify your own program for editing graphics files. Composer launches this application when you click the Edit Image button in the Image Properties dialog box that you access by right-clicking an existing image or by clicking the Insert Image button on Composer's toolbar (see the section called "Adding a Picture").

The next three options relate to how Composer expresses the relative sizes of text within the document you create. As you may have noticed, the main Composer window includes a drop-down list from which you can choose the font size for new text you type in or change the font size for selected text. (See the section called "Changing Font Size.") The numbers in this list will vary depending on which option button you select in the Composer preferences dialog box:

- **Show relative size as points.** The numbers in the drop-down list indicate the actual point size of the text. The point sizes available will vary depending on the font style you've selected.

- **Show relative HTML font scale.** The numbers in the drop-down list express the *relative* size of the font using a standard scale. In this scale, 0 is the size of text in the Normal style; negative values are progressively smaller, and positive values are progressively larger than the Normal font.

- **Show relative HTML scale and absolute "point-size" attributes.** This option allows both point sizes and HTML scale sizes to be displayed in the drop-down list. In other words, it combines the two options outlined above. The list shows the relative HTML scale first. If you scroll down the list, you can access the absolute point sizes.

Now on to Composer's Publishing options. In the left-hand category list, click the Publishing subcategory under Composer. (You might have to expand the Composer category by double-clicking it or clicking the plus sign.) The Publishing preferences dialog box appears, as shown in Figure 9-7.

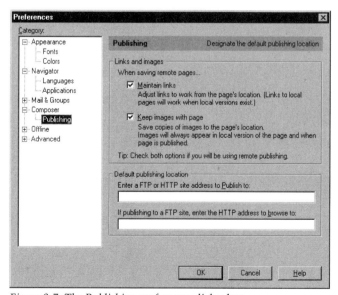

Figure 9-7: The Publishing preferences dialog box.

If you intend to place your Web pages on a remote server, or even a server on your own intranet, you need to fill this dialog box out very carefully. Some of the concepts may be new to you, so I'm going to go through each option in detail:

- **Maintain links.** Typically, you create your Web pages on your own machine before publishing them on a remote server. You may create a main HTML file that includes links to *other* HTML files on your own machine. What happens when you upload all this stuff to your server? How does the main HTML file know how to find the other HTML files now that they're no longer on your local machine?

  Well, if you leave this check box checked, Composer will automatically adjust the links in your files when it uploads them to the server.

  Showing how this process works is easier than explaining it abstractly. Let's say you have a file called main.html in a folder or directory called C:\home_page. And let's say that main.html contains a link to another file called pictures.html that is located in a subdirectory of C:\home_page called Pictures. In other words, you have two files: C:\home_page\main.html and C:\home_page\Pictures\pictures.html.

  OK, now pay attention here. When you publish your page, let's assume you upload your files to a Web server whose URL is http://www.server.com. The directory they've given you is user1, so the URL to your main HTML file, once you upload it, is http://www.server.com/user1/main.html, and the URL to your pictures file is http://www.server.com/user1/Pictures/pictures.html. Originally, your main.html file included a link to C:\home_page\Pictures\pictures.html, but since the Maintain links box is checked, Composer automatically adjusts this link to http://www.server.com/user1/Pictures/pictures.html. Your main file always knows where the pictures file is, and browsers won't get "File not found" errors.

TIP

While the Maintain links feature is very convenient for intermediate and advanced users, if you're a Web publishing beginner, you should keep all your HTML and associated files in a single directory and upload them all to a single directory on the Web server. Keeping things simple is the best way to avoid "File not found" errors in your pages.

- **Keep images with page.** If you keep this option checked, Composer uploads copies of your images to the server along with your HTML files. The images therefore will appear when somebody browses to your site as well as when you view your document locally. Again, if you're publishing on a remote Web server, keeping this box checked is usually essential.

- **Enter a FTP or HTTP site address to Publish to.** Typically, you upload your pages to a Web server using Composer's built-in FTP protocol. However, Composer also supports HTTP uploads. In either case, type in the URL for your publishing location, including the full path to your publishing directory. For example, your publishing location might be ftp://www.server.com/user1/public_html/.

- **If publishing to a FTP site, enter the HTTP address to browse to.** This address is the actual location of your Web pages, for example http://www.server.com/user1/public_html/. Filling in this information is essential if you have entered an FTP address in the previous field, which is usual.

When you are finished making changes, click OK to return to the main Composer window. Now let's get busy with the creative process itself. Netscape Communicator provides two convenient tools that make it easy to get started—the Page Wizard and page templates.

Creating Your Page Using Page Wizard

Our first order of business is to fire up Netscape Composer:

1. For this exercise, make sure you are connected to the Net, either through a direct connection or a SLIP/PPP connection with your Internet Service Provider.

TIP

The Page Wizard actually "lives" on Netscape's own Web site. If you are on an office intranet but are not currently connected to the Net itself, you will not be able to use this convenient feature. You should skip ahead to the section called "Creating Your Page Using a Page Template."

2. Click the Netscape Composer icon on your desktop. Alternatively, from any other Communicator module, click the Composer button in the Component bar. The Composer window appears, as shown in Figure 9-8.

Figure 9-8: The Composer window.

Now you're ready to start composing your page using the Wizard:

1. In Netscape Composer, click the New Page button, the one at the far left of the special Composer taskbar. A dialog box composed of five buttons appears, as shown in Figure 9-9.

Figure 9-9: The Create New Page dialog box.

2. Click the From Page Wizard button. Composer launches Navigator 4 and takes you to Netscape's Page Wizard site, as shown in Figure 9-10.

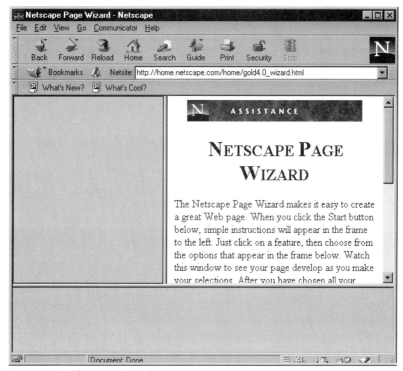

Figure 9-10: The Page Wizard.

3. Scroll down the frame that contains text, and read the description of the Page Wizard feature. When you're done reading, click the Start button. Now some instructions appear in the left-hand frame, as shown in Figure 9-11, and the right-hand frame contains a preview of the page you are building.

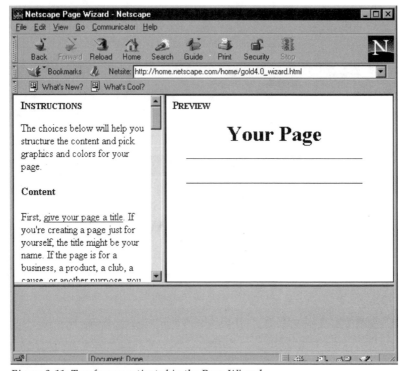

Figure 9-11: Two frames activated in the Page Wizard.

Scroll down the left-hand frame. As you can see, it contains several links that are actually options for customizing your document. Here's the rundown on how the three frames in the browser window will operate as you start to create your page:

- In the left-hand frame, you choose particular options you want to configure. We'll call this the *Options frame*.

- Once you click one of these links, the bottom frame will display various choices. For example, if you click a link labeled Background Color, various background color choices appear in the bottom frame. We'll call this bottom frame the *Selection frame*.

- The right-hand frame, where we started this whole process, shows you a preview of your Web page. As you choose new elements in the Option and Selection frames, this *Preview frame* is automatically updated to reflect your latest changes.

The left-hand Options frame always contains the same information. Therefore, if you don't like a change you've made, you can always go back and click that option again.

Let's go through the various options offered by the Page Wizard.

Titling Your Page

Everything's got to have a name, right?

1. In the Options frame, click the "give your page a title" link. The Choices: Title edit field appears in the Selection frame.

2. Enter a title for your page; then click the Apply button. As you can see in Figure 9-12, the Preview frame is automatically updated.

   ■ If you make a mistake or want to change your title, simply edit what you typed in the Choices: Title box, and click Apply again.

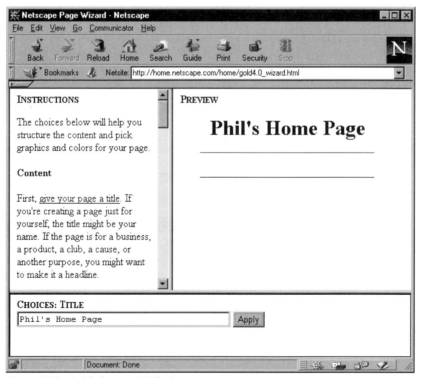

Figure 9-12: A title for your Web site.

Creating an Introduction

An introduction is the place where you tell people what your page is about. If you're just creating a page for your own use, the introduction is the place where you remind yourself of who you are.

1. In the Options frame, scroll down to the link "type an introduction" and click it. A new edit box appears, as shown in Figure 9-13.

Figure 9-13: The Choices: Introduction edit box.

2. Start typing. When you are satisfied with your introduction, click Apply. Once again, the Preview frame is updated with the new information.

Now comes the fun part: adding some links to other sites.

Adding Links

You probably already know what's in your own home page, so why not explore beyond your own little world by adding some links?

1. Scroll down the Options frame to the "add some hot links to other Web pages." Click it.

2. In the Selection frame, type a site name in the Name field and its URL in the URL field. In Figure 9-14, for example, you can see that I've entered a link to the Ventana Web site.

Figure 9-14: Adding the Ventana Web site to your page.

3. Click Apply. The link is added to your page.

4. You can enter as many new links as you want, clicking the Apply button each time. All these links are added automatically to your page.

OK, you've got your links. Now maybe you want to add some concluding remarks to your page.

Adding a Conclusion

To add some more text after your links, follow these steps:

1. In the Options frame, scroll down to the "type a paragraph of text to serve as a conclusion" link.

2. In the Choices: Conclusion box, enter up to 1,000 words.

3. As before, click Apply. The preview frame is automatically updated.

Let's add one last touch to this very basic page: a clickable e-mail address so people can contact you or so that you can send yourself the kind of hot messages I know you love.

Adding Your E-Mail Address

If you've been cruising the Web for a while, you've probably noticed that many pages include a link that lets you send e-mail to the creator of the page or to a site administrator. Click the link, and you're automatically transported to Netscape Messenger, where you can simply type a message and click the Send To field that is already filled in with the correct recipient. This special kind of link is called a *Mailto link*, and you can add one to your own page as well.

1. Scroll down the Options frame to "add an email link," and click it.

2. In the Selection frame, type in your full e-mail address, and click Apply. Your page now contains a new Mailto link.

Now that you've added some basic information to your Web page, you're ready to configure what it looks like.

Configuring Visual Elements

When you're ready to configure visual elements, your work gets fun:

1. Scroll down the Options frame to the "preset color combination" link, and click it. A number of color schemes appear in the Selection frame, as shown in Figure 9-15.

2. Select one of the color combinations. As usual, the Preview frame immediately reflects your choice. You can see in Figure 9-16 that I chose a combination that includes a gray background.

Figure 9-15: Available color schemes for your page.

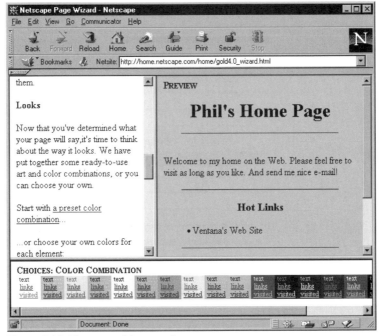

Figure 9-16: The page with new colors.

What if you don't like the color combinations available, or what if you want to add a background texture to your Personal Workspace? No problem. As you can see in the Options frame, the Wizard lets you choose custom colors for many display elements, including background color, background pattern, text color, link color, and visited link color. Simply click the appropriate option, and make your choices from the Selection frame.

Now scroll down and click the next link in the Options frame, the one that lets you choose a bullet style. As you can see in the Selection frame, several of the choices are actually animated GIFs. Instead of basic square or round bullets, you can use one of these graphics in your page for any bulleted lists you add.

Finally, the Wizard lets you choose a horizontal rule style. You know the drill: scroll down to the "choose a horizontal rule style" link, and click it. Now several choices for a horizontal rule appear in the Selection window, as shown in Figure 9-17. As with the bullets, several of them are animated. Some are even sort of Liberace-ish.

Figure 9-17: The horizontal rule option.

The horizontal rule you choose is the line that will separate the various areas of your page.

OK, you've added some information and some graphical interest to your page. Now comes the most important step: saving your work.

Saving Your Page

Saving is easy. When you've customized your page to your satisfaction, click the Build button at the very bottom of the left-hand Options frame. Immediately, the Navigator 4 browser window displays your new page, as shown in Figure 9-18.

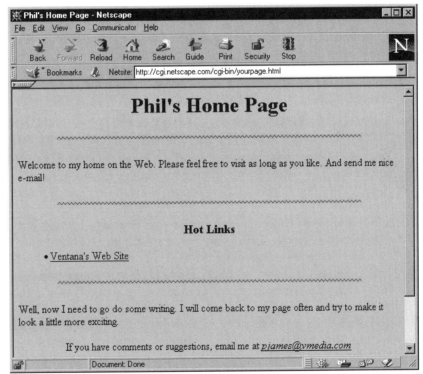

Figure 9-18: The Navigator window after clicking Build in the Page Wizard.

To save your page, simply press Ctrl+S or select Save As from the File menu. A Save As dialog box appears, letting you save your new file in any directory you want, either on your local hard drive or on a network drive. You may also change its name in the File name edit box. To edit your file some more, simply select Edit Page from the File menu. You are returned to Composer, with the current page available for more editing.

Naming Your Files

If you are planning to publish your pages on a Web server and want to make them accessible to the general public, you should name the top-level file (the one that people are supposed to see first, before clicking any links) **index.html** or **index.htm**. (Check with your system administrator or ISP about which extension to use.) Files with these names are treated a little differently by the Web server: they are displayed automatically when a user browses to your site. In other words, if you store your HTML files at http://friendly_server.com/~joe_blow/, users will see your index.html file just by entering that URL in their browser programs, without any filename explicitly specified. But if no index.html or index.htm file exists, the users will probably get a "File not found" error.

Creating Your Page Using a Page Template

Page templates are sample documents designed for specific purposes, such as a company newsletter or advertising for a small business. The idea is that you modify them for your own use, keeping elements of the original design and thus saving time over creating a page completely from scratch. You may be familiar with the concept of templates from your word processor.

Any Web page can serve as a page template; there is nothing really unique to them. However, using templates that are designed for that particular purpose is helpful. They will contain less nitty-gritty specific information and more broad design features that you can easily adapt to your own needs.

Netscape provides a number of page templates on its own Web site, and we will work with one of them now. However, the techniques discussed in this section apply to using any page template, whether it's one supplied by your MIS department and located on your office intranet or one you've developed yourself and are storing on your hard drive. Of course, to work with the templates located at Netscape's site, you have to be connected to the Net. Once you've established your connection, you can just follow these steps:

1. Run Composer by clicking its icon on your desktop or in the Component bar.

2. In the Composer window, click the far left New Page button. The Create New Page dialog box appears, as shown earlier in Figure 9-9.

3. Click From Template. The New Page from Template dialog box appears, as shown in Figure 9-19.

Figure 9-19: The New Page From Template dialog box.

4. As you can see, this dialog box lets you choose a local file to use as a template, or in fact a file located at any URL you specify. Since we're going to use one from Netscape's Web site, though, click the Netscape Templates button. In a few seconds, the Templates Page appears in a Navigator 4 window, as shown in Figure 9-20.

Figure 9-20: The Templates Page.

5. Read the text in the page; then scroll down and click the "My Home Page" link. Netscape then provides you with a template for a simple home page.

As you look over the template you've chosen, you can see that it includes some formatting and graphics elements that may be useful to you in your own page. Obviously, though, it needs a lot of modification. In the next section, we'll play around with the page in Composer, learning the most important of Composer's many commands.

To start editing the template in Composer, select Edit Page from Navigator's File menu. Composer appears, displaying the template as shown in Figure 9-21. Now would be a good time to press that Save button and save the file locally under whatever name you want to give it.

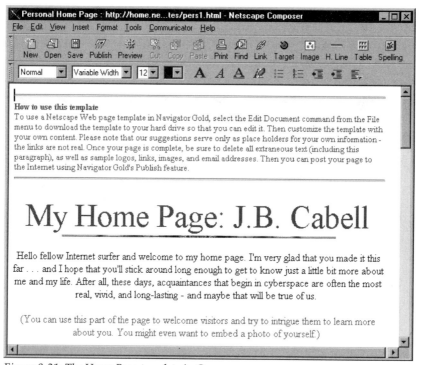

Figure 9-21: The Home Page template in Composer.

Rolling Your Own

The next section is about modifying a template, a Web document supplied by Netscape that can serve as a starting point for creating your own page. But if you are not starting with a template, you can also create a page from scratch. Just click the New Page icon in Composer, choose Blank Page, and either start typing or paste text in from any other Windows program. Once you have some material to work with, even just a word or two, the skills and commands covered in the next section will work for you just as well as they do for somebody starting from a template. The only difference between editing a template and editing a new blank document is how much material you start with. And, of course, something doesn't really have to be *called* a template to be used as one. A time-honored approach to creating Web pages is to take an existing one you like—from anywhere on the Web—and modify it sufficiently to call it your own. This approach is also an excellent way to hone your Web authoring skills.

One word of advice, though: as soon as you start working in your own document, save it right away to your hard drive (or a network drive) so you don't lose any of your work. To do so, click Composer's Save button or simply press Ctrl+S. Then select a location for your new file. Typically, you save all the documents that make up a particular Web page (text, graphics, sound files, and so on) together in a directory or folder. For example, you may want to save your first home page to the directory C:\home_page. This way, you can easily find your work if you want to modify it later. (You open Web files that already exist on your machine by clicking Composer's Open File button, the second from the left on the top toolbar.) In addition, this approach makes it easy to publish your work on a remote Web server. I'll cover this information later in the section "Publishing Your Page."

Modifying Your Page

Way back in Chapter 5, I showed you how to edit your e-mail messages so that they look just like Web pages. In this section, we'll cover many of the same Composer features in more detail, modifying your document until it looks exactly like you want it to. For the purposes of this exercise, we'll edit the template document we looked at earlier, but even if you're building a Web page completely from scratch, you'll use the same Composer features and commands. OK, let's get busy.

Editing Text

You're in the Composer window shown earlier in Figure 9-21. You've saved Netscape's home page template under a new filename and you're ready to start editing the content so that it's suited to your particular needs.

Composer supports the navigation keys that are typical in any Windows text editor, as shown in Table 9-1:

Navigation Key	Action
Left arrow	Moves the cursor left one character
Ctrl+left arrow	Moves the cursor left one word
Right arrow	Moves the cursor right one character
Ctrl+right arrow	Moves the cursor right one word
Up arrow	Moves the cursor up one line
Down arrow	Moves the cursor down one line
PgUp	Moves the cursor up one screen
PgDn	Moves the cursor down one screen
Home	Moves the cursor to the beginning of the line
Ctrl+Home	Moves the cursor to the beginning of the document
End	Moves the cursor to the end of the line
Ctrl+End	Moves the cursor to the end of the document

Table 9-1: Navigation keys in Composer.

TIP

The keys in Table 9-2 can help you edit a document faster, but if you forget them, you can access all the most important editing commands from the menus. And Communicator includes buttons for Cut, Copy, and Paste commands, just like common word processors. There's even a Find button for locating text within a document you're working on.

In addition, Composer supports a full range of keys or key combinations you can use to actually modify text, as shown in Table 9-2:

Key	Action
Backspace	Deletes the character to the left of the cursor
Del	Deletes the character at the current cursor position, or deletes selected text
Enter	Adds a line break, with a blank line below it
Shift+Enter	Adds a new line break, with no blank line below it
Ctrl+A	Selects the entire document
Ctrl+B	Changes selected text to boldface
Ctrl+C	Copies selected text
Ctrl+I	Changes selected text to italic font
Ctrl+Shift+L	Inserts a link at the cursor location
Ctrl+M	Increases the indent
Ctrl+Shift+M	Decreases the indent
Ctrl+S	Saves the file
Ctrl+V	Pastes the contents of the clipboard to the current cursor location
Ctrl+X	Cuts selected text
Ctrl+Z	Undoes the last editing change
Shift+Ctrl+Z	Redoes the last undone change
Shift+Ctrl+End	Selects text from the cursor position to the end of the document
Shift+Spacebar	Adds a nonbreaking space (a space that will not cause a line break)

Table 9-2: Text editing keys in Composer.

Now let's try out some of these keys. Using your mouse, move your cursor to the beginning of the line that reads My Home Page and click the left button. Now press the End key. Your cursor moves to the end of the line. Again using your mouse, click and drag over the name J.B. Cabell until it is selected (appears in reverse colors), as shown in Figure 9-22.

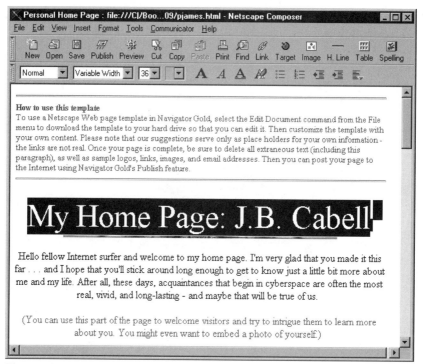

Figure 9-22: Some text selected.

At this point, you could delete the text you don't want, but replacing it is simpler. With the name still selected, just start typing your own name. The selected text is automatically replaced, as shown in Figure 9-23.

Using the keys listed in Tables 9-1 and 9-2, the Cut, Copy, Paste, and Find buttons, and commands on the Edit menu, you can modify all the text you want in the template document. But suppose after modifying the contents, you still don't like the way things *look*? Netscape Composer offers a full range of features for modifying the way text appears in a Web document.

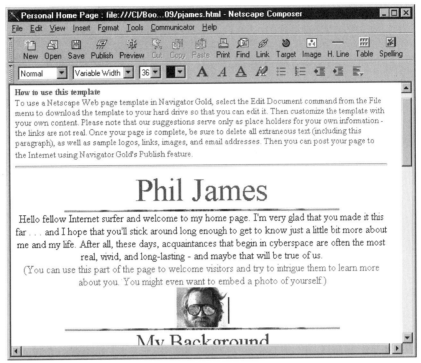

Figure 9-23: A new name.

Selecting a Style

The first control on the bottom of the two Composer toolbars is a drop-down list of *HTML styles*. Styles are tags that tell a Web browser or e-mail viewer to display text in a particular way. For example, a Heading 1 style tells the client program to display the corresponding text as a large header, usually surrounded on the top and bottom by some empty space. Let's change the style of the text we just edited:

1. Place your cursor anywhere in the line that reads Home Page: Phil James (or your own name). Since styles apply to an entire paragraph, you don't have to click and drag to select the line in order to change its style.

2. Click the arrow to the right of the drop-down style box (which now contains the Normal+ style tag), and select the Heading 1 item. Your

Composer window should now look something like Figure 9-24.

- Note that the text is now bold. This type face is a characteristic of the Heading 1 style, at least when it's displayed in Navigator 4. Composer shows you what the text in your page will look like in a Netscape browser, but it may look different in a different (non-Netscape) program because it is up to the client program to inter- pret HTML tags in a way that is appropriate to the system. A text-only browser, for example, will not be able to display a large bold font and may display all Heading 1 information set apart from other text and surrounded by asterisks, for example. These days, however, you're pretty safe assuming that for most people the page you're creating will look pretty much as it does to you in Composer.

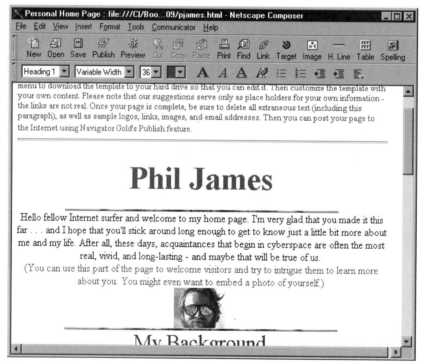

Figure 9-24: A new Heading 1 style added for the edited text.

Changing Fonts

Styles are a composite of different text display information, including relative size and positioning. But once you've chosen a style for a particular piece of text, you can tweak its appearance further, modifying font, size, color, and other characteristics. Let's change the display font for your name.

1. Click and drag your mouse across the words Phil James (or your own name) so that the entire phrase is selected (appears in reverse).

2. Click the arrow to the right of the Font list, and select Fixed Width. Your name will now look something like Figure 9-25.

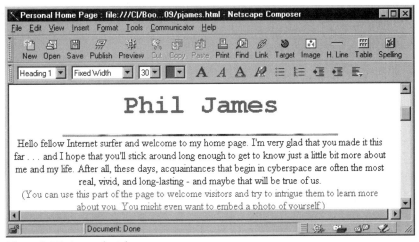

Figure 9-25: A new font for your name.

Changing Font Size

The next control lets you manipulate very precisely the relative size of your text. You can even select individual letters to create dramatic effects. In Figure 9-26, I've selected individual letters of my name. I've given the P a value of +1, the next letter a +2, and so on.

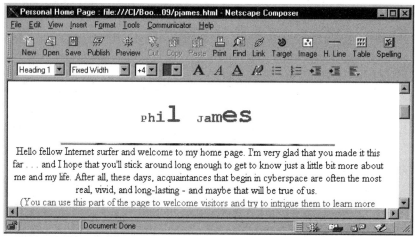

Figure 9-26: Fun with font sizes.

TIP

The drop-down list of font sizes may be configured to display relative HTML sizes, absolute point sizes, or both. See the section called "Configuring Composer" earlier in the chapter for a discussion of these options.

Play around a little on your own with custom font sizes.

Changing Font Color

I wish this book were printed in color so you could see what the next control does. Oh well, you can just try it on your own. Select some text from your page, and then drop down the list of colors, as shown in Figure 9-27.

Figure 9-27: The color list.

Now simply choose a new color for the text you've selected. Changing the font color is easier than painting your nails.

Adding Bold, Italic & Underline

Messenger makes it easy to add bold, italic, and underline text to your message. You do it with the three "A" buttons to the right of the color list. Here we go:

1. Click and drag your mouse to select your name once again.

2. Click the first two A buttons (bold and italic). Your window will now look something like Figure 9-28:

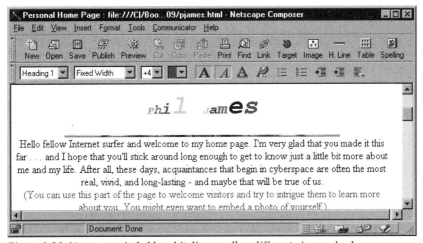

Figure 9-28: Your name in bold and italic as well as different sizes and colors.

Character Styles

Besides bold, italic, and underline, Messenger supports a number of other character styles such as subscript, superscript, and blinking text. To format text with these special attributes:

1. Select the text.

2. Select Style from the Format menu.

3. Choose the character style you wish to apply.

Don't like some of the character style changes you've made? You can always remove any styles you've added. Simply select the text you wish to "unstyle" and click the Remove All Styles button, just to the right of the Underline button. This feature not only removes character styles, it also removes any HTML links in the selected text.

Making a Bulleted or Numbered List

Let's make some more dramatic changes:

1. Place your cursor at the end of your name and press Enter.

2. On the new line, enter the phrase **A few things about me:** and press Enter.

3. On the next line, enter **Incredibly intelligent** and press Enter.

4. Enter **Warm and winning personality** and press Enter again.

5. Enter **Look like Antonio Banderas**. (Women may replace **Antonio Banderas** with **Melanie Griffith**.) Your page now looks something like Figure 9-29.

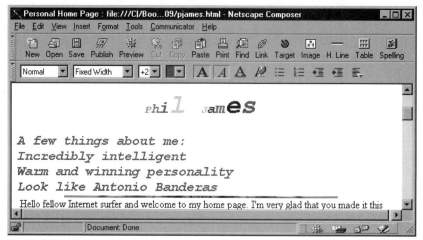

Figure 9-29: Some new text.

6. Click and drag to select the last three new paragraphs.

7. Click the Bullet List button. You'll see something like Figure 9-30.

Want a numbered list instead? Reselect the three new lines, and click the Numbered List button, just to the right of the Bullet List button. Voilà! People will *know* you're telling the truth because it looks so official.

Figure 9-30: A bulleted list.

List Styles

Composer includes some advanced options that let you adjust the appearance of your lists. To access these features, select all the items in your list by clicking and dragging. Then right-click, and choose Paragraph/List Properties from the context menu that pops up.

A dialog box appears with a List section in the center. In this List section, you can choose from a variety of styles, both for the list itself and for the bullets. You should experiment with these settings to see what looks best on your page.

If you've specified a numbered list rather than a bulleted list, you can also change the starting number of the first item in your selection.

Adjusting Indents

Composer lets you adjust how far a paragraph is indented. This feature is especially useful if you want to create multi-level lists. Check it out:

1. Select the numbered list you just created, and make it a bulleted list again. (Click the Bullet List button.)

2. Go to the end of the Antonio Banderas lie, I mean line, and then click your mouse and press Enter.

3. Enter **Two arms** and press Enter.

4. Enter **Two legs**.

5. Using your mouse, select these last two lines you typed.

6. Click the second of the two Indent buttons, the one with the *right* arrow indicating more indent. Figure 9-31 shows what you get:

Figure 9-31: A multi-level list.

You can use the leftmost Indent button to return the new items to the same level as the original three bulleted phrases if you want, or you can create yet deeper levels for your list. Feel free to experiment.

> **TIP**
>
> *You can also change the indentation by pressing the Ctrl+M and Ctrl+Shift+M keys.*

Changing Alignment

The last button on the bottom toolbar lets you specify the alignment for particular paragraphs. For example:

1. Scroll down the template document, and click your cursor anywhere in the paragraph under the "My Background" header, the paragraph that begins "I was born in a small town...."

2. Click the Alignment button, and then select the bottom of the three new buttons that appear, the Right Alignment button. The paragraph now looks like Figure 9-32.

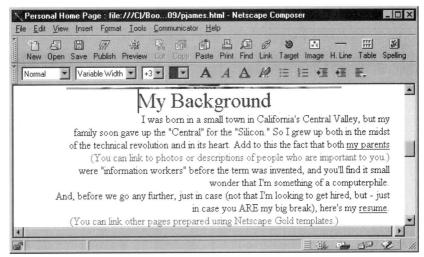

Figure 9-32: A right-aligned paragraph.

Netscape Composer lets you choose Left Alignment, Center Alignment, and Right Alignment. HTML does not currently support full or block justification, in which both the right and left edges of text are perfectly aligned.

The Preview in Navigator Button

Composer gives you a good "layout view" of your document, but it does not show you *exactly* what people will get when they surf to your page. Most significantly, in this special Netscape editing mode, you cannot click a link to jump to a new document—clicking in Composer is for editing the current file, not for hurtling yourself across the vast expanses of the Web.

In the next few sections, we'll work with adding links. To test these links, you'll have to leave the normal Composer window momentarily and view your document-in-progress in browser mode, just as any other client would view it. To do so, you click the Preview in Navigator button on the top Composer toolbar, the fifth button from the left. Once you've tested your links in the browser view, you can simply return to Composer for further editing.

Editing & Adding Links

The Web is about links, and of course you can use Composer to edit any links in the template document or to add new links of your own. In the "My Background" paragraph you just realigned, right-click the "my parents" link, and then select Link Properties from the context menu that pops up. A Link Properties dialog box appears, as shown in Figure 9-33.

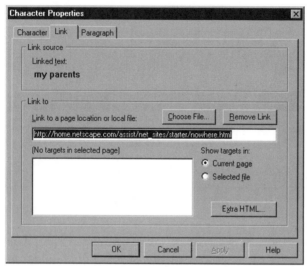

Figure 9-33: The Link Properties dialog box.

As you can see, the location of the linked file (a local file in this case) is already selected, so to change it, all you need to do is start typing. Alternatively, you can click the Choose File button to select a different HTML file from your own computer.

Linked Files & Relative Links

If you're like most Web authors, you've got more to say than you can fit in one HTML file. Typically, a Web site consists of several linked files. When people click a link in your main file, they are transported to a different file that gives more specific or detailed information about a particular topic. They can get back to the main file by clicking another "return" link.

So how do you keep these linked files organized as you're developing your Web site? The easiest approach is to keep them all in the same folder or directory on your hard drive, or in the same directory on a network drive. That way, you don't have to specify paths in the Link Properties dialog box shown in Figure 9-33. There is an added advantage to this approach: if you publish your pages on a remote Web server, Composer can automatically upload all these linked files to the same directory on the server. When a user clicks a link, the linked file will be in the right place. If your link had specified a particular location on your hard drive, the file might not be accessible to remote users—although Composer can be configured to adjust links during the upload process so that they're always valid.

You can also place linked files, including graphics, in subfolders or subdirectories of the main directory. For example, if your main HTML file is in your C:\home_page directory, you may want to store graphics in C:\home_page\graphics and other linked files in C:\home_page\more_html. When you specify these locations in the Link Properties dialog box, however, you should leave off the drive designator and just enter, for example, \home_page\graphics. That way, Composer can upload all the files to the same directory structure on a server. If your main HTML file is uploaded to the user1/home_page/ directory on a remote UNIX machine, the supplemental files can be uploaded automatically to user1/home_page/graphics/ and user1/home_page/more_html/, assuming those directories exist. Your linked files are located in the same place, *relative to each other*, no matter where you create or publish your site. By not specifying exact locations but only relative link locations, you're making sure that your Web site is portable to different servers, even if you don't use Composer to upload the files.

Of course, you can also create links to documents on completely different Web servers. To do so, you'd specify entire URLs, as in http://remote_server.com/directory/file.html.

But what about creating new links? That's just as easy:

1. Scroll down to the very bottom of the template document and press Enter a couple of times.

2. Click the Insert/Make Link button on the top Composer toolbar, the one with a chain link on it. Again, the Link Properties dialog box appears, as shown in Figure 9-34.

Figure 9-34: The Link Properties dialog box.

- Notice that this time no Link source or Link to text appears, since you are not editing an existing link.

3. In the Link source field, enter the words **Netscape Press Web Site**.

4. In the Link to field, type http://www.netscapepress.com.

5. Click OK. You are returned to your Web page, which now contains a link, as shown in Figure 9-35.

  - If you're an advanced user of HTML, you can add supplemental HTML commands to any link by clicking the Extra HTML button in the Link Properties dialog box. For example, you could add HTML attributes or JavaScript code right into the HREF tag that Composer creates.

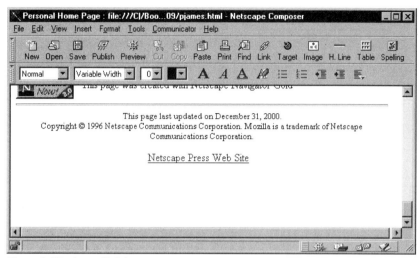

Figure 9-35: A new link in your page.

Composer includes a shortcut for turning text into links. Simply click and drag to select some text. Then right-click and choose Create Link Using Selected from the context menu that appears.

Drag & Drop Links

You can add links to your Web document in one other way: just drag them in!

Let's say you're cruising the Web with Navigator 4, and you find a site you like. You want to add a link to the site into your own page. All you have to do is drag Navigator 4's link icon, just to the left of the Netsite/Location box, into the Composer window. The link is copied directly into your page.

Instead of dragging the link icon, you can also simply drag a link from another page into the one you're working on. In addition, you can drag in links from the Bookmarks window and even from mail messages. If it's a link, Composer will take it!

Lastly, you can click the name of any HTML file on your desktop or in Explorer and drag it into the page you're working on. A link to that file is created automatically.

Adding Targets

Targets (also known as *anchors*) are different kinds of links. Instead of referring to a different HTML document, they refer to a particular location right within the current page. This capability can be useful when you're organizing a long document. Your reader clicks a link and is transported to the concluding remarks at the end of your page, for example, or back to the executive summary at the beginning. Let's add a target to the template page you've been working on:

1. Scroll to the section of the page titled "My Interests." Place your cursor just to the left of that heading.

2. Click the Insert Target button, just to the right of the Link button. A dialog box like the one in Figure 9-36 pops up.

Figure 9-36: The Target Properties dialog box.

3. Enter **interests** and press OK. You are returned to your page, which now includes a target icon next to the "My Interests" header.

   - This icon will *not* appear in your actual Web page. It appears only when your page is loaded in Composer to indicate to you the location of any anchors. You can also right-click the icon to change the properties, just as you right-click a regular link.

4. Place your cursor at the very top of the page, and click the Insert/Make Link button. The Link Properties dialog box appears, this time with your new anchor listed in the bottom text box as shown in Figure 9-37.

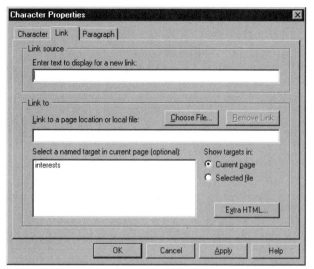

Figure 9-37: The Link Properties dialog box showing your new anchor.

5. In the Link source box, enter **Interests**.

6. Leave the Link to box blank.

7. Select the word interests in the bottom box. The link #interests is automatically entered into the Link to box.

   - The # character followed by the anchor name is the standard code for specifying a specific anchor location in an HTML file. Anchor locations may be included in URLs, too. For example, entering the URL http://www.phil.com/home_page/homepage1.html#interests in Navigator 4 would take you directly to the Interests section of the specified HTML file, assuming that anchor existed.

8. Click OK. You are returned to your page, which contains a new link as shown in Figure 9-38.

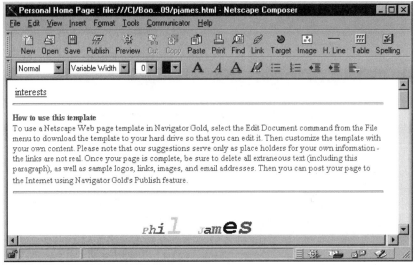

Figure 9-38: A new Interests link.

Clicking this new link in a browser window takes you down to the My Interests section of the document.

TIP

> *Remember, you can test any of these new links by clicking the View in Browser button.*

Adding a Picture

Just to the right of the Insert Target button is the Insert Image button. By now you've probably got this figured out: place your cursor where you want a picture in your document, and then click the Insert Image button. The button itself is pretty unassuming, but once you click it, you're faced with a pretty threatening dialog box, as shown in Figure 9-39.

Figure 9-39: The Image tab dialog box.

TIP

In this section, I'll show you how to add a new image to your page. But you use the same dialog box to change any of the properties of an image that's already in your page. To access this dialog box for editing your image properties, simply right-click the image and select Image Properties from the context menu that appears.

Don't worry, this dialog box is not as bad as it looks. Here we go:

- **Image location.** In the Image location field, you simply enter the URL of a remote picture you want to include in your message, or you can click the Choose File button and select a graphics file from your own hard drive or a network drive.

- **Edit Image button.** Once you've selected an image file, you can edit it with a graphics editor by clicking the Edit Image button. (To learn how to specify an external graphics editor that will be launched when you click this button, see the section called "Configuring Composer" earlier in this chapter.)

■ **Text alignment buttons.** The buttons in the middle of the dialog box are fairly self-explanatory. They control the spatial relationship between an image and the text that surrounds it. A number of configurations are available, and after pressing one of these buttons, you'll need to view your page in a browser window (click Composer's View in Browser button) to see how your choice looks.

■ **Dimensions.** Composer lets you adjust the size of an image you place in your page. You can set the dimensions either in pixels or in percentage of the window—you switch between these two units of measurement by selecting from the list box to the right of the actual dimensions. To return an image to its original size, click the Original Size button; to maintain the aspect ratio of an image—in other words to ensure that when you increase or decrease one dimension, the other dimension is adjusted proportionately—make sure the Lock width/height check box is checked.

■ **Space around image.** These settings are fairly self-explanatory. To add blank space around the image, set the top two boxes to a positive value. To add a solid border around your image, set the bottom box to a positive value.

■ **Remove Image Map button.** I'm sure you've already discovered that when you click a particular area in some images, you are transported to a different URL than if you'd clicked on a different area. The graphic at the very top of the Netscape home page is an example of this: click one part of the image and you get product information; click another and you are transported to the General Store. This movement is done through what is called an *image map*. An image map is a special supplemental file that associates areas of an image with corresponding actions. It is beyond the scope of this book to teach you how to create image maps in your own pages, but if you *do* know how to do it, the Remove Image Map button may be useful to you at times.

■ **Alt. Text/LowRes button.** Not all browsers are created equal. Some, such as Lynx, emphasize universality and portability over advanced features and display only text—no graphics at all. Lynx users will not see any of the pictures you add to your page. Fortunately, though, HTML lets you add a special *alt tag*. With the alt tag, you can specify some text that will display in place of the image on text-only systems. Let's say you're adding a picture of yourself to your page. Click this button and you can enter the words "picture of me" in the Alternate text box that appears. When text-only users view your page, they will know exactly what they are missing, and may even run out and buy a new browser. Note: This feature also makes your pages user-friendly for those people who have turned "Show Images" off in Navigator. Based on your *alt* descriptions, they can decide whether to display images for this particular page.

You access another helpful feature with this same button. You can specify an additional low resolution image that will load right away, while the main higher resolution image is still being transferred from Web server to browser. That way, your users won't have to wait too long before they see *something* on the screen. Typically, you'd specify a low resolution version of the same image.

- **Extra HTML button.** This button is for advanced users. It lets you add additional HTML tags or JavaScript for your image.

OK, let's add a picture. As you can see in Figure 9-40, I've specified a new image to appear at the current cursor location in my page. I have left all the other settings at their default values.

Figure 9-40: A new image specified in the Image Properties dialog box.

TIP

Remember, you can specify either a local file location or a remote URL.

Click Apply now, and the image appears in your page at the current cursor location, as shown in Figure 9-41.

Figure 9-41: The Web page with a new image.

Pretty simple, isn't it?

Actually, we can make it even easier. Read on!

After you drag a new image into the Web page you're working on in Composer, you will probably want to edit some of its attributes, such as size and exact position on the page. Simply right-click the image, and select Image Properties from the context menu. Additionally, you may want to save the image to your hard drive or a network drive under a new name. Again, right-click and select Save Image As from the menu that appears.

But what if you want to make the picture a link, so that when users click it, they are transported to a different URL?

With Composer, you can assign a URL to any image on your page. In the next section, you'll learn how to turn your images into clickable links.

Drag-and-Drop Images

Earlier you learned how you can drag links from other Web pages right into the Composer window. Well, you can do the same thing with images.

If you're cruising the Web with Navigator 4 and find a picture you like, click and drag it right into the Composer window. The image is immediately copied into your own Web page. **Note:** Make sure you're not violating any copyright restrictions!

In addition, you can click the name or icon of an image file on your desktop or in Explorer and drag it into the page you're working on. The image is immediately copied into your page.

But here's an even cooler feature: if you attempt to drag in an image that's not in GIF or JPEG format (common standards for the Internet and intranets), Composer may even convert it for you!

Let's say you have a BMP file you want to use in your page. But a BMP file may not display properly in some browser programs, and since it is larger it will transfer more slowly than a JPEG. When you drag a BMP file into your page in Composer, a dialog box appears that lets you choose a new name and a location to store the JPEG version of the file. Once you have selected a name and location, Composer then lets you choose what image quality you want. Make your choice, click OK, and your Web page now includes a brand new JPEG that's been converted from the bitmap you initially dragged in.

Making Your Picture a Link

Making your picture a link is a very quick procedure. Don't blink or you might miss it:

1. While you're still in the Images Properties dialog box shown in Figure 9-40, click the Link tab. The Link dialog box appears with your image specified in the Link source section, as shown in Figure 9-42.

Figure 9-42: The Link tab with image file specified.

2. In the Link to section, type in a URL or choose a local file that will be accessed when users click the image.

3. Click Apply. Your new image is now a clickable link!

TIP

> *There's a quick way to turn an image that's already in your page into a clickable link, or to modify the URL linked to an existing image. In Composer, simply place your cursor on the image and right-click your mouse. Then select Create Link Using Selected from the context menu that appears.*

We have only one more detail to deal with: positioning or *aligning* the image on the page.

Aligning the Image

OK, we're still in the Images Properties dialog box shown in Figure 9-40. Click the Paragraph tab this time. You see the tab shown in Figure 9-43.

Proceed directly to the Alignment section, and click one of the three option buttons, depending on whether you want your image to be centered on your page or aligned to the left or right margin. For the sake of this exercise, let's choose Right. Now click OK and you are returned to your Web page in the main Composer window, with a new image aligned to the right margin, as shown in Figure 9-44.

Figure 9-43: The Paragraph tab.

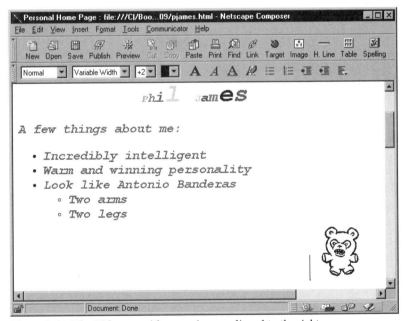

Figure 9-44: The Web page with a new image, aligned to the right.

You may want to add just a few more special elements to your Web page: *horizontal lines* and *tables*.

Adding a Horizontal Line

With all these fonts and pictures, your Web page is starting to look like—well, like a Web page. But what would a Web page be without those horizontal lines you see all over the place?

1. Place your cursor right after your name near the top of the page and press Enter.

2. In the top toolbar, click the Insert Horizontal Line button. You then see the page shown in Figure 9-45.

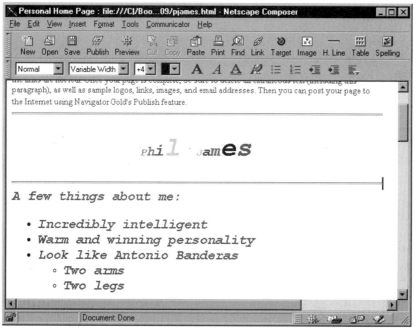

Figure 9-45: The page with a new horizontal line.

Don't like that line? Right-click it and choose Horizontal Line Properties from the context menu that pops up. The Horizontal Line Properties dialog box appears, as shown in Figure 9-46.

It's time to experiment again. Try different heights and widths. If you set your width to less than the width of your page, try different alignments. Or try using the 3D shading effect that's become ubiquitous on the Web. If you like what you come up with and want to set it as your default horizontal line, make sure the Save settings as default box is checked before you click OK.

Now we move on to one of HTML's most powerful features: tables.

Figure 9-46: The Horizontal Line Properties dialog box.

Adding a Table

We all know what tables are: things with rows and columns in them. You can easily spot a table in a Web page, so I'm not going to get into a lot of introductory fluff here. This section is going to be a learn-by-doing section. Here we go:

1. In Composer, with your Web template displayed, position your cursor just below the horizontal line we added.

2. Click the Insert Table button, the one at the far right of the top toolbar. The New Table Properties dialog box appears, as shown in Figure 9-47.

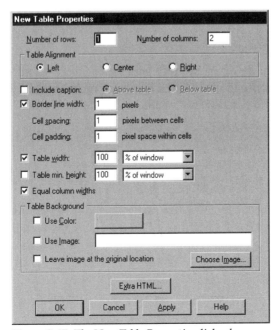

Figure 9-47: The New Table Properties dialog box.

3. Fill in the properties for your new table:

- Enter the number of rows and columns. For the purposes of this exercise, leave it at two each.

- In the table alignment section, click the Left option button if it is not already selected. Clicking this button will place your new table at the left edge of the page.

- For the purposes of this exercise, check the Include caption check box, and click the option button labeled "above." This feature will let you add a caption directly above your table.

- Enter a width for the table border. (Again, the default is fine.)

- Leave the cell spacing at 1 pixel as well.

- Cell padding refers to the minimum amount of space between any item within a cell (text, graphics, links, and so on) and the edge of the cell. You may want to adjust this setting occasionally to make your table look less busy, but for now the default is OK.

- The table width setting is just its initial width—you can stretch or shrink it once it's placed on your page. For the purpose of this tutorial, set the Table width value to 15% of the window.

- Table min. Height is what it sounds like: the minimum height for the table, no matter how little you add into its cells. Again, let's not mess with this setting.

- If you want your initial column widths to be identical, leave the Equal column widths option checked.

- If you want a new background color for the table, check the Use Color option and then click the button to the right. Select a new color from the palette that appears.

- The last two options let you choose an image instead of a solid color as the background for your table, and to specify whether the image file is left at its current location or sent along with the HTML file.

4. Click OK. You are returned to your page, which now includes a new table as shown in Figure 9-48.

Notice that your cursor is within the outlined area above the table. In this area, you add a caption, so start typing. How about entering the words **My new table**, as shown in Figure 9-49.

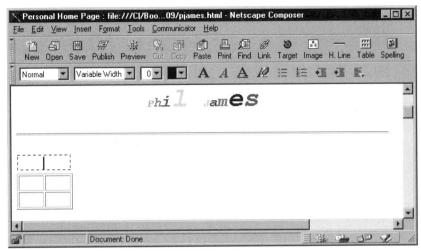

Figure 9-48: A new table.

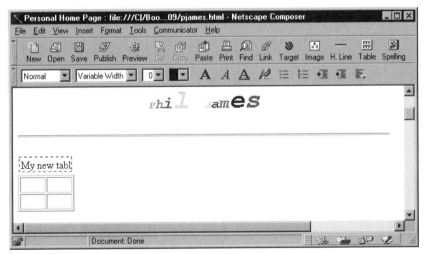

Figure 9-49: Adding a caption.

Hmm, doesn't look very good. The words don't fit very well in the box, do they? No problem. Place your mouse cursor on the right edge of the table; then click and drag to the right. You widen your table this way, as shown in Figure 9-50.

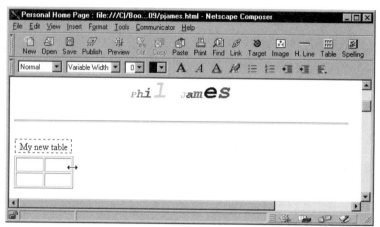

Figure 9-50: Widening the table.

This method is not the only way to widen the table, though. Individual columns widen to accommodate material (text, graphics, links, and so on) placed within them. Let's try widening these columns:

1. Make the table very narrow again by clicking and dragging the right edge leftward.

2. Place your cursor in the top left cell, and enter **Wideningthecolumn....** The column grows as you type, as shown in Figure 9-51.

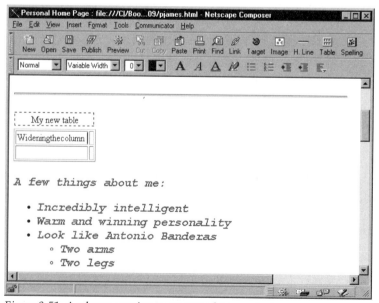

Figure 9-51: A column growing to accommodate new text.

Of course, you can also change the attributes of text in a table the same way you change the attributes of text *anywhere* in your Web page: just select it and start playing with the style, size, and font buttons. Again, your table will resize itself to accommodate your modified text.

To align text within a cell, simply select it and click the regular Composer Alignment button. You can then center the text or align it to the left or right of the cell.

Adding Images & Links to a Table

As I mentioned, text is not the only thing you can put into a table. Any element you can place in your Web page you can place just as easily in a table cell. Let's move an image from the main body of our Web page into a table cell:

1. Click and drag to select the image we recently added to the Web page, shown earlier in Figure 9-44.

2. Press Ctrl+X to cut the image. Alternatively, you can click the Cut button in the toolbar.

3. Place your cursor in the top right cell of the new table, and press Ctrl+V to paste the image. (You could also select Paste from the toolbar.) Your table now contains the image, as shown in Figure 9-52.

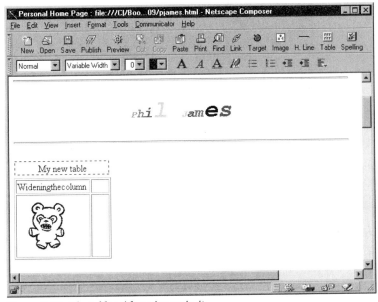

Figure 9-52: The table with an image in it.

What about links? You create them in tables the same way you create them in the rest of your page. For example, to make the new image a link, you follow these steps:

1. Right-click the image in the table.

2. From the context menu that pops up, select Create Link Using Selected.

3. In the Link tab that appears, fill in the Link to field as you would for any other link.

Row & Cell Properties

We've already set a variety of properties for the table as a whole. You can change them, by the way, by placing your mouse anywhere in the table, right-clicking, and selecting Table Properties from the context menu. Then select the Table tab, which looks just like the New Table Properties dialog box we saw earlier. You may want to change the number of rows or columns, for example.

But Composer also lets you change the configuration of individual rows and cells. For example, you can make every row a different color if you want, or even every cell! Let's take a closer look at these options:

1. Place your cursor inside a cell of the table and right-click.

2. When the context menu appears, select Table Properties. The Table Properties dialog box appears, as shown in Figure 9-53. Notice that this time it has three separate tabs: Table, Row, and Cell.

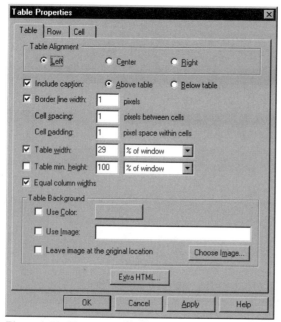

Figure 9-53: The Table Properties.

3. Unless you want to change the configuration of the table as a whole, click the Row tab, as shown in Figure 9-54.

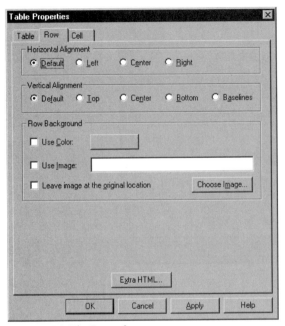

Figure 9-54: The Row tab.

In this tab, you can choose a variety of options for the entire row where your cursor is currently positioned. For example, you can adjust the text alignment so that all text within the row is aligned at the right edge, or you can adjust vertical alignment so that all text within the row sits on the bottom of the cells rather than hovering in the middle. If you choose Default for either of the alignment options, the row will simply "inherit" the alignment properties already established in the Table tab.

You can also choose a color for the row. Simply select the Use Color option, click the button to its right, and select from the palette that appears. As with the table as a whole, you can also specify a background image. When you've configured the row to your satisfaction, click the Apply button.

Now, you can change the properties for the individual cell at the current cursor position:

1. Click the Cell tab, as shown in Figure 9-55.

Figure 9-55: The Cell tab.

2. Select attributes for the individual cell:

- You're already familiar with the text alignment options, so let's leave them alone. "Default," in this case, means that the cell will inherit the text alignment attributes of its row; if the corresponding text alignment attribute in the Row tab is also set to Default, the cell will inherit the attribute of the table as a whole.

- Enter the size of your cell in the next two boxes. As you can see, a single cell may span multiple rows and columns. To see what this looks like, enter **2** in the right-hand columns box.

- In the next line, you can choose to apply a Header style to the text in your cell. You can also determine whether the text will wrap to another line when you reach the right edge of the cell.

- The rest of the options—cell width, height, and background color—are ones you've already seen in the Row and Table tabs. If you want to adjust the size or color of an individual cell, this is the place to do it. And again, you can even add separate images to individual cells.

3. After you've finished adjusting the properties of an individual cell, click OK to return to your page.

Figure 9-56 shows a table whose cells have been customized using the procedures outlined above.

Figure 9-56: A table with customized cells.

We've been buried in some pretty technical nitty-gritty for a while, and we're almost done messing up—I mean modifying—the home page template. But before putting it out into the world, you better check your spelling.

Checking Your Spelling

Cant spel wurth a dam? With Comunicater, that's rilly not an ishew.

See that button with the ABC and the checkmark on it? That's your personal spelling assistant. Click it and you can make your Web page read like it's been thoroughly worked over by Netscape Press' crack editorial team.

Figure 9-57 shows a section of the page with a few problem words in it.

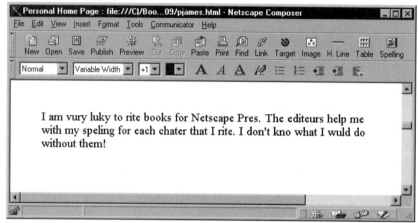

Figure 9-57: A section of the page with spelling mistakes.

Click the Check Spelling button and you see something like Figure 9-58.

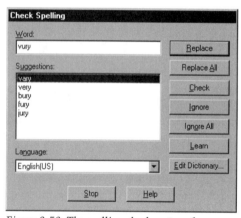

Figure 9-58: The spelling checker at work.

The spelling checker has found the first of the errors. If you've used Microsoft Word or any other major word processing program, this dialog box should look pretty familiar to you. It offers you an alternate spelling for the word, or in some cases a list of possible spellings. If you don't like the choice or choices it offers you, type in the correct spelling in the Change To box yourself. Here's what the various buttons do:

- **Replace.** The spelling checker changes the currently selected word to the spelling that is highlighted in the Suggestions box. Highlight the spelling you want to use before clicking the Replace button. You can also type a new spelling directly into the Word before clicking the Replace button.

- **Replace All.** The spelling checker changes every instance of this particular misspelling within your page.

- **Ignore.** If you click this button, the spelling checker doesn't bother correcting the selected word and instead goes on to the next misspelling it finds, if any.

- **Ignore All.** If you click this button, the spelling checker won't stop at any further words in your message that are spelled this way.

- **Stop.** Click this button to exit the spelling checker. It will not look for any further errors in your page unless you press the Check Spelling button again.

- **Learn.** If you click this button, the spelling checker adds the selected word, as it is currently spelled in your message, to a custom dictionary. Once it is added to the dictionary, the spelling checker will no longer consider it a misspelling when it encounters this word in *any* page (or e-mail message) you create. This can be useful for unusual proper nouns and specialized technical words that you use frequently.

- **Edit Dictionary.** This button lets you edit your custom dictionary directly, adding words that the spell checker will not flag as errors when it encounters them. For instance, if you often spell check Web pages that include your own e-mail address, you might want to add that address to the dictionary, as shown in Figure 9-59.

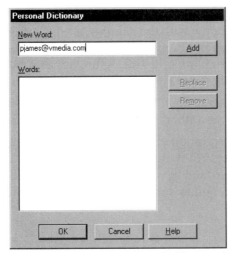

Figure 9-59: Adding your e-mail address to the Personal Dictionary.

You can also use this feature to *delete* words from your dictionary.

Figure 9-60 shows the section of the page after Communicator's spelling checker has done its job:

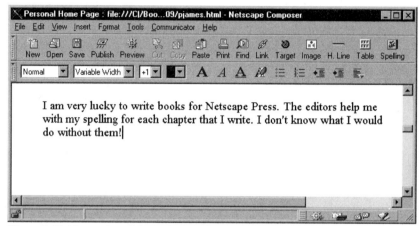

Figure 9-60: The section of the Web page after spell checking.

OK, we're in the home stretch now. You're almost ready to release your page on the unsuspecting public. But first, we must address a few broad, general options that affect various characteristics of the page as a whole, not just individual elements within it.

Page Colors & Properties

Let's do some more beautifying:

1. Still in the Composer window with the page we're working on displayed, select Page Colors and Properties from the bottom of the Format menu. The Page Colors and Properties dialog box appears, with the General tab selected as shown in Figure 9-61.

2. In the top part of the General tab, fill in a title for your page. If your own name doesn't appear as the author, modify that information as well.

3. You can enter a short description of your page, as well as some keywords and a classification. All these information fields will appear as special "Meta Name" tags within your document and may be used by browsers and by search engines such as Yahoo to help users find and classify the page.

Figure 9-61: The Page Properties dialog box with the General tab selected.

Now let's move on to Colors and Backgrounds for your page:

1. Click the Colors and Background tab, as shown in Figure 9-62.

Figure 9-62: The Colors and Background tab.

2. To change the overall color scheme of your message, select from the drop-down Color schemes list. The "Use custom colors" option button is automatically selected, and you are shown a sample of your new colors.

3. To change individual elements within the chosen color scheme, click any of the buttons for Normal Text, Link Text, and so on, and then select a new color from the palette that appears. Note that you can also change the background color of your page.

4. If you want to return to the default colors, click the option button at the top labeled "Use the Browser's color settings."

You can also specify an image, rather than a solid color, to use as the background for your message. To do so, follow these steps:

1. Check the Use Image check box in the Background Image section.

2. Click the Choose File button. A Select Image File dialog box appears, as shown in Figure 9-63.

Figure 9-63: The Select Image File dialog box.

3. Choose a GIF or JPEG file from your local hard drive or network drive and click Open.

TIP

To make your Web page reference the image file in its current location, check the "Leave image at the original location" check box.

As you work with these appearance changes, you can click Apply at any time to see what they look like in your actual page. Remember, reverting to your original look is as simple as choosing an option button, so you're in no real danger of messing up your page. If you like what you've done, though, and want to use your customized color scheme as a default in future pages you create, check the check box labeled "Save these settings for new pages."

When you're done with the Colors and Background settings, click the META Tags tab. It is beyond the scope of this book to cover advanced HTML commands, but on this tab you enter META tags and user variables. If you don't know what I'm talking about, take a look at Netscape Press' excellent book *HTML Publishing for Netscape*.

Click OK to accept all your Page Property changes and return to the main Composer window.

Saving Your File

Ow, just look at that page! I've demonstrated how you can turn a perfectly good template into a useless mess. But, hey, you can't learn to create Web pages if you don't get your virtual hands dirty. You've learned to manipulate text and graphics elements so well by now that you can continue working on the file on your own, adding and deleting and moving things around until you've got something you'll be proud to show the whole world. Well, to show your mother, anyway. But before you show it to her, make sure to save it. Just click the Save button, select a location for your file, and type in a filename.

Once you've saved your page the way you want it, you're ready to publish it. I'll show you how in just a minute. But before that, here's a short section for my geek readers on how to manipulate HTML code directly. Non-geeks may skip ahead to the section called "Publishing Your Page."

Editing Your HTML Source

As I mentioned earlier in the chapter, sometimes you may want to leave the comfortable Composer interface and plunge into the details of actual HTML code. You may want to tweak a value so that graphical elements line up exactly the way you want them to, or you may want to add some frames, JavaScript, or advanced HTML tags that are not available through Composer. Fortunately, Composer makes it easy to jump back and forth between a text editor and its own interface. Using the same template file, let's see how this works:

1. In Composer, with the template file we've been working on open, select HTML Source from the Edit menu. You will be asked whether you want to save your changes to the file. Click OK.

   If you haven't specified an external HTML editor in the Composer preferences, you will be asked to specify one now. See the "Configuring Composer" section near the beginning of this chapter.

2. Follow any instructions that appear for specifying an HTML editor. Composer will launch your external editor with the HTML source for your page loaded. Figure 9-64 shows the HTML source in WordPad.

Figure 9-64: HTML source file in WordPad.

3. Make any changes you want to the HTML code, and then click your text editor's Save command. For now, do not close the file or your text editor.

TIP

If your editor can save files in a variety of word processor formats, make sure to save your HTML file as ASCII text.

4. Go back into Composer. As soon as you select the Composer window on your desktop, a Reload File dialog box pops up.

5. To see the effects of the changes you made directly to the HTML code, click Yes. Composer reloads the page with your changes.

6. If you want to make more changes to the HTML code, return to your text editor and repeat steps 3 through 5. You can bop back and forth *ad nauseum* between your text editor window and the Composer window.

7. When you've made all the changes you want, close your text editor.

And now that you've tweaked your page to your satisfaction, it's time to go public!

Composer Plug-ins

Directly editing HTML code is only one option for tweaking your page and adding niceties that aren't available through the Composer interface. Netscape has actually provided a mechanism for incorporating new capabilities right into Composer: Composer plug-ins.

You already know about regular plug-ins and how they can be used to enhance the multimedia powers of Navigator. Composer plug-ins are very similar. They are special add-on programs that you can download from Netscape and other Web sites. Once a Composer plug-in is installed, the new feature it provides is listed right in Composer's Tools menu. For example, a plug-in might allow you to change selected text to small caps or some other special font. The command to do this will appear on the Tools menu along with the other Composer features. And, of course, you can have as many plug-ins as you want.

It is beyond the scope of this book to discuss Composer plug-ins in depth, but for more information check out Netscape's Home Page.

Publishing Your Page

You've been working for hours on your page, adding text and graphics, adjusting the relative position of various elements, creating tables.... At a certain point, you realize that the law of diminishing returns has taken effect, and you need to let go and let *other* people be dazzled by your creativity.

Of course, you can simply put your HTML files on a network drive where they will be accessible to others. That is the simplest way to publish your work, but as I mentioned earlier, it's not always the best. To really exploit the power of Web publishing, you need to publish your files on an actual Web server. And to do that, you use Composer's Publish button, the fourth button from the left on the top toolbar. Let's try it:

1. Make sure you are connected to your intranet or to the Net itself.

2. In Composer, and with a Web file loaded, click the Publish button. The Publish Files dialog box appears, as shown in Figure 9-65.

Figure 9-65: The Publish Files dialog box.

If you've followed the instructions up until now, the top section of this dialog box should already contain the title of your page as well as its actual filename. And if you've already chosen a default publishing site for your Web pages, the correct HTTP or FTP location field may be filled in as well. If it is not, you can click the Use Default Location button or even type in the correct address now. And if you have already uploaded files to various Web servers, you may be able to select the correct URL from the drop-down list.

Once you have entered the correct address to send your files, fill in any User name and Password information that's necessary to complete the upload. You can get this information from your system administrator or your ISP. If you're using an ISP's Web server, in many cases this information will be the same as for your regular SLIP/PPP account. Notice that Composer can also "remember" your password so that you don't have to type it in each time you upload files to your Web server.

In the bottom section of this dialog box, you can construct a list of *all* the files you wish to upload to your Web server. If your page contains images, you can choose to upload just the image files by selecting the left-hand option button. If you want to upload HTML or other files, click the right-hand option button. The window now displays all the files in the current directory or folder, and they are all selected for upload. You can click any individual file to *de*-select it, or click again to re-select it. In addition, you can use the Select All and Select None buttons to speed up the process of selecting files for upload. Remember, you must upload any local files you've created that are linked to your main file, as well as any image files that appear in your page.

When you're ready to send your files to the Web server, just click OK. That's all there is to it!

Moving On

In this chapter, you've learned how to use Composer to create and publish your own Web pages. Congratulations! You have joined the vanguard of modern electronic publishing!

Of course, I only scratched the surface of this very large topic. There are thousands of different ways to enhance Web pages with innovative design, multimedia, JavaScript, and little tricks that keep Web geeks awake all night. In the next chapter, I cover some of the powerful multimedia features available in Communicator, but mainly from the viewpoint of the browser rather than the Web author. If you want more in-depth information about Web authoring, dozens of books—maybe even hundreds—are available. Be sure to select one published by my friends at Ventana.

OK, on to some of the most exciting features of Communicator. By the end of the next chapter, you will indeed be a Web power user.

CHAPTER 10

Power Communicator 4

As you learned in the last chapter, Communicator is one of the most robust tools available for displaying a wide range of multimedia content. But the story doesn't end there. As new technologies develop, Netscape is quick to incorporate them. And Communicator even includes methods by which developers can tack new modules onto the program, seamlessly integrating powerful new multimedia features. This open architecture ensures that Communicator will stay current as the world at large comes up with ever more exciting ways to package information.

In this chapter we'll look at four ways in which Communicator is keeping up with all the changes in multimedia presentation:

- VRML 2.0 support, letting you navigate the three-dimensional virtual worlds that are starting to crop up around the Net. VRML 2.0 is the best legal way to get dizzy without leaving your desk chair.

- Plug-ins, which allow developers to extend Communicator's power in all kinds of imaginative ways. Plug-ins are software components you can add to Navigator as needed to process multimedia and other non-HTML files. Thanks to a couple of plug-ins, my computer is now playing MIDI music files off the Net while it displays 3D models of agricultural chemicals. OK, so I'm a geek.

- Support for the hundreds of Java applets available on the Web, as well as the thousands waiting to be written. Java is a full-featured, general-purpose programming language, and Communicator is designed to execute Java programs referenced in Web pages. This means that the ways to extend Communicator are virtually limitless. In addition, many Netcaster channels (see Chapter 4) are implemented in Java.

■ JavaScript is a much simpler language whose statements can be incorporated directly in Web pages to extend Navigator's capabilities. JavaScript can make sure you've entered a valid zip code in a Web form, make text scroll across your screen, or even replace the status information at the bottom of the browser window with a joke. I think of JavaScript as the tool of choice for "stupid Navigator tricks" (as well as some pretty clever Navigator tricks).

TIP

This chapter emphasizes the use of advanced presentation features in Navigator 4. But all the same multimedia power is available in Netcaster as well. For instance the same kinds of plug-ins that extend Navigator's capabilities also extend the power of Netcaster, and the Java and JavaScript features mentioned here apply to Netcaster as well. For more information on Netcaster, please see Chapter 4.

Feeling adventurous? Let's start right in with VRML.

VRML

First, how do you say it? Some people say V-R-M-L, carefully articulating each letter, but they're not the cool people. The cool people say *VER-MUHL*, with the stress on the first syllable just like in *thermal*.

And what exactly does it stand for? *V*irtual *R*eality *M*odeling *L*anguage. It's really a pretty simple concept. Just as HTML is a markup language that tells a Web browser to display various elements such as headings, italic text, and links, VRML is an extension (a special plug-in), which tells a Web browser to display various components of three-dimensional *virtual worlds*. These include objects that rotate or otherwise move through space in a "realistic" way, as well as graphical backgrounds that make you feel as if *you're* moving as you manipulate your mouse. To get technical, VRML is a standard for encoding computer-generated graphics into a file format for transmission across the Net or an intranet; it is also the standard a Web browser uses to interpret and display these graphics so that you can interact with them. Some people see VRML as an eventual replacement for HTML itself, offering a more intuitive and lifelike way of navigating the Web. (Personally, I think they're wrong, but my publisher sometimes has to remind me that the title of this book is not *Phil's Opinions, Vol. 1*.)

Moving Worlds? Live3D? Cosmo?

Here's some more terminology you may encounter, but first a little history.

Originally, Silicon Graphics (SGI) came up with Open Inventor, a file format that became the basis for VRML; they also developed QvLib, which was the software component responsible for "understanding" and interpreting the file. Gavin Bell of SGI then wrote the proposal for the VRML 1.0 standard. The standard was adopted, and developers began implementing it.

Of course as soon as version 1 of any standard is accepted by the technology community, somebody starts working on version 2. There have been several rival proposals, but the one that really caught on is called *Moving Worlds*. Developed and supported by a broad consortium of software and hardware vendors, it provides many new features including full motion, live content and animation, enhanced audio, and the ability to connect with databases. Most importantly, it has strong support for multiuser interactivity. You won't have to get dizzy alone any more.

Just as the HTML standard doesn't specify exactly what a heading or footnotes should look like in every Web browser, VRML doesn't specify exactly how to display graphical objects such as wire-frame models. Virtual worlds may look and feel a bit different from one VRML browser to another. *Live3D* is simply Netscape's own particular implementations of VRML 2.0; Cosmo is the implementation for 32-bit systems (Windows 95 and NT).

OK, let's go ahead and try some VRML navigation.

VRML Navigation

There are VRML sites you can get to right from the Netscape home page, but first we're going to try something even simpler. Netscape includes a sample VRML file with the program, so you can try your hand at exploring virtual worlds without even being connected to the Net. Let's try it:

1. From the Navigator File menu, select Open Page. Optionally, you can simply press Ctrl+O. The Open dialog box appears.

2. In the "Files of type" drop-down list at the bottom of the dialog box, select VRML Worlds.

3. Now navigate to the following directory: Program Files\Netscape\ Communicator\Program\Plugins\Cosmo\ui\.

4. Once you are in the correct folder, double-click on the file vrml.wrl, back in the dialog box and click Open. After a few seconds, a three-dimensional page appears, as shown in Figure 10-1.

Figure 10-1: Navigator 4 with VRML page.

Let's take a few minutes to get oriented. There are seven clickable labels along the bottom of the window: Walk, Spin, Look, Slide, Point, Lamp, and View. Each of these labels represents a different operational mode for your controls. In other words, if you click Slide, your mouse and keyboard might act differently in the window than they do when you click Walk.

And since you've got to walk before you can slide, let's start there:

1. Make sure the Walk mode is selected. (Modes are yellow when selected.)

2. Move your mouse around the window. Notice whenever your pointer rests on the large N, the words *Live3D Home Page* appear, as shown in Figure 10-2.

Figure 10-2: Link to Netscape's Live3D site in the sample VRML page.

This is a simple link to the Netscape Live3D home page. Links in VRML do not appear as underlined text, but as a temporary element in the graphic.

3. If you are currently connected to the Net, try double-clicking your left mouse button while the link is displayed. You are transported to the Live 3D site. Click the Back button to return to the VRML page. If you are running Windows 95 or NT, you can also click the Cosmo logo at the bottom right corner of the window to access the Cosmo home page.

TIP

At some VRML sites, you need to be in Point mode in order to see links to other URLs. For Point mode, simply click the Point label.

4. Now click your left mouse button and while holding it down, drag your mouse slowly around the window. Notice that you seem to move in relation to the images, as shown in Figure 10-3.

Figure 10-3: Moving around the sample VRML image.

As you drag to the right or left, you seem to move right or left in relation to the object.

As you drag up, you seem to move toward the object.

As you drag down, you seem to move away from the object.

TIP

You can also use your arrow keys to move left, right, forward, and back.

5. Ready for some fun? Try dragging with your *right* mouse button instead of the left. Immediately you see the power of VRML: you are now moving around the object as if it's three-dimensional (see Figure 10-4).

6. One more move: hold down the Alt key while dragging with the left mouse button. The object "slides" in the window in a two-dimensional manner. In other words, the up-and-down component of your mouse movement does not change your apparent distance from the object.

Figure 10-4: Three-dimensional movement.

TIP

In Walk mode, the A and Z keys slide you up and down.

7. OK, I was lying. There's still one more move I want to show you. Click the View label. The VRML window returns to its original state, as shown in Figure 10-1.

Lost in Cyberspace

I sure love that View label. I was born in the early fifties and never saw a video game until I was an adult. My idea of fast-paced action was when the Lone Ranger and Tonto discovered a hideout, one that looked suspiciously like the hideout they found in the previous episode. Now drop me into a VRML page, and in a matter of seconds I'm hopelessly lost, wandering the far reaches of space looking for something—*anything*—recognizable.

My kids, on the other hand, seem to find virtual worlds utterly familiar, warm, and homey. So if you were born before the Kennedy assassination, here's my big hint for exploring VRML effectively: bring a kid along, and if you can't bring a kid just keep clicking that View button.

Now let's check out some animation. Click your right mouse button and drag to the right until you see the image as three distinct objects: the Netscape logo, the set of geometric shapes, and the lamp. OK, let go of that right mouse button before everything slides off your screen! Now put your cursor over the lamp until the word "Headlight" appears. Click it and what happens is shown in Figure 10-5.

That's right, simply by clicking you have adjusted and turned on the lamp. It casts its light on the other objects, changing their appearance appropriately. In fact, if you move the objects around so that the lamp casts its light behind the Netscape logo, it lights it up like a rear-projection screen. This demonstrates some of the power of Navigator.

Want to turn the lamp off? You guessed it, just click Headlight again.

OK, enough of the baby stuff. Are you ready for some motion sickness?

1. Click the Look label.

2. Start looking around by dragging with the left mouse button. As you discover immediately, you are now moving through space very quickly.

Figure 10-5: Results of clicking the Headlight object

The way the labels work in different VRML worlds varies a bit. For example, try turning the lamp on again, clicking the Lamp label, and then playing with the up and down arrows just to the left of it. In this particular 3D world, the arrows act like a dimmer switch, and you can make the objects blaze with light or create a soft romantic mood. Well, almost. Anyway, that's how it works in *this* virtual world, but in another the Lamp label might simply turn underlining on and off! The only way to know what's going to happen is to click.

> **TIP**
>
> *Notice that each of the geometric shapes is also a control that affects the way you navigate this world. The red cube puts you into Walk mode, the green sphere puts you into Fly mode, and the blue cone puts you into Point mode. This use of custom objects as navigational controls is typical of Live3D worlds.*

The VRML Context Menu

One of the most powerful features of VRML is that it lets *you* control the way the graphic information appears on your screen. You can do this by clicking your right mouse button anywhere within the browser window. A Context menu pops up, as shown in Figure 10-6.

Figure 10-6: The Context menu.

From the Context menu there are a number of ways to reconfigure your navigation environment. I'm not going to cover all of these, mainly because they're a lot harder to describe than they are to explore. You can have some fun checking them out on your own, but here are a few things to try:

- Want to make your travels really wild? Select Bank when Flying from the Navigation submenu. Your imaginary craft will tilt in the direction of your turns.

- Getting too dizzy or confused? Select Stay on Ground when Walking from the Navigation submenu.

- Want to turn off the buttons at the bottom of the window for a better view of your virtual world? Uncheck the Navigation Bar item on the Options submenu.

If you want to preserve the changes you have made, simply click Save Current Settings As Default in the Options submenu.

What's the Point?

So far, VRML applications have concentrated on pretty, imaginative pictures. You can see some great examples of individual images at http://www.tcp.ca/gsb/VRML/vrml-modelshop.html. (Don't miss the rotating zebra head!) But what about more serious applications?

Well, just about everything you can do with ordinary HTML you can do with VRML as well. VRML pages can include links to other documents, enhance sites with sound and video, and even collect user information for online transactions. You can think of the added dimension as providing yet more ways to organize information.

In addition, VRML provides a visual analog for the "real" world. Imagine an online real estate company providing three-dimensional models of houses. You could check out the front yard, then the back yard, then go inside and wander through the rooms. You could click various appliances to find out what brand they are or how old they are. And think of the educational possibilities: kids in school wandering through three-dimensional depictions of the human body, clicking to get more information on their favorite organs.

No, you're not going to see that in 1997, but it's quite likely in 1998. VRML is just emerging from its "proof of concept" stage, and real-world applications haven't caught up with the technology yet. In addition, VRML pages are still pretty slow to load over modem connections. But for a taste of things to come, check out Netscape's own showcase site at http://home.netscape.com/comprod/products/communicator/multimedia/live3d/cool_worlds/index.html.

Plug-ins

Right out of the box (or the CD sleeve), Netscape Communicator lets you experience most of what is available on the Net. But as the Web becomes more popular and the technology improves, more sophisticated multimedia content is becoming available all the time. You just saw, for instance, how VRML is adding new dimensions to Web content—literally. Movies, desktop-published documents, and video conferencing are slowly making their way onto the Web as well. Not only are these new types of data putting strains on the infrastructure of the Internet, they are also forcing Web browsers to evolve from text and graphics displayers to real-time, interactive multimedia viewers.

Not to worry. Your investment in Netscape Communicator is a good one. The Netscape developers have come up with an open-extendible architecture that lets the program evolve as technology itself evolves. Through plug-in applications developed by independent software vendors, Navigator 4 and Netcaster enable you to experience most of what is currently available online.

Plug-ins extend Communicator's capabilities so that it can display or play a wide variety of documents and file types, such as Adobe Acrobat PDF (Portable Document Format) files, Macromedia Director movies, and MIDI music files. It uses what's known as its *Live Objects* technology to enable developers to create rich multimedia content for the Internet or office intranets.

Up until Netscape Navigator 2.0, Web users were required to configure separate helper applications that worked independently of their Web browsers to view and control most multimedia documents. Now when you download and configure plug-ins to work with Netscape Navigator 2.0 or later, the plug-ins effectively become part of the browser itself. Movies, sound events, presentation graphics, and more display directly in the Navigator 4 window. In fact, plug-ins are so well integrated with the program that you'll quickly forget you're using them.

How Plug-ins Display in Navigator 4

When you use a plug-in with Netscape Communicator, it may not always be apparent that the plug-in is a separate application. With helper applications, you always know when a graphics program or a media player starts because you see it display in a separate window. Plug-ins, however, can interact with Navigator 4 in one of three modes of operation:

- **Full-screen plug-ins.** Full-screen plug-ins are just that—plug-ins that take up an entire browser window. They are referenced in an HTML document with a link which the user must click in order for the results to be seen or heard. These are less common than embedded plug-ins.

■ **Embedded plug-ins.** Embedded plug-ins are referenced in HTML documents so that when a document is loaded, the plug-in activates and displays the object or plays the sound. Figure 10-7 shows a typical embedded plug-in, an interactive Shockwave tic-tac-toe game.

Figure 10-7: A plug-in tic-tac-toe game.

TIP

If you navigate to a site that contains an embedded image or animation for which you do not have the correct plug-in, you'll see a blank area with an icon that looks like a blue jigsaw puzzle piece in the middle.

As a Web author, you specify embedded plug-ins by using the <EMBED> HTML tag, as shown in the following syntax:

```
<EMBED SRC="movie.mpg", WIDTH=150, HEIGHT=250 AUTOSTART=TRUE>
```

In this example, when the user clicks on the plug-in reference on the Web page, an MPEG player activates automatically and plays a film clip named "movie.mpg."

■ **Hidden plug-ins.** Hidden plug-ins are ones that users cannot see or otherwise control, such as a plug-in that plays a music file in the background.

There are dozens of excellent plug-ins available for Netscape Communicator, and many of them are available in shareware or beta versions right on the Net.

Just to show you how easy it is to work with plug-ins, here's some more detailed information on one of the most exciting—the Macromedia Shockwave plug-in.

Shockwave & Netscape Communicator 4

The Shockwave plug-in lets you view Macromedia Director movies as well as FreeHand and Authorware multimedia files in Netscape Communicator. Developers can include this media in HTML documents by using the <EMBED> tag. Documents can even include more than one movie per HTML page.

When you access a site that includes a Director file, you can scroll through the Web page even while the movie is playing. You can interact with the movie by clicking on it, and you can enter text from the keyboard into text fields within the movie. And the movie itself can access information from the Internet and open URLs.

To download a copy of Shockwave, enter: **http://www. macromedia.com/ shockwave/download/plugin.cgi** in Navigator's Netsite/Location field and press Enter. Next, click the link Get the Shockwave Plug-in for Your Browser. On the next page, click the link for your appropriate operating system, such as Windows 95. You now can download the file by clicking one of the links provided.

After you download the Shockwave plug-in file, exit Netscape Communicator. This is very important. *Plug-ins may not install properly if **any** Communicator component is running!* Now double-click the downloaded file. This decompresses it and installs Shockwave on your system.

TIP

Macromedia currently offers two different Shockwave packages: Shockwave flash, which is useful for viewing smaller animations on the Web, and Shockwave Director, which is used by Communicator to play larger multimedia documents, interactive games, etc. You can also get both versions in one package by downloading Shockwave Essentials.

Once Shockwave is installed, you can start Netscape Communicator and test its new capabilities. One page that uses a multimedia image to enhance its appeal, unsurprisingly, is Macromedia's own Welcome page. The URL is: http://www.macromedia.com/shockwave/welcome.html, and what it looks like is shown in Figure 10-8, if you've installed Shockwave properly:

As you can see—and hear—Shockwave enhances Web pages not only with animation but also with sound and embedded HTML links. You can see other uses of Shockwave at the Macromedia's Shockwave Gallery, http://www.macromedia.com/shockwave/epicenter/, but Shockwave presentations are also sprinkled all around the Web.

Figure 10-8: The Shockwave Welcome page.

AutoInstall

What if you're browsing the Web and suddenly Navigator 4 encounters a file that it cannot display or play for you because you don't have the associated plug-in installed? There are a variety of different scenarios, depending on the programming of the Web page containing the link and on whether or not the file type is one that has been registered with Netscape. (Registration with Netscape allows a new plug-in for the file type to be installed automatically, via a special *AutoInstall* feature.) If it *is* a file type that has been registered with Netscape:

■ You may be asked to agree to a license and approve the installation of a particular plug-in. Once you approve the installation, the plug-in may be installed on your system automatically.

TIP

Some plug-ins include a special digital security certificate that you can view before the plug-in is installed on your system. This certificate assures you that you are getting the plug-in from its rightful vendor. Plug-ins that include a digital certifi-cate are known as signed plug-ins. *For more information on digital certificates, please see Chapter 12.*

■ The plug-in may be installed automatically right away, if you previously approved a digital security certificate (see Chapter 12) from the plug-in vendor. As soon as the plug-in is installed, you can see the Web page with the multimedia information rendered correctly.

■ You might be transported to Netscape's Plug-in Finder page, with the appropriate plug-in selected from Netscape's list. Just follow the direc-tions that appear, which will vary from plug-in to plug-in.

Non-automatic Installation

If the file type is *not* one that has been registered with Netscape, Figure 10-9 shows what you'll get.

Figure 10-9: The Unknown File Type dialog box.

In this case, click More Info. Once again, you'll be transported to the Plug-in Finder Page, as shown in Figure 10-10.

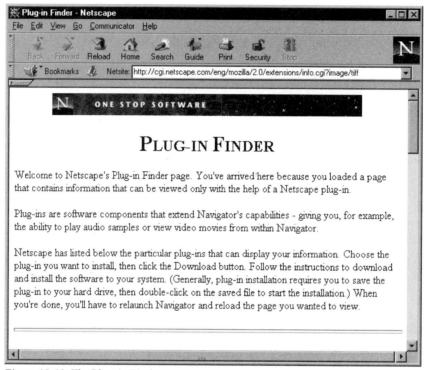

Figure 10-10: The Plug-in Finder page.

Of course you can always access the Plug-in Finder *before* you encounter a new kind of file, selecting whatever plug-ins may be useful or interesting to you. Simply click the Navigator Plug-ins link on Netscape's home page (http://home.netscape.com). Or, you can select About Plug-ins from the Navigator Help menu and then click the "click here" link near the top of the page.

If you scroll down the Plug-in Finder page, you'll see a graphical index of third-party plug-ins loosely arranged by function, as shown in Figure 10-11.

Start exploring from here and you'll find some pretty fascinating ways to extend Communicator's power!

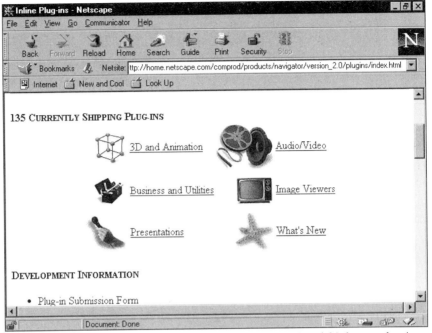

Figure 10-11: Netscape's Plug-in Finder page, showing the index of third-party plug-ins.

Finding Out Which Plug-ins You Already Have

Plug-ins are such an exciting feature that you may become a "plug-in fool" like me, downloading add-ons that make Communicator do everything except wash your socks. And, if you're like me, you won't remember what you've already installed and may download the same plug-in several times!

Fortunately, Netscape takes care of people like you and me. To see what plug-ins are currently installed, select About Plug-ins from the Help menu of any one of the Communicator components, or enter **about:plugins** (no space after the semi-colon) in Navigator's Netsite/Location field. The Installed Plug-ins information page appears, as shown in Figure 10-12.

Figure 10-12: The Installed Plug-ins information page.

As you can see by scrolling down the page, it includes the name of each installed plug-in, what kind of files it operates on (listed by MIME type as well as by file extension or suffix), and whether or not it's currently enabled. This is a good place to determine what version of a particular plug-in you have, too. There may be a newer version available that *does* wash your socks.

TIP

> *You can also get to Netscape's Plug-in Finder from here, by clicking the "click here" link near the top of the page.*

Java

When you get older and your grandchildren ask you about the good old days of the World Wide Web, you'll tell them about Java. You'll tell them that Java was the technology that got us one step closer to bringing real-time interaction between people on the Internet. Java not only enhances Web pages with impressive graphics, it enables software developers to create secure two-way Web applications in a straightforward fashion. These applications are called *Java applets*. Figure 10-13 shows an example of what a Java applet can do.

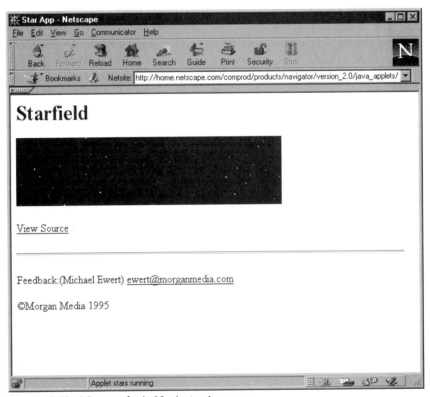

Figure 10-13: A Java applet in Navigator 4.

Many Netcaster channels (see Chapter 4) are also implemented in Java. Because they are written in a separate programming language rather than in HTML, they are able to provide a complete interactive interface.

So What Are Applets?

Java applets are the hottest new eye-candy on the Web. But what exactly are they? They are simply small applications written in the Java programming language. Yes, Java is an entire programming language developed by Sun Microsystems, Inc. (For the propeller-heads reading this, it's similar to C++ but without pointers.) Java lets developers create platform-independent multi-media applications for distribution on the Web. With Navigator 4, you can visit sites that include Java applets (or even full-blown applications) and actually run them.

Since Java applets are cross-platform, you run the same code on a Mac as you do on a Windows 3.1 or Windows NT machine. When you get to a Web page that includes Java applets, you don't have to choose which version to link to. And since Netscape was in the technological vanguard in supporting Java, you don't need a special helper application to interpret the Java code— Communicator does it all.

With traditional Internet and World Wide Web content, the focus is mainly one-way—from the server to the user. It's similar to the cable television that comes into your house. You can receive data from this cable, but you cannot transmit data back through it. We've seen that format allow for some two-way interactivity, but Java really opens up the possibilities. When Java applets are integrated with a Web browser, such as Navigator 4, you can experience live information updating, interaction with other users, and instant interaction with Internet servers.

References to Java applets are included in Web pages with the <APPLET> tag. Each applet is a separate software component that is downloaded with the page. A Java run-time application included in Navigator 4 executes the Java applet and enables you to interact with the applet.

As more and more developers acquire Java programming skills, and more and more people start using browsers like Navigator 4 that support Java, Web sites will begin to include them. In fact, they may become as plentiful as graphics and other files you encounter on the Web now. For this reason, you need to know how to interact with Java applets when you encounter them.

Interacting With Java Applets

When you arrive at a site that includes a Java applet, you really don't have to do anything special. Netscape Communicator does all the work. Information that Navigator needs for running the Java applet is embedded in the HTML documents using the <APPLET> tag. Netscape Communicator automatically downloads and interprets the applet. A complete download may take up to several minutes. Once the applet arrives on your machine, you interact with it per the individual applet's instructions.

Figure 10-14 shows a Java crossword puzzle that lets you actually enter words.

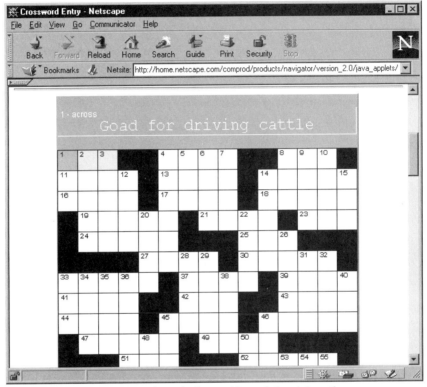

Figure 10-14: A Java crossword puzzle that enables real-time interaction.

If you scroll up the window you'll see that this Java applet (shown in Figure 10-15), like many others, includes a list of instructions:

```
How to play:
    1) The current word you are working on is highlighted in yellow.
    2) The current letter is highlighted in cyan.
    3) Click any letter to move to that word.
    4) <Spacebar> switches between across and down. It pivots around the
       current letter.
    5) <Back space> erases the current letter.
    6) Incorrect letters are drawn in red.
```

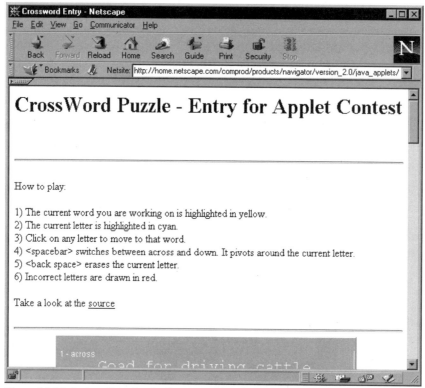

Figure 10-15: Instructions for the Crossword Puzzle applet.

As you can see, you fill out the crossword puzzle while it's actually displayed in Navigator 4. You can type in letters, delete letters, and move from one box to another using your mouse and keyboard. The main difference between this type of application and a crossword puzzle that may have appeared earlier on the Internet is that the Java applet lets you interact with it directly in Navigator 4. Previously you would have had to download a file that runs separately from Navigator 4.

If you're interested in taking a look at some more Java applets, you can do so by visiting one of the sites listed in Table 10-1. These sites include one or more applets that automatically display in the Navigator 4 window. Remember that most Java applets are interactive, so get in there with your mouse.

TIP

As you know, the exact locations of files on the Web often change. If you have trouble with any of the links listed in the table above, simply navigate to http:// www.javasoft.com:80/applets/applets.html and select from there.

Applet	Where You Find It
Blinking Text	http://www.javasoft.com/applets/Blink/example1.html
Curve	http://fas.sfu.ca:80/1/cs/people/GradStudents/heinrica/ personal/curve.html
Crossword	http://home.netscape.com/comprod/products/navigator/ version_2.0/java_applets/Crossword/index.html
Imagemap	http://www.javasoft.com/applets/applets/ImageMap/ example1.html
Modern Clock	http://www.wsrn.com/southern/java/DateClock.html
Pythagoras	http://home.netscape.com/comprod/products/navigator/ version_2.0/java_applets/Pythagoras/index.html
Simple 3D Viewer	http://www.javasoft.com/applets/applets/WireFrame/ example1.html
StarField	http://home.netscape.com/comprod/products/navigator/ version_2.0/java_applets/StarField/index.html
Traditional Clock	http://www.javasoft.com/applets/Clock/index.html

Table 10-1: Some Java applets and where to find them.

Another great site is the Gamelan Java Directory at http:// www.gamelan.com/. This Web site is full of links and resources to Java sites and development news. If you're serious about Java, either as a developer or end user, you need to check out this site every so often to see what's new on the Java front.

Signed Java

Typically, applets are written in a Java language subset that includes several security precautions. For instance, applets can't perform most file system access or file I/O routines.

There may be times, though, when you *want* to grant a Java applet more access to your system. For instance, you may want a Java applet at work to be able to update certain data files stored on your hard drive.

For both tightening and loosening security, Communicator supports what are known as *signed Java applets*. A signed Java applet is one that will not be downloaded to your system until you approve a special digital security certificate (see Chapter 12) that positively identifies the sender. If the Java applet performs any unusual function that could compromise security, you will be asked to approve this action as well. If you have run Communicator's Netcaster component (see Chapter 4), you may have already seen an alert like this. A Java Security alert informs you of what level of risk is involved in the access that is being requested, and it lets you click a button to grant or deny access. You can grant access for this Communicator session or for all subsequent Communicator sessions. If you decide to grant access to the holder of the certificate for subsequent sessions, Communicator keeps a copy of the digital certificate.

In addition, you can view detailed information about the requested access privileges by clicking a Details button.

What if you want to change these access privileges later? You can adjust the privileges allowed to Java applets on a certificate-by-certificate basis at any time. To adjust the Java privileges for a particular certificate you've already received:

1. Click the Security button or the security icon at the left of the status line in any Communicator component.

2. In the left hand frame of the Security page, click Java/JavaScript, as shown in Figure 10-16.

The scrolling list includes all the security certificates that you've already approved, presumably when launching a new signed Java applet. If you select a certificate from the list, you can then use the buttons on the right to:

- **View Certificate.** Click this button for a detailed view of the certificate.

- **Remove.** Click this button to remove the certificate from the list. Java applets from this point of origin will no longer be downloaded and executed automatically on your computer. Instead, you will be presented again with the option of approving a digital certificate.

- **Edit Privileges.** Click this button for the Edit Privileges page. In the Edit Privileges page you can choose which privileges you want to grant for this session only or for any future sessions; it also may let you choose privileges that are specifically denied. For more information, please see Chapter 12.

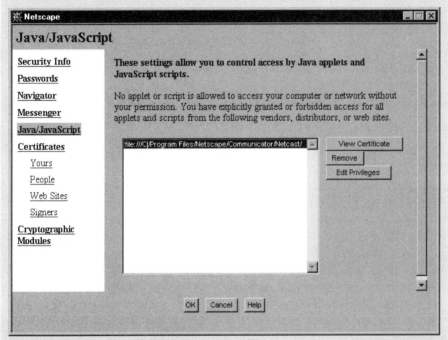

Figure 10-16: Java/JavaScript security options.

If you want, you can even disable Java completely in Netscape Communicator. To do this, select Preferences from the Edit menu of any component and then click the Advanced category. In the window that appears, uncheck the Enable Java checkbox. You can disable JavaScript here as well. Please refer to the upcoming section on JavaScript.

Creating Your Own Applets

For those interested in developing Java applets, you can obtain Sun's official documentation and the Java API (application programming interface) from http://java.sun.com/java.sun.com/aboutJava/index.html. Remember, this is a serious programming language. If you don't have any previous experience with C++ or a similar object-oriented language, now's the time to go out and buy a book about programming in Java.

Java is what's known in the computer industry as a "cool new feature." It's not just something that's needed to perform a particular task—it also looks toward the future and has a strong element of fun to it. What you can do with Java is limited only by your imagination.

TIP

For detailed technical information on a particular Java applet, click the Java Console item in the Communicator menu.

JavaScript

As you travel around the Web, you may notice some user interface niceties that don't seem part of regular old HTML. For instance, there might be some text in your Navigator 4 status bar that ties in with the Web page you're viewing. Or words may scroll across the browser window. Or when you type a bogus area code into a form, a message pops up telling you your entry isn't valid. Some of the following material may be of interest to you only if you are planning to create your own Web pages (see Chapter 9). Once you have a basic understanding of what JavaScript is, feel free to skip over the technical stuff!

If you wonder how the author of the Web page is pulling off these tricks, a good guess would be JavaScript. You can think of JavaScript as "Java Lite": a language that's less powerful than Java but easier to use. While Java programs are independent binary files compiled using special Java programming tools, entire JavaScript programs may be entered directly into an HTML page with a simple text editor. Communicator simply interprets the new commands along with the HTML. Table 10-2 points out some of the differences between Java and JavaScript.

Whoa! In case you're not a programmer, let me put that in plain English: Java is for the big stuff, JavaScript is for smaller effects. Java requires special development tools and a solid understanding of object-oriented programming concepts, while you can probably add some simple JavaScript to your own Web pages after a few hours of playing around, or even minutes if you cut and paste existing examples.

JavaScript	Java
Code is human-readable and embedded right in HTML file.	Java applets are separate from HTML pages.
Interpreted by Communicator—not compiled.	Applets are compiled before being placed on server.
Uses objects but does not support classes or inheritance.	Completely object-oriented. Applets are made up of object classes that support inheritance.
No need to declare data type of variables.	Strong typing: data types need to be declared.
References to objects checked dynamically at run-time.	Static binding at compile time.

Table 10-2: Differences between Java and JavaScript.

LiveConnect

LiveConnect is the Netscape technology that lets plug-ins, JavaScripts, and Java applets interact with each other. For example, thanks to LiveConnect, clicking a button in a Web page could start up separate video and audio plug-in files that are perfectly synchronized. Or it might start a brief movie, which could then trigger a sound file. In other words, LiveConnect allows for real-time integration of various separate media files and interactive JavaScripts or applets.

JavaScript Nuts & Bolts

There are two ways that JavaScript can be embedded in HTML scripts. First, a Web author can use the <SCRIPT> tag. Here's a simple example:

```
<HTML>
<HEAD>
</HEAD>
<BODY>
<SCRIPT LANGUAGE="JavaScript">
document.write("Everybody loves Communicator! (And the <I>Official Netscape
Communicator Book</I>, of course.)")
</SCRIPT>
</BODY>
</HTML>
```

Yep, you guessed it: what appears on your screen is the phrase "Everybody loves Communicator…". OK, you would never really *do* it that way, but at least this gives you an idea of how it works. As you can see, the SCRIPT tag is inside the BODY area of the document. Now just imagine that instead of using the predefined *document.write* function, we had used something more interesting. How about a function that scrolls the words across your browser window in rainbow colors?

Or here's a more practical example using a square function you define yourself:

```
<HTML>
<HEAD>
<SCRIPT LANGUAGE="JavaScript">
function square(i) {
    document.write("The number  to be squared: ", i,"<BR>")
    return i * i
    }

</SCRIPT>
</HEAD>
<BODY>
<SCRIPT LANGUAGE="JAVASCRIPT">
x = prompt("What number is to be squared? ", "number, please")
document.write("The result of this calculation is: ", square(x), ".")
</SCRIPT>
<BR>
The script is all finished calculating the square.
</BODY>
</HTML>
```

The result?

```
JavaScript Prompt: What is the number to be squared?
The number  to be squared: 2
The result of this calculation is 4.
The script is all finished calculating the square.
```

If you study the code a little, you can see that it defines the square function as one that will print the phrase "The number to be squared:" after accepting a number from the user via the built-in prompt method which asks "What is the number to be squared?", then multiplies that number by itself and returns the result. Once defined like this, the function may be used anywhere later in the document.

The <SCRIPT> tag is pretty convenient, but there is also an even more powerful way of working with the language: *event handlers*. This sounds pretty techie, but it's actually quite simple. Netscape Communicator obviously recognizes when a user performs some action such as clicking on a word or phrase. With JavaScript, you can associate chunks of code with actions (or events). In other words, when a user clicks on a word, JavaScript knows to do something. Take a look at this example:

```
<INPUT TYPE="button" VALUE="Add It Up Now" onClick="AddItUp(this form)">
```

This snippet of code executes a user defined function called AddItUp whenever you click the button labeled "Add It Up Now." It could be used as the last button in a form to add all the numbers you'd previously entered.

JavaScript can use *properties* such as "visible" and "color" to return your specified response. You might, for example, design a Web page that includes listings and descriptions of your products. Let's say you sell countertops, and each model of countertop comes in various styles, textures, and colors. Customers to your site may want to design a virtual kitchen by mixing and matching colors and textures with different countertops and other fixtures. With JavaScript, you can include a selector that enables users to adjust the colors and textures of specific countertops. You could create the entire site as a Java applet, but why not use Java only where necessary (such as for creating the virtual kitchen and countertop and the selector)? Then use JavaScript to change the colors and textures of the countertop in the applet.

There's no end to the kinds of fun things you can do with JavaScript. For instance, JavaScript can detect whether or not a plug-in is available and adjust the Web page accordingly. Suppose a page includes a fancy 3D-animated image that requires a plug-in you don't have. JavaScript could figure this out and substitute a plain old GIF or JPEG. JavaScript can even change JPEG and GIF images "on the fly." Imagine staring at a picture of Alan Greenspan that suddenly turns into Madonna. Graphics can change automatically at a particular interval or when the viewer clicks a button or icon.

TIP

For a more comprehensive and up-to-date user reference on JavaScript, see the JavaScript Authoring Guide at http://home.netscape.com/eng/mozilla/3.0/handbook/javascript/index.html.

Kiosk (Canvas) Mode

As I mentioned way back in Chapter 3, Navigator 4 supports a special "kiosk" mode (called *Canvas mode* by Netscape). When in canvas mode, you as a Navigator user cannot affect the display except through interface elements specifically programmed by the author of the Web page—in JavaScript. For example, take a look at Figure 10-17:

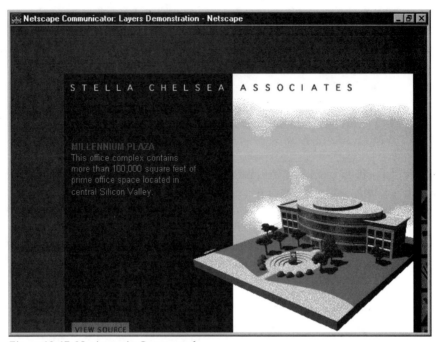

Figure 10-17: Navigator in Canvas mode.

A viewer can click any of the buttons or icons on the screen to access more detailed information but is effectively "locked out" of the Navigator software itself until he or she presses the Close Demo button (in an actual public setting this button would not exist).

And what are the JavaScript commands that you can put in a page in order to force Navigator into canvas mode? That's easy:

```
window.open('pageURL',
'windowName',titlebar=no,left=-1,top=-1,
width=screenWidth,
height=screenHeight,alwaysRaised=yes');
```

The above lines of JavaScript create a full-screen window without browser menus, scroll bars, toolbars, or other visual "chrome." Another *very* useful JavaScript trick.

Moving On

In this chapter we've looked at some of the advanced capabilities of Netscape Communicator; forward-looking extensions such as VRML that put you at the cutting edge of Web browsing. We've also seen how plug-ins and Java can extend the power of Communicator in ways that are hard even to imagine.

All this multimedia muscle is pretty impressive, but there's another area that Web browsers haven't touched until recently: real-time interaction with other Internet (or intranet) users. Imagine placing long distance phone calls over the Internet, talking to somebody in Tibet with no costs beyond what you normally pay for Net access. Imagine clarifying your conversation by typing messages to each other while you talk, or even sending each other text files. Imagine working together long distance by means of an electronic drawing board that lets you markup each other's ideas.

On second thought, don't bother imagining any of this: it's already available to you! In the next chapter, you'll learn how to take advantage of the interactive power of Communicator's Conference component.

CHAPTER 11

Netscape Conference

Some software is not only useful, but it's also genuinely fun to use. For decades now, we've been playing with variations on the old tin-cans-and-string phone that intrigued us as kids, and Netscape Conference has to be one of the coolest variations yet. Here are some of the things you can do with this exciting Communicator component:

- Talk to friends or business associates without ever paying a phone bill.

- Examine complete information on a caller before "picking up the phone."

- Type real-time messages back and forth with an individual halfway around the world.

- Place graphical information on a virtual White Board that both you and a remote Internet or intranet user can mark up and edit as you talk.

- Transfer files to remote users quickly and efficiently.

- Browse the Web collaboratively with a remote user, leading each other from link to link.

And as a bonus, many of these features are tightly integrated with other Communicator components.

What Is Conference?

Conference is a program that sends and receives voice and other data in real time over the Net or over an intranet. If you're not familiar with the term *real time*, here's what it means: when you talk, another user hears your voice right away, just as if you were using a telephone. You don't need to play a sound file. Conference also sends and receives text and graphical information in real time. In other words, you can call your mother and not only tell her what's going on in your life, you can also send her pictures of the kids as you speak. You can even draw circles and captions to make sure she knows which kid is which. And in return, she can send you the text of some favorite recipes as she tells you about them. Perhaps the best way to think about Conference is as a multimedia phone service.

Most of the services you've learned about in this book—e-mail, newsgroups, the Web itself—are client-server based. You use a client program such as Netscape Communicator to access information that's stored on a server. But Conference is different. It's a *peer-to-peer* service. You communicate directly with other individuals, not with servers storing the information they've created. Of course intranet or Internet servers are still involved in the process, but only to pass the information along transparently from user to user. You are immediately in touch with millions of geeks, nerds, and even some regular people all around the world.

Pretty amazing, isn't it? And remember, this whole process is accomplished using the Internet or an intranet. That means no phone bills. Go ahead, call that high-school buddy who's hooking into the Net from his mountain-top hut in Ladakh. (You can let me know by e-mail if there are no mountains in Ladakh.)

There is one slight catch, though: anyone you communicate with using Conference has to be running Conference as well. That's because the program uses special proprietary protocols to send and receive multimedia data as efficiently as possible. But since Conference is part of Netscape Communicator, this exciting new technology is rapidly becoming commonplace. Not too long from now you might hear some self-satisfied young businessman say, "Have your avatar e-mail my droid, we'll do Conference."

And that's when *I* move to Ladakh.

Hardware Requirements

In addition to the requirements for running the rest of Netscape Communicator, Conference has a few specific requirements of its own. Of course, you can use Communicator without it, but here's what you need to run Conference:

- A 486 or better machine running at a CPU speed of at least 50 MHz.

- For SLIP and PPP connections, a modem with a speed of *at least* 14,400 kbps; I highly recommend a faster modem for this feature.

- If you plan to use the voice features (in addition to the Chat, White Board, and collaborative Web browsing features), a Windows-compatible sound card with speakers and microphone.

TIP

For full-duplex audio conferencing (letting both parties speak at the same time), you need a full-duplex sound card and a driver that supports full-duplex operation. Most sound card manufacturers keep updated drivers at their Web or FTP sites, available for free download.

OK, let's get busy and actually run Conference.

Running Conference the First Time

You can start Conference by double-clicking its icon in the Communicator folder or program group, or you can simply choose Conference from the Communicator menu of any Communicator component. Either way, if this is the first time you've run Conference, the Setup Wizard appears, as shown in Figure 11-1.

Figure 11-1: The Setup Wizard.

> **TIP**
>
> *Notice also that as soon as you fire up Conference, a telephone icon appears in the tray area of your Windows 95 or Windows NT 4.0 taskbar. When you're connected to or are attempting to reach another Conference user, the handset turns red to indicate "call active." And if you right-click the icon, you can access the Conference window itself or Conference preferences. You can even select Do Not Disturb from the icon's right-click context menu to block any incoming calls.*

The first screen of the Wizard is a typical Welcome message; read it and click Next. Now you are presented with a list of hardware requirements for running Conference, but you already know them. Click Next again.

At last, you get to a dialog box in which you need to do some real work, the Business Card dialog box. It's shown in Figure 11-2.

Figure 11-2: The Business Card dialog box.

Filling Out Your Business Card

Want other users to know something about you when you call them? Sharing that information is easy with Conference. Now you can set up Conference's business card feature, which is kind of like caller ID on steroids.

In the Name field, type your—Wait a minute, how many times have you filled out a form like this? You can probably figure out what to do here just fine without me. After you've completed the form, it should look something like the one shown in Figure 11-3.

Figure 11-3: A completed business card.

But wait, there's more! Don't you want the world to know what you look like? Yes, you can actually add a picture to your business card. Here's how:

- To add a picture from a file, click the button just to the right of the Photo field. A standard file selection dialog box appears, letting you choose a picture from anywhere on your system.

- To add a picture that's already saved in the clipboard, click the button to the far right of the Photo field. The picture will be pasted in immediately.

In either case, your picture is plugged into your business card, and your completed form should now look something like Figure 11-4.

Figure 11-4: A Conference business card with my picture.

TIP

You probably already thought of this idea: it doesn't have to be a picture of you. It could be your company logo or even a favorite painting or cartoon. (Make sure you're not violating any copyrights, though.) And you've probably already thought of this idea too: if you locate some public domain photos, you can look just like Antonio Banderas or Michelle Pfeiffer for the day. This feature is ideal for people with delusions of grandeur, multiple personality disorder, or problems finding a date.

OK, you've completed your business card. Click Next and the Wizard pops up a Directory Preferences dialog box. Let's take a closer look.

Setting Up Directory Preferences

Figure 11-5 shows the Directory Preferences dialog box.

Figure 11-5: The Directory Preferences page of the Setup Wizard.

Notice that this page has two different fields for entering information. The first one is for the Dynamic Lookup Service (DLS) server you want to use. In Conference, you can initiate calls to an individual simply by entering his or her e-mail address. Conference then logs on to the DLS server and finds an actual Internet IP address that's associated with that e-mail address. For instance, if I tell Conference I want to call joe@some_company.com, the DLS server may send Conference the address 123.456.789.123, the actual IP address of Joe's computer. As long as Joe is currently running his own copy of Conference, the connection is established.

The default DLS server is dls.four11.com. You should probably leave this field unchanged unless you're on an intranet and your network administrator has given you a different server address to enter.

The other field on this page lets you specify a Phonebook URL. It is the Web page that appears when you click the Web Phonebook button in Conference. It lets you choose from among users all around the Net who are currently running Conference. Simply click a name and you're connected to that individual, ready to talk or to use any of Conference's collaborative features. This method is a lot easier than using an old-fashioned paper phone book. You'll learn more about the Web Phonebook later, but here's a sneak preview in Figure 11-6.

Figure 11-6: The Web Phonebook.

TIP

You should leave the Phonebook URL setting alone unless you know of a different Web Phonebook you can access.

How do all these people get into the Web Phonebook? They are all people who left the List my name in phone book option checked, as shown earlier in Figure 11-5. If you leave it checked, you too will be listed in the default Web Phonebook whenever you're connected to the Net and start Conference. Don't worry, you can change this option at any time later if you want an "unlisted number."

OK, click Next and we're on to the Specify Your Network Type dialog box.

Specifying Your Network Type

For Conference to operate at optimum speed and with the best sound quality possible, it needs to know the data rate of your Internet or intranet connection. Conference uses different types of audio compression—known as *CODECs*—depending on your connection type. As you can see in Figure 11-7, the Wizard lets you choose anything from a 14,400 kbps modem connection up to a hard-wired LAN connection.

Figure 11-7: The Specify Your Network Type dialog box.

After you have selected the appropriate option button, click Next for some questions about your sound card.

> **TIP**
>
> *If you have specified a LAN connection, the Wizard will pop up an extra screen that gives you some information about running Conference behind a firewall on an office intranet. If your office uses a firewall (see Chapter 12 if you don't know what I'm talking about), read this screen carefully.*

Detecting Your Sound Card

Figure 11-8 shows the sound card dialog box.

Figure 11-8: The Detecting Your Sound Card dialog box.

If your sound card is properly installed on your system, chances are that Conference has already found it and correctly identified it. Its name should appear in both the Microphone and Speakers fields. If you have more than one sound card in your computer, you may be able to choose from the drop-down lists. If no sound card at all appears on either list, your computer does not have a sound card, it is not properly installed, or it is not supported by Conference. You can still use Conference's non-audio features, but you will not be able to actually talk across the Net or your intranet.

TIP

If you have more than one half-duplex sound card installed on your system, you can use different ones for Microphone and Speakers. That way, you can realize full-duplex operation—while you're "talking out" one card, you can be listening to a voice "coming in" on the other card. Of course, it's simpler and more economical to use a full-duplex card and make sure you have a full-duplex driver for it.

Now click Next again. A dialog box labeled Testing the Audio Levels (Screen 1 of 2) appears. Read the text carefully. If you don't currently have a microphone attached to your system, click Skip. Otherwise, click Next to test and set your audio levels. Screen 2 of the audio testing portion of the Wizard appears, as shown in Figure 11-9.

Figure 11-9: Testing the Audio Levels (Screen 2 of 2).

You should read the instructions on the screen, but to understand what's going on, also read the following sidebar.

Dealing with Half-Duplex Sound Cards: The Silence Sensor

As I explained earlier, you can use two kinds of sound cards: half-duplex and full-duplex. With a full-duplex card, you and the person you're talking to via Conference can both speak at the same time, just as you can with a telephone. If either of you has a half-duplex card, however, you'll have to take turns, as with a CB radio. Netscape Conference handles half-duplex communication in two different ways:

1. You can simply click a Microphone button whenever you want to speak and then a Speakers button whenever you want to listen.

or

2. You can configure Conference so that it automatically switches between your voice and your friend's voice, without any intervention on your part.

Take my word for it, the second scenario is much easier! But a potential problem exists. Suppose your office is noisy. How does Conference know when it's you talking and not just the sound of your computer? Since Conference goes out of "listen" mode whenever it hears sound at your end, your friend might *never* get a word in edgewise.

➡

The Sound Sensor comes in at this point. See that blue dot inside the microphone meter shown above in Figure 11-9? That dot lets you set the minimum level of sound at which Conference assumes you are speaking; everything less than that level is ignored as silence. To set the level higher (in other words, if your environment is noisy and you want to make Conference ignore more ambient noise rather than interpreting it as speech), drag the red dot to the right.

OK, let's follow the instructions on the screen:

1. Click the small microphone button to the left of the upper panel. This way, you can check sound levels without actually being connected.

2. Try talking into the mike. You'll see green bars move to the right across the panel. The dark green indicates sound that is really too soft for a clear conversation; the maroon bars indicate the ideal volume for talking; and if you see red bars, you should get a job in a rock band.

3. If no green at all is showing when you're not talking, you can leave the blue Silence Sensor control exactly where it is. But if some green appears in the window, indicating significant ambient noise, you should drag the dot to the right until it is just above that level, as shown in Figure 11-10. That way, Conference starts to send audio immediately when you begin speaking.

Figure 11-10: A new silence level.

Once you have set the Silence Sensor, click Next and then click Finish on the last page of the Wizard. By the way, you can access the Setup Wizard at any time to change any of the options you've just set. In Conference, simply select Setup Wizard from the Help menu.

TIP

> *You can change the Silence Sensor setting at any time later without running the Wizard again. The blue dot control is right within the main Conference window.*

The Conference Window

As soon as you click the Wizard's Finish button, the Conference window appears on your desktop, as shown in Figure 11-11.

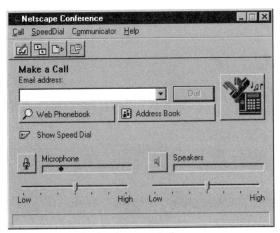

Figure 11-11: The Conference window.

Let's take a quick look around and get familiar with this new communications tool before we actually initiate a call. The Conference window is divided into three main areas, which I'll call the addressing area, the Business card button, and the Microphone and Speakers controls.

The Addressing Area

Near the top of the Conference window is the addressing area, which is composed of a drop-down list box, a Dial button, a Web Phonebook button, and an Address Book button. We'll work with all these elements in depth in the section called "Initiating a Call" later in this chapter. These controls let you find and dial remote Conference users.

Can I Use Conference to Call People Who Use Different Conferencing Software?

The short answer is: "Yes, you can!" Netscape Conference utilizes a recently adopted real-time conferencing standard known as H.323, and many of its features will be compatible with products from other vendors that follow the same H.323 standard.

The slightly longer answer is: "Your mileage may vary." Since this standard is new, not every conferencing or Internet phone package uses it yet, and others may implement H.323 only for some basic features. Trying to connect to somebody who uses a different software package is certainly worthwhile, though. If it doesn't work, tell that person to get Communicator!

The Conference Button

Now click the big colorful square button at the right side of the Conference window. You see something like Figure 11-12.

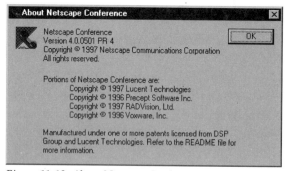

Figure 11-12: About Netscape Conference.

Hmm, why would the Netscape engineers devote such a big button to the mundane task of displaying this very ordinary About information? As you'll discover in a few minutes, everything changes when you actually place a call. If the person on the other end has a picture as part of his or her business card, the button displays that picture. And when you click the button, you see the business card itself, as shown in Figure 11-13.

Figure 11-13: The results of clicking the Conference button while connected to another user.

Thus the Conference button is the key to knowing when you're connected and when you're offline. But the Conference button also conveys a variety of other information:

- By default, Conference prompts you when a call comes in, asking whether you want to answer it or not. The Conference button indicates this "prompt me" mode by displaying a phone that looks like it's being taken off hook.

- If you change this setting so that Conference automatically answers all calls, the button depicts a phone that is clearly off hook.

- If you elect to put Conference in "Do Not Disturb" mode so that it answers no incoming calls, the image on the button becomes a "not" sign over the telephone.

TIP

The Conference icon in your Windows 95 or Windows NT 4.0 taskbar tray changes just like the Conference button, indicating these various states even when Conference is minimized. When you are connected to another Conference user, the taskbar icon depicts two connected telephone handsets.

And how do you switch between these three answering modes in Conference? From the Call menu, simply select Always Prompt, Auto Answer, or Do Not Disturb. You'll learn more about these features later, in the section called "Answering Calls."

The Microphone & Speakers Controls

Back in the main Conference window, notice the two horizontal black areas just below center. These two controls indicate where you'll see the volume level for your own voice and for the voice of the person you're talking to. Your voice is depicted in the Microphone meter; the person you're talking to is in the Speakers meter. You can adjust the mike sensitivity for your own voice by dragging the slider just below the Microphone meter, and you can adjust the volume of the "incoming" voice by dragging the slider just below the Speakers meter.

The buttons to the left of each meter are on/off switches. Click them to enable or mute either your outgoing sound or the sound of the person you're talking to. You know that Microphone or Speakers sound is on if you see a green display of the sound level in the respective meter. You can turn Microphone sound on even when you're not connected—this is a good way to set your sound level. (I'll talk more about sound level when I actually show you how to place a call.)

I told you about the Sound Sensor earlier. Although you may have adjusted it properly in the Setup Wizard, you can readjust it right here if you want. Simply use your mouse to drag the blue dot in the Microphone meter to the right or left.

> **TIP**
>
> *If you have a half-duplex sound card, make sure that autoswitching is enabled. To enable autoswitching, select Preferences from Conference's Call menu; then click the Audio tab. Near the top of the tab, make sure the Recording/Playback autoswitch check box is checked. As long as this option is selected, Conference senses when you're done talking and automatically switches to "listen" mode so your friend can get a word or two in before you start up again. No need to click the Microphone button when you want to speak or the Speakers button when you want to listen.*

Initiating a Call

When you initiate a connection to a remote user, you have to tell Conference how to reach that individual—or more specifically, that individual's computer. Conference needs the numeric IP address of the computer you're trying to connect to. (Remember, numeric IP addresses are the unique strings of numbers that positively identify every computer currently connected to the Internet or an intranet.) Of course, you're not likely to know your friends' numeric IP addresses, especially if they have SLIP or PPP accounts that assign them a new IP number each time they connect to the Net! So how does this process work?

Fortunately, Netscape Conference can look up IP addresses automatically by means of special directory servers. All you do is enter somebody's e-mail address. Conference logs on to a directory server and requests the current IP address that's associated with that e-mail address. If the person you're trying to reach has Conference running, the server can find his or her current numeric IP address, since Conference reports this information to the server when the program is launched.

So "dialing" an individual across the Net is as simple as entering an e-mail address, right?

Wrong! It's even simpler. Conference provides three different methods that further automate the process: The Web Phonebook, the Address Book, and Speed Dial buttons.

The Web Phonebook

Let's get right down to business. The Phonebook I am using in this example is located at out on the Net, so make sure you are currently connected. Launch Conference by double-clicking its icon on your desktop or by selecting it from the Communicator menu of any Communicator component. The main Conference window appears, as shown in Figure 11-11. Now follow these steps:

1. Click the Web Phonebook button. Navigator 4 is launched automatically, and within a few seconds the Conference Phonebook page appears, as shown in Figure 11-14.

Figure 11-14: The Conference Phonebook page.

2. Scroll down to the Viewing Users section of the page and type the beginning of your name in the edit box, as shown in Figure 11-15.

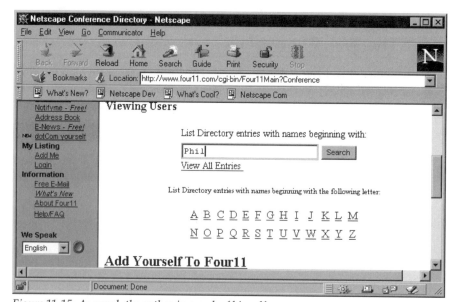

Figure 11-15: As usual, the author in search of himself.

- The default Web Phonebook will generally include your own name. This is because when you start Conference, it automatically reports your addressing information to this server. You can choose *not* to have your name listed in the Phonebook, or you can specify a different phonebook and DLS server to store your information. For instance, your office intranet may have its own server. To change either of these settings, select Preferences from the Call menu and then click the Network tab if it is not already selected.

TIP

You can also get a complete list of Conference users by clicking View All Entries, or you can click one of the letters of the alphabet to list all names beginning with that letter.

3. Click the Search button. In a few seconds your search results appear, as shown in Figure 11-16.

Figure 11-16: The search results.

4. If the list has several entries, scroll down until you find the individual you're interested in.

Notice that each Web Phonebook entry contains three fields, Username, Email, and Application. Let's examine each one separately.

- **Username**. If you click the individual's name, you will be presented with detailed information.

  Not only can you view the information, you can add it directly into your Communicator Address Book. (Why would you want to do this? See the section below called "The Address Book.") To add this individual to your Address Book, click the "get vCard" link. On the next page that appears, click the Add to Address Book button. The individual is added automatically to your Address Book.

- **Email**. If you click the individual's e-mail address, a Message Composition window appears (see Chapter 5) with the correct address already filled in. Just type your message and click Send!

- **Application**. In most cases, this field will contain the word "Conference." Just click it to initiate a Netscape Conference call to the individual.

Conference doesn't let you call yourself, so to try its communications features, you'll have to select a different name from the Phonebook. Use Navigator's Back button to return to the previous display. You can then choose a different initial letter for the names you want to show, or you can select View All Entries to see everyone who is currently using Conference. When you've found the name of an individual you want to call, simply the word "Conference" in the Application field.

What happens when you click Conference? For that answer, you'll have to wait for the section called "Establishing the Connection." Right now, I want to show you how the Address Book provides another convenient way to initiate calls.

The Address Book

The Address Book is one of Communicator's shared resources. You've probably used it in Messenger for sending an e-mail message or for creating a new list of recipients. Conference uses the exact same Address Book for initiating calls. Let's take a look:

1. Launch Conference by double-clicking its icon on the desktop or by selecting it from the Communicator menu of any Communicator component.

2. Click the Address Book button. The Communicator Address Book appears, as shown in Figure 11-17.

Figure 11-17: The Address Book.

3. Select a name from your list and click the Call button. That's all there is to it! Conference automatically initiates the call to this individual.

   ■ OK, it may not always be *quite* that simple. This will work just fine as long as the individual you're trying to contact uses the default Netscape Conference DLS server, the one you've already specified (generally netdls.four11.com). If you think you are more likely to find this individual on a different DLS server, you need to reconfigure the Address Book entry as follows:

4. Double-click the Address Book entry you want to reconfigure. The card for that individual appears, as shown in Figure 11-18.

Figure 11-18: The card for an Address Book entry.

5. Select the Netscape Conference tab, as shown in Figure 11-19.

Figure 11-19: The Netscape Conference tab.

6. From the drop-down list, select either Specific DLS Server or Hostname or IP Address.

7. In the second field, enter the address of the DLS server, the domain name for the individual's machine, or the numeric IP address of the individual's machine.

A reconfigured Netscape Conference tab should look something like Figure 11-20.

Now just click OK. The Address Book entry you selected can now be used by Conference. Just select it and click the Call button. To see what happens next, move ahead to the section "Establishing the Connection."

Figure 11-20: A reconfigured Netscape Conference tab.

Entering Addresses Directly

The Web Phonebook and the Address Book make it easy to "dial" individuals across the Net, but sometimes you may want to enter an e-mail address—or even a domain name or numeric IP address—directly. You can simply type an email address right into Conference's email address field. Then just click the Dial button to complete your call.

If you want to type in a direct IP address, you need to put it in parentheses, as shown in Figure 11-21. This way, Conference knows you're not specifying an e-mail address and won't try to go contact a DLS server to translate it.

Figure 11-21: Conference with a direct IP address entered.

> To avoid typing the parentheses, select Direct Call from the Call menu and then just type in the IP address.
>
> If you don't know the numeric IP address of the machine you want to connect to, but you know its fully qualified domain name, you can also enter this information directly in either the email address field or the Direct Call dialog box. If you enter it in the e-mail address field, you need to surround it with parentheses, just like the numeric IP address.

Speed Dial Buttons

In addition to the Web Phonebook and the Address Book, Conference provides a third and even more convenient way to initiate calls: Speed Dial buttons. They are exactly like the speed dial buttons you may have on your telephone: just press one and the next thing you know you're talking to your mother, stockbroker, or main squeeze. (Don't start talking until you know you've hit the right button.)

OK, let's get busy:

1. In Conference, click Show Speed Dial. The Speed Dial buttons appear, as shown in Figure 11-22.

Figure 11-22: The Speed Dial buttons.

2. Right-click the Speed Dial 1 button. The Speed Dial Edit dialog box appears, as shown in Figure 11-23.

Figure 11-23: The Speed Dial Edit dialog box.

3. Complete the dialog box:

- Fill in the name of a person you call frequently. This name will actually appear on the Speed Dial button.

- Fill in his or her e-mail address.

- Leave the DLS server field alone unless you know the name of a different DLS server that stores the addressing information for this individual.

- If you want to use the Speed Dial button to connect directly to a specific machine rather than look up the individual via a DLS server, type in the numeric IP address or fully qualified domain name address for the machine. You do not need to surround this address with parentheses. (See the sidebar called "Entering Addresses Directly" above.)

4. After you've completed the dialog box, click OK. You are returned to the Conference window, which now includes a newly labeled Speed Dial button, as shown in Figure 11-24.

Figure 11-24: The Conference window with a new Speed Dial button.

To initiate a call, simply click the Speed Dial button you have just created.

TIP

To clear a Speed Dial button, select the name of the button from the SpeedDial menu; then click Clear from the submenu that appears. You will be asked if you really want to clear the contents of the button. Click OK. You can also edit the contents of a button at any time by right-clicking it.

Establishing the Connection

OK, you've just clicked a name in the Web Phonebook. Or you've selected a name from your Address Book and clicked the Call button. Or you've clicked one of your Speed Dial buttons. Or you've entered an address for a direct call. What happens next?

In Figure 11-25, you see the Pending Invitation that appears while you're waiting for somebody to accept your call.

Figure 11-25: The Pending Invitation message.

If you want to cancel the call, simply click the Cancel call button. The remote user you're trying to reach may cancel the call as well, in which case you'll get a Call Status message like the one shown in Figure 11-26.

Figure 11-26: A Call Status message indicating that the remote user refused the call or simply did not answer.

But what happens when the remote user accepts your call? It's very very simple: no messages, no dialog boxes, just the ability to communicate. Figure 11-27 shows what your screen looks like now.

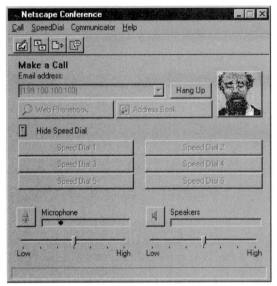

Figure 11-27: Conference after a connection has been established.

The Business card button may show a picture of the remote Conference user, and clicking it displays that individual's card, as shown in Figure 11-28. You can even learn about the remote user's hardware and software configuration by selecting the System tab.

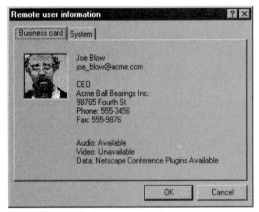

Figure 11-28: The business card for a remote user.

Of course, the remote user has your card too. You have just exchanged business cards without even knowing it.

More importantly, though, you can now talk to each other. To learn how to do that, read on!

TIP

If either you or the remote Conference user does not have a sound card properly set up, you will still get a window that looks like Figure 11-27 when you connect, and you can still view each other's business cards. The Conference status line, however, will indicate that audio communication is not possible. Of course, you can use Conference's non-audio features: chat, the White Board, file transfer, and collaborative Web browsing.

Leaving Voice Mail

If the individual you're trying to reach is not currently available—perhaps because he or she is not currently running Conference or is already connected to another Conference user—Figure 11-29 shows what you'll get:

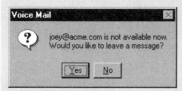

Figure 11-29: The Voice Mail dialog box.

If you click No in this dialog box, you are simply returned to the Conference window. But if you click Yes, a voice mail recorder pops up, as shown in Figure 11-30. This utility lets you record a sound file that will be sent to the individual via e-mail.

➡

Figure 11-30: The voice mail recorder.

To record your message, click the red-dotted Record button and start talking. Click the Stop button when you are finished. To listen to your message before you send it, click the Play button. If you don't like what you hear, click Record again and talk some more. When you've created a message you're satisfied with, simply click Send.

Once you click Send, a new Message Composition window appears, as shown in Figure 11-31.

Figure 11-31: A new Message Composition window with the voice mail file attached.

Notice that the To field already contains the address of the person you were trying to reach. (If you weren't using a valid e-mail address, you can edit the To field now.) Your voice mail file is already embedded in the message. You can add some text if you like, or simply click the Send button.

Figure 11-32 shows what your recipient sees, assuming he or she is using Messenger.

Figure 11-32: A received e-mail message containing voice mail.

To listen to the message, your recipient simply clicks the Play button. The special voice mail control also includes a Stop button, a Pause button, and a slider to adjust the volume.

This is what is known in the industry as a VCF (Very Cool Feature).

Once You're Connected

After you're connected to another user, follow these steps carefully:

1. Talk.

2. Listen.

3. Repeat steps 1 and 2 until you're tired of the conversation.

Pretty technical stuff, huh? As you talk, watch the green level indicators for a while. If either voice is too loud or too soft, you can adjust the microphone sensitivity and audio volume while you're conversing. And if somebody fires up the vacuum cleaner, you can tweak the Silence Sensor as well, moving that blue dot further to the right.

Audio Settings

If you're having problems with the audio in Conference—for instance, if you can't hear your colleague well even after adjusting the Speakers level—take a look at Conference's Audio settings. You get there by selecting Preferences from the Call menu and then clicking the Audio tab. A button in this tab lets you access Advanced audio settings. **Note:** You must hang up any active Conference session before you can modify most of the Audio preferences.

Getting into the nitty-gritty of all the available adjustments to your audio is beyond the scope of this book, and most of them are very dependent on what kind of connection you have. Fortunately, the program itself includes some good detailed information that you can read by clicking the Help button. You should be able to find the answer to any concerns right there.

All good things must end. So what about hanging up? Either participant can do it. All you do is click the Hang Up button.

Now you know all about initiating calls to remote Conference users. But what about answering calls?

Answering Calls

As you might guess, answering calls is *really* easy. Remember, though, that to answer calls you must have Conference running—or a smaller supplemental program called Conference Attendant that I'll talk about in a minute, in the section aptly called "Conference Attendant."

Figure 11-33 shows what you see onscreen when somebody calls you via Conference:

Figure 11-33: The Call Invitation dialog box.

Of course, your speakers ring like a phone at the same time this dialog box appears.

Notice that the Invitation dialog box specifies the name of the person calling you, and separate buttons let you accept or reject the call. If you reject it, you're back in the idle state. If you accept the call, your window will look just like it did when you initiated a call. You're ready to start talking.

Suppose you're the gregarious type and want to answer all incoming calls without even clicking the Accept button? That's easy. From the Call menu select Auto Answer.

But now suppose you're busy writing a book about Netscape Communicator and don't want to be bothered by incoming calls. For that, there's Do Not Disturb, one of my favorite Conference features.

Do Not Disturb

To activate the Do Not Disturb feature, simply select Do Not Disturb from Conference's Call menu. Selecting this option makes you unavailable for incoming calls until you switch back to Always Prompt or Auto Answer. When the Do Not Disturb feature is activated, the Business card button includes a big "not" sign, as shown in Figure 11-34.

Figure 11-34: The Conference window with Do Not Disturb activated.

The phone icon in the taskbar tray is overlaid with a red "not" sign as well.

Conference Attendant

You may not want Netscape Conference sitting on your desktop at all times, simply waiting for calls to come in. Of course you can minimize the program, but Netscape provides a neater way to save screen real estate: Conference Attendant.

Netscape Conference Attendant is a supplemental feature that acts as a sort of watch dog, waiting for Conference calls. Once one comes in, the usual Conference interface appears on your screen.

To start Conference Attendant, double-click the Netscape Conference Attendant icon in the Utilities subfolder of the Communicator folder. A small Conference icon appears in your taskbar tray, but that is the only sign that Conference is running. But don't worry, unless you've selected Do Not Disturb, the Attendant won't miss your calls.

If you right click the Conference Attendant icon in your taskbar tray, a context menu appears. From this menu you can:

- Launch one of the other Conference features (Whiteboard, Collaborative Browsing, File Exchange, or Chat). I'll cover these features in the next few sections of this chapter.

- Select your answering preference (Always Prompt, Auto Answer, or Do Not Disturb).

- Change your Conference Preferences.

- Show the normal Conference window.

- Exit Conference completely (including Attendant).

TIP

Once Conference Attendant is running, closing the normal Conference window does not shut it down. It remains loaded, ready to answer your calls and to provide you this alternative access to Conference features. To unload Attendant, you must select Exit Conference from the context menu.

So far I've shown you how to get connected with Conference and how to use the software as a long-distance voice phone across the Net. But Conference offers much, much more. In the next few sections, I'll cover the White Board feature, collaborative browsing, file exchange, and chat. Rather than follow the order of the buttons on the Conference toolbar, we'll work through these features in an order that makes it easier to understand the concepts behind them. Let's start with Chat.

Chat

In geek-speak, chatting doesn't mean talking. It means typing messages back and forth in real time. America Online, for instance, has specialized chat rooms where you can have typed conversations with people of like interests. (And if you can't find a chat room for some of your stranger interests on AOL, your interests are very strange indeed.) Chatting is very different from leaving messages on a newsgroup or some online service. The "real-timeness" of chatting gives it a quality of immediacy and vibrancy much like voice conversation. And obviously, it's a great means of communication for people with hearing or speech disabilities.

The Conference Chat feature even lets you send entire text files. You can be conferencing with somebody about a particular legal document and send the text itself as you speak!

TIP

Even if you don't have a sound card, you can communicate with other Conference users using its Chat and White Board features.

Let's give it a try:

1. Connect with a Conference user following the step-by-step instructions in the section "Initiating a Call" earlier in this chapter.

2. Click the Chat button, the one that depicts a document and a conversational "balloon." The Chat window appears, as shown in Figure 11-35.

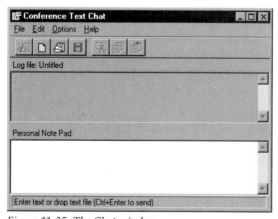

Figure 11-35: The Chat window.

By default, Conference is configured so that the Chat window pops up as soon as the Conference user at the other end tries to chat with you. If you do not like this behavior (in other words, if you don't want to feel "pushed" into a chat without explicitly requesting it yourself or agreeing to it by voice), select Options from the Chat menu and select Pop Up On Receive to remove the checkmark.

3. Type a word or sentence in the white Personal Note Pad pane. After you've completed it, send it by pressing Ctrl+Enter or clicking the Send button at the far left in the toolbar.

   ▪ Notice that as soon as you send your text, it appears in the upper Log panel, prefaced by the label **local user>**. Text you receive from the individual you're connected to also appears, prefaced by the label **remote user>**. The Log panel keeps a running record of your entire chat, including what you type and what the other Conference user types.

The Conference user at the other end of the connection doesn't see anything you type until you press Ctrl+Enter or click the Send button. This feature gives you time to think about what you're saying. That's good, since both parties can keep a log of the entire chat!

The two of you can keep chatting indefinitely, and you can keep *talking* at the same time. You can facilitate communications by cutting, copying, and pasting text in the Personal Note Pad, and you can even copy text from the Log and paste it into the Note Pad. What a great way to remind people of what they said a few minutes ago! All these editing tools are available via the usual editing buttons at the top of the Chat Tool window.

Including Text Files

This Chat feature gets its own section because it's one of my favorites. Including text files while you're chatting is really very simple: you can paste entire text files into the Personal Note Pad by clicking the Include button (the third from the left) and selecting the file you want to include. Figure 11-36 shows you the result.

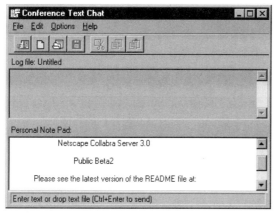

Figure 11-36: The Personal Note Pad with an included text file.

You don't need to follow any special procedure for sending included files: pressing Ctrl+Enter will do the trick.

Log Files

At any point while the Chat window is displayed, you can save the contents of the Log to a file by clicking the Save button. You might want to name your log file with the date of the chat session and the name of the other chatter, as in 4-1Joe. You can also start an entire new log file by clicking the New button.

TRAP

Unless you save your current log file, the information in the Log panel will be lost when you select a new file.

Leaving Chat

When you're finished chatting with your fellow Conference user, simply close the Chat window. This action does not break your connection; you can keep talking as long as you want, and you can start chatting again simply by clicking the Chat button in the Conference window.

And now, on to the White Board.

The White Board

You can think of Conference's White Board as Chat on steroids. It lets you share not only text messages, but also graphics and even screen captures of whatever's on your monitor right now. Or you can think of it as a paint program that two people work in at once, collaboratively creating rich, colorful content even though they might be thousands of miles apart.

If you've ever used any paint program, such as Microsoft Paint (which comes with Windows), you'll have no trouble figuring out the White Board. Covering every detail of its operation is beyond the scope of this book. I'll just hit the important points as well as some interesting features that aren't immediately obvious. After that, I think you'll find it's the kind of feature that's a lot more fun to learn by using.

Starting the White Board

To start the White Board, follow these steps:

1. Connect with a Conference user following the step-by-step instructions in the section "Initiating a Call" earlier in this chapter.

2. Click the White Board button, which looks like an artist's palette. The White Board window appears, as shown in Figure 11-37.

TIP

By default, your White Board also pops up as soon as the individual you're connected with starts working with his or her White Board. If you don't like this behavior, uncheck the Pop Up On Receive option from the White Board's Options menu.

Now you can start adding elements to your White Board using the various tools and the width, fill, and color options at the left-hand side of the window. You can also add text by selecting the Text tool (the button with a big "T" on it) and choosing your font size and style at the top of the window. For example, Figure 11-38 shows my White Board with a few simple geometric shapes and some text.

Figure 11-37: The White Board window.

Figure 11-38: My White Board with some important stuff on it.

> ### TIP
>
> *Notice the White Board's scroll bars. You are not limited to what you can fit within the window. This virtual White Board is less like the kind of white board you buy at an office supply store than it is like an endless roll of drawing paper.*

You might be wondering what's going on at the other end of the Conference connection. Here's the scoop:

- Everything you draw or paint appears on the remote White Board exactly as it appears on yours. Not only that, it gets there right away. If your Conferencing friend starts unleashing his or her artistic talents, you'll see that artwork right away too.

- Text that's added to the White Board using the Text tool, on the other hand, is sent after you press Enter. This feature allows for a combination of collaboration and effective written conversation. The White Board is a truly collaborative feature that adds a new dimension to the phrase "it's almost like being there."

And, of course, the two of you can keep yacking away into your microphones as you create your collaborative masterpiece. Kids could entertain themselves for hours with this feature. So could I.

> ### TIP
>
> *Don't like what's on your White Board? Of course you can delete parts of the window using the Erase tool, but you might want to get rid of the whole thing. Simply select Clear White Board from the Edit menu. Remember, though, that you're erasing it for your fellow Conference user as well!*
>
> *And what about if you're convinced your collaborative masterpiece will some day sell for millions at Sotheby's? Just click the File Save button.*

Pasting Images onto the White Board

One of the most interesting uses of the White Board is to share graphical material that's already been created. Imagine talking to somebody a thousand miles away and suddenly saying, "Here, let me show you a picture of my kids!" Or your cats or your motherboard.

To paste an image onto the White Board, follow these steps:

1. Click the File open button at the top left of the White Board window.

2. Using the standard Open dialog box that appears, select a file from your hard drive or a network drive. Notice that you can choose files from among seven different graphics formats.

3. Click the Open button. The dialog box disappears, and you are returned to the White Board window.

4. Your White Board cursor is now a crosshairs, and an outline shows the size of the graphics you selected. Move the outline to the location on the White Board where you want to place it.

5. Once you have decided the location for your graphic, click the left mouse button. The new image is pasted onto the White Board, both locally and remotely.

TIP

You can also drag and drop graphics files directly onto the White Board. Simply select a file from anywhere on your hard drive, and hold down your left mouse button while dragging it into the White Board window. When you let go of the mouse button, the crosshairs cursor and outline appear as in step 4 above.

Screen Capture

The White Board also includes a screen capture facility. You can capture a snapshot of a window, your entire desktop, or any region of your screen and then paste it onto the White Board. Think of how useful this capability can be in technical support settings. Instead of trying to describe how that brand new game is spewing unrecognizable garbage all over your screen, why not *show* it to the technical specialist?

Here's how to place a screen capture onto the White Board:

1. Select one of the options from the Capture menu. Selecting Window lets you choose any window currently on your desktop; selecting Desktop captures your entire desktop; and selecting Region lets you choose a screen region to capture.

   ▪ For this example, go ahead and select Window. As soon as you do, the White Board is temporarily minimized, and a crosshairs cursor lets you choose any window currently on your desktop.

2. Position the cross-hairs cursor over the Conference window and click. The White Board pops back up. Your cursor now includes a movable outline indicating the size of the captured image.

3. Move the outline to the location on the White Board where you want to place it; then simply click. An image of the Conference window now appears exactly where you indicated, as you can see in Figure 11-39.

Figure 11-39: A new screen capture on the White Board.

Markup & the Pointer Tool

As a convenience for collaborative work, the White Board distinguishes between static material in what's called the *image layer* (screen captures and images loaded from disk) and *markup* (anything you add to the White Board using the various drawing tools). If these terms are unfamiliar to you, here's an example. Let's say you place a new image on the White Board to get your friend's feedback. Using the drawing tools, he puts a bunch of circles and arrows all over your picture, creating something like Figure 11-40.

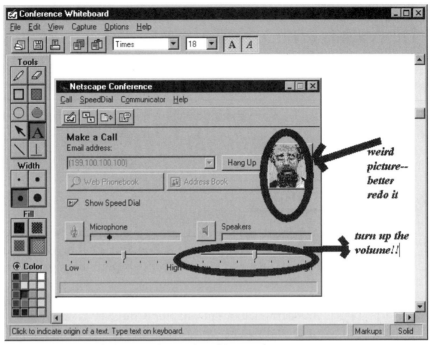

Figure 11-40: A marked-up graphic on the White Board.

And now let's say you think his comments are completely bogus. Wouldn't it be nice to get rid of what your pal added without getting rid of the original picture?

Well, you can! Just select Clear Markups from the Edit menu, and you're back to ground zero, a nice clean screen capture just like the one in Figure 11-40. You can also erase portions of the markup using the Eraser tool, without deleting any of the underlying graphic. You also can clear your own markups just as easily.

Conference's White Board offers another feature that's especially useful for collaborative work: the Pointer tool. You select the Pointer tool by clicking the arrow button in the left-hand tool bar. It then lets you place an arrow pointer anywhere on the White Board. But this highly visible arrow is not fixed in place like the other graphics tools such as lines and circles. If you still have the Pointer tool selected and you click your cursor somewhere else, the arrow moves to the new location. Thus, as you discuss the various elements on your White Board with another Conference user, you can point to them. You can think of the Pointer tool as your virtual index finger.

> **TIP**
>
> *If you suspect that you and the person you're conferencing with are not seeing the same stuff on your White Board, you can make sure by selecting Synchronize Page from the Edit menu.*

I could say a lot more about the White Board, but you'll have more fun exploring on your own. Let's move on now and take a look at the File Exchange feature.

File Exchange

In the section on Conference's Chat feature, you learned how you can paste text files right into your online conversation. But what if you want to send files that aren't text—for instance, spreadsheets, graphics files, or even entire programs?

The classic way of transferring files across the Internet or an intranet is via FTP, which you learned about in Chapter 8. But FTP is neither immediate nor direct. It requires that you log on to a special FTP server and deposit your file, which can then be retrieved by another individual who has access to the same server. Not only does this procedure add extra time to the process, but the majority of Net users do not have access to FTP servers that they can upload to and use in this way.

Enter Conference's File Exchange facility. It is one of my favorite features in all of Communicator, and what's more, it's so simple that I can demonstrate it in a few paragraphs.

OK, let's assume you're currently connected to another Conference user. In fact, let's pretend it's your editor, and she has just said, "Phil, I can't wait till later for those new chapters—I need them *this instant!*"

"OK," you respond weakly, "I'll send them right now."

And here's what you do next:

1. Click the File Exchange button, the one that shows a page with an arrow. The Netscape File Exchange window appears, as shown in Figure 11-41.

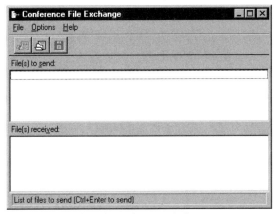

Figure 11-41: The File Exchange window.

2. Click the Open button, which is the middle button on the toolbar. The Add File to Send List dialog box pops up, as shown in Figure 11-42.

Figure 11-42: The Add File to Send List dialog box.

3. Use the controls in this standard file open dialog box to navigate to the directory that contains the file you want to send. Select it and click Open. You are returned to the File Exchange window. The file you've just selected appears in the top File(s) to Send pane, as shown in Figure 11-43.

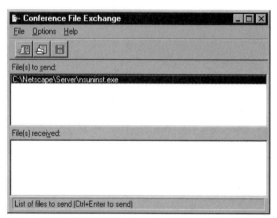

Figure 11-43: The File Exchange window with a file waiting to be sent.

4. Want to send more files? Simply repeat steps 2 and 3, adding as many files as you want. Figure 11-44 shows the File Exchange window with several files.

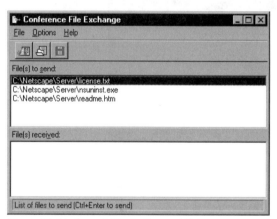

Figure 11-44: Several files in the send list.

TIP

To remove a file from the send list, simply select it and press the Del key. Don't worry, pressing this key doesn't delete the file from your hard drive—it only tells Conference not to send it.

5. Click the Options menu. If you're sending ASCII files, select ASCII; if you're sending binary (non-text) files, select Binary. You should also select Binary if you're sending a mixture of ASCII and binary files.

TIP

A Compress item also appears on the Options menu. Clicking this option tells Conference to compress, or shrink, the files you send; they are automatically decompressed at the other end. If you're sending short files across a relatively fast network connection, you might want to turn compression off to speed up initiating the transfer.

6. When you're ready to send your files, simply click the Send button. The files are sent across the Net or intranet to the remote Conference user. Unless you want to send more files, you can now close the File Exchange window.

And what happens when you *receive* a file from a remote Conference user? No matter what you're currently doing in Conference, the File Exchange window pops up, with the new files listed in the bottom pane, as shown in Figure 11-45.

Figure 11-45: The File Exchange window with several new received files.

TIP

If you don't want the File Exchange window to pop up automatically, click Pop Up On Receive in the Options menu to uncheck this feature.

You can now save these files to any folder on your hard drive or on a network drive. Here's how.

1. In the list of received files, select the name of the file you want to save.

2. Click the Save button on the toolbar. The Save Received File dialog box appears, as shown in Figure 11-46.

Figure 11-46: The Save Received File dialog box.

3. Navigate to the folder where you want to store the file, type in a new file name if you want, and click the Save button. The file is saved in its new location, and you are returned to the File Exchange window. As you can see in Figure 11-47, the received list no longer contains the file you just saved.

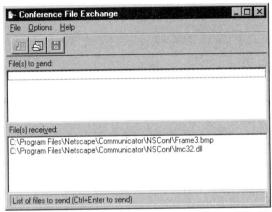

Figure 11-47: The received list after saving one of the files.

4. Repeat steps 1 through 3 for every file you want to save. After you're finished, simply close the File Exchange window.

Collaborative Browsing

OK, a short play:

[A man in a room, sitting at computer. Enter co-worker, who stands behind the man's chair, staring over the man's shoulder at the computer screen.]

Co-worker: Watcha doin', man, surfin'?

Man [*uncertainly*]: Oh, just catching up on some work.

Co-worker: Looks like yer surfin' to me.

Man: Well, maybe a little.

Co-worker: Whoa, cool picture, dude. I didn't even know Jesse Helms *knew* Heidi Fleiss.

Man [*clicking mouse quickly*]: Never mind that. Here, let me show you some really cool sites.

Co-worker: Well, awright, we're surfin' now!

[Man clicks from Web site to Web site. Co-worker continues to look over man's shoulder for next three hours, gurgling happily as audience slowly exits theater.]

This scene must get repeated thousands of times a day. Once you know a little bit about getting around the Web, you become a tour guide for your friends. And now, thanks to the collaborative browsing feature built right into Conference, you can be a *remote* tour guide.

Collaborative browsing is really a pretty simple concept. Using this feature, you can direct a remote Conference user to a specific Web page. That means you can use the multimedia documents that you both view simultaneously as the basis for your Conference discussion. As soon as you click a link, the remote user is immediately taken to the same site. It's as if you were controlling the remote user's copy of Navigator 4 yourself.

Let's give it a try:

1. Following the steps outlined earlier in this chapter, launch Netscape Conference and establish a connection with a remote user.

2. Click the Collaborative Browsing button, which depicts two windows with pointers in them. The Collaborative Browsing dialog box pops up, as shown in Figure 11-48.

Figure 11-48: The Collaborative Browsing dialog box.

3. Click the Start Browsing button. The remote Conference user is informed that you have requested a collaborative browsing session and is asked to join. Assuming he or she agrees to join by clicking Open Navigator, Navigator 4 is launched on both systems.

4. Simply cruise the Web using any of the techniques discussed in Chapter 3. Wherever you go, your colleague goes as well. Take a moment to savor the feeling of power this feature gives you.

Of course, your power is by no means absolute. *Either* party can cancel collaborative Web browsing at any time. Here's how:

1. Click the Collaborative Browsing button again. You are returned to the Collaborative Browsing dialog box, but it looks a bit different now, as shown in Figure 11-49.

Figure 11-49: The Collaborative Browsing dialog box during an active Collaborative session.

TIP

If your browser and your partner's browser are not currently displaying the same Web page, click the Sync Browsers button. That will assure that you are both viewing the same URL.

2. To end the collaborative browsing session, click the Stop Browsing button. The remote user is informed that you have terminated the session. Remember, though, that you are still connected via Conference and can resume collaborative browsing—as well as any other Conference facility—at any point.

Who's Leading?

Collaborative Web browsing is like ballroom dancing: One of the partners is always leading, and the other follows. But Conference lets you switch these roles very fluidly. Take another look at Figure 11-49 above. If you uncheck the Control the Browsers check box in the middle of a session, your partner becomes the lead. As he or she moves from site to site, you are dragged along.

You can switch back and forth like this as often as you want. But remember that the "follower" cannot assume the lead unless the leader has relinquished it. In other words, you can *uncheck* the Control the Browsers check box when you're in the role of leader, but you cannot check it when you're not.

Moving On

Now that you're familiar with Netscape Conference, I'm sure you'll come up with all kinds of interesting ways to use it. And I think you'll agree that with its flexibility and dazzling combination of features, it is potentially one of the most *fun* Communicator components.

Real-time conferencing is one of the hottest new trends on the Net, as well as on office intranets. But there's another important trend as well: an every-increasing interest in security. As more and more companies set up shop on the Web, more and more of us will start purchasing all kinds of products electronically. I don't know about you, but when I type in my credit card information, I want to make sure it gets to the right place without any side trips onto some hacker's hard drive. Netscape Communicator provides some of the most robust and flexible security features available, and in the next chapter we take a close look at them.

CHAPTER 12

Communicator Security

The Internet has had a colorful history. The military started it, the academic world helped to develop and refine it, and thousands of individuals began using it for everything from research to interactive games. Then, as with every other innovation, people figured out ways to make money with it. Online transactions are now commonplace. And as the Net has grown and become more commercialized, security has jumped to the foreground as one of the most important. It goes without saying that the administrators and users of office intranets have their own very serious security concerns as well.

Whether you're shopping online or sharing sensitive company information with one of your co-workers, Communicator offers the most powerful and flexible data security of any commercial communications program. In this chapter, you'll learn how to use and configure Communicator's security options for your own specific needs. But first, understanding a little about the underlying issues and technology might help.

Security on the Net & on Intranets

When I was a kid, the mix of technology and commerce was already cause for panic. "Some companies encourage you to order products by telephone," complained the news media. "When you place your order, they'll try to get you to tell them your credit card number instead of mailing a check. Don't do it!" they warned. "Don't give *anyone* your credit card number over the phone!"

Twenty-something years later these fears seem quaint. The American public has become used to home shopping and 800 numbers and has clearly decided that convenience is worth a little risk. Did the nightmare scenarios come true? Did unscrupulous employees at companies all over the country steal thousands of credit card numbers and spend all your money at the track? Of course not. Most employees want to keep their jobs.

Security is about people, not technologies. No matter what methods you use to transfer information, somebody can steal it if he or she wants it badly enough. Germany under Hitler was home to some of the world's cleverest cryptographers and information scientists, and yet the Allied powers were able to crack the secret codes. Right now hundreds or perhaps even thousands of workers—telephone sales agents, customer service representatives, data entry personnel, managers, bank tellers, system administrators—have access to your financial records or your credit card information. The operator could even listen in on your phone calls. And yet how often do you get ripped off?

The people who handle Internet transactions are really no different from the workers who already know or have access to your credit card numbers. Let's dispel a few myths:

- The Internet is *not* a den of hacker-thieves looking for a quick buck. There are easier ways to steal.

- Sending data across the Net does *not* give everyone on the Net access to that data.

- Most businesses set up shop on the Net because it offers a new, cost-effective point of sale, *not* because it enables them to collect more personal information about their customers—although this is an increasing problem.

- The Internet is *not* a leaky old boat full of giant security holes that can never be plugged.

That said, the security of information on the Net is still an important issue. Even though the biggest security hole is people rather than software or hardware, and even though abuses have been exaggerated by weekly magazines and so-called news shows, nothing is wrong with making the Internet as secure a medium as possible for financial transactions. And, of course, if you're on an office intranet, you want to make sure that neither the outside world nor unscrupulous individuals within the company have access to trade secrets or sensitive personnel information.

Netscape, recognizing from its inception as a company that commercial transactions were the Next Big Thing on the Net and that intranets were the Next Big Thing in the business community, has taken a lead in bolstering the security of transmitted data. In this chapter, we'll take a brief look at how Communicator addresses security. After that, we'll get into the nuts and bolts of actually *using* the security features available to you.

Communicator & Security

To understand what Netscape has done to address security issues, you have to understand the issues it is addressing. In other words, in what ways is it even possible to improve Internet and intranet security?

Information traveling between your computer and another machine, such as a Web server, is routed from node to node—or machine to machine—until it finally reaches its destination. It may pass through a handful or even dozens of computer systems. At any one of these sites, a technically proficient but unscrupulous individual can access the stream of data for ulterior motives. Somebody could eavesdrop on you, collecting personal or financial information; somebody could copy your intellectual property, such as a great new idea for a patent; or somebody could even change your data before it reaches its destination, causing all kinds of mayhem. The Internet itself provides no built-in mechanism for preventing such activities, nor do intranets.

Netscape's response to this lack of security was to develop the *Secure Sockets Layer (SSL) protocol*. The SSL protocol enhances Internet security in four ways:

- It provides a mechanism for server authentication. That means you can be sure you're really connected to the site you intended to connect with.

- It provides for user authentication as well. A secure Web site can make sure it's really dealing with you, not some cheap imitation.

- It provides privacy by using a powerful encryption technique on transmitted data.

- It provides data integrity, ensuring that the information you send arrives exactly as you sent it.

If you think about this situation for a moment, you'll realize that for SSL to work, both ends of the link—the client and the server—must run software that supports these features. If your Web browser encrypts your credit card information, for example, the server you're talking to must be able to decrypt it. Currently, SSL is supported by Netscape Communicator and all of Netscape's Web servers, which are rapidly becoming a standard for businesses on the Net.

How does SSL work? The Internet and intranets can be seen as layered sets of protocols. In Chapter 1, you learned that everything rests on TCP/IP, the protocol suite that actually divides your data into packets and ships them out to the right destination. Above this layer are application protocols such as Telnet, FTP, and HTTP. They are the support protocols for the various services available on the Net. SSL actually provides a new protocol layer, situating itself between TCP/IP and the application protocol, HTTP in this case. That way, it is not dependent on any of these other protocols to do its job. Figure 12-1 illustrates how a message you type is processed by the various protocol layers and then travels across the Net to a Web server that "unprocesses" the information.

Figure 12-1: A secure message sent to a Web server.

SSL uses a powerful mechanism known as *public key encryption* for protecting data. Each secure Netscape server has its own unique pair of digital keys, which are really just long strings of random bytes. One of these keys is private and kept secret at the server site; the other is made public. When you send a message to a secure server, it is encrypted and automatically includes the public key for that site. The private key at the server end must be the one that "fits" this public key; otherwise, your data will not be decrypted and you will not be able to communicate. Since these pairs of keys are guaranteed to be unique, you can be certain that your information has reached the right destination before it is decrypted.

Can't Some Hacker Crack SSL?

Sure, hackers can break anything. The issue is just a matter of how much work it takes.

SSL uses authentication and encryption technology that was developed by RSA Data Security. The standard "export" version of Netscape Communicator, which is required by the United States government to use a weaker version of encryption than the U.S.-only version, relies on what is known as RSA's "40-bit key RC4 algorithm." Even in this weaker implementation, the security is pretty impressive. Let's say your neighbor knows you are about to transmit your credit card number. He goes outside with a ladder and a bunch of equipment and manages to capture the encrypted data from your phone line. If you're a forgiving sort of person, you should go out and warn him that it takes an average of 64 MIPS-years to break the code. If he gets a 64-MIPS computer to work around the clock on deciphering your information, he'll probably have the answer in about a year. By that time, your credit card will be maxed out anyway.

Of course, this scenario is assuming your neighbor doesn't know much about you and is trying to crack the code by trying millions of random combinations. Using various heuristics—educated guesses—the time can be greatly reduced. If you're concerned and want to use the very strongest security available, get the 128-bit U.S.-only version of Communicator. In fact, some financial services, such as Fidelity, require this stronger version for stock trading and other transactions. You can get more information on obtaining it from the Netscape home page.

Site Certificates

In conjunction with public key encryption, SSL offers another level of security called *site certification*. Here's how it works:

To operate in secure mode and use the features of SSL, anyone who sets up a Netscape server in secure mode must have requested and been sent a special digital certificate, a unique pattern of bytes that "unlocks" these features. Before issuing a certificate (which, of course, is sent encrypted), a special certifying authority makes sure that the requesting organization is "for real."

A secure server may include its site certificate along with any data it sends you, whether it's a Web page, a Netcaster channel, a Java program, or even a simple e-mail message. Data that's sent along with a digital certificate—also known as a digital signature—is called *signed* data. Based on the identity of the sender, you may choose to reject certain features of the information. For example, you may not want to grant an unknown party access to your hard drive via a signed Java applet.

A site certificate also includes the organization's public encryption key so that Communicator can automatically transmit encrypted information back to the site.

Digital certificates, in conjunction with public key encryption, help to protect you from fraud, pranks, and theft of intellectual property.

Personal Certificates

Communicator also supports Personal Certificates. They are just like site certificates, but they positively identify individuals running Communicator rather than organizations running a Netscape server. A personal certificate assures a secure Web site that you are really you. A certificate can make it unnecessary for you to type in a name and password each time you access a secure site—the Web server gets much more complete authentication information automatically from your personal certificate.

A personal certificate also enables others to send you encrypted e-mail, since your certificate includes your unique encryption key. And, of course, you can't send encrypted e-mail to others unless they've already included *their* keys in digital signatures.

Communicator allows you to have several different personal certificates. Within the next year or so, you'll even be able to obtain personal certificates that are specific to particular payment methods. You may have a Visa personal certificate, for example, as well as a MasterCard one.

You learn how to obtain personal certificates later in this chapter, in the section called "Getting a Personal Certificate."

Passwords

OK, let's say you have several personal certificates. That means you might be able to log on to a secure site without typing a special password—the software handles authentication for you. But suppose somebody else can access your machine. Since the authentication process is automatic, hasn't this whole system made online transactions less rather than more secure?

Not really. If you think that somebody else might access your machine, Communicator lets you create a personal password that you must type every time you launch the program. You can change this password as often as you like, and there is no way for another user to discover it. In fact, it is so secure that it may even cause *you* some headaches: if you forget what it is, there is no way to find out, and you have to get all new personal certificates!

Security Alerts

Most of Communicator's security features are set into motion automatically. For example, once you fill in credit card information and click the Submit button in a form from a secure server, your information is automatically encrypted as it makes its way across the Net. Because of this automation, you must know when you are in fact communicating with a secure server and when you're not. Fortunately, Communicator lets you know with special messages called *alerts*. By default, Communicator lets you know when you're in the following situations:

- You're entering an encrypted site.
- You're leaving an encrypted site.
- You're viewing a page that includes a mix of encrypted and unencrypted data.
- You're about to send unencrypted information to a site.

In addition, Communicator warns you when you're about to download a Java applet or JavaScript code that uses your system resources in any way that may compromise your security. You may have already seen one of these warnings, or Java Security alerts, if you've run Communicator's Netcaster component. Communicator can even warn you before you download a signed plug-in or before a server tries to store any information in the form of "cookies" on your machine.

TIP

Cookies are pieces of system or configuration information transmitted between a Web server and the browser software and then stored on the client machine. Cookies enable a Web page to adjust its display or other configuration options for particular clients that connect, but they may also be used to trace exactly what documents a user accesses on the site. In other words, they can be useful in developing a "click profile" of a user, and some people feel this capability is an invasion of privacy. To change your cookie settings—that is, to disable them or activate an alert when they are sent to your machine—select Preferences from the Edit menu of any Communicator component and then click the Advanced category. These options are also covered in Chapter 3, in the section called "Advanced Preferences."

Firewalls & Proxies

You've probably read horror stories about hackers who get online only to sabotage or destroy data. As the new information technologies mature, acts like these probably won't have the same thrill they used to, but cyber-criminals will never disappear completely. For this reason, businesses, universities, government agencies, and other sites that have sensitive data on their networks are forced to think of ways to keep these types of users away. Firewalls are software and hardware solutions that provide a layer or several layers of protection between the Internet and a local network. These layers are designed to keep the bad guys out, but they also restrict users within a network from getting out on the Internet directly. For this reason, *proxy gateways,* or simply *proxies,* were created to enable users to work through firewalls and access the outside world.

Proxies are security features deployed by many businesses. System administrators set up proxy gateways so that users on an intranet or other LAN are not actually connected directly to the Internet. Instead, any Internet data they send or receive is handled by the proxy computer, which passes the information on. The proxy may be completely transparent, allowing all data in and out of the organization and simply monitoring activity, or it may be part of a firewall that restricts both inbound and outbound access in various ways. The proxy settings in Netscape Communicator allow the program to pass on a network request to an outside agent through a firewall, which performs the request for Communicator. The proxy agent then returns any Internet information to Communicator.

When you use a Communicator component through a proxy gateway, you might think you're on the Internet even though you really aren't. Proxy gateways are implemented based on the type of service in use, such as FTP, Gopher, WAIS, news, and HTTP (the World Wide Web). Each URL access method can send its requests to a different proxy.

How does this system work? Typically, when you try to access a particular kind of network server, you specify its address—or click a link that includes the address. Communicator then sends a request to the server using a particular software *port number* associated with that kind of network service. For example, the port usually associated with FTP is 21, so Communicator sends messages to an FTP server specifying port 21. The server then knows that FTP is the service required. With a proxy server in use, though, Communicator does not send its request or a standard port number directly to the actual Internet server. Instead, it sends its request to the proxy server's address with a special port number that's unique to the proxy server itself. The proxy server then sends the request on to the appropriate Internet server, using the usual port number for that service.

Configuring Proxy Settings

Before configuring proxy settings, your first task is to ask your system administrator whether a proxy is even necessary or available. If you're running Communicator on an internal network from behind a firewall, you need to know the URL of the file your network uses for automatic proxy configuration. Or if your system administrator has not enabled automatic configuration, you need the proxy port numbers for each network service supported by your proxy server. This data is necessary for filling out the Proxies category in Communicator's Preferences. To get to the correct dialog box, click Preferences in the Edit menu of any Communicator component. Then expand the Advanced category by double-clicking it and select Proxies. The Proxies page appears, as shown in Figure 12-2.

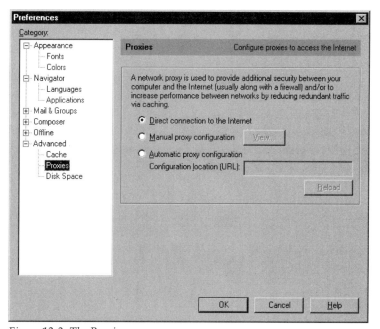

Figure 12-2: The Proxies page.

The Proxies page includes the following items:

- **Direct connection to the Internet**. Configures Netscape Communicator to run without a proxy. This option is the default setting.

- **Manual Proxy Configuration**. Allows the most flexible configuration of proxy gateways for each type of URL. If you want to configure the proxy settings yourself, use this option, as described in the section "Configuring a Proxy Manually."

■ **Automatic proxy configuration**. Instructs Netscape Communicator to configure your proxies automatically based on a configuration file designed expressly for your proxy server. Click the radio button, and then provide the file's URL in the Configuration Location (URL) field.

Configuring a Proxy Manually

To set a proxy using the Manual Proxy Configuration choice, follow these steps:

1. While you're still in the Proxies page, click the Manual proxy configuration radio button.

2. Click the View button to display the Manual Proxy Configuration dialog box, as shown in Figure 12-3.

Figure 12-3: The Manual Proxy Configuration dialog box.

■ The long list of proxies should be blank unless already configured by your network administrator. The Port settings will all have zeros in them, with the exception of the SOCKS host port, which should read 1080. If you see some other data already listed, stop and ask someone whether you're using the proper settings. If so, you're done.

3. Fill in each of the proxy fields with the following information:

- **HTTP**. Enter the Internet address of the system running the proxy software and the port number for HTTP protocol access. When these addresses are set correctly, you'll be able to access Web pages and sites.

- **Security**. Enter the information for your Secure Sockets Layer (SSL) protocol resource.

- **FTP**. Enter the Internet address of the system running the proxy software and the port number for FTP protocol access. When these addresses are set correctly, you'll be able to access anonymous FTP sites.

- **SOCKS**. If your network uses a SOCKS Host gateway as part of a firewall, enter its Internet address here.

- **Gopher**. Enter the Internet address of the system running the proxy software and the port number for Gopher protocol access. When these addresses are set correctly, you'll be able to access Gopher menus.

- **WAIS**. Enter the Internet address of the system running the proxy software and the port number for WAIS protocol access. When these addresses are set correctly, you'll be able to access WAIS databases.

TIP

You can put the Internet addresses for multiple hosts in each field. If your network administrator provides you with multiple proxy addresses for each protocol, you should separate them with commas. Do not use wildcards for multiple addresses!

4. Your network may be configured to allow you to access certain sites directly, without going through a proxy. If so, enter the addresses for these sites in the Exceptions box. The format of these entries is the Internet address followed by the port number for the allowed protocol. For example, the standard port number for Gopher is 70, so to allow direct access to the Gopher server at pjames.com, you would enter **pjames.com:70**. You can specify multiple sites in the Exceptions box, separating them with commas.

> **TIP**
>
> *Unless you have a photographic memory, take this book or page with you when you talk to your site administrator. Have him or her fill out the correct addresses and ports for each setting. Then enter them yourself in your copy of Netscape Communicator. Why? Because you need to make sure all these settings are perfect before trying to use Communicator. Otherwise, you'll experience problems and won't be able to access anything on the Net.*

5. Click OK to save your changes.

Once you've got your proxy all set up, you should be able to connect to the Internet via your company's LAN. Give it a try by clicking the Home button. If you can't connect this way, you'll need to talk once more to your network administrator. Every network is configured a little differently, so we can't give you any easy answers here.

Now that you have a broad overview of Communicator's security features, let's see how these features work in some individual Communicator components, starting with Navigator 4.

Security in Navigator 4

The first thing to understand about security in Navigator 4 is the concept of *secure* and *insecure* Web pages. An insecure Web page is one that has not been encrypted and does not include a digital certificate assuring you of the source. A secure page is encrypted and includes a certificate. The vast majority of Web pages are insecure; there is simply no need to ensure the privacy or authenticity of most Web communications, and the security safeguards aren't worth the slight amount of extra time they would add to the transfer of the information.

> **TIP**
>
> *Netscape considers data security of utmost importance, and the Communicator development team was still busy tweaking security features as this book went to press. Consequently, you might find some very slight "holes" or inconsistencies in this chapter where option screens had not been finalized. The differences are mainly cosmetic, however, and you will be able to figure everything out very easily by following the procedures outlined here.*

If you click the Security button or the Security icon on the status line when visiting a typical Web site, you'll get information like that shown in Figure 12-4.

Figure 12-4: Security Info for an insecure Web page.

As you can see, Communicator has correctly identified this page as unencrypted. In addition, the Verification section of this dialog box does not indicate that a digital certificate was included with the page. But you *can* get some more information about the document. Try clicking the Open Page Info button. You will see something like Figure 12-5.

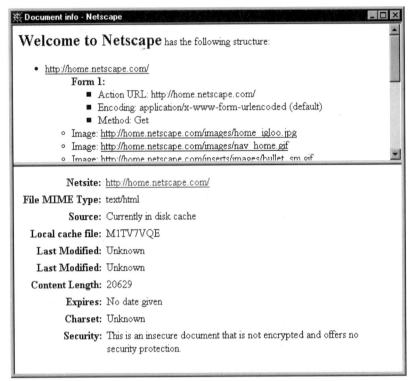

Figure 12-5: The Document info page.

The top frame of the Document info page identifies the actual documents currently displayed in the Navigator 4 window, including the URLs for the HTML file itself and for any inline graphics. The bottom panel is composed of a miscellany of information about the files, including security information. As you select a file in the top frame, the bottom frame gives you information about that specific file.

Scroll through the bottom panel to view information about the file you have selected. Not all this information is directly related to security issues, but even the more general items can help you determine the authenticity of a document. Here's a list of the fields and their meanings:

- **Netsite** or **Location**. This field simply provides the URL of the file.

- **File MIME type**. For an HTML file, the MIME type is text/html. For graphics, it will depend on the graphic format.

- **Source**. This field tells you how Netscape Navigator 4 is currently accessing the file. In many cases, it will have been cached to disk, and Communicator will indicate it is reading the cached version.

- **Local cache file**. This field indicates the name of the file on your local hard drive that contains the source for the cached document.

- **Content length**. This field simply indicates the size of the file, if available.

- **Expires**. This field indicates when the cache file expires, based on your Preferences settings.

- **Charset**. This field indicates the character set used by the document. In most cases, the Charset will be iso-8859-1, which is the technical name for ISO-Latin (the character set used for Western European languages). Obviously, if the file is a graphic, the charset will be unspecified or labeled unknown.

- **Security**. This field indicates the type of security used for this document. In this case, it's an insecure document, so this field reads "This is an insecure document that is not encrypted and offers no security protection."

TIP

For graphics files, several additional fields include specific information about the format and resolution of the image.

And now for a totally different experience, let's visit a secure site.

1. Make sure you are connected to the Internet, either directly or through a SLIP or PPP connection with your access provider.

2. Launch Netscape Navigator 4.

3. Click your mouse inside the Netsite/Location box at the top of the window to select the URL http://home.netscape.com/.

4. Replace this URL with **https://www.att.com/**, the URL for AT&T's secure home page. (No, that's not a typo. To access documents on secure servers, you type **https** instead of **http** in the protocol section of the URL). A Security Information alert appears, as shown in Figure 12-6.

Figure 12-6: Security Information alert.

Whenever you are presented with a notification dialog box like this, you have the option of unchecking the Show This Alert Next Time check box. If you uncheck it, a corresponding check box is unchecked in the Navigator security preferences window, making it a default *not* to show the alert. You can also change this option *directly* in the Navigator security preferences window. You'll learn how to make this change in a few minutes, in the section unsurprisingly called "Navigator Security Preferences."
Note: If the site you are accessing attempts to send you several documents—for example, if it includes multiple frames—you may be presented with several of these Security Information alerts.

Once you've responded to any alerts, the AT&T page itself finally appears in the Navigator 4 window, as shown in Figure 12-7.

Since this site is secure, the Security button—as well as the Security icon in the status line—now depicts a locked paddle lock. Go ahead and click either the button or the icon. The Security Info page for this site appears, as shown in Figure 12-8.

Figure 12-7: The secure AT&T page.

Figure 12-8: Security Info for the AT&T secure Web site.

The top portion of the page informs you that this document is encrypted and that it is "signed" with a digital security certificate. To view the contents of the certificate, click the View Certificate button. The View a Certificate window appears, as shown in Figure 12-9.

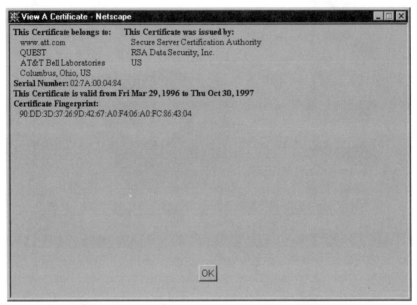

Figure 12-9: The View a Certificate window, showing the certificate for AT&T's secure site.

Let's take a closer look at some of the information in the certificate:

- **This Certificate belongs to**. The certifying authority RSA requires that each applicant for a certificate submit a registered organization name and a variety of other identifying information. Obviously, if you think you're at an AT&T site, but the owner of the Digital ID is not AT&T, you may have found a security problem.

- **This Certificate was issued by**. For now, this field should indicate that the certificate was issued by RSA. Other organizations might be involved in the certification process in the future, but if this field reads something like "Hacker d00d," you probably should not submit your credit card number.

- **Serial Number**. As you might expect, this field indicates a unique number assigned by the certifying authority.

■ **This Certificate is valid from**. As an added protection, digital certificates are issued for set lengths of time. This field indicates when the current certificate expires.

■ **Certificate fingerprint.** This field indicates a special digital signature that helps assure the authority of the certificate.

You shouldn't need to access this information very often, but if you suspect a security problem, the View a Certificate page offers you ample opportunity to play digital detective.

Now click OK to return to the Security Info page, as shown earlier in Figure 12-8. Once you're there, click the Open Page Info button this time. The Document info window appears, as shown in Figure 12-10.

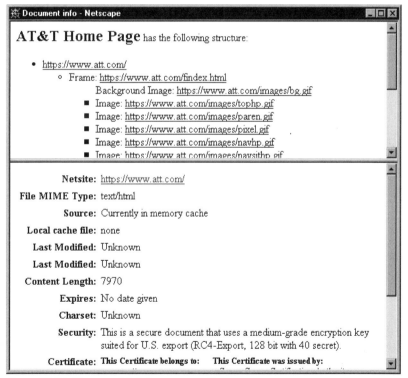

Figure 12-10: Document info for a secure site.

This window looks pretty much like the Document info we saw earlier for an insecure site, but if you scroll down to the bottom of the bottom frame, you'll see that the Security field now indicates the type of encryption being used. In addition, a new Certificate field includes the same information you saw in the View a Certificate window, as shown in Figure 12-11.

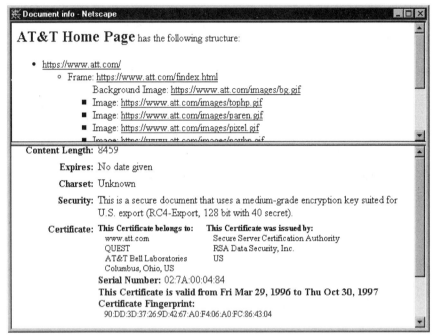

Figure 12-11: Security information in the Document info page.

Of course, you can view this information for any file listed in the top frame. Simply click the URL to see the specific information.

Now that we've seen how Communicator's security features work at a particular Web site, let's examine some of the configuration options available to you.

Navigator Security Preferences

Communicator provides a number of options that let you tailor Navigator's security features for your particular needs. For example, if you're on a small office intranet and are very familiar with all the material you access with Navigator 4, you may want to turn off some of the alerts.

To configure the Navigator 4 security preferences, follow these steps:

1. Click the Security button in any Communicator component that includes it. Optionally, click the Security icon in the status line. The Security Info page appears.

2. In list at the left of the window, click Navigator. The Navigator security preferences window appears, as shown in Figure 12-12.

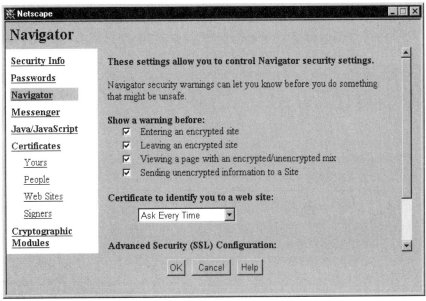

Figure 12-12: Navigator security preferences.

Earlier in the chapter, you saw that Navigator 4 pops up special security alert messages to inform you of changes in the security status of your connection. Leaving these alerts enabled is a good idea, but the top section of this dialog box lets you turn off any that you don't want to see. Here are the results of unchecking each of these boxes:

■ **Entering an encrypted site**. Unchecking this box means that you will not receive notification when you are about to access a document on a secure server. If you spend a lot of time on secure servers and know what you are doing, you might want to uncheck this box.

■ **Leaving an encrypted site.** Unchecking this box means that you will not be notified when you are about to *leave* a secure server and access a document that is not secure.

■ **Viewing a page with an encrypted/unencrypted mix.** Unchecking this box means that you will not receive an alert when you are about to access a document that contains both secure and insecure information.

■ **Sending unencrypted information to a site.** Unchecking this box means that you will not receive notification when you are about to submit information insecurely over the Net or your intranet. If you do a lot of online shopping and are concerned about credit card fraud, I would not recommend unchecking this item.

I mentioned earlier that you can obtain a digital security certificate of your own; in the section called "Getting a Personal Certificate," I'll show you how. With your own certificate, you can electronically sign your e-mail messages, assuring your recipients that it's really you. You also can use a certificate to identify yourself to Web sites that require user authentication. In this case, a digital certificate acts like a password, except that it is more secure and completely automatic. You don't need to type anything to identify yourself to the site.

I also mentioned earlier that you can have several different personal certificates, and the next option in the Navigator security preferences dialog box lets you choose how to handle this situation. The drop-down box in the middle of the page contains at least two choices:

■ **Ask every time.** Select this option if you want Navigator to ask you which certificate to use every time a Web site requests your certificate.

■ **Select automatically.** Select this option if you want Navigator to send a certificate automatically, without asking you which one.

The rest of the drop-down list is composed of any personal certificates you've obtained and installed. You can select any one of them from the list to designate it as the certificate that's sent whenever an identifying certificate is required.

The bottom section of the Navigator security preferences dialog box lets you check which versions of SSL you want to use. It also lets you configure them to use a variety of different encryption algorithms. Unless you know what you're doing and have very specific reasons for disallowing any of the protocols or encryption types, you should *leave these settings alone!*

Note: SSL 3 has several advantages over earlier implementations. Besides being more efficient, it includes an extra encryption mechanism, better digital certificate management, and better support for hardware devices.

Certificates You've Accepted

Once you've accepted a certificate from a Web site, it is saved on your system. Communicator lists all the certificates you've accepted and lets you view their details even when you're not connected to the particular site. You can also tell Navigator what action to take when it encounters another document originating from the holder of any one of the certificates you've collected. For example, you might want to *reject* any pages from the holder of a particular certificate.

Follow these steps to view certificates you've accepted from Web sites:

1. Click the Security button or Security icon in a Communicator component. The Security Info page appears.

2. In the list on the left, click Web Sites, under the Certificates category. The Web Sites' Certificates dialog box appears.

After selecting a particular certificate from the list, you can use the buttons to delete it from your system, verify it (determine whether it is still a valid certificate or whether it has expired), or edit the actions Navigator takes when you are sent a page from the holder of this certificate.

Certificate Signers (Certifying Authorities)

Security certificates are granted to Web sites—as well as to individuals—by special certifying authorities or *signers*. These authorities can be compared to notaries public—they check the identity of the applicant and then assure that the digital certificate they assign is unique. You can instruct Navigator 4, as well as other Communicator components, to react in various ways to digitally signed information based on the identity of the certificate's signer. And guess how you know the identity of these certifying authorities? That's right, they have certificates too!

To view signers' certificates, follow these steps:

1. Click the Security button or Security icon in a Communicator component. The Security Info page appears.

2. In the list on the left, click Signers, under the Certificates category. The Certificate Signers' Certificates dialog box appears, as shown in Figure 12-13.

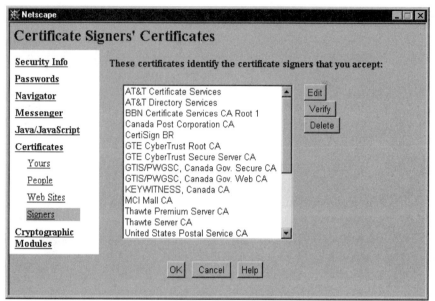

Figure 12-13: The Certificate Signers' Certificates dialog box.

3. Select a certificate from the list.

4. To delete the selected certificate, click Delete. To verify it (determine whether it has expired), click Verify. To edit the action Communicator takes when it encounters a certificate signed by the selected certifying authority, click Edit. The Edit a Certification Authority dialog box appears, as shown in Figure 12-14.

Check boxes in this dialog box let you do the following:

■ **Accept this Certificate Authority for Certifying network sites**. Checking this check box means that you will not automatically reject Web site certificates signed by this certifying authority.

■ **Accept this Certificate Authority for Certifying e-mail users**. Checking this check box means that you will not automatically reject certificates included with e-mail if they are signed by this authority. (See the next section called "E-Mail Security (S/MIME).")

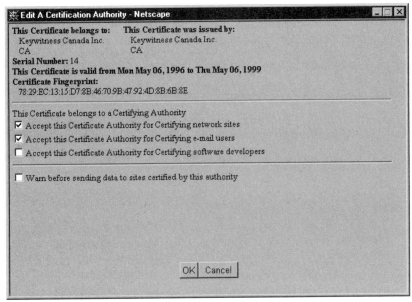

Figure 12-14: The Edit a Certification Authority dialog box.

■ **Accept this Certificate Authority for Certifying software developers**.
Checking this check box means that you will not automatically reject
certificates included with Java objects, plug-ins, and software upgrades if
they are signed by this authority. (See the section called "Java &
JavaScript Security" later in this chapter.)

■ **Warn before sending data to sites certified by this authority**. If you
check this check box, Communicator will pop up an alert before you
send any data (for example, in a form) to a site whose certificate is
signed by this certifying authority.

Now that you've seen some of Communicator's security features that are
specific to Web sites, let's move on to an area where just about everybody
cares about privacy: e-mail.

E-Mail Security (S/MIME)

As we start using e-mail for financial transactions and other sensitive communications, the privacy of our messages becomes increasingly important.

Communicator's Messenger and Discussion Group components support a standard known as S/MIME (Secure MIME) for digitally signed and encrypted e-mail messages. S/MIME can assure you that messages you send and receive are authentic and have not been read anywhere between their point of origin and their final destination. In this section, I'll cover the basic features of S/MIME as implemented in Messenger.

> **TIP**
>
> *If your incoming e-mail server is an IMAP server (rather than POP3), it may support encrypted connections, automatically encrypting information it sends you. If your network administrator has told you that this is the case, select Preferences from Messenger's Edit menu and then click the Mail Server category. Check the very last check box, "Server supports encrypted connections (SSL)," in the Mail Server dialog box.*

Let's start with sending signed and encrypted messages.

Sending Signed & Encrypted Messages

Messenger lets you send *signed messages* that include a digital security certificate assuring the recipient that the message did in fact come from you, or at least from somebody sitting at your computer. Like site certificates, personal digital security certificates are issued by special certifying organizations. Getting a personal security certificate can be compared with getting a passport from the Post Office, except that it is a "cyber-passport" and you can obtain one electronically, using Netscape Communicator, of course. Later in this chapter, in the section called "Getting a Personal Certificate," I'll show you how to obtain a new personal security certificate, but for now let's assume you already have one. Here's how you attach it to your e-mail:

1. Follow the steps outlined in Chapter 5 for creating a new e-mail message.

2. In the Composition window, click the Sending Options tab, as shown in Figure 12-15.

Figure 12-15: The Sending Options tab.

3. Check the check box labeled Signed.

4. Send your message by clicking the Send button.

TIP

After you check the Signed check box, a signature tag appears as part of the icon on the Security button.

That's it! And what does the recipient see when he or she looks at a signed message? I'll cover that information in the section called "Receiving Signed & Encrypted Messages," but for now let's move on to sending encrypted messages.

As you learned earlier, encrypted messages are scrambled using a special *algorithm*, or formula, so that they cannot normally be read at any point between your computer and your recipient's computer. In encrypting your message, Messenger uses a key that's part of your recipient's digital security certificate—that's how your recipient can *de*crypt it at the other end. Yes, you have to have received a signed message from an individual before you can send that individual an encrypted message. You do not necessarily need your *own* digital certificate to send encrypted e-mail, but without one nobody will be able to send *you* encrypted messages.

Getting a Recipients' Certificate from a Directory Server

Your recipient may have added his or her digital certificate to an LDAP directory server on your intranet—or even to a large public directory on the Net. If that is the case, you can obtain the certificate—and send encrypted e-mail—without already having received a message signed by your recipient. Here's how:

1. In Messenger, click the Security button or the Security icon on the status line.

2. On the left side of the Security Info page, select People under the Certificates category. The Other People's Certificates dialog box appears.

3. Click the Search Directory button. In the next dialog box that appears, select a directory server from the drop-down list, type in the e-mail address of the person whose certificate you want, and click the Search button. After a few moments, a Search Results dialog box appears listing any matches.

4. To save any certificates that were found, click OK.

You can now send encrypted e-mail to your recipient.

To send an encrypted message, follow these steps:

1. Follow the steps outlined in Chapter 5 for creating a new e-mail message.

2. In the Composition window, click the Sending Options tab, as shown earlier in Figure 12-15.

3. Check the check box labeled Encrypted.

4. Send your message by clicking the Send button.

TIP

After you check the Encrypted check box, the paddle lock icon on the Security button appears locked rather than open.

Receiving Signed & Encrypted Messages

What happens when you receive a signed and/or encrypted message? Check out Figure 12-16.

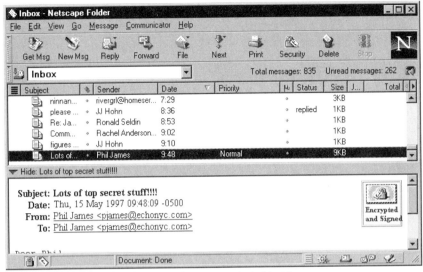

Figure 12-16: A signed and encrypted message selected in Messenger.

The Messenger window looks different in several ways:

■ The Security button now depicts a locked paddle lock (indicating an encrypted message) with a tag hanging from it (indicating that it's also a signed message).

■ The status line paddle lock is now locked, and the "signed" icon appears to its right.

■ Just to the right of the usual headers, the message itself contains a special "Encrypted and Signed" icon.

TIP

Remember, signing and encryption are related but independent S/MIME features. You may receive messages that are just encrypted, or just signed. In these cases, the icon will, of course, be slightly different.

The whole idea of signed messages is that you can verify the identity of the sender. Obviously, the mere presence of these new icons doesn't necessarily give you the assurance you need. When Immigration agents ask you to verify your identity, they usually want to see a bit more than your passport's blue and gold cover. Well, go ahead and click the new icon within the message, or the Security button, or the paddle lock icon on the status line. Any one of these actions has the same result: it opens up the message sender's electronic passport. A new Security Info window appears, providing detailed security information, as shown in Figure 12-17.

Figure 12-17: The Security Info for a signed and encrypted e-mail message.

To see more identifying information about the message sender, simply click the View button. The details of the individual's security certificate appear in a new window, as shown in Figure 12-18.

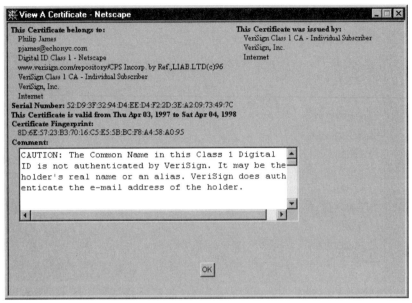

Figure 12-18: The View a Certificate window.

Note: Several classes of personal digital certificates are available, graded (and priced) according to how positively they identify an individual or organization. A Class 1 certificate does not positively identify the individual who holds it—the certifying authority has not done any background work to match the stated name with the person applying for the certificate. In fact, you can even get a Class 1 certificate using an alias or nickname instead of your real name. Class 2 certificates, on the other hand, require positive identification using a real name. The View a Certificate page tells you what class certificate this is.

Click OK after you've finished viewing the sender's security certificate. Now that you've received the security certificate, you can send encrypted e-mail to this individual.

Messenger Security Preferences

Back in the Security Info window, as shown in Figure 12-17, click the Messenger category at the left side. A new dialog box appears, as shown in Figure 12-19.

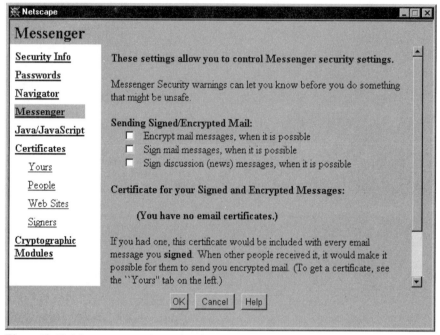

Figure 12-19: Messenger security preferences.

By checking the respective check boxes, you can activate the following options:

- **Encrypt mail messages, when it is possible.** If you check this check box, Messenger will encrypt all outgoing messages as long as you already have a digital security certificate for the recipient.

- **Sign mail messages, when it is possible.** If you check this check box, Messenger will digitally sign all outgoing messages as long as you already have a *personal* (your own) digital security certificate.

- **Sign discussion (news) messages, when it is possible.** If you check this check box, Messenger will digitally sign all outgoing discussion group messages (see Chapter 6) as long as you already have a personal digital security certificate.

In the drop-down list near the center of this window, you can choose which personal digital certificate you want to use for your encrypted mail. (You may have several different digital certificates from different certifying authorities.)

As you already know, other individuals can't send you encrypted mail unless they have already received your personal certificate, which contains the special encryption key that will be used to encrypt messages in a way that only you can decrypt. Typically, your recipients will have your certificate because you've sent them signed messages. But you can also make your certificate available by publishing it as part of your identifying information (e-mail address, and so on) on an LDAP directory server on your intranet or even on the Net itself. To do so, click the Send Certificate to Directory button. Then select a directory from the drop-down list that appears, and click the OK button. Now anyone who accesses you by means of this directory will be able to send you encrypted e-mail.

At the bottom of the page, a button lets you select what S/MIME ciphers (encryption algorithms) to use. Covering the specifics of different ciphers is beyond the scope of this book, but please don't play around with this option unless you really know what you're doing!

Since I keep mentioning personal security certificates, maybe it's time to go get one.

Getting a Personal Certificate

A personal certificate enhances your online experience in various ways:

- It lets you digitally sign e-mail messages so that others can be assured of your identity.

- It lets you receive encrypted messages.

- It can serve as an electronic passport, automatically identifying you to private or secure Web sites. At many of these sites, you won't need to type a username or password as long as you have a personal certificate.

OK, let's get one!

1. Make sure you're connected to the Net.

2. Launch Communicator, and click the Security button or Security icon. The Security Info page appears.

3. On the left side of the page, click Yours under the Certificates category. The Your Certificates dialog box appears, as shown in Figure 12-20.

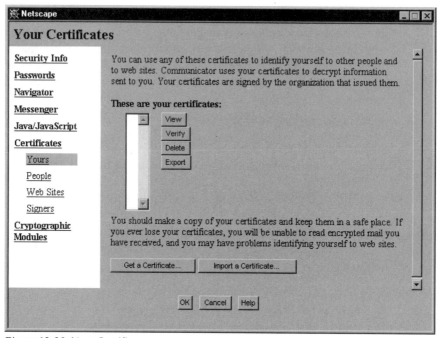

Figure 12-20: Your Certificates.

4. To obtain a new personal security certificate, click the Get a Certificate button. Netscape's Client Certification page appears in a Navigator 4 window, as shown in Figure 12-21.

5. Read the page and then click a link to one of the certifying authorities listed. VeriSign is the best known provider of individual certificates, so you might want to click that link.

Once you've reached the home page of a certifying authority, follow all the directions for obtaining a certificate (sometimes called a digital ID) very carefully. They can be complex! Since the procedure will vary depending on what class certificate you want, I'm not going to go into the details here. Prices for different kinds of certificates vary as well, so you might want to shop around.

Toward the end of the process of obtaining and installing your new certificate, you will be given the opportunity to make a copy of it. This is something you should definitely do! If something goes wrong with your software, and you have to do a complete reinstall, you need to be able to retrieve your certificate.

Figure 12-21: The Client Certification page.

OK, Figure 12-22 shows what the Your Certificates dialog box looks like once you've installed a new personal certificate.

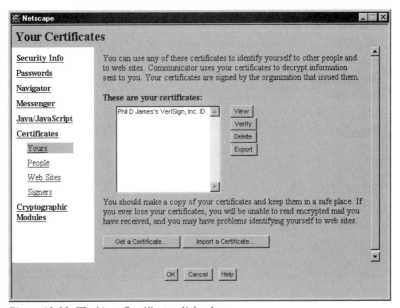

Figure 12-22: The Your Certificates dialog box.

Now you can use the buttons to the right of the certificate list to view your certificate, to verify it (make sure it has not expired), to delete it, or to export it (copy it to a file for safekeeping). Once you've exported a certificate, you can always reinstall it in Communicator using the Import a Certificate button at the bottom of this dialog box.

You've got your own personal certificate now—maybe even a few of them. What's to keep somebody from walking over to your machine and sending all kinds of interesting messages using your certificate? Passwords come in handy at this point.

Passwords

Once you have a personal certificate, you might want to protect it from unauthorized use with a password. To do so, follow these directions:

1. Once again, click the Security button or Security icon.

2. At the left side of the Security Info page, click Passwords. The Passwords dialog box appears, as shown in Figure 12-23.

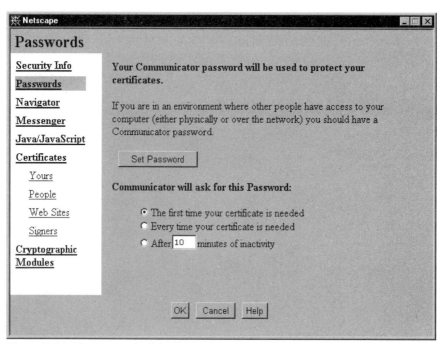

Figure 12-23: The Passwords dialog box.

3. Select one of the Communicator will ask for this Password option.

   ▪ Select "The first time your certificate is needed" if you want Communicator to ask you for your password only once per session, the first time you need to use it for signed e-mail or when it is requested by a Web site.

   ▪ Select "Every time your certificate is needed" if you want Navigator to ask for your password each time it transmits your personal certificate information.

   ▪ Select "After 30 minutes of inactivity" if you want Navigator to ask you for your password after 30 minutes of idle time. You can also change the number of minutes if you want.

4. To actually set your password, click the Set Password button. The Setting Up Your Communicator Password dialog box appears, as shown in Figure 12-24.

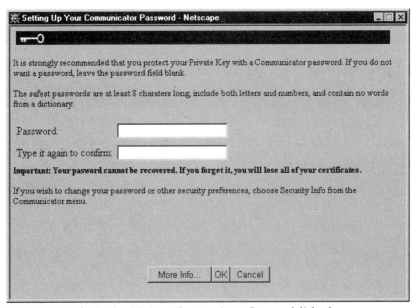

Figure 12-24: The Setting Up Your Communicator Password dialog box.

5. Type in your new password and click OK. You are returned to the Passwords dialog box.

To change your password at any point, return to the Passwords dialog box and click Set Password again. Then fill out the Change Password dialog box that appears. To eliminate your password entirely and work without one, leave the New Password field blank.

We have only a few more security issues left to discuss. By far the most important of these is how Communicator deals with Java and JavaScript.

Java & JavaScript Security

As you have learned in various chapters throughout this book, Java is a programming language that extends Communicator's capabilities and provides new multimedia elements or even entire interfaces. Java programs, or applets, are referenced in Web pages or channels. They may be downloaded automatically by Communicator and then run locally on your machine. Because you are in effect running a new program that you know nothing about, Java may in rare cases create havoc on your system or pose security risks.

JavaScript is a simpler language than Java, and it has more built-in security. It is used for lots of small "special effects" within the browser window, things like scrolling marquees and kiosk mode. In spite of its additional security, you might still have some concerns in highly sensitive situations.

To disable Java or JavaScript in Communicator:

1. Select Preferences from the Edit menu of any Communicator component.

2. From the category list that appears on the left, select Advanced. The Advanced preferences dialog box appears, as shown in Figure 12-25.

3. To disable Java, uncheck the Enable Java check box.

4. To disable JavaScript, uncheck the Enable JavaScript check box.

Figure 12-25: Advanced preferences.

TRAP

If you disable Java, you will not be able to run Netcaster!

Other Advanced Options

The Advanced preferences dialog box also includes several other options related to security:

- **Enable style sheets**. Style sheets are collections of formatting and layout information that may be stored for reuse by multiple Web pages. In most cases, you should leave this item checked.

- **Enable AutoInstall**. Communicator includes an exciting new feature whereby new plug-ins (see Chapters 7 and 10), upgrades, or other extensions to the program may be installed automatically. You don't need to request or install the software yourself.

Once you've approved an electronic security certificate that appears on your screen identifying the source of the software, the files simply download, unpack their virtual bags, and make themselves at home on your computer. A typical example: Navigator encounters a multimedia file that requires a special plug-in to display properly. You are asked to approve the installation of the new plug-in, which then installs itself automatically on your system. Within minutes or even seconds, the multimedia file is displayed correctly in the browser window. In cases in which using this feature imposes a security risk, you may want to uncheck this check box.

- **Send e-mail address as anonymous FTP password**. When you log on to anonymous FTP sites to browse and download files (see Chapter 8), the convention is to send your e-mail address as the password. But you may not want to spread your e-mail address around. In most cases, you should not check this box; Navigator will generate a password for you.

The bottom section of this window deals with *cookies* and whether you want Navigator to accept them. Cookies, in this case, are bits of information that a Web site stores on your own hard drive. This capability enables the site to "remember," from session to session, information that's specific to your use of the site. For example, you may have chosen a particular color configuration on the site or a category of information that you want to access each time. Cookies enable Web page designers to do things that would be very clumsy otherwise, but not everybody likes the idea of them. They may be used, for example, to provide advertisers and other collectors of demographics with information about the trail of pages at their site you have visited.

This dialog box lets you deal with cookies in one of three ways. You can accept them; you can accept them only if the information they contain is sent back to the originating Web site, not to some other URL; or you can reject them.

Signed Java and JavaScript

Typically, Java applets that are downloaded to your machine are written in a subset of the Java language that includes several security precautions. For instance, applets can't perform most file system access or file I/O routines. And JavaScript, as you learned in Chapter 10, is even more restrictive in terms of security.

There may be times, though, when you want to grant a Java applet more access to your system. You may want a Java applet at work to be able to update certain data files stored on your hard drive, or you may want to use Communicator's Java-based Netcaster component, which needs to store channel information on your system.

For both tightening and loosening security, Communicator supports what are known as *signed Java* applets and *signed JavaScript*. A signed Java applet is one that will not be downloaded to your system until you approve a security certificate that positively identifies the sender. Similarly, signed JavaScript will not be executed without your approval. If the Java applet or JavaScript code performs any unusual function that could compromise security, you will be asked to approve this action as well. A special security alert asks you to approve a digital certificate and to allow a specific kind of access to your system. Let's say an applet needs to read files from your hard drive. In this case, the alert will let you select among the following options:

- To view the details of the digital certificate, in other words to get more information about the organization or individual distributing this Java applet, click the View Certificate button.

- To view more information about the special access this Java applet is requesting, select the action from the list and click the Details button.

- To grant this specific access for this *one Communicator session*, select the Grant button.

- To grant this specific access for any applets from this same distributor, check the "Remember this decision…" checkbox at the bottom of the page before clicking Grant. In this case, the digital certificate is saved to your system.

- To deny the specifically requested privileges, click Deny. The Java applet will not be downloaded to your system.

When you have selected the appropriate choices, click OK. Assuming you have allowed the specific access to your system, the Java applet will now "do its thing."

Let's take a closer look at what you get when you click the Details button. Figure 12-26 shows a typical Java Security's Target Details window that appears.

Figure 12-26: A Java Security's Target Details window.

As you can see, this dialog box lists exactly what access privileges the application is requesting. It's a good idea to take a look here before clicking Grant.

What if you want to change these access privileges later? Assuming you've checked the "Remember this decision.." checkbox before clicking Grant, you can adjust the privileges allowed to Java applets on a certificate-by-certificate basis at any time. To adjust the Java privileges for a particular certificate you've already received:

1. Click the Security button or the security icon at the left of the status line in any Communicator component.

2. From the list on the left, select Java/JavaScript. The Java/JavaScript dialog box appears, as shown in Figure 12-27.

Figure 12-27: Java/JavaScript dialog box.

The scrolling list includes all the security certificates that you've already approved, presumably when launching a new signed Java applet. If you select a certificate from the list, you can then use the buttons on the right to:

- **View Certificate.** Click this button for a detailed view of the certificate.

- **Remove.** Click this button to remove the certificate from the list. Java applets from this point of origin will no longer be downloaded and executed automatically on your computer. Instead, you will be presented again with the option of approving a digital certificate.

- **Edit Privileges.** Select a certificate from the list and then click this button for the Edit Privileges page, as shown in figure 12-28.

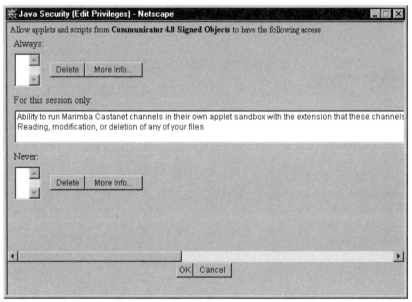

Figure 12-28: A typical Edit Privileges page.

In this dialog box you can choose which specific privileges you want to grant for this session only or for any future sessions. You may also be able to deny specific privileges.

Signed Plug-ins and Upgrades

With Communicator, plug-ins and even upgrades to the program itself may be installed automatically. Simply click a link to start the upgrade process—or, in the case of a Netcaster channel that's dedicated to upgrading your software, you may not even have to do *anything*!

Obviously, this kind of automation is a great convenience, but it imposes certain security risks. When you enhance Communicator with plug-ins or automatically upgrade a piece of software, you want to be sure you're getting the new code from the appropriate vendor or distributor rather than from Hackers 'R Us. For this reason, many automated plug-ins and upgrades are digitally signed, just like Java objects. Prior to allowing any modification of your software, you may be asked to agree to a license and to approve the installation of a particular plug-in or upgrade. Once you approve the installation, the installation proceeds. Or, if you already have a certificate from the vendor or distributor, the plug-in or upgrade may be installed automatically right away.

The Most Powerful Security: Common Sense

There is no question that Netscape Communicator provides very powerful protection from theft, fraud, and abuse of sensitive electronic information. I applaud Netscape for working so diligently toward making online commerce a safe and sensible option. I wouldn't be surprised if electronic transactions become the norm a few years from now. SSL and digital certification are paving the way for this new way of doing business.

But you already possess an even more powerful security tool: your common sense. I hate to get Forrest Gumpish on you, but here are a few things your mama should have always said:

- If you don't know anything about a company, don't send it your money. If you need more information, what better place for doing the research than the Net?

- Don't send sensitive information if the document doesn't include an e-mail address or a phone number you can use to get back in touch if you experience problems.

- Expect some sort of acknowledgment of any online transaction. If you don't receive one, get in touch with the company right away.

- Read the fine font.

- Disorganized Web pages could indicate sloppy business practices as well.

- If something looks like a scam, it just may *be* a scam.

Add these truisms to SSL, and you've got *real* security.

Moving On

By this time, we've covered most of the features of Netscape Communicator, and you're well on your way to becoming a savvy veteran of the Net or your office intranet. (With the accelerated sense of history imposed by electronic media, becoming a savvy veteran of anything takes only a week or two.)

Since Communicator is such a full-featured suite, chances are it provides all the communications power you need. But just in case you're on an office intranet and could use a few extra facilities such as integrated group scheduling and centralized administration of workstations, the next chapter introduces you to a special premium edition of the software that's specifically tailored for enterprise solutions: the Professional Edition.

CHAPTER 13

The Professional Edition

Throughout this book, you've explored the many features available in Netscape Communicator and seen how they can enhance your online experience. Using the Communicator suite, you may feel as though you've delved into every nook and cranny of the Net or your office intranet.

But if you're part of a corporate environment or a large collection of networked computers, you may feel that your online needs are not quite being satisfied—that you're looking for something to keep you even *more* in touch.

For example, if you're working on a corporate network you may find that you need to be a little more aware of what's going on with your coworkers. You might want to know who's having a meeting when, or you might need to know when your network administrator decides to change the name of the mail server. You might even need to connect to some old mainframe the company insists on keeping around.

Netscape Communicator Professional edition was designed specifically for the corporate environment. In this chapter, we'll look at Communicator Professional and what it offers that regular Communicator doesn't. By the end of this chapter, you should have a good idea of which version you need.

An Overview of Communicator 4 Professional

When your program has a name like Netscape Communicator Professional, you may feel like you've got to put on a tie and ID tag before even firing it up!

Fortunately, Communicator Professional doesn't require very much formality. Nor is it very different from Communicator. Its core components are the same, but it adds a few applications to aid corporate users and those who use an intranet. These additional components are Netscape Calendar, Netscape IBM Host-On-Demand, and Netscape AutoAdmin.

Netscape Calendar

Did you ever have one of those lousy days? You make an appointment for a business meeting with Alicia and Chris, only to discover a day later that Chris is getting his hair cut at the same time you've scheduled a meeting. Or you make an appointment to visit Jill, only to get a phone call later as Jill discovers she's spending that entire day at a seminar.

Scheduling appointments within a company can be a huge pain. Everyone's got different schedules, and before computers, coordinating those schedules took lots of phone calls and a small legion of administrative assistants.

Netscape Communicator Professional makes coordination much easier by including Netscape Calendar. Netscape Calendar is a scheduling and calendar application that can support up to 100,000 users! Finally, you can coordinate with everyone from the company president to the folks in the mail room.

TIP

To use Netscape Calendar, your intranet must have a Netscape Calendar Server. For more information on this software, visit Netscape's home page at http:// home.netscape.com.

Here's how this system works. When you launch Netscape Calendar, you're asked to log on to the Calendar server. After you've logged on, you're presented with something that looks like a Web page, except that it includes a special scheduling facility, as you can see in Figure 13-1.

Figure 13-1: The opening Netscape Calendar screen.

TIP

If you don't like the way the Calendar looks in Figure 13-1, you have a choice of several different types of displays, including weekly and monthly displays.

Scheduling an event for yourself is as easy as double-clicking in the time area that you want to schedule. For example, if you have a vendor meeting at 11 a.m., you'd double-click 11 a.m. After you do that, you're presented with options that allow you to indicate the length of the meeting, where it will be located, what resources it will take, and so on, as shown in Figure 13-2.

Figure 13-2: Adding an event to Netscape Calendar.

Here's the feature that really saves you time and headaches. You can add the names of other people to the meeting you're scheduling—as long as they also have accounts on the Calendar server. And once they've been added, you can have Netscape Calendar automatically check their calendars for possible scheduling conflicts. No more calls back and forth and constant checking of your daily organizer. Instead, Netscape Calendar checks possible conflicts for you. (If you can't give up your paper organizer, don't worry about it; Calendar can print your schedule in 150 organizer formats.)

If a conflict *does* occur, other participants in the meeting have a chance to suggest their own meeting times, which will also be checked for conflicts.

Worried about planning meetings and then letting everyone know? Calendar prompts you to send e-mail to users letting them know that an item has been added to their calendars, as shown in Figure 13-3.

Often when you're scheduling meetings, you'll find yourself working and meeting with the same group of people over and over again. To meet this need, Netscape Calendar offers a group manager. The group manager allows you to put the names of several people into a group and then assign meetings for the group as a whole instead of manually assigning each person. Groups can be private, publicly accessible, or accessible to group members only. Group allocation of resources, as shown in Figure 13-4, still lends itself to the handy automatic schedule checking that Netscape Calendar offers.

Figure 13-3: Alerting meeting attendees to the next great gathering.

Figure 13-4: Creating groups for easy resource allocation.

The whole point of meetings is to get something done, to make decisions, and to assign tasks. Netscape Calendar contains an integrated task manager so you can manage not only the meetings, but also the tasks they generate. Using the task manager, you can assign priorities, access levels, percentages of completion, and due dates. Your tasks appear on the main calendar page, like the one shown in Figure 13-5, when you first open Netscape Calendar.

Figure 13-5: Creating a task list with Netscape Calendar.

In short, Netscape Calendar takes a lot of the pain out of scheduling meetings and tracking tasks. It helps ensure that everyone in your company is on the same page at the same time.

But what if your conflict is not with someone else's schedule, but with the way your company stores data? What if you're working on a PC-based network but need to access data from one of your corporation's ancient 3270-based mainframe systems? In that case, you need the second component of Netscape Professional Edition: Netscape IBM Host-On-Demand.

Netscape IBM Host-On-Demand

Netscape IBM Host-On-Demand is a lobotomy for your computer. Don't panic, though—it's only a temporary lobotomy. The Host-On-Demand application allows your computer to emulate a 3270 "dumb terminal."

TIP

A dumb terminal, *or just plain* terminal, *is the piece of equipment that lets you access information and programs on a mainframe computer. A terminal looks something like a PC, but it doesn't actually run programs itself. It only lets you send commands and other information to the mainframe and then displays the result.*

Your corporation might still be using 3270-based mainframe systems. And you might need to access data on that mainframe system. In the past, you'd have had to use a stand-alone terminal to access the information on the mainframe. More recently, you could use a type of software program called a 3270 emulator, which also worked as a temporary lobotomy, making your very smart computer as dumb as a dumb terminal and able to talk to the 3270-based mainframe in a language it could understand.

Netscape IBM Host-On-Demand is a 3270 emulator integrated right into Netscape Professional. With this emulator, you can open a session with a mainframe computer while using your Web browser. In some cases, using this emulator can substitute for a Telnet session—for example, you can use the IBM Host-On-Demand to access the Library of Congress catalog, as shown in Figure 13-6. You can launch the 3270 session either from within Navigator or in a separate window, as shown in Figure 13-7.

Figure 13-6: Checking out the Library of Congress from within a Web page.

Figure 13-7: A separate window for a 3270 session.

The 3270 sessions are established with TCP/IP, the protocol you're already using to connect to the Internet or your office intranet, so establishing a connection isn't difficult. Once the connection is established, Host-On-Demand gives you access to keys normally found on a 3270 terminal through an onscreen keypad. And if you get stuck, help is available in a familiar HTML format so you can read and access context-sensitive help topics.

Now you've learned how to painlessly schedule meetings at which you can share information, and you've learned how Communicator Professional Edition can let you access information even from very different computer systems like mainframes. The final additional component included in Communicator Professional is Netscape AutoAdmin, which makes sure that everyone on the corporate network is using the same configuration and the same helper applications to retrieve and process information.

Netscape AutoAdmin

You're on the Internet. You're also on an intranet. You use your Web browser to access company information as frequently as you check out The Dilbert Zone. One day, though, you find yourself unable to send out corporate e-mail or read the corporate newsgroups.

Apparently, your intranet administrator had to change the name of the mail server, and she didn't get around to telling you. If a situation like this has ever happened to you, you might want to tell your administrator about Communicator Professional's AutoAdmin.

> **TIP**
>
> *AutoAdmin works in conjunction with an administration tool called the Netscape Mission Control. Information on this software is available at the Netscape home page (http://home.netscape.com).*

Instead of relying on the slow and often unreliable "sneakernet"—where the system administrator contacts each user and tells him or her about changes in the intranet setup—Netscape AutoAdmin automates the process.

With AutoAdmin activated, every time you launch Communicator Professional, it queries a central configuration URL that is set by your network administrator. The configuration URL can contain updates to your copy of Netscape Communicator, including the server addresses, home page URL, and proxy settings (critical if your corporation changes its firewall information).

AutoAdmin also includes a facility called AutoUpdate, which allows network administrators to update Communicator files and components. For example, an administrator might want to implement a new plug-in for all corporate users. AutoUpdate allows the implementation to occur automatically across the network instead of forcing the administrator to install every copy manually. Components can be secured by digital certificates (see Chapter 12), which assure that only authorized software and components are being used on the corporate intranet.

Is Communicator 4 Professional for You?

Communicator Professional includes all the same components as the regular version of the product, but as you can see, it also includes some enhancements that can really optimize online communications in a corporate setting.

But beware! Netscape Calendar isn't going to do you any good unless you have access to a Calendar Server on your corporate network. In the same way, Netscape AutoAdmin isn't going to do you any good unless your network administrator has used the Netscape Mission Control to set a central configuration URL. Only IBM Host-On-Demand will work without specialized server software. Don't purchase Communicator Professional with the expectation of using the Calendar and AutoAdmin features unless you've touched base with your network administrator and know what to expect. But if your corporate intranet is properly configured, Communicator Professional helps you work more quickly and efficiently.

Moving On

By now you know how to communicate with your co-workers—and with the world—using Netscape Communicator. You've learned how to view Web pages, how to subscribe to channels, how to send e-mail and participate in discussion groups, how to collaborate in real time using Conference, and even how to start creating your own media-rich content. *Whew!* Now let's relax a little bit and have some fun.

The next—and last—chapter of this book highlights some of my favorite Internet sites. Of course, you can find plenty of great sites using links built right into Communicator: the What's New and What's Cool lists, the Netscape Guide, and the search engines on the Net Search page. But it always helps to have a few pointers from someone you know, or at least from somebody who wrote a book you're reading. Now let's get cruising—or surfing—or whatever the term is this year!

CHAPTER 14

My Favorite Net Resources

This is a chapter for those of you who are connected to the Internet itself, either directly through a LAN connection or via SLIP, PPP, or ISDN. But if you are not currently connected to the Internet, this chapter may make you hurry up and do something about that.

Now that you can use Netscape Communicator effectively, it's time to get out there and discover some really cool sites! You already know the best ways to get started:

- Netscape's own What's Cool page.
- Netscape's What's New page.
- Some of the large Internet directories such as Yahoo!
- Netscape's Destinations page.

These are great resources. But I thought I'd let you in on some of my own favorite pages and hangouts. This is a very personal list. It is by no means exhaustive, as that would be impossible, nor have I attempted to cover a broad range of topic areas. These are sites that we've found useful, instructive, inspiring, amusing, or just a bit peculiar. I've divided the entries into categories and listed them in alphabetical order, from Art to Windows 95. But hypermedia tends to defy categorization. If you don't find a site you're looking for under one category, try a related one. And if you have purchased the version of this book that comes with a CD-ROM in the back cover, you can browse an electronic version of this chapter, clicking on links to go directly to sites that interest you.

Except for e-mail and newsgroup resources, I've included an address in the standard URL format so that you can use it directly in Netscape Navigator 4. For many of the Gopher sites listed, I've also included path information. This path simply guides you to the appropriate area by following the Gopher's menu system.

A word of warning: The Internet is constantly under construction. A site that was there yesterday may have outgrown its current server and moved, or the person maintaining the site may have decided it was too much trouble and closed it down. All of the addresses included were accurate at time of publication, but it wouldn't surprise me if some sites had moved or closed down since then. Yes, the Internet really *is* that changeable! In many cases, if a site has moved, you'll be able to get to the new location through a link that's kept at the old location. And you can always try looking for the site using Navigator's Net Search page. But if a site's gone, sometimes it's just plain gone. The best advice is simply to move on. There are plenty more out there!

> **TIP**
>
> *Don't forget to create bookmarks, toolbar icons, or desktop shortcuts for your favorite sites!*

The beauty of the Net is that you can't get too lost, so feel free to follow paths that lead away from our suggestions. With Netscape Communicator and a willingness to explore, you'll soon be discovering all sorts of wonders that I've never even heard of!

Art: Visual

@art

Type: WWW

Address: http://gertrude.art.uiuc.edu/@art/gallery.html

Summary: An interesting "gallery" of new visual art that explores some of the possibilities inherent in the Web. This site is a must-see for electronic artists as well as anyone interested in visual information and Web design.

Australian National University Art History Server

Type: WWW

Address: http://rubens.anu.edu.au/imageserve/

Summary: Michael Greenhalgh, professor of art history at Australian National University, compiled this collection of over 2,800 print images from the 15th to 19th centuries and another 6,000 images of classical and European architecture and architectural sculpture. Some highlights: a tutorial on the Palace of Diocletian at Split, a survey of the architecture of Islam, and a tour of classical sites in Turkey.

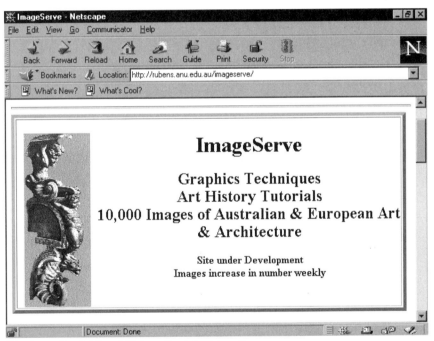

The Australian National University Art History Server.

Carlos' Coloring Book

Type: WWW

Address: http://ravenna.com/coloring

Summary: A fun site, especially for younger kids, though they will need lots of help from an adult. By pointing and clicking you can choose virtual crayons and color in any one of several pictures. This is great for artistically challenged people like me, because there is no way to color outside the lines. After your masterpiece is finished, you can download it.

Fractals

Type: FTP

Address: ftp://csus.edu/pub/alt.fractals.pictures/

Summary: Tons of fractal images in GIF format. They're arranged in directories by date; as of this writing, the latest is 1991, but there's a lot of cool stuff.

Fractals Fractals Fractals . . .

Type: WWW

Address: http://www.bhs.com/ffo/intro.htm

Summary: Yes, another fractals page. I never get tired of them, and so this is a favorite site. Here you can find over 500 beautiful computer-generated graphics as well as links to other fractal sites. Enjoy.

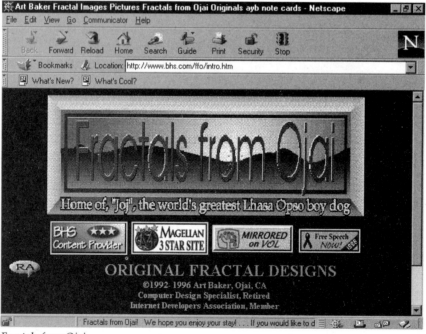

Fractals from Ojai.

Gallery of Interactive On Line Geometry

Type: WWW

Address: http://www.geom.umn.edu/apps/gallery.html

Summary: Use Kali to learn about the 17 crystallographic symmetry groups of the plane. This work is similar to that seen in some of M. C. Escher's woodcuts. Play a pinball-style game to explore the effects of negatively curved space. Much more involving symmetry groups and angle geometries. This page is maintained by the Geometry Center at the University of Minnesota.

Institute of Egyptian Art and Archaeology

Type: WWW

Address: http://www.memst.edu/egypt/main.html

Summary: Take a color tour of Egypt or view the exhibit of Egyptian artifacts at the University of Memphis. The Institute of Egyptian Art and Archaeology is part of the Department of Art at the University of Memphis.

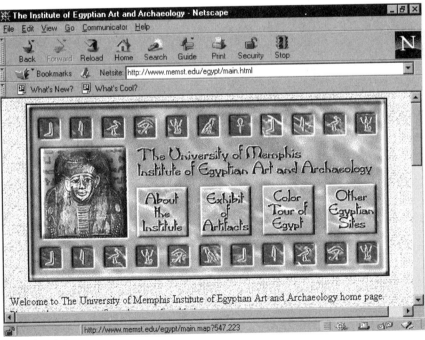

Egyptian Art.

Kaleidospace

      Type: WWW

   Address: http://kspace.com

  Summary: A commercial site, but well worth a look. Independent artists gather here to display and sell their work.

Kaleidospace.

Origami

      Type: FTP

  Address: ftp://nstn.ns.ca/listserv/origami-l/

  Summary: Learn new folding techniques, get display ideas, tips, and bibliographies. Subscribe to mailing lists by sending e-mail to origami-l-request@ntsn.ns.ca.

Strange Interactions

Type: WWW

Address: http://amanda.physics.wisc.edu/show.html

Summary: An online art exhibit by John Jacobsen. From his artist's statement, "My work is an attempt to give a concrete aspect to the subconscious." Definitely worth checking out!

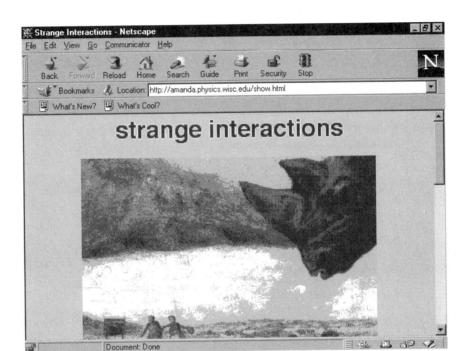

Strange Interactions.

The Thing

Type: WWW

Address: http://www.thing.net/thingnyc

Summary: Serious talk about serious contemporary art. I like to have a glass of red wine in my hand when I visit this site.

WebMuseum

Type: WWW

Address: http://watt.emf.net/

Summary: Great art classics right on your computer screen! It takes a while to download some of the paintings, but it's still quicker and cheaper than flying to Paris.

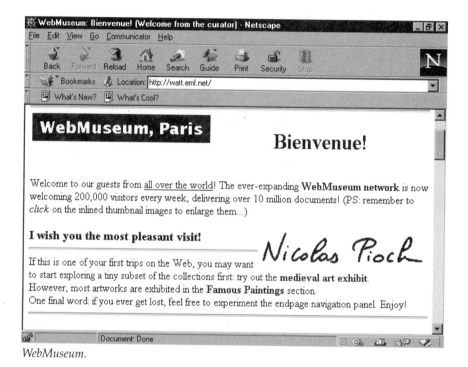

WebMuseum.

The Whitney

Type: WWW

Address: http://www.echonyc.com/~whitney/

Summary: The Whitney Museum in New York is one of the most important showcases for contemporary art. Besides information about the museum itself, special electronic exhibits, and a museum store, this site also includes an excellent collection of links to other art-related sites on the Web.

Some Related Newsgroups

alt.artcom   rec.arts.misc

alt.postmodern   sci.fractals

rec.arts.fine

Arts: Multidisciplinary

BOMB Magazine

Type: WWW

Address: http://www.bombsite.com/

Summary: The print version of BOMB Magazine has been around for a while and great for the whole time it's been around. The electronic version is equally interesting, full of inventive visual art and literature by important writers. BOMB also features a variety of fascinating interviews. If you're in the arts, don't miss this site.

The Fluxus Page

Type: WWW

Address: http://www.panix.com/~fluxus/

Summary: A grab-bag of art, music, and writing by the Fluxus pioneers of the early sixties (George Maciunas, Wolf Vostell, LaMonte Young, Yoko Ono, Philip Corner, etc.) and by later neo-Fluxus artists. A must-visit site for anybody interested in the history of contemporary art or interested in forms of expression that are innovative and fun at the same time.

Fluxus Online.

IAMfree

Type: WWW

Address: http://www.rahul.net/iamfree/

Summary: This "Internet Arts Museum for free" offers interesting art, music, and literature in a virtual museum setting. All of the work included was specifically intended for this form of free Internet distribution.

Internet Arts Museum.

Life With Father

Type: WWW

Address: http://gertrude.art.uiuc.edu/ludgate/the/place/stories/ life_with_father/Life_With_Father.html

Summary: This is a poetic, autobiographical story-with-pictures by the artist Joseph Squiers. It shows some of the possibilities for highly personal and highly professional artwork on the Web.

Megadeth, Arizona

Type: WWW

Address: http://hollywoodandvine.com/Megadeth/megadeth.html

Summary: A well-designed and media-rich site maintained by the band Megadeth. Some of the highlights include a "HorrorScopes" service and a set of links to peculiar freeware programs. This is a good site for those who like their entertainment slightly spooky.

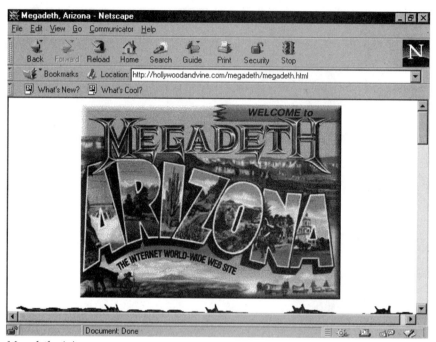

Megadeth, Arizona.

Postmodern Culture

    Type: WWW

  Address: http://jefferson.village.Virginia.EDU/pmc/

  Summary: Postmodern Culture is an interesting, heady e-zine exploring recent developments in culture and the arts. It includes some poetry and fiction as well as essays.

Books, Literature & Zines

Alternative-X

    Type: WWW

  Address: http://www.altx.com/

  Summary: This is *the* place to visit if you want to catch up on recent trends in literary fiction, especially the so-called "avant-pop" phenomenon. This site includes stories and polemics by such great, innovative writers as Derek Pell, Euridice, and Harold Jaffe. Rather than playing with the visual possibilities of HTML, Alt-X serves up prose by the bucket-load, so if you're a literary type, there's an excellent bang/buck ratio.

Alternative-X.

Amazon

Type: WWW

Address: http://www.amazon.com/

Summary: Amazon.com has quickly become *the* online store for locating and ordering hard-to-find books. I'm into some pretty obscure literature, but I can usually find what I want here and have it delivered within days. Amazon also features discounts on selected titles and a very easy-to-use Web interface. These people do Web commerce right!

The Asylum

Type: WWW

Address: http://asylum.cid.com/

Summary: This adventurous site exploits the interactive possibilities of the Web. It includes collaborative stories and poems that you can add to as well as a "lite brite" that lets you exercise your imagination by creating pictures out of little circles of color.

Basement Full of Books

Type: FTP or WWW

Address: ftp://ftp.greyware.com/pub/Literature/BFoB/ basement_full_of_books.txt http://www.sff.net/bfob/

Summary: Get autographed books (with personal inscriptions) directly from their authors. Lots of science fiction authors like Ursula K. Le Guin, Harlan Ellison, David Brin, and Joe Haldeman. The list is updated every month. You get a short synopsis of each book, along with ordering information.

You can also get this list by sending an e-mail message to mail-server@rtfm.mit.edu. Put "send usenet/news.answers/books/ basement-full-of-books" (without the quotes) in the body of the message.

Bookstore List

Type: WWW

Address: http://www.cis.ohio-state.edu/hypertext/faq/usenet/books/ stores/top.html

Summary: This site presents, in hypertext form, lists of the best bookstores around the world. (They are taken from Usenet FAQs.)

Bordeaux and Prague

Type: WWW

Address: http://www.freedonia.com/~carl/bp/

Summary: Carl Steadman, the creator of the Bordeaux and Prague page, is a story writer and artist whose unusual work was influenced by postmodern French thought and Situationism. He uses the richness of HTML to present complex works effectively and with humor. This material is not everybody's cup of espresso, but I love it!

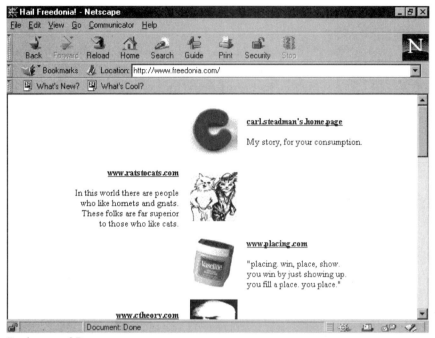

Bordeaux and Prague.

Feed

Type: WWW

Address: http://www.feedmag.com

Summary: Cultural, political, and artistic commentary with a technological bent. Good solidly designed site.

Foxy

Type: WWW

Address: http://www.tumyeto.com/tydo/foxy

Summary: Got a teenage daughter? Send her here. Oh wait a minute, you *are* a teenage daughter? Check it out!

The Hypertext Fiction Page

Type: WWW

Address: http://www.ugcs.caltech.edu/~benedett/hyper.html

Summary: A good introduction to the theory and practice of hypertext fiction, including a few interesting examples. This page is maintained by students at Caltech.

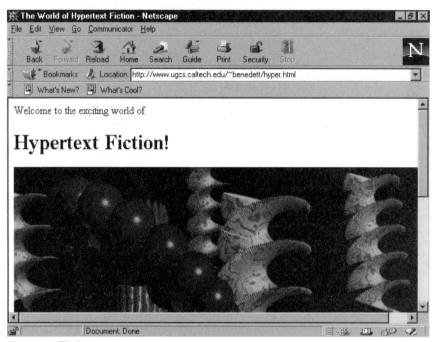

Hypertext Fiction.

Libido Magazine

Type: WWW

Address: http://www.indra.com/libido/cover3.html

Summary: In its print version, *Libido* is one of the best and "classiest" magazines that focuses on erotic art, photography, and writing. The electronic version is just as good. This is erotica for people who are not afraid to think.

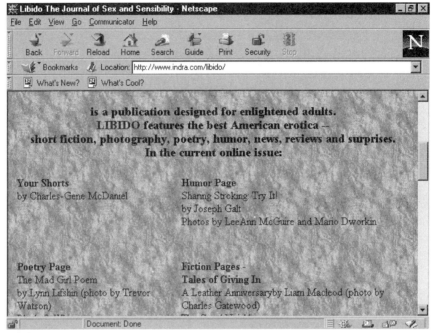

Libido.

The Nancy Drew Page

Type: WWW

Address: http://sunsite.unc.edu/cheryb/nancy.drew/ktitle.html

Summary: I love this site! Nancy Drew from a historical perspective. From a psychological perspective. From a sociological perspective. From an artistic perspective. This is pay dirt for pop culture fans and deconstructionists. By the time you're done here, you'll know Nancy better than you know yourself.

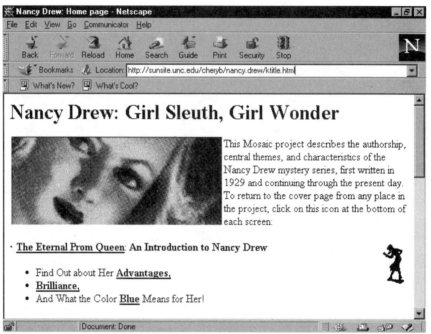

Nancy Drew, Eternal Prom Queen.

Online Fairy Tales

Type: FTP

Address: ftp://info.umd.edu/inforM/EdRes/ReadingRoom/Fiction/FairyTales

Summary: I always enjoyed telling my kids stories when I put them to bed, but quite often I couldn't remember exactly how a particular fairy tale went and ended up improvising my own bizarre plots. If only I'd had Internet access I could have FTPed to this site and quickly brushed up on any of the almost 100 tales provided!

STIM

Type: WWW

Address: http://www.stim.com/

Summary: This is one of the most interesting new zines on the Web. It features good solid writing, lots of ear and eye candy, and some excellent regular columns including Daniel Radosh's perceptive analyses of the Web itself.

Urban Desires

Type: WWW

Address: http://desires.com/

Summary: An *excellent* and intelligent zine full of provocative articles, interviews, reviews, and artwork. The masthead says it all: "An Interactive Magazine of Metropolitan Passions."

Word Magazine

Type: WWW

Address: http://www.word.com/

Summary: No, this has nothing to do with Microsoft Word. It's a big, intelligent New York–based zine that emphasizes high-quality writing and colorful graphics. It's sort of an East Coast *HotWired*, but with more of an emphasis on the arts and pop culture and less of an emphasis on things cyber. Definitely worth a look!

Word magazine.

Some Related Newsgroups

alt.books.reviews	bit.listserv.literary
alt.books.technical	misc.writing
alt.etext	rec.arts.poems
alt.mythology	rec.arts.prose
alt.usage.english	rec.mag
alt.zines	

Business

Downtown Anywhere

Type: WWW

Address: http://www.awa.com/

Summary: Businesses can establish a Net presence in this virtual community. But it's not all business. Lots of Net and general reference info. Check out the library and newsstand, museums, the financial district, the sports arena and, of course, Main Street.

Marshall Space Flight Center Procurement Home Page

Type: WWW

Address: http://procure.msfc.nasa.gov

Summary: Advanced procurement information and small business assistance documents. Learn about federal streamlining initiatives. Pointers to other federal procurement sites such as the Johnson Space Center and Kennedy Space Center home pages.

Contact: Jim Bradford
GP01/Procurement Office
NASA/Marshall Space Flight Center
Huntsville, AL 35812
205/544-0306
jim.bradford@msfc.nasa.gov

STO's Internet Patent Search System

Type: WWW

Address: http://sunsite.unc.edu/patents/intropat.html

Summary: Do a title search through all U.S. patents issued since 1970.

Patent Search System.

Some Related Newsgroups

> alt.business.misc
> alt.business.multi-level
> misc.entrepreneurs

Computing

Free OnLine Dictionary of Computing

Type: WWW

Address: http://wombat.doc.ic.ac.uk/

Summary: Searchable dictionary that includes terms related to general computing, programming languages, networks, domain theory, acronyms, computing history, and just about anything else that has to do with computers.

Global Monitor

Type: WWW

Address: http://nccr.monitor.ca:80/monitor/

Summary: A cool electronic mag loaded with computer-related info.

Global Monitor magazine.

PC's and Macintoshes

Type: Gopher

Address: gopher://wiretap.spies.com

Path: Wiretap Online Library / Technical Information / PC's and Macintoshes

Summary: Lots of articles and tips for both PC and Mac users.

Toll-Free Numbers

Type: FTP

Address: ftp://oak.oakland.edu/pub/misc/telephone/tollfree.num

Summary: Toll-free numbers for a bunch of computer companies.

Toll-free number index.

UNB Graphic Services Desktop Publishing Resource Base

Type: WWW

Address: http://degaulle.hil.unb.ca/UNB_G_Services/GSHomePage.html

Summary: Plenty of plugs for UNB's services, but enough pointers to clip-art collections, font banks, and other DTP resources to make it a valuable site.

Virus Information

Type: FTP

Address: ftp://oak.oakland.edu/pub/misc/virus

Summary: Technical information about most known viruses. Includes DOS and Mac data.

Some Related Newsgroups

alt.cad.autocad	comp.misc
alt.cyberpunk.tech	comp.theory
alt.privacy	comp.virus
clari.nb.general	comp.sys.misc

Culture & Diversity

American Memory From the Library of Congress

Type: WWW

Address: http://rs6.loc.gov/amhome.html

Summary: A nicely done glimpse of America's past, including collections of photographs, text, and even sound recordings. Lots of material on American culture and history, most of it from special collections of the Library of Congress.

Native American Net Server

Type: Gopher

Address: gopher://alpha1.csd.uwm.edu

Path: UWM Information, Native American Net Server

Summary: Articles and cases on Indian law, book reviews, job openings, education, Native American newsletters, even Native American fonts.

Contact: Michael Wilson
University of Wisconsin at Milwaukee
mwilson@alpha2.csd.uwm.edu

Resources for Diversity

Type: WWW

Address: http://www.nova.edu/Inter-Links/diversity.html

Summary: This page has links to the African Studies Web, Chicano-LatinoNet, Disability Information, Diversity at the University of Michigan, the Inter-Tribal Network for Native Americans, the Latin American Network Information Center, Minority Online Service (MOLIS), Omni-Cultural Academic Resource, Gay/Lesbian Resources, and Women's Studies at the University of Maryland.

Resources for Diversity.

Women's Resource Project

Type: WWW

Address: http://sunsite.unc.edu/cheryb/women/wshome.html

Summary: *Women's studies:* Pointers to women's studies programs at several colleges and universities. *Women and literature:* Bios of female authors from Harriet Beecher Stowe to Marge Piercy, from Jane Austen to Maya Angelou. A guide to women's resources on the Net.

Women's Resource Project.

Some Related Newsgroups

> alt.discrimination
>
> soc.culture.african.american
>
> soc.women

Education

Higher Education Resources and Opportunities

Type: Telnet

Address: telnet://fedix.fie.com

Login: new

Summary: The Minority OnLine Information Service is an online database service with all sorts of information about scholarships, grants, fellowships, conferences, research opportunities, and other opportunities for minorities and women.

Hillside Elementary School

Type: WWW

Address: http://hillside.coled.umn.edu/

Summary: Every student in Mrs. Collins's sixth grade class has created his or her own home page. Lots more planned for this site, a joint project of Hillside Elementary School in Cottage Grove, Minnesota, and the University of Minnesota College of Education.

Reading Disabilities

Type: FTP

Address: ftp://ftp.spies.com/Library/Article/Misc/disable.rd

Summary: Extremely clear and well-written paper, "Neuropsychological Bases of Educational Disabilities," by Robert Zenhausern, Ph.D., professor of psychology at St. John's University. It's a scholarly paper, but its style makes it accessible to the lay public.

Schoolnet Resource Manual

Type: FTP

Address: ftp://schoolnet.carleton.ca/pub/English/Manuals/

Summary: This is a huge file with about a kazillion pointers to science, technology, and education resources on the Net.

The manual's directory is full of Net information. Check out the Big Dummy's Guide to the Internet, Electric Mystic Guide to Internet, FTP Introduction, E-Mail Intro, Gopher_FAQ, Internet Basics, and Guidelines-Netiquette.

U.S. Department of Education

Type: WWW

Address: http://inet.ed.gov/

Summary: Get press releases and information about funding opportunities, speeches prepared for the U.S. Secretary of Education, Teachers' and Researchers' Guides to the U.S. Department of Education, and links to other educational resources.

Entertainment

The East Village

Type: WWW

Address: http://www.theeastvillage.com/

Summary: *The East Village* is the premier example of an entire new category of Internet entertainment: the Web soap opera. Of course instead of suburban neurotics the regulars in this drama are a bit closer to home, or to home page: they are Noo Yawkers dealing with the vicissitudes of passionate bohemianism. The producers have really done a good job with this. Let's hear it for the Internet, offering us better and better ways to keep from getting any work done.

Ski Vixens From the X-Dimension

Type: WWW

Address: http://www.atlas.organic.com/atlas/multi/vixens

Summary: Another soap, campy, funny, and silly. A great way to spend your morning at the office while you're waiting around for lunch.

The Spot

Type: WWW

Address: http://www.thespot.com/

Summary: This is probably the most popular of the new Web soap operas. You feel like the ultimate voyeur as you look into the diaries and journals of a group of people that seem very, very real.

Environment

Ask-a-Geologist

Type: e-mail

Address: ask-a-geologist@octopus.wr.usgs.gov

Summary: Ever wonder what kind of rock is the most common in your area? How the mountains were formed? When the next earthquake is likely to hit your town? I'm not sure how the U.S. Geological

Survey has time for this, but if you send your question to the address above you'll receive an answer within a couple of days. And since this service is free, you won't lose your chert. (Sorry about that.)

Cascades Volcano Observatory Home Page

Type: WWW

Address: http://vulcan.wr.usgs.gov/home.html

Summary: Arm yourself with information about volcanoes and other natural hazards. Get hazard assessments and warnings during volcano crises. Find out about the International Volcano Disaster Assistance Program. Links to Alaska and Hawaii volcano observatories.

The EnviroLink Network

Type: Gopher

Address: gopher://envirolink.org

Summary: As you'd guess, this site is full of information about ecology, environmental groups, endangered species, and environmental law.

Institute for Global Communications (IGC)

Type: Gopher

Address: gopher://gopher.igc.apc.org

Summary: From the welcome message: "IGC runs four computer networks known as PeaceNet(TM), EcoNet(TM), ConflictNet, and LaborNet. IGC is the U.S. member of the Association for Progressive Communications, a 16-country association of computer networks working for peace, human rights, environmental protection, social justice, and sustainability."
TIOTS! (This is one terrific site!)

Contact: Institute for Global Communications
18 De Boom St.
San Francisco, CA 94107
415/442-0220
igc-info@igc.apc.org

Ozone Depletion

Type: FTP

Address: ftp://rtfm.mit.edu/pub/usenet/news.answers/
ozone-depletion/

Summary: FAQ files about the depletion of the ozone layer are posted
monthly. There's a special section for the Antarctic ozone hole.

Students for the Exploration and Development of Space

Type: Gopher

Address: gopher://seds.lpl.arizona.edu

Summary: This site includes the latest information about celestial events as
well as a wealth of material related to space exploration.

The Virtual Desert

Type: WWW

Address: http://www.well.com/user/vegas/desert/Top/index.html

Summary: If you love the American desert as much as I do, you'll love this
Web page.

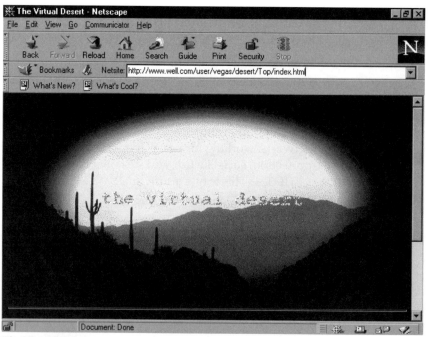

The Virtual Desert.

Some Related Newsgroups

bit.listerv.biosph-1

sci.environment

Finance

Credit Info

Type: FTP

Address: ftp://rtfm.mit.edu/pub/usenet/news.answers/
consumer-credit-faq/

Summary: Is Mastercard better than Visa? What is a secured card? Do I want
a fixed-rate or floating-rate card? Why is a discount better than a
rebate? The answers to these and many other burning consumer
questions can be found in the consumer credit FAQ, which was
compiled from questions asked on the misc.consumers
newsgroup.

Economics

Type: Gopher

Address: gopher://nysernet.org

Path: Special Collections:Business and Economic Development

Summary: If the world of business is your world, have a blast exploring
these resources. Among them: a FAQ on advertising on the
Internet, the Basic Guide to Exporting, Commerce Business Daily,
and a U.S. Patent database.

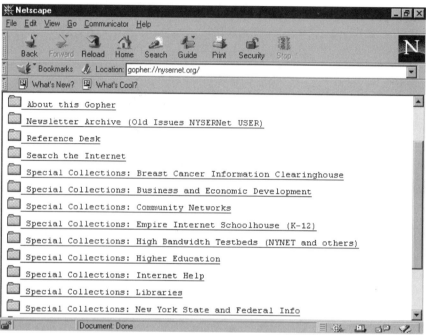

NYSE Gopher.

Some Related Newsgroups

clari.biz.currencies.us_dollar

clari.biz.finance

clari.biz.economy.world

Food & Drink

1-800 Truffle

Type: WWW

Address: http://www.truffle.com

Summary: Are you feeling down lately? Or is there someone nearby who seems to need something a little more substantial than a bouquet of flowers? If you understand that chocolate is a necessity for happiness, 1-800 Truffle will hook you up. Use your credit card, and bliss will be on its way to your doorstep.

Cat's Meow 3

Type: WWW

Address: http://alpha.rollanet.org/cm3/CatsMeow3.html

Summary: Looking to create your own home brew? This site is guaranteed to turn you into a beer afficionado. (And allow you to throw great parties.) Beer recipes are listed by category such as pale ales or wheat beers. If you are just getting started there are detailed instructions on how to turn your kitchen into a brewery.

The Chocolate Lovers' Page

Type: WWW

Address: http://bc.emanon.net/chocolate/

Summary: Lots of links to information about everybody's favorite designer drug.

Cooking Light Online

Type: WWW

Address: http://www.pathfinder.com/cl

Summary: Based on the popular magazine, this is a good place to go when you are trying to be healthy. If you get really good at cutting calories in your recipes you can join their contests to win money and trips. But when you go on that trip make sure you maintain that light attitude.

DineFind

Type: WWW

Address: http://www.dinefind.com

Summary: Are you on the road frequently? Find yourself eating in too many Sheraton hotel lobbies? Check this site out before you leave next time. Sponsored by the National Restaurant Association, it offers searches by city, type of cuisine, or price.

Epicurious

Type: WWW

Address: http://www.epicurious.com/

Summary: This is a great place for any food lover to start. Not only is it the home of Gourmet and Bon Appetit online, it also includes Conde Nast Traveler online. Dream of traveling to exotic places while looking over beautiful recipes, why would anyone want to go elsewhere online?

HOT HOT HOT

Type: WWW

Address: http://www.hot.presence.com/g/p/H3/

Summary: No, it's not another one of those virtual sex sites you keep reading about. This one's a highly organized list of hot sauces from around the world. If you like your food spicy, check this out!

Hot Hot Hot.

The Italian Internet Winery

Type: WWW

Address: http://www.ulysses.it

Summary: If you are looking for information about Italian wines, this is the site to visit. The information is included in both English and Italian. Search by varietal and then plan a trip to one of the regions. There are over 75 wine touring itineraries planned to pick from. Or just order some wine straight from the producers.

Mama's Dining Room

Type: WWW

Address: http://www.eat.com

Summary: Whether or not you are an Italian by blood or by food association, this is a site for anyone who enjoys Italian food. The plate graphics alone are enough to inspire you to cook a meal that would make Mama proud. For those that are just learning Italian food there is a pasta glossary. Or if you are really ambitious, try the Italian lessons over RealAudio.

Over the Coffee

Type: WWW

Address: http://www.cappuccino.com/

Summary: If you're a coffee lover, it's all here. Coffee trivia and factoids, a travelers' guide to coffee houses, a list of coffee-related Usenet groups, a coffee recipe collection, lists of coffee (and tea) books, a glossary of coffee terminology, and resources for coffee professionals.

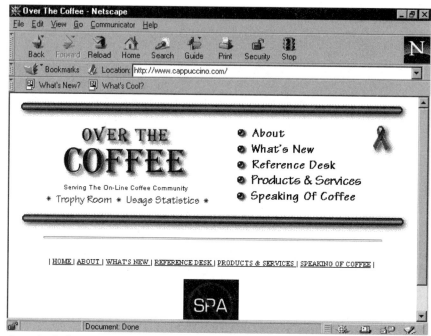

Over the Coffee.

Patriots' Trail Girl Scout Council

Type: WWW

Address: http://www.ptgirlscouts.org/

Summary: I've listed this Boston-area scouting page with other food-related Web sites because it lets you order your cookies online! Of course, the Scouts advise that you should support your local troop first, but if nobody comes knocking on your door and you've got a Thin Mints jones that just won't go away . . .

The Real Beer Site

Type: WWW

Address: http://realbeer.com/

Summary: If you want to hear about Coors and Anheuser-Busch products, watch football; if you want to find out about micro-breweries and carefully hand-crafted beers, check out this Web page. The emphasis here is on old-fashioned *quality*, and there is a wealth of information about beers from all areas of the country.

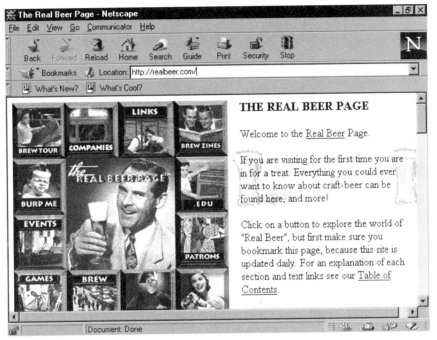

Real Beer.

Recipes

Type: FTP

Address: ftp://gatekeeper.dec.com/pub/recipes

Summary: A collection of over 500 recipes.

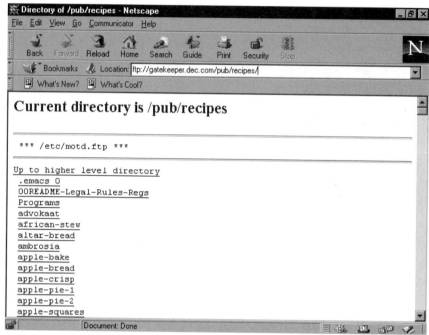

Recipes.

The Recipes Folder

Type: WWW

Address: http://english-www.hss.cmu.edu/recipes.html

Summary: If you're a vegetarian, you'll feel right at home here. If you're a flesh eater, you'll have to put up with the following subject headings: "Vegetarian Stuff," "Dead Animals," and "Things Possibly Involving Dead Animals and Possibly Not." Whatever your culinary predilections, this is a terrific list of recipe sources.

The Single Malt Page

Type: WWW

Address: http://www.dcs.ed.ac.uk/home/jhb/whisky/

Summary: I hate to admit it, but I've spent a lot of time at this site. Here you can learn everything there is to know about fine, single malt Scotch whiskey, or *whisky*, as they say over there. This is a serious, professionally designed Web page that includes a clickable map of the different whiskey-producing regions and even an Excel spreadsheet! As a concession to the nonpurists of the drinking world, there is even some recently added information on blended whiskeys.

Whisky!

Vegetarianism

Type: FTP

Address: ftp://flubber.cs.umd.edu/other/tms/veg

Summary: All kinds of info for vegetarians and would-be vegetarians—FAQs, recipes, and so on. Another vegetarian resource to check out is the rec.food.veg newsgroup.

Veggies Unite!

Type: WWW

Address: http://www.vegweb.com

Summary: A searchable index of over 900 vegetarian recipes. Links to other nutrition and health sites.

Western Culinary Institute

Type: WWW

Address: http://www.westernculinary.com

Summary: So many people dream of going to culinary school that I decided to include one of them here. Look at some pretty impressive examples of just what you can learn. One of the best things about this school is its location, Portland, Oregon. Just think of all the fresh salmon and local riesling you can sample in your classes!

Yan Can Cook

Type: WWW

Address: http://www.channela.com/food/yancancook/main.html

Summary: If you are looking to try your hand at Asian cuisine, Yan can help you along. Based on his television cooking show, this site features recipes and tips for cooking in a wok. Yan also takes you on a culinary tour through China.

Some Related Newsgroups

alt.college.food
alt.folklore.herbs
alt.food.fat-free
alt.gourmand
alt.support.diet
rec.crafts.winemaking
rec.food.cooking

rec.food.historic
rec.food.recipes
rec.food.restaurants
rec.food.sourdough
rec.food.veg
sci.med.nutrition

Fun & Games

Chiba Woo

Type: WWW

Address: http://sensemedia.net/sprawl/

Summary: What do you get when you cross a MOO with a Web document? A WOO, of course. As you may know, a MOO is an interactive online game with object-oriented extensions. This site is an interesting experiment in extending MOOing to the Web. It also contains some excellent links to other sites.

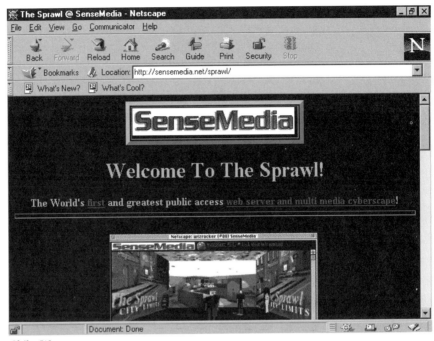

Chiba Woo.

Ferret Central

Type: WWW

Address: http://www.optics.rochester.edu:8080/users/pgreene/central.html

Summary: I keep threatening to get one of these wonderful animals, and after browsing this site, which includes a thorough FAQ, beautiful photos, and links to other ferret-related sites, you might want one too. Remember: *They are not rodents!*

Fly With Us!

Type: WWW

Address: http://www.interedu.com/mig29/

Summary: Have you ever wanted to climb into the cockpit of a MiG-29, roar down the runway, and then fly at supersonic speeds to the edge of space? We're not talking virtual reality here, this is the real thing! For a price—make that a *hefty* price—Fly With Us!, Inc., offers you a first-class vacation in Russia that includes a flight with a "co-pilot" who hopefully knows more about the aircraft than you do. The Web site provides you with a description of the various vacation packages and even an in-flight video clip. I dare you to do this!

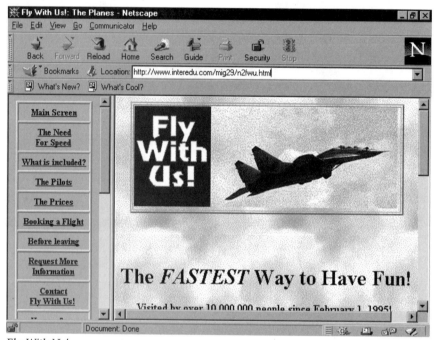

Fly With Us!

Games Domain

Type: WWW

Address: http://www.gamesdomain.com/

Summary: If you have any interest in games, check out this page. It has links to Usenet groups and games FAQs, a Walkthroughs link that can get you unstuck from several popular games, and over 100 links to games-related Web pages and FTP sites.

Hollywood Online

Type: WWW

Address: http://www.hollywood.com/

Summary: This is the place to find out about the latest Hollywood movies. Not only does it include listings and discussion boards, it exploits the multimedia power of the Web by offering up sound clips and video trailers.

Hollywood Online.

Killer List of Video Games

Type: Gopher

Address: gopher://wiretap.spies.com

Path: Wiretap Online Library/Mass Media/Games and Video Games/ The Killer List of Video Games

Summary: Get the inside scoop on your favorite games through files like Definitive Arcade Video Cheats, SEGA Genesis Secrets, Killer List of Video Games, Home Video Games History, and (yes, this is for real) The Rules of Tiddlywinks.

Sony

Type: WWW

Address: http://www.sony.com

Summary: As you would expect, this is a large, well-done, slick site that includes lots of information on movies, CDs, concerts, electronic equipment, and so on. It's a nice mall to visit.

Sony (no baloney).

Ultimate TV

Type: WWW

Address: http://www.ultimatetv.com/

Summary: Want to find out what's on tonight? TV Net can tell you! This page also includes a wealth of TV-related information and links to other sites. Put your computer near the couch and you'll never have to get up again.

Ultimite TV.

Virtual Vegas

Type: WWW

Address: http://www.virtualvegas.com/

Summary: Lost Wages is one of those love-it-or-hate-it cities. Since this site does a nice job of capturing all the gaudiness and tackiness, I suspect it may be one of those love-it-or-hate-it Web pages. There are layers of annoying registration forms to get through, and the process is made even slower by traffic (Virtual Vegas has received some mass-media attention). Once you're there, though, you'll see a well-crafted piece of glitzy Americana.

Viva Las Virtual Vegas.

WebMind Crosswords

Type: FTP

Address: ftp://rtfm.mit.edu/pub/usenet/news.answers/crossword-faq/

Summary: Crossword aficionado heaven. Guides, diction-aries, solution tips, software info, and so on.
Also try ftp://pub/usenet/news.answers/puzzles/faq for a collection of mindbenders.

Zarf's List of Interactive Games on the Web

Type: WWW

Address: http://www.leftfoot.com/realgames.html

Summary: Just what it sounds like. A good hotlist.

Health, Medicine & Recovery

Americans With Disabilities Act

Type: Gopher

Address: gopher://scilibx.ucsc.edu

Path: The Library/Electronic Books and Other Texts

Summary: Get the full text of the 1990 Americans with Disabilities Act.

Dr. Greenson's Gastrointestinal and Liver Pathology Home Page

Type: WWW

Address: http://www.pds.med.umich.edu/users/greenson/

Summary: Just what you've been waiting for! It even includes pictures of a GI Case of the Month and an Infectious Case of the Month. I'm thinking of making a musical of this page.

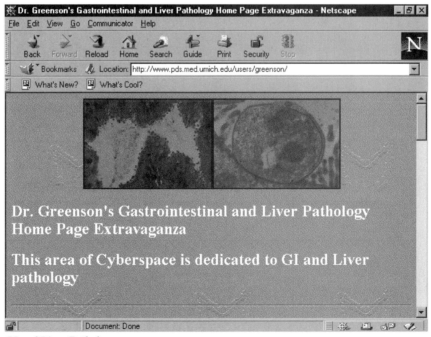

GI and Liver Pathology.

The Heart Page

Type: WWW

Address: http://sln2.fi.edu/biosci/preview/heartpreview.html

Summary: All kinds of physiological information about the human heart, with great illustrations. No, you won't learn how to keep people from breaking it.

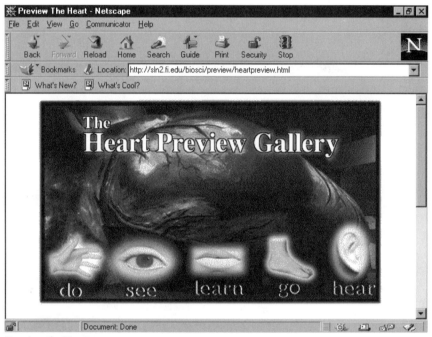

Preview the Heart.

Institute for Molecular Virology

Type: WWW

Address: http://www.bocklabs.wisc.edu/

Summary: Info about the AIDS virus, 3D images and animations of virus structures, 2D electron micrographs of viruses, online virology course material, phone book of virologists on the Net, and virology-related journal articles.

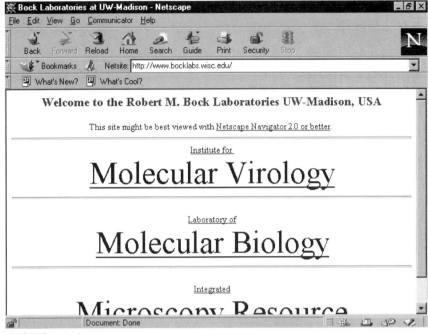

Bock Laboratories.

Midwifery and Birth Information Page

Type: WWW

Address: http://www.efn.org/~djz/birth/birthindex.html

Summary: This is my wife's favorite Web site. It includes articles on midwifery as well as prenatal and postnatal care. This is not a flashy site, but it's full of valuable information that can't be obtained elsewhere.

Midwifery, Pregnancy, and Birth-Related Information

National Toxicology Program (NTP) Home Page

Type: WWW

Address: http://ntp-server.niehs.nih.gov/

Summary: Established by the Secretary of Health and Human Services "to coordinate toxicology research and testing activities within the Department, to provide information about potentially toxic chemicals to regulatory and research agencies and the public, and to strengthen the science base in toxicology. In its 16 years, the NTP has become the world's leader in designing, conducting, and interpreting animal assays for toxicity." The annual plan describes current work being done in carcinogenesis, toxicology, genetic toxicology, and chemical disposition.

National Toxicology Program.

New York State Breast Cancer Information Clearinghouse

Type: Gopher

Address: gopher://nysernet.org/

Path: Special Collections: Breast Cancer Information Clearinghouse

Summary: A great resource for breast cancer patients, family members, and health professionals. Lots of info on treatment and rehabilitation, a list of names and phone numbers of support groups throughout the United States, and pointers to other cancer resources.

Psycoloquy

Type: WWW

Address: http://www.w3.org/hypertext/DataSources/bySubject/Psychology/Psycoloquy.html

Summary: An electronic journal sponsored by the American Psychological Association. Contains reports on new ideas and findings in all areas of psychology. Contributors solicit peer feedback, and contributions are refereed by members of Psycoloquy's Editorial Board.

Usenet: sci.psychology.digest

Or, to get articles automatically, send e-mail to listserv@pucc.bitnet or listserv@pucc.princeton. edu. Leave the Subject line blank and put the following in the body of the message: **sub psyc *Firstname Lastname*** (where *Firstname* and *Lastname* are your own names, *not* your Internet address).

Sexual Assault Recovery Service

Type: Gopher

Address: gopher://wilcox.umt.edu

Summary: Documents and discussions on dealing with sexual assault experiences and prevention.

You can also Telnet to selway.umt.edu and use the login *health*.

12-Step

Type: e-mail

Address: muller@camp.rutgers.edu

Summary: The purpose of this group is to share experiences about 12-step programs.

The Wellness List

Type: mailing list

Address: majordomo@wellnessmart.com

Summary: This list includes discussions of health, nutrition, wellness, and life expectancy. Lots of healthy recipes, nutrition and fitness-related product announcements, book reviews, and nutrition-related position papers.

To subscribe, send the following one-line message in e-mail: **subscribe wellnesslist *your name*** (where *your name* is your full name, *not* your e-mail address).

Some Related Newsgroups

alt.folklore.herbs	clari.tw.health.aids
alt.health.ayurveda	misc.fitness.misc
alt.med.cfs	misc.health.diabetes
alt.support.diet	talk.politics.medicine
bit.listserv.c+health	sci.med.aids
clari.tw.health.misc	sci.med.pharmacy

History

The History Resources Page

Type: WWW

Address: http://history.cc.ukans.edu/history/WWW_history_main.html

Summary: The University of Kansas maintains this excellent collection of links to history resources around the Net. If you can't find out about it starting from here, it might not have happened.

Time's Man of the Year

Type: WWW

Address: http://pathfinder.com/time/special/moy/moy.html

Summary: Each year since 1927, *Time* magazine has chosen somebody to appear on the cover as Man of the Year. Can you guess who was chosen in 1984? That's right, Peter Ueberroth. How about 1955? You guessed it, General Motors president Harlow Hubert Curtice. Once you get past the overwhelming male bias, this is actually a pretty interesting stroll down memory lane. While the articles about the individuals are informative, this site really says more about our values, about what types of achievement we have considered important over the course of recent history.

Man of the Year Home Page.

Some Related Newsgroups

alt.history.what-if	alt.war.civil.usa
alt.revisionism	bit.listserv.history
alt.war	soc.history

Humor

VibeComics

Type: WWW

Address: http://www.vibe.com/vibecomics/

Summary: *Vibe Comics* is a well-done, idiosyncratic personal humor zine. It always makes me laugh, and sometimes it even makes me drink.

VibeComics.

Cartoons

Type: Usenet

Address: alt.toon-pics

Summary: Download pictures of your favorite cartoon characters.

The Comic Strip Page

Type: WWW

Address: http://www.unitedmedia.com/comics/

Summary: The home for United Artists cartoons.

The Comic Strip. (Copyright UFS, Inc. 1995. Reprinted with permission of United Features Syndicate. All rights Reserved.)

The Corporation

Type: WWW

Address: http://www.thecorporation.com

Summary: I'll just let this site speak for itself: "Now, using the **Internet**®, our proprietary worldwide network of large computing devices and cables, we are able to manufacture and distribute fresh, modern humor products faster than ever."

The Unofficial Tank Girl WWW Site

Type: WWW

Address: http://www.cs.ucl.ac.uk/staff/b.rosenberg/tg/index.html

Summary: Tank Girl is a creation of Jamie Hewlett and Alan Martin. On this page, you'll find a gallery of Tank Girl pictures, a Tank Girl FAQ, and everything else you need to be Tank Girl–literate.

Tank Girl.

Some Related Newsgroups

alt.comedy.british	rec.arts.comics.strips
alt.comics.buffalo-roam	rec.humor.d
alt.comics.superman	rec.humor.funny
alt.fan.firesign-theatre	
alt.fan.wodehouse	
alt.fan.tank-girl	
alt.folklore.college	
alt.humor.best-of-usenet	
clari.feature.foxtrot	
rec.arts.comics.marketplace	

Indexes, Hotlists & Search Tools

Archie Request Form

Type: WWW

Address: http://hoohoo.ncsa.uiuc.edu/archie.html

Summary: Archie is a utility for locating files at anonymous FTP sites. You used to need your own Archie client to connect with an Archie host, or alternatively you could Telnet to a site that provided a text-based UNIX client. Now it's much simpler. This site lets you specify your request in a simple Web form and then does the rest of the work for you.

Archie Request Form.

ARGUS ClearingHouse for Subject-Oriented Resource Guides

Type: WWW

Address: http://www.clearinghouse.net/

Summary: A well-organized collection of hotlinks, grouped by subject area.

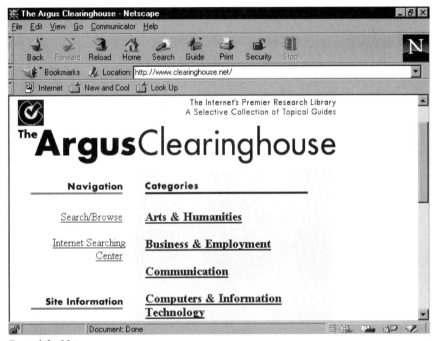

Best of the Net.

Best of the Web

Type: WWW

Address: http://wings.buffalo.edu/contest/

Summary: This is the Academy Awards for Web pages, voted on by thousands of Internet users. There are a variety of categories, and you can jump right over to the winners via the provided hotlinks.

CityLink

Type: WWW

Address: http://www.usacitylink.com/

Summary: More and more city governments and civic organizations are establishing a presence on the Web. CityLink points you to many of these. It also includes a wide range of information that may be important to travelers. For instance, the New York link includes a brief guide to treating gunshot wounds.

The USA CityLink Project.

Cool Site of the Day

Type: WWW

Address: http://cool.infi.net/

Summary: On the Web, as in "real life," there's always someone who's willing to tell you where to go. This home page includes a new link each day to a particularly interesting and original site. There are also links to previously chosen cool sites.

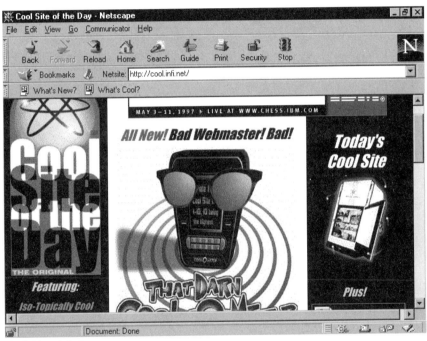

Cool Site of the Day.

ECHO!

Type: WWW

Address: http://www.echonyc.com/

Summary: This is a collection of interesting home pages by members of the Echo online service. The documents vary from technology hotlists to experimental art.

ECHO!

The ElNet Galaxy

   Type: WWW

   Address: http://www.einet.com

   Summary: ElNet Galaxy is an easy-to-use and thorough hotlist. A good starting point for Web novices.

E-ZINE LIST

   Type: WWW

   Address: http://www.meer.net/~johnl/e-zine-list/

   Summary: John Labovitz maintains the most thorough and up-to-date list of electronic zines currently available.

451f

   Type: WWW

   Address: http://hakatai.mcli.dist.maricopa.edu/451f/index.html

   Summary: Another great collection of Web links.

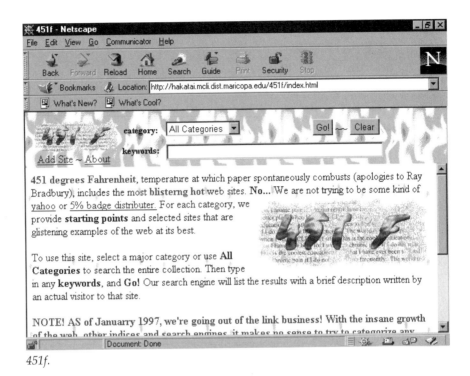

451f.

Harvest

Type: WWW

Address: http://harvest.cs.colorado.edu/

Summary: This is one of the best Web "search engines," including indexes of home pages, public domain software, newsgroups, and so on. It is easy to use and thorough, one of the best places to go when you want to "harvest" specific information.

Index Librorum Liberorum

Type: WWW

Address: http://www.fourmilab.ch/

Summary: John Walker has amassed a large, interesting collection of public domain electronic texts, technical papers, and programs. Not only does he make these materials available to you, he has organized them so that it's easy to find what you're looking for.

Infomine

Type: WWW

Address: http://lib-www.ucr.edu/govpub/

Summary: Links to a variety of federal government Web sites.

Infoseek

Type: WWW

Address: http://www.infoseek.com/

Summary: This claims to be the largest set of searchable indexes to WWW pages and to USENET newsgroups. After a quick look around I have no reason to doubt it. Infoseek also maintains indexes to over 80 computer periodicals. A great place to start your research.

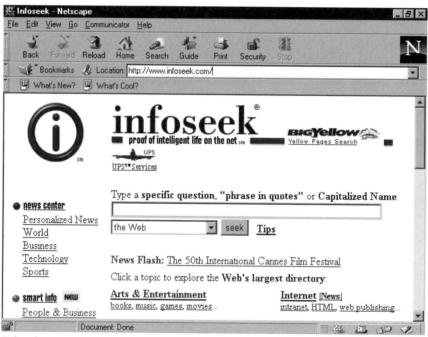

Infoseek.

Internet Resources Meta-Index

Type: WWW

Address: http://www.ncsa.uiuc.edu/SDG/Software/Mosaic/ MetaIndex.html

Summary: This page has links to most of the resource directories and indexes on the Net.

The Internet Services List

Type: WWW

Address: http://www.spectracom.com/islist/

Summary: This is Scott Yanoff's absolutely huge list of World Wide Web hotlinks. It is well-organized and updated regularly. Another great place to start browsing!

InterNIC Directory

Type: WWW

Address: http://ds.internic.net/

Summary: InterNIC provides several very large searchable databases of Internet resources. Definitely worth checking out.

Justin's Links From the Underground

Type: WWW

Address: http://www.links.net

Summary: This is an almost legendary hotlist of interesting and unusual Internet sites.

TILE.NET/*LISTSERV*

Type: WWW

Address: http://www.tile.net/tile/listserv/index.html

Summary: There are hundreds of special-interest e-mail lists, but how do you find them? This site provides an organized overview of what's available.

Lycos

Type: WWW

Address: http://www.lycos.com/

Summary: Lycos lets you search for specific Web documents based on keywords you enter. It maintains a database of over 800,000 URLs. There are some other interesting resources here as well, including a list of the frequency of over six million words used on the Web. Lycos is one of those facilities that's almost too good, presenting you with more information than you really need, but it's a great resource if you use it carefully to narrow down your search.

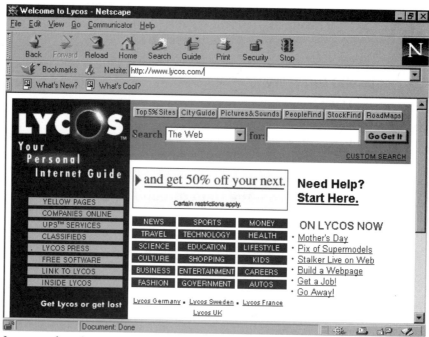

Lycos search engine.

Mirsky's Worst of the Web

Type: WWW

Address: http://mirsky.com/wow/

Summary: Not all of us have the time to cruise around the Web each day looking for the worst sites we can find. Fortunately, Mirsky does. Actually, some of his award winners I found more interesting than atrocious. I wonder what that says about me?

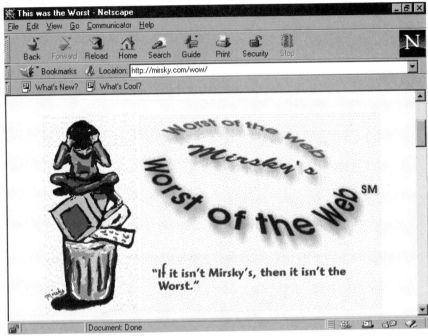

Mirsky's Worst of the Web.

The Mother-of-all BBS

Type: WWW

Address: http://wwwmbb.cs.colorado.edu/~mcbryan/bb/summary.html

Summary: Links to just about everything on the Web. You can perform a WAIS search on the Bulletin Board.

Nexor Public Services

Type: WWW

Address: http://web.nexor.co.uk/public/welcome.html

Summary: Yet another good search tool, letting you find information on the Web by keyword.

The Rumor Mill

Type: WWW

Address: http://asylum.cid.com/

Summary: A small, highly selective collection of fun and bizarre hotlinks.

The SenseMedia Surfer

Type: WWW

Address: http://www.picosof.com:8080/html/scott.html

Summary: This is one of my favorite hotlists. It includes links to hundreds of different sites in many different categories. A great place to begin a day of Web surfing.

The Source

Type: WWW

Address: http://hakatai.mcli.dist.maricopa.edu/smc/ml/source.html

Summary: A great selection of philosophy, religion, and psychology resources.

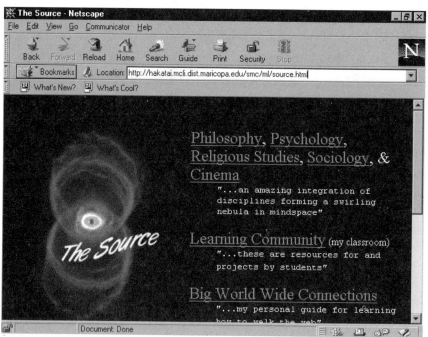

The Source.

Special Internet Connections

Type: FTP

Address: ftp://ftp.csd.uwm.edu/pub/inet.services.txt

Summary: A *huge* list of Internet resources, updated regularly. Better than a lot of other resource lists because it gives descriptions of each site. Print it out and start browsing—there's enough to keep you busy at least until the next edition of this book comes out.

Also available by mailing list by sending a subscription request to yanoff@csd4.csd.uwm.edu. The list is also posted regularly to several Usenet newsgroups including biz.comp.services and alt.internet.services.

The UCMP Subway

Type: WWW

Address: http://www.ucmp.berkeley.edu/subway/subway.html

Summary: A large hotlist of interesting sites, presented in a slightly unusual way: "The subway will take you to many virtual destinations throughout the Internet. Below you will see a map. Please touch a place on the map and you will receive a seat on the next train." Yes, yet another travel metaphor for browsing the Web!

UNC-CH Heliocentric Information Map

Type: WWW

Address: http://sunsite.unc.edu/heliocentric.html

Summary: I'll bet you didn't know that the University of North Carolina, with its SunSITE, is the center of the information universe—or at least the information solar system. Check out this interesting example of Web design, which provides lots of valuable information as well.

Vibe's World Map

Type: WWW

Address: http://www.vibe.com

Summary: While this seems to be mainly an ad for Timex, it is actually a pretty useful page. Click on any area of a world map and you will be presented with a comprehensive list of Web sites in that area. Since it's Timex, you also get the local time.

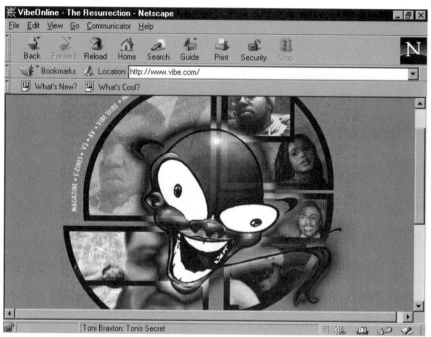

Vibe's World Map.

Virtual Town

Type: WWW

Address: http://wwwcsif.cs.ucdavis.edu/virt-town/welcome.html

Summary: Plenty of good Web links presented in the form of a virtual town. You click on the area that you want to visit.

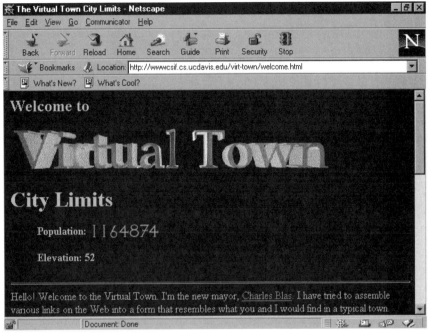

Virtual Town.

Washington & Lee University's Netlink Server

> **Type:** WWW
>
> **Address:** http://netlink.wlu.edu:1020/
>
> **Summary:** Links to high-level Internet sources, database of links to public login Telnet sites, WWW servers, WAIS servers—tons of stuff!

The Webcrawler

> **Type:** WWW
>
> **Address:** http://www.webcrawler.com/
>
> **Summary:** This excellent search engine indexes the contents of Web documents, so you can find pages that contain a particular word or phrase.

The Web's Edge

Type: WWW

Address: http://kzsu.stanford.edu/uwi.html

Summary: "UnderWorld Industries' Cultural Playground." Lots of alternative stuff. Check out "Stream of Conscience," an art/poetry Webzine.

What's Hot and Cool on the Web

Type: WWW

Address: http://kzsu.stanford.edu/uwi/reviews.html

Summary: Lots of cool (and hot) alternative-type stuff.

What's Hot and Cool.

NCSA What's New

Type: WWW

Address: http://www.ncsa.uiuc.edu/SDG/Software/Mosaic/Docs/whats-new.html

Summary: Get the latest Web info here. Descriptions of and links to new home pages.

NCSA What's New.

World Birthday Web

Type: WWW

Address: http://www.boutell.com/birthday.cgi/

Summary: Andy Warhol said that in the future everybody will be famous for 15 minutes. Well if you're a Web traveler, you can be famous for at least an entire day. Enter your name and birthday here and you will appear in the birthday list on that day. If you enter a URL for your home page, a hotlink to that site will be included as well.

The World Wide Web Consortium

Type: WWW

Address: http://www.w3.org/pub/WWW/

Summary: This is one of the best starting points for exploring the Web, although the sheer volume of information can be overwhelming.

The World Wide Web Consortium.

World-Wide Web Worm

Type: WWW

Address: http://wwww.cs.colorado.edu/wwww

Summary: The "WWWW" is becoming one of the most popular tools for searching the Web. It is extremely flexible, allowing regular expression searches on URL, subject, and content. In spite of its flexibility, it's not difficult to use, and the site even includes a straightforward tutorial.

Yahoo!

Type: WWW

Address: http://www.yahoo.com (or Net Directory button)

Summary: Yahoo! may be the best-known of the large public hotlists sprinkled around the Web. It includes a good search facility, and since it allows users to enter new sites it is always up-to-date. This is an excellent place to start exploring.

Internet Stuff

A Beginner's Guide to HTML

Type: WWW

Address: http://www.ncsa.uiuc.edu/demoweb/html-primer.html

Summary: Learn to create HTML documents that can be placed on the Web.

Community Computer Networks: Building Electronic Greenbelts

Type: FTP

Address: ftp://ftp.apple.com/alug/communet/

Summary: Steve Cisler's excellent overview of community networks examining what kinds of information and services can be found on these systems, what groups are running community networks, and cost aspects. The essay discusses current models for community networks and the impact these networks have on their local (physical) environment.

Contact: Steve Cisler
Apple Library
4 Infinite Loop
MS 304-2A
Cupertino, CA 95014
408/974-3258
sac@apple.com

Good Internet Books

    Type: Gopher

  Address: gopher://nysernet.org

     Path: Special Collections: Internet Help/Good Books About the Internet

Summary: A great list of books about the Net. There's a short summary, the ISBN number, and the price.

Internet Society

    Type: WWW

  Address: http://info.isoc.org/

Summary: The Internet Society was created in 1991 to be the international organization that promotes global cooperation and coordination for the Internet and its technologies. Individuals and organizations can join. There's a great general info Internet FAQ.

  Contact: Internet Society
org-membership@isoc.org
800/468-9507 (U.S. only)
703/648-9888

Internet Society.

Internet Web Text

Type: WWW

Address: http://www.december.com/web/text/index.html

Summary: Created in spring of 1994 (but updated since) by John December for a course in Computer-Mediated Communication at Rensselaer Polytechnic Institute. His goal: to create an interface students could use to familiarize themselves with the Internet—how to use it, how to find information, how to connect with people. He makes use of icons to create memory aids to remembering sources. This page also has links to lots of online Internet guides and resources, such as *Zen and the Art of the Internet*.

Contact: John December
decemj@rpi.edu

NCSA Mosaic

Type: WWW

Address: http://www.ncsa.uiuc.edu/SDG/Software/Mosaic/ NCSAMosaicHome.html

Summary: Download the latest release of NCSA Mosaic, get installation and configuration instructions, info about bugs and bug fixes, FAQs, and an online users' manual. Also get graphics viewers, HTML editors, Pkunzip, and winsocks.

Why Are Internet Resources Free?

Type: Gopher

Address: gopher://wiretap.spies.com

Path: Wiretap Online Library / Cyberspace / Why are Internet Resources Free?

Summary: Ever wondered why you can get to most of the stuff on the Net without having to pay? This article explains it all for you.

Some Related Newsgroups

alt.answers	alt.security.pgp
alt.culture.internet	bit.listserv.new-list
alt.culture.usenet	misc.answers
alt.newbie	misc.legal.computing
alt.online-service	news.software.readers

Jobs

Federal Jobs

Type: Gopher

Address: gopher://gopher.Dartmouth.EDU:70/11/Careers

Path: Job Openings in the Federal Government

Summary: Lists of federal job opportunities and information that'll help you apply for a federal job.

Online Career Center

Type: Gopher

Address: gopher://msen.com

Path: The Msen Career Center/The Online Career Center

Summary: You can post your resume and search job lists at no charge, get career counseling, and connect with recruiting agencies.

Contact: occ@mail.msen.com

Some Related Newsgroups

bionet.jobs   misc.jobs.misc

bionet.women-in-bio   misc.jobs.offered

biz.jobs.offered   misc.jobs.offered.entry

info.wisenet   misc.jobs.resumes

misc.jobs.contract

Journals & Zines

Boardwatch Magazine

Type: WWW

Address: http://www.boardwatch.com/

Summary: A taste of what's in the print version of this wide-ranging monthly about BBSing and the Internet.

Boardwatch Magazine.

Career Magazine

      Type: WWW

    Address: http://www.careermag.com/careermag/

   Summary: Tired of cruising the Net and want to get a job instead? Need money to support your online addiction? About to get fired for playing games on the Web instead of selling widgets? You need to check out this site quickly.

Career Magazine.

Computer Mediated Communication Magazine

Type: WWW

Address: http://www.december.com/cmc/mag/current/toc.html

Summary: An interesting electronic magazine filled with information and opinion about the technology and culture of the Internet.

dimFLASH

Type: WWW

Address: http://www.well.com/user/futrelle/dflash.html

Summary: An interesting zine with excellent graphics and hotlinks to other peculiar sites.

Editor & Publisher Interactive

Type: WWW

Address: http://www.mediainfo.com/edpub/

Summary: This is an extensive and constantly changing list of newspapers that offer online services. The list only covers large mass-media papers, not zines or electronic newsletters.

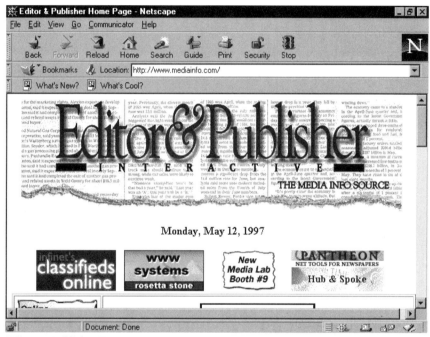

Editor & Publisher Home Page.

The Fiore Report

Type: mailing list

Address: sept4yu@ix.netcom.com
(send e-mail saying you want to subscribe)

Summary: Sex therapist Tony Fiore writes this monthly electronic newsletter that offers advice on improving or enhancing your sex life.

Fringeware

> **Type:** WWW
>
> **Address:** http://www.fringeware.com/
>
> **Summary:** Fringeware is an interesting bunch of people in Austin who offer cutting-edge cyberinfo, cyberart, and cyberproducts. This is the place to go when *Wired* looks tired.

HotWired

> **Type:** WWW
>
> **Address:** http://www.hotwired.com/
>
> **Summary:** This is one of the biggest tourist attractions on the Internet, a sort of new-media Disney World for plugged in twenty-somethings. You'll find a little of everything here, though most of the material focuses on various aspects of cyberspace itself.

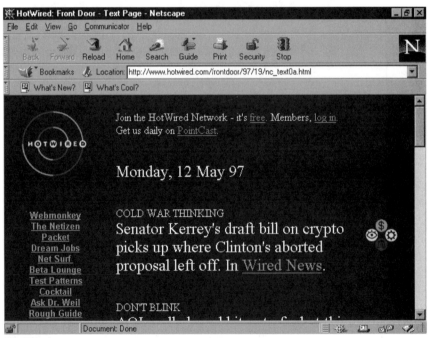

HotWired.

iWorld

      Type: WWW

    Address: http://www.iworld.com/

  Summary: This is the Web home of Mecklermedia, the folks who publish *Internet World*. Here you can find a special hypermedia version of the magazine.

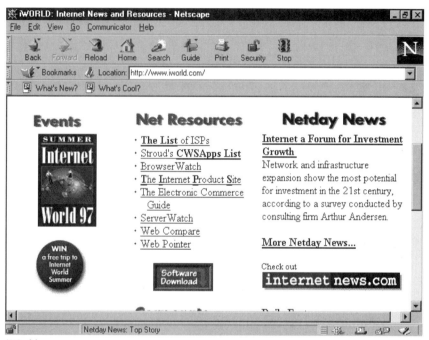

iWorld.

Link Digital Campus

      Type: WWW

    Address: http://www.linkmag.com/

  Summary: In addition to the interesting *Link* zine, this site contains a thorough index to student publications from universities around the country. A valuable resource!

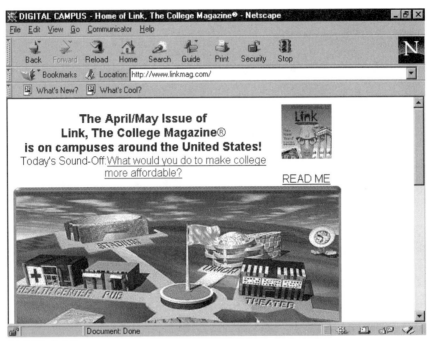

Link Digital Campus.

Mediamatic

Type: WWW

Address: http://www.mediamatic.nl/home.html

Summary: This is an interesting Dutch magazine about interactive media and its cultural implications. Well-written and well-produced.

Mercury Center

Type: WWW

Address: http://www.sjmercury.com

Summary: Many newspapers now offer electronic versions. This is one of the best, developed by *San Jose Mercury News*.

Mediamatic.

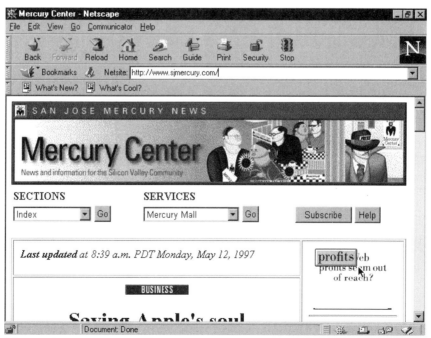

Mercury Center.

The Netly News

Type: WWW

Address: http://www.pathfinder.com/Netly

Summary: Internet expert Josh Quittner runs this one. "There are 35 million stories in cyberspace. We give you a new one every day." That's the basic idea, a new and usually excellent feature article every day, mainly about Web and Internet issues.

Netsurfer Digest

Type: WWW

Address: http://www.netsurf.com/nsd/index.html

Summary: This is an interesting electronic zine about the Net and interactive communications. Zines like this are popping up daily, but this one has more substance than most.

Netsurfer Digest.

Ziff-Davis Publishing

Type: WWW

Address: http://www.zdnet.com

Summary: Ziff-Davis is the General Motors of computer magazine publishing. This site lets you access *PC Magazine* and eight others.

Kids

The Cisco Educational Archives

Type: WWW

Address: http://sunsite.unc.edu/cisco/cisco-home.html

Summary: Lots of hotlinks to Web pages of interest to school-age kids as well as teachers.

Disney

Type: WWW

Address: http://www.disney.com/

Summary: I'm no fan of the empire Walt and Mickey built, or of all the saccharine pap the company churns out these days to make a buck or two zillion, but I have to admit this is a well constructed and colorful site. With a dearth of family oriented Web pages, it's an OK place to stop by with the kids on a rainy day.

Explora-Net

Type: WWW

Address: http://www.exploratorium.edu/

Summary: This is the home page for the Exploratorium, a fascinating hands-on science museum in San Francisco. It includes areas of interest to both children and adults.

Global Show-n-Tell

Type: WWW

Address: http://www.telenaut.com/gst/

Summary: It is difficult to find good sites for younger children on the Web, but this is one of the best. It's an interactive exhibition of children's art; everything on display was created by kids and e-mailed in. I'd like to see more ideas like this!

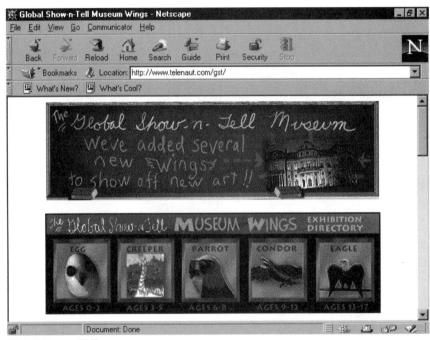

Global Show-n-Tell.

Interesting Places for Kids

Type: WWW

Address: http://www.crc.ricoh.com/people/steve/kids.html

Summary: This Web page includes links to literally hundreds of entertaining and educational sites for children. Don't stick them in front of the TV, drop them off here!

IPL Youth

Type: WWW

Address: http://ipl.sils.umich.edu/youth/

Summary: This is the kids' section of the University of Michigan's Internet Public Library, and it's a wonderful site. Kids can submit their own stories to a contest, check out a book, explore math and science, chat about books they like, even submit questions to authors.

Yahooligans

Type: WWW

Address: http://www.yahooligans.com/

Summary: This may be the only kids' site you ever need. It's the junior version of Yahoo!, with hundreds of neatly categorized links to other pages. A great starting place for exploration on a rainy afternoon.

Languages

Esperanto-English Dictionary

Type: Gopher

Address: gopher://wiretap.spies.com

Path: Wiretap Online Library / Articles / Language / Esperanto English Dictionary

Summary: Next time your boss tells you what to do, why not answer in Esperanto!

Foreign Language Resources

Type: WWW

Address: http://www.itp.berkeley.edu/~thorne/HumanResources.html

Summary: This is a large collection of links to sites that can help you learn a foreign language.

Human-Languages Page

Type: WWW

Address: http://www.june29.com//HLP/

Summary: This page currently contains more than 100 links to over 40 different languages. Tutorials, dictionaries, software, and literature.

Japanese/English Dictionary–Gateway

Type: WWW

Address: http://www.wg.omron.co.jp/cgi-bin/j-e

Summary: This page is also available in Japanese. The dictionary entries can be viewed with text-based browsers or with Japanese text sent as images.

Travelers' Japanese with Voice

Type: WWW

Address: http://www.ntt.co.jp/japan/japanese/

Summary: Learn some simple Japanese before that next business trip.

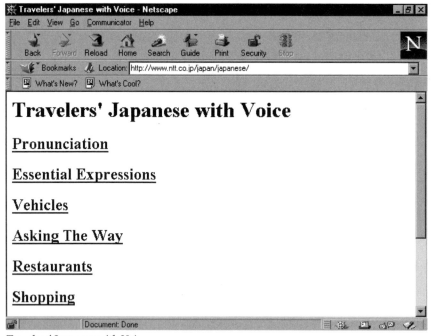

Travelers' Japanese with Voice.

Some Related Newsgroups

>alt.chinese.text
>alt.japanese.text
>k12.lang.francais
>k12.lang.russian
>sci.lang
>soc.culture.esperanto
>soc.culture.french

Law

Advertising Law Internet Site

Type: WWW

Address: http://www.webcom.com/~lewrose/home.html

Summary: Legal aspects of marketing. Stuff about infomercials, home shopping, and 900 number regulations. You can also get FTC guides and consumer advisories.

Criminal Justice Country Profiles

Type: Gopher

Address: gopher://uacsc2.albany.edu

Path: United Nations Justice Network / U.N. Criminal Justice Country Profiles

Summary: Find out how the criminal justice system works in different countries.

Legal Information Institute

Type: WWW

Address: http://www.law.cornell.edu/

Summary: Get information about recent Supreme Court decisions, search an e-mail address directory of faculty and staff at U.S. law schools. Lots of links to other law-related stuff.

Some Related Newsgroups

bit.listserv.lawsch-l

clari.news.usa.law

misc.int-property

mis.legal

misc.legal.computing

Miscellany: Unclassifiable Wonders

The Advanced Nerdity Test

Type: WWW

Address: http://gonzo.tamu.edu/nerd-backwards.html

Summary: If you're reading this book instead of *Proceedings of the ACM* you're probably not a total nerd. On the other hand, if you're reading this book at all, you're probably a little bit of one. Find out just how nerdy you really are.

Animals

Type: FTP

Address: ftp://rtfm.mit.edu/pub/usenet/news.answers

Summary: You'll find all sorts of animal stuff here. A few of the subdirectories to check out:

> cats-faq
> pets-birds-faq
> fleas-ticks
> dogs-faq

Celebrity Slugfest

Type: WWW

Address: http://slugfest.kaizen.net

Summary: Do you ever wake up feeling like there'd be nothing better to do today than throw Fabio a punch? Here's your chance! Choose your celebrity, take a swing. Requires Shockwave.

The Digital Confession Booth

Type: WWW

Address: http://anther.learning.cs.cmu.edu/priest.html

Summary: It's so much easier this way. And, you can scroll through everybody else's sins, too!

Find-the-Spam

Type: WWW

Address: http://www.smalltime.com/nowhere/findthespam/findthespam.cgi

Summary: Some people have too much time on their hands, and I'm glad they do. This is by far the goofiest, stupidest Web page I've come across. I love it.

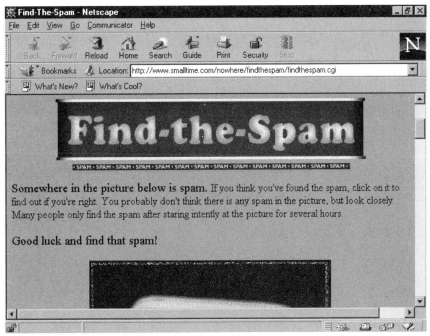

Find-the-Spam.

The Froggy Page

Type: WWW

Address: http://frog.simplenet.com/froggy/

Summary: This is one of my favorite sites. It includes many beautiful photographs of frogs as well as a variety of frog-related information. From the Froggy Page you might also want to jump to Sandra Loosemore's home page, which contains some other interesting links.

The Grouchy Café

Type: WWW

Address: http://www.echonyc.com/~cafephrk/cafe.html

Summary: This is a warm friendly hangout with a real sense of *place*. Cafephreak, the proprietor, serves up recipes, anecdotes, information on coffee, a list of angst-ridden teenage books, fun artwork, and the memorable advice "Never fall in love with a lesbian who read Sartre instead of Judy Blume. She will rip out your heart."

The Grouchy Café.

Hacker Barbie

Type: WWW

Address: http://www.catalog.com/mrm/barbe/barbe.html

Summary: An amusing and interesting home page focusing on a transformed and far more interesting version of Mattel's Barbie doll. Not for everybody, but I really enjoyed this site.

InterJackie

Type: WWW

Address: http://www.echonyc.com/~interjackie

Summary: A sort of cyber-club from the people who publish the always interesting *Verbal Abuse* magazine. Great graphics.

Mr. Edible Starchy Tuber Head

Type: WWW

Address: http://winnie.acsu.buffalo.edu/potatoe/

Summary: Yes, this is what it sounds like. You add various features to a potato-shaped outline, coming up with "hilarious" distorted faces. This is where you come to relive a vital part of your 1960s childhood.

The MIT Gallery of Hacks

Type: WWW

Address: http://fishwrap.mit.edu/Hacks/Gallery.html

Summary: At MIT the word "hack" means a clever prank such as putting a phony police car on top of the Great Dome (Building 10) on the last day of classes. Many descriptions of hacks are accompanied by photographs. This site is an inspiration to college students everywhere.

Net Chick Clubhouse

Type: WWW

Address: http://www.cyborganic.com/People/carla

Summary: "Psst!—Over here! We're in the Net Chick Clubhouse—spreading gossip, telling secrets, relishing pop culture, luxuriating, and playing hard." What more could you want if you're a Net Chick?

Paul Haas' Appliances

Type: WWW

Address: http://hamjudo.com/

Summary: Paul Haas is a UNIX consultant. He also maintains a Web page that includes constantly updated information on his refrigerator (temperature, contents) and hot tub (temperature, contents). This is the age of information. Can you really afford to miss any?

The Personal Death Clock

Type: WWW

Address: http://www.speedoflight.com/techs/ray/death

Summary: The Web knows everything! At this site you enter some information about yourself and quickly learn exactly when you're going to pop off. I discovered that I will start my dirt nap on October 21, 2026, exactly 937,914,265 seconds from now. But that's OK. The Death Clock also told me that Rush Limbaugh has only 843,478,991 seconds left. That means I'll have over 94 million seconds in a Rush-free world!

The Really Big Button That Doesn't Do Anything

Type: WWW

Address: http://www.wam.umd.edu/~twoflowr/button.htm

Summary: This is another one of those useless sites, a giant push button that does not respond to your clicks. It includes, however, numerous philosophical musings on the nature of the button, and it allows you to add your own. A great site to visit if you've already figured out every other way to waste time.

SCHWA™

Type: WWW

Address: http://fringeware.com/SchwaRoot/Schwa.html

Summary: I've always felt that the Internet wouldn't really be the same without Schwa. This crazy alien conspiracy think-tank typifies the wide range of viewpoints available to Netsurfers. Crackpots are one of America's greatest products, and I'm glad they have a voice on the Web.

The Really Big Button.

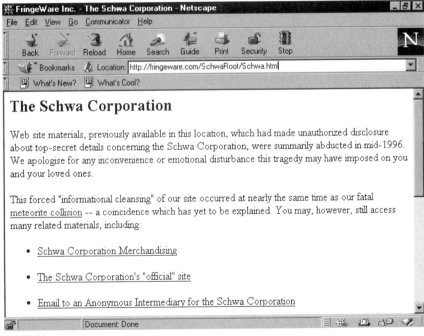

SCHWA.

SpingoWorld

Type: WWW

Address: http://www.echonyc.com/~spingo/SpingoWorld

Summary: A fun and very unclassifiable site that includes chatting via Time-Warner's Palace. Lots of sounds, too.

The Surrealist Compliment Generator

Type: WWW

Address: http://pharmdec.wustl.edu/cgi-bin/jardin_scripts/SCG

Summary: This Web page presents you with a unique randomly generated compliment each time you reload it. For instance, the first time I visited it told me, "Sound barricades into rolls of peanut butter when you speak." It was the nicest thing anybody had said to me all day, so I decided to try again. This time I got, "Ever so slightly, you remind me of a staircase falling exotically into a sea of spilled macaroni." There is also a slightly more serious side to this site, as it includes lots of fascinating information on the Surrealist Movement in the arts.

The TiReD-WiReD Server

Type: WWW

Address: http://www.cs.odu.edu/~bianco/bin/
tired-wired.cgi

Summary: Every month devoted members of the *cyber-hipoisie* thumb as quickly as they can to *Wired* magazine's TiReD-WiReD list to find out what's cool to be talking about this month and what's oh-so-five-minutes-ago. This site offers an amusing take off on this cyberculture chestnut, an almost Dadaist list generated by some secret mathematical formula. Good clean fun.

Multimedia

Index to Multimedia Information Sources

Type: WWW

Address: http://viswiz.gmd.de/MultimediaInfo

Summary: Links to film and video resources, media archives, MPC specs, cable regulations, desktop publishing, art, music, zines, publishers, MIDI, MPEG, satellite TV, Nielsen ratings, the Billboard chart, hypertext and hypermedia, multimedia software, newsgroups, and about a zillion other multimedia-related resources. Multimedia FAQ heaven and lots of conference announcements.

ITP

Type: WWW

Address: http://www.itp.tsoa.nyu.edu/

Summary: New York University's Tisch School of the Arts sponsors this Interactive Telecommunications Program for students who want to explore the latest communications technologies from a creative perspective. And on the ITP Web site, you can see some of their most interesting projects. There's a lot of good work here. In fact, from time to time you'll find something here that's as fresh and exciting as anything on the Web.

Silicon Graphics' Serious Fun Page

Type: WWW

Address: http://www.sgi.com/Fun/fun.html

Summary: As you would expect from this pioneering high-tech company, this site is loaded with fascinating computer-generated images and video clips.

Serious Fun with SGI.

Music

Addicted to Noise

    Type: WWW

  Address: http://www.addict.com

Summary: The title says it all.

Classical Music

    Type: Usenet

  Address: rec.music.classical.performing

Summary: Lots of interesting and serious discussions (low garbage ratio).

The Mudcat Cafe

Type: WWW

Address: http://www.deltablues.com/dbsearch.html

Summary: A searchable database containing words and music to thousands of folk songs collected by Dick Greenhaus and friends.

Hyperreal—the Techno/Ambient/Rave Archive

Type: WWW

Address: http://hyperreal.com/

Summary: The Rave Archive will take you to the alt.rave FAQ, The List of Rave Lists, and pointers to tons of Rave home pages.

Contact: Brian Behlendorf, founder of the SFRaves mailing list brian@hyperreal.com

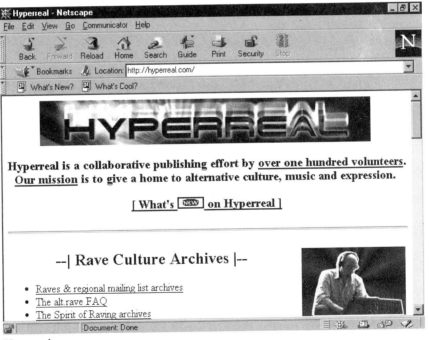

Hyperreal.

Internet Underground Music Archive (IUMA)

Type: WWW

Address: http://www.iuma.com/IUMA/

Summary: IUMA is a huge catalog of artists, albums, and songs, including reviews and many MPEG samples. This site keeps getting bigger and better. It was founded by Rob Lord and Jeff Patterson to showcase unsigned musicians. Listen to clips from over 140 independent rock bands.

Intrrr Nrrrd

Type: WWW

Address: http://nervecore.com/e-zine

Summary: A classic. "Saving souls with punk rawwk since August 1994." What else can you say?

Knitting Factory

Type: WWW

Address: http://knittingfactory.com

Summary: The Knitting Factory is both a performance space and record label in New York City. For many years they have been devoted to some of the most interesting music around, including the work of adventurous composers and performers who bridge whatever gap there used to be between innovative jazz and avant-garde "classical" music.

Random Band Names

Type: WWW

Address: http://www.terranet.ab.ca/~aaron/band_names.html

Summary: Everyone who has started a band, except maybe Courtney Love, has struggled with the difficulty of coming up with a good name. Should you be "Stuck Pig" or would "Timex Junk-Monkies" make more sense? This site solves the problem by offering you a unique randomly generated band name. If you're not musical, you could probably use it as your handle on AOL or some other information service.

SonicNet

Type: WWW

Address: http://www.sonicnet.com

Summary: One of the most popular music sites on the Web, SonicNet, features great visuals, news and reviews, and RealAudio sound clips. Alternative rock is the style here.

The DJ

Type: WWW

Address: http://www.thedj.com

Summary: This site lets you choose from 50 channels of music, just as you would tune a radio. The big difference: *NO COMMERCIALS!* The only catch is that you need RealAudio 3.0 and at least a 28.8 Kb/sec connection.

The Ultimate Band List

Type: WWW

Address: http://ubl.com/ubl/ubl.shtml

Summary: Want to find the Nick Cave Web site? This claims to be the largest listing of Internet resources for specific bands, and I have no reason to doubt it. What makes this a great site is that it can be updated by users and that it includes not just Web links but links to all kinds of resources: lyric files, newsgroups, mailing lists, digitized songs, and so on.

VANGELIS—The Man and the Music

Type: WWW

Address: http://bau2.uibk.ac.at/perki/Vangelis.html

Summary: Pictures, sounds, and digitized film sequences. Biographical information, as well as info about his solo and collaborative works, including motion picture scores.

Violin and Bow Makers

Type: WWW

Address: http://www.eskimo.com/~dvz/
violin-makers.html

Summary: Get a regularly updated list of e-mail addresses for bowed
stringed instrument makers throughout the United States. There's
a short bio for each person. This site also includes info about The
American Federation of Violin and Bow Makers.

The Voodoo Lounge: Rolling Stones Web Site

Type: WWW

Address: http://www.stones.com/

Summary: Be the first on your block with a "black polar fleece ear warmer
with embroidered tongue." Yes, folks, this is where you'll find the
official Stones merchandise catalog. Also tour schedules, music
clips, picture collections, and interviews.

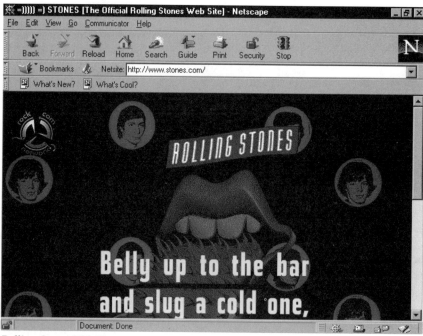

Rolling Stones Web Site.

WNUR-FM Jazz Information Server (The Jazz Web)

Type: WWW

Address: http://www.acns.nwu.edu/jazz/

Summary: Discographies, jazz media info (radio stations, etc.). History of jazz, live performance schedules, biographical info on artists, FAQ, lots of info on other jazz resources.

Some Related Newsgroups

alt.emusic	rec.music.bluenote
alt.guitar.tab	rec.music.celtic
alt.music.a-cappella	rec.music.christian
alt.music.filk	rec.music.classical
alt.music.jewish	rec.music.country.western
alt.rock-n-roll.hard	rec.music.funky
alt.rock-n-roll.metal	rec.music.indian.misc
rec.music.afro-latin	rec.music.marketplace.cd

News

Commercial News Services on the World Wide Web

Type: WWW

Address: http://www.jou.ufl.edu/commres/webjou.htm

Summary: Links to all the newspapers on the Net, campus as well as commercial, and to other newspaper and journalism-related resources.

The New South Polar Times

Type: WWW

Address: http://139.132.40.31/NSPT/NSPThomePage.html

Summary: Do you ever wake up wondering what's going on at the South Pole right now? Before this Web site opened its virtual doors it wasn't very easy to get the latest news from the bottom of the world, but it's fascinating stuff. You won't read about OJ, Newt, or Whitewater; instead, it's scientific research and life in one of the most beautiful and difficult environments. In more ways than one, this is a truly cool site.

The Onion

Type: WWW

Address: http://www.theonion.com

Summary: When you get bored with the "real" news—who doesn't?—check out this very funny parody of serious journalism. Just the headlines make me chuckle.

Our World News

Type: WWW

Address: http://www.ourworldnews.com

Summary: This is solid journalism from a Black perspective. Our World News covers both national and world news, presenting stories clearly and thoroughly.

Occult

Dark Side of the Net

Type: mailing list

Address: carriec@eskimo.com

Summary: Subscribe to this list if you want to find out about all sorts of occult-related resources, including stuff about vampires.

To subscribe, send the following one-line message in e-mail: **subscribe dark side of the net *your name*** (where *your name* is your full name—*not* your e-mail address).

Freud's Studies of the Occult

Type: FTP

Address: ftp://ftp.spies.com/Library/Fringe/Occult/freud.occ

Summary: Freud actually dug into paranormal studies, and this paper gives all the spooky details.

Occult

Type: FTP

Address: ftp://ftp.funet.fi/pub/doc/occult/

Summary: Lots of pictures and documents—everything from astrology to wicca to magic.

Real Astrology

Type: WWW

Address: http://www.realastrology.com

Summary: Horoscopes for the rest of us. It doesn't matter if you believe in the stuff or not, Rob Brezsny is a writer with a wonderful upbeat style. I've known hardcore astrology-haters who love this page.

Online Services

Echo

Type: WWW

Address: http://www.echonyc.com/

Summary: Echo, an online service in New York structured somewhat like the WELL, has often been compared to a salon where artists and media professionals gather for stimulating conversation. This is not far from the truth. Echo has its own unique style and culture, "very New York" according to some users and certainly very different from most Internet forums. The Web site gives you a small taste of this uniqueness.

The WELL

Type: WWW

Address: http://www.well.com/

Summary: The WELL is a large West Coast online service that for many years has provided users with some of the most stimulating conferences in cyberspace. The Web page is like a snapshot, giving you a good picture of the unique WELL culture. This site is full of fascinating information and links, definitely worth a visit.

The WELL.

Politics, Government & Social Issues

ACLU

Type: WWW

Address: http://www.aclu.org/

Summary: Even if I completely disagreed with the beliefs and aims of the
American Civil Liberties Union, I would still highly recommend
this page. It is well organized, colorful, and thought provoking.
In addition, it contains many valuable links to other political and
human rights resources. The ACLU page is one indication that
the Web has come of age, that it is able to deal with serious
material as effectively as it presents the latest eye candy to Net
surfer dOOdz.

Amnesty International

Type: WWW

Address: http://www.amnesty.org

Summary: News, contact information, and software pertaining to the organization for prisoners of conscience everywhere.

Contact: Hilary Naylor
AIUSA PeaceNet Coordinator
hnaylor@igc.apc.org
Amnesty International USA
500 Sansome St. #615
San Francisco, CA 94111
415/291-9233

Anarchist Electronic Contact List

Type: WWW

Address: http://www.cwi.nl/cwi/people/Jack.Jansen/spunk/
Spunk_Resources.html

Summary: Spunk Press maintains this collection of anarchist and alternative resources. Newsgroups such as alt.society.anarchy, alt.society.revolution, and misc.activism.progressive. A Marx and Engels Gopher hole. Alternative literature and mailing lists.

Bibliography of Senate Hearings

Type: FTP

Address: ftp://ftp.ncsu.edu/pub/ncsu/senate/

Summary: Monthly bibliographies of Senate hearings.

The California State Senate

Type: WWW

Address: http://www.sen.ca.gov

Summary: As you would expect from the most computer literate state in the nation, California has done a great job making important government information available to the public. Here you can search for pending bills in a particular area of interest, view the actual content including proposed changes, get updates on the bill's status, and so on. If you leave an e-mail address you will be notified automatically when the bill's status changes. It would be nice if every state provided this service!

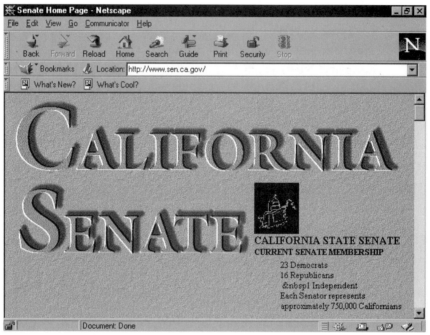

The California State Senate Web Site.

Censorship

Type: FTP

Address: ftp://ftp.spies.com/Library/Article/Rights/censored.bk

Summary: A list of books that have been banned, burned, or otherwise challenged in the last 15 years.

Center for Civic Networking

Type: FTP

Address: ftp://ftp.std.com

Path: Choose /associations/civicnet

The CIA

Type: WWW

Address: http://www.odci.gov

Summary: Yes, they're here too. The World Fact Book, included at this site, is an excellent reference for general information on specific countries.

Declassified DOE Documents

Type: WWW

Address: http://www.doe.gov

Summary: The Federal government recently declassified hundreds of Department of Energy documents, including those dealing with nuclear experiments and the possible exposure of American citizens. Not only has the DOE made these documents available to professional researchers, they've put them up on the Web with an online index. Now you can find out the *real* reason you have three arms.

DIANA: An International Human Rights Database

Type: WWW

Address: http://www.law.uc.edu:80/Diana/

Summary: This site is dedicated to "completing the pioneering work in human rights information of Diana Vincent-Davis." It's a searchable database of human rights and law-related resources. As of this writing, there were over 10,000 pages available, with the volume increasing daily.

The FBI

Type: WWW

Address: http://www.fbi.gov/

Summary: Now that J. Edgar Hoover's gone they might not be everywhere anymore, but they do have their own presence on the Web. This is a surprisingly interesting home page. Of course there's a long warning not to copy their opening logo.

The FBI.

Fedworld

   Type: WWW

   Address: http://www.fedworld.gov/

   Summary: Fedworld serves as a clearinghouse for information on federal
   agencies. It also contains links to dozens of government sponsored information servers. An important resource.

Government Documents

   Type: Gopher

   Address: gopher://wiretap.spies.com

   Path: Government Docs (US: World)

   Summary: Get full text files of government acts such as the Americans with
   Disabilities Act, the Brady bill, and the Fair Credit Reporting Act.
   This area also has world constitutions, as well as NATO and
   White House press releases.

The MoJo Wire: Mother Jones Interactive

Type: WWW

Address: http://www.mojones.com/mojo_interactive/
mojo_interactive.html

Summary: The Mother Jones Interactive page is organized into ten "campaign" areas such as Making Our Democracy Work, Waging Peace, Curbing Violence in America, Fostering Diversity and Community, Improving Our Nation's Education, and Keeping the Media Honest. You'll find articles from *Mother Jones Magazine*, resource guide listings, and "chat" rooms.

National Child Rights Alliance

Type: WWW

Address: http://linux.hartford.edu/~jerry/ncra.html

Summary: A collection of documents about the NCRA and issues pertaining to child abuse.

Contact: Jim Senter
JIMSENTER@delphi.com

Silent Witness

Type: WWW

Address: http://gn2.getnet.com:80/silent/

Summary: Wanted Posters go interactive! This site is not tremendously relevant unless you live in Phoenix, but it demonstrates an interesting new use of the Web. Police reports are presented with photographs, sketches, and lots of information. Viewers are encouraged to call in anonymous tips if they have any information about the particular crime or missing person. I suspect this idea will spread to other cities.

Silent Witness.

SLATE

      Type: WWW

      Address: http://www.slate.com/

      Summary: This is Microsoft's initial foray into the world of mainstream politically oriented journalism. A hair left of center, this paper-magazine-in-Web-clothing reads a lot like *Harper's* or the *Atlantic Monthly*. Yeah, the kind of stuff your dad called "a good read." If you like hearing what pundits have to say about the state of the world, curl up in front of your monitor and enjoy.

United Nations

      Type: Gopher

      Address: gopher://nywork1.undp.org:70

      Summary: Info about UN conferences, session highlights and press releases, UN System directories, UN Development Programme documents, links to other UN and related Gophers.

United States Department of Justice Home Page

Type: WWW

Address: http://www.usdoj.gov

Summary: Links to several Justice Department organizations concerning litigation, investigatory, and law enforcement offices. Also pages for various DOJ issues and links to other Federal government and criminal justice information sources.

U.S. Bureau of the Census

Type: WWW

Address: http://www.census.gov/

Summary: Census Bureau news releases, population information and projections, tips on genealogy, financial data for state and local governments and schools, and summarized demographic data.

The Census Bureau.

The U.S. Constitution

Type: WWW

Address: http://www.law.cornell.edu/constitution/
constitution.overview.html

Summary: Yep, just what it sounds like. See it while it lasts.

U.S. Department of Health and Human Services

Type: WWW

Address: http://www.os.dhhs.gov/

Summary: A starting point for accessing DHHS organizations. Cancer and
AIDS related information, NIH grants and contracts, molecular
biology databases, poverty guidelines, and links to other federal
government resources.

U.S. Government Today

Type: Gopher

Address: gopher://wiretap.spies.com

Path: Government Docs (US & World) / US Government Today

Summary: Current membership lists for the House and Senate, phone and
fax numbers for members of Congress.

Voice of America (VOA)

Type: Gopher

Address: gopher://gopher.voa.gov

Summary: Check out the International News and English Broadcasts radio
newswire reports. You'll get daily reports, features, and docu-
mentaries on worldwide news events.

Contact: Chris Kern
202/619-2020
ck@voa.gov

Welcome to the White House

Type: WWW

Address: http://www.whitehouse.gov

Summary: As of the writing of this book, this is still where Bill and Hillary live. Tour the White House, check out Al Gore's favorite political cartoons, download a picture of Socks, read the electronic citizens' handbook, get detailed info about Cabinet-level and independent agencies, daily press releases, briefings on economic and environmental policy, information on government funded child care and disaster assistance, and lots more.

Some Related Newsgroups

alt.activism	alt.society.conservatism
alt.censorship	alt.society.revolution
alt.politics.greens	bit.listserv.politics
alt.politics.libertarian	bit.org.peace-corps
alt.politics.media	talk.politics.soviet
alt.save.the.earth	talk.politics.theory

Privacy

PRIVACY Forum

Type: WWW

Address: http://www.vortex.com/privacy.htm

Summary: Discussions of privacy in the information age. This directory includes all issues of the Privacy Forum Digest, as well as lots of related reports and materials.

The home page gives complete instruction for subscribing to the PRIVACY Forum.

Type: FTP

Address: ftp://ftp.vortex.com/privacy

Type: Gopher

Address: gopher://cv.vortex.com

Path: *** PRIVACY Forum ***

Privacy Information

Type: WWW

Address: http://www.eff.org/

Summary: The latest information on personal privacy online from the Electronic Frontier Foundation.

The Electronic Frontier Foundation.

Reference

IoQtus

Type: WWW

Address: http://pubweb.ucdavis.edu/Documents/Quotations/ homepage.html

Summary: Jason Newquist at the University of California at Davis has put together a comprehensive quotations resource. It includes his own quotations list and pointers to a whole bunch of other quotations sources.

Contact: Jason Newquist
jmnewquist@ucdavis.edu

Online reference works

Type: WWW

Address: http://www.cs.cmu.edu:8001/Web/references.html

Summary: A great collection of links to dictionaries, geographical information, legal and governmental references, phone books, and other reference resources.

Religion & Spirituality

The Bhagavad Gita

Type: WWW

Address: http://www.cc.gatech.edu/gvu/people/Phd/Rakesh.Mullick/gita/gita.html

Summary: The Hindu scripture in the original Sanskrit. Each chapter is a separate PostScript document. An English translation and a summary are also available from this page.

Catholic Resources on the Net

Type: WWW

Address: http://www.cs.cmu.edu/Web/People/spok/catholic.html

Summary: Some of the sections: Liturgy and Worship, Scripture, Writings from the early Church, Vatican II documents (1962–1965), selected papal encyclicals and pronouncements, history and culture, and related resources.

Full text of several books such as *Confessions of St. Augustine*, *The Imitation of Christ*, and *The Practice of the Presence of God*.

Electric Mystics

Type: Gopher

Address: gopher://wiretap.spies.com

Path: Library/Articles/Religion

Summary: Complete bibliography of online religious studies resources. Electronic documents, conferences, serials, software, and archives.

Hindu Names

Type: FTP

Address: ftp://ftp.spies.com/Library/Article/Language/hindu.nam

Science

Alfred Wegener Institute for Polar and Marine Research

Type: WWW

Address: http://www.awi-bremerhaven.de/

Summary: The Alfred Wegener Institute has laboratories in Bremerhaven and Potsdam, bases in the Arctic and Antarctic, and research ships and aircraft. Lots of GIFs, maps, and charts of the polar region. Includes a detailed hydrographic atlas of the Southern Ocean. There's a database of polar and marine related docs on the Web, pointers to other WWW servers related to polar, marine, and global change research.

AMSAT: The Radio Amateur Satellite Corporation

Type: WWW

Address: http://www.qualcomm.com/amsat/AmsatHome.html

Summary: If you're one of those people who makes and launches satellites in your backyard, this is *the* site for you.

Avion Online

Type: WWW

Address: http://avion.db.erau.edu/avion/avionhome.html

Summary: The first online aviation/aerospace newspaper. The Space Technology section covers activity at Kennedy Space Center, including shuttle launches and landings. The Aeronautica section routinely covers activity in the aviation and aeronautics industry, including aviation trade news and special flying events.

Center for Coastal Studies

Type: WWW

Address: http://www-ccs.ucsd.edu/

Summary: The Center for Coastal Studies is a research unit of UC San Diego's Scripps Institution of Oceanography. You'll find all sorts of studies on subjects like global warming, long-term climate change, earthquake prediction, coastal protection, and sediment management.

Type: Gopher

Address: gopher://gopher-ccs.ucsd.edu

Comet Shoemaker-Levy 9

Type: WWW

Address: http://www.jpl.nasa.gov/sl9/

Summary: When Comet Shoemaker-Levy 9 collided with Jupiter in July 1994, it was the first time the collision of two major solar system bodies was observed and recorded. This page contains lots of background information and animations, and takes you to photo files from NASA and world-wide observatories. There's a whole section full of links to other Comet Shoemaker-Levy home pages (currently there are seven).

Lunar Institute of Technology

Type: WWW

Address: http://sunsite.unc.edu/lunar/index.html

Summary: The Lunar Institute of Technology was established in 2032, and its School of Starship Design is renowned throughout the Solar System. If you are one of the lucky few to attend this prestigious institution, you will participate in the design of a manned inter-stellar vehicle. Pick a specialty—Mission/Operations, Structure/Shielding, Payload/Sciences—and become part of the design team.

My description may be somewhat tongue-in-cheek, but you'll find some serious science here.

The Mercury Project

Type: WWW

Address: http://cwis.usc.edu/dept/raiders/

Summary: Ever since the first text-based adventure computer games, we have been the masters of virtual worlds, engaging in all kinds of exciting activities from the comfort of our desk chairs. But no matter how deeply we immersed ourselves in these alternate realities, a part of us always knew they weren't really real. What if you could type something on your keyboard and have an immediate effect on a robot made of wires and metal, not just electronic information? Well, the Mercury Project lets you do just that. In real-time you control the movements of a robot arm that's busy excavating an actual physical site as part of some academic research. Not exactly Star Wars, but it's a fascinating project that demonstrates the power of the Internet and makes you feel like you're driving a big electronic bulldozer.

The Myers-Briggs Test—Kiersey Temperament Sorter

Type: WWW

Address: http://sunsite.unc.edu/jembin/mb.pl

Summary: Take this short psychological test to determine what makes you tick or tock. For instance, I found out that I'm the same kind of guy as Socrates, Gerald Ford, and Henry Mancini.

The NASA Newsroom

Type: WWW

Address: http://www.gsfc.nasa.gov/hqpao/newsroom.html

Summary: All sorts of NASA press releases, press kits, status reports, fact sheets, and official statements.

NASA Online Information

Type: WWW

Address: http://mosaic.larc.nasa.gov/nasaonline/nasaonline.html

Summary: NASA's home page, huge and full of interesting information. It includes links to specialized FTP sites, Gopher sites, and much much more.

Numerical Aerodynamic Simulation: The NASA Supercomputer

Type: WWW

Address: http://www.nas.nasa.gov/

Summary: This is the ultimate computer geek page, full of information on the NAS large-scale supercomputing system used by NASA and other agencies. It is a rich and fascinating site.

Primate Info Net

Type: Gopher

Address: gopher://night.primate.wisc.edu:70/11/

Summary: This entire gopher is devoted to primate biology. You'll find stuff about animal welfare legislation and behavioral patterns. Lots of newsletters and discussions.

Smithsonian Institution's Natural History Gopher

Type: Gopher

Address: gopher://nmnhgoph.si.edu

Summary: This Gopher contains newsletters, projects, and lots of pointers to other natural history resources. If you're interested in botany, vertebrate zoology, biodiversity, biological conservation, global volcanism, or anything else involving natural history, check out this cool site.

Space Movie Archive

Type: WWW

Address: http://www.univ-rennes1.fr/ASTRO/anim-e.html

Summary: We're not talking science fiction here. We're talking solar eclipses, meteorology, and space exploration. (With some science fiction thrown into the mix for good measure.) Tons of animations and instructions for getting animation viewers if you don't already have one.

Type: FTP

Address: ftp://ftp.univ-rennes1.fr/pub/Images/ASTRO/anim

Space Movie Archive.

United States Geological Survey

    Type: WWW

  Address: http://info.er.usgs.gov/

  Summary: Geologic map of the United States and information about public issues, education, and environmental research.

Midcourse Space Experiment

    Type: WWW

  Address: http://msx.nrl.navy.mil

  Summary: A GUI system developed at the Backgrounds Data Center in Washington, D.C., to "bring visualization to its databases of multiple remote sensing platforms." Users can query, visualize, and analyze geophysical and celestial data and metadata.

The VISTA Midcourse Space Experiment.

Some Related Newsgroups

alt.sci.planetary	bionet.women-in-bio
bionet.genome.arabidopsis	sci.astro
bionet.genome.chromosome	sci.astro.hubble
bionet.molbio.ageing	sci.bio.ecolog
bionet.plants	sci.astro.planetarium
bionet.photosynthesis	sci.bio.tcchnology
bionet.population-bio	sci.engr.chem

Science Fiction

J. R. R. Tolkien Information Page

Type: WWW

Address: http://www.csclub.uwaterloo.ca/u/relipper/tolkien/
rootpage.html

Summary: This page, put together by Eric Lippert, is an amazingly complete Tolkien resource. In addition to FAQs, there are book lists, newsgroups, language resources, info about the Tolkien Society, a Middle-Earth map, Noldor and Great Houses family trees. There are several query tools.

Contact: Eric Lippert
relippert@descartes.uwaterloo.ca

The Klingon Language Institute

Type: WWW

Address: http://galaxy.neca.com/~soruk/tlhIngan/

Summary: In learning most foreign languages, there is no substitute for visiting the actual country. If you want to learn Klingon, however, there is no substitute for the Web pages maintained by the Klingon Language Institute. Even if you're not a *Star Trek* fan you'll get a kick out of this site, a labor of love for some very dedicated Klingon enthusiasts.

Speculative Fiction Clearing House

Type: WWW

Address: http://thule.mt.cs.cmu.edu:8001/sf-clearing-house/

Summary: Science fiction, fantasy and horror archives, authors, awards, conventions, zines, and newsletters. Also resources for SF writers.

Unofficial Xanth Page

Type: WWW

Address: http://www.best.com/~wooldri/xanth/

Summary: For fans of Piers Anthony's Xanth world novels. Some highlights: a cheat list for Companions of Xanth, a Qbasic program that allows you to generate Xanth-like talents, the Piers Anthony FAQ, a Xanth family tree, the Xanth calendar, and a color image of Piers and his dog.
Newsgroup: alt.fan.piers-anthony

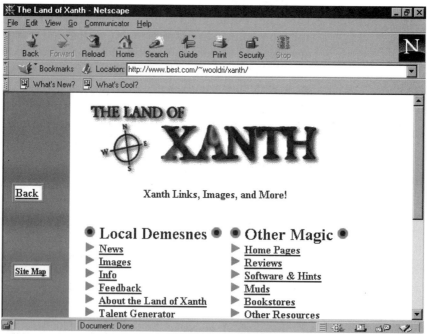

The Magic of Xanth.

Shopping

Aircraft Shopper Online

Type: WWW

Address: http://aso.solid.com/

Summary: Looking for a P51 Mustang fighter? Or is an old DC-3 more your style? Or do you want to sell your rusting 172 and upgrade to something a bit newer? Whether you want to buy or sell a plane, this is the best place on the Web to get started.

The Classified Advertising Page

Type: WWW

Address: http://www.imall.com/ads/ads.html

Summary: Whether you're looking for a computer, a job, or a date (or even if you're looking for all three), this is the site to visit. The listings, many of them links to Usenet newsgroup announcements, are well organized and current.

The Future Fantasy Bookstore

Type: WWW

Address: http://futfan.com/

Summary: Digital maintains this excellent online book catalog full of SF and fantasy titles. This is probably the best Web source for this kind of material.

Hall of Malls

Type: WWW

Address: http://nsns.com/MouseTracks/HallofMalls.html

Summary: I *hate* malls! Malls fall somewhere between rats and taxes on my list of the 10 Worst Things in the World. But I have to admit that electronic malls on the Web aren't *quite* so annoying—at least you're not bombarded with endlessly repeating Muzak versions of "Little Drummer Boy."

　　If there's something you can't get online, it's probably pretty hard to get any other way. Malls are springing up all over the Web. And because there are so many malls, the Web has generated a new kind of virtual hell: the meta-mall, somewhere you can go to choose which mall you want to visit. Here it is, a glimpse of the Jetsonesque future. Shop till your hard drive drops.

Offworld Metaplex

    Type: WWW

  Address: http://offworld.wwa.com/

 Summary: Oh no, a cyber *theme* mall! Let the mysterious Mr. Sin lead you through a "unique shopping experience." There's actually some pretty neat stuff here if you're in a consumerist mood.

The Virtual MeetMarket(sm)

    Type: WWW

  Address: http://vmm.ravenna.com/

 Summary: "Wild and crazy netsurfer dude seeks female UNIX tigress for some fun with a SUN." That sort of thing.

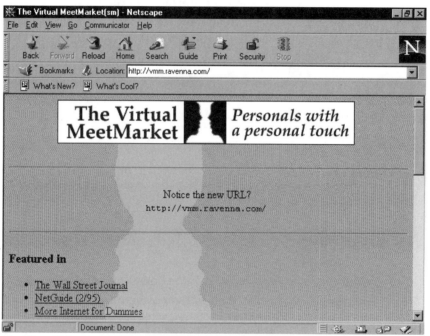

The Virtual MeetMarket(sm).

Showbiz

Elvis Lives!

Type: WWW

Address: http://128.194.15.32/~ahb2188/elvishom.html

Summary: Created by superfan Andrea Berman to "honor his cultural and musical legacy." Take a tour of Graceland, inspect Elvis's shopping list, and check out the results of an online seance conducted in January 1994.

Gossip

Type: Usenet

Address: alt.showbiz.gossip

Summary: Don't get bogged down with the facts—this is pure unadulterated gossip.

Sports

Aquanaut

Type: WWW

Address: http://www.aquanaut.com:8080/

Summary: Everything scuba—a database of diveable shipwrecks, reviews of dive gear and equipment, reviews of popular dive destinations, and underwater pictures.
Newsgroup: rec.scuba

Footbag WorldWide

Type: WWW

Address: http://www.cup.hp.com:80/~footbag/

Summary: Footbag is a new sport, similar to the game of Hacky Sack. Get tournament results, equipment information, images, and video clips of footbag action.
To join the mailing list and chat with other players at all levels, send e-mail to ba-footbag-request@cup.hp.com (include your first and last name somewhere in the message).

George Ferguson's Ultimate Page

Type: WWW

Address: http://www.cs.rochester.edu/u/ferguson/ultimate/

Summary: Ultimate Frisbee is a non-contact team sport. Get the official rules and tournament handbook here.

Hawaii's NHL Home Page

Type: WWW

Address: http://maxwell.uhh.hawaii.edu/hockey/hockey.html

Summary: Welcome to the world of hockey. From here, you can get to all of the NHL team home pages, the NHL Statserver, game schedules, and Stanley Cup info. Currently, there are plans to provide daily statistical updates on teams and players.

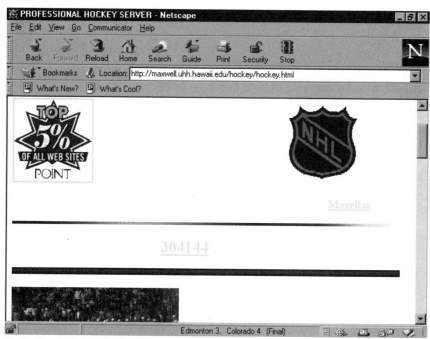

Professional Hockey Server (Author: Richard Crowe, The University of Hawaii at Hilo).

Korfball

Type: WWW

Address: http://www.earth.ox.ac.uk:80/~geoff/

Summary: Korfball is a mixed team sport that's kind of like basketball, but without backboards or dribbling. Get the latest information about this rapidly growing sport.

Mountain Biking

Type: WWW

Address: http://xenon.stanford.edu/~rsf/mtn-bike.html

Summary: Info about biking trails in various parts of the United States, as well as a link to a mountain bike page in the UK.

NBA.com

Type: WWW

Address: http://www.nba.com

Summary: My 11-year-old son lives here. This site solves the problem of what to do with your life when the game is over.

Orienteering and Rogaining Home Page

Type: WWW

Address: http://www2.aos.Princeton.EDU:80/rdslater/orienteering/

Summary: Get out your old scout compass and hit the road. Announcements about these two popular sports, federation and club information, and links to related pages.

The Running Page

Type: WWW

Address: http://sunsite.unc.edu/drears/running/running.html

Summary: Info about upcoming races, race results, places to run, running related products, and running publications.

Check out the Exercise Trails Network. Members of the American Running and Fitness Association have been contributing maps of their favorite running and exercise trails. You can get a free map by contributing one of your own, even if you're not a member. Otherwise, maps cost $1.

Volleyball World Wide Service

Type: WWW

Address: http://www.volleyball.org/

Summary: This page was created by Tom Jack, a software design engineer who coaches volleyball in his spare time, as a way of centralizing information about the sport. You'll find FAQs, info about the volleyball newsgroup, equipment, TV coverage, and coverage of Olympic and professional teams. Because Tom lives in Cupertino, California, there's lots of info about classes, clubs, tournaments and such in the San Jose/San Francisco area. Links to volleyball sites throughout the United States.

Contact: Tom Jack
taj@cup.hp.com
408/447-4239

Star Trek

Star Trek Files

Type: FTP

Address: ftp://ftp.spies.com/Library/Media/Trek

Summary: Tons of Trek-related files, including a Klingon vocabulary and a *Deep Space Nine* bibliography.

Klingon Language Institute

Type: WWW

Address: http://www.kli.org/

Summary: The Klingon Language Institute was founded in 1992 "to promote, foster, and develop the Klingon language, and to bring together Klingon language enthusiasts from around the world." You'll find sound files, information about their postal course and how to subscribe to the mailing list, and a fascinating background on the development of the language (it's one of the few artificial alien languages actually developed by a trained linguist).

Klingon spoken here.

Strange Usenet Newsgroups

alt.angst

alt.barney.dinosaur.die.die.die

alt.buddha.short.fat.guy

alt.flame.roommate

alt.food.sugar-cereals

alt.geek

alt.happy.birthday.to.me

alt.pantyhose

alt.religion.santaism

alt.spam

alt.tasteless

alt.wesley.crusher.die.die.die

talk.bizarre

Technology

Telecom Information Resources on the Internet

Type: WWW

Address: http://www.ipps.lsa.umich.edu/telecom

Summary: A plenitude of pointers to telecommunications Net resources. It's all here—voice, data, video, wired, wireless, cable TV, satellite. You can find info about aspects of telecom issues, from technical to public policy, from economic to social impacts.

Contact: Jeff MacKie-Mason
jmm@umich.edu

Theatre & Film

Drama

Type: Gopher

Address: gopher://english-server.hss.cmu.edu

Path: Drama

Summary: Play scripts, drama-related materials, reviews, Shakespeare info. Follow path to Shakespeare-Glossary for glossary of Shakespearean terms.

Girls on Film

Type: WWW

Address: http://www.itp.tsoa.nyu.edu/~gof/

Summary: In case the title these folks have given their site doesn't clue you in on what it's all about, maybe the subtitle will help: "Chicks. Flicks. Politicks." This freewheeling and unpretentious Webzine dissects recent movies from some interesting perspectives. A recent issue also included Worst of '96 awards for "Movies that Made Us Embarrassed to Be Alive."

Home Page of Theatre

Type: WWW

Address: http://www.cs.fsu.edu/projects/group4/theatre.html

Summary: Follow the links on this page to find myriad theatre resources. Some highlights: Ray Bradbury's Theatre Episode Guide, ruins of the Roman Theatre, The Fire Sign Theatre, and Computers in Theatre.

Screenwriters' and Playwrights' Home Page

Type: WWW

Address: http://www.teleport.com/~cdeemer/scrwriter.html

Summary: As of this writing, this page is still under construction, but there are already lots of resources for screenwriters and playwrights. There's a guide to screenplay structure, scripts, discussion groups, and tips from the pros.

Weird Movie List

Type: FTP

Address: ftp://ftp.spies.com/Library/Media/Film/weird.movi

Summary: Alphabetical list of weird movies, with descriptions. You can also get this list via Gopher. The address is wiretap.spies.com, then choose Wiretap Online Library / Mass Media / Film and Movies/ Weird Movie List.

Travel

City.Net

Type: WWW

Address: http://www.city.net

Summary: Good information on the largest and best-known cities around the world.

Clothing Optional

Type: FTP

Address: ftp://rtfm.mit.edu/pub/usenet/rec.answers/nude-faq/beaches

Summary: When you're tired of computing naked, why not head for the great outdoors? Lists of clothing-optional beaches, hot springs, parks, and resorts worldwide.

Downwind

Type: Telnet

Address: telnet://downwind.sprl.umich.edu:3000

Summary: Traveling? Why not check out the current weather and the forecast for your destination city.

The Global Network Navigator/Koblas Currency Converter

Type: WWW

Address: http://bin.gnn.com/cgi-bin/gnn/currency

Summary: This page is updated weekly. By default, the page shows the currency rates of over 50 countries relative to U.S. currency (e.g., one U.S. dollar is worth 1.3605 dollars in Australia). To get currency rates relative to another country, just click the country you want.

The Hawaiian Islands

Type: WWW

Address: http://www2.hawaii.edu/visitors/visit.hawaii.html

Summary: This one's maintained by the Hawaii Visitors Center. There's a link to each of the islands.

The Jerusalem Mosaic

Type: WWW

Address: http://www1.cc.huji.ac.il/jeru/

Summary: Listen to the song of Jerusalem, view Jerusalem from the sky, read about events in the history of Jerusalem.

Local Times Around the World

Type: Gopher

Address: gopher://austin.unimelb.edu.au

Path: General Information and Resources/Local Times Around the World

Summary: Connect to computers in cities around the world to get local time reports.

Mapquest

Type: WWW

Address: http://www.mapquest.com

Summary: This is one of the most useful sites on the Web. You tell Mapquest your origin and destination, and it plots your exact route, giving you unbelievably detailed driving instructions. For some cities, it can even get you to the exact address you're looking for! Don't leave home without checking out this site.

The Perry-Castañeda Map Collection

Type: WWW

Address: http://www.lib.utexas.edu/Libs/PCL/Map_collection/ Map_collection.html

Summary: This is a great collection of electronic maps from the Perry Castañeda Library at UT. It even includes National Park maps and a map of the South Pole. Needless to say, there are maps of Texas, too.

Subway Maps

Type: Gopher

Address: gopher://vishnu.jussieu.fr

Path: Indicateur des metros (don't worry, there's a file in English too)

Summary: Download color maps of the Paris and Lyon subways.

UT-LANIC

Type: Gopher

Address: gopher://lanic.utexas.edu

Summary: This is the University of Texas Latin American Network Information Center. Here you can access a wealth of information about Latin America, including catalogs, databases, FTP archives, other gopher sites, and so on.

Virtual Paris

Type: WWW

Address: http://www.paris.org/

Summary: Well, it's not quite the real thing, but it's a lot cheaper.

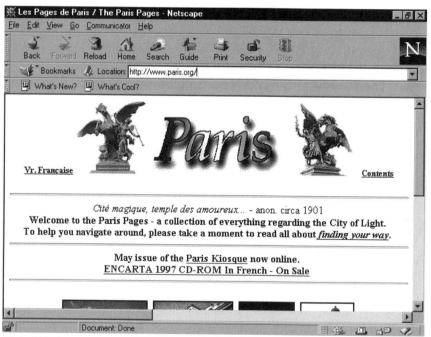

Virtual Paris.

Virtually Hawaii

Type: WWW

Address: http://www.satlab.hawaii.edu/space/hawaii/

Summary: This is a NASA site that includes lots of remote sensing satellite and aircraft images of Hawaii. It also provides real-time satellite data and links to several related pages. While it's not exactly the same as sunning on a beach in Maui, this is a great educational site.

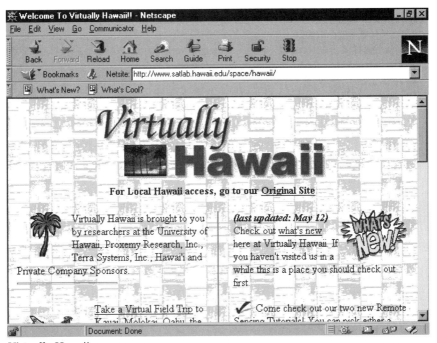

Virtually Hawaii.

Welcome to Eurogopher

Type: WWW

Address: http://www.sunet.se/eurogopher/eg.html

Summary: This is a great starting point for information about Europe.

A Related Newsgroup

rec.travel.marketplace

Utilities & Specialized Information

The AT&T 800-Number Directory

Type: WWW

Address: http://www.tollfree.att.net

Summary: This is a wonderful convenience that I use all the time. Simply type in the name of a company and you will be presented with the 800 number much more quickly than you could look it up in a phone book.

Electric Postcard

Type: WWW

Address: http://persona.www.media.mit.edu/Postcards/

Summary: This is a great idea, really exploiting the interactive possibilities of the Web. You choose from a large collection of "postcards," beautiful and interesting graphics files, and address one to a friend. Your friend can then log into this site and, based on a tracking number, pick up the postcard you "sent."

FedEx

Type: WWW

Address: http://www.fedex.com/

Summary: This site is about as sexy and inspiring as the U.S. Senate, but it lets you find out where your package is.

The IRS

Type: WWW

Address: http://www.irs.ustreas.gov/prod/

Summary And you thought you could get away from them on the Web! Actually this is a very useful site that provides forms, instructions, and answers to common questions. ("Do I really have to give you my money?" "Yes.")

The Jargon File

Type: WWW

Address: http://www.phil.uni-sb.de/fun/jargon/index.html

Summary: This is a huge index of jargon, especially tech-speak. After a few hours here you'll sound like you know what you're talking about.

The Mortgage Calculator

Type: WWW

Address: http://ibc.wustl.edu/mort.html

Summary: Back in the days when text-based DOS programs ruled the PC world like primitive insects, I had a utility for everything. In fact, I sometimes had several different programs for the same job. Then Windows came along, and disk space became as precious to me as Manhattan real estate. Thanks to behemoth programs like Word and Excel, not to mention Windows itself, there was no longer room for directories full of little one-job tools. Fortunately a wealth of simple utilities is available on the Net, and this flexible mortgage calculator is a good example. I find it quicker to click over to this URL via a bookmark than to load up a local copy of Excel!

NewsHound

Type: e-mail

Address: newshound-support@sjmercury.com
(send a message requesting information)

Summary: This is an electronic version of a clipping service. You tell them what you're interested in, and NewsHound keeps an eye out for articles that match your search criteria. It then sends you the information via e-mail. There is a monthly charge.

Stanford Netnews Filtering Service

Type: WWW

Address: http://woodstock.stanford.edu:2000

Summary: This is an interesting service for those who don't have access to a Usenet news server or who don't want to weed through the thousands of newsgroups looking for what they want. The Stanford Netnews Filtering Service lets you specify areas of interest; it then sends you Usenet postings, via e-mail, based on those criteria.

Taxing Times

Type: WWW

Address: http://www.scubed.com/tax/tax.html

Summary: The only things that are certain in life are death, hard disk crashes, and taxes. This site can help you with one of those.

Xerox PARC Map Viewer

Type: WWW

Address: http://pubweb.parc.xerox.com/map

Summary: Another great example of how hypermedia can be used effectively on the Web. You are presented with a map of the world. Click on an area and it zooms in. Click again and it zooms in some more. You can also search by keyword. This is a well-designed tool that's great for putting geography in perspective.

Weather

National Weather Service Forecasts

Type: Gopher

Address: gopher://wx.atmos.uiuc.edu

Summary: Weather reports by geographical region as well as by weather type.

Web Info

A Beginner's Guide to HTML

Type: WWW

Address: http://www.ncsa.uiuc.edu/General/Internet/WWW/ HTMLPrimer.html

Summary: Once I started cruising the Web, it wasn't long before I wanted to start putting up my own pages. The HTML markup language that's used to create Web documents is not at all difficult, especially with some of the specialized editing tools. And to help you get started, NCSA provides an excellent hypermedia tutorial. You'll be creating simple documents in a matter of hours.

Building a Corporate Web

Type: WWW

Address: http://www.webcom.com/~wordmark/sem_1.html#home

Summary: Wordmark Associates has put together this informative and well-thought-out hypermedia seminar for corporations wanting to establish a presence on the Web. I recommend that you read this information *before* designing your commercial Web pages.

Building a Corporate Web.

The PERL Page

Type: WWW

Address: http://www.cis.ufl.edu/perl

Summary: PERL stands for Practical Extraction and Report Language. It is a flexible and fairly easy-to-use programming language that's especially suited to manipulating text. It is often used for developing CGI gateways on Web servers. This site will get you started on creating your own PERL scripts.

Broadcast

Type: WWW

Address: http://www2.infi.net:80/talker/

Summary: For those of you who can't get enough of yaking online, here's another interesting Web-based chat program. Looks interesting.

Virtual "Separator Bar" Collection

Type: WWW

Address: http://inls.ucsd.edu/y/OhBoy/bars.html

Summary: No, this is not a hotlist of virtual drinking establishments. The bars we are talking about here are the horizontal rules that most HTML authors use to break up sections of their document. Instead of letting Web browsers display their default plain-vanilla line when you specify an <hr> tag in your page, why not ship a colorful, interesting, beautiful graphic bar instead? This site includes more horizontal rules than you'll ever use.

WebChat

Type: WWW

Address: http://www.irsociety.com/webchat.html

Summary: WebChat is an exciting new Web-based facility for live conferencing or chatting. You can see a .GIF picture of the person you are chatting with, and you can place .GIFs and Web hotlinks in your messages.

WebChat.

Web Page Design and Layout

Type: WWW

Address: http://www.yahoo.com/Computers/World_Wide_Web/
Page_Design_and_Layout

Summary: This is a great place to start if you're looking for ideas and advice
on designing your own HTML home page.

Wow, The Web is BIG

Type: WWW

Address: http://www.mit.edu:8001/afs/sipb/user/mkgray/ht/wow-its-
big.html

Summary: This site offers frequently updated statistics on the size of the
World Wide Web, based mainly on the flow of traffic. You'll be
surprised at how popular the Web really is!

The WWW FAQ

     Type: WWW

  Address: http://www.boutell.com/faq/

 Summary: This list of frequently asked questions is one of the best places to start learning about the Web. It is thorough, well-organized, and updated frequently. A good place to visit if you feel lost or confused or if you simply want a fuller understanding of how the Web works.

Windows 95 Pages

Dylan Greene's Original Windows 95 Home Page

     Type: WWW

  Address: http://www.dylan95.com/

 Summary: "In addition to my other sources of timely information, I have been selected to become a ClubWin WebMaster. This means that I will be receiving periodic updates on new content and information from the Windows 95 team. For you, that means you will always be able to find the most recent information here, at Dylan's Windows 95 Pages."

Win 95-L Windows 95 FAQ

     Type: WWW

  Address: http://www.primenet.com/~markd/win95faq.html

 Summary: These questions and answers were compiled from responses to newsgroup posts and from the two mailing lists forums: WIN95-L, a general discussion group and WIN95-NET, a networking issues group.

Windows 95 InterNetworking Headquarters

     Type: WWW

  Address: http://www.windows95.com/

 Summary: This site was featured in *PC World*'s September 95 issue as "The Site To See" about Windows 95.

The Windows 95 QAID

Type: WWW

Address: http://www.kingsoft.com/qaid/

Summary: QAID is an acronym for Question Answer Information Database, and it more than fulfills its promise. According to Mike Dixon, who compiled these pages, "The QAID Pages contain tons of useful information, both documented and undocumented—comments from users of the QAID—Tips & Tricks—News and rumors—Dozens and Dozens of Questions and Answers and Information and instructions listed by topic."

Windows 95 Tips

Type: WWW

Address: http://www.process.com/Win95/win95tip.htm

Summary: A terrific and growing set of tips to help you work with and customize Windows 95.

Glossary

access privileges   A user's rights on a host. Typically users are allowed to create or edit files only in their home directories and its subdirectories, though they can run programs from public directories.

account   An agreement with an organization allowing you to take advantage of various services. For instance, an account on an e-mail server lets you log on to send and receive e-mail. Accounts are often protected by *authentication*, requiring that you type in a user name and password.

activate   To make a window the active one by clicking on it.

active window   The window with the highlighted title bar, where the user is currently interacting with a program.

ACU   *Automatic Call Unit*. Fancy word for a modem.

address area   The area in Messenger's New Message window where you can edit your list of e-mail addresses.

Address Book   A Communicator feature that lets you store individual e-mail addresses and address lists.

Address Book Card   An electronic record of an individual's name, e-mail address, etc., often used in e-mail. Also known as a vCard.

address list   A list of e-mail addresses. The address list lets you send e-mail to many individuals at once without entering each address.

addressing   The assignment of unique names or numbers to every node on a network so that information doesn't get misdelivered.

agents   Search tool that automatically seeks out online information based on your queries. Also called intelligent agents, knowbots, and droids.

algorithm   The step-by-step process a software program uses to produce its results.

alias   An alternate name used in place of a "real" one. Rather than using your real name to log in to a system, you probably use a shorter alias. Commands can also have aliases. For instance, you can create command files on a UNIX system so that instead of typing **ls -al** to see all the files in your directory, you could just type **dir**.

American Standard Code for Information Interchange   *See* **ASCII**.

anchor   In HTML, the target of a link, usually in the same document. It is sometimes also used to mean any link.

application protocol   A **protocol** that "sits on top of" the underlying transport layer of a communications system. For example, **FTP** and **Telnet** are application protocols that format data in particular ways and use the services of the lower-level **TCP/IP** transport layer.

Archie   A network service used for locating files available at **FTP** sites that accept anonymous logins.

ARP   *Address Resolution Protocol.* Protocol used on a network for mapping Ethernet addresses to IP addresses.

ARPAnet   A wide area network developed in the 1960s by the Advanced Research Projects Agency of the U.S. Department of Defense. It links government and academic networks around the world.

ASCII   *American Standard Code for Information Interchange.* This standard assigns a binary value to common text and control characters. ASCII is used for manipulating text in a program and for transmitting text to other devices or systems.

ASCII file   A human-readable file made up only of letters, numbers, and symbols. An ASCII file contains no formatting except tabs, linefeeds, and carriage returns. Also known as a *text file.*

assigned numbers   The usual port numbers for well-known Internet services such as **Telnet**, **FTP**, and so on. For instance, hosts usually wait for Telnet connections on TCP port 23, for World Wide Web connections on port 80, and for Usenet news connections on port 119. These assigned port numbers are how the host knows what kind of connection is being requested.

asynchronous transmission   The transmission of data without special timing information. Each character you transmit is made up of several bits of information. In asynchronous communications, the characters are "packaged," usually by special start and stop bits, so that the receiving hardware or software knows when it has received an entire character. This way, the interval *between* characters doesn't have to be fixed, and information can arrive at any time. *See also* **synchronous transmission**.

Attachment   A text or binary file included with an e-mail message.

attachment encoding   The method used to encode an attached binary file so that it can be delivered to the recipient via any intermediary systems without being corrupted.

attachments list   The list of attached files that will be sent along with an e-mail message sent.

attribute (text)   The display characteristics of text. Text attributes include bold, italic, underlined, and so on. In **World Wide Web** documents, text may be tagged with a wide variety of attributes using **HTML**.

AU sound   Audio format developed by Sun and used for sound files on the Web. Netscape browsers play AU files using the helper program NAPLAYER.

authentication   The process of identifying a user to determine if he or she should have access to a particular computer system. Name and password prompts are a form of authentication.

authoring software   Any software that lets you create HTML or other multimedia documents.

bandwidth   The range of frequencies that can be transmitted over a network, limited by the hardware. Higher bandwidth allows more information on the network at one time.

baud rate   The number of signal changes per second as data is transmitted from one device to another. For instance, 110 transitions per second from a high frequency to a low frequency on a phone line would be 110 baud. Each signal change may signify one bit of data (for instance, high frequency to low could signify 1, low to high could signify 0); if a signal changes in multiple ways (frequency, amplitude, etc.), it may signify multiple bits of data. In the first case, baud rate would equal **bits per second**; in the second case, bits per second would be higher than the baud rate. The difference between baud rate and bits per second is a common icebreaker at nerd parties.

BBS   *See* **bulletin board system**.

BCC Short for *blind carbon copy*. A copy of an e-mail message that does not include information about who the other recipients are.

binary Numbers composed of combinations of two different digits, specifically 1 and 0. In the context of this book, binary data means information that may contain the full range of combinations of binary digits in a **byte**, as opposed to information that contains only the limited range of information that is displayable as text. Bytes of **ASCII** text contain only seven significant **data bits**, as in 1011001, while programs, graphics, spreadsheet files, and so on, contain eight significant data bits per byte, as in 10011011.

binary file Any file, such as an executable or graphic, that cannot be read as text, usually containing characters that have eight rather than seven significant data bits and are therefore beyond the range of **ASCII**. In some cases binary files need to be encoded as seven-bit files in order to be transmitted across certain systems (*see* **attachment encoding**).

BIND *Berkeley Internet Name Domain* server. This is the DNS server on BSD and related UNIX systems. *See also* **DNS**.

BinHex A file format, used mainly in the Macintosh world, for storing and transmitting binary data as **ASCII** text. This format is useful for transferring 8-bit data over 7-bit networks or data paths, or for including binary files as part of mail messages. Among UNIX and PC users, **UUENCODING** is more common.

bit A *binary digit*, the smallest piece of information that a computer can hold. A bit is always one of two values, written as 1 or 0 and corresponding to the on/off state of a digital switch or the high/low state of electrical impulses. Combinations of bits are used to represent more complex information, such as **ASCII** text or commands to the computer.

bitmap A representation of an image as an array of bits.

bit rate The rate at which bits are transmitted, usually expressed as a certain number of **bits per second**, or bps. *See also* **baud rate**.

bits per second *See* **bit rate**.

bookmarks In Netscape browsers, a means of permanently storing the **URL**s for sites you want to revisit.

bridge (1) A device or a combination of hardware and software for connecting networks together. (2) Something that goes over troubled water. *See also* **internet**.

browser A software program, such as Netscape Navigator 4, that is designed for accessing documents on the World Wide Web, or HTML documents on an intranet.

bulk cipher An **encryption** method used to encrypt large quantities of information.

bulletin board system (BBS) An electronic version of the old cork bulletin board—a place to leave and collect messages and files. A modern BBS is really like a whole collection of bulletin boards, with different sections covering different areas of interest. Users can generally exchange public as well as private messages, and many BBSes include extensive areas for distributing shareware or public domain software.

byte A combination of **bits** used to represent a single character. In the world of personal computers, a byte is eight bits long.

cable A bundle of wires or fiber strands wrapped with insulation and used to connect devices.

cache   An area of memory or a file used to store frequently accessed instructions or data. A memory cache is used to reduce hard disk access time. Memory and file caches are also used by Web browsers and other online programs to store images or data that rarely change; thus, a large home page does not have to be re-sent each time a connection is established.

carrier   A steady background signal on a communication channel used to indicate that the system is ready for the transmission of data. The carrier is then modified to represent the data transmitted.

CC   Short for *carbon copy*. A copy of a message sent to a secondary or additional recipients.

category   In the context of Netsape Collabra discussion groups, a subdirectory used to organize similar groups.

CCITT   *Consultative Committee on International Telegraphy and Telephony.* This is an international standards-setting body that makes recommendations for international communications technologies.

certificate   *See* **digital certificate**.

Certifying Authorities   Organizations that distribute **digital certificates**.

CGI   *Common Gateway Interface*. A standardized technique that lets Web clients pass information to Web servers, and then on to other programs that process the information. When a Web site accepts the information you enter into a form, it is using CGI.

channels   Collections of information, usually including multimedia files, that are downloaded and then stored locally on your system. Subscribed-to channels may be updated on a regular basis so that they contain the latest information available from the provider. In Communicator, the **Netcaster** component is used to subscribe to, view, and configure channels.

Channel Finder   A Netcaster feature that lets you preview selected **channels,** which you may then subscribe to.

character entities   In HTML, special symbols that stand for other characters. Character entities begin with an ampersand (&) and end with a semicolon (;). For example, *>* in an HTML document would appear on your screen as > (greater than).

character set encoding   The encoding methods that enable software to properly interpret characters and symbols from a variety of languages. To view Web pages that use the standard English alphabet, for instance, you choose the Latin1 character set.

check box   A Windows 95 and Windows NT control that lets you choose a particular option by clicking. Once you click, an X or checkmark appears in the check box; click again and it is cleared.

CIX   *Commercial Internet Exchange*. CIX is an agreement among Internet service providers allowing them to make the Internet available to commercial traffic.

Clear To Send   A signal from a **DCE** to a **DTE** indicating that circuits are ready for data transmission. *See also* **DCE; DTE.**

clickable image   In a Web page, an image you can click in order to access a different URL. *See also* **image map**.

client   A computer or a software program that can access particular services on a network. The machine or the software that provides the service for a client is called a **server**. For instance, an e-mail client would request received mail from an e-mail server.

client pull   A method specific to Netscape products whereby a Web client can request the Web server to send it a particular set of data. *See also* **server push**.

client/server architecture   A system in which a **client** program establishes a connection with a **server** and then requests information or services. *See also* **client; server**.

client write key   The software key used to encrypt data written or transmitted by the client in a **client/server** system.

Clipboard or clipboard   An area of memory where objects (data) are placed when a user carries out a Cut or Copy command or chooses a menu option. This data can then be passed to another program.

Collabra   The component of Netscape Communicator that lets you view and respond to intranet discussion groups as well as **Usenet** newsgroups.

column heading   A Windows 95 and Windows NT control that displays data in a multicolumn list.

combo box   A standard Windows 95 and Windows NT control that combines a text box and a list box.

command button   A control used to initiate a command; also known as a push button.

command prompt   A set of characters or a symbol that indicates where you type in commands. The DOS C:\ prompt is an example of a command prompt.

Communicator   The Netscape software suite that currently includes **Navigator** for Web browsing, **Messenger** for e-mail, **Collabra** for reading or participating in discussion groups, **Composer** for creating HTML documents, and **Conference** for interacting in real time with other individuals on the Net or on an intranet.

Component bar   The Communicator control that lets you access the various components of the program (**Navigator**, **Collabra**, etc.) by clicking on icons. The Component Bar may be anchored to the status line of the various Netscape programs, or it may "float" on your desktop.

Composer   The Communicator component that lets you create and edit HTML files.

Conference   The Communicator component that lets you interact in real time with other individuals across the Net or an intranet. Features include full-duplex voice communication, chat, file transfer, a special graphical whiteboard for collaborative design and planning, and collaborative Web browsing.

computer name   On Microsoft networks, a unique name of up to 15 characters that identifies a particular computer on the network.

configuration registry   In Windows 95 and Windows NT, a database that stores information about a computer's configuration as well as the configuration of various software. The registry may be edited by using the program *regedit* in Windows 95 or *regedt32* in Windows NT.

connect time   The amount of time you're connected to a host or to a service provider.

connection   A link between two computers for the purpose of transferring or sharing information.

container   Any screen object that holds other objects; for instance, a folder.

content-type   The MIME name for particular types of files to be transferred by e-mail or the Web. For instance, the content-type for a GIF file is **image/gif**. *See also* **MIME**.

control   Any window object that lets you interact with a program by selecting an action, inputting data, and so on.

Control menu   The menu that pops up when you click the icon at the top left of a program's main window. It contains commands such as Move, Size, Maximize, Minimize, and Close.

cookie   A piece of system or configuration information transmitted between a Web server and the browser software and then often stored on the client machine. Cookies enable a Web page to adjust its display or other configuration options for particular clients that connect.

crawler   *See* **spider**.

cross-platform   Describes software that can be used on more than one operating system, such as Windows, Macintosh, and UNIX.

CSLIP   A common variant of the SLIP protocol that uses compressed IP headers. *See also* **SLIP**.

cyberspace   A slightly dated term referring to the entire world of online information and services. It was originally coined by the writer William Gibson.

daemon   UNIX-speak for a program that's always running on a server machine, waiting for requests for a particular service. For instance, an FTP server daemon sits and waits for an FTP client to connect and request files.

data   Information used or processed by a software program.

data bits   Bits that carry information as opposed to control information. For example, the bits in the middle of a **byte** might signify a text character and are, therefore, data bits, while the bits at the beginning and end of the byte merely mark the beginning and end of the data.

Data Carrier Detect (DCD or CD)   A signal from a **DCE**, such as a modem, to a **DTE**, such as a PC, indicating that a communication channel has been established with a remote device. *See also* **DCE**; **DTE**.

data-file object   An object representing a data file (spreadsheet, document, image, sound clip, etc.) in the file system.

Data Terminal Ready (DTR)   A signal from a DTE to a DCE indicating that it's ready to receive and transmit data. Usually, a modem keeps DTR high as long as it's turned on. *See also* **DCE**; **DTE**.

DCE   *Data Communication Equipment*. A device used by a **DTE** to transmit and receive information. Your modem is a DCE.

DDE   *See* **dynamic data exchange**.

decode   To translate electronic information back into its original form. Unlike decrypting, decoding does not need any special key. *See* **encoding**.

decrypt   To translate electronic information back to its original form through the use of a special electronic key that insures privacy or security. *See* **encryption**.

default   In software, the "out of the box" value of a configuration option. The software will use this value unless the user explicitly indicates a different one in a setup program, property sheet, or .INI file.

desktop   The visual work area that fills your screen and holds the objects you interact with, such as icons, the task bar, and so on. The desktop is a container (or folder) that can also be used as a convenient place to access files.

destination directory   The directory to which you copy, move, or download a file or files.

device driver   A program used by the system to access devices such as video cards, printers, and mice.

dialog box   In Windows 95 and Windows NT, a box that appears on your screen requesting your input; it engages you in a *dialogue* with the software. It may contain edit fields, check boxes, list boxes, radio buttons, and so on, and it stays on your screen until you click its Cancel or OK button.

dial-up networking   A facility built into Windows 95 that allows users to link to a network or to the Internet using phone lines. Similar to **Remote Access Dialer** in Windows NT.

digital certificate   A unique electronic key that identifies you and authorizes you to access secure Web sites. Also, a digital certificate may be included with an e-mail message, identifying the originator of the message and allowing it to be encrypted. *See also* **personal certificate, site certificate**.

digital signature   The inclusion of a digital certificate (for instance with an e-mail message) that matches a key you hold, allowing decryption.

dimmed   A button, menu item, or other control is dimmed or *grayed* (displayed in light gray instead of black) to indicate it represents an option or command that is not currently available.

direct connection   A permanent connection between a computer and the Internet as opposed to a temporary dial-up or **SLIP/PPP** connection.

directory   1. A structure on a disk that contains files or other subdirectories. Also sometimes referred to as a folder. 2. A collection of names, addresses, and other contact information stored as part of a directory service, useful for looking up individuals for e-mail.

directory service   An Internet or intranet service used for looking up e-mail addresses or other contact information.

directory tree   A hierarchical display of a disk's directories and subdirectories.

DLS server   *Dynamic Lookup Service* server. A server that provides the e-mail addresses of and other information for people who want to be included in the list—in other words, a server that acts as a sort of phonebook.

DNS   *Domain Name Service*, an Internet service that returns the appropriate **IP address** when queried with a **domain-name address**.

dock   To configure a toolbar so that it no longer floats, but lines up with the edge of a window or pane.

document (World Wide Web)   On the **World Wide Web**, a file or set of related files that can be transferred from a **Web server** to a Web **client**. The document may contain text, graphics, sound, or hyperlinks to other documents.

document encoding   *See* **encoding**.

document window   A window that lets you view the contents of a document.

domain   A collection of associated computers on the Internet, given a specific domain name that is used as part of the Internet address. For Windows NT Server, a domain is also a uniquely named collection of computers that share a domain database and security policy.

domain-name address   The "plain English" address of a computer on the Internet, as opposed to its numeric **IP address**. For instance, www.echonyc.com is a domain-name address.

download   To get a file or files from a remote computer; the opposite of **upload**.

draft   A message that you're still working on, that is stored in a special holding area (the drafts folder in Netscape Messenger, for instance) until you're ready to send it.

drag   To move a mouse while pressing and holding one of its buttons. Dragging is used to move or resize objects on the screen. (Also known as "drag-and-drop.")

droids   *See* **agents**.

drop-down combo box   A Windows 95 and Windows NT control that combines a text box with a drop-down list box.

drop-down list box   A Windows 95 and Windows NT control that displays a current text selection, but that can be opened to display the entire list of choices.

drop-down menu   A menu that is displayed from a menu bar.

DSU   *Digital Services Unit.* The piece of equipment that enables transmission of data in synchronous digital connections to the Net.

DTE   *Data Terminal Equipment.* A device that serves as the originating point or the final destination of information. Typically, a computer or a terminal is a DTE.

dynamic data exchange (DDE)   The exchange of data between programs such that any change in the data in one program affects that same data in the other program. For instance, if spreadsheet data are shared via DDE by Word and Excel, any changes made to the data in Excel will also appear in the Word document.

edit field   *See* **text box**.

electronic mail   A network service for transmitting messages from one computer to another. Also called *e-mail*.

ellipsis   The "..." added to a menu item or button label to show that the command needs more information to be completed. When you choose a command with an ellipsis, a dialog box appears so you can enter additional information.

encoding   The technique used for storing or expressing data. For instance, text may be stored via ASCII encoding or some form of encoding that uses compression (such as ZIP). In Web browsers, document encoding refers to the translation of incoming characters into display fonts. For instance, you may set Netscape browsers to Japanese encoding so that information in a Japanese HTML document will be correctly displayed.

encryption   A method of **encoding** information for secure transmission. The data can be read in its original form only after it has been decoded. *See also* **public-key encryption**.

environment variable   A symbolic name associated with a string of characters used by an operating system or programs for its own informational purposes. For instance, the environment variable GIF_DIRECTORY could be set to C:\GIF so that a graphics program knows where to look for GIF files. Typically, you set an environment variable by using the Set command at a command prompt or in a batch file. In Windows NT, you can use the System option in Control Panel to define environment variables.

Ethernet   A hardware system and a protocol that is commonly used to connect computers on a LAN.

external viewer   A separate program used by a **World Wide Web** browser to display graphics or to play sound or video files. After downloading a particular media file, the Web browser launches the external viewer program appropriate to the type of file. In order for this to work, you must configure your Web browser with the names of the external viewer programs you have on your system. Another term for external viewer is **helper application**.

extension   The period and characters at the end of a file or directory name, often used to indicate the type of file or directory. For instance, INDEX.HTML includes the .HTML extension to indicate it is an HTML document.

extranet   A TCP/IP network that links businesses to customers, suppliers, etc.; part of an enterprise intranet that is made available to the outside world for marketing or other specific purposes.

e-zine   A zine, or small non-mass-market magazine in electronic format. Some e-zines are text files distributed via electronic mail or posted on a BBS; others are Web pages with extensive graphics and even sounds.

FAQ   Abbreviation for *frequently asked question*. FAQs are lists of frequently asked questions (and their answers) in a particular topic area. For instance, a Windows NT FAQ would help users understand the basics of using Windows NT by providing answers to common questions. Most mailing lists and network newsgroups regularly provide updated FAQs. It is important to read the FAQ for a particular newsgroup before beginning to post messages.

file   A named collection of **ASCII** or **binary** information stored on a disk or other storage device. Files include text, programs, databases, spreadsheets, graphics, and so on.

file server   A computer that provides storage space for files and applications that may be shared by network users.

file system   In an operating system such as Windows 95 or Windows NT, the structure used for storing, organizing, and naming files.

file transfer protocol   Any **protocol** for transferring files from one computer to another. A file transfer protocol usually includes provisions for making sure the data was transferred without errors and for resending any blocks of information that were corrupt.

filter   A facility for automatically organizing your received e-mail into separate folders. When your e-mail program retrieves messages that match criteria you've specified in a filter (for instance a particular name in the From header), it can automatically store those messages in a particular folder instead of your **inbox**. It can also delete the messages immediately.

finger   A UNIX program that lets you retrieve basic information about an Internet user or host. Finger is available via the Web at various sites.

firewall   Software and/or hardware that places an electronic barrier between an internal network and the Net, allowing only controlled access. This protects the network from access by the outside world and may also be used to monitor or limit the Internet activities of employees in an organization.

flag   A characteristic of a file that may restrict its use in particular ways. A file may be flagged read-only, for instance. Also, a special designation for an e-mail message. Flagged messages may be found quickly in a list of messages.

flame   A public message on any electronic forum, such as a **BBS** or online service, that personally attacks another user. Usually a flame is in response to an earlier message. If the user who has been flamed responds with another flame, or if other users jump into the fray, a "flame war" ensues. Flaming, though common in **Usenet** newsgroups, is generally considered an obnoxious waste of other users' time and of network bandwidth.

folder   A container that holds and organizes objects, typically files or other folders. On the desktop, a folder may represent a directory in the file system; other folders within it are equivalent to subdirectories.

font   A particular style for displayed or printed characters, including the shape, weight, slant, and so on.

font size   The size of a **font**; typically represented in units of measurement called *points*.

FQDN *Fully Qualified Domain Name.* The full domain name of a computer on the Internet, including both the host name and the domain name. *See also* **domain-name address**.

frame A portion of a Web browser window that may contain a different document from other frames within the same window.

frameset An HTML page that contains several **frames**.

FTP Abbreviation for *File Transfer Protocol.* A particular file transfer protocol that is common on the Internet. It is also used as a verb, as in, "FTP me that file, wouldya?"

full duplex A communications link in which both ends can transmit data simultaneously, as in a telephone conversation. In situations where you are working interactively online, full duplex communication lets a remote host echo back to you each character you type so that you can see what you're writing as you work. *See also* **half duplex**.

FYI *For Your Information.* A series of technical documents on various Internet-related topics, available at many public FTP sites. *See also* **RFC**.

gateway A device or the software that links networks that use different protocols. For instance, a Novell network might have an Internet gateway that "packages" information into the **TCP/IP** packets required for Internet communication. The term *gateway* is also used in a very specialized sense to mean a program on a **World Wide Web** host that accepts and processes information sent by a Web client. For instance, a document on a **Web server** might display a form in which you can type your name; the gateway program would then enter your name in a database.

GIF (Pronounced "jiff.") Abbreviation for *Graphic Interchange Format.* This is a format for compressed graphic files developed by CompuServe and Unisys.

Gopher A menu-based client/server system for exploring information resources on the Internet. A Gopher client is seamlessly built into Web browsers, so you don't need a separate Gopher client program.

GopherSpace All of the information presented by a **Gopher** server, in the form of directory and file menus.

grayed *See* **dimmed**.

half duplex A communications link in which both ends can transmit and receive data, but not at the same time. Half duplex communication is like two-way radio or CB, where only one person speaks at a time. In situations where you are working interactively online in half duplex, you will not see characters you type echoed to the screen unless you set your communications program to echo them locally. *See also* **full duplex**.

handle An interface element added to an object to enable the user to move, resize, or reshape it.

handshaking The initial negotiation and the exchange of control information between a **DCE** and a **DTE** or between two DTEs in a communications link. Handshaking is necessary to make sure both devices are ready to transfer data and can "understand" each other. *See also* **Data Carrier Detect; Data Terminal Ready; XOFF; XON**.

hardware handshake A protocol whereby a **DTE** tells the connected computer to start or stop sending data. Typically hardware handshaking is implemented by raising and lowering the voltage on the DTR (**Data Terminal Ready**) line in the cable that connects the **DTE** and **DCE**. *See also* **XOFF; XON**.

header Text within a Web page that indicates the main point of the document or of a section within it. Headers often use the specific HTML heading styles. *See also* **message header**.

helper applications   Programs that a Web browser such as Netscape Navigator 3.0 uses to perform tasks such as displaying particular types of graphics, playing sounds, or initiating Telnet sessions.

history list   In Netscape Navigator 3.0, the list of Web documents you've displayed during the current session.

home page   The **HTML** document you choose to display when you open a **Web browser** such as Netscape Navigator 3.0. It may be located on your own hard drive or on a remote **Web server**. Home page can also refer to the top-level document at a particular Web site.

host computer   A computer that a user can connect to in order to access information or run programs. A user may log in locally using a **terminal** or remotely using a computer and phone lines or the Internet.

host name   The name clients use to access your Web server or other Internet server. For instance, your Web server's host name might be www.acme.com.

hotlist   In a **Web browser**, a user-built list of frequently accessed **World Wide Web** sites. Also, an **HTML** document consisting of hotlinks to Web sites or other Internet resources.

HTML   Abbreviation for *Hypertext Markup Language*. A "markup language" for indicating attributes and links in a Web document. An HTML **tag** may tell a Web browser program how to display a piece of text or a graphic, or it may direct the browser to another file or document.

HTML message   An e-mail message formatted using **HTML** rather than **plain text**. Also sometimes referred to as a **rich text message**.

HTTP   *Hypertext Transfer Protocol*. The **protocol** that World Wide Web **clients** and **servers** use to communicate with each other.

HTTPS   A variant of HTTP that provides security for transferred documents.

hyperlink   *See* **link**.

hypermedia   **Hypertext** that also includes nontext information such as graphics, video, or sound.

hypertext   Text that is organized by means of links, or jumps, from one piece of information to another. The reader can move among related topics by clicking on tagged words or phrases.

IAB—*Internet Architecture Board*. The organization that decides on Internet standards.

icon   An image used to represent an object such as a file or program.

image map   A graphic in a Web document that lets you click on certain portions in order to activate particular **URL**s. It has an associated map file that identifies these hot spots. *See also* **clickable image**.

IMAP   *Internet Message Access Protocol*. A protocol that lets you access your e-mail messages on a remote server machine instead of retrieving them and viewing them on your own computer. The most common implementation of IMAP is IMAP4. It provides an alternative to **POP3** e-mail servers.

inactive window   A window with which you are not currently interacting. Its title bar is not highlighted, and it receives no keyboard or mouse input. *See also* **active window**.

inbox   In Netscape Messenger, the folder where new e-mail messages are stored by default after retrieval from a POP3 or IMAP server.

inline images   Graphic images contained within **World Wide Web** documents. An inline image displays automatically as part of a document when it is retrieved; a non-inline image must be retrieved by clicking on a **link**.

intelligent agents   *See* **agents**.

internet   A larger network made up of two or more connected LANs (**local area networks**) or WANs (**wide area networks**).

Internet   The huge worldwide Internet made up of cooperative networks and using **TCP/IP** protocols to offer a variety of services.

Internet access provider   A business or organization that provides Internet access to consumers, often via dial-up **SLIP** or **PPP** connections. Also known as an **ISP**, or Internet service provider.

Internet address   *See* **IP address**.

Internet presence provider—An Internet-connected business that provides equipment and services to customers without equipment or technical expertise.

Intranet   A network of connected computers that uses the same protocols and provides many of the same services as the **Internet,** but which cannot be accessed by the public. For instance, a corporation may have an intranet for its employees.

IP address   Also called *Internet address*. The unique address for each computer on the Internet. The IP address appears as a set of four numbers separated by periods.

ISDN   *Integrated Services Digital Network*. The telecommunications standard that supports digital transmission of voice, video, and data over phone lines.

ISOC   *Internet Society*. Organization that was formed to support a worldwide information network. The ISOC sponsors the **IAB**.

ISP   *Internet Service Provider*. Another term for an **Internet access provider**.

IPP   *See* **Internet Presence Provider**.

Java   An object-oriented programming language developed by Sun Microsystems. It allows developers to create applications that may be run from within Web browsers such as Netscape Navigator 3.0.

JavaScript   A set of commands that can be added to HTML files to add functionality to Web documents. JavaScript is useful for scrolling text, data validation in forms, etc.

JPEG   A format for compressed graphics files. JPEG graphics are commonly used as part of **World Wide Web** documents.

kbyte   *See* **kilobyte**.

kilobyte (K)   1024 (2^{10}) **bytes** of data. Thus, a 64K file consists of 65,536 bytes.

knowbot   A software program that can retrieve information from a variety of electronic sources when you give it a set of search parameters. Same as **agent**.

LAN   *See* **local area network**.

LDAP   *Lightweight Directory Access Protocol*. A protocol that lets individuals search directories on the Net or an intranet. *See also* **directory service**.

link   A special hidden **tag** in an HTML document on the Web. It includes the **URL** for another file or document, or for another anchor point within the same document. When you click a word, phrase, or graphic that's tagged as a link, Netscape Navigator 3.0 automatically retrieves the appropriate target.

list box   A control that displays a scrollable list of choices.

Live3D Netscape's **VRML** technology.

LiveConnect Netscape technology that allows Navigator plug-ins, Java applets, and JavaScript to communicate with each other.

local area network (LAN) A group of computers connected together by cable or wireless transceivers so that users can share resources such as database files, programs, printers, and so on. *See also* **wide area network**.

log file A file that is automatically generated by software, indicating events that occurred such as errors, attempts to access your server, etc.

log in To identify yourself to a remote system or network by typing in your login name and password.

login name The name you use for security verification when you call into a remote system.

login prompt The prompt (usually *login:* or *name:*) a remote host uses to tell you it's ready for you to type in your login name.

logon script A file containing simple commands that automate the process of logging on to a server, **SLIP** or **PPP** account, or other computer. In Windows NT, the files SWITCH.INF and MODEM.INF are logon scripts that automate the process of logging on to a remote machine using the **Remote Access Dialer**. In Windows 95, logon scripts generally have a .SCP extension and are associated with particular **Dial-Up Networking** connections using Microsoft's Dial-Up Scripting utility.

log off To tell a remote host system or a network, using the appropriate commands, that you are terminating interaction. In many cases, logging off will also break the communications link to the remote machine.

log on To tell a remote system or network, using the appropriate commands, that you are initiating a session.

mail headers The informational fields at the beginning of every e-mail message, indicating sender, recipient, time and date sent, etc. Mail headers may not be visible in an e-mail program, but they are used by the program to organize messages.

mail host An Internet or intranet server that sends e-mail for you and/or temporarily stores your incoming messages. A client program like Messenger sends e-mail via a mail host and retrieves new e-mail from a mail host.

mailing list A list of e-mail addresses. Messages sent to the list are actually sent to every member of the list individually. Mailing lists are useful for disseminating information to established groups of individuals, or to subscribers who want ongoing information in a particular area of interest.

mailto link A special kind of HTML **link** whose URL includes an e-mail address. When you click a mailto link, Communicator pops up a New Message window with the recipient's address already filled in. Mailto links are useful for soliciting response to a Web page.

maximize To expand a window to its maximum size. *See also* **minimize**.

maximize button The button used to maximize a window. In Windows 95 and Windows NT 4.0, it is the second button from the right in the title bar.

megabyte (MB) 1024 **kilobytes**, or 1,048,576 bytes.

menu bar A horizontal bar at the top of a window (between the title bar and the rest of the window) that contains menu choices. *See also* **drop-down menu**.

menu button   A command button that displays a menu.

menu item   A choice on a menu.

message box   A window that appears to inform you of something, for instance that a connection has been established or that an error has occurred.

message area   The part of the main Messenger window that displays the actual contents of the currently selected e-mail message.

message body   The main content portion of an e-mail message, distinguished from the **mail headers**.

Message Center   In Communicator, the window that displays a list of e-mail and discussion group folders.

message flag   *See* **flag**.

Message List window   In Communicator, the window that displays a list of received e-mail and discussion group messages.

message status   How a message has been handled so far by the e-mail software and an individual recipient. For instance, a message's status may be new, unread, read, replied to, or forwarded.

message thread   *See* **thread**.

Message window   In Netscape Messenger and Collabra, the window that displays the actual contents of an e-mail or discussion message.

Messenger   The Communicator component that lets you send, retrieve, and organize e-mail messages.

MIME   *Multipurpose Internet Mail Extensions*. MIME is a convention for identifying different types of **binary** information, such as images or sounds, and thereby indicating the appropriate programs for viewing or playing this information. MIME is used in attaching binary files to e-mail messages so that they can be displayed or played automatically when received.

minimize   To minimize the size of a window; in some cases, this means to hide the window. *See also* **maximize**.

minimize button   The button used to minimize a window.

modem   Short for *modulator/dem*odulator. A hardware device that connects your computer to other computers using analog telephone lines.

modem command   An instruction, typed from the keyboard or transmitted automatically by a software program, that tells a modem to perform some action. For instance, the command ATH0 tells a modem to hang up the line.

moderated discussion group   A discussion group that only includes messages that have been seen and approved by a discussion **moderator**.

moderator   An individual responsible for viewing and approving discussion group postings before they are made available to the group as a whole.

Mozilla   This word stands for "Mosaic meets Godzilla." It is the name for the early Netscape products and for the Netscape-specific extensions to the HTML language. It has also become the Netscape mascot. The word and the associated image appear frequently in Netscape products.

MPEG   *Moving Pictures Expert Group*. MPEG is a standard format for compressed video files, sometimes known as "desktop movies." MPEG files may be part of **World Wide Web** documents, but they require a special **helper application** for viewing.

MUDs and MOOs   Text-based multiuser interactive games, accessed using specialized software or via **Telnet**.

multiple selection list box   A special list box that's used for multiple independent selections.

multiuser system   An operating system, such as UNIX, that lets more than one user at a time access services.

My Computer   A Windows 95 and Windows NT 4.0 object (icon) that represents all of your local data storage.

Navigator   The Communicator component that lets you browse the Web or HTML documents on an intranet.

NCSA   *National Center for Supercomputing Applications.* NCSA is the department of the University of Illinois where the Web browser Mosaic was developed. Mosaic was the forerunner of all modern graphically based Web browsers.

Netcaster   The Communicator component that lets you display and configure **channels**.

netiquette   Proper behavior on the Net (derived from etiquette).

Netscape Security Advisor   A Communicator feature that helps you maintain and organize your digital keys and certificates, as well as showing you the security status of documents you access.

Netsite   The label for Navigator's Netsite/Location field when you accessing a Web site that uses one of Netscape's server programs.

network   A collection of interconnected computers. Each attached computer runs its own software processes, whereas in an unnetworked **multiuser system**, users run all processes on the central host computer and use terminals simply to interact. A network lets users share information as well as devices such as printers, disks, and modems.

network administrator   In an organization, the individual who is responsible for configuring and maintaining the network. This is the person to talk to if you have problems with a direct "hard-wired" connection to the Internet.

Network Neighborhood   A Windows 95 and Windows NT 4.0 folder that includes objects stored on a network file system.

New Message window   In Messenger, the window that lets you compose, edit, and send e-mail and Collabra discussion group messages.

newsgroup   A special forum that allows users to exchange messages (postings) in a particular area of interest. These messages are accessible by all members of the group. Some newsgroups, like the Usenet newsgroups, are accessible to the public; others, like those on Collabra servers, may be private.

news host   The computer that stores discussion group messages and makes them available to all memebers of the group.

NFS   *Network File System.* NFS is a set of protocols developed by Sun Microsystems for allowing computers running different operating systems to share files and disk storage.

NIC   *Network Information Center.* The organization responsible for supplying information about the Internet.

NNTP   *Network News Transport Protocol.* The protocol used by news hosts and client programs like Collabra to transfer discussion group messages over the Net or an intranet.

NNTP host   *See* **news host**.

NOC *Network Operations Center.* The organization in charge of the day-to-day operations of a network on the Internet.

node Any computer or other device on a network that has its own unique network address.

NTFS A **file system** that can be used under Windows NT. It supports a variety of advanced features including system recovery.

object An entity that you manipulate in some way to perform a task. (Is that vague enough?) Typical objects are **icons** or **folders** on the **desktop**.

offline Not currently connected to a remote computer or a network; not currently on the Internet or office intranet.

online Currently connected to a remote computer or network.

option button A control that allows a user to select one choice from a set of mutually exclusive choices (also known as a *radio button*). *Compare* **check box**.

outbox In Messenger and similar e-mail client programs, the folder that stores outgoing messages before they are actually delivered. For instance, when you work **offline** any messages you compose are stored in the outbox until you go **online**.

packet A block of information that has been "packaged" with address information, error-checking information, and so on, for transmission on a **network** or on the **Internet**.

parameter A variable that affects the results of a command. For instance, in the command *dir /p, /* p is a parameter.

parity A crude system of error-checking used in data communications. For most scenarios these days, your communications software should be set to "no parity."

parsed HTML HTML files that are read and manipulated by separate software on a server machine after the server software has answered a client request for the document. Using parsed HTML, for instance, a program could customize a Web document based on who requested it. Parsed HTML is also known as server-parsed HTML and SHTML. Often HTML files that will be parsed end with the extension .SHTML instead of .HTML.

Perl *Practical Extraction and Report Language.* A programming language first developed by Larry Wall for UNIX systems. Because of its power in pattern matching and in handling strings, it is often the language of choice for creating **CGI** programs.

personal certificate A digital **encryption** certificate for which only you hold the decryption key. If you "sign" an e-mail message with your personal certificate, the recipient can then encrypt messages he or she sends you. *See also* **digital certificate, site certificate**.

pixel The smallest unit of graphic information on a computer screen. Graphic images are usually measured in pixels, and a pair of pixel coordinates can indicate an exact point within an image.

plain text Text that doesn't contain any special formatting such as HTML tags.

plain-text message In Messenger, an e-mail message that contains HTML tags and that hasn't been encrypted or encoded.

plug-in Software programs that extends the capabilities of Netscape Navigator. For instance, a plug-in may let you view PostScript files right within the browser window.

PNG *Portable Network Graphics.* A standard for highly compressed graphics files that may include trillions of colors, multiple layers of transparency, and searchable text information.

POP *Point of Presence.* The local dial-up node an Internet access provider makes available for its customers.

POP3 *Post Office Protocol, version 3.* The protocol used by Netscape Navigator 3.0 and other e-mail programs to retrieve messages from your e-mail server. *See also* **SMTP, IMAP**.

pop-up menu A menu that appears right at the location of a selected object (sometimes called a *shortcut menu*). The menu contains items related to the selection.

pop-up window A window with no title bar that appears next to an object and provides information about that object.

port (1) A hardware connector on the back panel of a computer where you can plug in a serial, parallel, or network **cable**. (2) A unique number assigned to a particular Internet **service** on a host machine. For instance, most **MUDs** and **MOOs** require that you Telnet to a host using a specific port different from the standard Telnet port number. You can usually specify a port number as part of an Internet address, as in *lambda.parc.xerox.com 8888*.

POTS *Plain Old Telephone Service.* What it sounds like; the current analog phone system, as distinguished from ISDN and other digital technologies.

PPP *Point-to-Point Protocol.* This is a protocol that lets a computer link to the **Internet** by calling in to a service provider using a modem and a standard telephone line.

properties Characteristics of an object defining its state, appearance, or value. Often used to mean a program's settings.

property inspector A viewer that displays the properties of the current selection.

protocol A set of rules for interaction between software programs on a network. Protocols may include requirements for formatting data, for passing control information back and forth, and for error checking.

proxy A server that allows communication with the outside world (for instance the Internet) through a **firewall**. When a client behind a firewall requests a specific Internet service, the request actually goes to the proxy, which then relays it on.

public-key encryption An **encryption** method that requires two unique software keys (one public and one private) for decrypting the data, making it secure across public networks. Pretty Good Privacy (PGP) is a well-known public-key encryption system.

query string The word or phrase you pass to a Web search engine.

QuickTime A multimedia file format developed by Apple. It is often used for video clips or "movies."

quoted-printable A **MIME** type for binary data that has been specially encoded to seven-bit ASCII text so it can be transmitted across a variety of networks. The recipient's software must then decode it back to binary data.

radio button *See* **option button**.

random access memory (RAM) Computer memory that temporarily stores information; for instance, software code that you've loaded by launching a program or data that you're processing. Generally, the more of it, the better!

read-only memory (ROM) Computer memory containing data that cannot be changed by the user and that remains even when the computer is turned off. ROM is used for storing your computer's BIOS, for instance, which is the code that lets you boot up and that performs a variety of low-level functions.

refresh   In Netscape Web browsers such as Navigator 3.0, the command that reloads a document into the browser window from a disk or memory **cache**.

regedit   A program in Windows 95 for editing the **configuration registry**. In Windows NT this program is called regedt32.

registry   *See* **configuration registry**.

reload   In Netscape Web browsers such as Navigator 3.0, the command that reloads a document into the browser window from its original local or remote source.

remote   Any system that you can connect to by using only communications devices rather than just local wiring.

Remote Access Dialer   A Windows NT program for connecting via ordinary phone lines or **ISDN** to a remote computer, often used for **SLIP** or **PPP** connectivity.

remote computer   A computer you link to via telephone lines, satellite, or other communication links.

resolution   The density of an image, expressed in dots per inch.

restore button   The button that replaces the maximize button once a window has been maximized. It lets you return the window to the size it was before maximizing.

reverse lookup   The process of looking up the domain name of an Internet-connected computer when all that's known is the numeric IP address. For instance, you may have a numeric IP address assigned by a **SLIP** or **PPP** access provider, but no associated domain name. When you try to log in to certain security-conscious FTP sites, the host software looks up your domain name via DNS reverse lookup. If it can't find one, you are not allowed on the system. *See also* **domain-name address**.

RFC   *Request for Comments*. An RFC is a proposal or report electronically distributed via the Internet, usually for the purpose of elucidating or helping to define a new Internet technical standard.

rich text   Text that contains HTML or other special formatting. *See also* **plain text**.

rich-text message   A message that includes encoded, encrypted, or HTML-formatted content. *See also* **plain text message**.

robot   *See* **spider**.

root directory   The top-level **directory** on a disk such as your hard drive. For example, C:\ would be the root directory of your C: drive.

RS-232   The standard used by your serial port. RS-232 lines are the individual pins and wires that make up the hardware interface, such as the send data line, the receive data line, and the various hardware handshaking (or hardware flow control) lines.

RTF   *Rich Text Format*. A file format that can be read by many word processing programs across all platforms.

RTS/CTS   *Ready to Send/Clear to Send*. In an RS-232 serial port, the two lines that allow two devices to signal each other when they are ready to send or receive data. This process is known as **hardware handshaking** or hardware flow control. *See also* **RS-232**.

script   A software program that doesn't need to be compiled. It is run by another program "as is," in human-readable form. *See also* **logon script**.

scroll bar   The control that lets you move the image or text within a window either horizontally or vertically to view data that is not currently visible.

search engine   A program on the Net that lets users search for online information. Typical search engines include Infoseek and Alta Vista, both available from Netscape's Search page.

security key   A special file that is needed in order to access a secure document. *See also* **public key encryption**.

server   A computer or a program that provides a particular service on a network or on the Internet. Typical services include file access, printing, e-mail, **FTP**, and so on. The computers and software that access servers are called **clients**.

server push   A technique specific to Netscape products whereby a Web server can initiate the transmission of data to the Web **client**. Server push is often used for animation or sound. *See also* **client pull**.

server write key   The software key used to encrypt data written or transmitted by the server in a **client/server** system. *See also* **client write key**.

service   A specialized function or utility provided by a **server**.

service provider   An organization, usually commercial, that provides connections to the Internet.

session   A connection between two machines on a network or on the Internet.

SGML   *Standard Generalized Markup Language.* A high-level standard for the electronic publication of information. **HTML** is a subset of SGML.

shell account   An account with an access provider that lets you access a text-based system for performing routine Internet tasks. You connect to a shell account via Telnet or a dial-up terminal emulation program. Some Internet access providers let you put your own Web pages on their server using a shell account.

shortcut   A desktop icon that can be used as a quick way to launch a program or document. Another word for *hotlink* in a WWW document.

SHTML   *See* **parsed HTML**.

signature   A text file that contains any information that you want to attach regularly to your e-mail messages and network news posts. A signature is usually less than five lines long and contains contact information.

single selection list box   A list box that lets you choose only a single item from a list.

site certificate   A **digital certificate** that lets you send an encrypted message to all recipients at a particular site. *See* **digital certificate**, **personal certificate**.

slider   A control that displays a continuous range of values and lets you choose one.

SLIP   *Serial Line Internet Protocol.* Like **PPP**, this is a protocol that lets a computer link to the Internet by calling in to a service provider using a modem and a standard telephone line.

S-MIME   *Secure Multipurpose Internet Mail Extension.* A secure version of **MIME**, useful for insuring e-mail privacy.

SMTP   *Simple Mail Transfer Protocol.* The most common protocol for sending e-mail messages over the Internet. *See also* **POP3**.

snail mail   A form of messaging that utilizes carbon-based materials to create and address human-readable data, which is then transmitted over a complex network of streets and air routes by human entities known as "postal employees."

snews   Part of a domain address indicating a secure news (discussion group) server. For example, snews.whatever.com would be a secure news server, while messages on news.whatever.com would not be automatically encrypted.

sockets   A software mechanism that allows programs to communicate locally or remotely by setting up endpoints for sending and receiving data. The application programmer does not have to worry about the nuts-and-bolts details of how the data travels from one point to the other, as that is taken care of by the operating system or other resident software. The Windows Sockets API (**Winsock**) uses this concept.

SOCKS   A protocol that lets a host server on an internal network access the Web through a **firewall**.

spam   Unsolicited messages that are sent to many e-mail recipients or posted in several discussion groups. Spam is an aggressive electronic version of junk mail and is considered an egregious violation of **netiquette**.

spider   A program that wanders around the Web looking for new content. Links to new sites that it finds may then be added to large directory documents such as Yahoo. Spiders are also known as robots, wanderers, crawlers, and WebCrawlers.

spin box   A control that displays a limited range of values and lets you choose one.

SSL   *Secure Sockets Layer.* A version of the **HTTP** protocol that includes encryption. SSL allows for the secure transfer of sensitive information across the Net, as in financial transactions.

string   Geek-speak for a set of characters. Your name, for instance, is a string.

symbolic link   A name that does not refer to an actual object but points to another name. For instance, on an FTP site, a directory list might include the entry WINDOWS, even though there is no WINDOWS directory at this level. The WINDOWS entry could be a symbolic link to a directory buried much deeper in the file system, such as /pub/micro/pc/GUI/windows. Symbolic links provide convenient shortcuts to actual objects.

synchronous transmission   A method of transmitting data that uses a special timing signal to ensure a set time interval between any two characters. *See also* **asynchronous transmission**.

tag   A special code used in an **HTML** document to indicate how a piece of text or a graphic should be displayed by a Web browser; it may also establish a **link** to another document.

target   The reference the browser "jumps to" when a user clicks on a link. The word is usually used for references within the same document.

TCP/IP   *Transmission Control Protocol/Internet Protocol.* TCP/IP is a set of protocols that applications use for communicating across networks or over the Internet. These protocols specify how packets of data should be constructed, addressed, checked for errors, and so on.

Telnet   A program that lets you log in to a remote **host computer** and access its data and services as if you were using a text-based **terminal** attached locally.

terminal   A keyboard and display screen used to access a **host computer**.

terminal emulation   A software program that lets you use a personal computer to communicate with a **host computer**. It transmits special commands and interprets incoming data as if it were a terminal directly connected to the host.

text box   A control that lets you enter and edit text.

text file   *See* **ASCII file**.

text-only   Containing no visual information other than human-readable **ASCII** text. When you **Telnet** into a UNIX system, for instance, your user interface is text-only, as distinguished from the graphical user interface of systems like Windows.

thread   A software process or task. Operating systems like Windows 95 and Windows NT allow for many threads to occur simultaneously.

title bar   The horizontal bar at the top of a window that includes the window name. The title bar also acts as a handle that can be used to drag the window.

title bar icon   The small icon at the top-left corner of the title bar. You can use it to display the pop-up menu. Double-clicking this icon closes the program.

TN3270   Protocol and **terminal emulation** used to make a Telnet connection to IBM mainframe systems. Using TN3270, your computer behaves like a 3270 terminal rather than the VT100 usually used in standard Telnet connections.

toolbar   A control that provides a defined area for a set of other controls such as icon buttons, drop-down list boxes, and so on.

traffic   Data traveling across a network or across the Internet.

tree control   A control that lets you display a set of hierarchical objects in an expandable outline format.

upload   To send a file to a remote system; the opposite of **download**.

URL   *Uniform Resource Locator.* A URL is a specially formatted address that a Web browser uses to locate, retrieve, and display a document. The URL includes the Internet address of the data, where it is located on the Web server machine, and what kind of transport protocol is required to retrieve it. URLs are contained in the **hotlinks** within **HTML** documents; they may also be specified by the user of a Web browser "on the fly."

Usenet   A large collection of networked users who communicate using the UNIX-to-UNIX Copy Protocol (UUCP) rather than **TCP/IP**. Usenet is connected to the Internet by gateways, and many Internet users are familiar with its broad range of discussion forums known as newsgroups.

UUCP   *UNIX to UNIX copy.* An older set of network commands for sending and receiving data on dial-up networks.

Uuencoding   A standard for encoding binary data that allows it to be transmitted as 7-bit ASCII information; it is then *UUDECODED* into its original binary form.

VCard   *See* **Address Book Card**.

virtual server   A server that appears like a separate server to clients, but which actually runs on the same machine and uses the same server software as other servers. For instance, the Netscape FastTrack server lets you set up www.server1.com, www.server2.com, and www.server3.com all at once. Somebody logging onto www.server2.com would access different information from somebody logging onto www.server1.com.

VRML   *Virtual Reality Modeling Language.* VRML is a specialized language that allows for the creation of three-dimensional user interfaces that can be accessed via Web browsers such as Netscape Navigator 3.0.

WAIS   *Wide-Area Information Server.* WAIS is a specialized Internet client/server system for re-searching information in Internet databases.

WAN   *See* **wide area network**.

wanderer   *See* **spider**.

Web   Short for **World Wide Web**.

Web browser   A program for retrieving and viewing **HTML** documents on the **World Wide Web**. Also known as a Web **client**.

WebCrawler   *See* **spider**.

Web document   Any document available on the **World Wide Web**.

Webmaster   The individual in charge of developing or administering a Web site.

Web server   A computer that stores Web documents and allows **Web browsers** to retrieve them over the Internet using the **HTTP** protocol. Also, the software that makes this possible.

Webtop   A Netcaster **channel** that's anchored to the desktop and often used as a primary user interface. Other channels may appear within the Webtop.

wide area network   A group of computers and/or networks connected to one another by means of long-distance communication devices such as telephone lines and satellites, rather than just through local wiring. *See also* **local area network**.

widget   In HTML geek-speak, an object in a Web document that accepts user input. Examples are check boxes, radio buttons, drop-down lists, and so on.

wildcard character   A character used when you specify a filename; it is a variable that stands for any other valid character or characters. The question mark (?) stands for a single character, while the asterisk (*) stands for any string of characters in the filename. For instance, *.*txt* means "any file that has the .TXT extension"; *??.txt* means "any file that has a two-letter name and the .TXT extension."

Windows NT Server   The version of the Windows NT operating system that provides centralized network management and security as well as additional connectivity options.

Windows NT Workstation   The version of the Windows NT operating system that provides operating and networking functionality, but without centralized management.

Winsock   *Windows Sockets API*. A software "toolkit" that lets Windows programmers access **TCP/IP** services using a standard interface. Any Internet programs that use this standard, such as e-mail clients, Web browsers, and so on, will work under Windows 95 and Windows NT.

workgroup   On Microsoft networks, a collection of grouped computers with a unique name.

workstation   In Windows NT, a computer running the **Windows NT Workstation** software.

World Wide Web (WWW)   An Internet service used for browsing hypermedia documents; the "Internet within the Internet" formed by all the Web servers and **HTML** documents currently online.

WYSIWYG   *What You See Is What You Get*. A description of data that already looks like the final output as you work on it. For instance, a WYSIWYG HTML editor like Composer lets you move graphic elements around the page rather than typing in HTML code.

XOFF   A special character that's used to control the flow of information between a **DCE** and a **DTE**. When one device receives an XOFF character from the other, it stops transmitting until it receives an **XON**.

XON   A special character used to control the flow of data between a **DCE** and a **DTE**. *See also* **XOFF**.

Index

http://www.vmedia.com

VENTANA

Official Online Marketing With Netscape Book

$34.99, 544 pages, illustrated, part #: 1-56604-453-7

The perfect marketing tool for the Internet! Learn how innovative marketers create powerful, effectove electronic newsletters and promotional materials. Step-by-step instructions show you how to plan, deisgn and distribute professional-quality pieces. With this easy-to-follow guide, you'll soon be flexing Netscape Navigator's marketing muscle to eliminate paper and printing costs, automate market research and customer service, and much more.

Official Netscape Guide to Online Investments

$24.99, 528 pages, illustrated, part #: 1-56604-452-9

Gain the Internet investment edge! Here's everything you need to make the Internet a full financial partner. Features an overview of the Net and Navigator; in-depth reviews of stock and bond quote services, analysts, brokerage houses, and mutual fund reports. Plus a full listing of related financial services such as loans, appraisals, low-interest credit cards, venture capital, entrepreneurship, insurance, tax counseling, and more.

Official Netscape Guide to Internet Research

$29.99, 480 pages, illustrated, part #: 1-56604-604-1

Turn the Internet into your primary research tool. More than just a listing of resources, this official guide provides everything you need to know to access, organize, cite and post information on the Net. Includes research strategies, search engines and information management. Plus timesaving techniques for finding the best, most up-to-date data.

VENTANA

Official Netscape Messenger & Collabra Book

$39.99, 408 pages, part #: 1-56604-685-8

Windows, Macintosh • Intermediate to Advanced

The Power of Web-based Communications—Without a Web Site!
Stay in touch with customers; promote products and services visually; share the latest market trends—with simple Internet dial-up access! This step-by-step guide helps you harness Netscape Communicator's e-mail, newsreader, HTML authoring and real-time conference tools to achieve faster, more powerful business communications—without the effort or expense of a Web site. Learn how to:
• Integrate Messenger, Collabra, Conference and Composer for efficient business communications.
• Distribute eye-catching, HTML-based marketing materials without a Web site.
• Use the Net to gather, organize and share information efficiently.

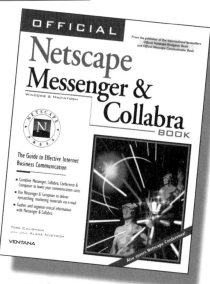

Official Netscape Composer Book

$39.99, 600 pages, part #: 1-56604-674-2

Windows • Beginning to Intermediate

Forget about tedious tags and cumbersome code! Now you can create sophisticated, interactive Web pages using simple, drag-and-drop techniques. Whether you want to create your personal home page, promote your hobby, or launch your business on the Web, here's everything you need to know to get started:
• Step-by-step instructions for designing sophisticated Web sites with no previous experience.
• JavaScript basics and techniques for adding multimedia, including animation and interactivity.
• Tips for businesses on the Web, including creating forms, ensuring security and promoting a Web site.
The CD-ROM features a wide selection of Web tools for designing Web pages, adding multimedia, creating forms and building image maps.

Official Netscape Plug-in Book, Second Edition

$39.99, 700 pages, part #: 1-56604-612-2

Windows, Macintosh • All Users

Your One-Stop Plug-in Resource & Desktop Reference!
Why waste expensive online time searching the Net for the plug-ins you want? This handy one-stop reference includes in-depth reviews, easy-to-understand instructions and step-by-step tutorials. And you avoid costly download time—the hottest plug-ins are included! Includes:
• In-depth reviews & tutorials for most Netscape plug-ins.
• Professional tips on designing pages with plug-ins.
• Fundamentals of developing your own plug-ins.

The CD-ROM includes all the featured plug-ins available at press time.

VENTANA

Microsoft Windows NT 4 Workstation Desktop Companion

$39.99, 1016 pages, illustrated, part #: 1-56604-472-3

Workstation users become masters of their own universe with this step-by-step guide. Covers file management, customizing and optimizing basic multimedia, OLE, printing and networking. Packed with shortcuts, secrets, productivity tips and hands-on tutorials. The CD-ROM features dozens of valuable utilities and demos for Windows NT. Innovative web-site designs, reference information, wallpaper textures, animated cursors, custom utilities and more.

Microsoft Office 95 Companion

$34.95, 1136 pages, illustrated, part #: 1-56604-188-0

The all-in-one reference to Microsoft's red-hot suite is a worthy sequel to Ventana's bestselling *Windows, Word & Excel Office Companion*. Covers basic commands and features, and includes a section on using Windows 95. The companion disk features examples, exercises, software and sample files from the book.

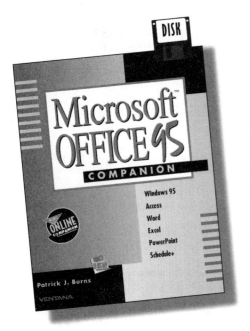

SmartSuite Desktop Companion

$24.95, 784 pages, illustrated, part #: 1-56604-184-8

Here's "Suite success" for newcomers to the critics' choice of business packages. This introduction to the individual tools and features of Lotus' star software packages—1-2-3, Ami Pro, Approach, Freelance Graphics and Organizer—has been updated for the latest versions. Features new enhancements for Windows 95. The companion disk features sample exercises and files that follow the lessons in the book.

VENTANA

The Comprehensive Guide to SmartSuite 97

James Meade
$34.99, 528 pages, illustrated, part #: 1-56604-651-3

Here's Suite relief for business users at all levels. Step by step, learn to use applications together, work collaboratively, and maximize Internet and intranet connectivity. Packed with tips and shortcuts.

For Windows 95/NT • Beginning to Intermediate

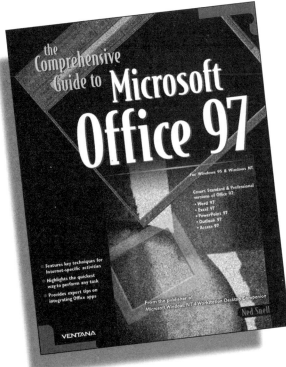

The Comprehensive Guide to Microsoft Office 97

Ned Snell
$39.99, 848 pages, illustrated, part #: 1-56604-646-7

The "right-size" guide to the world's hottest suite! Easy enough for beginners, yet in-depth enough for power users. Covers all five applications, plus tips, shortcuts, Internet techniques and more.

For Windows 95/NT • Beginning to Intermediate

Official HTML Publishing for Netscape, Second Edition

$39.99, 800 pages, part #: 1-56604-650-5

Windows 95/NT, Macintosh • Intermediate

Make the Most of the Latest Netscape Features!
Learn how the latest developments in Netscape Navigator and
HTML enhance your ability to deliver eye-catching, interactive Web
pages to a broad audience, and how to harness new technologies to
create a compelling site. Includes:
• Playing to Navigator's hottest features, including tables, frames,
  plug-ins and support for Java applets.
• Guidelines for designing great Web pages.
• New material on style sheets, sound, multimedia and databases.

The CD-ROM contains an example Web site on the Net, sample
JavaScript, clip objects, backgrounds and more.

Official Netscape JavaScript 1.2 Book, Second Edition

$29.99, 520 pages, part #: 1-56604-675-0

All platforms • Beginning to Intermediate

Brew up instant scripts—even if you're not a programmer!
Learn all the skills you need to perk up your Web pages with multimedia
and interactivity. Fully updated for Netscape Communicator, this bestseller
now includes:
• Basic programming techniques.
• Tips for using existing scripts and building your own from scratch.
• Nearly 200 script samples and interactive tutorials online.

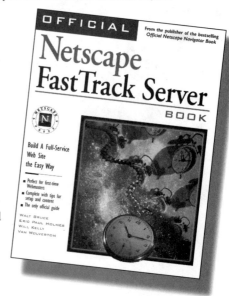

Official Netscape FastTrack Server Book

$39.99, 600 pages, part #: 1-56604-483-9

Windows NT • Intermediate to Advanced

Turn your PC into an Internet/intranet powerhouse!
This step-by-step guide to the hottest server software on the Net
provides all the instructions you need to launch your Internet or
intranet site, from technical requirements to content creation and
administration. Learn how to exploit FastTrack Server's high-
performance server architecture to easily create and manage customized web sites. Plus, enhance your site with FTP and Telnet;
ensure security for online transactions; and import and convert
documents.

VENTANA

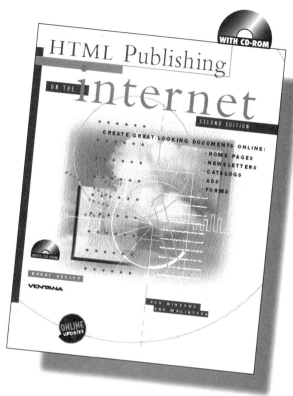

HTML Publishing on the Internet, Second Edition

$39.99, 700 pages, illustrated, part #: 1-56604-625-4

Take advantage of critical updates and technologies that have emerged since this book's bestselling predecessor was published. Learn to create a home page and hyperlinks, and to build graphics, video and sound into documents. Highlighted throughout with examples and templates, and tips on layout and nonlinear organization. Plus, save time and money by downloading components of the new technologies from the Web or from the companion CD-ROM. The CD-ROM also features HTML authoring tools, graphics and multimedia utilities, textures, templates and demos.

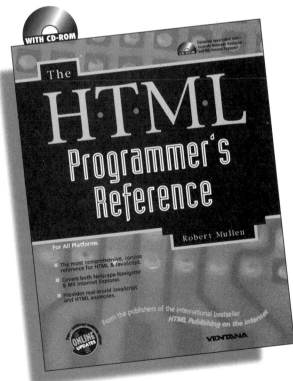

The HTML Programmer's Reference

$39.99, 376 pages, illustrated, part #: 1-56604-597-5

The ultimate professional companion! All HTML categories, tags and attributes are listed in one easy-reference sourcebook, complete with code examples. Saves time and money testing—all examples comply with the top browsers! Provides real-world JavaScript and HTML examples. The CD-ROM features a complete hyperlinked HTML version of the book, viewable with most popular browsers.

VENTANA

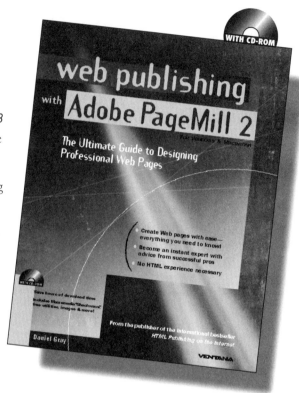

Web Publishing With Adobe PageMill 2

$34.99, 480 pages, illustrated, part #: 1-56604-458-8

Now, creating and designing professional pages on the Web is a simple, drag-and-drop function. Learn to pump up PageMill with tips, tricks and troubleshooting strategies in this step-by-step tutorial for designing professional pages. The CD-ROM features Netscape plug-ins, original textures, graphical and text-editing tools, sample backgrounds, icons, buttons, bars, GIF and JPEG images, Shockwave animations.

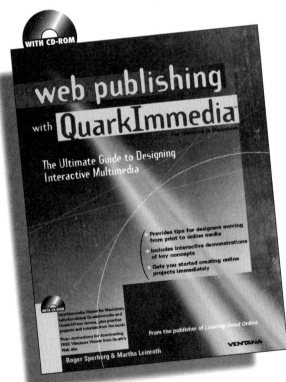

Web Publishing With QuarkImmedia

$39.99, 552 pages, illustrated, part #: 1-56604-525-8

Use multimedia to learn multimedia, building on the power of QuarkXPress. Step-by-step instructions introduce basic features and techniques, moving quickly to delivering dynamic documents for the Web and other electronic media. The CD-ROM features an interactive manual and sample movie gallery with displays showing settings and steps. Both are written in QuarkImmedia.

VENTANA

The Comprehensive Guide to Corel WEB.GRAPHICS SUITE

$49.99, 696 pages, illustrated, part #: 1-56604-614-9

Create spectacular web pages, incorporating sophisticated graphics and animation! Every component of CorelWEB is highlighted with an introduction, tools, tips and tricks, and a sample project. The Suite features tools for editing web pages, creating animation for web pages, designing 3D worlds and converting word processing files to HTML. Plus an illustration package based on CorelDRAW 5—along with 7,500 Internet-ready clipart images in GIF and JPEG formats. The CD-ROM includes images, textures and shareware for web designers.

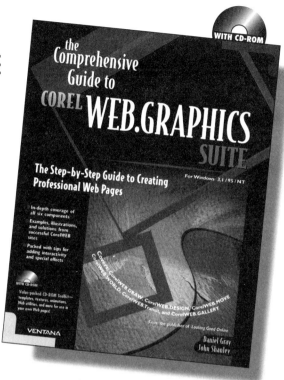

The Comprehensive Guide to Micrografx Webtricity

$49.99, 672 pages, illustrated, part #: 1-56604-607-6

Make your site soar with interactive excitement--and save time and money doing it! Micrografx Webtricity provides the drag-and-drop tool palette--this easy-to-follow, practical guide adds instructions, ideas and professional guidelines. Learn to design sophisticated, eye-catching graphics, optimize your files for the Web, create dazzling 3D effects and animations, catalog the hundreds of graphics files included in Webtricity, and much more. The CD-ROM features in-line viewers for dozens of formats, plus additional web-site utilities and images.

VENTANA

To order any Ventana title, complete this order form and mail or fax it to us, with payment, for quick shipment.

TITLE	PART #	QTY	PRICE	TOTAL

SHIPPING

For orders shipping within the United States, please add $4.95 for the first book, $1.50 for each additional book.
For "two-day air," add $7.95 for the first book, $3.00 for each additional book.
Email: vorders@kdc.com for exact shipping charges.
Note: Please include your local sales tax.

SUBTOTAL = $ _____
SHIPPING = $ _____
TAX   = $ _____
TOTAL   = $ _____

Mail to: International Thomson Publishing • 7625 Empire Drive • Florence, KY 41042
☎ **US orders 800/332-7450 • fax 606/283-0718**
☎ **International orders 606/282-5786 • Canadian orders 800/268-2222**

Name _____

E-mail _____ Daytime phone _____

Company _____

Address (No PO Box) _____

City _____ State _____ Zip _____

Payment enclosed ____VISA ____MC ____ Acc't # _____ Exp. date _____

Signature _____ Exact name on card _____

Check your local bookstore or software retailer for these and other bestselling titles, or call toll free:

800/332-7450
8:00 am - 6:00 pm EST

Technical support for installation related issues only provided by Ventana.
The Ventana technical support office is open from 8:00 A.M. to 6:00 P.M. (EST)
Monday through Friday and can be reached via the following methods:

World Wide Web: http://www.netscapepress.com/support

E–mail: help@vmedia.com

Phone: (919) 544-9404 extension 81

FAX: (919) 544-9472

America Online: keyword **Ventana**